THE TERRA AUSTRALIS INCOGNITA
PURGATORY

Paul David Adkin was born in England in 1958. His family emigrated to Melbourne, Australia, in 1965. He graduated with a Drama and English degree from Rusden State College in 1979. After leaving university he started a career in theatre as a writer, director and actor. His play *The Jack and Jill Story* was performed at the La Mama Theatre in Melbourne and was published by Anthill Theatre Press in 1981. In 1983 he left Australia, and spent a year teaching English in Japan before travelling extensively around Europe, settling finally in Madrid, Spain, in 1986. In Madrid he formed his own theatre company. He now writes in Spanish and English.

His other published novels are *Art Wars* and *When Sirens Call*. He is currently working on *Eternity,* the second part of the Terra Australis Incognita series, and his philosophical work, *Dismantling the Paradigm* is also expected to be published before the end of 2016.

Much of his essayistic work can be found on his blog:
pauladkin.wordpress.com
His author's website is:
www.pauldavidadkin.com

PURGATORY

a dramatized account of the first attempt to reach the
TERRA AUSTRALIS INCOGNITA

by

Paul David Adkin

This is a work of historical fiction and depicts fictional characters as well as authentic historical ones. The historical characters are based on the lives of real personages and use their real names. Sailors' log books were consulted carefully in the development of the historical plot. Esoteric details are usually elaborations of historical claims made in primary sources. The non-historical characters are the products of the author's imagination.

ñubooks

Avenida Manzanares, 96, 1ºD

28019, Madrid, Spain

ISBN 978-84-608-7794-3

This is the first print edition.
Revised and corrected from the first digital edition,
originally published in digital form by ñubooks 2008

Thanks to my very good friend W. M.,
who was the original *impulse* for this fantastic and terrible voyage,
and to C. J.,
who seemed to be the only who believed it would ever reach a
destination.

CONTENTS

First Attempt

PURGATORY

the smooth-card-cover was caressed then bent
    fleshy fingertips gently flicking the frontispiece underneath
                               it hung

      miserable millisecond suspension,
    supported by material stiffness
before omnipresent gravity pressed
    and thumb
    and index finger
had to be applied
                      to clutch
     rub, pull and peel it back again
    and in so doing
uncover this...

and you are here at last
    i feel your breath brushing each word
                  caress the wood-pulp page and unfurl it
      let crinkled fingertips fondle the edge, flicking it up
    it wobbles, slips and floats
peel it i say, peel
      exertion
    push yourself
if you want to reveal...

Part One: An Alchemist

"The fantastic is what carries a person into the infinite
in such a way
that it leads him away from himself
and thus prevents him
from returning to himself"

SOREN KIERKEGAARD
The Sickness unto Death

Exordium (The Fool)

It was a *resurrection,* one of the grinning doctors said. A resurrection of consciousness. After *sixteen years,* he emphasised. Sixteen years of watering my vegetable state had made me a houseplant for them. My *return,* murmured one of them, was as shocking as a suddenly singing aspidistra. And I had been *lucky,* confessed a young nurse. Just hours before I reanimated my doctors had been overheard contemplating *pulling the plug.*

I was told that I was an amnesiac. There had been an accident. I had had a fall whilst fishing, from a high and slippery boulder onto jagged rocks. *Brain damage,* they said, and told me about a spear-like splinter of stone that had opened a hole in my skull, poking deep into my cerebrum. Into the thalamus. Permanent damage: if one of the doctors had not decided to experiment on me, inserting electronic implants into the region. There had only been a *slim* chance. *Sixteen years in a coma is a long time,* they reiterated.

Recuperation of perception had come in a silent explosion of white light, but it burned and blinded instead of revealed.

When my eyes had adjusted, the source of illumination became a long, cold white bar. *Fluorescent* - I told myself, and shuddered at the sound of it in my mind. A *word* – I realised, but was hardly sure *how* I had realised it. Then another term – *Shit* – made a mental testimony to that surprise. My other senses also emerged. There was a creaking noise beneath me, the springs and joins of a hard, cast iron bed. Around me an ugly, constant music of murmuring voices, punctuated by a clanking clamour and the thuds of indiscernible objects colliding, or an annoying squeak of rubber sole footsteps on linoleum.

Soon after I was sniffing as well, sniffing rubber, or vomit mixed with antiseptic. Tactile sense recognised the presence of something strapped over my nose and mouth, and olfactory clues merged into a sound – *an ox-y-gen mask.*

Eventually someone lowered something over my eyes and forms sharpened. A fine tuning of images that made me more comfortable, and I nodded to express it. Nodded because, although I could think in words I was still unable to speak. That had to be managed through therapy.

It took months before I could pronounce my first words. Not only did the mechanisms of speech need to be reconstituted, I possessed vocabulary but they had to instil grammar, imposing a time-space that made no sense to me anymore. I had come from a past that I could not be sure had existed, moving into a future which was forever forming. With glasses on more things constituting my immediate reality could be confirmed. I could see plastic tubes and cables leading to a continuously soft-humming machine - *plugged in* – which lead me to a realisation with subject, predicate and copula - *I am in ho-spi-tal* – provoking a sudden terror and an attack of epilepsy. They were quick to come. Falling on me to inject sedatives: *Part of your brain is swollen.*

And they strapped me to the bed. Years ago now, in the 1960s.

I was conscious, yet that consciousness was still an enigmatic thing. I had become conscious of consciousness, but is that what consciousness is?

When I looked into a mirror I saw a scarred face that I knew was mine, I had no problems with that. Even the first time when I looked I knew, and the doctors told me that this was a good sign. Also later, when I confessed to feeling very alone and admitting to having a clandestine interior-existence which none of them seemed to be aware of, they told me that this was a *normal* thing.

But from where did my consciousness evolve? *From nowhere*, the first doctors I talked to told me. They said that it had never actually left me. It had merely become *dormant* ... or deceased? Didn't the fact that I could remember nothing mean that it had died?

It only seems that way, they reassured me. *The essence of you is still the same* ... But that did not help ... *The relationship between your consciousness and what you are conscious of is not so different from a plant to the ground in which it its rooted* ... said one of them. Yet how could that make sense to me? Was not my problem precisely that I felt uprooted? ... *Consciousness is a fundamental property of all living things* ... So I was alive. Very comforting. But did that mean that when I would be dead I would have no consciousness? ... *That is a religious not a scientific question* ...

Eventually I was introduced to the neurologist who had brought me round. His name was Dr Magoon. When he interviewed me he explained that some of the routes channelling information through my cerebrum had been cut: "Although in some cases," he said: "It seems your brain has developed new vias of communication. You have regained consciousness, but a *new* kind possessing an acute logic. You scored highly in the Intelligence Quota test and both of your languages have been preserved – English and Spanish – although you still cannot use either of them properly. But that will come. This is cause for some hope, Valentín. It means that one day a more concrete section of your memory could return. Although it would probably not be exactly the same memory you had before, you are still Valentín..."

Then began a briefly refreshing period. I began to receive *visits*. Strange visits, from *strangers* who wore different clothes and were gentler than any of the hospital staff. When they spoke it was in soft whispers, so seductive after the rasping grunts that I had been obliged to grow so accustomed to. Sometimes they spoke in languages unknown to me, although they seemed to expect me to understand.

I never complained. Their mere presence was enough to console me. When I could understand and contribute, our conversations were deep and rich. They kept me amused for hours at a time with long stories, educating me, filling in the gaps opened by my amnesia, explaining the tragic course of human history, of the bitter-sweet fruits of our species' variegated cultures. And none of this seemed peculiar until I was quizzed about *my distance* by one of my concerned doctors.

He was trying to interview me at the same time that I was receiving a *visitor*. When I explained that I had not been listening to him because I was busy conversing with a German historian who spoke perfect English, and who was standing beside my bed and explaining the Peloponnesian war, he became anxious. He reported the incident as a problem. Different doctors came to examine me and I was once more transformed into the hospital ward's main focus of attention. These new teams of specialists decided that I needed to be subjected to more tests.

They shaved my head and attached wires to my bald scalp. Afterwards they informed me that what I was seeing were *hallucinations*, and rubbed their chins in a concerned way. *The anomaly is probably caused by an overdose of adrenaline* - they explained - *because your damaged kidneys* – that was the first thing I knew about that - *are unable to expulse adrenaline from your body at a normal rate. This creates an adrenaline overdose, causing a chemical reaction which plays tricks on your brain.*

However, the aberration had a very interesting *incredible* side. The information imparted by my *visitors* seemed, as far as anyone could deduce, to be perfectly accurate.

And so, according to my doctors, *your mind has created a race of phantom beings who seem to be able to dig into, what has become, for some reason, forbidden areas of your damaged brain, and in so doing they resurrect information.*

This inspired a heated argument. Some thought that the *madness* was actually restoring my memory. For this reason, they argued, it should have been allowed to persist, perhaps even be encouraged. However, others thought that was a barbaric notion. *Madness* was *madness*, it should never have been encouraged. Finally, they decided to ask me for *my* opinion. When I told them that I was actually thankful for my *visitors*, they decided to prescribe drugs. A daily dose made the *visitors* vanish, and by this means I was able to remain in the *real* world of everyone else.

After six months or so, I was taken outside. Wheeled out. A tremendous dazzling light forced my eyes shut. I opened my throat to gasp. My first real breath of real air. A crisp early morning air hit my lungs and I writhed in the wheelchair. The nurse mistook ecstasy for discomfort. He wanted to take me back. I had to yell. Then a sharp heat sliced through the chill atmosphere and pricked me. The sudden warmth of a cloud liberated sun.

My first sun. I had imagined it. I had conceptualised it before seeing it; an orange egg yolk in my interior eye. Something that could be stared at. So far from the truth. Now I was experiencing the blinding brilliance of truth *... Do not look on me for you will go blind! ...*

When it was thought that I had recovered enough, I was taken to a house which was said to be my *family house*, or my *home*. It was a dull, autumn morning. We went in a van, crossing a murky river to enter what I was told was a very *well-to-do* suburb of the city. The property, abandoned for nearly two decades, was conspicuous. The garden around it had become a dry and thorny jungle.

"An eyesore for the neighbours," complained the lawyer who accompanied us. A moist and pinguid young man in a grass green suit with orange shirt and a narrow, stripy, red tie. The firm he worked for had been in charge of the estate and of my inheritance of it.

"I thought you people were taking care of the maintenance," accused the doctor who accompanied me.

The lawyer nodded sarcastically: "Nothing unauthorised. We're a law firm. We know what kind of trouble improvising can get you into," and then swore. A curling rose stem had tugged and ripped his jacket.

I was pushed through that jungle in my wheelchair, hoping the thorns would scratch me too. The house was massive and sturdy. Thick stone and stucco walls, painted grey-blue and peeling. It was high, with two floors and a tower. The large brown and scaly tiles gave it a saurian feel. Its large, lead-lighted, cracked and broken paned windows made it weeping sad. I was handed crutches and nurses stood by me as I clumsily hobbled across the veranda and inside, where it was dust.

The lawyer had organised some cleaners but they had only just begun.

The doctor complained and shook his head: "This doesn't help ..."

When they had been wiped he showed me pictures of my parents. Both had died.

The sad news evoked not a ripple of emotion. What could death mean to me?

I was the son of Spanish immigrants. But my parents had not emigrated for economic reasons.

"Contrary to the norm." The doctor's stern voice insisted.

They seemed such a handsome couple, with a handsome, happy son; all the photos of him as a child or young adolescent, too bright and handsome to be the scarred and crippled creature that I had become. They too were too handsome to be the progenitors of the monster. Sadness squeezed my throat and made me gasp.

The doctor looked at me compassionately: "It's hard, but you must," and continued with biography.

Both had been professionals. My mother was a cellist; I have since heard recordings of her melancholy interpretations. My father had been a civil engineer. They had both been inspired pacifists, recognising an imminent tragedy in Spain and in Europe: I had to re-learn what that implied. They had run as far away from the old continent as possible. Interesting, I was told, that they had chosen Australia as a destination rather than the Hispanic Americas. That had been 1933, when I was two years old, the year Hitler came to power. I had to relearn what that meant.

My mother had suffered her own accident shortly after I had had mine. But hers had been fatal. Two catastrophes in short succession. The terrible bouts of depressions that were ignited in my father eventually lead to his suicide.

"This desperate act was understandable," the doctor assured.

As for myself, I was informed that I had been a brilliant scholar, obtaining a Bachelor of Arts degree in philology and history. I was still at the university working on a doctorate when I had had my fall. They showed me notebooks; full of a tiny handwriting that looked nothing like the giant scrawl I have now. That was my unfinished thesis, I was told; sketches of a project describing the Spanish exploration of the Pacific. One notebook had a title, *The Terra Australis Incognita*.

Several months later I was walking without crutches and my epilepsy seemed to have disappeared. I had been taught the fundamentals of a domestic life: how to cook, clean and iron. This made me ready, they said, to move into that house.

Being alone for the first time that I could remember was comforting. I had very few problems. Nevertheless, my doctors maintained a continual surveillance.

"You are a more than fascinating model," one of them eulogised, although I was hardly flattered: "Despite all the damage you've got an extraordinary capacity. If you work, you could still make important contributions. You should finish your thesis."

In order to push me further along these lines Dr Magoon introduced me to an aged and trembling man who said he had been my professor of history at university. This new acquaintance sniffled, coughed and puffed on a pipe, while he claimed, over and over again, to have had great hopes for me. He had even met my mother.

"Who had pushed you," he told me: "Such a beautiful lady, and an excellent musician. Both she and you entertained me, one evening, with a rendition of a cello sonata. Brahms. Your mother's playing was superb," and then, just in case I should confuse my vocation: "*Your* gift was not music, but history," followed by: "Have you looked at your work on the Terra Australis?" and after I had confirmed that I had: "Would you not consider renewing it?"

The work. *This* book. Although then it was not really this. I had hardly begun at all, merely a few score pages. In any case it was obviously going to be something very different, straight forward, *historical*. In the beginning it was an empty and barren space, beckoning me to lose myself in it. Empty, like me, and in that respect a familiar friend.

The Pacific Ocean in which the Terra Australis lay was both huge and invisible. There had been three crossings made by bobbing Spanish boats betwixt the years 1567 and 1606. Somnolent endeavours, culminating in the voyage captained by Torres. This had sailed through the strait separating Australia from New Guinea that now bears his name, his drifting vessel almost caressing the Australian mainland, only four miles distant on the larboard side. They had had the rabbit-ear Cape York Peninsula in sight for three days, yet no one aboard apparently ever suspected it could have been the same Terra Australis that they had been dreaming about for so many years. As if the dream-become-reality had been unbearable. No further attempt was ever made, and the aim of my thesis was to try and uncover the reason why. In any case, it was the book which sent me back to the country of my birth.

"There are so many gaps that cannot be filled, not here," I complained to my old professor.

He scratched his bearded chin: "Then you must leave ... Go to Spain." Which really meant *"go home."*

This did not seem so difficult. My doctors had been tracing relatives and had located my mother's only brother in Madrid. I had written to him and he wrote promptly back inviting me to stay with him.

When I told the old professor he slapped my back: "Then you have no excuse."

He advised me on how to finance the trip and helped me obtain a grant. This was conceded swiftly and generously. Then, all that remained was the letting of the house in my absence. Packing brought no remorse, amnesia meant no roots to extract. The idea of returning to my homeland seemed to make my awakening more complete and I could start to imagine a future, the future that they had told me could be imagined. My mind was beginning to become what they called *normal* and everything then seemed to be absolutely straight forward.

Until I met Estrella.

I. My New World

Spain, November 1970: still in the insalubrious grip of its moribund dictatorship.

When I arrived at my uncle's, I was greeted with apprehension. The main scar down the side of my face is deep and twists my head into a bulging potato. As I came in the door, the faces expressed obvious regret. I suppose one expects a nephew or a cousin to resemble oneself. Between us there seemed to be none, neither physical nor spiritual.

I likewise shuddered. The home I had entered was a much too tiny and noisy flat in the centre of Madrid. Murky old with an oozing wall, mildewed mustiness. Furniture was wooden and upright hard, producing stiffness. Decoration: miserably catholic. Tearfully kitsch Christs and Virgins offered a gaudy colour that did nothing to brighten the grim, grey-green walls enveloping their family of six. My uncle and his wife lived with their son and his wife, and their two infant children. And then I arrived, to study and write.

When we had shaken our mutual disappointment away and replaced it with insincere smiles, they embraced me in unaffectionate hugs, brushing their cheeks against mine to give me pseudo-kisses that blew past my ear into the air. A tingling desperation surged through me. The situation was abysmal.

But it was not just my family who rejected me. My clumsy spastic limp, its spasms and twitches, seemed to make me a monster for most people. In the street some would stare, while others obviously averted their gaze. My speech also bewildered them. Although my understanding of Spanish was excellent, I had to struggle with the grammar in the same way that I had fought with English grammar, and my vocabulary usage was dictionary derived rather than learnt through conversations. Social contact was therefore disastrous and had to be avoided.

At first, my uncle and his family treated me with resignation. As if I were a cruel burden that had dropped into their midst but had to be carried. But they were most devout Catholics and it seemed to that Catholicism that God had sent me to them for a reason. A reason that demanded an acceptance of me, but *acceptance* was as deep as their feelings for me were allowed to go.

I went to church with them once. I wanted to experience the ceremony, but, in the end, I found it repulsive. So much hypocrisy in the dogma. Such little *humanity*. I never returned, not even when invited to weddings or baptisms. They resented this and gave me lectures about how a Spaniard *should* act. Of course this made cohabitation tough.

Nevertheless, in the short time I stayed with them we usually avoided each other quite successfully. During the day I was always in the library, in reading rooms, hunched over badly lit desks. By the time I had arrived home I had an aching head and smarting eyes, hardly in any mood for trivial conversation. But this was not a problem. They had usually finished their supper and were preparing for bed.

When I finally announced that I had found some alternative lodgings in a small attic flat of my own, they were visibly relieved.

My uncle offered very little information about my parents. My mother had been the radical *black sheep* of the family: which meant *enlightened*, I thought. He told me that he knew next to nothing of my father other that he had been an only child, like me, and that his parents had died young, like mine. I tried to trace information myself. This turned out to be an absurd mission. My family names: Lopez (from my father); Valle (from my mother). Both too common. There was a multitude of possibilities, but nothing concrete. Most of the files were in church archives.

When I tried to uncover them an elderly priest with no teeth explained: "During our glorious leader Franco's illustrious crusade, the iniquitous reds ravaged and burned so many of our temples, eradicating so much of our heritage."

In an official sense my family had never existed. And I gave up.

Then came *the Academy* ...

It was Estrella who introduced me. Estrella: *young,* fresh out of university, yet full of a self-confidence that I completely lacked. She was the author of a thesis on the philosophy of dreams, submitted when only nineteen. Her ideas were delivered with a difficult lucidity. I know the beginning of it off by heart: *"We dream when we are asleep, they say. Do we? When we dream we are really abandoning the void of sleep and in this way dreaming itself is an awakening. While we dream we are moving from pitch dark into light. From non-being into being ..."*

When read by her it was a melancholy dirge. Passionate theories of dreams and being, dreams and non-being, of sleep, space, time, gravity, and light. They were interior indagations that meant so much to me: this victim of a sixteen-year snooze. She told me once that I was perhaps the only one who could really understand. The Regime's stodgy machinery had to reject it. Her paper was too radical to receive official encouragement. Estrella, though a genius, was just a girl.

"A girl with a very *un-female* mind," they decided. Not a particularly fine role model for Franco's women.

"When your society rejects you for what you are," she expounded once: "One either becomes a recluse or looks for something else. I would have left Spain - it's hard, but I would have found a way - if I hadn't come across *the Academy*." And her beautiful eyes were briefly masked by a slow blink.

For those who could not understand the spiritual connection between her thesis and my life, it must have seemed strange when that wonderful girl attached herself to a twitching scarred stranger like me. Perhaps my doctors would have said that her brilliance distanced her from her peers, establishing a preference for older friends. My forty was a sweetly withered age for her. She herself once described us as a pair of freaks.

"Misfits," whispered through a sigh: "We do not belong in this world. It's the wrong time and space for us, although I think we would feel out of place in any country," then after reflecting on this last word: "People place too much faith in the concept of nations. Most people are strangled by it and they can't even see it. They slowly choke to death thinking it's the cigarettes they smoke. Even in democracies people are wheezing."

She discovered me in the library. She had secretly studied me for hours in the reading room, but claimed it had been a spontaneous impulse to follow me into the coffee shop.

She came with a tray and rattling cup. I was trying to get a spoonful of sugar into my tea, but I was suffering an attack of some Parkinson's like spastic tremors that were spraying it across the table. At first I thought she was a waitress come to clean the mess. Of course I was embarrassed. When I looked up she shivered. A fringe of black hair flicked across large but dark, deeply mysterious eyes. She had her own little hand outstretched to take the spoon out of my useless grip and finish the simple chore. But she too was trembling, and apologised for her audacity.

"I'm sorry to bother you ... But I'd like to talk," her voice was deep, emphasising the profound substance below the soft, sweet face: "I couldn't help but notice what you've been reading ..."

My eyes must have flickered with the contortion of my mind – *what had I been reading?* – But before I could adjust my brain, she twisted a ring off a finger and laid it on the table. When I saw it my pulse raced. A whoosh of steam from a coffee machine elongated my gasp, as if I had just been shown something that used to be mine, a sad suffering loss suddenly cured. I reached forward to inspect the design. I knew straight away what it was, but not because it *was* really mine, but because it bore a familiar seal – *why familiar?* The ring gleamed, a precious gold. As I rubbed it I noticed her chest heave, her throat gulp, the features of her face had been opened by a deep inward fear. Perhaps she was considering that I might not be the friend she had assumed me to be.

I pinched the rim and turned it to examine the markings. Two circles, like a wheel, with groups of squiggles between them, resembling simple zodiac signs, yet not exactly, and there were only eleven. Within the inner circle ran two perpendicular lines, although one of these had the form of a tower. There were two parallelograms traversing it, one with an arc beneath it as if it were a balcony.

"The secret seal of Solomon," it assibilated out of my mouth on a whisper. My spine tingled and hairs on my arms and the back of my neck pricked up. I must have seen it in the books she had been referring to. The dusty esoteric tomes full of myths and legends concerning King Solomon's mines I had on my desk. Books I had been reading for the *Terra Australis*, because that was what the Spanish had been searching for when they crossed the Pacific; that was why they had baptised their new world *the Solomon Isles*.

I had to shake my head. I could not remember seeing the seal on any page, let alone the name of it.

The face before me was damp, her nostrils dilating, her deep brown eyes, brilliant and fixed. Her top lip shivered and her brow tightened as she prepared to affirm something preposterous: "We have met before ... In a dream ..."

Perhaps we had, in my coma ...

I stared at her, trying to remember. The concept seemed quite logical to me then, and the more I stared the more vaguely familiar she became. Her left eyebrow arched, both eyes huge. Then she reached forward and stroked her finger down my deepest scar: "It must have been a terrible accident," she sucked in her bottom lip: "Could it be that we are worming through the same field?" A low, but softly melodious, seductive whisper.

I was dumbfounded – *worming?* – new association. I knew what worms were. But its function as a verb? I had to consider it carefully before I said *yes*.

We left the library and went to a handsome, art-nouveau café. There we drank a bottle of red Catalan wine. Dizzying. The young girl's intricate mind, sliding into my own upon spiralling currents of alcohol. Her lopsided smile was sardonically sexy in an otherwise pulchritudinous face, hypnotically bobbing amidst the ubiquitous undulations of the furnishings around us. When she leaned to one side, wood carved ocean waves on the oak panel behind her emanated from the brushed curves of her black hair. On the other side the waves were flames, and, when she sat straight, flower stalks twisted upward from her head. Yet through all this sensory vertigo, I was able to maintain a semblance of dialogue, sharing what I knew of our common *field*.

She asked me about my scars and I explained my story and my amnesia to her as best I could. I think she was moved by it and I imagined a kind of bonding between us. However, when the wine was finished she turned her wrist to examine her watch, clutching her small and red leather shoulder bag to her stomach and straightening her back in the same instant. My heart sank. It was obvious she was making ready to leave.

"But we must meet again. There is a conference at the Academy, next Wednesday ... perhaps you would be interested?"

It took me some seconds to register what this meant. That she was inviting me to go with her. To be together again. The realisation forced my affirmation out through a splutter.

We arranged to meet in the afternoon at the Retiro, Madrid's most central park, by a statue of Lucifer: "They say Madrid is the only city in the world with a monument to Satan," she boasted and grinned: "The effigy is mounted deep in the heart of the Retiro. Not easy to find."

She was right. I was stumbling with my staggering limp along sandy tracks through budding-green woods for almost an hour before I did.

It was early March. The cloudless sky sun already strong: inspiring crowds. Crowds: along the paths, on the lawns, under the trees, around the pond or rowing on the pond. Happy crowds, leisurely strolling. All carefreeness, despite the ubiquitous police and priests and the stifling gloom of the dictatorship. However, it was this happiness that terrified me. A fear of seeing the monster that I was manifested in someone's squinting-pained recognition of my deformity. It made me hurry with my head down and I lost my way in the maze of paths.

When I eventually found the courage to ask for directions, I did it badly. Instead of enquiring where the statue of *the fallen angel* was, I quite innocently asked for the way to *Satan*. I really did not understand the semantic shift and the terrible connotations that that name could have. The male member of the middle-aged couple I had consulted, straightened his immaculate suit and snarled, while the woman shook herself in a bird-like way, before mumbling something about *locos*. This seemed to inspire the macho beside her to curl his upper lip up and snort phlegm into his throat as if he were going to spit in my face. But before he could his partner tugged his cuff and they carried stiffly on.

It was only by accident that I managed to finally arrive. I was expecting to stumble on it in some recondite corner. If I had not looked up I would never have seen it, for it was standing proudly alone, in the midst of a wide rotunda.

I approached it from the east, an avenue of elms. The sun was already low and almost behind the statue, producing a halo. A lead coloured statue. It had been twisted out of bronze upon a white stone pedestal which was also a fountain. Twelve gargoyles' heads were vomiting water through beaks or savage sharp teeth, each with a cringing, frill-necked basilisk and baby crocodile under webbed, amphibian claws.

I had no preconception, as I am told that most others do, of what Lucifer should have looked like, so I found nothing strange that he should be such a handsome youth. A winged athlete, curly haired and as beautiful as any angel, but suffering. He was strapped to a rock by a squeezing python. His mouth wide open, an anguished but silent howl as he gazed painfully in the direction of tomorrow's rising sun. I walked around. Studying it. Oblivious, at first, to Estrella. Of course she was already there, sitting in the shade of a huge plane-tree.

A priest crossed my path. He stopped when he saw me. I suppose from his perspective I was emerging from Lucifer's pedestal. His jaw suddenly dropped and he began to shiver. I straightened myself and stiffened my spastic arm. This calmed him and gave him enough confidence to continue. But, as he edged carefully past me, he clutched a crucifix and pulled a white handkerchief from some pocket in his black soutane to wipe his brow.

Estrella waved from her tree and ran to me, stretching up to kiss me through a panting breath on each cheek. As she lowered herself I took her hand and rubbed her Seal-of-Solomon ring, hoping, as I did, that its magic would transform me into the figure towering over us, and, beautified, I would lift her chin and give her a deep, proper kiss. But what did I know of kisses then?

I enquired about the statue: "What is he falling from?"

Estrella, who was still ignorant of the extent of my ignorance, misunderstood the question, expecting it to be needing a deep reply. Instead of pronouncing that *he had fallen from God's grace*, she explained an astrological significance of *Lucifer*: "He is the morning-star, the brightest in the night sky, who must surrender his status each morning to the rising sun. He is suffering," she explained: "Because he needs to rise again. His vitality cries out for *rebirth*." Which reminded me of my own condition.

I clutched hold of the term *vitality*. The word and Lucifer's image, making me spurt some ridiculous, philosophical babble: "As this statue was p-p-perused," I stammered: "Thoughts began emerging to me ... concerning the possibility of the existence ... of an absolutely necessary being ... that the Universe itself is ... something necessary ... as is everything in that Universe."

Yes, ridiculous babble. But, nevertheless, it inspired Estrella to embark on a monologue regarding absolute purposiveness and human destiny that confined our concentration all the way to the Academy.

Estrella's Academy was situated in the banking district of Franco's Madrid, just behind the calle Alcalá. The building containing it was palatial, with clean classical lines and an occasional modernist twist. The entrance was framed by a stone portico with columns and a slogan in Latin: *a caelo usque ad centrum*. Their official *raison d'être* was for the acquiring and sharing of knowledge. A brave but dangerous practice in the Regime.

That first *date* was attending a conference on diachronic linguistics: *Phonological aberrations in the Spanish of sixteenth century America*. Estrella timidly suggested it, no doubt because I had told her that I had studied philology, omitting to add that it had been in a past life that I had completely forgotten. Of course the lecture would be unbearable, but I did not care. I just wanted to be with Estrella.

The general foyer was a huge and cold, open space. Ionic pillars marked the way to a wide marble staircase, rising toward a triumphant Minerva.

"Apart from Lucifer and the statues of Franco, this city is full of goddesses," Estrella sighed. *And virgins* – I thought, recalling the church and mass I had attended with my uncle.

Estrella carried on: "Yet despite the veneration of the symbolic, real women are loathed."

She guided me through lead-lighted glass doors. On the floor, a huge block of yellow marble from which another woman's smooth naked body half emerged. I crouched down and stroked it.

Estrella snorted: "Some artist's idyllic nymph."

"But irresistible," I added.

She shrugged her shoulders, knelt down next to me and we rubbed the cool stone together: "If we warm her, perhaps she will escape from her marble prison," and then: "Like Pygmalion," an idea which made her pensive and her voice dropped: "But I hope not. If she emerged you would fall in love with her."

Which was probably the first time she had ever indicated a more than Platonic affection for me. Expectancy brought a lump of clogged emotion to my throat. I wanted to cry out – *No, don't be stupid ... you are perfect, why should I need anyone else?* – but I did not dare.

The conference was held in a mostly wooden room with high ceilings and a creaking parquet floor. Huge and brilliant chandeliers were suspended by heavy, rusty chains.

"We'll do anything for illumination," she laughed.

But despite the luxury, hard wooden chairs were our only seating option, and the room itself was far more interesting than the lecture. I very quickly lost track of any cohesive argument. The technical terms were new to me, and impossible to grasp. Added to this was its ridiculous duration, some two hours, so by the end I was yawning and wriggling in my seat, concentrating on some ornate interlaced bands that decorated the skirting-boards while trying to keep my spastic arm still.

Afterwards Estrella was nervous and embarrassed: "I'm sorry, it must've been awful for you."

"Oh n-no," I lied: "It's very interesting for me to have linguistic problems known," which probably sounds like a strange way of speaking but that was how I tended to construct my spoken sentences: "My r-re-search is ... will be ... helped, of that I am assured ... thank you," and then: "... but ... err ... is linguistics alone being discussed here?"

And she laughed: "No, not at all," and put her arm around my shuddering one to calm it as she led me into the vestibule: "The Academy is an umbrella for a wide variety of cultural expression in the arts and sciences. In a sense," and she pointed to all the redwood doors, each bearing an embossed title: "... it's a university," then paused, tilting her head a little, her mouth curling into a piquant smile: "Although I find this ridiculous place far more stimulating than the university ever was," then looked suddenly solemn: "You see we have more freedom here. Would you like to come again?"

Our second date was to a huge cocktail party in the palace ballroom. The guests were mainly men in tuxedoes, I had also hired one for the occasion. Estrella was wearing a long white dress, tightly clinging around her body, spreading into bell lips over her feet. The cut made her look taller and slimmer and the whiteness made her black hair pitch. There was music. Very serious at first, no dancing of course. A piano had been raised on a small stage. Chopin sounded familiar, but Debussy and de Falla were new to me.

Estrella explained the music and who the other guests were. We took a plate to gather snacks on and were given a glass of champagne from a passing waiter. After a while I felt uncomfortable. I seemed to receive unfriendly snarls whenever we passed anyone. When I confessed this to Estrella she hung her head slightly. Her voice came up peeved: "Yes, they're so snobbish. They think their group is really special. They only accept *great* minds, they say," then she looked up at me, with a frown and ringing-urgent sincerity: "But how do you define a great mind?"

I shook my head. Not the slightest idea. But her own attitude was puzzling: "You say ... said... that these people are ... were ... liked by you."

She grinned: "I like *some of them.* I've some very good friends. But most of the people here are ..." and she leaned to my ear: "Arseholes." Her eyes flashed with naughty glee and she tapped her own bottom when I looked puzzled.

Then I literally bumped into one. Dr Hilario de Coca. He was a short man, but stiffness and formality made him appear taller. I accidentally struck him with a hyperactive elbow as we passed. He spun around, glaring at me in a fiercely piercing way that made me avert my eyes.

Estrella stepped between to introduce us. She explained that the man I had hit was the doyen, which merely highlighted my clumsiness. He ran a hand across his well-oiled hair, pressing it down and back around an ample, shining forehead. I held out my hand. It did not shiver that time. I felt relieved. He took it with the same hand that had wiped the grease, squeezed it rather than shook.

"Any friend of Estrella's is a friend of the Academy," a hissing whisper: "You must feel privileged, for she has the most perceptive intellect," stressing the word *perceptive:* "It's been taken for granted that if you are with her, you must be equipped in a similar way. She is most selective, which is very important. We must not sully what is good, eh? A clean mind is the reflection of a clean soul. We have to keep them polished, if we are ever to conquer the future," and smirked, but then quickly let go of my hand as if it had burnt him, blurting out the strangest question: "Time and all events are servants of the will, don't you think?"

I started to consider an appropriate response, then realised I had not understood but began excogitating a reply anyway.

In a pause in my bumbling, Estrella dragged me aside: "Don't bother. He's crazy. The product of centuries of family in-breeding" she chortled. But I did not understand the irony. She smirked: "The blood of barons, which certainly facilitated his graduation in medicine," again I missed the implication, then: "I suggest you don't cough in his presence, he's a specialist in pulmonary diseases," eventually registering my utter confusion: "I mean - I couldn't think of anything worse than to feel his cold hands on my chest," I shook my head: "Oh for God's sake Val! He's an arsehole!" which finally drew a chuckle from me.

"Aren't you worried by that?" I asked: "To be belonging to a group which is directed by an arsehole."

She whispered: "I'm used to it ... I live in Franco's Spain."

Then suddenly, the piano music made an abrupt change of tempo; to jazz. At the same time Estrella caught a glimpse of something out of the corner of her eyes and made off in that direction, dragging me with her.

As we moved, a group of older men intercepted us. One of them looked up at Estrella, aghast: "Did you organise this farce?"

Estrella laughed: "No, but I wish I had..."

I recognised the men from the conference on diachronics. They recognised me too, and wanted me to *add my grain of salt* to an argument about evolving phonologies.

Unfortunately, I had not understood what the phrase *adding a grain of salt* implied, never mind the rest. I needed Estrella. But when I turned to her she had gone.

The situation was embarrassing, the men in front of me really did expect an opinion. Luckily my spastic arm erupted and I dropped my plate. Then, crawling between legs while scooping up crumbs and shards of china, I escaped.

I had to rise up on tiptoes in order to locate Estrella again. She was standing in a corner with another woman, who was older than her, and very handsome, with long, red hair. I stretched my neck and saw that Estrella was also up on tiptoes. She put her hand up making a scooping gesture. I pushed past tuxedoes. Estrella's huge dark eyes were a beautiful gravity. I leaned forward and she slipped her arm under mine.

"Val, I want you to meet Inma, a friend," her eyes guiding me to equally delicious wells, but pale green: "Inma Fernández."

Who stood up. She was considerably taller than Estrella, almost as tall as me. She wore a black dress, a bell cut like Estrella's, but with a deeper, more revealing cleavage. Her head tilted toward me, proffering a kiss inviting cheek. I suppose I slipped, it felt like I was pushed, the rest was instinct. I dropped to one knee and, with the same movement, reached out, took Inma's hand and pecked that instead.

Estrella roared. Inma leaned back. A flash of what I thought was horror swept across her face. I was expecting her to scream. Instead, she caught her breath and laughed: "A gentleman," husky.

I felt dazed. I turned to Estrella for support but she had a wry smile, and it made me feel ridiculous: "Where did you learn to do that?" It seemed to be scolding.

Inma leaned forward and I was able to detect a faint constellation of freckles across her nose: "Be every act an act of love and worship." It was as enigmatic as Dr de Coca, but I felt less foolish and sensed that I had been approved. She smiled and I noticed that one of her front teeth was crooked, which in turn made me realise that I was noticing these defects because she was so perfect. The husky voice scratched me again: "I'm sorry that I missed you at the conference the other day. I would have liked to have been there. Linguistics are part of my field. Although I'm not so hot on diachronics," and grinned, in a way that seemed to insinuate something.

Then I realised that I still had the broken bits of plate in my other hand. I felt myself blush and laid the rubble onto a passing waiter's tray. He also snarled at me.

Estrella began to sketch a background: "Inma is a teacher," and put an arm around her friend's back, resting a hand on her shoulder. The white and black dresses, the red and black hair, became a universe of opposites: "She taught me the sublime pleasure of reading verse. My literature teacher ..."

"At a terrible nun's school," annotated Inma. And shivered around a puckering smile.

"Don't worry Val, she's not a nun," and they laughed together.

Estrella gazed admiringly across the other woman's profile before darting up to give her a little peck on the cheek. Then: "That was in our home town. In Galicia," which drew a sudden shadow across her face. She became thoughtful and had to hurl gravity away by flicking her head. When the black fringe had settled again on her pale brow: "She also taught me philosophy," her chin trembling with chest-straining pride: "Not officially," and she blinked herself into a more modest composure: "Philosophy in Franco's schools means Catholic theology," then staring back at Inma's pouting chin: "I owe much of my thesis on dreams and time to her," Inma's eyelids dropped and she shook her own self-esteem away. Estrella's voice began to chirp: "From the Pre-Socratics to phenomenology, with a good dose of oriental mysticism on the way," and then through a laugh: "All done on the side of course."

It was Inma's turn to flick her hair: "Your heterodox homework," and they gurgled again.

Inma was a mentor for Estrella. She had introduced her to the Academy. But more importantly she had brought the girl to Madrid and had managed her *premature* entry into university at a tender sixteen. Like every other member of the Academy, Inma had her specialities. A degree in philology as well as literature: French, German, Latin, and academic Greek - not to mention a near perfect grasp of English. But her real expertise, her philosophy, had been self-taught.

Estrella put an arm under Inma's and the other under mine. Maintaining the wry smile, she pulled us around. There was another beaming grin in the corner. A short, white haired man with a soft face, Don Enrique Villeplein.

He was nearly eighty, I was told, though physically lithe and mentally lucid. A non-conformist. Instead of the black bowtie that all the men had, his neck was wrapped in a sky blue, silk cravat. He held a white, knobbed ivory cane, which seemed more for the purpose of fashion than support. Inma informed me how he had made a fortune as a wine grower before dabbling in mining, afterwards turning to chemistry and the creation and perfection of pharmaceutical products. He wrapped my hands in his own and, through an impish smile, in a soft, low voice: "You haven't come to take these lovely women away from me have you?"

I sighed: "Oh no ... I am ... have been ... sent ... sent to write a book."

"Yes, I know. Estrella has told me. Similar themes."

Similar, yes. He meant Estrella's new project – *The Lure of the Better (a study in the psychology of exploration in the Renaissance)*.

"P-Perhaps the same book," it occurred to me then: "Oh yes... the same thing is ... is being written ... yes ... but a pencil is used by me ... and by her ... a pen."

Nobody laughed at the joke I had tried to make. It did not matter. Everything felt warm and wonderfully united. They talked. I listened. Conversation was mainly academic. It occasionally drifted into politics. They discussed the dictator's waning health and a student movement that could become a transition. Their voices dropped too, and they huddled, as if conspiring.

After a while Estrella and Don Enrique stood up and started pacing around. They turned their backs to us. I looked down to a small pack of business cards that had been accumulating over those busy days and started to try and memorise them, but a hand grasped my chin and yanked it up. It was Inma, staring deeply into my eyes, frowning. Her breast heaved. She leaned towards me. A nasty smell. Whisky on her breath.

"Estrella has told me about your ... your amnesia," and licked her top lip before biting it.

"Oh," and I probably bit my own lip: "Please ..."

"Don't worry. If it's a secret, it's safe with me."

Which seemed to accuse me. I felt guilty. Defensively: "It shouldn't be called a secret ... It's just that ..."

"No. I understand. Better not to bring it up ... I only wanted to ... it's stupid but I ... I have the strangest feeling that I've met you before ... a long time ago I suppose, no idea where. It's very strange. I'm not sure why, but, obviously, even if I had met you, you wouldn't be able to remember it anyway, would you?" and she looked relieved. But the nonchalance of my strange reply obviously pained her.

"Is it ... was it ... in a dream?" I asked: "Were you there with Estrella?"

"Why?" she stammered.

"It is said ... was said by her ... that she was there too," which choked Inma. She looked across at Estrella, who was locked in her conversation with Don Enrique. When she looked back at me her face was bright red, which made me blush as well: "I'm s-s-sorry..." I stammered.

But she shook her head: "No, it's not a problem ... just a feeling. Let's forget it."

And I did. It did not seem important. But I had met two women and they had both made the same remark. From then on I decided to pay more attention to my dreams.

II. Lucid Dreams

The first *experiments* were conducted at a dinner party in Estrella's little, sparsely furnished flat. That was weeks after the ball. The sitting room was cramped, illumination was gentle. Her white walls were tinged with a soft yellow, emanating from a simple shaded lamp sitting on a low coffee table.

We could either sit in a frayed armchair or on a ragged sofa. Both had been especially adorned for the fiesta, happily draped with rainbow coloured blankets and smothered by chaotically variegated cushions. Food was spread out on the floor, on a green and white checked mantle. Plates, resting amidst the curling wave creases of the ocean tablecloth, bearing mounts of green-blue olives, pink and ruddy cold meats, or the yellow to gold cheeses or potato omelette; all of them awaiting their imminent destruction. Which soon came. Hands thrust in. Moistened teeth clamped and chewed.

Six of us were there that night: Estrella, Inma and I; Tomás Puigsegur, who was a writer friend; also Francisco Arizmendi, called *Paco el rojo* or *Red Frank* because of his socialist ideas, as well as a strange character called Vicente. The latter was wrapped in a tight, black, polo neck jumper, frog eyes looking towards each other, bulging from a pale face under pitch and curly hair.

To provide music there was a valve radiogram which gave off its own soft light and hum. It was then that I first heard-felt the *duende*-genius pain of flamenco song, but there was also psychedelic stuff; imported underground records that had been smuggled into the fascist state, along with other psychedelic stimulants. That was the first time I heard Frank Zappa and Jimmy Hendrix, and the first time I got truly *stoned*.

Estrella's friends were not only music lovers, they were also heavy drinkers, and had brought their own supplies. Plenty of beer, wine and other alcohol: and there was hash to smoke.

It was a like a rest cure for me. After only a few puffs my spastic arm was almost stilled, and afterwards I kept my own supply for medicinal reasons.

Perhaps the term *symposium* would have been more appropriate than *party*, for besides the drinking and smoking there was also serious discussion and even *readings*. At first the conversation was dominated by Vicente and Francisco, who were arguing politics, discussing the rising student and clandestine trade-union movements and a possible overthrow of Franco and his censors: "If he doesn't die we'll have to seize power."

Inspiring a bobbing flat hand from Vicente. His grim voice: deep, with a galloping rhythm: "Patience/patience/his days/are numbered. Have you not seen/how he shakes?" Which was followed by a suggestion to *read*: "Is it true/that we have/poets/here?"

Inma proposed that Estrella read first. But Estrella had not brought anything of her own, instead she had some of Inma's poems. She would recite them if Inma wanted.

"Please do."

Estrella unfolded a page and cleared her throat:

"The air we breathe
flapped into our soul by blue-birds' wings -
an avian freedom
It is swallow made oxygen that lifts us
above the camel-trodden desert"

Tomás sighed.

Afterwards Francisco was asked to read. Inma knew he had brought a story with him. She pressured.

At first there was a pseudo-protest: "Stream of consciousness," he warned us: "Very strange."

It was. He called it "political" and guzzled rum between each sentence. Inma and Estrella laughed and applauded. Tomás also seemed interested, though his eyes kept wandering back to Estrella. Vicente smoked a joint and remained grim. He complained that it was pointless writing such things that could never be published. I became bored and drowsy. Estrella had to explain it to me: that it had been a story full of anti-Franco sentiment, allusions which I was incapable of grasping. Inma said that she would copy the manuscript because she actually enjoyed doing transcripts.

"Transcripts or translations," she said forcefully, almost proudly: "There is no better way of understanding how another writer thinks than by copying what he or she writes," and then turned to me: "Compiling history must be like that too," she said: "Yet, so awfully difficult deciphering all those ancient squiggles," which I affirmed with a nod. Then she said that she was going to translate Francisco's stories into English or French, and that she would try to get them published overseas: "Because Vicente is right, it would be impossible here."

"One is never a prophet/in one's own land," quoted Vicente.

The discussion turned to the writer, Julio Cortázar. About a story he had written in which a man is sitting in an armchair with a velvet headrest in his study with his back to the door, looking out onto a park while reading a novel in which an assassin stalks his lover's husband, slowly creeping up to him as he sits in his study, in an armchair with a velvet headrest, his back to the door, attention immersed in a novel about an assassin who ...

"Infinite regression," someone said.

The idea of the assassin must have registered a rather oblique connection in Estrella's mind and she told us a story about a cruel family. Self-confession it was. Her brother and cousins used to often beat her up when she was a child: "And I felt so defenceless," she whimpered and ran a hand down her left arm: "In a sense coming to Madrid was an escape. But now my brother is here too ... I mean close ... In Toledo ... as if he had followed me south."

"But at least he doesn't hit you anymore, does he?"

"Not physically."

I could not imagine how anyone could have beaten Estrella, how anyone could have dared to. To me she seemed so strong.

Then Inma: "Estrella and I have been studying Hebrew."

Vicente coughed: "You're not/going to become ... Jews/are you?"

They all laughed. I did not have the faintest idea why.

Inma commented on Estrella's dress, which she said that she liked. It was *sexy*, someone said. And no one disputed it. I think all of us there, except for Vicente, were in love with Estrella in some way.

Eventually the focus turned to Tomás.

Tomás Puigsegur was a rookie psychology professor: radical minded, but also timid, awkward and moody. He tended to avert his gaze from eye-contact, which probably had something to do with Estrella being there. His terrible infatuation for her was obvious. She told me that they had known each other for several years. They had studied the same subjects at the same university in Madrid, but that was after he had returned from the USA. When Estrella met him he had completed part of his course at a university in California. It was there, Estrella told me, that he learned to be radical. He often bragged about that time, and about the mind-opening drugs that he had taken. Drugs which were so hard to obtain in Spain. Tomás's appearance, like his mind was *radical*.

He had long brown hair and a beard, wore denim shirts and flared jeans, but he was a slow, clumsy speaker, his tongue even thicker in his mouth than mine, and this obstructed his attempts to be *cool*.

Yet Tomás became important in the shaping of my own destiny for none of these reasons. The important thing was his knowledge of hypnotism. And, despite his stutter, that night he intrigued us with long stories.

"I once saw a g-girl, no bigger than our little Estrella, lift quite a hefty g-g-guy ... over her head ... with one f-finger ... Under hyp-nosis."

It motivated discussion. Estrella and Inma provided the classical background.

"Hypnosis comes from the Greek Hypnos" explained Inma, exaggerating the final sibilant: "No doubt familiar to Estrella."

Who confirmed it: "God of sleep."

"Son of Nyx or night. And Thanatos, who was death."

"Lived in the underworld ..."

"In a misty cave on an island between the waters of forgetfulness and oblivion."

There was a shiver down my amnesiac's spine.

Both Francisco and Vicente had their own hypnosis stories. But the point of reference returned to the expert Tomás. Eventually he brought up the idea of hypnoregression.

"Altered-State Therapy ... Hypnotic Regression techniques that can access ... err ... bring forth ... repressed m-memories."

Which made me gasp. It was the first time I had ever heard of such an idea.

I was gulping wine. It went down the wrong way. Estrella stood up, leaned across and thumped my back. She was laughing. My hand began its uncontrollable shake again but only briefly.

I asked Tomás, through coughs and splutters, if this kind of psychotherapy was common.

"Yes," he replied: "Really f-far too common ... It is poorly un-derstood ... mis-used ... quite dangerous if c-carried out by an in-experienced practitioner."

Then the question that was really troubling me. The scars on my face seemed to tighten and pull. I wiped my nose on my sleeve: "Is it used for treating amnesia victims?"

"Most definitely," he said: "Although it does not always work ... Am-nesia is a d-delicate ... a ... err ... com-plicated p-problem."

– *Complicated: but even so, why had my Australian doctors never ever tried this out?* –

Of course Tomás did not know then that *I* was an amnesiac. The only person I had told was Estrella, who, as far as I knew, had only violated this pact once, with Inma.

Estrella had sat down again, staring and smiling at me. She rubbed a finger around the rim of her wine glass, making it ring. Tomás became watchful: trying to interpret signs.

The pitch of the rubbed glass intensified and filled the room, until Vicente suddenly reached forward to squeeze Estrella's hand.

Tomás shuddered. We insisted that he continue. He took a deep breath, obviously worried about something, but the opportunity of being able to perform in front of such an attentive audience was too good to be missed: "I've b-been in-vestigating a n-n-new and re-volutionary technique," delivered like a solemn confession: "Based on massage, rather than the old ... err ... swinging w-watch routine."

I took a deep breath and looked at Estrella. Her eyes were electric. She nodded at me, but I must have merely gaped. I knew what she was insinuating but felt frozen before the need for initiative. She recognised my cruel-fear and smiled sadly back before taking my fate into her own hands and encouraged Tomás to give us a demonstration. My neck and jaw tensed as I croaked out my own commitment.

Vicente loved the idea: "We have/a guinea-pig!"

Tomás erupted: "Guinea-pig! I have n-not been proposing a p-party game ... Hypno-Regression is a very s-serious ... err ... s-serious thing."

"But you *have* studied it, haven't you?"

It was Inma. Her look and tone stripped him. He turned red while the others, inspired by Inma's offensive, also egged him on. He shivered, stuttered, then acquiesced. The others applauded, but his agreement came with conditions. He stipulated that we meet some other day, at the university, where he would organise a more *scientifically safe* environment.

I considered this. It sounded reasonable. But Inma was shaking her head, slowly, authoritatively: "If we're going to go through with this, then we'll have to do it right here, tonight." Then turned to me, winking at me, which I did not understand at all: "Won't we Valentín?"

I nodded. An automatic reaction. I did not feel confident enough to plunge into the debate. Or perhaps it was because I was not properly stoned yet. Or maybe I was, and the drug inspired me to keep my distance.

Estrella backed Inma up for me. They wanted to witness such an experiment, if I was willing to endure it.

Under pressure Tomás gave in, but absolving himself of responsibility and making a sour comment about everyone's motives. He accused us of possessing an underlying scepticism. Then he told me to take my shoes and socks off.

This made me anxious – *Did he want to humiliate me? Demonstrate that I had scars on my smelly feet as well?* – Estrella looked compassionate. Inma firm. Vicente was enjoying my disgrace. Francisco was bored and yawned.

I untied laces and stretched cotton. When the three missing toes on my right foot were revealed I felt a stir. Vicente grimaced. Tomás looked saddened, Estrella and Inma fascinated. Then Tomás ordered me to lie face upward on the floor. I removed my glasses and stuffed them into my shirt pocket. It would be easier if I could not see features.

Incense was lit and Gregorian chants moaned from a recording that

Vicente had chosen. Estrella and Inma began to massage my feet and hands, but Vicente refused to help. He sat up with his arms folded across his chest, complaining: "You can't/expect/me/to do that ... I'm not/a pooftah you know!" Provoking a guffaw from Estrella.

Francisco had fallen asleep.

"It's fine," whispered Inma: "He doesn't snore."

Tomás himself concentrated on my forehead, mesmerised for an instant by my scar. Then he dripped oil onto it, rubbing in a clockwise direction. His intention was to stimulate what was left of my atrophied pineal gland or what he called *the third eye*. His tremulous reasoning: "This is ... err ... is a remnant, of something primitive ... used to be a s-sensory organ, a key to the psyche, grown obsolete with evolution. Now a third eye would be a dis-advantage, like schizo-phrenia is. But, although the third eye has vanished, the nerves still exist, and can be activated through mas-sage. It re-opens a door. The door linking us to the in-finite." All pure theory. He had never conducted the experiment before. But, amidst the Gregorian drones the girls rubbed and he moaned soft instructions: "Re-lax ... relax your shoulders ... your knees, ankles, feet ... f-f-f-feel your body becoming heavy ... heavier," he insisted: "Re-lax ... You are air ... but your body is heavy, oh so heavy ... and you ... you are oh so light ... like a f-feather."

What he had really expected I do not know, but instead of a sense of satisfaction he was given an abrupt shock as I came excitedly out of my trance, gasping, clenching his arm and proclaiming what I called, in my excitement, a *miracle*.

The initial sensation had been wonderful. I had felt my *self* floating, approaching the ceiling, then hovering there. I had tried to turn and rolled over a few times. As I did there had been the shock of seeing my own body below me, still on the floor, eyes open and staring back up at me on the ceiling. Tomás and the girls were around it, rubbing. And I saw it all with incredible clarity, even without my glasses. It had been tremendous, inspiring a sharp electric snap and I became a rocketing rollercoaster tripper, dipping through long, fluorescent, rainbow rods of irradiation that flashed past an otherwise blurred and dimmed universe. Dimming universe, dimming into blackness. A sticky pitch slowed me, tugging me into it to envelop and immobilise me with its consistency. All was black. I tried to move but, without a point of reference there can be no movement. I, the subject, was fixed, still. Only my thoughts were able to confirm my existence, but even they became clogged, as if anaesthetised, inspiring a restrained paraplegia-panic: the agony of the coma-victim again, aware of his void-bound condition, in the hell-space of nothingness – *if there is nothing to perceive, why am I here?* – The anguished question received an immediate response. A physical response, if that can make any sense in a non-physical world. It was as if some swift Mercury god's hand shot into the mire and tugged me free. There was a tremendous gush which filled my *out-of-body-ears* with cat whining cries over a general breaking-surf sea-gush – *did I use to live by the sea? Is it taking me back to where I come from?* – In any case I felt that I were being lead somewhere *important*, that it really was a winged god or angel that had me, dragging me toward a distant, end of the tunnel light. A swelling circle, becoming blinding bright then dulling as it grew massive. Reds and yellows melting into oranges and browns, sharpened by shadows and more variegation, into images. Forms. Objects. Furniture, I realised.

The tugging god left me – *in a room* – I told myself – *my home?* – I wondered – *Am I home?* –

The prospect calmed me. The warm orange light emanated from a flaming hearth. This was covered by something metallic. A black web – *a grill* – There was a metal rod lying before it – *a poker* – rolling through grey powder – *through ash* – rolling as if blown by a fierce wind – *impossible, if there were such a wind in the house, it would have blown the fire all over the place* – The poker's tip near the flames was glowing red. I looked up. Above the black grill was a large black iron pot, swaying vigorously on a metal chain – *could this be my mother's kitchen?* – A popping staccato, then a scuffling undercurrent. Animated figures. Life-forms. Small, brown, bear-like creatures. Not animals, too dextrous, they had to be human – *two of them* – I realised – *could one be my mother?* – No, they were both men – *Strange men* – I thought at first. Oddly dressed. Long hair poked out like straw from under pointed leather caps. Long robes, worn open at the front, wafted audibly over the wooden floor.

Billowing shirts underneath, tucked into brown-red tights. Stockinged legs that ran down to pointed, soft leather slippers – *like medieval wizards* – whose activity was also strange. They were busily throwing balls of what looked like horse manure onto the fire – *this cannot be home* - When the lumps ignited, the water in the pot began to boil – *not home, but where?* –

The men's clothes gave clues, but more precise information came from the barrels.

Barrels with dates stamped onto them. They were all roughly marked the same – *1526, 1527* – It was no ordinary kitchen. The swaying and sliding objects indicated a tilt from right to left and left to right – *a ship* – I passed through walls, flittered out from the kitchen, that we should probably call a galley, to a tiny space: a cabin. A book was open on a table. Its pages splattered with black, nebula dots of dripped ink, decorating flourishes of data scribed in antiquated Spanish. It was difficult to decipher, but it was not my first experience of such calligraphy. The book was a log, I realised. I found entries describing position: "... off the east coast of the *Java Maior,*" – *The Great Java* – and I knew, from my own research, what that meant. Translated into modern terms, the ship was sailing in the Pacific Ocean, to the north-east of New Guinea.

The space changed again. I was wrenched out onto the deck. There was a purple dawn. A man was emerging from the hull and clambering up to the poop. On top, stretching the clicking joints of his arms and yawning through a massive full beard, he groaned and complained that his breakfast had not been brought to him in his cabin.

Another haggard creature, lying on the deck, craned his neck up to look lazily: "Mornin', Captain," he groaned, before his head sank back to floorboards.

The captain sniffed and grimaced – *a stench of alcohol* – I deduced. Empty bottles were strewn over the deck and snoring seamen were collapsed under the fading stars.

Then there was a wooden thump, followed by a succession of clomps. A man running. Filthy bare feet. White shirt open. Filthy bare chest. He jumped onto a ladder and pulled himself monkey-like up. When his chin drew level with the captain's toes, he strained his neck and looked up into the captain's beard. Panting.

The captain pushed his own chin into his neck: "Well, Cook! There ye are! And, where's me breakfast then?" Muffled by constriction the voice sounded ominous.

The man at his boots gulped: "Cap'ain..." and gasped: "There's somethin' yer should know. Sometin' to see ... come ..." then clambered, baboon-like down.

The captain pouted, pulled a black cloak around himself and followed.

In the galley again; the fire in the stove had burned down to a blanket of smouldering embers. The captain looked phantom-like. Blue wisps of smoke curled. He stared through me, his gaze pensive, but electric, and shuddered. Instinctively I turned and saw what had surprised him. He was looking into the hearth. Something was wriggling under the ashes. A lizard thing. It crept out and scurried away. But he did not watch where it went, he was startled by something else. The cook went straight to it. He put on a leather glove and reached right in, digging his fingernails under. A metal plate. He peeled it out. One large round piece. Wafer thin, but under the grey veneer of ash, there was ... gold.

On top, a sailor, coughing himself into consciousness, sprang up and carried himself convulsively forward to vomit overboard. An arch of lumpy bile splattered onto the sea and became fish food ...

The captain was now back in his cabin, sitting on a low stool, scratching his beard. Four other men were squeezed together in a huddle in front of him. The cook was also there, standing nervously under the low ceiling in a corner, gripping a tangled bundle of linen. The captain made signs to him, indicating the removal of the white sheet to unfurl the golden disk. His finger jolted up, commanding the disk to be lifted and leaned against the wall. Once erected the officers and navigators stood back and contemplated it in a bewildered silence ...

On the poop above, the steersman gazed out over the gloomy sea. Radiant Venus was low over the silver line of the horizon, much brighter than dull Mercury to its left. He rang the bell. The rest of the crew stirred.

Dirty hands on the ends of hairy arms, scooped water from barrels, splashing gaunt faces.

Exposing themselves to the morning sea air, they evacuated litres of renal streams overboard.

They looked sheepish. Someone timidly admitted to having drunk an entire week's ration.

It had been a long and animated celebration, thought to have been well justified. They had spent months visiting strange islands in uncharted waters that they had grown miserably sick of, and now it was time to head for home.

Home. After a profitable mission; their hold was brimming with exotic spices. Each sailor would receive his due share.

But, despite the occasion, their revelling had reached ridiculous extremes and the captain would be furious. The day's work would be made doubly intense; quadrupled by their throbbing, churning hangovers.

No one had an inkling of their commander's real obsession ...

The captain scraped away slag with his staff. The other men in the cabin squinted and swallowed hard.

That wafer thin veneer certainly looked like gold. The captain ordered the cook to lift it while he ran the tip of his pole over it. The others leaned forward to make out the complex pattern of squiggles on the surface of the plate.

"'Prodigious," the captain hissed.

The others looked nervously around. I caught a glimpse of their minds, each one asking himself where such a treasure could have come from. They had not boarded any ships, and there had been no palaces or temples on the islands they had plundered ... or not as far as they knew.

The captain encouraged the cook to explain: "Where did it come from, whelp? Out with it!"

The cook wiped his dripping nose with a dirty hand, then sniffled: "From the oven, Cap'ain." But it only made the others more perplexed.

The captain, elaborated: "It was forged," then, struggling for an adequate adjective: "...fortuitously," the word being strong enough to open the captain's face into a wide grin. When he realised that the others were still bewildered he gesticulated with his staff: "Heat has smelted minerals separating precious stone from the mundane clay on the bottom of our ship's oven," inspired enough to come to a sublime conclusion: "An accident, nay, pray señores, a miracle."

The others scratched chins or testicles, trying to grasp the real basis of so much passion. Until, dismayed by the glory, they demanded a more pragmatic explanation: "How, Captain?"

But instead of replying the commander added another question: "Where did the mud for our clay stove come from?"

Simplicity made everyone more comfortable: "From the islands?"

Then the cook, grinning huge and scratching his already red neck: "I raked most of it me'self, señor. Off the bottom of the river running into the south of the bay."

"The islands ..." it was a retarded bellow. The captain was now ecstatic and he began poking his staff, as if to indicate directions: "We have just left a place where rivers are encrusted with precious metals. And not ordinary nuggets. Heed these markings, señores ..."

I would have groaned if I had had substance. The squiggles were similar, perhaps the same as those on Estrella's little ring ...

"This is a special, *spiritual* treasure," whispered the captain through clenched teeth: "We have been to the legendary lands once mined by King Solomon himself. We have been to Ophir!"

Madness ...

"Or time travelling!"

Inma excitedly threw the fantastical proposal in, as soon as I had finished my description. Tomás assumed she must have been inspired by the wine.

"Yes," she said: "The wine. Or no! ... What does it matter what inspired me!? No, his accounts are really so much like something Estrella was working on in her thesis." Estrella sat up, but said nothing - if it was in her thesis, then Inma would have to explain it: "Dream consciousness and time," Inma pleaded: "Or rather, the idea that dream consciousness exists in a space outside of time."

"Is what you are ... s-s-suggesting ... that ... in our dreams we have the capacity to time travel?"

"That is what is suggested by Estrella's thesis, yes. What you have provoked, Tomás, is a kind of lucid dream, a conscious entry into the subconscious, which makes a consciously perceived experience of time travel possible. In a normal dream we can't control the moment that we are in, but Valentín's *lucid dream* experience was controlled and framed in time, even though he was out of time. It was controlled and framed in a time and place in the past."

Vicente laughed: "In time/out of time/That's a good one."

The idea made Tomás thoughtful. He reached into a bowl of sunflower seeds. Cracking shells and scooping out seeds with his tongue.

Inma went on: "In time, out of time, yes. He has been allowed to enter an impossible world, and, in a sense, while he was out of his body he was also existing *outside* time itself."

Estrella had a different hypothesis. Explained simply: "It sounds like he's describing a past-life regression. Don't you think so Tomás?"

He nodded, though he was looking down at the sunflower seeds in the palms of his hands, resting in his lap.

She continued: "The hypnosis has dug up Valentín's past incarnation. Someone who had once been on that ship."

Vicente chortled sarcastically.

Inma protested verbally, but gently: "Had he? But if he had who was he?" and the two women exchanged smiles - *knowing* smiles I think they say.

Estrella gave a resigned nod and Inma turned to me: "I mean if you had been someone you would have had the point-of-view of the past incarnation, but yours was a fly-on-the-wall's perspective. Let me stick to my original postulate: you time-travelled in a lucid dream."

I straightened my glasses and scratched my chin, unsure what to think. Then Francisco suddenly came out of his sleep, and began a slurred shouting: "Down with the *Caudillo*! Death to Franco!"

Inma hugged him. Pressed his ear to her heart. He smiled, then suddenly fell unconscious again, his head drooping and dropping off her breast.

It made us all laugh, except Tomás. He was still stewing over what had been said.

Then, spitting shell segments into a bowl: "But ladies ..." he spluttered:

"Why do you assume ... that ... that he really did *ex-perience* this other past t-time ... Ex-perienced or imagined it? ... it's not quite the s-same I'm afraid," and he laughed, spitting out more shell, pouring himself more wine: "He says himself that it was as if he had returned to the books he had been r-reading in the library," and he held out the palms of his hands, expressing irrefutability: "Otherwise please tell me," he said turning to me: "T-tell me where you went ... where you think you were!"

"I have told it," I insisted: "The Pacific, yes ...1520 something ... yes."

"On a sh-ship ... heading from New Guinea going eastward!"

"Yes," I confirmed.

"You just happened to find a sh-ship ... a Sp-panish ship ... in un-explored waters ... in an un-known part of the world!"

We were getting angry. Shouting. Estrella hushed us: "Quiet down, please. Before some snitching neighbour has the Guardia Civil around."

Tomás remained tense. Even if he accepted the historical possibility of what I had seen, and allowed for the notion of lucid-dream time-travel, he could not rationalise my account of a veneer accidentally forged in gold and bearing a Solomonic inscription identical to the one on Estrella's finger: "A purely symbolic manifestation, from the s-s-subconscious ... what F-Freud would have called *latent con-tent* ... or repressed wishes, if you like," and gave me a *knowing* and *accusing* look: "...un- .... err ... absolutely un-real."

I began to give in, taking it seriously was madness and I recalled my *visitors* whilst I'd been in the hospital. The doctors had called me *mad*, and I didn't want to be mad again. To explain myself to my new friends, I needed to tell them my story. This brought the detail of my amnesia out, as well as the other neurological problems my brain damage had caused. When I admitted to having suffered epileptic fits, Tomás was furious.

"Do you realise w-w-what we have been p-p-playing with? The consequences could have been i-i-i-irreparable," he shouted and, wrenching his coat from Inma, literally walked out of the argument.

Of course he never submitted to conducting any further experiments. And everything would have ended there, but ...

*   *   *

The coincidental events of the following days seemed uncanny. The next evening, I was sitting, waiting for Estrella in a café opposite the Academy. I had made a point of forgetting the experience of the night before and passed the time watching girls walk by, comparing them to the image I had of Estrella. I was considering *beauty* because I had asked myself why Estrella seemed beautiful to me. In those days, meanings of concepts were still problematic – *What is the meaning of meaning?* – I often asked myself, as well as other futile questions. But they seemed less futile than worrying about the strange vision I had had from Estrella's living room floor. When Estrella eventually arrived at the café, she came striding in, as beautiful as I had been imagining her, and exuberant. A slip of paper dangled from her fingers. This was the programme outlining the evenings activities at the Academy. She stopped in front of me, standing, holding the programme up in front of my face: "Read," she said.

I did. The doyen, Dr Hilario de Coca, was announced to be delivering a lecture at nine o'clock. The title: *Pacific Gold: sailors' myths from the time of the Austrian Kings.*

"The time of the Austrians, beginning with Emperor Carlos V. The 1520s. Pacific gold. Exactly what you saw."

I shrugged my shoulders: "If it must be said so," with apathetic aridity. I did not care. I was thinking about the absolute treasure that she was, nothing else.

Estrella sat down. A silent change of plane. Eyelashes brushing the edges of her fringe. Electric intense eyes.

She was not going to leave the night before alone: "What you experienced was fantastic."

I shrugged shoulders again: "But impossible to be proven."

This made her squint, expressing a painful thought. Her voice squeaked: "Why?" and she gave a frustrated sigh and stood up again, holding her hand out to me: "Let's go to the lecture... I've got a funny feeling it's going to be very interesting."

I ignored the hand and pushed my glasses back up the bridge of my nose: "Interesting? Why should it be considered interesting? Has it been deduced by you that the existence of a mystery ship that discovered King Solomon's mines in the Pacific in the 1520s will be confirmed by Dr de Coca?"

"No, of course not. But you're still writing your thesis, aren't you? And I'm writing mine. Or have you forgotten about that?"

The implicit accusation stung me, forcing a stutter: "N-n-no ... But it's d-de Coca ... Was I not told ... by you ... that de Coca was a lung specialist."

This made her laugh: "Yes, he's a trained doctor. But as far as I know he prefers to spend his time on the humanities. History is a hobby for him, yet I don't think that we should presume from that he'll have nothing interesting to say."

I shook my head: "Yet it was pronounced ... by you yourself ... that he was considered to be ... an *arsehole*."

"And he is ... a huge arsehole. But, who knows? He might actually be able to shed some light." And she grabbed the lapel of my jacket and pulled me up. I had no choice I realised. I gulped down my beer and followed her.

There were about a dozen people in the main lecture room, which meant that it was almost empty.

Dr de Coca had already begun when we stumbled in. His shiny head just came over the lectern. It tilted up and he acknowledged our arrival with a bitter glare.

We bumbled apologetically but also noisily into the centre of one of the back rows. I crossed my legs and arms and unashamedly studied the time on my watch. I was expecting nothing more than an inane session, but it soon became clear that that orator was not the same de Coca I had elbowed at the party.

The initial image I had had of him was of someone who exuded rather than expressed and he had seemed unguent and unsavoury. But at the pedestal that porous nature closed, his oiliness dried, solidified and he became marble. His movement as a speaker was minimal, and the power of his gestures were enhanced by that concision. The gesticulations were elaborated by the right-hand only, while the left remained tightly trapped in a trouser pocket. Arm and eye were co-ordinated, his gaze fierce. When he caught an audience member's glance his flashing orbs were unflinching gateways to a disconcerting inner authority and no one could return his stare for long. The speech engrossed, although his voice was dry at times, overly affected at others, and it was his calculated use of the pause which enriched his delivery to give it real expression and drama. He would raise an arm like a symphony conductor and freeze, filling his soul with cold emotion that would chill us.

Of course my reaction must have been tainted by my own affinity to his themes. I was soon able to appreciate how much extensive research the lung doctor had carried out. And he had uncovered material which was quite bewildering.

But it also struck me then that no one there would have understood what de Coca was telling us as well as I did. My head began to nod along with his affirmations. At times I had to clap his conclusions, at others moan a discrepancy, but I was always totally involved. I dragged out a pocket book and began scribbling. There was a particularly thorny point about the explorer Torres that I wanted to debate with him, but he did not invite questions at the end.

We applauded enthusiastically and Estrella dragged me up to the doyen, but De Coca did not remember me and I had to be presented again, the new introduction being appended with details about our shared affinity. His eyelids drooped and he seemed to become oily again, obviously contemplating a forthcoming, unsavoury request: "So you would like to pick my brain, would you?"

I opened my mouth with the intention of expressing my point about Torres, but before I could get a syllable out Estrella had leapt ahead with her own answer to his question.

"Yes," she confessed: "In a sense." I felt a rush of anxiety and shook my head, but Estrella continued: "Valentín has been researching this field for many years," which relieved me, but then she suddenly went on a totally unexpected tack and began excitedly blurting out the story of our experiment in hypnosis with Tomás.

I couldn't believe that she was doing such an inane thing. It sounded even more foolish when she was telling it. What interest would this *doctor-historian* have in such a fantasy? I protested, but de Coca did not flinch: "No, please, let her go on," he said wiping sweat from his brow onto an already grey handkerchief: "This is most interesting. Astral travel you say. Through time."

Estrella nodded: "Well, lucid-dreaming time-travel actually. To the sixteenth century. To the Pacific," she insisted.

As she did Dr de Coca's mouth curled into a smirk and I expected cruel sarcasm or bitter scorn, but instead he rubbed his chin: "Have you been able to ascertain accuracy?"

"Not exactly," she confessed.

"Not at all," I murmured.

Estrella hurled in over the top of me again, drowning me out: "It's difficult. But we want to try. It'll take time of course ... patience."

Dr de Coca extended his arm and lay the same hand on my shoulder. This he rubbed, then patted: "Patience, yes. I can understand your anguish. Perfectly natural. But you must be encouraged, it's so easy to dismiss incredible ideas. All great ideas were incredible to begin with. Let's not begin cynically," and as he said this his head jerked back and his eyes rolled.

I did not know what to think. Was he saying that to be kind?

A man in overalls came in to clear up and switch off the lights.

Dr de Coca caught his breath: "Wouldn't it be better if we continued this conversation in a more private place? But not now, there are things I must do. Tomorrow perhaps, come to my office." And we nodded.

That office was windowless and dark. There was black furniture and a deep burgundy carpet on the floor. Soft light from a table lamp on his desk was the only source of illumination. The walls had been adorned with a Spanish flag and three pictures: a humourless Franco, a portrait of a suffering Christ with a grizzly crown of bloodied thorns, and one of Salvador Dalí's more catholic compositions. De Coca beckoned us to sit down and poured a whisky for me without asking if I had wanted it. Estrella coughed. He turned to her: "You don't drink scotch, do you?"

She puckered her lips: "Well I do actually."

He poured another glass. She stood up and snatched it out of his hand. It was the first time I had seen Estrella get upset so quickly. Strange, after all, we were there because of her enthusiasm. If she was angry why did we stay? The realisation made me feel fidgety. Dr de Coca poured his own drink then sat behind the desk in front of us, as if to interview us for a job, or interview me. It became obvious that he was ignoring Estrella. His voice, however, was languid: "So you are working on the explorers as well. Which ones in particular?"

I took a deep breath: "Mendaña and Quirós ... Torres."

He scratched his bottom lip: "Such an interesting time, and sad, sometimes it makes me so sad ... (*I kept nodding though I did not know why*) ... with a little bit more imagination our forefathers would have had another continent."

"More imagination and more money," Estrella rectified.

De Coca gave her a long, hard and aggressive stare. Then he turned back to me. Softening: "What do you think about Sarmiento de Gamboa?"

The directness of the unexpected question made me nervous, but I did know a little: "It's believed, by some, that the Pacific attempts were instigated by ... by him, but I don't think so."

"No?!" the interruption was savage. I became unsettled.

"N-no ... err ... that myth was spread by himself."

"Was it? And you are sure it was a myth?" I squirmed. He was unrelenting: "What if I were to tell you that I've uncovered information indicating that Pedro Sarmiento de Gamboa really did have an accurate map; that he really did know where he was going. That in fact he was the only one who did. What would you say to that then?" which left me stammering until he suddenly twisted the subject: "This man who hypnotised you ..."

"Tomás Puigsegur," blurted Estrella.

"Tomás Puigsegur ... umm ... and he's a member of the Academy?"

I looked at Estrella. She nodded. I nodded. De Coca rubbed his thumbs together: "This is very interesting."

I was anxious for an opinion: "So it is believed by you, that what I saw was real?"

He closed his eyes: "Well I've been thinking carefully about what you told me yesterday. It's the first time I've heard such a thing."

He was insinuating a complete change of face. My spirits sank. Estrella seemed to sense it too, she lurched in: "But yesterday you indicated that you thought the possibility of astral travel was feasible. Have you changed your mind?"

De Coca snorted: "Oh, it's a very subjective phenomenon. All I can say is that if we assume that your experience is real, then it could be of great value to our common cause. There are many troubling details that might be uncovered. Of course we cannot prove them, but is that important?"

Then he became sticky: "The control of the future depends on our discovering the past." He frowned: "Let me give you time to think about it. How's your research financed?"

"I've been given a grant," I said: "For a year."

"Which must be half-expired," he insisted. I nodded. Estrella was shaking her head; she knew what was coming. De Coca scratched his nose: "I could probably provide funds for you, if you agree to make an alliance on this. Share information. That's what you want, isn't it?"

I kept nodding: "And it will be allowed for the documents to be seen by me ... the documents it was said you had about Sarmiento de Gamboa?"

He grinned: "Oh yes, of course," and then his dull eyes seemed to brighten: "*Give forth thy light to all, without doubt.*"

When we left, night time, collars up, walking into a freezing wind down a damp wide street to the Metro station, Estrella was fuming: "What a mendacious man," I had to trot along to keep up with her. She kept yanking at the strap of her bag to stop it slipping off her shoulder: "He thinks he can buy us, as if we were prostitutes." I hung my head. It sounded so terrible now. Then she suddenly stopped and grabbed the lapels of my coat to stop me. Her lips were determined-stiff: "He's going to take this from us, if we're not quick." Which I didn't really understand. I must have had an imbecile grin. She shook me: "We've got to do it!" I shrugged – *Do what?* – She read my mind: "We've got to repeat the experiment, just as de Coca suggested. But without Dr de Coca." The madness again. I shook my head. But she insisted: "If Dr de Coca thinks this is worth pursuing then I think it's worth pursuing. He's an arsehole, but he doesn't waste his time. He really thinks you're on to something, that's why he's offering you money. Let's look for ourselves, Val. Ourselves," and she reached up, around my neck, pulled me down to her, lifted my glasses and pushed her lips against mine to give me a deep kiss. I almost collapsed – instinctively reaching for her breast to hold me up. She pulled away to an arm's length, still holding my hands, shaking her head: "Not here," she said: "Let's go to my place."

III. Lifting the Veil

Estrella was frowning impatient. Breakfast was already prepared. She had created a work plan: "The library opens at nine o'clock."

"A *f-fascist* design," I whined, blowing steam from my coffee.

She had a mouthful of cake and had to keep her lips tight shut while burping a kind of retarded laugh. When she had swallowed she pulled a comically serious face and put on a pompous, politician's voice: "Well, if there's a strike or something and it's closed when we get there ... (*eyebrow arching*) then we'll go to a café ... (*thrusting a statesman's finger in the air*) and have vermouth in long glasses."

I remembered her naked, standing in front of the bed again: "And at night?"

"At night you travel," which must have made me look disappointed. She seemed to register this and her own face stiffened into something angry, yet only for an instant before melting and squeezing into a coquettish pucker and she blew air across the scar down my cheek.

We began enthusiastically, but fascist's plans never really work. The breaks with crimson red vermouth, paling on thawing ice, became longer and longer, and research and writing dwindled.

As for our so-called experiments in the timeless dimension of lucid dreams, usually we went to Estrella's little flat rather than my tiny one because she had room enough for me to lie on the floor. Me, supine on her rug. She, kneeling over me, kneading. Prodding fingers running over my temples and around the furrowed space between scars on my forehead. Circling before attacking my pineal gland centre: "Relax," she would murmur, and squeeze a groan out of me.

Objects were secretly planted, goals for my astral body to seek out and identify. At first we used playing cards, although our imaginations were very quickly inspired into more pleasurable realms, and we started to give each hidden item a sexual or drug orientated connotation. The experiments became a game, or a foreplay ritual, yet successful, and my intrepid astral searches for Estrella's underwear did enable us to affirm an out-of-body movement through *space*. But repeating the excision into the past was far more difficult.

Estrella had an ice cube between her teeth that she was running over my bare belly when she mumbled a denouncement of my lack of faith: "You're questioning your own possibilities," then after crunching the ice: "Why?"

I thought she was joking: "My mind is made to think, but when thought is evoked Tomás Puigsegur appears, umming and ahhing and spitting out sun-flower seed shells."

So Estrella changed our strategy: "Think small. Just take little hops."

In order to do this, I tried to whirl my astral body around itself, holding my head down and flicking my feet over me. In this way I could flitter back a few hours, then a few days, but keeping to the same space, Estrella's flat.

Nevertheless, it was impossible to determine if such observation was real.

I could bring nothing back, merely observe. If one goes into the future one can say: *I saw you do such and such,* and time will confirm it, but if I say: *I saw you did such and such last night,* you will think I am talking about a memory.

Blind faith alone maintained our indagations, until my Ferris wheel propulsion was thrown off its axis and I felt myself being tugged into another space, Inma's flat, where I had never been, and where I saw a concrete, personal scene between Estrella and Inma that had never been revealed to me.

I could perfectly describe the room I had never been to. Inma was sitting at a table. There was a candlelit dinner. Plates, empty, but dirty, and a bottle of wine, also empty. Inma was standing, at times she began pacing. Estrella took a long, last suck on a fat cigarette before extinguishing the stub on one of the plates. Tears were rolling down her cheeks, but she was not *crying*. However, she sniffled before she spoke: "Why should I feel this remorse you talk about, for someone who has escaped?"

Inma whimpered. Then: "No Estrella, the word is *dead*. You have to face that. It's normal to cry. Normal. Good. It's good for you; necessary. Necessary for the soul."

"Yes, you're an expert on the soul, aren't you?"

"Please Estrella, don't be sarcastic with me. You have no right. You wouldn't be here if it wasn't for me."

"Not tonight. I invited myself."

"Do you want to go?"

"Yes ... No ... Let's talk about something else. My father's dead. OK, he's dead. And I want to forget him."

"Have you been writing?"

"Yes."

"Read me something."

Estrella was visibly embarrassed when I recounted this. She confirmed it. Or what she could remember of it. Her father had died of a cancer almost a year before and the conversation was vaguely familiar to her. Yet I never told her about the rest of my observation. That I had stayed while she began one of her poems, listened and watched how she choked half way through the recital. I did not remind her of how Inma had leaned forward and embraced her, nor say how I had watched her run a hand through Inma's long, red hair; how Inma had stroked her cheeks, her temples, her brow; how she had taken a handkerchief and dried the tears from Estrella's face, and kissed her: a deep, passionate kiss ...

Perhaps it was jealousy or a fear of treading too roughly on her private world that prevented me from revealing that part of the vision. Or perhaps I really enjoyed having this secret information. Nevertheless, I think I wanted Estrella to feel comfortable in every way.

Then the real heat came.

Madrid: a furnace in summer.

At home the fridge was an imperative. Beer and chilled gazpacho, electric or handheld fans and cold showers kept our blood from boiling. But heat and failure also made us even more apathetic, and the experiments practically stopped. We had made no more real progress and it seemed unlikely that we ever would.

Until Inma suddenly became involved, appearing on one of the hottest nights I can remember.

Estrella and I were lying naked on a humid mattress on the floor. Our hearts seemed to pump oxygen instead of blood, stifling the throat. A red scarf was draped over a table lamp, scorching the white wall and drowning our skin and minds in sensual light. When the knock came Estrella picked herself slowly and groggily up. I straightened my glasses to sharpen the image, fast enough to catch her small breasts wobble then suddenly disappear beneath the short, sky blue satin robe that was wrapped over them. This whispered as she tied it, nicely tight and its hem crept up. Just high enough to reveal curving grey shadow lines, mesmerizingly distorted as she tiptoed to the door.

Inma was in a white cotton dress that was drooping damp, its light nature heavy with sweat. The suitcase at her toes revealed intentions. She slid it forward with her foot. Claiming the flat.

No excuse for being there was proffered other than she wanted to be with us, but Estrella told me later that she had been quarrelling with her boyfriend, Francisco. Estrella never said *yes* to her, but after sharing cheek kissing greetings Inma went straight to the couch. Her usually pretty face was drawn. Grey-black smudges under each eye.

Estrella fetched her a drink. A small bottle of beer. Inma emptied it in four silent gulps. Then she opened her case and unpacked a long, salmon pink, satin cloth. As she unfurled it she looked down at me on the floor, running her gaze along the flimsy sheet that covered me to confirm my nakedness with a knowing smile. Then, suddenly lifting her own dress over her head, she began to wrap herself up in the satin.

"A sari," she sighed while smoothing out creases. Estrella sat down on the sofa next to her and rubbed it against her own mustard cheek. Inma explained that she had spent the spring studying *yoga* and preached its virtues: "It's changed me...," and then: "It could change you as well."

Estrella clutched her own oriental robe self-sufficiently and sniggered:

"Please Inma, no evangelism. Not if you really want to stay."

The sari woman laughed and draped more cloth over her fire-red hair: "No, no evangelism. I've come here to work," which was the last thing I wanted to do just then, but Inma was adamant. Her nostrils dilated and her voice dropped. She ran her toe over the hairs on my arm: "Yoga: a discipline designed for escaping the illusion of time."

I stretched myself out on the mattress: "How?"

"First by controlling the continuity of moments," and she unwrapped the sari. Her skin was nicely tanned and damp, gleaming softly in the lamp light. Her body was thinner than I had estimated, but not too thin. She sucked air up, tightening her diaphragm, flattening her stomach and inflating her chest. She straightened her back, her breasts rising firm, and she pulled her feet up onto the couch to cross them in front of her, her wrists resting loosely on her knees, slowing her breathing while mine increased. I was meditating on differences, losing myself in the chore of comparison, when my hardening penis suddenly prodded the sheet up. Inma laughed: "The first thing you must learn is how to control that," and took my breath away with a hard ambiguous stare. The rest of what she said seemed to be transmitted telepathically. I cannot remember her lips moving: "This technique must be developed until your breathing becomes part of the inhaling and exhaling of the great cosmic cycle itself. Dedication and discipline, the idea is to make your breathing rhythmical." I told her that I thought that breathing *was* rhythmical and she shook her head. Her long, red hair flicking across her face: "Not usually. What we intend to do, is organise the chaos so that the circulation of the psycho-mental forces is no longer anarchic. By working this way on our breathing we are working directly on our own experience of time. Let each breath be longer, deeper, slowing your rhythm gradually down, allowing the gap between inhaling and exhaling grow longer each time."

This then flowed into a series of strenuous stretching exercises that left me sitting upright with my legs crossed and my wrists resting on my knees. My penis was flaccid again at last, and it was at that moment that Inma and Estrella came alongside me, all fingers and air, rubbing a sweet smelling hot ointment on my forehead; blowing a series of soft sounds: "Sahh ... ahhh .... sahh .... ahhh ... ar ... miento ..." Until I gradually understood that it was a word, his name: "Sarmiento ..." which became:

"Sarmiento de Gamboa ... Pedro Sarmiento de Gamboa ..." and I realised that Inma had got her way. She was making me work, and I was gone.

I dropped away into the pitch space behind my eyes until I was buoyant in a starless night sky, just like I had been before, without points of reference, infinite and devoid of force. Eventually the invisible winged-god's hand came again, snatching and shoving me about into an upright position. The blackness brightened, not much, but instead of pitch it became murky, until there were traces of real light: a cloud shrouded moon's beam coming in through an open French window. A breeze, curtains fluttered. The light hit the floor then curled over a bed. There was a bulge under a sheet from which came a breath, a slight snore, this mingling with an exterior symphony: frogs, crickets. A warm night, but not as hot as the one I had come from. A cockerel was crowing, despite the darkness. I moved to the window and stepped onto a balcony two storeys up. It overlooked a street running down to a square. A long-haired rat, huge, scurried along the lane. Otherwise there was stillness, maintained for some time, until a shrill human whistle, out of nowhere, echoed. This announced a chorus: a clip-clop-clopping accompanied by a tonk-conk-clonking of bells. A goatherd taking his flock out. A bucolic orchestration that faded, replaced by the louder, uglier disturbance of a rattling, thumping wooden cart. This bounced, shook, creaked. Then the machine suddenly burst into the square and there was a tremendous reverberation created by the open space, until the cart had crossed, drawing to a halt at the end of the lane. Cessation of movement outside seemed to inspire interior action, and the lump under the sheet in the bed suddenly sprang up.

The moonlight sliced one side of a face. It was a man's face: one wide-open, startled eye. He took a deep breath and held it, listening carefully. One of the animals pulling the cart snorted, but otherwise the town remained still and silent.

Quiescence calmed him and he slipped back under the sheet. I approached and hovered over him. Still too dark to distinguish anything, but another gravity dragged me down, a new darkness suddenly opening below me. I assumed that Estrella and Inma had sent me there. I heard their voices again.

"Down ... Down ..."

Then that sweet sound became something else, something masculine. Harsh and hasty phrases ran over and into each other like the ramblings of an excited mind. A new light illuminated the darkness, defining a new space slowly filling with figures.

The first prominent image: a ghostly pallid woman's face was glowing out of a frame of fire-red hair – *Inma!* – I thought.

She was up on bare, white feet and standing still in a long, cream, linen nightshirt. There was a tie at the neck, she undid it solemnly. I tried to speak to her. She sensed it and put a finger to her lips. Her chest heaved, tiny breasts, still a girl – *not the Inma I knew* –

She whimpered. Her little green eyes were red and moist. There were tears as she began to peel off her smock: vanilla ice shoulders, protruding collarbone, frail ... but these suddenly thickened, became fleshy, stronger.

The red hair had darkened, the pale skin was tanned and fattened and her face was transformed also, achieving bigger, rounder, happier features. The frock fell to the floor. She now had large, heavy breasts and round thighs.

She kicked the garment from her ankles and stepped out, forward – *towards me* – I thought, then remembered where I was. It was towards *him*, towards *his* centre, towards *his* mind's eye.

It was not Inma, this was *his* mind, not mine.

She wiggled her hips and grinned. A gap had spread between her teeth and I had the sensation of him running his tongue, a wet tongue, over her soft skin.

– *Payta! My darling* – his mind's voice sighed.

– *Payta, not Inma* – I realised. Then he – *Saliva and salt* – It was a groan.

He was imagining himself with his head trapped between Payta's thighs, staring up at her as he licked.

Her hair became algae; her clitoris a long clam's siphon snaking out from between black sea urchin spikes. Snaking, then hardening and becoming fatter, swelling into something else - *a penis* –

He looked up, beyond, to her shrivelling breasts, a metamorphosis that made his imagination chortle – *Ah! Dear Conde, Señor Viceroy* – he sighed – *My patron-whore is quite splendid today* –

The voice in his mind chortled and the vision exploded into an orgy. A nymph dancer approached, the transparent cloth of her gown hanging over bulging collarbones, falling over breasts and pubis. She pranced around to the twangs of a lute, dropped flower petals onto slowly bobbing heads that moved between open laps. The metamorphosed girl, now Count, stood up. A full fleshy body, with a fuller, fleshier, sagging belly that had been decorated with body paint. A body mural of alchemical and astrological symbols. The chest above it was also a full and flabby pair of little breasts. Flesh that drooped from rings of neck flab, upon which a pallid moon face shone amidst a curtain of frosty white hair, tickling his naked shoulders. A little grisly and pointed beard and thin moustache encircled his enormous toad-mouth grin, stretching his fat, pink cheeks. Arms passed a wine sack to him. He lifted it and his belly shook as he guzzled a splashing gush. Then he gasped and laughed while the scene became weightless, evaporating and elevating the rippling Count and his orgy into a starry sky.

The Jelly-Count, his arms spread with a splashing full chalice in one hand and a dripping slice of bread in the other, wheezed as a crimson line drew itself across his throat.

Next to him was another young woman: long, black hair, Asian eyes, honey coloured skin.

She bore the same red line across her neck, a thin slice, opening to reveal a pink gash as neck and head separated. Both heads, his and hers, were rising.

Then, a cacophony of shouting and banging as the sky filled with a multitude of still howling, severed heads. Screaming cannon balls were crashing in slow motion into a wooden wall that had suddenly risen up on the horizon.

Each head was a rubber ball bouncing back off the wall with a cry, and each new wave of heads came faster than the one preceding it. Dreadful constancy, hurtling balls of light.

Their screams were piercing, an unbearable blasting, bawling clangour, stroboscopic and dissonant. It made me dizzy. I wanted to get away, without knowing how.

I was starting to panic – but then... expulsed, as if vomited into a corner of the room, which was brighter now, so I could clearly see the man whose mind I had just possessed, hunched up on his bed, shattered by the nightmare and whimpering – *I had dreamt my way into his dream* – I realised.

The sun had risen. But he had his head turned, so I still could not see his face.

He stretched and prodded the mattress, reaching for someone. He rubbed his eyes and looked around, sighed, then mumbled: "Not enough from me. You had to go unto your other whore's bed ... Idiot!"

Dogs were barking outside. Murmuring men's voices coming from within the building. He slowly lifted himself, turned, leaned over and spat into a chamber pot on the floor. His face was visible at last. His stare fixed on the space where I was standing. I shuddered. He didn't flinch. He was looking right through me, to a crack in the wall.

Red faced. Long, reddish, wine coloured hair. Trimmed beard. Hair that concealed or mitigated the effects of scars.

The right side was particularly marked. Part of his cheek and temple had been burned. There was a stain, gleaming pink, as if polished, and creased into permanent blisters: some of them pimples, others vermiculate tracks going nowhere.

From that side he looked plastic, but even his warmer, left profile was disfigured. A deep furrow crossed his brow from the bridge of the nose, stretching sharply upward then slightly down again towards the ear, fading away at the temple.

Under the brow were his eyes: large, lazy, drooping lids. A long nose almost stroked his fleshy lips.

He grimaced. His body was stiff and reluctant to stretch itself. He pinched the skin over his ribs and groaned through obvious pain: "I warned you. Or perhaps you went there because I forbade it. Because I told you your cuckold temperament would destroy you. Did you think you needed to annihilate yourself in order to redeem yourself? Typical of you, sirrah."

He curled back onto the bed, pulling his nightshirt over his neck: "And the girl? What've we done? Oh, that this were but a sorry nightmare." The voice was whimsical: "And if you do not return, how'll I get my ship? Westward to Ophir," then wild again: "A pox on your cock, señor! I've been patient for a decade, whilst you! You cannot even wait a single evening. Can she be that beautiful in your eyes? Is your heart so riddled with the cholera in your creaking codpiece?! Damn you, señor! We're ruined!"

Westward … The search for King Solomon's Mines – *It had to be him* –

"If the experiment works. I can still save you, but the uttermost patience is required."

Experiment? He looked down from the bed. A light, sky blue fabric was crumpled on the floor. He sat up and reached for it, lifted and stroked its silky smooth texture before draping it mournfully over his head. Then he stood up and the scarf, bleached pale by the moonlight, made his sleepy advance theatrical, like an apparition.

He went to a table cluttered with cards and crumbs, an upturned glass and a little, metal box. Sitting his bare arse on a short stool, he pried open the tiny case. A silver tinderbox. He struck a light from it, setting it to a candle. The stiff, black wick took the teardrop flame. This elongated into a rising, gold fulguration, illuminating a mirror lying there that I had not noticed at first. This took the light and the forms it revealed as its own.

When he saw himself reflected in the flat instrument his hand went for it, fingers clamping its rim to lift it. His wrist twisted and the mirror twisted. Angle shifted the image, panning down from the shawl over a claret coloured fringe to his face. As he did, he began nervously patting the mantle he had collocated there. Unhappily placed it seemed. He frowned and grimaced while his fingers made a gathering fist to yank it off.

Then there was a pause. A drawn and tired face contemplated itself. He gasped, immediately reaching for the discarded fabric again, to drape it once more over his head only to rip it away again. Then he repeated the sequence. The rhythm gaining momentum, until it became frantic, climaxing when he squeezed the light shawl into a ball and made a particularly violent gesture with an obvious intention of hurling it out of the window.

But it had arched through the air no more than a metre before it suddenly unravelled and floated sadly down to the floor.

With the same vertebrae wrenching movement that had hurled the cloth, he wedged the mirror in his mouth, clamping the glass with his teeth, and growling over it. Breath, inspired condensation: "What devil's trick is this?" then flicked his head and spat the mirror out: "Now my magic does not work."

He began patting his face, pinching and pulling skin and beard, before crouching down on his knees and crawling on all fours to the mirror, now cracked. He stared at the distorted reflection, sighing and shaking his head. Glazed his eyes were – *Potions and exotic herbs* – I thought before glancing back into the drugged mind. A tremendous image came at me, gushing blood from an open, quivering vein. I leapt out again.

He sighed and stood up, then went to the French window and stepped onto the balcony. He squinted and put a hand over his grey brow to shade his eyes against the just risen, dazzling sun. There was a hustle and bustle as short, shadowy forms, a gaggle of honking geese, lumbered around a doorway below the balcony. They waddled around an upturned cart toward a mound of bulging Hessian sacks.

"Fie!" he shouted, muffled by a hand.

There was something within the pile, between the sacks. Naked limbs. Five were visible. Two people. Two hirsute man's arms. One girl's. One man's leg, one girl's, poking out, as were the heads. The girl was face down. Long, black and filthy hair. The man's head, propped up by one of the sacks, stared straight up at the balcony. Wide open eyes almost popped out of their sockets. Cold orbs, like filthy ivory, bulging. Between them a bent and broken plasticine nose. Underneath this was a long, white moustache curving into a thick frosted beard. A pale tongue protruded, drooping limply: a taciturn plea for succour.

"Fie!" he shouted again. He turned pale. Nauseous: "Fie!" the features were bent and broken, but it was still possible to discern identity even from the balcony. It was the same face from the dream. The same head that had been severed then by his imagination – the white moon face of the jelly-belly Count.

He bit his lip and had to gasp for air, holding tight onto the balustrade to stop himself from falling: "Fiiiieeee!" rasping, guttural.

Men came running out, some of them still pulling jackets and boots on. They approached the sacks, whistling and waving arms to scare away the geese. These were protesting, hissing, some of them snapping back at legs. A pack of dogs joined them. They sniffed around, excited, snapping at the snapping geese and running around the legs of the men. Some of them had to be kicked.

There were shouts when the men saw the body. Hands were thrust into the pile. Grappling with Hessian. Heaving.

The sacks came away. One of them burst open.

Sacks of sand. They uncovered the figures. Filthy. The girl was naked.

One man sniggered, another lifted her head and it came away.

He screamed and dropped it. A dull potato thud on the ground.

Other men groaned and put arms over noses and mouths while other hands dug out the Count.

His corpse was in a filthy nightshirt, both bodies had been covered in shit. The rescuers lifted arms over their noses again.

The jelly-belly Count was quickly recognised. Shocked cries. More people came. Part of the group lifted him. Some hands grappled with the nightshirt, while others slipped underneath, pushing up. The body floated upward and forward, through the door under the balcony.

I turned back to the man on the balcony above them. He raced back into the room, to a large wooden chest, and flung the lid open. He grabbed an indiscriminate bundle of clothes, then turned to the table and blew out the candle. Stomping feet and voices could be heard coming up the stairs. He raced back out onto the balcony. The latch on the bedroom door turned.

He looked down at the woman.

In his mind's eye it was a woman.

I saw her from there. Then looked again ...

Not a woman at all ...

A big, black dog. A bitch with sagging teats.

One of the men put the dead dog's huge and filthy head in a sack. Others wrapped the body in a blanket.

Then they ran away with her, her black limbs flopping out as they ran.

For the drugged-crazed man on the balcony they were still white arms and legs that were dangling. He watched them go, disappearing across the square, then stepped back, bent his knees, down, then up to enable a huge leap over the balcony railings and down, to the sacks.

The door opened. The dead Count's head poked through first. Then they all came in. Each one was shouting comments, instructions or complaints: "The Viceroy..." "I can't believe it" "... poor soul ..." "he does not breathe." "Find the surgeon!" "Foul act ..." "no accident surely ..." "the Viceroy ..." clumsily manoeuvring the corpse onto the bed.

The still warm bed. They laid him out on it. But nobody seemed to notice the heat, or at least they did not worry themselves about it. They were not detectives: "He is cold..." "poor soul..." "too late for the surgeon..." "dead cold..."

Down below on the ripped and burst sacks, a sandy figure was dressing.

I came hurtling back, coughing and asthmatic, as if my own lungs had filled with sand. The sight of the corpses had been nauseating, but memory of the image of the man throwing himself over the balcony made me want to laugh, yet without the air for it. Estrella held my head up and Inma gave me a glass of water. I drank it. My breath came back with a cough.

"He has been seen," I told them through splutters and tears: "Oh yes... It must've been him ... I'm sure of it ... Sarmiento de Gamboa," and then: "The girl is thought to be dead, he thinks her dead ... yet he's mad, she's really a dog ... But the Viceroy's real ... and is really dead ... the Conde de Nieva, that's how he's known ... oh yes: dead, dead! 'Tis the end of a plan!" Yes, I actually said it like that.

"What plan?" my mesmerizers asked in unison.

Then Estrella: "The *Terra Australis*!"

"Yes," but I was shaking my head: "And no. There was something ... something else."

"What?"

I shook my head again. I did not know, still did not understand what I had really witnessed.

I shuddered and reached out for Estrella. She helped me to my feet. Kissed me. Inma reached forward and stroked my hair: "Now you must tell us everything," she said: "And Estrella will write it down. We have to record it all. Your memory this time will be fixed, recorded. Everything you saw. I know you're tired, but we must."

I sighed, swallowed: "Yes, we must."
And Estrella set up the typewriter.

IV. A Costa da Morte (Galicia)

An hour later and the remains of my voice was a lingering echo punctuated by a resilient click of typewriter keys.

Despite the lateness of the hour, the room seemed more stifling than ever.

Estrella got up and pushed the open windows wider apart: a vain attempt to catch a breeze, but it just seemed to make the stillness even more pronounced. She herself, with her arms outstretched between the panes, stiffened, as if she were imagining herself frozen, perhaps hoping that she would melt.

All three of us were drenched, our minds tired and slow. Inma leaned back into the sofa and stretched her own arms upward and out. Her head lolled and her long red hair bounced against the back of the couch.

Estrella went to the fridge and brought back beers for each of us, rubbing her own cool bottle against her forehead. Inma did the same on her throat. Then Estrella crouched down next to me on the mattress. She sighed and a gave me a tired, sorrowful, basset hound look. I guzzled beer then picked up the pages of the typed report: "Was it worth it?"

Inma chortled: "Worth it? Now I know how they felt at NASA when Armstrong stepped onto the moon," and when I looked blankly up at her: "Don't tell me you've never heard about that?" I shrugged my shoulders. She threw her hands up, shaking them: "But you've got so much to learn," she laughed: "Before you'll ever be ..." and then stopped, her lips curling into a stupid smile and I realised that she had stopped because she was about to say something which would have offended me.

"Before I'll ever be regarded ... *normal*." I concluded for her.

Which at least forced a consoling hug: "Oh Val ... It's not an insult. We love you precisely because of that, because you're not normal. Don't we

Estrella?"

Who nodded and droned: "Yes, we love you because you're our very own Neil Armstrong," and when I cringed: "Don't worry, I'll tell you all about it later."

Inma smirked: "Perhaps you should go and see him on the moon yourself. It was only two years ago."

The joke seemed bad taste. I took it seriously: "It's not that easy," I whined: "Finding Sarmiento has been difficult enough," and then: "But now that I've seen him what good is it?"

Estrella lit a joint and blew a smoke ring that floated spirit-like into my face. I closed my eyes and shook my head to disperse it. When I opened them again she had also moved, risen and gone to the sofa, curling up beside Inma with her head in her lap.

I groaned: "I was sent too close. It's no use ... no use at all."

Estrella sighed again, while Inma slurped beer and burped gas: "No use?" She passed Inma the joint, then lifted her head and shook it. Her dark fringe was plastered against her brow and temples.

"Not much..." I insisted.

Inma was up on her feet, a smoke-filled breath held in her lungs. She passed the joint to me. When her hands were free she vomited blue air and gesticulated wildly, her hands cutting sharply through the languid atmosphere. Her pitch slashed: "What did you expect?"

My voice was a bombinating return to the dull mood: "It was too subjective. A distance needs to be maintained. How can any sense be made of any of this?"

Inma slumped back into the couch: "That dead man you talked about. This jelly-belly Count. You called him the Viceroy. The Conde de Nieva. You said he was historically real, didn't you?"

"Yes... Historically real..."

"How did he die?"

There was a prickly itch at the base of my spine: "It was a mystery really. Most probably he was murdered."

"A murder mystery," her eyes brightened and she wriggled. But the idea did nothing to enthuse me.

I remained monotonous and scratched: "More like a ghost story. What are your thoughts about that for a theory? That they were ghosts that were seen ... that I don't travel at all ... the tormented spirits are sent *to me*."

Inma sniggered and became sarcastic: "Perhaps they want you to solve their mystery for them. Revenge a terrible injustice."

"Yes. Well, it is not certain to me that it's my desire anymore."

"Ah, Val. You're hot and tired," and then she crouched down on the mattress beside me. She ran her fingers through my sweat-damp hair, then leaned forward and gently snaked her tongue along my scar.

Estrella stirred and my heart fluttered, but she seemed oblivious to Inma's sensual affection. She rubbed her tired eyes, puffed on the joint and coughed: "What else do you know about this Count, Val?"

"Not much. He had been designated the position of Viceroy ... of Peru ... Sarmiento was by him employed. He was made the court astrologer."

Inma puckered her lips and softly moaned: "Astrologer? I thought you were looking for an explorer."

"Yes ... but the explorer was an astrologer."

"So perhaps there's some magic in this mystery."

"No doubt. Sarmiento was an alchemist ... and a necromancer."

Inma smirked: "A real man. What else do you know about him?" then with an unsavoury puerility: "This sounds like it's going to be fun."

Fun! - but I restrained the impulse to complain. Estrella did it for me, thinking aloud, a dreamy drone: "History is just a glimpse through an opaque veil, but we've opened it. Light pours through. We're one step closer to an undiscovered truth. It could be fatal rather than fun." Which I could not understand either.

The idea of truth as something dangerous seemed absurd then. I tried to fix myself with a more mundane and concrete idea, expressed as a question: "Do you think that the Viceroy was killed by Sarmiento?"

The 'yes or no' answer that my interrogative demanded was evaded.

Inma, thumb sliding over her teeth: "Our hero Sarmiento seems to be quite mad. Although I suppose if we looked into anyone's drowsy mind they would seem deranged."

"Drug-drowsed mind," I corrected.

Inma readjusted her course: "You said the Count died in 1564. When was Sarmiento born?"

"1527."

"In Peru?"

"Oh no," fingertip bumping over a creased brow: "In Spain ... Galicia."

There was a sudden guffaw. Inma and Estrella together. Then Inma: "Galicia ... My, my! I had no idea ... a neighbour."

And then I remembered. I had been told: "Oh yes... You're from Galicia."

"A fishing village in La Coruña." Which was enough of a coincidence. The matter should have been dropped there. But Inma was inspired: "Let's go home." Estrella shuddered. Inma laughed: "The north-west is much cooler in August. Of course Val will have to sleep in my old teacher's flat." Estrella gulped for air. Recognising her anguish, Inma put a reassuring arm around her and elaborated: "I'll stay with you, at your mother's."

Estrella groaned: "It's so complicated."

But Inma ignored the complaint and span around to me: "You've got to meet her family, Val. Estrella, he must!"

I also groaned. Galicia: a land of cliffs I had heard. My head ached. I recalled my fall, the fall I could remember nothing of. I groaned again. It was not just the idea of cliffs that made me anxious, the family: birth, parents, ancestors. Just hearing the words made my throat swell. I also had to gulp to get air: "No families."

Inma would not have realised how those concepts troubled me, but Estrella did. We had talked about it often enough. She gave me a compassionate glance, which was reciprocated. Yet Inma persisted: "But it's such a fabulous excuse for a break. It'll be so good to get out of this heat ... get some clean sea air," provoking a sigh: "And you can take your notes with you, Val. Refresh your memory." – *oh, my memory!* – "Oh, Val! Have you ever seen the sea?" I had, but from an aeroplane, or in that astral dislocation that took me to the ship. I could not remember ever having *experienced* it. She insisted, exploiting the heat and our discomfort: "If you want to understand explorers you need to get some saline oxygen into you. Fill your lungs with some of Sarmiento's air. Which part of Galicia was he born in?"

"Pontevedra."

"Then we'll go there. Who knows what you might find at the original scene of the imbroglio."

What could I say? I expected Estrella to save us, but in the morning, when I saw that she had started packing, I dragged my suitcase out and packed as well.

The Galician coast: six hundred kilometres away. The trip turned out to be complicated and stressful. We had to travel with Estrella's elder brother, José María, the same one she had complained had used to beat her. He was a civil servant posted in some public works office in Toledo, which was close to Madrid so he often came up and slept on Estrella's couch. I was warned never to mention the fact that sometimes I slept over too. Estrella wanted to give him the impression she was still a good catholic girl, who would be a virgin until her wedding night.

But I never actually met José María until the day that we were leaving.

That morning Inma and Estrella left me alone with him while they prepared provisions for the journey. He was stiff and sour faced, and never really smiled, not even when he laughed, although the first thing that struck me about him was his reaction to my deformity.

When he first stood before me I had the impression that I was one of Bosch's monsters that I had seen in the Prado, but observed by a jocund schoolboy. He seemed to find an ugly satisfaction in the bizarre twists of my face.

Contact helped me to comprehend the terms *bigoted* and *chauvinistic*.

He was a misogynist, and conversation with him was often maddening. An addiction to black tobacco had given him a rasping voice, blown through a gurgling throat. He hardly listened. Dialogue became crazed soliloquy.

Because we were travelling with women, *women* became his favourite topic of conversation: "Confused, capricious creatures - have completely lost the art of modesty (*cough*) Take Inma for example (*expectorate spasm*) such an arrogant fox (*gurgling laugh*) which has been rubbing off on my little vixen sister." I grimaced, he grinned: "No offence to you of course (*expulsing phlegm into a handkerchief*) I see that you two are very close," and put his arm around me and patted my shoulder: "But I've always found my sister too boyish, not feminine at all (*cough*) And you know why?" he actually paused for a while as if expecting a response:

"Because she lacks modesty. It's modesty that makes girls feminine. If Estrella had modesty she would be a gorgeous little thing, there can be no-doubt about it (*wheeze*) Perhaps you can do something about that, now that you're with her. Make her more modest (*he scratched his testicles*) It gives women a feminine equilibrium I say, and have always said it (*sniffle*) You can tell a lot from the way a person moves (*cough*), especially a woman (*snort*) They have to take especial care of their walk, the way they wiggle their backsides (*cough*) because, a woman that moves with too much exaggeration can easily be mistaken for the kind of woman that she really doesn't want to be (*wheeze*) if you get my drift. Then she gets into trouble and we men get blamed, don't we now!?" and he winked at me as if I should have been in complete agreement.

Later Estrella told me that he had been denounced several times for sexual aggression, though nothing had ever come of any of the charges: "A pretty face and decent gestures, that's what a woman should have (*wheeze*)" For some reason I nodded, a grave mistake, it encouraged further verbiage: "She should have a discreet laugh (*snort - scratching testicles*) Loquacity is always reproachable. Silence a virtue."

I wanted to escape and stupidly suggested that we helped the girls prepare the picnic basket.

This provoked a passionate objection and a perfect excuse to elaborate on his thesis, expounding convictions regarding the incontestably slavish role of the *weaker* sex.

To demonstrate, he shouted to his sister, ordering her to bring some bottles of beer and prepare snacks for us. Estrella, unfortunately, came with the order, laid it out in front of us, even pouring the beers into our glasses. Then she switched on the radio for us.

José María coughed, grinned and winked at me. He slapped Estrella's behind as she bent over. She turned around. Looked horrified, but said nothing. I said nothing either.

I thought the radio was going to be a relief, but Franco was on, delivering some bombastic, patriotic diatribe.

José María reacted dramatically. Unexpectedly ridiculing, even cursing the dictator. This seemed much better than our abysmal conversation, so I joined him, swearing and blowing comic raspberries at the radio, until

Estrella came rushing in. She grabbed my arm and dragged me into the kitchen.

"Don't say anything against Franco!" it was low, firm. I was shocked. For a moment I thought she was standing up for the dictator: "What has José María been telling you?" a harsh whisper. Even Inma looked uncharacteristically agitated.

"Nothing is ... was said about F-Franco until your b-brother started ... started a-a-abusing him."

Estrella turned to Inma: "I told you this was a stupid idea."

Inma hung her head and rubbed her forehead. Then, after taking a deep breath leaned towards me: "Just don't talk to him, all right? He's a fucking *informer*."

Then Estrella: "He's been testing you. Don't worry he does it to everybody. As long as you don't tell him anything about the Academy. He doesn't know anything about that yet."

Inma: "He *mustn't* know anything!"

Which made me angry: they could have at least been kind enough to have mentioned it before abandoning me with him. The informer's presence complicated things, of course. If we really wanted to hunt down Sarmiento's family home, we had to invent a reason for making a detour to Pontevedra. I suggested telling the truth. Inma blew a loud raspberry: "The truth is the last thing we can tell José Mari. His perverse pleasures obtained by spoiling everyone else's plans."

So thinking again: "Does it have to be him driving?"

She screwed up her face: "Can *you* drive?"

I was slumping: "We could catch a bus..."

Inma smirked and turned to Estrella: "He doesn't know anything, does he?" then back to me: "Estrella can't travel without permission ... a permit ... That she has, but it has been granted on the condition that she goes with her brother ... We're stuck with him ... and if we want to go to Pontevedra he's going to have to take us there, unless you want to risk a run in with the Guardia Civil."

Estrella was starting to look absolutely fed up, but the final excuse came from her. Very dubious I thought, but it worked. They told José María that I was very fond of boiled octopus and that they therefore wanted to take me to the best restaurant for octopus in Spain, which, they said, was in Pontevedra. It was a mad enough kind of reason for a detour to inspire him. He never made the slightest protest. He too was very fond of boiled octopus.

We left early. Estrella and Inma had their hair arranged differently. Inma's was tied up in a bun at the back while Estrella's had been wound into plaits. So conservative. So suddenly.

It was a stifling slow drive in a stifling little slow car, trudging across the hot, flat Upper Castilian plain. Stiff or non-existent suspension coils made each bump bone rattling.

The car shook, shaking us, the exhausted motor's constant loud complaint numbing our minds and mitigating conversation which was forced to sink into the car seat upholstery.

Luckily for us it drowned out José María as well. We could listen without hearing a word of his arguments, staring blinkingly out through smarting, wind slapped eyes to contemplate sameness.

The monstrous oatmeal landscapes, wheat filled, yellow, fields, made occasionally vertical by lonely melancholy oaks. Or the more massive but always distant Moorish watch towers that had become bed bases for storks. Occasionally a whirling dust cloud, churned up under scores of cloven hooves. A rude disclosure of an awkwardly ordered army of scraggy, merino sheep.

Finding himself unnoticed, and thus peeved, the driver invented a better way of asserting his presence and suddenly made a completely unannounced stop by the side of the road.

Without saying a word, he clambered briskly out and went around to the back of the car.

A huge shotgun was slid out from under a sack in the boot with as much mystery as a magician conjuring up a rabbit. The thick barrels were tugged, opening the breach, then slammed shut again before trudging smugly off across dry ochre soil in search of hare or quail.

Some quarter of an hour and several surprisingly gentle popping explosions later, he came back with an example of each and stuffed their blood smeared corpses into an ice cooler that he insisted would sit on the back seat between the women.

"Violent acts against harmless creatures is his forte," Estrella had murmured whilst he had still been away, rubbing her cheek and contemplating a shivering kite that was probably hovering over some twitching field mouse: "As if he were some kind of perfect creation whose God-given purpose was to eradicate vermin."

Inma was stoical, Estrella less so. She was mostly grumpy and her dark mood draped all of us. When we crossed the *sierra* and sank down into Galicia we were refreshed. The coastal region was greener and cooler, just as Inma had promised, and our spirits lifted.

We arrived in Pontevedra the following afternoon, after spending the night in some mosquito infested, Orensian river town.

Estrella suggested parking the car in the old part of the city-centre, and she and Inma left us *men* alone while they went off in search of a hotel.

This meant that I had to stand by José María at a greasy bar in a dingy tavern while he defended my deformity against the bewildered stares of the locals. There we indulged in the local *fire-water*, my bigoted chauffeur complementing his glass by wallowing in the recitation of his own misogynists' jokes. But it seemed that my incomprehension was funnier than the stories, and each of my gormless reactions inspired a burst of outrageous laughter, immediately before he would give my arm a rock hard, *friendly* punch.

"You're a funny man, Val," he would burble, like thick treacle: "A funny man." That time he called me *Val*, but later I became *Quasimodo*, although never in front of Estrella.

By the time the girls had returned I was groggy and José María exuberant. They had to drag us out. I responded to Estrella's tug by trying to suck her lips. She looked horrified and pushed my face away with a flat slapping palm: "Uh, uh ... no ... this is the real world, Val ... you have to control yourself in public places."

Then after checking into the hotel that had been found, Estrella and Inma insisted that we should have coffee and go for a stroll around the town. It was cloudy, at times drizzling, and José María protested. But not enough and he easily gave in and joined us, which had not been desired.

We had been hoping he would have indulged himself in his usual siesta, for the intention behind our walk was to visit Sarmiento's house.

I went arm in arm with Estrella, my hot and slightly drunken mind sailing in the bliss of her sweet-soap smell. She was pressing up against me, her breast against my elbow. I rubbed it like a hopeful teenager, but she did not respond in the way that my hopeful-teenager will was hoping she would.

After a while though, she was squeezing and tugging the muscle in my arm, and her hand was suddenly in front of my nose, pointing the way to a large, grey, stone building, accompanied by a whisper: "There it is," stopping us, while Inma deliberately walked on ahead with José María.

The old house was a mansion erected in the midst of a spacious, but neglected garden, swamped in long and dead dry grass and deformed and thorny bushes.

There were few trees, but two twisted olives stood at the entrance like crippled guards. The chain locked gate consisted of sharp, spear tipped, iron railings which continued on as a high rusted fence.

I was drawn to this, and when I curled my fingers around the bars, their brittleness and coolness, and a chill breeze emanating from the building, surged through me.

I shivered but my pulse raced and pumping lungs made me dizzy.

Perhaps it was some high or low blood pressure, but it felt as if the house had taken possession of me. My vision in particular became unnaturally acute and nauseatingly telescopic. I gulped to keep vomit down while my perception zoomed in on some huge slabs of speckled, lichen splattered limestone, then rose along mortar tracks up the walls to a flat, parapet roof which had a tower sprouting from it with embrasures and gables, as if possessing battlements.

I reached out, or imagined I did, to run my fingers over a cluster of relief figures. A lamb was strung up in a sling beside a crowing cockerel. There was a wolf resting beside a reclining goat. Above this a dragon munched its own tail, which pointed toward a serpent dangling from a lion's mouth, and next to this were a chained eagle and a winged god.

I imagined myself digging my nails into the mortar cracks, pushing and lifting myself to the top.

There I found a small and narrow window in the tower. A figure within, misshapen behind blurring glass, but I could tell it was a woman. She had long hair, a smudge with a tinge of red. I wanted to go to her and get away at the same time.

The double impulse froze me.

She smiled. At me?

No. She was looking out, through and past me to something else, something that was in her own place and time.

Things darkened around me and I was inside, alongside her. She had her head bowed and her long, hot hair was masking her face, until the redness parted, revealing a fulgent green like a cat's eyes caught in torch light.

Her eyes: yet from across what kind of space? I reached out to touch her but something hit my hand and pulled it back. I could get no closer, but when I swallowed I could taste her, or taste a memory of her.

Her breathing was rasping under her hair, yet I could feel it against my cheek. It was damp, smelling of mildew and ... death ... She reached out and put her arms around me, but her breath smelled like shit.

I tried to leap away, but the arms were real. It was Estrella hugging me. We had not moved from in front of the fence. I looked to the tower, so distant, impossible to discern anything. My cheek smarted as if it had been slapped. Estrella was rubbing her hand: "You can't *journey* now, we have company," and looked up the street to José María who was scowling.

That night we went to the restaurant that was supposed to serve the best octopus in the world. The pink flesh of boiled tentacles was all around us.

As each of us chewed on the soft, rubbery meat Inma enriched us with science: "Did you know that octopuses have three hearts?" José had potato in his mouth that sprayed out with unbelieving air. Some of it hit Inma's cheek. She wiped it away and snarled at him: "That's three more than you'll ever have."

He chewed and swallowed the attack before countering with baseness: "How many dicks do they have?" and snarled back with his fork upright.

Inma became mockingly seductive: "I don't know, but they have a big brain, located in their large head, not in the pudenda. But you wouldn't get jealous about that now, would you? Your brain works perfectly well between your legs, or should I say between your buttocks?"

Sitting across the table from Inma was unsettling. Her green eyes disturbed, as if they had their own invisible tentacles, snaking out to trap. One side of me wanted to tell her about what I had seen at the house, another that this was absurd, while a third that perhaps it was dangerous. At times my mind drifted into a space alone with her.

Of course Estrella must have sensed it too. But she did not say anything.

Later, as Estrella and I lay secretly in bed together, I ran my nose along her spine and let my tongue wag out, licking salty-sweet balls of sweat from within the valleys between her shoulder blades, and thought about what Inma's breasts must have felt like; what it would have been like to have tasted *her* sweat.

We stayed only one night in Pontevedra. Our efforts to prolong the visit were useless. We tried to invent excuses, but the city was really too small to warrant a long stay and José María seemed to be growing suspicious of our motives. I tried to impose my free will, claiming to be quite happy to stay on my own. But Estrella's brother would have none of it and the next day we were all in his car again, moving north up the coast, to the fishing village on the rugged *A Costa da Morte* that they called their home town.

This was the most rugged part of the Iberian Peninsula. We were greeted by a squall. Slashing, smarting arrows of gale-hurled rain slapped redness into our cheeks.

Estrella warned me to be careful, but not just of the weather: the little town was full of citizens loyal to the Regime.

At first I did not appreciate what she meant, the whole of Spain was full of loyal citizens to the regime, but when I had become immersed I understood. There are loyalties and there are *loyalties*. Franco's dictatorship was a triumph of Catholicism and the Catholic family as a patriotic mask. Fascist Spain was an autocratic government of the Cross, and in this town in particular, the Passion Play had become a way of life. Each day was a climb to Calvary. The streets were steep and narrow pathways where every journey had to be a painful procession and each villager had to anticipate his or her own crucifixion. Eternally downcast, hauling lugubrious airs.

Catching eye contact was difficult, but on the few occasions that I did, a squinting, troubled gaze would express an inward snarl or shudder. There, Estrella's soft voice, which had always seemed to have a warmth in it, dropped into a monotonous dead drone: "Nearly everyone here loses someone from their family every year ... so they're always in black, especially the women."

Estrella's family house was up on its own Calvary hill. Huge and noble: overlooking the village, as if to dominate it. To dominate the dullness of it all with its own dullness: "Welcome to our dreary palace."

It was a sturdy edifice and one of the oldest in the region, a gothic revival of even darker and more mysterious times. Dampening drizzle darkened and the grey skies made its grey walls greyer.

The doorway was a keel arch entrance, an ivy overgrown, lofty curve, the convex running into the concave. We passed through into an enormous entrance hall. A cold, stone womb, warmed slightly by the creak of the black oaken floor under our shoes.

Feeble light dropped through leaded-light panes, falling over a tiny woman, Estrella's mother. Grey eyes dim-glazed. A fleshy white lily collapsed from spreading fingers as she rose from her armchair throne.

She stepped forward, lifting stiff arms to make room for her daughter's embrace. And then there was a bustling commotion, voice and movement whirling around us.

Women everywhere. Women in black, cringing at the proximity to my scars before embracing me. Severe hugs. Dry kisses on cheeks.

The last to reach me was the tiny mother. As I bent down to kiss her, my gaze dropped to an ancient tapestry carpet, worn and worm eaten.

I followed its embroidered pattern; faded fleur-de-lis and decrepit fishes whirling around a colourless rose.

Images that disappeared under a huge and heavy table.

White dominoes were scattered across it, and a book lay open at a medieval picture of a moon's passage through the signs of the zodiac. But a framed photo grabbed the bulk of my attention.

I let the mother go, stepped forward and as I picked the picture up the room was suddenly gripped by seconds of frozen silence.

My thumb slipped along the kitsch rococo frame while I examined the image it enclosed. There was a young, stiff couple with a child on the deck of a ship. A gale was obviously blowing into their faces. The man's hair was spiking up, the woman's dropping. Only the child's was intact, plastered down with some pinguid substance.

They posed with enormous, genuine smiles, but in the same instant a flash blew the image up, animating it. The man in the photo seemed to rise and the bitter cold air blew out and through me.

I shivered. There was a tremendous crash. I screamed a violent curse. And then, remembering where I really was: "I am sorry," I whispered.

But Estrella's mother was already terrified. I turned back to her, looked into her trembling face. Each wrinkle on it suddenly became a gorge of information that I absorbed implicitly.

Her life was streaming before my eyes, too fast to absorb any more than the emotional state of it. I pulled her tightly to me. She started to weep. I kissed her forehead, then sighed: "Your husband was very much loved." And then I was on the sea again ...

A man who I did not recognise was desperately trying to grab hold of the taffrail. Slipping, he dropped, taken by a dark, lead-grey wave. Vanished – *man overboard!* – I let loose of the woman lest she should be dragged under too and reached away, grappling for something more solid, something to hold me up ...

Estrella's arm. She was incredulous and also trembling. My own voice came out deep, strange, and rasping: "He's dead... has been taken... by the sea... d-dragged... from a fishing boat."

There was silence. Somebody gasped and then burst into tears. A sister. I sensed her leave. José María blurted a stifled protest: "What the...!?"

Estrella and her mother were cataleptic: disaster in each frozen muscle. A disaster which seemed to hang on a collective interval between inhalation and exhalation, as if all our lungs had become frozen.

Like an eternal yogi moment, but it was the yogi aspirant, Inma, who was the first to exhale and move, coming quickly toward me, rapid heels clanking against the wooden floor. She thrust her hand forward, took mine and, without saying a word, lead me out into air, which was heavy with a threat of storm.

We went down some stone stairs, then a slate slab path running down to a cobblestone street that curled around the hill to the village, to a claustrophobic lane: pink, blue and yellow facades of two-storey cottages, a line of green shutters, cast iron hoops for terracotta plant pots nearly always bearing pink geraniums.

Eventually we stopped at some cracked concrete steps before a simple wooden door and Inma rummaged for some keys.

A jangling struggle to insert one in the lock, turned it when it was in, metallic clunk. She had to push hard. Wood was swollen by damp, hinges rusted by salty air.

The air inside was thick. Inma rushed to jerk open curtains and windows. Oxygen blew through from the other side straight off the Atlantic Ocean sea.

She took my hand and lead me up a dusty concrete staircase to the simple *teacher's* room that I was to be sleeping in. Musty yellow. She began to tug off my clothes and ordered me to lie down on a small, hard bed, under an eiderdown patterned with blue twisted flames.

The next morning Inma returned to fetch me and escort me back to the house up on the hill. There we all gathered in a huge and cold kitchen for breakfast.

Estrella had two sisters, one younger, one older, still living with their mother. Each were dressed in mourning. In the doorway the elder one, Asunción, was arguing with Estrella.

She was a dour faced woman who José María called *la monja* (the nun) although she was actually the only one in the family who had a living spouse, and two children what's more. These siblings ran in and sat down panting at the kitchen table. Asunción was scolding Estrella for not wearing black as the mourning ritual demanded. Estrella just ignored her.

The younger sister, Cristina, was preparing the breakfast with her mother. She seemed happier, although she had an infantile character that contradicted her very ample woman's body. Asunción left Estrella and joined the two women at the stove.

Then José María came in. The women fussing. It was as if they worshipped him.

I asked Asunción where her husband was. It was the wrong question.

"Probably in bed," and she almost spat out the last word. Estrella told me later that they were separated and that her husband was living with another woman in the village, although he was said to be very ill. Most of the conversation over breakfast centred around similar gossip, but about other local families. No one said anything about my strange introduction.

It was Estrella who broke the ice, after breakfast. We were walking alone in the fields around the village. She demanded clarification: "What happened yesterday?" staring at yellow gorse.

The implicit accusation made me also turn my gaze downward: "I don't know. It was as if ghosts were dragged before my eyes."

"You have to be careful here."

"I was not able to prevent it," then stopping. A halt that demanded eye-contact: "It's not your opinion that I acted deliberately, is it? ... I didn't want it ... How could I? It must be thought that I was mad."

She flicked her fringe, her eyes flashing, threatening fury. But when she let loose the breath it was a sad sigh: "Mad, no. They are very superstitious; they all are in these parts. If you say you saw ghosts they'll believe you, and think of you as either a prophet or a devil," then the vapourish voice gathered substance and sank into a region more grave: "From now on they'll be watching you carefully, judging you continually, waiting for your mind's eye to open again and give them some insight into things that are too painful for themselves to recall."

"But ... what did I t-tell to them? That a man was seen in my mind f-falling overboard?" Realisation of the absurdity returned confidence: "Yet it was a cancer that killed your father."

Provoking the flicking of her head again, and a tired but also patronising laugh: "No, that's right. You didn't see my father. No one thinks that either. They think you saw my other brother, my other brother, Paco. He was a fisherman. Captained his own boat..." returning to gravity again: "He died almost exactly a year ago tomorrow. There's going to be a funeral service ... that's why José María decided to come."

I sighed: "But I was not told any of that..." and then I became angry: "Why did no one tell it to me?! I thought we came for me!"

Estrella shuddered. The idea of me seeing ghosts did not inspire her. It did not inspire me. I had opened my subconscious, now I had to question whether I would ever be able to close it again.

We walked for almost an hour, not stopping until we had arrived at a field full of cows, brown and dappled. I looked at their faces and I recalled the vision I had had: the figure on the ship. And then my mind was filled with ruddy brown hair and I realised that it had not been Estrella's brother either. It had been another death. There had been a reddish brown beard with frosted white bristles, droplets of water hanging from the tips. Then I saw his clothes. No contemporary tragedy. It had come from a much deeper place. Him. It had to have been him ... It had been Sarmiento.

Inma's little teacher's flat was in a house erected on a small peninsula, rising with the line of the cliff. The bedroom looked directly out over the sea. Once I made the mistake of peering out and into the abysmal drop. The whirling vertigo was so strong that I vomited.

Nevertheless, as far as our work was concerned, there were also some positive details, at least at first. The cooler temperatures made writing more comfortable, and the vulnerability to the elements helped provoke excisions. Yet these advantages were quickly mitigated by the abundance of problems.

In order to write I needed isolation, but the social atmosphere was claustrophobic. Although in theory I had been given my own little flat, privacy was impossible. People were constantly appearing to take me somewhere and Estrella's mother was forever insisting that the *stranger* be introduced to a different uncle or aunt who in turn would undoubtedly invite me over to their house for a meal of the boiled octopus they had all heard that I loved so much. Suffocating. I longed for *freedom*.

Freedom. Because of my amnesia, because of my naïveté, because of my obsession with my work. It took me some time to comprehend what the word meant, or more precisely what lack of freedom meant. However, a run in with Franco's paramilitary police, the *Guardia Civil,* helped push me in that direction.

It was nothing really, just a routine check in a bar. I was a stranger. And an ugly one. The police seemed to find my scars quite amusing to contemplate. After several long seconds of deprecating examination, they wanted to know who I was, so they checked my papers. There were two of them, two clichés: one was stiff and lanky, the other one barrel like; Don Quixote and Sancho Panza. Both of them had typical handlebar moustaches, the characteristic three-cornered hat and phallic stiff shotguns slung over their shoulders. As they had approached I had almost burst out laughing. Estrella elbowed me in the ribs. She was terrified. They checked my passport and Inma and Estrella's papers too, then interrogated us. It was brief, but humiliating. Afterwards Estrella exploded: "I can't stand it. They treat us like we were smugglers."

José María, smug, gave a sarcastic rejoinder: "In these parts everybody's a smuggler. They probably asked for your papers because three people looking so honest reek of suspicion."

We were to spend a month in Galicia, but after the first few days the situation had become already unbearable. Contact with Estrella's family helped me to understand the essence of Franco's dictatorship. The Catholic family was a microcosm of the Catholic Regime. But it was also the *real* world, I told myself, and it made me appreciate how difficult social interaction was for me.

My amnesia had left me poorly equipped for coping with life. I gradually came to discern the rules and began to comprehend the need for learning them, that there was no option but to follow them, and it was a painful process.

Estrella and Inma, who had spent a lifetime absorbing the Regime and learning strategies for coping with it, seemed to observe my frustration with a kind of sympathy. Nevertheless, I could not have expected Estrella's family to be so rigid and different from her.

Eventually I confronted her with it.

"Yes, we're different, very different," she confessed: "I suppose that's why I don't mind living so far away from them."

"But how can people of the same family be so dissimilar?"

"You never knew your parents, never had any brothers or sisters. Perhaps you would have been different too. Most families have their black sheep."

She took me into her dead father's study. It was an octagonal room, one of the biggest in the house and jutting out from the rest of the building.

The walls were lined with bookcases, some of them glass cabinets. All of them full. It was impressive.

"So your father was well read?"

She shook her head: "No, not really. I don't think he would have opened many of these old tomes. They were gathered by my great-grandfather. My father was a businessman, as was his father, but my great-grandfather was supposed to have been different, a black sheep like me. They say he was crazy, and a Jew. A Jew who wanted nothing to do with his culture or his religion. So they said. But actually these shelves have dozens of works in Hebrew and the man obviously had a secret passion for the kabala." Then she began pulling some down, laying them on the thick, oak desk in the middle of the room: "When I was a little girl I used to come in here and look for picture books. Now I search for esoteric treasures. Yet I'm sure the most interesting would be these Hebrew texts that I cannot read."

She ran her fingers across a yellowing, scabrous page that she had opened.

I put my arm around her: "You've never wanted, to learn?"

"Oh yes, of course I have. But I've never found the time, and something tells me that I never will. Unless I can find a way to live a thousand years."

I picked up one of the hefty volumes and ran my fingers across the binding: "They are ... have been ... well kept."

"My mother makes sure they are properly cared for, as safe as in any museum. She appreciates their value. Occasionally she sells one or two, but luckily for me she is not a greedy woman. Some of my own books at home come from here too."

"I would love to work here," I told her.

She shook her head: "Impossible. My mother couldn't bear it. Since father died she's never allowed any man in here. You shouldn't be here now," then she went to the door, opened it slightly and peeked out, before signalling to me that the coast was clear. I shuffled out, my head down.

I was grateful to have seen the room. It made sense of Estrella. But the prohibition of such a close and perfect space just upset me even more. I needed to be outside but the weather would not let me. Tremendous, disturbing winds. Constant sheets of pouring rain washing against my mind.

And across the village in my teacher's room it was far worse: the persistent, maddening crash of the ocean right under my window, smashing my brain. Or my *matted green carpet*: the mounds of stinking kelp that the receding tides left to dry on the rocks below. Factors which created an excited but also melancholy condition. I was depressed two days out of every three, and, even worse, I began suffering epileptic fits again.

In a sense though, illness allowed a reprieve. When pain made me unbearably morbid Estrella's family left me alone. And I did suffer physical as well as psychological pain there. There was an agonising bout of food poisoning which kept me in bed for days. Estrella blamed it on the oysters. But whatever the provenance, it became a fertile source of haunting visions. *Visions* which were not the same as my experience of *journeys*. They were a kind of hallucination accompanied by a nausea.

That nausea made me sharply aware of my body, whereas my out-of-body journeyings allow me no sense of the corporeal. *Visions* are always accompanied by an intense vertigo, whereas with my *journeys* this is not necessarily the case. Contact in *visions* is like contact with a ghost, a door to another dimension is opened but I never go through it. When I *journey* however, I am hurled through to the other side.

One long afternoon in my sick-bed, febrile and wanting to vomit, the room around me dissolved into another place: a long hall, at the end of which sat a woman, who was a complete stranger to me. She was sitting on a low stool, or at least I guessed so from her posture, because the seat was hidden by the folds of her long black dress.

The cut of her costume was elaborate, indicating nobility, and fashioned in the style of the renaissance. Her head and limbs drooped: an emanating misery. This sense grew stronger the more I watched her.

She was fanning herself, a red fan with a white dragon painted on it. With each flick of her wrist she appeared to grow larger. The faster she fanned the quicker she grew.

Realising that this was absurd I suddenly lifted myself up in the bed and looked behind me, thinking that by doing so I could get a grip on my distorted sense of perspective. However, when I did, I discovered that the headboard had vanished and that the rear wall had also opened out, so that the corridor was now incredibly long and even seemed to dip, as if the floor were curved and I was balancing on the edge of a globe. Then from the other side of the corridor I could make out movement. Someone was approaching. A young man. He walked past my bed, toward the woman on the stool, going down on one knee in front of her. Her dress sighed and swayed. She dropped her head further, resting it on the kneeling man's shoulder. As she did the angles that made up the hall began to distort, becoming liquid, then began to whirl. My stomach churned and instinct pushed me to the edge of the bed. I leaned out and vomited into a bucket that I knew had been left there. As the green bile splattered onto plastic the hallucination vanished ...

In a sense all my visions were like that. At first I thought they told me nothing. Only with time did I encounter the substance around the gaps that they filled. But the Galician sojourn was not just a time of hallucinations. It was there that I also had my first, non-induced, out-of-body experience.

It happened one afternoon as I was strolling alone along the cliff tops. Inma, Estrella, and her family had gone to mass. I had gone to the cliffs without thinking. When I reached the edge panic set in, a mixture of exhilaration and unnerving anxiety. Exposure to the gale blowing off the sea, taking in the air and cleansing my lungs while marvelling at the flight of seagulls, had excited me. But this was amplified by a sudden recollection that it had been at such a place where I had had my fall. Looking down at the rocks below caused a violent, spinning nausea, and then my mind suddenly left me.

The epileptic fit probably lasted but a few minutes, but the scene into which I was propelled went on for hours. There was a bright flash, as if a bomb had exploded in my face, and a wind caught me and lifted me so I was suddenly hovering hundreds of metres high. Although still anxious about the cliffs and rocks, the vertigo had left me and I felt lucid.

Below me was a figure. From the distance between us he was no bigger than a tick on a small rock, but I knew, whether through intuition or paranormal perception, that it was him. I tried to approach. Arduous, the winds were tugging every which way, and there was a constant, chilling howl. Cries of thousands. Dead souls, dead sailors, dead fisherman: hurled there on stormy nights, impaled on half-submerged skerries. Perhaps my own dead memory was there somewhere. It seemed that I were attached to something, a gossamer web rooted within some invisible apogee. And so I used, or I imagined I did, the weight and mass that I could not possibly have possessed to swing near him. A certain distance down, a certain proximity gained, but then I was always tugged up again when I had reached my limit. I was forced to be excessive, the only viable option. I grabbed hold of him as I passed through, threw an anchor down when I was within. I *possessed* him.

He was clambering along the edge and my entry almost provoked a tragedy. There were spasms and he stumbled, wavering right on the brink. I feared his sudden death. Absurd. Of course I knew that he didn't die then. I knew his story. I was witnessing history, already written.

He shook his head to regain control then moved away from the precipice. Panting, he was, and stumbling through deep, spongy bracken. I went with him, in his mind. The music of his thoughts was around me, within me.

The voice I heard then is the same as one of the voices I hear now. It was ... is ... sometimes an echo in the back of what I thought was my own mind; sometimes louder than my own inner voice. That is when it is the most troublesome, when I confuse it with myself and forget what *I* sound like. Of course he thought in old Spanish, but this was sometimes Castilian and other times Galician. Sometimes there were only sounds, but more often than not there was a barrage of images: the food he ate, usually stinking cheeses or greasy fish served on cracked platters in dingy taverns, washed down with beers and ciders. Sometimes wines, cups of sack. Occasionally he was alone, but usually he was with company. Ruddy, drunken countenances, glazed eyes, picaresque smiles with tongues of bawds, laughing and winking at me as if they actually knew I was there. There were lovers, prostitutes, fair hot wenches letting long, heavy skirts of flame coloured taffeta drop, laying themselves down on mattresses of straw. Yet only one woman's image ever repeated itself. The same one I had seen in the window at his house. When she appeared I sensed a rush of emotion.

At other times there were memories of the wars: blood smeared swords and soldiers, armoured cavaliers on horseback with long lances. Foot soldiers with pikes and harquebuses, crested helmets, old crossbowmen and teenage boys banging drums. There were shots, gunpowder, screams, fire.

Of course thinking with someone's thoughts makes it easy to know how they are motivated. It was not at all hard for me to deduce why that youthful Sarmiento was on the cliff top. On his way to visit someone ... an old man. And he was walking because he had a secret to conceal and did not want to draw the attention to himself that the sight of a lordly rider would have brought. His pulse was racing, too fast, he was almost breathless. At first I thought it was a nervous anticipation of the visit ahead, but I eventually came to realise that he was permanently cautious. He was constantly turning his head and looking back because he believed that he had someone stalking him.

Then I left his mind. It was tiring ...

From on objective point again, I watched him clamber up onto a path.

A long sword dangled from a leather baldric and slapped against the pig skin pantaloons that covered his calves, against his knee high boots. He marched along the crunching sandy path until it forked. Squawking gulls mocked his deliberating meditation. Oblivious to them, he slipped his hand under his shirt, and equally oblivious began to tweak something. Uncertainty inspired a tug and a leather tube emerged through the open neck.

He untied its calf gut bow. Inside was a parchment. He slid it out and started to unravel it, but when the gulls began to clamour, flapping above his head, he seemed to take this as a warning and pushed it back, lower down, under his breeches.

Air and liquid rumbled audibly through his intestine and he rubbed his hand over his belly.

The bifurcating path: he would have to make a decision. One direction ran down the cliff to a village nestling in a little bay. It could be clearly seen from the cliff top. He could even discern the village square packed with a crowd.

Voices were occasionally blown up to join the racket of gulls. A street festival. A safe place to immerse himself in. A multitude would guarantee anonymity and the empty space in his digestive tract was demanding a meal.

The crowded village was a pressing, pushing place. A dancing, singing, clapping crowd accompanied by annoying bag-pipes and drums. But there was food, albeit on filthy stalls.

A stinking stench of fish. Huge, cold and bewildered eyes, gaping mouths, bellowing-mute screams for succour.

His foot squelched in a lump of something that had been flung or carried there by some animal. Flies buzzed up and around him. He swallowed one, spat, then pushed forward looking and sniffing around for an alternative. Black rats, chased by boys with sticks, ran across his path, over his feet.

There were beggars on the ground. Food scraps and vomit lay at their feet and knees, if they had them. The limbless ones kept their polished stumps exposed, like tiny, oiled buttocks poking at the passing crowd. Next to these were the glazed, white, marble eyes of the blind and a chorus line of pathetic drunks squirming and gulping their pleas. Rasping, solemn groans sallied from them all: "Please señor ... for the love of God." There were flies on the food and on the beggars. On their faces, trotting happily between lips, sucking saliva. Free to drink what they wanted – *beggars give generously to their parasites* –

Smoke drew Sarmiento to a grill, barbecuing enormous sardines. He bought two. Wafted the flies away. Ate them with bread. Another stall offered spicy dishes. Minced and pickled pork. He hurried a portion down with one hand while his other remained on the parchment under his shirt. That must have been of great importance. He maintained an oblique glance from one side to the other, never looking at his food, not noticing that most of the meat was dropping to the ground.

Two dogs came out, sniffing and lapping at the refuse. Then three boys pummelling each other bumped into him. Jolting, pushing. He pushed back, then kicked. One of the boys screamed and they all darted away. He gulped, obviously needing a drink after the salted fish and spicy pork. There was a wine seller opposite the barbecue. But reaching for his purse on his hip, he found himself pawing the air. A solitary leather strap dangled, untied or cut. The purse had gone.

His first reaction was to drag out his sword to slice anything or anyone near him. But frustrated good sense channelled the rage into a simple kick at a black cat. This managed to dodge the blow and spat at his intention while he stumbled off balance and his red face crashed into a bundle of sparrows and young pigeons which were tied and dangling from the frame of a stall.

He looked across the square. The wine seller – *And me without a centimo!!!* – He wanted to scream – *Circumstances leave me with no other option* – he deduced – *I will have to recuperate losses* –

The wine seller was doing a fair trade: pouring cups, handing over bulging goatskin sacks, taking the barter, bending down, reaching, distributing change.

Sarmiento was at the back of the stall in a flash. A narrow lane running out of the square would serve as an escape route. It was going to be easy.

The booming wine seller's voice was relating a tragic tale of a fishing accident: a terrible storm had wrecked three boats.

Sarmiento clicked his knuckles in preparation, then crouched, sliding his hand under the stall's cloth backdrop. It fell straight onto the money box. It was heavy, but he managed to lift it and put it under one arm. He turned towards the lane, then paused. He was still thirsty. A wine sack dangled from the frame of the stall. He unsheathed his sword and slipped its tip under the leather thong attached to the sack. One quick flick and it was off the nail and sliding down his sword, over his arm and shoulder. Then he was away, up the lane, out of the village, and back up the cliffs.

He stood on the edge, at the top, obviously enjoying the tremendous force of the wind. But the theft could not have gone unnoticed, so he turned and bent his back in order to look downward to the ascending track, where he was expecting a pursuer.

He untied the scarf from his neck, laid it on the ground and emptied the contents of the cumbersome money box into it. Folded again, the neckerchief became a big purse attached to his belt. More comfortable, he threw the empty casket over the cliff and watched it disappear into the surf before struggling across the bracken onto the narrow path. At first he ambled forward, the coins in his scarf purse rattling as he went, but then his knee joints clamped and his nose curled up. Something unsavoury had been dragged to him on the wind. I caught a sense of it myself. A sour smell. Urine. He turned around to confirm the suspicion. To his right, on a rise, but off the track, was a white steed. It stood quite still, only its long tail quivering slightly. The rider had his back to him, head up on a stretched neck and searching the other way. Sarmiento, knowing that he was still unseen, felt the wind blow into his face: they could not have smelled him either.

He threw himself into the bracken, stuffing the wine skin under his shirt. That would have been more incriminating than the coins. His hand rubbed against the tube that he had strapped against his chest but he hardly thought twice about it then. All he was worried about was the wine. If they caught him he would probably have to spend a morning in the market place with his ankles trapped in the stocks ...

I approached the rider, who was scratching his neck. Nearer I could hear the hum of his mind. He was indeed looking for Sarmiento. But he was not from the village, and he was not after the wine or the coins ...

When Sarmiento caught a better glimpse he shuddered. A limp left hand suggested familiarity, a tear in the black cloth of his sleeve confirmed it. Limp because Sarmiento himself had slashed it with a knife.

A horsefly buzzed, then settled on the white mare's flank, jabbing its proboscis deep enough to make the animal stir. The rider yanked at the reins in protest and the bit dug into his mount's neck. Bubbling foam became long gobs of slime, dripping or splattering from the jaws. The mare snorted, its shivering lips curling up until the rider gave way, allowing it to descend and trot down onto the path.

Sarmiento froze. The rider's hand dropped from the feathered cap he had been holding and darted towards his waist.

Sarmiento found himself gasping for air, expecting to hear the crack of a musket and feel the heat of a bullet. But instead of drawing his gun the rider settled again on the horse's reins, giving them a sharp tug with both hands.

The animal whinnied, pranced around, then trotted away, vanishing behind the hill.

There, there were three other horsemen. They murmured something to each other. I thought, then, that they were talking in the Galician dialect, but now I know they were speaking Portuguese.

V. Terra Mater

When I came around from the attack, my mind was a shattered mess of fragmented changes. Pictures flashed past, at times fusing into kaleidoscopic mosaics. To confuse me even more, the scene I had returned to was much the same as the one I had just left. The same screeching gull cliff, same shrubs shivering in the same ocean cooled wind, and so at first I did not realise that I was back.

That had to be confirmed by an experience of physical sensations: taste and smell; pain. There was a smarting sensation in my hands and arms and on the side of my face. I was lying in some low, prickly bushes on the cliff edge, scratched by spicules and bleeding. I lifted myself, exhilarated and exhausted, moving back, onto the path running down towards the town.

But then there was a painful shock, like an electrical charge. The world went black. I felt myself jerked forward out of myself, toppling over. Right over, plummeting down into an abyss illuminated by bright flashes of fluorescent lights. Then everything went black, but only briefly before a swelling glow appeared in front of me. It was dull grey blur, and as I fell into it, a gale with rain, blew against me.

I was *journeying* again ...

Sarmiento was in front of me, still with the same wine sack and bulging scarf purse.

It was the same day that I had hardly just left from, but now it was dusk, and raining heavily. He was running down a slope, storm drenched and filthy with the streaky globs of mud that splashed up from each slapping step. One hand struggled with the jangling scarf sack of money, while the other maintained contact with the tube under his shirt.

At the bottom of the slope was a grey farmhouse. A red door was closed, the paint peeling. A wisp of smoke curled out of a chimney.

Sarmiento's breath grunted over the rush of rain and his feet squelched in his waterlogged boots. The ground was like butter. He slipped over, stood up, then slipped over again.

The third time he lay back in the mire and roared. This seemed to stop the rain: a sudden and absolute cessation. He gasped and laughed and scrambled up.

A cool but clearing breeze blew past and the valley in front of him became silent. He whistled three times, piercing in the empty atmosphere. Each emission filled it.

A wooden clunk came from the house and the door slowly creaked opened.

A girl. Some cloth flicked out also, a walnut brown skirt, brushing against a black puddle before a tiny hand pulled it back in. Then the girl leaned out, wrapping a twisted white scarf around her bare neck. One hand was under the elbow of another trembling figure. A man with a white beard was staggering beside her. He wore a tight, ruddy skull cap and a long frockcoat.

Seconds later Sarmiento had reached them, panting, and laughing through each puff. The girl and the old man looked concerned. Sarmiento gave a spraying, wet dog shake. The girl screamed through a tight throat and a screwed up face. Cloth rustled. Sarmiento squelched straight past them into the house. He was shivering, so he went directly to the fireplace and the warmth of the blaze. Blue wisps of evaporating steam off his filthy ruddiness gave him a diabolic air.

He pulled off his boots and water splashed out. The girl lifted her heavy dresses and hurried for a mop while the old man sank into a large armchair. When Sarmiento's booty had been poured onto the table, the old man grimaced, then started to pile the coins into towers. Behind him, closer to the hearth, Sarmiento stripped, carefully removing the leather tube from inside his trousers and wrapping it in his brown jacket. He had a good, trim body. The girl came back. Her face, reddened by movement and fire, beamed. She picked up a dirty rag, fell on her knees and mopped the floor, unperturbed by their visitor's nakedness.

Over the fire were two iron cauldrons. In one was a simmering, ochre stew, while the other was brimming with steaming water. The girl went into a dim corner and dragged out a clanking tin tub. Sarmiento lifted the pot of water off its hook and emptied it into the makeshift bath. Some of it splashed out and hissed in the fire, other drops scalded his testicles.

He yelled. The girl laughed. The old man grunted and lifted one of the coins to the light. While Sarmiento splashed and scrubbed himself in the tub and the girl stirred the bubbling stew on the fire, he remained perfectly still, only his eyes shifting slowly to follow a black cricket that was struggling up the wall. No one said a word.

When Sarmiento had finished he wrapped himself in a large towel.

The girl set the table then dished out the supper: a steaming mixture of honey coloured tripe, shrivelled spinach and yellow chickpeas, all swimming in a gravy, ochreous because heavy with paprika.

The three of them sat down and ate, sipping white wine from porcelain bowls. After devouring all the solid matter Sarmiento got to work on the gravy. He rubbed thick chunks of bread over the plate and it was clean before the others had hardly started. He burped, farted. The girl laughed again, air blown out of fat red cheeks, rubbing through lips to make their own farting noises. As she did she covered her mouth, but more as a barrier against the bits of chewed chickpea spluttering out than the rude noise.

When the old man had finished his plate, the girl stood up and went to a cupboard. Sarmiento watched her carefully, obviously trying to make out the line of a body. He turned to the old man and nodded approvingly. The old man grunted, deprecating Sarmiento's reaction.

The girl reached into the cupboard and pulled out a jar full of a clear liquid drowning a pale green lizard. She poured some of this potion into a small terracotta jug and brought that to the table. Then she emptied a little of it into each of the men's empty drinking bowls. They each gulped it down in one take.

Suddenly there was a pounding on the door.

It startled them all. The old man pushed the coins into a pouch in the lap of his frock coat, some of them spilling out and rolling under the table. Meanwhile, Sarmiento fished his sword out from the bundle of belongings. He put the rest of the bundle under his arm and crept nervously, still clad only in a towel, to the doorway. He swallowed as if to encourage himself, probably considering the precariousness of his naked chest and bare feet, then nodded to the girl, indicating that she could open the door.

She was cautious and trembling slightly. A quavering voice enquired who was there.

The hurried, anxious reply, a low throb, muffled by the door, was obviously familiar to her. Her nervousness bubbled into joy. Her mouth curled into a huge grin, diaphragm pushed air up, spluttering out as a raucous laugh. Her trembling arm became a firm, thrusting limb. It shot to the latch. Fingers and thumb, in a co-ordinated twist, flicked the lock and yanked the door open. Then the hand was outside, reaching to grapple and quickly pull the one out there towards her.

A young man, he was saturated, with a long pitchfork in one hand. Too long, it became momentarily stuck in the doorway as he was being pulled through. He also had a shorter and thicker pole in the other hand. This became entangled with the pitchfork and some of his fingers were caught in between. He yelled. The girl laughed again.

When he was in, she embraced him and kissed him on the cheek. Then she ran for a towel to dry his hair. The old man looked worried. The servant girl was sheepish and apologetic: "My brother, señor."

The youth stumbled forward, his head nodding. A gormless smile. His words came out slow and monotonous both in pace and pitch: "I've come for 'er. Our mother sent me. Most foul indeed, out there. Fie! Only Beelzebub would be glad in't. No weather to be walking home alone in, and the worst of it are the curs and cutpurses about. Swift 'n' subtle. Today, in the village, they were sharking. Probably a dozen of 'em. The worst rank of men. As eager to cut a good girl's virtue as slice away a money bag. Portuguese said some. Probably still around these parts. Camped somewhere. Must be on our guard, señor. If I were you I'd keep the door well locked tonight."

The old man turned on his stool and the coins rattled. Sarmiento coughed, as if to conceal it. When he did the youth turned and acknowledged the other young man with a nod. Sarmiento nodded back but his towel dropped. The shock nearly made the brother topple over. The girl squealed with joy, her brother, lowering his pitch fork, raised his club. The girl pushed it down.

Then she went behind the old man. He pulled some of the coins out of the pouch and dropped them into a pocket in her apron. She smiled and curtsied in front of him and before Sarmiento, who was still trying to wrap the towel back around his waist. Dragging a shawl over her head she took hold of her brother's club and wrapped an arm around one of his.

Finally, she opened the door and they disappeared into the cold night. The rain had stopped, but the wind had picked up.

Sarmiento watched the door shut. Then he turned, grinning and scratched his chin while fondling his testicles under the towel. His deep, rough whisper was conspiring: "Where did you get the wench?"

The old man, his gaze still fixed on the table, groaned. His gurgling voice dripped out between shallow breaths: "Magdalena, her name. A damsel she is, not a wench. And if you were civil, which you're not, and knew courtesy, which you obviously don't, you would lay those lascivious thoughts o'yours aside. Her sweet body was not contrived for groping devilfish hands," and he wiggled his own fingers as he said this: "She's my helper. Has been for a full year. And an apprentice"

"Apprentice girl!" followed by a guffaw.

"Don't scoff at me lad! A wonderful scholar she is. If you did but learn with her speed. Ignorant when she came, but full of promise," he lifted himself up off the chair: "I've already taught her to read and write Latin." He shuffled to the bookshelves, pulled a notebook out, and spread it open: "Her script. Pretty, isn't it? She gives new purpose to my own labour. She has become part of my alchemist's chore."

Sarmiento laughed: "Which is why you recruited me, or have you also forgot it?"

"No. Forgot it, no. But you are opposites. You're iron, while she's clay. The results will be most different. E'er but I had more girls like her. Yea, her possibilities are limited by her sex, yet, mark me, the strangest thing is … that I have learned so much indeed from her."

"The wench teaches?"

"Yea. O yes! She teaches. What she has learned from her own mother. I am well acquainted with the entire family. Although the mother is a widow now … and a witch."

"Witch?"

"With all the charms, toads, beetles, bats. Yes, the girl has tutored me well enough to know her mother's recipes ... her elixirs ... cures. Why not? Old as I am, erudite as you may think me to be."

Sarmiento scratched his scrotum again through the towel and then coughed.

This seemed to trigger a similar but more violent response from the old man, indicating something serious in the lungs. He had to sigh and close his eyes for a moment. His face: wet clay, jaundiced and folded, each wrinkle was a dark furrow. He stayed perfectly still for so long that I began to wonder if he had not died. When he did recover it was quite sudden. His eyes shot open and he took a deep breath. His bilious complexion paled and became something more salubrious. He even looked younger, but serious: "I received your news (*sighed*) Tragic (*looked hard at Sarmiento. The next phrase was mumbled*) Be careful what you write. A letter is by no means the most discreet way of communicating (*then the tone sharpened again*) Learn to write in code. Spies are everywhere these days."

Sarmiento looked incredulous: "How, Rodolfo! (*so the old man's name was Rodolfo*) I have to question your justice. Spies who can read Hebrew!?"

Rodolfo spat something out and wiped it on his shirt: "Aye, of course there are! Do you think you're the only cultured man in this world?"

Sarmiento shrugged his shoulders: "It does not matter much. They're already closing in," then, obviously sensing old Rodolfo's blood race, nonchalantly scratched a bit of bread from his tooth, teasingly: "They had me in a tavern in Lugo. I had to put my sword to them."

"You killed them?"

A miserable frown: "Oh, but I had! There were four of them. I jabbed one's liver and sliced an arm or two. Then I had to run."

"Were they French?"

"No, Portuguese," which made Rodolfo gawk, but fiercely. Sarmiento's gaze turned down and mumbled the rest into the backs of his hands: "And worse still. I saw them again, today, on a hill. By chance. They missed me, but they're close."

Rodolfo's voice rasped across his sudden-dry throat: "Then we must be careful... and quick."

I never read the letter they had been talking about. I would not have understood it even if I had. But snippets of conversation that I picked up have told me that it related news of the death of a mutual friend, always referred to as Don Nicolás. He was another of Rodolfo's pupils, older than Sarmiento, but had accompanied him to the University of Alcalá. They had studied Latin, Greek and Hebrew, and had travelled through Spain together, ravaging libraries and scavenging alchemical texts to be copied or even stolen and taken back to Rodolfo. Afterwards, they enlisted in the Emperor Carlos V's armies, campaigning in Italy and Flanders together, until Nicolás was killed at the battle of Metz. Before dying he had given Sarmiento the sealed parchment that was now wrapped up in his jacket.

"Well then ... may we see it?!" Rodolfo spluttered.

Sarmiento twitched. He reached down to the pile of clothes on the floor and fished out the leather tube. This he opened and dragged out a paper cylinder, pausing to brush some crumbs off the table-top before unrolling it there. As he spread it out he recalled the thick hand streaked by blood and mud that had given it to him: the rasping, gasping voice of Don Nicolás, his jacket ripped, a deep gash, his liver poking out. Sarmiento looked away and shuddered. When he had been able to endure his rolling stomach and turn back, Don Nicolás was already dead.

Rodolfo saw the young man shiver and guessed why: "Man is body ... and soul," he whispered: "And the soul ... immortal is."

But instead of cheering it depressed.

Then the old man squinted and dragged a candle closer. The room filled with prancing shadows, but the men remained completely still, momentarily frozen. The image that had been revealed was a world map. Rodolfo was the first to thaw. He ran a shaky finger along some of the lines. These went every which way: some straight, others anarchic. The finger moved south-southeast tracing a coastline. Quite obvious which coast it was, quite obvious to me. Chartered in minute detail. Its angle, distorted, stretching too far, but it was still a faithful representation: "Ptolemy's Quarta Pars," he murmured: "Catigara, in the Indian Sea."

In the first instance I felt a shudder of sheer amazement. Then confusion. He was running his finger along the east-coast of Australia.

My heart sank. The snaking lines seemed to hiss, lift off the page and gravitate towards me, running up to my neck and choking me. I had to remind myself of where I was, or was supposed to be, of the time, the

1550s, which was more than two hundred years before Cook's discovery.

How could I have been gazing on a chart of a place that had never been reached? Impossible.

All the hours I had spent believing that I was really experiencing something momentous, were now rendered absurd. I tried to return to real consciousness. To the real world. And suddenly the term *real* became an essential concept. Reality: the antithesis of madness. If I believed what I had been seeing, I was mad. It made me imagine hospitals again.

My return was not at all smooth. For a while I felt as if I were taking continual steps backwards. Yet what was moving was neither my physical nor astral body but something else. I was swamped in a cold, black inner space. I looked out but my sensors had dulled. The exterior made no sense while the interior, though freezing dark, was comforting. For a while there seemed to be peace in the depths. Later I would understand that this sensation had been termed *depression*.

My mind told me that it had started to rain and that I was getting wet, that I should move. But the nadir peace retarded the will. It stirs slowly at the bottom, little more than gentle bobs, trying to generate self-movement, self-power. When it cannot, it turns into a death wish and the depression becomes dangerous. The dull will becomes fixed to the nadir: a will to nothing. To lie and rot and waste away and become compost for the field on which I knelt.

Then, suddenly, the horror of exposure. Estrella and Inma had found me, calling to me. They seemed so distant from my hollow refuge, but I was suddenly grabbed. They took hold of my arms and forced me onto my feet. I could sense their wills gradually infusing my own reason. The dulled mind in my numbed brain began to tick over. It moved my legs. And with time they got me back to the little house and into bed.

Once the journeyings began in full swing, my life fell into eternity. An instant of normal time could be an entire day on the *other side*. The result was that I was spending more time *there* than here. But, for what?

There became my reality: what would now be called a *virtual reality*. I was *there*, watching, but I was not *living* there. I was wasting my time. *There* was a delusion. The delusional world of the impossible map.

Thinking became problematic as it led to involuntary propulsions. Only by not-thinking could I protect myself from the *journeys*. For the rest of the time we spent in Galicia, I hardly left my bed. I tried not to think. But, it is impossible to stop thinking.

After some ten days of self-imposed silence, Estrella and Inma managed to coax an explanation from me. I told them about the absurd map and at the same time announced a decision to abandon the experiments with journeyings. My new conviction was to finish the book in the traditional way. I would write a history drawn up from historical research, as all legal historians do.

This pronouncement visibly disturbed them both. Neither could be convinced that the witnessing of an incongruous chart proved fallaciousness and necessitated the project's abandonment.

Inma turned on me: "I don't, can't understand you! You want to give up just because you've seen a map."

"The error ... of everything ... is ... has been ... denounced," I argued in anguished staccato.

Then Estrella: "No, it hasn't! Reality is always more complex. Nothing can denounce everything. As for the map it doesn't prove a fallacy, quite the contrary. Dr de Coca himself claimed to have proof that Sarmiento had such a map. He told us that. Isn't this scene precisely what we are really looking for?"

My brow must have knitted, resisting: "I don't know what is really being looked for." Then: "But, until concrete proof is seen by me, in this physical world ... until then, the *other* cannot be believed."

Estrella squeezed her lips, cutting the circulation, making them pale: "And so if we can prove that the chart you saw was probable, would you continue?"

"Of course I would," I told her: "But it *is* impossible."

The point became a catalyst exposing all of our incompatibilities. Daily doses of catholic-fascism from José María were getting to me. Galicia was a pressure cooker that threatened to explode in our faces. It had opened my eyes to the dictatorship and I suddenly saw fascists everywhere. And while we argued even Estrella seemed to be a fascist. A lack of criticism of the regime implied acceptance.

Eventually I let loose a direct accusation: "You and your ... Nazi friends

... I am made ill by them!"

Estrella was becoming estranged from me and I knew it, but could nothing to prevent it. I knew she felt sorry for me, but I also knew that she would have to keep a safe distance from me. During the time she did spend with me however, she was always comforting and trying to heal.

There was still some space for some tender moments between us.

"Depression, melancholy: an aspect of your soul," she told me once: "It has much to do with the eternal in you. A sense of infinity can do nothing but sadden. You despair because, perhaps for the first time since you came out of your coma, you're realising the absolute ephemeral nature of everything. But you must come to terms with this. The eternal is a concept that you can sense but can never have and *that* is what causes despair." Then turned to me: "But you can do nothing to change it."

So, I was condemned: "The law of God, or the law of physics?"

"If God exists then God created the laws interpreted by physics."

"Yet, physics is defied by my experiences."

Which seemed to shake her. Her face twitched, gathering into a smile: "You defy the physics that humans have discovered. But that's not really the same as defying the physics of God."

"If God exists."

"If God exists."

"And if He doesn't?"

"Then you're defying nature, but what is nature?"

"Physics, biology ... Science."

"And much more, Val, much more," applying the brake: "Nature is also everything we don't understand, everything we don't know."

I changed gear: "Like love."

Making her smile again: "Love? You want to talk about love?"

"No ... But the way it is felt ... by me ... about you it could be talked about, and perhaps the word *love* could be used."

"And does that mean that you love me?"

"Perhaps. What do you think?"

I could see that the idea was a horrible one for her. But she stayed with it. Even smiled into it: "If you want to use the word *love*, please do. It will make me very happy."

"Then the word is understood by you?"

And she laughed: "Yes ... well, perhaps ..." then thinking: "Well, no, it isn't; but that doesn't matter. The important thing is that I can feel the sentiment, feel it without understanding it. There are some things that can only be felt." She hugged me: "Like this for example," and kissed me: "That doesn't need to be *understood*. It is lingering. You will remember it for, I don't know how long, but you'll remember, and when you've forgotten that, and this conversation, perhaps then you'll know that you no longer love me."

I was unbearable then. Estrella had to endure me as best she could. Most importantly she helped me to endure myself. Despite the fact that she had distanced herself from me, I rediscovered her and it was that rediscovery that brought me around. That she didn't run away from me in my delusions and depressions, that she could persist with me in the quagmire of myself without any guarantees that I would ever be bearable: what did that indicate? Absolute foolishness or great character? Or perhaps it even proved that she did love me, that I loved her, and that it was reciprocated, although also impossible.

We returned to Madrid.

VI. Initiation

————

(a) choose

———————

When the work on my thesis resumed, I concentrated on the historical research to restore self-confidence to what was, after all, an historical project. As such I refused to *journey* and made an effort to keep myself anchored in normal time.

Estrella took charge of her own research, into maps. She knew that in order to prove that what I had experienced was not a delusionary hallucination, each journey had to be concordant with historical data, and she was determined to find that data. She was convinced that there would have to be a trace of Rodolfo's map somewhere. Something that historians had overlooked, that would prove the chart's probability and reveal the authenticity of my journeyings.

"History is like doing a jigsaw puzzle without the box, and without most of the pieces." It was suggested in the street, while we were trotting quickly through a shower on our way to the library. I was fighting to keep the umbrella balanced; she was jogging beside me: "And once historians have located all the straight-edged pieces and completed the frame, they become complacent. But, the difficulty of the puzzle is in the centre, where it might all be sky or sea."

"Or might all be lost ... The pieces I mean."

"Accepting that most of the pieces are missing, doesn't imply that the difficult ones in our hand have to be thrown away as well. Historians may assume it's better to have an incomplete picture than an unconfirmed one."

"That is what is thought by me, as well."

"But you're wrong, Val. Why should *we* ignore them? We see things differently, beyond what the academics see. You, Val, with your vision, you've picked up one of those difficult pieces that an historian might discard, but we're not going to do that. What we're going to do is re-think and re-do the puzzle. Build the picture up from the lonely piece we hold in our hands. If we can find just one other piece that fits ours, maybe we can draw a trail that joins this centre to the frame." We stopped under the library's grey portico. I shook the umbrella to get the water off.

I must have grimaced: "I'm not sure that will be swallowed by my sponsors."

"Ok. But if that *is* the case then it's essential to prove the error! That the piece we found does not belong to the jigsaw we're doing at all."

"And, how can that be done without the picture on the box to confirm it?" I noticed her wilting: "After all ... it's possible for *significance* to be read into almost anything ... if we try hard enough to do so."

Her faith made her untiring. The National Library was open twelve hours a day and she made sure we were there from opening-time till close, searching each and every cross-reference that had the slightest relevance. Her persistence bore fruit. Estrella herself uncovered the information. She flicked over a page and the soul-destroying map suddenly made perfect sense.

She had stumbled on it in a glossy journal. It was not purely accidental, but she had not been really expecting it.

I was at a table in an annex to the main reading room. There was a scandalous commotion. She screamed. I knew it was her. I sat up and saw her hurtling towards me, the open magazine flapping from one hand.

Three bulky librarians came bustling over to deliver caustic reproof. They crashed into each other. She laughed. They were not amused.

Ignoring them, she spread open the relevant pages on the lectern in front of me and pressed them flat before running a finger over several key lines. I laughed. We laughed together. Someone hissed.

We controlled ourselves, but it seemed incredible then.

The lines on the page, from an English Historians' Quarterly, were part of a lengthy essay by an Australian called McTierny. They elaborated a theory - his theory - proposing that the Australian east-coast had been *secretly* discovered, even chartered, not in the 18th or 17th centuries, but in the 1520s. It had been mapped by the Portuguese, decades before Sarmiento had unfurled his portolan in front of Rodolfo. There was a revolutionary imbroglio to support my observations. What I had seen was possible, was probably real! McTierny had even included copies of charts to prove it.

I hugged Estrella. We jumped and danced, and they threw us out of the library, although they did allow us to photocopy the essay beforehand.

Later, we wrote to the author in Australia. Hiding our real reasons and objectives we sent him a sketch done from memory saying it was a copy of a chart stumbled on in a flea-market and asking him to try and verify its authenticity. He promptly and politely wrote back, complaining that he could not make a definite judgement without seeing the original, but suggested that it was very likely a version of the Dauphin map attributed to before 1536. This, he proposed, had probably been traced off Portuguese charts by spies working for the French cartographer Desceliers. He enclosed his own photocopies of these maps, each was the same as the one on the parchment that I had seen Sarmiento unfurl.

The mention of the French made Estrella stir: "Remember where Sarmiento got his map," and she traced a finger along the backs of the twenty-four volumes of an encyclopaedia.

"From Don Nicolás," I reminded her: "Whoever he was."

"At the siege of Metz. Where is Metz?"

"In the Lorraine province," I told her.

"In France," she concluded.

"Well not exactly," I corrected her: "Now it is, but then it was part of the Holy Roman Empire."

"But it was close to France, and Sarmiento and Nicolás were linguists, they could have easily slipped over the border." The idea thudded into me, causing a momentary *journey*. I saw a younger Sarmiento, not yet bearing his scars, alert, his hand on his sword, ready to draw. Behind him was an older, taller, thinner man, moustached and rummaging through boxes of parchments. As he unrolled one a repressed cry of joy jerked out.

"Aye! A pox on the French! They'll be puking when they find this little gem missing from their treasure trove."

I shook my head and the scene vanished as quickly as it had come. I grabbed Estrella's arm. She hugged me. There were tears in her eyes. She told me that I had been gasping and clutching my chest, and that she had thought I must have been suffering a heart attack. I laughed: "No, no... I'm fine. And so are you." The *journeys* would be renewed.

This was some months after our trip to Galicia. During my time there, alone in Inma's bed, in my depression, I had endured, and subsequently ignored, many *journeys*. Projections that had been pushed aside by short-term memory lapses or conscious decisions to erase what I was convinced were ugly hallucinations from my mind. However, hallucinations or not, memories of them occasionally oozed back into my consciousness. Most of those recollections were awful. It seemed that my memory chose what it did or did not want to keep.

Nevertheless, with the discovery of the map's authenticity and the decision to continue our lucid-dream research, it also became requisite to return to the danger zone and recover what had been pushed aside. I felt an uncomfortable gut reaction. I am talking about recollecting the most painful scenes. To go back *there* was alike to opening the door once more to one's worst nightmares. Of course, for a brain as scarred as mine, the effects of such stimulus could have been tragic.

* * *

The laboratory in the cellar: windowless dark. Illumination was restricted to one corner where a soft, red, pulsating glow emanated from the interior of a small kiln.

Pedro Sarmiento was there, and Rodolfo was behind him, in shadows, hand on heart, mumbling instructions: "Apply this science to your industry. Your sacred duty; to transform; improve the human condition." Rodolfo's philosophy was his work. His collaboration with nature would accelerate the process of change: "What nature has done; we can also do, by copying her procedure. What required centuries in subterranean solitude, we can manage in an instant." Or, on the contrary, nature's process could be slowed down: "By learning how things are transformed, one can also preserve."

Sarmiento leaned over the furnace, slowly tending its stoke-hole. Bundles of kindling were shaken out from rattling goatskin sacks. After a while he made a sudden reverse movement and yanking one of the burning sticks back he went over to a desk and lit a thick, pink candle. Next to this was a clay beaker; his melting-pot, the crucible. He filled it with a lump of cold, damp, mucus-covered dirt that had been scooped out of a bronze chalice. This he mixed with a handful of yellow powder passed on by Rodolfo.

The old man's voice droned while he swung a censer and Sarmiento joined his song, almost creating harmonies, before spitting three times into the crucible and stirring it with the tip of a circling dagger.

With time what was solid became a runny, squelching slime.

I looked into Sarmiento's mind and saw memories of another face. His father's, I realised. It was more severe than Rodolfo's, and instead of sitting by books it was hovering over a table while podgy fingers fondled coins. A materialist. His grey eyes were glazed. His mouth, downward drawn by the weight of demands. They were spiritually opposite, but the hermit-alchemist and Sarmiento's father had once been the closest friends: "We whored together," Rodolfo once told him, although the smile the memory had brought was quickly stifled by realisation of the declaration's impropriety: "But later we became very different and distant men. Your father was a well-to-do merchant and respected citizen. Me, a wretched Magus," and his creased face drooped even more.

"Yet he sent me to you," said Sarmiento, frowning to emphasise his sincerity: "He told me there was no wiser man in the Empire," which made the old alchemist's cheeks redden and he turned to hide the weakness.

"He sent you here because he'd no idea how to quell your fiery soul."

"I was not apt for his commerce?"

Rodolfo shook his head: "Better to enrich yourself than have all the tables of your life laid by the gold of inheritance," and then, sniffing: "Did you know that your mother wanted you to be a priest? You've much to thank for your father's stubborn-mule atheism."

This made Sarmiento laugh: "Why, Rodolfo, I think you are proud! Are you suggesting your own wisdom to be greater than that of God?"

"Priests do not learn God's wisdom. Monks are instructed in the kissing of Pope's rings. They learn philosophy by repetition, not by logic. But an alchemist experiments, observes. We know our task is the most difficult of all, perhaps impossible; and therein lies the spirit and beauty of it. Is that proud talk?"

The flesh stretched upward on Sarmiento's face, creating a huge smile: "Yes, very proud. but beautiful, beautiful pride," and he laughed while Rodolfo shook his head again.

"You shall live a prodigious life, if you work, Pedro: *labor omnia vincit.* Yes, it's in your stars; in your palm." Sarmiento sniggered and spat again into the crucible. Rodolfo persisted: "An exorbitant destiny." Sarmiento stood up, reached to a shelf, pulled down a bottle and poured liquor into two beakers. Rodolfo took a swig of the drink while Sarmiento grinned and stirred the stuff in the crucible some more: "You'll be tragic; or tragicomic," went on Rodolfo: "But significant; like Columbus ... who believed ... who knew ... as one day you will know. Oh yes, still you don't appreciate it, but, it will be."

The wind outside suddenly blew into a frenzy, shaking the roof. Rodolfo caught his breath and went to the bookshelves, his arms trembling as he tried to lift a huge tome. He started to slide it along, but then suddenly stopped; panting breath desperately trying to fill shrivelled lungs. Sarmiento was quickly up to relieve him. He had to take a deep breath himself, bending his knees when the massive book dropped against his chest: "How do you move these normally?"

"Oh, I seldom do," wheezed the old man: "Not anymore. If I have to I usually get Magda to." Sarmiento's eye-brows rose, expressing scepticism, but Rodolfo nodded emphatically: "Oh, she's a strong young lass alright."

Then he flicked a gnarled hand, indicating to Sarmiento to bring more books. Each one thudded down and Sarmiento wiped dust off their undulating damp covers before presenting them for Rodolfo to spread open.

As paper was parted and stretched, maps of the world were exposed. Each double page was a hemisphere-enclosing rectangle. Lines, latitudes, and still impossible to measure longitudes, intersected, forming

115

quadrangles that were in turn cut by the radiating, polyact tracks of compass-roses, or the too complex description of chaotic, indented coasts. Rodolfo leaned forward, his head was inclined down and his pale, weak eyes were flickering and straining as his fingers traced the ink trails, searching for blemishes: "There. Look! Just here and here," and then: "Ophir exists. Though they have it wrong. Each one mistaken. They have it in divers' places. But, it must be there!" Quoting scripture: " *'And the navy of Hiram bought gold from Ophir ... four hundred and twenty talents ... and brought it to king Solomon'* "

Something metallic creaked. Somewhere, beyond, other hollow, metal objects rattled.

Rodolfo clipped pince-nez onto his thin nose.

Awe inspiring was the line stretching down from the *Java Maior* and enclosing the Terra Australis. Rodolfo squinted at its delineation while recommending far-sightedness and in whispers he advised Sarmiento to look beyond: "Beyond the knowledge of this time. Beyond the New World. Ponder the newer, impossible world that is this chart," and stroked a fingertip across lines depicting two small isles, very near to the northern coast of the Terra Australis: "Mark me lad, this is the future and the end of history." He quoted biblical prophecy, Isaiah: "*Behold I create new heavens and a new earth.* The New Heavens imply the Southern Hemisphere. A different sky with different stars. And then we must take into account the movement of empires. Since Babylon, power has moved from east to west. The next great empire after Spain will be in the Americas. After that ... where? The New Earth will be in the south and the west. The further west you go the newer the world will be. Until you can go no further west without beginning again, no further south." He ran his finger again along the coast of the map and shuddered and coughed: "I pray you ... mark me ... and mark this ... for this serpentine stain describes our destiny," and opened his hands to caress the line: "This cartogram land, depicted here, will be where the New Jerusalem, for centuries in awesome wonder, will be contemplated."

Sarmiento sighed: "So far off," then farted: "Rather like a dream than a certitude," sniffed: "Wow! That, troth, is real!"

Rodolfo laughed: "Aye! Your gas is real, 'n' the rest is a dream. A dream. Oh, how often I have thought the same. But no, not true. That dream is more real than your foulest fart, marry! 'Tis written as they say, and it will come to be. And when it will, henceforth ships will leave its ports, to sail for the mysterious Isles around it. For Ophir and for Tharsis. To trade with angels and saints. To equip the Paradise with all the precious minerals needed to build the marvellous new and holy cities to be edified therein," which left him breathless. He waved the palms of his hands slowly over the map: "Search well for them, Pedro."

"Then teach me how to see, pray."

"If you blend your cunning with occult sapience, you'll find out."

"Then I'll do it. But first I'll need a boat."

"Aye, and that'll not be easy. For first you must sail *here,*" and he prodded: "This chart will lead you to the Terra Australis easily enough. But Ophir and Tharsis will be more difficult, they are a magic place. It's no accident that no one has seen them since Hiram's time. If this map bears them, that is an illusion. No map bears them for they have no fixed place. As difficult to manage as a drop of mercury."

<hr />

(b) impregnate

<hr />

The memories returned with vivid precision. Another time, in the same sixteenth century Galicia. A bright spring morning. I was looking up a deep verdant valley, up a snaking central stream to later flatten and sail cleanly across well soaked, grassy hills. But just when it all seemed to be smooth going, my perspective was violently blocked by trunks of trees. Brown-black boles, speckled by the shiny light green splatters of new-born leaves, and exaggerated by the brilliance of the just risen sun that was replacing a full moon that I could still sense.

The stream, that had spent millennia cutting the land, gurgled and frothed over rocks, coursing fast and with enough power to shove the blades of a creaking mill. Then, coming from behind this, next to a path, Sarmiento appeared with the servant girl Magdalena. They had a white line between them which they began to pull, and I eventually realised they were twisting a drenched sheet to squeeze the water from it into a wide basin. Behind them, other sheets had been stretched out between wooden stakes in the ground, catching the morning dew. To the left was a grazing ram, on the right, a prancing young bull. Magda's arms tensed, her teeth grinding. There was a gap between the incisors: "Twist!" and then: "If you please, señor."

The material between them curled around, knotting up, thick and tight. The liquid gushed out, splattered into the basin. Magda gasped. Sarmiento was also breathing heavy, excited by the young woman's heaving breast. They unravelled the sheet. A relief. Magda felt thirsty. She licked her dry lips. They shook the sheet, their eyes fixed on each other. Magda recalled something and looked away. The man maintained his stare. Magda swallowed again: "Don Rodolfo tells me you have been campaigning, señor. With the king no less."

Sarmiento slowly closed his eyes, as if some excruciating image or idea had wafted through his head. He grimaced but nodded:

"Aye, at Metz."

"Metz? ..."

The town's name shoved me into another darker scene. Suddenly a grey sky, blackening and blending into the pitch line of the horizon and a black land that ran into it. Below me was a charcoal earth, and smouldering parts of broken trees jutted out. The only colour came from flames: the pockets of fire clinging to black wood like vibrant, variegated parasites. Skeletons of houses with their leeches of flame. But there were also burning torches, wafted by men roaming the field: the destroyers of the field, defenders of the town. Metz: the town was there, converted into a fortification. The fort of Metz: a deep black ditch surrounded it, rising into grey, earthen ramparts to make the wall a dirt-slope. Behind it there was another kind of smouldering: poking, prickling sticks. The black cannons of the city's defence, themselves propped up on platforms of packed, grey earth.

Then it began to snow, slowly and softly at first. The cavalry and grumbling foot soldiers of the besieging army were rattling slowly forward, already tired. The white snow mitigated the solemnity of the otherwise black scene. Sarmiento would have been there, on horseback somewhere, amongst the thousands. Ten thousand horsemen, I remembered having learnt somewhere. Sixty-five thousand foot soldiers. Formidable: but they would never take Metz.

"Metz señor? If you please ..."

Magda's question returned me to the green and sunny morning. Sarmiento sighed, his shoulders drooping. Then he twisted the sheet again, violently expressing a violent memory. Afterwards more relaxed: "Metz. Aye, a long way away indeed. On the other side of France. A part of the Empire called Lorraine."

"Lorraine?" as if the sound of the name itself had inspired a dream.

Sarmiento shook his head, denying any romance: "Far indeed."

"And you walked there, señor?"

"Nay, I walked back. I went there on a horse."

"And why did you walk back?"

"You ask too many questions," and he shook the sheet again.

Magda held on firmly: "I'd like to travel," and became languid: "Next year I'll go to the shrine at Santiago de Compostela."

"I was in Metz to suffer a war, not a pilgrimage."

She straightened herself and frowned: "No doubt of that, señor. But pray, what was it like? I'd so love to hear of it, if you please."

"There was a siege. There's hardly aught to tell."

"No brave stories?"

"We spent the winter there. Cold, enough to gall our kibes and freeze our balls off. I, a cavalryman of course, there's not a lot for the cavalry to do at a siege. We drank beer with Italians and Germans, consorting with 'em. We played sharking games. Sometimes I won and sometimes I lost. But that was most dull indeed. Always a wall betwixt our faction and theirs. A futile scheme ... futile."

"Don Rodolfo always speaks badly of the wars too, señor."

"Yes, but that's because his bones are old and his blood has iced in his veins. A good rumble can liberate the soul. But when you're tottering and feeble like our old Don Rodolfo then it's easy to forget about that."

"You enjoy a fight then?"

"Aye, I do," and he suddenly grabbed her hand and pushed it between his legs: "And I always keep my lance's tip well oiled."

She pulled away, slapped his cheek with her other hand: "Just because I'm a working girl, doesn't mean that I'm a whore."

"Oh, sirrah, you misjudge me intent. I'd no intention for paying you, I'd thought you were giving it away," which provoked a harder slap from the opposite direction.

Sarmiento rubbed his mouth, checking that he still had his teeth: "Well met, lass. If I want your virtue, I'll have to be more subtle."

"Verily so, señor."

"And if I was to spark your passion with tales of incredible bravery?"

"Then I'll listen, but promise nothing."

Sarmiento began staring at her again. She had to speak to break the tension: "Did you kill many, señor?"

"One or two."

"Frenchmen? Protestants?"

"Italians and Germans. Catholics. Metz was a defeat. Not a single noble soul in the whole Empire's army. We all went with cutpurses' dreams of filling our money bags. And came back with 'em empty."

"Troth, señor! You intend to win my virtue with an empty purse?!"

"No ... Yet let me seduce you with truth. War's an honourable abomination, or at least it's become so. We were in Metz to plunder, and yea, if we'd breached the wall we would've ... but we did not, and instead we had to freeze and rot in the fields outside."

"But your bravery? Were you not about to talk of that?"

"Oh, good faith, but have I not? Can you imagine anything more valiant than to survive the sufferings of the loser? That was my courage!"

"And your scars?"

"Aye," and he ran his finger over the side of his face: "This caught the edge of a German captain's blade, who I'd well sharked at cards. Much pain and blood there was, verily I say."

And Magda laughed then: "You're a scoundrel if ever there was one." He leaned forward and drooled while Magda became serious again: "Don Rodolfo also tells me you're to go away," there was regret in her voice: "On a voyage, to explore and discover."

"Rodolfo told you that!"

"Yes, señor," she laughed: "But not to worry. Your secrets are safe enough with me."

Sarmiento was furious: "I thought my secrets were to be safe with Rodolfo. Yet it seems he spurts them out like custard."

"It's Don Rodolfo's secret too. And I'm, his confident."

"So it'd seem. But don't you see the danger in't."

"Danger, señor?"

"Yes!" and he dropped his end of the sheet and reached forward to grasp her hand. When he did she instinctively clenched it so he had to wrench it open, stretching her fingers out. Then he softly stroked her palm. She gasped. He pulled her closer to him, lifting her hand to study the grey lines across it. Her breast began heaving again.

"You divine from hands?" He frowned. She persisted: "Well?"

"Lo, you don't possess a fortunate destiny I'm afraid."

Which made her pull away: "Then tell me nothing," tears welled up, her voice choked with emotion: "If my fate's a ruin, then I have no choice but than to tempt it."

This silenced Sarmiento - *Had Rodolfo told her that?* -

In silence they picked up a new dry sheet and tied its corners tight to other stakes in the ground, so that it was stretched out like the other sheets. Having managed this, they hoisted the basin of water and carried it to the house. Still in silence.

Rodolfo met them in the doorway. He lifted his arm and a trembling finger indicated the way down the fifteen steps to the windowless cellar: "No dalliance if you please," he croaked and passed a candle to Sarmiento: "The preparation must be swiftly done, otherwise the water will be contaminated."

A still had been erected in the cellar's gloom. Surprised mice scurried over the tables and around instruments and then seemed to evaporate. Drooping spouts elongated by snaking tubes poked out of the bulging bodies of retorts. Hefty glass vessels, arranged and glowing, were illuminated from beneath by the flames of stoves. In one of these, a thick and silvery liquid simmered. Rising balloons of vapour stretched and rose, shivering on the surface before popping in spasmodic rhythm: each bubble exploding into an unperceived semi-second of arching drops, showering away from the dark but ephemeral crater on the surface.

The couple descended into that symphony of ebullition and, lifting the basin, they carefully poured the collected dew through a funnel into one of the retorts. When it was empty Magda put her hand on Sarmiento's, indicating that he should loosen his grip, then took the basin away herself. Contact tickled her palm and tickled his arm. Chests heaved again. Eyes met. The basin dropped. He clenched her breast. She gasped, gritting teeth. He groaned, buried his head, biting her neck, losing himself in her long hair. Her arms wrapped around his waist, under his jacket, hands over his shirt, lifting it, wrestling for flesh.

Then a sound shocked them.

Rodolfo, hobbling on the floorboards above.

Magda whimpered. Sarmiento kissed her. Air.

Rodolfo's wheezes were audible, they turned into a cough.

Magda panted and pushed Sarmiento away.

The coughs upstairs grew uglier.

The girl scurried up, Sarmiento behind her.

Rodolfo was slumped in a large chair. The coughs had turned into wheezes again, but had become more desperate in their thinness. The choking man waved a hand.

Magda hurried to a cupboard and lifted out a phial and a golden bowl. She uncorked the bottle and poured a brown liquid into the bowl, slipping the rim between Rodolfo's trembling lips. He slurped it. Half the contents were swallowed the rest spilt down his shirt, but within seconds he had grown calm again. He took Magda's hand, patted it and stroked it. He thanked her and asked her to make his bed. He would lie down after breakfast. A morning siesta.

When Magda disappeared, Sarmiento lifted the bowl and examined it in a beam of sunlight that was crashing through the door. It dazzled: "Why do you always consume your elixir from this same receptacle? Is it imbued with therapeutic qualities?" and he turned it to examine a strange inscription.

"From the Orient," droned Rodolfo as if bored: "From the Cathay of Marco Polo. I too am ignorant of the language. But the artist was well versed in the alchemical *Opus,* and in the amalgamation of gold and vermilion." Then he reached for the phial, uncorked it and invited Sarmiento to sniff: "This is my own invention, mixed by Magda's subtle hand, under my instruction."

Sarmiento grimaced: "You should not teach her such things. I mean it for her sake not ours. They'll burn her for a witch if they ever know of it."

"Burn her?" and he shook his head: "For a witch?" and sniggered: "Aye lad, that they burn the servants of Hecate is true enough, but do you know the reasons for sizzling so many hags and their warlock kindred?" and laughed: "Burn a witch for being a witch?! No, lad! Justice is more subtle. I swear on Hermes' rod, seldom do they burn a witch because she's mixed a devil's brew." Then he took his golden bowl and poured water into it from a jug on the table. But instead of drinking he stared into the liquid, as if meditating on its substance: "I was in Pamplona... a good quarter of a century ago, at the witch hunt there. A famous case: two little girls of nine and eleven, suffering some lunacy of mind. Sweet little whelps. They were employed by the Empire to shark a kingdom," and he looked up grinning at Sarmiento: "Aye! It was a convenient moment for our Emperor Carlos, still young and ambitious. So when those green-eyed urchins appeared, all febrile and claiming to be possessed by Hecate's will ... it was the Inquisition's first idea to send the kids home. But the girls insisted and claimed to be repentant of their malady. They begged pardon and offered to turn their malefic powers against the same evil kindred that had possessed them. Can you imagine it? The Inquisitors, slathering and rubbing their hands, suddenly realising what a marvellous tool had dropped into their midst. The little girls promised that they had an irrefutable test for unveiling evil. That they could separate the devil's chaff from Christian corn by a mere glance at the suspects' left eye," his own eyes gleamed: "*The left eye* – they lied – *revealed all* – There could be no better trial, no better armament for our Emperor Carlos to condemn the friends of the upstart Navarran king and consolidate annexation of that reluctant throne," and he sighed and shook his head: "The Inquisitor Avellanda took charge of the case and lead the prodigal daemon girls, with an escort of some fifty foot soldiers, around the Navarran towns. They claimed to be in search of Beelzebub's kin, but really they were hunting the local king's cronies," and he laughed: "The left-eye test was employed with an artist's diligence and those little girls condemned, most freely, without compunction, every left eye they saw. Till hundreds were tortured, tried and killed. Hundreds," and he paused giving Sarmiento time to properly imagine the totality of the *auto da fé*: "But witches? What does our

Emperor care for the devil! Heresy is a marvellous excuse, and if the scheming rivals of our lord happen to have a tell-tale gleam in their left eye ... to the bonfire with 'em!" Then he uncorked the phial again and took a swig: "No, lad. Witches are not tried for being witches." Then: "Little Magda is a clever girl. If she can learn it is my duty to teach."

"But she's a girl still. With a girl's tongue. Her destiny is not in science, but as a mother. Her duty as a woman is to engender heirs."

"Heirs? Can one be heir to poverty? Knowledge will help her rise."

"It will damn her."

"And you? You take my sapience all right. Are *you* damned?"

"I am a man!"

Rodolfo sniggered and moved into the kitchen, beckoning Sarmiento to follow: "Boys are engendered by a hotter and drier seed than girls who are cooler and damper, and it's true that there's much less force in coldness than in heat, and in dampness than dryness, and this is the reason why a girl takes longer to be formed in the womb than a boy. But the fact that girls are slower does not mean that they cannot go forward. The inferiority of the female will is determined by many factors, but not by natural science. And even if it were, or even construed by divine plan, I would challenge it. That's why I am an alchemist!" He opened up the oven and the bread was baked: "Time, for some breakfast."

Sarmiento was still unconvinced: "Haven't you read her palm? Hers will not be any fortunate life."

"Her left hand is miserable, yet her right suggests great hope!" and he scooped out the bread, dumping it onto a cutting board. Each slice was steaming. Sarmiento was peeved: "I'm not hungry," then: "I've too much ambition. But am not sure what I need do."

"Then do me a favour," grunted Rodolfo: "*Materia Prima* ... Go and gather some. We've a long day ahead of us. This afternoon we make gold. Is that not what you want?"

But Sarmiento was still unsettled. It took him a second to consider what Rodolfo was telling him. When he had absorbed it he became agitated. His voice dropped: "Aye señor. And I would fetch your Materia Prima, if I knew what to look for."

Rodolfo laughed: "Lo, it's simple enough," and his eyes gleamed: "Within the grasp of both rich and poor," he saw Sarmiento's eyebrows climb and he laughed: "It can be reached as easily by one who travels, as by one who remains fixed," rubbing his hands: "Something that is exuded ... and trodden on," and he laughed again.

I remembered I had remained by Rodolfo watching Sarmiento go out perplexed into the yard. There were chickens and two fat and snorting pigs, all of them with their heads down, scavenging scraps. Then a sudden noise made us look across to where a door on the other side flew open. Magda came hurrying out, lifting her skirt and squelching her feet. She was splashing, barefoot, through the cold, sticky, green mud; anxious, in pain.

I looked into her own thoughts: confused, anguished, desperate. A hefty lump of congested matter was trying to pass through her bowel. She was worried that it would escape in the house so she had tightened her sphincter. This had just blocked the passage and the air had curled back upwards to churn the gizzard.

She had to halt and double over. A long but quiet groan, then she pushed herself away from a granite wall and stumbled over to the shining trunk of an enormous fig tree filling one corner.

Low-lying branches forced her to crouch but, lifting her dress, she let loose a stream of steaming, almost liquid excrement. It splattered out, slapping over itself. A nigrescent clod of mashed potato - *Ink of baby-squids, lunched on yesterday* - she remembered, mesmerised. Over its surface was a viscid membrane of colourless mucus that had been showered by the waters automatically gushing forth with the release of the sphincter. Caught by a golden beam of sunlight, it gleamed. Joyful disencumberance. Her jaw dropped, allowing the voicing of a sensual moan as the ever-hungry hens trotted over to get their fill of the delicious morsel. An audacity which seemed to mesmerise her and, as she contemplated their advance she reached drowsily and innocently for the fowls' drinking bowl. Pulling this to her, she rested it on the flat of her palm, beneath her sex, while her free hand splashed water against the dirty crease between her buttocks. Lap, lap.

When she saw *him* she toppled over in silent surprise, falling away from the black mash and landing instead on a heap of well matured, purple-brown figs. These squelched and split apart, emitting a zymic gas that made her mouth and nose curl back. She looked up, straight into Pedro Sarmiento's approaching, enlarging face. His eyes shone as if announcing lewd violence – *I could scream* – she thought. But she was misinterpreting his intention. He was not concerned with her or the figs, but with the effluvium.

He recalled Rodolfo's instruction – *Materia Prima: something that is exuded and trodden on* – It simmered. He sighed. His senses reeled and his imagination transported him. The black pile turned into a dark silhouette against a pink, dawn sky in which the sun was rising, the blackness becoming brown and green. The mound, a mountain island rising out of a dead-calm sea. Within an instant he was on it, filled with a sense of completeness, at one with the infinite.

But then he was suddenly brought back. A hand on his shoulder. Rodolfo's hand. His dry laugh: "Many have thought like you, but you won't find it there." Then seriously: "Be patient. Time equips the worthy with wisdom. One day you'll see it and you'll know what it is; and remember that it's one thing only, though the four elements are all contained there."

*   *   *

Excavating memories of memories from my sickbed in Galicia resurrected other traumas. It became obvious how much I had forgotten, and I began to wonder how I had lost so many recollections. It was as if my brain had become a sieve, or at least on the outer surface. Things eventually stuck, nevertheless the idea caused anxiety. It suggested my amnesia could have been recurrent. I did not want to return to the abyss. So I began to study and practice methods of mnemotechnics. It was suggested that I had to make a copy of my fragile mind, something to fall back on if I became lost again. I bought myself a cassette recorder and began storing detailed, narrated accounts of each day before going to sleep. These were typed up later. This security calmed my anxiety, and for a while I was able to work normally again. But then the complications and stress returned. This time, Inma.

She rang. I told her that Estrella was not with me but at home, and that she should try calling her there. She told me she did not want to speak to Estrella. She wanted to speak to me, wanted to *see* me, *alone*. She was agitated. Insistent: "We must."

I was busy writing. I would have gone to her if I could have deduced her needs, but she would tell me nothing on the phone and I did not want to complicate things with Estrella. I told Inma that it was impossible to see her alone. She was anxious and incredulous.

"How can you say that after what happened?" accusingly.

"After what h-h-happened?"

"What happened at home. In the village."

What had happened? I could remember nothing significant, other than what I have already described here. She gasped and hung up – *What had happened?* I had hardly seen Inma since we had returned from Galicia – *What had we done? What kind of psychological guilt did I possess that made me obliterate the memory of it?* –

When I saw Estrella again I asked her if she had seen Inma. She replied with a very curt *no*, which obviously made it clear that she did not want to discuss it. When I told her that Inma had rung me she turned pale.

After the shock had subsided: "What did she want?"

"It was desired by her ... to talk to me."

Then she put on jealous airs: "Huh! What are you telling me this for?" and began to play-act the role of a betrayed lover. But I could see right through it. She was not jealous at all. She was covering up something else. I made a concerted effort to recall.

Inma ... And then the ghostly horror started coming back ...

There had been a time when I had been lying in bed, the creaky-soft bed in her musty yellow teacher's flat. I had been depressed and partly absent, listening to voices which I at first thought had come from an adjacent neighbour's room. They had all been women's voices. At first I had assumed they were strangers but suddenly I had recognised Inma's husky tone and then Estrella, and I had understood that part of my consciousness was on the other side of the town, at Estrella's mother's house. There had been an argument. Estrella against the rest. She sounded desperately sad, at times sobbing. But those voices had arrived on a muffled distant signal and I could not understand much at all. Soon everything had all been drowning and fading as I had found myself journeying again, back to the fields in Rodolfo's lush valley ...

A baby lamb. Lost. Magda lifted it up and cradled it in her arms. It pushed its snout and nestled its head between her breasts. Sarmiento was lying behind her, under an oak tree, in the shade, like a Little Boy Blue with only one shoe on and a long stalk of green grass dangling from his mouth. Fresh and innocent. It must have been midday; the sun was well up. A cow came waddling slowly past. Its belly huge, because pregnant. The calf inside wobbled from one side to the other according to the gait of its mother.

Magda suddenly dropped the lamb and, clutching her own belly, dropped to her knees. Sarmiento spat out the grass and stood up. He paused, considering if there was any real emergency or not, until Magda groaned. He hobbled to her in his one boot and lifted her chin to look into her lacklustre eyes: "What's the matter with you then?"

Large lids sank over the sad orbs. Her voice was also heavy: "Nothing."

"Nothing?"

The tone rose with the lifting of eyes: "It's just that when that heifer went past, so heavy with child ... it's just that I remembered my own birth, troth."

"Your own birth?"

A doubt-expressing flutter of her pupils, preceding a dubious: "Aye."

Sarmiento guffawed: "Impossible."

She pushed away and lifted herself. Indignant: "So they say. Yet I can do it," then looking skyward as if at a vision: "There's no disease half as painful as the torment my mother endured when she squeezed me out. It's been confirmed."

Sarmiento rose to her: "You shouldn't condemn the miracle of birth. It's a woman's privilege."

"Woman's burden," and she sighed and began fingering an amulet around her neck: "I will never marry."

The man's voice crashed: "Then you'll have to a nunnery go."

"I'll be an alchemist, señor."

Which made Sarmiento laugh again, but more sensitive and sad this time, expressing futility:

"And the Inquisitors will catch you and incinerate you."

"Burn me for not marrying? Then I'll marry a man like Don Rodolfo. If I could marry someone like him, I mean someone like him when he were younger of course, then he'd treat me right, I'm sure."

Sarmiento's eyebrows shot up: "You mean wed an alchemist?"

"No, I mean marry a humanist."

And the man's tightening brow gathered his entire face into an expression of patronising ridicule: "And do you know what a humanist is?"

"A kind man, señor. Terrible hard to find," Sarmiento looked smug and this seemed to puzzle her. He challenged elaboration of her thesis. She obliged: "Don Rodolfo told me that a humanist is a benevolent man who believes in the virtues of being kind," this made one of Sarmiento's eyebrows arch: "A humanist, said he, believes that love between a man and a woman is the greatest virtue. Benevolence, Don Rodolfo told me, grows with the intimate relationship. If the friendship is accompanied by honesty, then there can be no other more perfect union."

Which provoked a snort: "So the old man fancies you, eh!"

Magda trembled: "I love the man like a father."

"Or like a grandfather," he hurried in, then smiled, his pitch deepening: "No. I love him too. He's been a second father to me."

Magda pulled the amulet up from around her neck and stuck it between her teeth: "For me he's the father I never had. My real dad died in the Emperor's infantry. Fighting for Austria and Castile." A memory that provoked a dreamy look in Magda, and then a disclosure: "Rodolfo says you have a map."

Sarmiento's jaw dropped. He ordered Magda to repeat what she had just said. When she did he slapped her: "You should not know of it!"

She wiped the pain away from her red cheek: "Why? Do you think I cannot keep a secret? Because I'm a girl!?"

"Yes!"

"You're so cruel ..."

"Yes," but then his attention was drawn to her amulet as it bounced on her chest. Magda thought he was staring at her breasts and crossed her arms over them.

Nevertheless, he reached forward and inspected the images and inscriptions engraved on the pendant: "The woman under the star, lascivious dress ... dear Venus... accompanied by cupid, his bow and seductive arrows. And on the reverse side ... a magic square, seven by seven, the numbers add to one hundred and sixty-five. What powers does it imbue you with?"

"Powers?"

"Don't feign false innocence. Don Rodolfo's told me about your witch's craft."

"And will you be my Inquisitor then?"

Leaning forward. Her lips edged towards Sarmiento's, but, before they could touch, a sharp cry reverberated through the valley. Magda sprang back from Sarmiento so fast that she toppled over on the grass. It was Rodolfo calling.

"Stay well clear of him ..." hissed the old man: "He's more devil than human."

Magda had still not completed her panting approach. The remonstrance confusing: "Why do you say that, m' lord? Didn't you tell me before that he was *eminent*?"

"Aye, lass. Precisely. It's the evil spirit in 'im which is his peculiarity. He's part of Universal Destiny. But do not attempt to understand. I've spent a life-time trying and I'm still more ignorant than wise. Greatness is hardly ever good ... destiny never kind."

"Then I'll love him and change destiny."

"You'll love him ... and be damned."

"He will go soon?"

"Yes."

"And then my grief'll simmer. My heart's a crucible, my sorrow a furnace. As it bakes there'll be a slow, soul transmutation ... into gold!"

"Ah!" he sighed: "You are such a delicious morsel. if only I could rekindle an appetite for ye!" and he ran a bony finger across her cheek. Then he grunted and swallowed phlegm: "Come. We've a lot of work to do. The firmament today is perfectly aligned ... for miracles."

* * *

I remembered that when I returned there had been a tingling shock. Inma had been sitting at the end of the bed, her hands like a huge almond cupped in her lap. Her head had been tilted forward, her hair a gushing waterfall over her face. The posture added gravity to her voice: "You shouldn't have come here."

I had coughed. Bewildered: "But you had me brought. I had not wanted to come, not at first … you insisted."

I remember she did not look up. The only expression came from shoulders and voice. A slow gasp: "Yes … Yes, I did … but it was a mistake … you shouldn't be here."

"Then I'll be gone. I'll get the bus."

Which made her head snap back though her eyes remained masked by the red veil of her hair: "No you can't. They won't let you."

"Then why am I being told to go?"

"You'll have to sneak out, leave when they're asleep."

It seemed a bad joke: "What? Walk to Madrid?"

"You can walk to Coruña … about two hours … or three. Stay off the roads, they may go after you. In Coruña you can catch a morning train. There's one at five o'clock."

My reaction was ironic: "And if some inquisitive Guardias should be met?" I smelled something burning then and realised she had a smoking joint resting between her fingers. She passed it to me: "Don't take any dope with you."

I sucked it. Blew blue smoke against the darkness: "Am I in danger?" and passed the joint back to her.

"No … Perhaps … I don't know," pushing her hair back, exposing a pallid smile: "I want you to go for Estrella's sake," brushing stubborn strands behind her ear: "She can't bear you being here." Then she turned her head, to hide her thoughts I deduced.

"For Estrella's sake, or for your sake?"

She ignored the question and pushed her fingers through her hair, twisting it tight before releasing it again. The red bundle remained an instant, then unravelled, bouncing on her shoulders. Her fingers wriggled through the air and took my hand. Cheerful now: "Last night I saw you in a dream."

I sat up: "You've been seen by me in dreams too. But it's not really you. You're someone long dead."

"Funny thing to say. I've often felt that, that I've been long dead." She smoked again; blown out with the blue air: "Do you love Estrella?"

"Yes, I do."

She leaned over and kissed my forehead: "I'm glad. I love her too."

The door opened. She had my head in her hands. I saw her grimace caught by the light. A black silhouette was in the doorway. José María, as if announcing the time for an execution: "My mother wants to see you."

Inma stubbed out the joint in an ashtray at the side of the bed. Then she stood up, straightening her dress, wavering slightly as if dizzied by the sudden ascension: "Shit!"

José María slapped her. She ran out. I wanted to hit José, but my arm was frozen. Nevertheless, I managed to whine a complaint: "This is her h-house."

He lifted his nose and sniffed: "And her home is in our town ... and certain things are not permitted here."

I did not dare ask anything else.

(c) purify

I never took Inma's advice. Was I too afraid to? I certainly lost the will to do anything more than stay in bed. But not even the autistic isolation of my depression could protect me. Once I had opened the gateway to my soul I could not lock it again. For those who knew how to get in, I was an open field. And, some people obviously wanted to get into my paddock.

The worst of the memories came back. One particular night, I was alone in that bed in Inma's flat, gazing vacantly out of the window. There had been a jaundiced, full and rising moon. Women's voices floated in, as if through the wall. Estrella's sisters. I wasn't sure what they were saying but I was gripped by an anxious feeling that they were coming for me - *they want to get in* - I told myself - *they want to take me* — I felt the presence of someone in the room with me and I reached for a walking stick that I sometimes used and kept by my bedside.

However, when I turned with the stick raised ready to strike, it was Rodolfo's girl, Magda that was there. Her tanned face was leaning over me. Within its frame of brown-black hair, her eyes glazed and distant. She leaned back, illuminated from below. A flickering candle painted a bright warm mask, rubricating patches between shadows. Rodolfo was beside her. His hand on her shoulder pulled her back, while he pushed his own face forward into the candlelight. His quavering voice: "You must comprehend what has been decided for you. Each element is subject to generation and corruption. Ponder upon it. Learn the anatomy of the natural world and its separation into the elements."

"Yes, speak ... tell ... tell us all."

It came out as a chorus. Not Magda, but Estrella's sisters. Not their time, but mine – *Get out of my head!* – I tried to shout.

"Tell us!" they insisted.

"Behold the generation," whispered Rodolfo. He held a candle in one hand, illuminating a flat plate of shining rock at the bottom of a retort.

Gold, I realised. They had made gold.

"From this we will forge your protecting rings!" said Rodolfo to Sarmiento, who also leaned into the frame around them, reaching forward to pick up the retort and smash it.

The gold pulsated. Sarmiento grabbed it, then pulled his hand back: "It burns!"

"It's not ordinary."

Magda was on her knees, drawing something around them on the floor – *a pentacle!* –

On the floor around the bed, around *my* bed, around *the teacher's* bed.

Magda looked up. Not Magda now, it was Inma, sobbing.

Around the bed, outside the pentagram, was a circle of candles. It was not Magda who had drawn the pentagram, but Inma - *Inma!* - and Estrella's sisters were also there now – *had Inma let them in?* –

The older sister was standing, the other kneeling, and Estrella's mother was in an armchair watching from the corner - *they are going to burn me* – then panic, but I could not move.

The moon outside, now ivory white and gigantic, was pressing against the window, freezing me.

Dizzy, nauseous. My stomach quaked while my heart had become the lung cramping size of my chest. Each beat took my breath away. A face leant over me. A moustache, dark and pointed, curling upward.

José María disguised as Salvador Dalí.

I started to float upwards. Stiff. Paralysed. My left ear resting against the hairs of his moustache.

"*The formula*," he said in English: "*Give us the formula.*"

My own lips were opening, against my will. I could realise that I had a will, but it wasn't my own anymore. I snapped my mouth shut.

He became angry, insistent: "*Tell us!*"

Then the sisters leaned over me: "*He resists*," said Asunción: "*Let me...*"

My teeth, gnawing, grinding, until an excruciating pain forced a tremendous scream. Pain from my appendix. A large fluffy stork was perched on my chest, picking at my flesh. It had pulled a hole through my side: "*Estrella!*" I screamed, but she was not there: "*Inma, help me!*"

All I could hear then were Inma's sobs and Estrella's mother's persistent drone: "*Tell us ... tell us ...*"

But what did they want to know?

The sobbing soothed me, made me drowsy. I drifted again ...

On the other side it was warm, nice, relaxing – *distance will protect me* – I thought – *while I am here I have escaped* –

Rodolfo, Sarmiento and Magda were ecstatic within their own pentacle in the alchemist's workshop, chanting mumbled prayers in Latin.

There was a stove and a crucible between them, white smoke like a fog. Slashes of light escaped through gashes.

Sarmiento, with crucible tongs, was working a piece of gold, inserting it through a gap. Heating, softening, withdrawing it, handing it to Rodolfo. The old man grunted and grappled the tongs, stretched the soft metal then cut and curled it. He bent over a pimpled lump of rock wedged into a vice. Pince-nez wobbling. Sarmiento handed him another little piece of gold. He lay this over one of the pimples on the rock and began tapping. The gold between rock and shaping hammer flattened. Old Rodolfo coughed, took a burin and began scraping it. Geometric shapes, cuneiform text ...

Then I remembered José María and the sisters - *was this what they were asking for?*

Did I tell them? I don't know. And even if I did, I don't know if I was really betraying anyone or anything. This was a once-forgotten memory, complicating reality even more. If at times I doubted experience, how could I trust memory? An image returning from the past, returning from an oblivion. How can the amnesiac trust memory? ...

Rodolfo dipped the finished work in a beaker of water. It hissed, vapour, cooled. More mumbling, droning. Magda was in a trance, never breaking the rhythm of the chant ...

Reality, projection, hallucination. The two scenes continued to dissolve and run into each other. Magda's chanting becoming Inma chanting. Chanting through her sobs. Monotonous, disturbing. I was still levitating. Anxious, I looked down. To the witches' circle around the bed. They were now all naked and José María sat cross legged over my chest, like a Buddha on my lung cramping heart, in front of the stork that was still dipping its huge beak ...

The house in Galicia became liquid, hardening into Rodolfo's house. Estrella's mother liquefied then solidified again as the old alchemist in a wooden armchair, spotlighted by rays of a just risen sun.

I was still floating, and Rodolfo's kitchen was whirling around me. Magda entered through a scraping heavy door gasping: "Señor!" Rodolfo was slow to turn. When he did Magda sighed: "Are you well, señor."

His eyes, liquid-sad. I floated close to them. Their moisture touched me, made me shiver. But he smiled: "I've no need for you here ... today ... It is best that you be gone."

I zoomed around, could feel the girl's urgent pulsing heart: "And Don Pedro, señor?"

The old man smirked: "Departed ... To Santiago de Compostela," and an image of Sarmiento, patting and stroking the hind quarters of a yellowish horse, flashed through his mind. Then memories of the conversation with Sarmiento before his departure ...

"Go to Compostela. Take this mare. I've had her for thirteen years, hardly ever been mounted at all. My knees are not for trotting any more. Magda's brother has sometimes had the pleasure of her. Otherwise she's

practically untouched. So be kind."

Sarmiento was prodding her legs: *"She has windgalls."*

"Yes, but she'll get you to Compostela, if you don't race her. Go, and keep your wits and sword sharp. The Portuguese you saw on the hill; they'll be looking for you."

"And if they find me I doubt that I'll survive long. They are four, on fine Arabs, while I am alone and on this ancient hag."

"Which is why you must use your sword and forget about being a gentleman."

"Oh, I've never been a gentleman. But didn't you say these rings would protect me?"

"Yes, they will. The rings and your stars."

"So what is there to worry about?"

"Nothing. Live happily and long, Pedro. Happily, and long..."

"But please, señor, why? Why has Don Pedro gone to Compostela?"

"Because he has a mission there, girl. At the Cathedral," the last word echoing away through the walls.

"The Cathedral, señor?"

"Aye," then: "Leave me!" inexplicably cruel. He made a firm, almost violent gesture which sent her scurrying home.

Sarmiento in Santiago, Santiago de Compostela: to the cathedral. A stork on the cathedral with an eel in its beak. A stork on my chest, my appendix black-red and slimy.

"Take us there!" ...

It had become dark. Rodolfo was in his chair, wrapped in a rug. There was no fire, only cold white moonlight illuminating him. Magda entered, as before. The door scraping, as before. Rodolfo still deathly still. Magda gasping again. Then the old man suddenly came out of his trance: "What are you here for!"

The girl stammered: "I've brought you your supper..."

"Get out!"

But, as she shied towards the door again, he raised his arm, pressed a finger to his lips and listened carefully. There was a gust of wind. Leaves whooshed. Then, what he had been listening for; a horse whinnied ...

A sound which turned into whines. My own whines. The hallucination of the stork munching on my innards had stopped only to be replaced by another imagined torment. My flesh began to itch, a hot urtication that I could not scratch. I looked out of the window and used the cold light of the moon to soothe me and escape to the other side. A ghost's existence suddenly seemed better than the torture. With intense concentration, I leapt and liberated myself. The sharp, caustic heat of pain dampened into a liquid experience as I floated away from the physical through a black ocean that was neither warm nor cold. For the first time the blackness was desirable. An equanimity. Until, I was reeled in like an exhausted fish toward an illumination which I soon realised came from candles on a table.

(d) prepare

A man was with his back toward me, leaning over a table with one hand flattening an enormous open book. In the other was a shivering quill, scratching words onto a parchment which flapped in a breeze from an open window - *did I bring the breeze?* - It made the flame of the candles shudder, shadows flicker. The man reached down, lifted something. Bone-white and dry. Bone-white, the irony in the tautology made me shudder like the candle flames as I realised that it was bone; the bone of a human skull, used as a paper-weight.

I wanted to flee again, but I was fixed, as if I had been blown into a strip of transparent adhesive tape. Then the living head turned and I felt the breeze blown back at me.

I could not discern his face at first. Although he had turned, it was away from the light and all I saw was shadow. But it was as if he were scowling at me; as if he sensed my presence and was resentful of it.

A thumping noise echoed through the room. He twisted back, dropping the quill as he did, then reached forward and wrenched a candle from the table top. Hot wax dripped and he grimaced before impaling the stem onto the spike of a copper holder. The banging persisted. Banging on a door.

He shuffled forward, reached for the latch, lifted it and pulled. The door creaked. The candle was lifted to illuminate a face. Sarmiento, in a black cap – *Sarmiento, yes, Sarmiento* – A realisation that made me apprehensive again - *they want me to find* him – I realised – *they have sent me to find* him – José María twirled his Dalí moustache and grinned – *"Thank you"* –

Sarmiento was immediately recognised by the man in the room: "Cousin!"

Sarmiento embraced him, his exuberant voice thrown through an enormous grin: "Pablo!"

Cousin Pablo lifted the candle.

What I had thought was a blanket was really a cassock. A ring of hair encircled a shiny patch of pink skin; his tonsure. Pablo was a friar.

He proffered a chair, insisting that Sarmiento sit.

When he did, he lay a hand unwittingly down on the dry skull paperweight, the shock of which made him jump.

The friar laughed, then pushed the candle under his face to create a long shadowed death-mask: "Boooo!"

Sarmiento doubled over. The priest sniggered and shook his head, before sitting the skull on top of some green apples and adorning its greying occiput with a bunch of purple grapes. Sarmiento roared at the ridiculous image.

Sitting, facing each other, they grasped each other's hands across the huge open book that covered the flat, wooden surface. Staring into each other's eyes, until Sarmiento reached further forward and began to fondle the friar's cassock. He ran a finger upward to stroke his cheek. A soft cheek on a soft, feminine face: "Fray Pablo, Pablo Martín, and a Franciscan no less. But you will still be my cousin!"

"Aye Pedro. Cousins," and he took a deep breath then sighed. Histrionic: "Yet our destinies are so distinct. You serve the belligerent Mars, I, our good Lord Jesus. What happened to us?" and flicked his head slightly with the interrogative.

Sarmiento shook his. His voice was low and tinged with sarcasm: "What happened to *you*?" and leaned back in his chair, his arms rising to clasp his nape: "Before we were both of us sinners. It is you who has changed."

Fr Pablo's eyes brightened and he sighed: "Oh yes, Pedro, changed I am. Grown tired of the lust for flesh."

Sarmiento pursed his lips lasciviously: "Did you get so much of it?"

Pablo sighed again: "So much ..." and then closed his large almond eyes: "Life at the university was different," he murmured: "Ignoble."

"Ignoble?" a snigger and smirk. The alchemist scratched his scar: "We were monsters."

"Fiends," and the tonsured head shook. But he laughed as well, though a nervous giggle, and the end of it was abrupt. His eyes closed once more. His mouth straightened then curled up again with the opening eyes into another smile. This was sublime: "Now I am a man of God."

Sarmiento leaned back on his stool, took a deep breath, sighed, shook his head, then, in a funereal voice: "Made a priest by the plague," which seemed to strike a nerve.

The lump in the friar's throat bobbed sharply upward, expulsing a tremulous: "What?"

"If death hadn't so suddenly blown his pestilent breath into your parents' bed you would still be a sharking, fornicating whelp like me."

But the warm smile returned to the cousin's lips: "It was divine will."

Sarmiento gasped: "And do you not think it cruel?"

"God cannot be cruel. Only in the material sense is death a problem," which agitated Sarmiento. The priest leaned over the table and reached forward with both arms, rubbing Sarmiento's shoulders: "We must accept death as natural and good," and had a certain sensuality in his smile now, which brought Sarmiento's thoughts back into the immediate space.

He ran his palm across the huge book on the table top: "You also read the wrong book."

"Wrong book?"

"The wrong Erasmus."

The priest threw his arms in the air: "Erasmus? Me? I've never read Erasmus."

Sarmiento's dark eyes gleamed: "Verily you did cousin. How quickly one forgets."

Fr Pablo stood up, began to pace: "Erasmus, no, impossible."

"But you did. And it impressed greatly. His *Eulogy for the monastic life*."

"Eulogy?"

"Yes, written while he himself was in the monastery ... you read it."

The friar sat down again. Slumped, his eyes twitching as he tried to grasp the truth behind the accusation: "Umm ... I did read a eulogy, yes."

"Written by Erasmus."

"How strange."

"So there is still hope for you."

"Hope? For me?"

"That you'll escape, like Erasmus did. You should read his other books: *The Praise of Folly*."

"I would rather have my toenails ripped out."

"Oh come now Pablo, a book, troth, cannot be that bad," which petered out as he caught his cousin's eye. For a moment there was an uncomfortable silence. Sarmiento reached forward and ran his index finger along the line of the friar's lips: "Never have I such sweet kisses enjoyed."

Horror swept across the other's face: "Shut your mouth!" then, after taking a deep breath, a whining: "Please cousin. I have taken vows; I will atone for my sins."

"And my sins?"

Anger turned into enthusiasm: "I will atone for them too if you'll permit it," pulling the cassock's hood over his head, hiding anger, or embarrassment: "Though it would be better if you could appease God yourself. You will always be a blasphemer. And I will always love you for it. And through my love you will be saved."

Sarmiento reached forward and pulled his cousin's hood up and over his head. It was a tender gesture.

The friar responded. They reached over the table and hugged each other again.

"Have you been home? To Pontevedra I mean." Pablo asked while slurping a juicy pear.

"Briefly, to see my poor mother." And then terrible silence, until: "You went to my sister's funeral?"

"Aye, and your father's," which was whispered: "Too soon after the first tragedy. We all felt it," then shuddered, as if recognising the inappropriateness of such self-pitying empathy: "Of course your distress is reasonable."

Sarmiento's diaphragm tightened with his jaw, and his breath was only allowed to trickle out: "It took weeks for the news to reach me," sighing: "Mother said he had a brain fever, brought on by Dolores' tragedy, and that it was the madness that killed him."

His eyes gleamed wet-sad and the priest looked away from them, down to the rivers of wood grain on the warmly lit table. He rubbed his thumb against the flow and tried to sound cheerful: "Your father, God bless him, was a man torn betwixt an insatiable lust for the gambling life of commerce, and the anguish of suffering eternal condemnation from his Maker."

Which only provoked bitterness: "Did you confess him then, cousin?"

An ambiguous accusation that opened the priest's face and body: "No."

The resentful tone persisted: "Then why do you presume my father to have been a Christian man? Let me tell you that he believed in nothing but his purse," and the priest winced as if expecting to receive spittle: "My mother had plenty of fearful faith. She prayed for her husband's and children's souls. If my father had a conscience it was her. Though little good did such an alchemy do for either of them," and he took another deep breath to settle an evolving tremor in his voice: "I've seen my father sad-mad-drunk and slapping her when she preached him morality. He could not bear it. Once he even put the tip of his sword to her throat to stop her nagging."

Fr Pablo shook his head: "I always found him a gentle, well-mannered man."

Sarmiento gritted his teeth: "His was a seasonal character, but it could whirl from spring to winter in a matter of moments," and snorted: "I'll never forgive him for selling my sister to that monster, fie!" then rubbing the knuckles of a clenched pink fist: "He thought he would make more gold from the transaction, even though the whoreson bastard was famous for never sparing the stick on anything," and laughed, but ironically sad: "They even say he once whipped his own mother."

"She was his step-mother, actually," a statement which the priest was immediately regretful of and cringed. Sarmiento shook his head. The priest twisted back into the original flow of conversation. His pitch, moralistic: "You should not blame your father. He invested so much in your humanist's education."

Sarmiento's hands shot up to the nape of his neck: "He sent me to university to become a learned man. To speak Latin and read Greek, to memorise verse and philosophy ... but for what? To leave me, as he did, without an inheritance."

And glared.

Fr Pablo blushed: "I did not know."

To change the subject Sarmiento reached down, picked up a leather satchel and pulled out a large and heavy, leather bound book: "I'm looking for a Jew, now converted, called Canches. Have you heard of him?"

"Canches? Yes. Strange fellow, but then all Jews are. What do you want with Canches?"

"Another old and strange fellow called Rodolfo gave me this book," and he opened it. "Full of a Chaldean script which he nor I can cipher. He thinks that Canches may."

The friar ran a trembling finger across a page: "No Christian pen wrote this."

"No cousin. It's very old, pray. Copied from something much older. And saved, once at least, from some mad Pope's bonfire." He slammed the book shut, almost trapping his cousin's finger: "But we cannot say if it's either the devil's book or some great and holy text until we have it translated, can we cousin? That's why I must take it to Canches."

"Then we'll find him in the morning."

Sarmiento picked up an apple, crunched it, and: "But there's another reason too why I've come (*crunch*) I've been told you're planning a trip to the Americas."

"Aye (*Pablo Martín bit into another pear*) To New Spain (*slurp*) I have been offered the post of secretary with the Bishop of Tlaxcala."

"Then you'll be writing cousin?"

"Epistolary material."

Sarmiento inspected the apple, as if looking for traces of a worm: "And your poetry?"

"I have no time for such distractions now."

"Distraction? It used to be your great passion!"

142

"My passion now is the passion of the Lord."

"Yes, you *have* changed. Perhaps I'll not like you anymore," and he crunched the apple again.

"Then, so be it. If your black heart cannot bear the good and righteous path I follow."

"My heart's dark, yes. Or at least to you. Because you cannot see. It's bathed in another kind of light (*crunch*) We're both of us looking for the same mystery, cousin, the only difference between us is that I choose to look everywhere."

The friar smiled knowingly and slurped his pear: "It's obvious you've been with the hermit."

Sarmiento guffawed: "And obvious that you've been in the cloister." Then leaned over the table, reaching forward as if about to grab the friar's throat: "These studies of yours: these scriptures may make a man stubborn in debate, but, do they not tire your mind with their sterile subtlety? Where's their inspiration?"

"If you cannot feel it, you'll never understand why I am going to the Americas."

"Why are you going?"

"There are so many green souls there to gather in. Innocent and pure they say, and they've suffered much for the Empire."

Sarmiento nodded: "Our dear most catholic Empire (*crunch*) But haven't we all suffered that?"

"The church is recruiting teachers."

"And if I were to go with you?"

"To teach?"

"No. I've other plans. I go to explore."

"Ah, I see, and take your Mars with you. The captain becomes a Conquistador."

"Something like that."

"And who, do you think, will you help, cousin?"

"I will help myself."

"How generous!"

"I've done my service. I've just come back from Hell. It's a long way hence and freezing. Now I want a warm place to thaw my codpiece in."

"How can you complain like this? Do you really think you are an unfortunate man?"

"What do you know of it, cousin? One cannot know the evil of it until you've confronted it yourself."

"What is your suffering compared to Christ's?"

Sarmiento ignored that obvious interrogative: "Freezing and starving we were, whilst our darling Emperor, Don Carlos, drank himself into a melancholy stupor, numbing his gout with German beer. A disaster cousin, and I was a part of it. I need more hope."

"Consider God (*slurp*) He will not ..."

Sarmiento resorted to blatant interruption: "A New World. *That* is what I seek. My world (*crunch*) where I'm my own lord ... where there'll be neither Emperor nor God." And he pinched the stem of the eaten apple and let the core dangle.

"Blasphemy. To seek a Godless place. And you would that I went with you?"

"To New Spain. My final hope is somewhere much further. I'll be the new Columbus. But do not worry cousin, I'll not drag you with me; will not oblige you to go anywhere that you do not wish (*crunch*) So, marry, what misgivings have you? Would it not be better to have a friend to travel with?"

"Aye, Pedro, yes, yes. But we've changed, remember that."

"Do you fear me for my hard heart?"

"You have corrupted my soul once (*gulp*) yet I've scorched that evil and I have risen (*slurp*) intact (*slurp, slurp*) stronger (*gulp*) You'll not sully my spirit again."

"Strong man, Fr Pablo (*crunch*) You have your God and good faith (*crunch*) So fear me not and travel with me."

"I've made plans to sail the next month. On the night of San Juan. If you want to, then come, and if you feel a need to find God then let me show you to him. We sail from the port of Vigo ... the barque named *El Rocío*."

"I'll be there."

"And tomorrow we call on Canches."

"Ah yes, tomorrow Señor Canches."

Tomorrow Señor Canches ... and then it was tomorrow: the morning, warm, but gloomy. The sky was grey and there was a soft drizzle. I was in the street. A door opened and Sarmiento and his cousin appeared. They covered their heads and went into a square in front of the cathedral.

Despite the miserable weather it was a beehive of activity: pilgrims in rough cassocks, bearing scalloped shells on their hikers' staffs, shuffled up the steps to the holy sanctuary. Others stopped by dripping canvas covered stalls that sold relics. There were fragments of supposed saints', of their clothes or body parts, their bones and hair, pieces of dried saints' skin, their blood and spittle, even sperm. Sarmiento clutched his cousins hand.

"What do these pilgrims really search for?"

The friar tilted his head and his top lip curled up at the side. His teeth clenched as if he were pulling at some sinewy lump of squid: "The definitive answer to the mystery of the universe."

Sarmiento seemed unaware of the ironic tone: "Most noble pretence that."

Pablo's head moved sluggishly from side to side. The next phrase came out of a moan: "Aye, if only they were noble. Most of them come for the picnics along the way. They no longer come to die."

"To die!?" as if he had just been roused from a deep sleep.

"Yes," said Pablo, and squinted as if trying to see the ghosts in the street ahead of them: "It used to be the popular belief that annihilation on the road to Santiago de Compostela would assure the Eternal Life with God that every Christian should strive for. To drop dead was considered good fortune," and sniffled, wiping his nose with his rough cassock's sleeve: "Now, there is none o' that. They talk of penance, false penance. Really they think only about the prestige and the picnics ..."

Travelling exhausted me, but pulling myself out of the journeying only plunged me back into the hallucinogenic torture that was being meted out in my mind by Estrella's family.

The stork left me, but now it had been replaced by a succubus version of Estrella's fat faced younger sister, Cristina. In the hallucination she had a huge mouth that was breathing into my face, whilst, with a flicking, licking tongue, she probed my ear. I felt like my ear was a snail shell and she were a toad searching for meat, worming inside to lick on my brain. Then I felt a tickling all over my body, as if there were spiders, or other small creatures, running over it. But the spiders were actually tendrils of hair belonging to the second sister, Asunción. She had taken over the wound opened by the stork and was chewing on my liver herself. Her hair flicking over my naked body, slashing my skin as her head jerked with her tugging, gnawing jaw. At times she would look up at me, her eyes rolling back, white in their sockets as she chewed or sucked somnolently on my organ. A raspberry-yoghurt spittle, frothing from the corners of her mouth. The whole time this was happening, the mother's droning voice, Inma's sobbing or José María laughing and applauding were constant.

I looked down at the pentacle. They were deliberately possessing my mind and directing my will by imprisoning me there ... in the pentacle.

I tried to control my floating state to get my body outside of the blazing pentagram, but it was impossible, and if I ever got close to the flames they seemed to sear me, drawing screams from me. It was easier to go back. So, I did ...

A wide tree-lined path curled before me. Birds, excited by the rain and the creeping and sliding creatures it brought forth from under stones, were chirping, swooping down, bobbing about on the ground. Then the finches suddenly leapt up and circled Sarmiento and his cousin who were following the road out of town.

"Do you know this Canches?" asked Sarmiento.

"Not well. I've told you what I know," but then: "He lives alone. Another hermit like your Rodolfo."

Sarmiento sniggered and slapped his companion's back: "Like you, cousin."

"Me, alone?! My family is enormous. It's you who seems the lonely one, Pedro."

"Good company is hard to come by these days," and he laughed.

Then we were at Canches' house. Another lonely cottage in another green valley. The same sky, the same drizzle. Sarmiento and Pablo Martín were still on the winding path. A flock of ravens took off in front of them - white meat in their black beaks, some of it dropping as they left, had been lifted from the mangled corpse of a rabbit. Sarmiento stepped over it while Fr

Pablo slipped on a rotten and maggot ridden plum. While still at a fair distance from the cottage the friar lifted his nose and complained that it reeked of a stable: "Yet Canches has never kept animals."

Sarmiento sniffed too, then looked down at the path: "It would seem that our hermit does like to entertain," and he traced the outlines of horseshoe prints left in the damp earth around about: "Four invites?"

Fr Martín crouched down and examined a lump of horse dung: "And the revellers have not long gone. This shitten stuff is fresh."

Inside the house there had been more than a party. Things had been turned over, objects smashed, books knocked off shelves, their pages ripped out.

"Someone has been looking for something," mumbled Fr Pablo, more to himself than Sarmiento. Then: "I think we should assume that the objects searched for were of some value."

"Aye, Brother," and he picked up a leather bound book that had fallen open: "But they missed what I've come for." He thumped the book down on a table, pointed to the symbols, a cuneiform script next to terms in Greek: "A lexicon, cousin! Exactly what I need to translate my book," and then, mumbling: "But did they find Canches?" And suddenly turned ghostly pale.

He had to get back to Rodolfo: "I need my horse."

Sarmiento arrived back at Rodolfo's after nightfall, soaked - *Already too late* - deduced from the lack of light coming from the cottage. He stood in the doorway and tried to strike a match, but his tinderbox was wet. He stretched his arms and reached around, fumbling like a blind man.

Of course he could not see what I could. He could not see the mess, but he quickly began to divine the extent of it as he tripped over invisible books, slipped on spilt food and oil, stumbled against upturned furniture. He could not see the corpses that had been left, but there was so much to smell; the food and oil. The corpses were upstairs and he moved straight upstairs, slipping and reaching. His boots caked in mud and oil. He reached out. He knew where Rodolfo's bed had to be: he touched it, patting it, fondling upward to the headboard, and he found the pillow. The pillow, still over Rodolfo's face. Smothered, lifeless face. He ran his fingers under the pillow and over the features. A stiff, cold protuberance: the old man's nose. He patted, sighed, recognised that the mouth was open, tongue poking.

Magda was a mess. Sarmiento stumbled and accidentally kicked her. She lay on the floor in a pool of blood. This was dry on the surface, but Sarmiento stepped on it, breaking the coagulated top and he slipped on the thick but still liquid bottom. Her blood.

He sniffed, then ran his fingers over her. She had her mouth open too. But he pushed his finger into an opening further down, a cold gash. He dragged his finger along it, inside it, where her throat should have been. A mouth under the mouth, a mouth in the throat, and then realised that he had his finger in a gash that had been opened.

Her throat had been impaled.

He began to pant. He ran his hands over the rest of her body. Her legs were splayed, her dress up. He could feel her sex. Cold, dead sex. They had raped her first. The suspicion drew a loud moan. He pushed her legs together and pulled her dress down. There was a tear, hardly noticeable, it rested on his cheek, but he quickly brushed it away. Then he reached for her face again and pushed his fingers into that natural gap which was her mouth.

He started fishing for something under her tongue, something hard and metal. It was as if he had known it had to be there. He pinched it, pulled it, lifted it out, then clenched it in his palm.

He knew what it was. Her pendant. The lucky charm with the seal of Venus.

He bowed his head, stretched his arms and felt his way out ...

And then I was back ... back there ... there .... in the room, heavy, in Inma's bed. I actually felt well and good, as if I had emerged from a deep, restful sleep. I searched for my tormentors, expecting them to be there, but I was alone. I ran my hand over my belly, feeling for the open wound and my liver. There was nothing. I sniffed. There was a vague scent of incense.

I got up off the bed, down on my knees and inspected the floor. However, there was no trace of the drawn pentagram, or the spilled candle-wax that should have been there.

No trace at all of the witches' circle. Only an insubstantial whiff of fragrant gums

– *So it was a dream* – I thought. And then - *even if it wasn't, I should forget it* – and clambered back into the bed, wrapping myself up in the damp sheets ...

And I did forget it, but after recalling it again it chewed on my conscience – *Inma had warned me. She told me to escape. What if it hadn't been a dream?* – It began to torment me and kept me awake.

I decided I had to tell Estrella. José María had to be denounced, I was sure, even if it had been a mere dream, there had still been a conspiracy against me. But, *for what reasons*? And there was another crucial question left hanging – *Why had Inma drawn the pentagram?* –

I was certain of only one thing; now I had remembered the event, I could not ignore it.

When I got to Estrella's flat, I heard voices from the other side. When I knocked they stopped.

Estrella opened the door savagely. But when she saw it was me, she hugged me. Her heart pounding into me.

There was a man with her; pacing, gnawing finger nails. He was familiar, but at first I could not recall from where. He held out a hand. It was probably the blotches of blue ink on his fingertips that brought recognition.

Francisco Arizmendi, *Red Frank*. He was there because of Inma. He ran a hand through his hair and asked me if I had seen her. I slowly shook my head.

Estrella pushed herself away from me and, released from my arms she wrapped herself in her own. A straight jacket of limbs. She shivered, which evolved into a quake, exploding as a burst of moaning anguish and tears.

We took her and sat her down on the sofa. Gasping, she looked up. Not to me but to Francisco: "José María said Inma had wanted to borrow his shotgun."

It came out as a barrage that seemed to batter against Francisco and he exploded: "And the fucking idiot gave it to her?!"

"No, no ... he didn't ... he wouldn't ... he's been staying here with me this week ... his shotgun was here, but now it's gone ..." then maintaining her lungs full to calm herself before, with a lower pitch: "José's at the police station now, reporting it."

Then Francisco turned to me. His lips curling, pulling a mask of incredulous anguish: "She's fucking vanished," and then turning back to Estrella: "Why? That's what I fucking-well want to know. I don't trust that brother of yours. What's he up to? I saw him on my way up here. I told him she'd gone missing. He was cool as ice. Said that she would show up sooner or later. So cool your brother. Didn't seem to give a fucking damn."

Estrella, now centred by her breathing, tried to calm him. She embraced him and asked me to fetch a cognac.

Francisco's machine-gun monologue persisted: "I knew she had a problem. I could feel it. Why didn't she say anything to me? Your brother's capable of anything. The fascist creep."

I recalled Inma's anxious voice on the phone: "She called me a few days ago..." then a nausea rolled through my stomach, followed by an image. Red liquid spurting from a woman's face, over me. I reached out to protect myself, tried to wipe the imagined blood from my eyes. And I stammered: "She's in trouble," and then I blacked out ...

When I surfaced I was on the floor. Estrella was leaning, panting a sour whisky-breath over me. I grabbed her throat: "She's dead," I croaked, and she croaked back, trying to get air through the larynx that my hand had viced. She slapped me and I let go, my head thumping against the floor. Red Frank roared. White palms of hands descended, became clamps on my yellow shirt and he lifted me. I felt and heard cloth tear, the urgent release of popping buttons. But concern for my shirt disintegrated into his red-black throat, swamped by his rasping, spittle-throttling cry: "What are you saying arsehole? Inma dead?!"

I tried to break loose with a shoving forearm, rendered useless by the gravity of his rage. I could hardly get air out. He was on my chest. Nevertheless, my voice remained surprisingly calm: "Yes," and then: "No, not Inma ... someone who looked like her ... the one who looks like her ..." which made him pensively confused, and lighter, so I pushed him away, getting up on my knees and clutching Estrella's hips. I continued my discourse across the hanging waves of her dress: "I saw her before, at the house in Pontevedra ... there ... her ghost ... She's dead ... Sarmiento's sister is dead…" then turned back to a dumbfounded Francisco: "I'm sorry … she looked like Inma … so much like Inma …"

The scene I had witnessed; Sarmiento returning home. Dishevelled clothes, torn and grubby. His shirt was open and his bare chest heaved. His face febrile. Splashes of dirt. He was ushered into a room by a servant girl, also panting. Mouths curling down. Voices low. A woman sat in a solitary chair, completely in black. When she saw him, she said his name, opened her arms, but did not rise. He embraced her. She wept. He clutched her cloak, squeezed it and ran his filthy hand through her hair: "Oh mother, I'll have his gizzards for it!"

Her voice, kept low, but quaking through tears: "No, lad. Do nothing, I beg you. There is naught that can be done now."

But he fell back on his knees. Leaning backward, clenching his shirt.

The force of the explosion was again retarded by the tension in his neck, but each word sallied forth with a hornet's intuition: "There be the satisfaction of vengeance."

She staggered out of the chair. Her cap dropped and her grey hair burst free. She grabbed his throat. Her eyes wide open. Hissing through gritted teeth: "Thirst not for it, the evil done must be forgot…"

The redhead girl who looked so much like Inma, had been Sarmiento's sister. She was dead. Murdered. I had to piece the story together from a series of short flashes. Different times. Different spaces…

Pedro Sarmiento had been talking to Magda. He was calm then. His voice was soft and sad: "I dream of my sister every night, and carry her before my eyes, in my mind, when I'm awake. I contemplate her at my table with each meal. She walks with me wherever I go and I talk to her at all times of the day, in every place …"

And then Magda: "Then let me be her …"

Her name had been María Dolores and she had been murdered in her bed. In her husband's bed.

Rodolfo, with a cold voice as he rubbed his hands: "How vile those who do not love their wives. Marriage has to be a binding law of love and affection. They must, for love of God, learn and struggle to make the life of the spouse easier. A more tranquil existence and full of pleasure. That is marriage. Lo, your sister was flung onto a most abominable bed."

And then the image of the monster: the husband. Hirsute and huge, everything hirsute and huge. He was pulling off his clothes, revealing how hirsute and huge he really was. She, in their bed, laughing nervously. Then he pounced on her, walloped her: "The woman must never laugh," then another slap when she whimpered: "Verily, it is a most indecent habit, and one of whores." And he tore and ripped off the smock she was wearing. Her small girl's breast trembled. Blood trickled from the side of her mouth. He spat at her, crept forward, pushed his penis into her mouth.

Fr Pablo Martín: "The sexual act must be correctly channelled. Copulation should occur only betwixt married persons and with the sole aim of procreating ..."

The huge and hirsute husband, still bellowing and slathering: "You are mine, slut. *Debitum coniugalem*!"

Then María Dolores at the confessional. A tubby, balding priest snorting advice: "The good wife should submit to the sexual exigencies of the husband. If not she is committing sin and her mother even more, for having failed to teach her daughter her obligations ..."

Fr Pablo Martín: "Sexual relations are prohibited on Sundays, during menstruation and pregnancy, and during lactation. If not, they are worse than beasts. As for the act itself: it should not be indulged in with too much frequency, it is bad for the health. The couple must copulate facing each other, and the hands and mouth should not be used ..."

María Dolores began to gag on the penis being pushed down her throat ...

A monotonous voice: "Ejaculation outside of the vagina is a sin ..."

While the hirsute husband's hand took hold of his huge penis as it pulled out of María Dolores' mouth. He tugged it and it spurted over her face. She screamed. He slapped her again ...

"You must use the generative organ of your body. All else is a sin ..."

And the huge penis was shoved into the girl's little anus ...

"... a mortal sin! And the woman consenting to it is just as much a sinner as the husband performing it ..."

María Dolores was screaming until he wedged a cloth between her teeth, like the bridle of a horse ...

"Lo, my daughter, do not consent to this great sin! You must fight it, that is your obligation! ..."

Her hands thrashed behind her until he caught them both in one of his and squeezed the wrists tightly together ...

"Even if your husband, for not consenting to such a heinous abuse, should cut your throat; even that is better than enduring the sin, for as your life thus escapes you, you have the comfort of the knowledge that you die a martyr and that you win the prize of eternal life!"

Fr Pablo Martín: "Women have an enormous and uncontrollable sexual appetite. They exhaust their husbands *in seriatim*. Women seduce, manipulate, corrupt and are by nature unfaithful ..."

She lay naked on the bed, exhausted and trembling. Her eyes were swollen. A tooth had been knocked out of her bloody mouth.

A servant boy stood over her, staring at her naked and bleeding sex, but she was too dazed to react ...

"A man can freely kill his adulterous wife. This is not a crime."

The boy's hand with a wet cloth, wiped the blood from the girl's mouth. She sighed, but did not smile.

"Marry hussy! If I were your husband, I would give your feet and hands such a beating that you would remember it for a long time to come."

And the knife dropped and cut. And María Dolores was dead.

Part Two: The Alchemist and The Inquisition

VII. New Spain

(a) solutio

a warm gale heaves betwixt our souls
rising with the moon
   a mad-rushing breeze along a phantom plane,
past us and every other carbuncle pocking the surface
   it lifts
with the battered-bruised yellow-full face,
    arriving with the retreat of that sadly surrendering sun
      both orbs tilting,
         one up, the other down,
      as if they were fixed on a wheel's transparent smooth rim
    with an unseen golden rod between.
the heaving wind: a hurricane cacophony
         the scorching assassin in his high-voltage chair roars
    goodbye to the already dead moon
which is mighty huge tonight, say some,
   a relative deduction,
     even their raised and tightly-closed little fists
would cover it...

has my departure not infected us all?
   they accuse me of selfish-cruel flight,
but i left to bring us together
we cannot take chances
   you are not so distant

it is your breath i feel in my heart,
   that warm gale
heaving betwixt our souls
        open yourself -
i am there...

I fingered the soft paper that these words had been scribbled on. They were not just lines on a page, but sounds, scales to lead me, music to lift me. I was shoved; into her world, into their world, into *his* world ...

Flying-fish splashed out, shivered in the air, then plopped back. Sarmiento, sitting, nose down towards the pages of some thick, wind-fluttering book, reading or scribbling notes. Another book was under his fingers. The book he had taken from Canches's cottage. He pushed them aside to rise and stand at the prow; leaning against the rail, his arms folded tightly across his chest, his hands squeezing the lapels of his mud-brown doublet together. He was shivering, just like the struggling, air traversing fish he contemplated. But it could not have been so cold; his brow was moist and it gleamed, his gaze squinting, pained because enduring the gold white flashes of a still summer sun on the ocean.

A sharply still profile cut a blurred edge into my view. Fr Pablo, hands clasped, spatula-flat, in prayer: "*Blessed be the light and the Lord of truth ... Blessed be the day and the good Lord who brought us it.*"

Near them was a young woman, baby faced, her fleshy torso wrapped in a white, blood splattered apron. She had a long knife clutched in a thick, pale fist, and at first I thought she was about to hurl it at the venerating friar. But instead of skewering Fr Pablo's heart, a rude grunt was pushed up her throat and she thrust the blade into a large, pink fish in her lap. There was a slight squelch when she shoved the iron down into the belly, then sliced. This piscine victim had been dragged away from another dozen in a wicker basket, so while the one was butchered, twelve others were flapping with gaping, silent howls of agony that the woman had obviously grown insensitive to.

In front of her was another man in tight purple stockings, nervously pacing the deck. His white lace collar and cuffs fluttered in the sea breeze.

He had a high, black hat, black handlebar moustache and a beard that he rubbed, as if wringing problems from it. In his other hand he gripped the aureate embroidered lapels of a dark blue jacket, ignoring a delicate gold crucifix that dangled nearby.

Alongside his stomping trajectory, sat a mature, handsome *lady*; elegant, but stiff, in a conspicuously large and elaborately fashioned armchair. Her head was bowed, a white veil drooping with a slight tremble, sometimes blown up by the wind, exposing her countenance. Her eyes contemplated her fingers, which were pale and cupped over creases in her dress. She ignored the man, but they were obviously together, married and well-to-do. She, like him, was over dressed for a ship's deck; layer on layer of fabric, a black gown, high, white lace collar. Even sitting it was obvious she was tall and strong, which emphasised her husband's tenuity. Then she moved slightly and straightened her neck to catch air. Her chest was heaving into a too tight bodice. At one side of her stood a dark skinned woman, obviously a slave, who fanned. On the other side was an even darker boy, who watched the pacing, high-hatted gentleman with some anxiety.

Fr Pablo leaned back against the taffrail, observing the couple and their slaves, even wondering about them, then looked past to the rest of the passengers. Most of them were lying out of the sun under a tarpaulin. A lute was plucked. One man was standing, singing a slow, sorrowful song: "*Dime, tristee coraçón, ¿porqué callas tu pasión?*"

Those nearest the singer were silent and contemplating. Sarmiento was also affected by the dirge. He sighed and, despite the obvious heat, shivered again.

Then the man in the high black hat, also inspired, waved his hand and roared out his own despairing lament: "A prison this ship. If they'd told me I'd be sleeping on such an 'ard and narrow plank, in such a shallow and narrow cabin I'd not've paid 'em." And snorted: "Cutpurses they were, who sold us this passage." Grunting: "Oh, what an idiot I was to give away good money for this." And he pulled a handkerchief from his sleeve to wipe his brow: "The 'eat inside," and gulped: "... 'n' when they turn on the pump and move the putrid waters ... the stench, as if from some opened devil's arse," coughing: "Insufferable."

But Sarmiento's mind was far away from that reality: in a memory, long ago, when the already dead were still alive. A memory, from a child's perspective, staring up a rising street. Grey stone steps that climbed and twisted, only to disappear behind the adobe brown wall of a building. Then a squeal, and coming down the steps another child in a white, cotton shirt and linen cap, with a long, grey dress fanning out and rustling. She bobbed down rather than ran: one step up, two steps down. She was chuckling, exuberant, and suddenly burst into a sprint with arms outstretched. A large, gaping grin. The front row of milk-teeth had a wide gap. She reached out to the observer. He called out: "*María Dolores... Lola-Lolita, my little Lolita!!!*" The girl was giggling through her panting breath as the onlooker embraced her: "*Oh Pedwo, Pedwo!!!*" and she sank her infant head into the slightly older Sarmiento's shoulder ... sunk ... and arms clutched ...

... until a whirlpool caught the memory and dragged it into hell. His same sister, now almost grown up, with a huge knife wobbling in her throat. He put his hands under her dry hair and pressed his fingers into her cold, hard head. Her young dead-face, pale and gaping like the fish in the fishmonger's basket. He shook his head and grimaced. His chest heaving. Fr Pablo saw this reaction, guessed the cause, and sighed.

Meanwhile the man in the black hat was pouring himself a goblet of sack. His whining continued: "If we don't catch a plague it'll be God's miracle, pray."

Loud enough to invade half the ship. Sarmiento put his hands over his ears and shut his eyes. Fr Pablo turned away from his cousin and confronted the grumbler, admonishing his whingeing. That one, offended, agitated his head and turned to the young woman slicing fish. He mumbled something indiscernible into her large soft breasts. She grunted, straightened her back, and wiped sweat off her brow with the back of her bloodied hand. The fish in front of her had its head off. There were dark, almost black clotted streaks on the knife.

Fr Pablo returned to Sarmiento and reached forward. He too imagined his cousin's sister alive. But, in his mind's eye, it was a different face, more dour. The green eyes that Sarmiento had always imagined were now grey. When he ideated her dead, it was as a box being lowered into her grave. He sucked oxygen to inspire courage. His hand dropped lightly onto the alchemist's shoulder: "It's wrong to flagellate yourself for a world's injustice."

A twitch flickered in Sarmiento's cheek. He dragged phlegm from the cavities around his nose and mumbled as he spat over the side of the ship: "Fine morality to come from a friar."

Which was enough condemnation to ignite a brief but painful whirl in Pablo's head. For no conscious reason he squeezed the shoulder he was holding, pushing against it to support himself, and grimaced: "We're all hypocrites," his chin went down then flicked up again, hissing: "Do you really think it'll be any better where we're going?"

Sarmiento felt the ship's yaw under him. He had to grip hard onto a rail to retard the desire to drown: "I'm not looking for justice!" but then the catharsis came: "Two women I've loved, both have been fair of form, and both have died. Both with a blade in their neck. Can it be that it was written in the stars of my birth? Oh, I've looked for it all right," and the sun was obscured by a small cloud, making it dismal. He ran both hands through his hair: "Ah, but cousin, don't think because of what I say that I'm weak. Don't think that it'll make me a good God-fearing man because of some cruel fate," his jaw clamped and the next came out through gritted teeth: "If I *am* cursed, and the women I love must die; then so be it." Then, relaxed by luscious images of women to love: "It'll not stop me from lusting; not until the entire sex is murdered and gone, only then would I cease to yearn ..." and he moved away toward the stern.

A barrel was thumped, followed by a restrained roar, rasping through tense chords and gritted teeth. Not Sarmiento, it was the man in the black hat. He was hopping around on one leg, precariously balancing the goblet of wine in one hand while he pulled at the boot on his raised foot with the other. A tiny, tremulous rodent had appeared further down the deck where it had paused to scratch its snout. He flung the boot at it: at nothing, the mouse had already disappeared before it left his hand. Clomp. Inspiring cockroaches to scurry out from cracks.

But the boot bounced and skidded across the wet deck into the naked back of another man, well fed and huge. Under exercised meat, become flab, wobbled. He had been playing cards and was therefore sitting; a dim lump, grey in the gloom of a mast flung shadow. The impact inspired quake rippled up his back and neck and became a facial twitch. Then a backward reaching arm slapped fattened leech palps of fingers onto the point of contact. He rubbed, detecting abnormality, then winced himself up on the creaking joints of a pink ham arm and the almost non-existent knees of elephant legs. He turned out of the shade, into the light. A purple stain ran down from the smooth shaven scalp of his massive barrel head to decorate an already fiercely bristled face with the silhouette of a scorpion. An almost diagonal running slit of a mouth yawned open to release a penetrating monosyllabic roar and the tension taught blood-full digits on his hand darted to a huge and cold scimitar that had been pushed through and held tight by a girdle.

The black hat quivered and the sack in the jiggling goblet splashed over the rim.

Sarmiento was almost between them. He remained calm with an eyebrow lifted. One hand was on the hilt of his sword, the other up to his mouth, sucking one of his rings. He caught the rolling massive tall and bald man's eye. Glared at him with a tragic message. The giant's rubber jaw melted and dropped and he let go of the handle of his sword. He grunted, then cursed and, shaking his head, hurled the boot back at the man in the black hat before returning to his game.

The recipient took the blow unflinchingly. His hat fell or was blown off and he staggered as the ship lurched. Otherwise there was just a snort and a gulp. His eyes slid across to acknowledge the alchemist's tacit intervention. Then he put his goblet down, pulled on his boot and took three steps forward. His hair pricked up porcupine-like as his head nodded stupidly in front of Sarmiento: "Please señor. Allow me to present meself. Don Gabriel Mateos y Díaz, at your service," then with a brisk, flicking gesture: "As for this lovely creature over 'ere. She's me wife, Doña Rosa."

Sarmiento started shivering again. Fr Pablo, who seemed to have missed all the action and was still stuck with the idea of the *assassin-husband,* hooked his arm under Sarmiento's and dragged him away. The man, who was waiting for recognition, received this gesture as an insult. His lip curled, but the friar was oblivious.

Pablo pressed his hanging wooden crucifix to his sternum. His voice gently blown and sweet: "That he went unpunished is wrong. But blood-revenge would have merely enlarged the circumference of the sin…"

Sarmiento pulled himself away and reached down to the deck to recover Don Gabriel's black hat for him, scooping it up and flinging it like a discus into the breeze. But too hard and it hurled straight over the deck. Nevertheless, he had heard the friar and, as he watched the spinning ring of felt cut its way through the air, he shouted into the same wind to boomerang his questioning reply back: "And is it a sin to hurry a sinner unto Hell!?"

Don Gabriel watched his hat disappear with a look of complete incomprehension. And when Sarmiento's cry reached him he mistook it for a madman's insult.

On the other side Fr Pablo clenched his fists: "Agghh!" through jaws clamped by gritted teeth. It was the friar's turn to suffer a vision. A blade in his own mind had slashed, a crimson sluice had also opened. He squeezed his eyes shut to retard tears, then opened them wide again, staring into the breeze: "Last night you were rambling in your sleep about a black leopard," but did not see Sarmiento's feline snarl of contempt. It was his own welling emotions that made him rapid: "By vengeance you can palliate his evil deed by reciprocating it, but that does nothing to eradicate it," and he sucked to gather spittle: "Yet don't trouble yourself too much. God will have His justice even if earthly judges ignore it - and His wrath will be awesome!"

The monologue's progress was cut off by Sarmiento, who suddenly turned toward the sniffling orator, revealing the black leopard, gnashing teeth face of a real madman. He grabbed his cousin's throat, hard enough to produce an audible choke and, leaning to his ear, he whispered: "Know you why my sister was killed?"

Pablo wrenched himself free with a desperate hand. Smarting moist eyes expressed triste bewilderment. He had to cough useless air out of his chest to splutter, angrily curt: "The s-servant boy was accused … but … everyone knows it was the husband."

Sarmiento leaned his brow against his palm and groaned: "No, you're wrong cousin," staring at the frayed edge of his sleeve, he spat his own drop of wetted salt into the ocean: "It was most definitely the page."

Pablo's mouth became a gape.

Sarmiento's voice dropped even further, but affirmation of the detail seemed to calm him. The next sound was a much gentler kind of rasping, on the exhalation: "A man told me in a tavern. In Lugo."

Fr Pablo shook his head: "And do you believe a drunk, prithee?"

The alchemist maintained the whisper: "He wasn't drunk. Most definitely sober," and scratched a nut-shard out from a tight marriage of teeth. The top row was exposed when his upper lip curled: "I believed him because he told me that he'd paid the boy himself."

"To kill María Dolores?" emphatic, raising the tone again.

Sarmiento had to bring it down, transporting the grubby fingernail from his teeth to his lips, which he traversed: "Sshh ..." then an even softer whisper: "No, not to kill her. But to steal what he thought was in her house. Something the man who paid him wanted dearly." Then the finger was away and the lips were pressed right up against the friar's ear: "The boy searched for it. My sister found him ransacking her room. She tried to stop him and he wedged his knife into her throat."

Pablo's lips quivered. His own tone dropped to a murmur as well: "Devil's work. But what was he looking for, pray?"

The question brought Sarmiento's eye-brows up: "Something extremely valuable for the man who paid him. Or should I say for the men who paid the man who paid him." And he pulled up the cylinder containing the map that was under his jacket, just a glimpse, but enough for his cousin to understand what was being referred to: "My sister died because she was my sister. Do you cognise my anguish now?"

Pablo grimaced, but recognised that if his cousin did feel pain it was more from pride than love. Nevertheless, despite the impurity of it, the plot intrigued: "And this man sat with you and told you that he'd had your sister killed?"

"Aye..." expressing finality, but he was unable to endure the pause that ensued and hurried on: "I would've killed him then," he boasted. The next phrase trickled: "But he had friends." Then leaning close again, as if by exhaling the conspiracy he could redeem himself of it: "There were four of them. All clad the same, in black. Foreigners. Portuguese," the last sibilant hissed: "We fought. I slashed his arm, a deep enough cut, it bled in spurting jets. The others tried to restrain me," and he felt the mother sea tugging him towards it: "My dagger caught one of their cheeks. Then when the other customers in the tavern heard my attackers squeal in Portuguese they were all against them, throwing things at them, forcing their stumbling retreat," and he scratched his frayed cuff: "Since then I have been ever-so-carefully on my guard. If they find me they will chisel out my gizzards, troth."

The friar shut his eyes to the last vicious image. His voice came out slow and tremulous: "Has this something to do with Canches's disappearance?" Sarmiento merely nodded.

Pablo shook his head, whispering as softly as Sarmiento had done: "And the death of Rodolfo ... and that girl ..." Then squeezing Sarmiento's shirt, where the parchment was: "What is it? A map?"

Sarmiento pushed a rigid index finger against his cousin's twitching line of lips: "It's my secret cousin. Pray, a fatal secret that I must only know myself," ignoring the blow such a rejection had just dealt to the friar: "It's killed too many of my friends, I would not have it kill you also."

A scream. The woman with the fish. Her fat and trembling arms were in the air, mouth wide open, screwing up her face.

Sarmiento hurried to her. He bent forward and reached down for the long grey fish that had been dropped. His hands were under its back, holding its sliced and open belly up. Then he sat down and ran a finger along the gash, poking and parting the lips of the wound. The pink flesh inside was drawn tight over a thick skeleton. He flicked out an egg sack and a spleen.

The fishmonger woman, caught enough breath to blurt out a syllable: "Look!"

Sarmiento parted the gash wider until he could see it. He reached in for it, levering it out with a flicking finger. It looked like a fat, pale grub at first. The woman threw a cloth to him. He used it to wipe the extracted object.

She screamed again. It was obvious now what it was: "This is a terrible bad omen, señor ... Terrible bad!" and she turned her head away, unable to contemplate it.

Sarmiento was frozen; engrossed. Fr Pablo leaned forward, his jaw down, the tip of his pale tongue poking out. Stillness. Until Sarmiento, obviously sensing the friar's mounting horror, suddenly jerked and flicked the object into his cousin's face. The friar gasped and leaned back so quickly that he actually toppled over. Sarmiento laughed. Then he cracked his knuckles and lifted the little, fat white thing for all to see.

It was a finger, human, that had been cut off just above the knuckle. Sarmiento held it higher to catch more light, and twisted it. It gleamed. There was a ring on it. He smiled and mumbled to himself: "Fate has the most peculiar fashions for distributing gifts." Then pulled the ring off, smirked, and rubbed it while he laughed and patted his clambering cousin's shoulder: "See this cousin," and pointed to the disc on the ring. There was an engraving. A dim figure of a man, dressed in what seemed like ecclesiastical robes with a star over his head, reading a book: "The sign of Jupiter. A lucky charm. It promotes increase. Very good for business, and very good for keeping the heart calm in moments of dire peril," and he slipped it on his own finger.

"Do you think that's wise?" remarked the friar, his eyes bright with gleaming anxiety: "The last finger to bear that devil's ring was itself chewed off. Hardly the best of luck I'd say."

"God works in mysterious ways."

"As does the devil."

"Then I will tempt them both. Now I have three magic rings, cousin. They make me invincible."

Fr Pablo guffawed while Sarmiento's mouth curled into a rippling-strange smile. In Sarmiento's mind, his adult sister, in a long pink dress, was wielding a huge and heavy sword. Air filled his throat, making his eyes bulge. He reached forward and grabbed the friar's hands, squeezing them together at the wrists. The physical contact seemed to release the air: "Scoff not, and stay by me. You too will benefit greatly from it, sirrah."

Then the image of María Dolores became mere colour. A brief flash of brilliant red. Painful red. The light was accompanied by a mournful sound. Her dying scream: first shrill, then choked, finally gurgling, until colour took form.

Her, sitting over a desk. A writing cane scratching parchment. Behind her: a grey, hooded figure, whispering. Ambiguous sex. Dictation. The words, a verse – *her verse* – I thought, meaning Inma's …

from my cave i look out across my desert, to your arid plain:
  are we not united by landscapes?

the hot, dry land is like our hot, dry hearts and thirsty souls

step out and we are surrounded by horizons:
*   jagged rocks and pricking thorns constitute our paths;*
roads infested by snakes and scorpions,
*   flanked by weed and cacti -*
which is why we stay put.
*   in my cave i stand naked before a magic mirror,*
but i cannot see my breasts –
*   it is therefore a portrait that i send you...*
*   this image pierces your skull, becomes embedded in your consciousness.*
look
*   into the mirror,*
*   past me,*
*   past my nakedness,*
and you will find my soul...

A verse that became a gushing whirlwind of light in the realm of anti-physics. Dizzying. More choking fish, spread out on dry land. The beauty of their silver scales spoiled by freckles of sand. One of the fish flicked itself, a spastic leap, and vanished. Or so I thought, until I realised that I had vanished. That I had been flung again into open air, hurled through a sky, then dropped.

In the desert: not my desert, not hers even, but Sarmiento's desert. He and his cousin had arrived, in Mexico - on an open, ochreous plain ...

The back of a black haired boy. A sweat stained shirt filled by a heaving chest. His mud brown outfit was almost a camouflage. He stood, nearly straight, tilting to the left. The arm that side was weighed down by a thick stick. His other arm was up, his hand shading his eyes. Then he bent to the right, reached down and picked up a rock. This was meant for a long eared, tawny hare that was trembling beside a shivering, toasted tumbleweed. But the boy's attention was urged away; redemption for the leporine animal. From the bottom of the dry valley a dust cloud churned up from behind a dark, covered carriage. Before it a paling, flavescent strip: the road.

I swooped down, speed blurring the landscape below me. My target, the stage-coach. Hovering alongside it, I was close enough to discern the peeling paint on the door. The Hapsburg's bicephalous eagle was engraved there, one half of it red, the other yellow. Four dark figures lurched on top. Two looking forwards, the others back. And one of the front facing ones pulled on reins. Closing in I looked inside. There were four more bobbing figures, dark and difficult to discern in the penumbra of the vehicle, but I sensed familiarity. My hero with his cousin, and, opposite them, the lordly whinger from the ship and his wife, sitting silent, each one distant from the other.

Outside, in a ditch by the side of the road, a man was waving his arms, and kept waving them until the coach had come to a standstill. There was a chestnut lump on the ground behind him, a horse with open but lifeless eyes and a gaping mouth. Doña Rosa gasped, while her husband actually chuckled. Fr Pablo opened the door and stretched out: "A problem, señor?"

The dusty man outside had stopped waving and had begun wrestling with a hefty leather saddle which he clutched within the ark of an arm. When he had balanced himself, he trotted to Fr Pablo. His olive green doublet and hose were creased. He was sweating, but his voice was loud, youthful, and optimistic: "There's been an accident (*squinting to discern*) Father (*embarrassed chuckle*) My poor horse fell, broke its leg. I had to kill it (*sucking his lip gormlessly while proffering his hand*) I'm an engineer (*then, obviously realising the inappropriateness of a full introduction, retracted the outstretched arm*) With your permission, I'd like a ride. To Tlaxcala."

"We're going to Tlaxcala."

The young engineer clapped his hands. His stupid smile broadened: "Then I'll get on top," and lowering his head and mumbling: "With permission, Father."

Fr Pablo began gesticulating wildly: "Oh no. On top no. Come in and sit with us," and leaned out to help him lift the saddle to the driver, who was helped by Don Gabriel and Doña Rosa's slaves.

Sarmiento grimaced. His cousin glared at him, forbidding comment. He pushed him aside to make room for the stranger who was climbing in, stepping on a grumbling Don Gabriel's toes. Fr Pablo slammed the door, then slapped it and the carriage jerked.

There was no room for three on the same side, so they became all elbows and sweat. Nevertheless, the engineer and Fr Pablo maintained their stupid smiles, beaming faces that did nothing but amplify the gloom of the surrounding countenances.

Sarmiento still had his fever. He was radiant and anguished. Don Gabriel and his wife were also miserable. Fr Pablo introduced them to the new passenger, then presented himself. All of them grey with dust.

Doña Rosa was uncomfortable and made an obvious effort not to wriggle and not to complain. She had large, round, brown, but bitter eyes. A long nose almost touched a top lip. Stern, she was, and absurdly employed in the Sisyphus-chore of brushing her dress, which revealed a pattern of bees until the next cloud blew in on them. Sometimes she slapped dirt off her husband as well. Whenever she did his top lip would curl up, exposing crooked yellowing teeth, and he trembled as she whipped his jacket with a handkerchief. He had a cloak draped over one shoulder: yellow, under the grey. It bore a dark pattern of tiny, curling serpents. The rest of his suit was a deep burgundy.

The friar stiffly turned his neck to examine the profile of the man squeezed next to him. After a minute of close inspection, his voice, itself pulverulent, croaked through the thunder and rattle: "You said that you were an engineer, señor"

The young man's nescient smile had never left his round, bright face. He tweaked a finely groomed moustache and scratched a line of beard that covered the crease of his chin. Sweat dripped down his forehead from under his flat, green cap: "Fernando Magariño Rodriguez, Father ... At your service (*and tilted his head forward, a circumstantial bow*) Engineer, yes. My duty in this New World is the construing of its roads and bridges," and smiled just as the coach bounced, making his jaw clap up, trapping his tongue. He grimaced, and sucked in case of blood.

The friar, gripped by empathy, grimaced too, then reached under his cape and pulled out a wine-skin. This he proffered to Fernando, who shook his head. He had his own sack and reciprocated the gesture.

Pablo insisted: "This is Castilian wine. And a very salubrious one."

"But you're in New Spain now, Father. So take this Mexican vintage. I insist on the invitation being mine."

Which obliged. Fr Pablo tilted his head back, but, after squeezing a jet down his throat, choked and spat. The engineer roared. The woman moaned quietly, the friar's ejection had stained her dress.

Sarmiento, who had been staring outwards, turned, shivering. His face was moist and gleaming, and despite the heat he had his cloak wrapped well around him. The engineer took his sack back from the friar, gulping down his own ration before passing it on to Sarmiento: "It'll do your fever good."

Sarmiento squeezed a jet as the others had done and coughed and spluttered as his cousin. He offered the sack to Doña Rosa, who waved a frantic hand in negation.

Fernando laughed: "There's nothing like this in your Spain. It's called *pulque*."

Don Gabriel in front of him smiled and made an obvious gesture of acceptance, taking the sack without making a sound. He guzzled three jets and licked his lips before returning the brew with a satisfied grin and nod to Fernando who took another swig himself.

The engineer's narrow eyes squeezed closed. They were Asiatic features. He shook his head but did not cough. Then he looked gravely at Sarmiento and his voice dropped: "How you shiver, señor! You seem to have acquired the local ague, a most nasty friend. The fever will return every four days. Be warned señores, there's a lot here to die from. Though with your prayers, Father, I'm sure you'll be all well blessed."

Sarmiento coughed and spluttered, as if the sympathy had inspired an attack. He drank some water from a leather canteen and coughed again while Pablo persisted with the engineer: "So you know this country and its customs well."

"Aye, Father. My history begins, like most biographies must, with my progenitor," and took a deep breath: "He was a natural of Estremadura and Badajoz, and like his son, yours truly, a humble engineer by trade," the chest deflated: "Suffering the ignoble effects of a penury imposed by the gambling debts of his own dear but unfortunate brother, he caught a boat and sailed unto this New World. To the Hispaniola. But that isle was then already ruined by the tyrant Columbus and his Genoese clan (*sucked his teeth*) Finding the place well damned and beyond remedy, he considered the more virgin conquest, whose coasts were just then discovered by Grijalva (*eyes widening, brows and tone up*) and embarked with the most noble and famous conquistador, Cortés himself, no less. Do you attend?"

"Oh, heedfully," hastened Fr Pablo.

Sarmiento, broke the rushing pace with a low and drawling: "They say Cortés looked after his fellow *Estremeños* very well."

The statement, obviously sarcastic, provoked a moment of uncomfortable silence. But it was Don Gabriel rather than Fernando who seemed the more upset. His sallow cheeks were sucked in as he sniffed then lifted his bearded chin. His voice, rasping: "Troth, señor. Envious tongues look for all possible demerits. If Cortés chose to be surrounded by 'is countrymen that was 'is own election," and he licked his top lip and caught Sarmiento's eye. The alchemist did not falter, his own fierce stare absolutely unrepentant. Don Gabriel had to look away, to Fernando: "Most of us'd do the same," he went on: "We can be understood better by them who speak our own language, can we not?" and winked at Fernando, gulping air. A gesture which the engineer seemed to immediately understand and he passed on the sack of *pulque*.

Fr Pablo gave his cousin an accusing look, obviously disapproving of his provocation. But Fernando waved a hand to dismiss the contention and continued: "Think what you will of Cortés, but it cannot be denied that it was a more than glorious campaign which he led, to disperse, by Christian arms, the cruel and gloomy pagan cloud that had been hanging over this land, and to so bravely raze the Mexican king Montezuma's old capital of debauch and terror."

Sarmiento scratched his neck, mumbling: "Destroying what has been called the most beautiful city ever seen on this earth."

Ignored by Fernando: "And when Cortés, afterwards, contemplated the city's ruins; imagining the enormous task of rebuilding ahead of them, it was my very own father that he commissioned." Then threw his arms in the air: "You attend not!"

Fr Pablo, whose attention was just drifting outside, blinked hard and spluttered: "Oh good señor, but we do."

"Then regard this, prithee, that it was my very own father who was employed as one of the overseers working alongside Alonso García Bravo.

One of the illustrious group of men who were responsible for the construction of the glorious Christian city that's now the capital of this new and most catholic world."

Sarmiento coughed: "May God bless him."

"Aye! Well said," continued Fernando, oblivious to the irony in Sarmiento's pitch. But then his glorious tone saddened: "For he's been long dead. My father's current labour; building naves in heaven's cathedrals."

Fr Pablo clapped his hands: "Oh surely, señor! More blessed and good travail there cannot be!"

"No truer sentiment felt Father," which was expressed over a sigh.

The friar clutched his wrist: "Then you are Mexican born?"

"Mestizo. My own mother, my good dad's second wife, a piece of virtue, now also dead some five years hence, was herself a Mexican."

"Most truly well at home then," said the friar through a smile.

"Aye, the ghosts that haunt these dry rocks, are my ancestors, pray."

Sarmiento yawned while Fr Pablo turned to Don Gabriel: "And you, señor? Your history?"

Drawing a wry smile from the lordly passenger: "My history, Father? If you want," and then he looked straight and purposefully at Sarmiento, recalling for an instant how his dear black hat, had cut a sad arc through the air before plummeting over the side of that ship: "But then I'll have to admit to you that I'm from Medellín, no less," and sucked his front teeth: "From that western part of Castile that we call Estrem-a-dura." A challenging stare, screwing up his nose: "Which makes me, I should think, an *Estremeño*." Sarmiento groaned, but out of the window. Don Gabriel continued: "And a countryman of Don Hernán Cortés. Me father too was one of his own men. I was brought 'ere after the conquest, as a lad, and 've lived 'ere ever since. I'm me mum's eldest living son now, and master of me father's land. As for the reason for this journey that I am now returning from, that lies in the bosom of this woman wit' me. For I went to Castile to marry, and bring 'er back 'ere," and he laughed, nervously.

Sarmiento wriggled and turned toward the *Estremeño's* wife. A wisp of fair hair curled out from under her shawl: "And it's obvious, señora, that *you* have no Mexican blood."

But it was her husband who replied: "Me wife is from Burgos, 'erself, the daughter of noble parents. She's come from a ..." his eyes widened, realisation of an accident. He had to struggle to get the next word out: "c-convent ..."

And then the woman. Deep, dry voice and unexpected: "He means I was a nun, señores. In a Castilian convent. Of course, I escaped."

The friar sat up and instinctively grabbed his wooden crucifix. Don Gabriel and the engineer were also uncomfortable and wriggling. The woman drew the veil away from her face. Her lip curled up. She caught Sarmiento's eye, the corner of his own mouth rising, then she turned to the friar: "Don't worry, Father, I am not a renegade. I was forced to the convent at a tender age. Since then I have to admit that all paternal affection has abandoned me. The convent, señores, is a prison, marry."

Her face was slapped. Don Gabriel: "We're in a foul mood today!" Then to Pablo: "You must excuse me wife, Father, but it's been a long and tiresome journey. Verily, she must be exhausted, poor mouse."

Doña Rosa rubbed her smarting cheek: "Tired I am. But not too tired to speak. And not too tired to protest a husband's violence!"

The engineer reddened. The friar was also wriggling now. Sarmiento grinned, obviously enjoying the sudden radical shift whilst the woman thrust forth with a lip shivering snarl: "If I say that a convent is a prison, then I know what I'm saying, for I was twenty years locked up in one."

"Married to the Lord Jesus Christ!" spluttered out Fr Pablo, punctuating each syllable with a blink.

"And now divorced. With the Pope's blessing, señores."

Don Gabriel softened the tone: "Please, Father, let me explain the legitimacy of this base sounding circumstance. My wife, as I said, is the daughter of the Duke of ..." Almost a whisper, broken by screaming rage.

"Was the daughter! I have no parent now ..."

Dissipating into her husband's insipid composure: "...'er parents decided that a nun's life was to be good for her."

Then the wife's fire also dropped into something monotonous, but still full of spite: "And still at the tender and innocent age of only nine my irrefutable marriage was consummated."

" 'Cause ..."

The tedium gained pace again, as if imitating the rumbling rhythm of the coach: "Because with three other sisters, the good Duke realised that his economy did not extend far enough. It was therefore felt necessary to give up his wine and venison or sacrifice a daughter to save on the cost of her dowry." Then through clenched teeth: "Of course, being the great man he was, he chose the latter."

Sarmiento scratched his chin and laughed.

Don Gabriel frowned: "Please m' dear, you do yer cause no justice. Let me explain. M' wife was never comfortable in the convent. For years she petitioned 'er release. Somethin' more than frowned upon," Fr Pablo nodded: "But wit' the colonisation of these Americas it was necessitate to export good Christian women and have 'em bedded, I mean wedded."

"The family is the backbone of Christian society," punctuated the friar, made radiant by the realisation.

"Aye Father (*nodding*) 'n' so when me wife did petition a release of her vows to the good Lord Jesus in order to marry this man before ye, who is not without some considerable standing here in the Americas; when she offered to participate in this new society, in its Christianisation and moral formation, of course the Pope was most 'appy to bless such a virtuous plea." The edge of the wife's lips had curled down again. Crimson rage. She stared outward. Then gasped. The *Estremeño* snarled, his voice deep with offence: "She does not appreciate 'ow lucky she is, señores. But she will soon enough, troth, when she sees 'ow rich 'er 'usband is. We'll soon ... God willing ... a fortune make. After our wedding we passed through Seville. There, I managed to procure a deal wit' the Jorges."

And paused with his eyebrows raised, awaiting some applause or gaping expressions of astonishment from his audience. But only Fernando knew who the Jorges were. He was nodding and sucking his lips, which seemed to express approval.

When Don Gabriel realised that Sarmiento and the friar were ignorant, he guffawed: "But, señores, ye must've 'eard of the Jorges!"

"Probably the most powerful merchantmen in the world," squealed Fernando.

"And I've done a deal to distribute the esteemed company's goods throughout the Puebla and Tlaxcala regions."

"Sounds like a most profitable industry that one, good señor."

"Fie, yes!" roared Gabriel, forgetting that there were priests and women present.

But the friar was equally enthused by the enthusiasm and he clapped: "Pray, do tell. What items will you be importing?"

"Oh, the Jorges deal with almost anythin' yer could want. Primarily wax for candles, Flemish fabrics for the clothes of gentlemen and ladies, Castilian wine and olive-oil ... and slaves."

Which made Fr Pablo gulp: "Slaves ... You are selling slaves."

"Not selling them, Father. Distributing them."

Then the chirpy Fernando: "Oh, everyone's selling slaves these days. Personally I cannot think of a more profitable enterprise."

Spurring on Don Gabriel's boast: "If we're to build civilisation in this pagan land, then we must 'ave workers. 'Ow do you think Rome was built, troth? With slaves, fie!"

"There are more slaves here than you would think. Many arrive unregistered," squeaked the informed engineer.

But Fr Pablo was also informed: "Risking enormous penalties."

"Well worth it," sniggered Gabriel: "The profits you can get from a boat-full of good strong niggers, is enormous!"

At which point the engineer decided it would be more prudent to change the subject. He straightened his back and leaned forward, tugging Sarmiento's sleeve to grab his attention, then: "And you, señor? What is your reason, pray, for being here?"

Sarmiento fondled the folder in his lap: "I've come to write a book."

"You're an author then, marry."

"Of sorts. But no poet. My book'll be an almanac."

"Then you're an astrologer!"

"That's my science, yes. Astrology and geomancy."

"Geomancy?"

"Like you, I study the lie of the land. You, so that it may be changed. I, in order to divine an esoteric message," and he pointed to the dry plain: "Each rock's significant. Like the stars they mark our destiny. When you move one to build your roads, you're changing destiny."

"For the better, I trust."

"I'd hope it, señor."

"And your almanac?" asked Doña Rosa: "A Mexican almanac?"

Sarmiento nodded: "My intention's to study the firmament from the top of Popocatepetl itself. They say it's a Holy Mountain for the pagans."

Doña Rosa stared, then dropped her gaze. She looked into her own open hands resting upward in her lap and spoke softly: "I believe there is an astrology within men and women as well as without. A microcosmical sun and moon, and all the rest of the planets, are carried about within us," then looked into Sarmiento's gaze. An aggressive stare, but the voice remained soft: "Would you let me see this almanac then?"

Sarmiento wriggled: "They're just notes, madam. You'd not understand them."

"I have lived a nun's life remember. With plenty of time for meditation and thought on the most metaphysical issues."

Don Gabriel blew a ridiculous raspberry, then guzzled more of Fernando's *pulque*. Ignored by Doña Rosa: "Pray, do not underestimate my intellect because of my sex."

Sarmiento scratched an eyebrow: "I would not, madam."

Then Doña Rosa's husband, sarcastic: "Yer'd be right not to. She's a most modern woman. Well versed in many things ... 'Er skill at cards is most formidable," which inspired a squeal out of the engineer and he clapped his hands. Don Gabriel shook his head: "I'd advise ye not to challenge. Not boldly. She'd shark the shirt off you."

Which was delivered with obvious spite.

Doña Rosa ignored this. She leaned forward to Sarmiento and whispered: "Then come, let me see this almanac, if you have nothing to hide."

Sarmiento slowly, reluctantly, passed the folder to her. She took it, undid the ribbons that bound it and pried it open with great respect. She fingered the parchment and sighed: "Some of this is most profound."

"It's the fruit of much observation, and some fair amount of experimentation."

Then she passed it back to him. But with her thumb tightly pressed against some lines of text, written like a verse. This seemed to highlight it, as if she wanted to communicate the same idea to Sarmiento. The lines read thus:

... To a fair port you have arrived
though its gates seem locked, i have the key
and will open the passage
if you raise your sail tonight ...

Which turned into words on another page ... the words that *I* was thumbing ... in *my* hand ...

* * *

"Are you all right ..."

The voice made me shudder. So loud it was. So close. I looked up from the slip of paper. Over the table. Where was I?

"Are you OK?"

His face looked familiar but it took me time to place it. I had been away so long it seemed.

"For a few seconds then I thought you were going to be away for good."

... A few seconds ...

And then I remembered. There was a cup of tea in front of me, hardly drunk. I touched it. I could still feel the heat even through my gloves. Only a few seconds that had seemed like hours, days. I looked back at the slip of paper. The words had sent me there. A hand came down on mine: "Are you sure you're all right?" It squeezed me. Firm. Who was he? Where was I? "Shall I call a doctor?"

Then: "Red Frank!"

"Francisco Arizmendi," he corrected me, whispering.

"Ah yes, Arizmendi ..."

I had forgotten him, forgotten so much about him and them. He looked so different. He had put on so much weight, his belly hiding his belt buckle. Much fuller face. His hair had receded, on top just a wisp, and frosted. There was an equally frosted moustache. He had glasses.

"Well, don't you have anything to say?" The question accused. Why? What did he want from me? Trying to remember what I had tried so hard to forget: "I've come to get you out of here," he blurted.

"How is general Franco?" I thought and asked with a smirk.

He leaned back in his chair: "He died fifteen years ago..."

For some reason I looked at my wrist. Perhaps hoping that a watch would tell me which year it was. But there was no watch.

Francisco continued to drop hints: "There were elections last month. The Socialists have gained a third term. Gonzalez re-elected."

I sniffled: "So you are happy."

He grunted: "Not really. I voted for the communists."

Why were we talking politics? I sniffled again, then remembered the piece of paper I was holding: "This handwriting. It's Inma's?" I queried.

"Yes."

"She's alive."

"Yes."

"Is she seen ... by you?"

"No, she lives in Mexico."

"Where's Estrella?"

"She's in Madrid."

"Is she happy?"

He gulped and leaned back again: "I don't know. I mean, I suppose so," then: "She's got a good job, lecturing at the university ... and she's married ... with a kid ... a little girl." Which made him halt suddenly: "She didn't want me to tell you that ... not straight off."

I sniggered. It struck me how strange his presence was: "It is still thought by her that I'm enamoured?"

"She's a psychology professor. She knows she must be careful. We don't know exactly why you're still here."

Which angered me: "Oh, no! You came here to ... to visit me?"

He snorted and shook his head: "No. I came here to get you out. We want to get you out." Then, after a pause: "Do you want that?"

I felt my throat fill with choking emotion, but could only manage a dull: "Perhaps."

"Let us take you back, Val. They won't ever be able to treat you like this again."

A surprising statement: "What do you know? How am I treated?"

He frowned: "How?" blew air between half-closed lips: "You should know better than me," then, scratching his head: "Like a Chinese Emperor." and he sniggered. I must have looked perplexed; I did not understand his joke. He persisted: "You know, they treat you like a King-God, keeping you locked away from the world, protected from it."

"I am," I said, and smiled to myself: "I have to be. The Universe is being saved by me."

Which he thought was a joke too and laughed: "Most of us are content to save ourselves. Or used to be," then became solemn: "Everyone's just trying to look after themselves these days. It's a sad world."

"So you came here to have some words of wisdom uttered to you from the King-God?"

Which made him snarl: "Not at all."

"And you just thought you'd drop in, eh?"

"Not at all. I told you I've come to get you out. We've been trying for years, but now that de Coca's dead, things are facilitated somewhat."

This made me shudder, stammer: "Dr de Coca is dead? B-b-but he can't be. It's impossible."

He stood up. Reached out to me: "Come on. It's nearly over. There's just some paperwork left to be done. You have to sign a few documents and then you're free."

I felt myself slip into a well of futility: "That's what has been told me ... when they brought me here." And then: "Impossible ... I cannot be moved ... I'm mad."

"Oh yes, mad all right. You're in a mess, man. A fucking mess!" and he sat down again. His voice lowered, softened again and he took my gloved hands: "But that doesn't mean you can't live a normal life. The world is full of schizophrenics. A whole planet of lunatics. You don't have to stay hospitalised."

"And where are *they*, on the street?" I said: "My situation has been turned into something ... most precarious ... I'll be safer here."

He threw his arms in the air: "Look, I really think you're OK. There are other doctors who think that too. If you were mad, we wouldn't be talking like this. You're really all right, we would've had you out of here years ago if Dr de Coca hadn't vetoed it. This is *his* hospital. Did you know that?"

Yes, I did. But the only important thing anymore was my work. I told him so. He reacted violently, shouting: "But you were working for him, after everything he did to us ... to you. He picked your brain; washed it. Now it's time for you to catch up, but you've got to leave."

Which was confusing. I suddenly had a sense that I had forgotten something terribly important, which made me sorry for myself, and depressed: "I've been a long time alone." I had to take a deep breath to hold back tears: "My work has been aligned to my madness ... and both my work and my madness demand isolation," my hands trembled: "Although I am here in this institution, I am alone. Yes, you're right, like a Chinese

Emperor. Terribly old." He shook his head and sniggered. I was angry: "No ... you don't know ... you can't know how long it's been ... An eternity ... but that can't be discussed ... I was told before receiving you that there are certain things that cannot be talked about."

"Who told you?"

"They did."

"I told you, Dr de Coca is dead."

"There are others."

"But none are as important, or should I say *as powerful?*"

"Yes, you should ... powerful ... yes, very ... and they are as powerful as him, caution must be applied. If I leave my life is in danger," then I remembered something: "You've always been a brave man, Francisco, but don't risk your life for me now, it's not worth it."

He leaned back and sighed again: "One big mystery."

"It's business. Big money to be made. You should appreciate that."

He received the irony with a wry smile: "You're not mad at all, are you?" Then a young, tall man in a white coat who I call my Guardian came over and stood beside the table. Francisco laughed: "I suppose this means it's time for me to go, huh. Just when things were getting interesting." Then he passed me a card with his name and address on it: "You should drop me a line, Val. Let me know how things turn out," and smiled. He reached forward and seemed to run his hand over my bald scalp, but I could not feel it: "Who shaved your head?"

The question seemed impertinent. I reached for his hand to pull it away, but the muscles in my fingers had a sudden cramp, and the arm began to jerk about pulling my whole body with it.

He watched all this with an expression of horror. Then: "Can I get you something?"

I screamed the negation, reached forward and grabbed his cuff. When I whispered into his ear, the voice rasped: "Tell Estrella to come. And if she can't, then tell her a letter will be sent ... if an address can be given for her," and my eyes must have glowed with an energy that seemed to frighten him: "An address cannot be given for her, can it?" He shook his head: "She doesn't want it known, does she? In case the mad-demon should visit." Francisco shuffled uncomfortably. Realisation of his frustration calmed me: "No, of course not. It's very difficult, but it can be appreciated. She has to be so cautious. Now that you've seen it, you know what it's like too ... or can imagine how hard it is, can't you?" He nodded. The same wry smile. I insisted: "Tell her to come."

He nodded again: "I will. But it'll take some days. At least a week. It's a long way here. And it's so inaccessible."

(b) red dragon & white eagle (The Lovers)

Francisco left with my Guardian, leaving me to myself. The door slammed behind them, a tremendous crack, but that was not the door ...
I was back in the coach again.

This shuddered, tilted, reeled and heaved, the occupants bounced and everything was tumbling over and over and they roared as they tumbled with it, filling the space with desperate cries full of confusion and ghastly anticipation, until the rolling stopped with the same shudder that had started the chaos. Screams became whimpers which quickly evolved into coughs as the space then filled with billowing dust. Coughs then groans, and eventually curses. The carriage had tumbled into a ditch.

Sarmiento looked up at the back of Doña Rosa's head. She was sandwiched between the alchemist and her husband, her mouth gaping open and shut like the spasms of a just caught fish. Her shawl had come off, releasing her light brown hair. Loose, it tickled her nose and cheek, and she tried to relieve this by flicking her head back. Her hair whipped around, swiping and slapping Sarmiento's face. He murmured a protest and she turned to him to see what was wrong. He was exhilarated in his fevered state, but instead of suffering he was grinning and even softly laughing at the situation.

He looked straight into her dark brown eyes, and felt the anxiety surge through her body as it pressed against him. They breathed on each other. She was panting hard. Those above them also wiggled and rolled, pushing down on them, pressing her harder into him, and she gasped as the clamping vice of bodies pushed the wind out of her. Sarmiento moaned and stretched his neck forward until he could lick her cheek.

Her eyes widened in horror and I was expecting a cry of protest, but she drew a deep breath, held it, and said nothing. Sarmiento licked her lips. She still said nothing. The driver began to lift them out. In the commotion Sarmiento squeezed her breasts. She shuddered, then pushed her knee into his kidneys and spat at him. The spittle sat still for an instant on his cheek before making a slow effervescent slide towards his lips. He wiped it off with his sleeve, then struggled to get his hands on her again.

But she was rapidly moving away from him. A thick hand under her arm was pulling her up and out through a bright opening.

She squealed at the unnatural tugging of ligaments. Her legs kicked helplessly, and her feet slammed into Sarmiento's face in a rapid barrage of dull blows. He squirmed below her; one arm up to protect his face while the other stretched downward to retrieve his folder of notes. These had been wedged between an upturned seat and the carriage door handle.

Release.

Sarmiento clenched his folder tight under his arm and cringed in the sunlight.

Don Gabriel and Doña Rosa's slaves were sitting in a ditch, the boy with his arm around the girl who was rubbing a naked and swollen ankle and sobbing. At the same time the driver and his assistant were chasing after the horses which had broken loose in the accident: whooping and whistling at the snorting, clip-clopping animals.

All the other passengers were moaning and dusting themselves. All ached, but no one was badly hurt. Don Gabriel straightened his frilly ruff and called his slave boy over to brush his coat and lace cuffs. Fernando pulled out a delicately embroidered handkerchief, dragging it over the brown sweat on his brow and stiff neck. Doña Rosa straightened her dark veil and rearranged the pleats in her dress.

Fr Pablo grimaced. The intense radiation on his shaven pate made his scalp smart and the arteries at the back of his head began to swell, provoking a dull but constant pain. He lifted the hood on his cassock and gestured to the others that they should likewise protect themselves.

Don Gabriel shouted to the slaves who began searching the ditch and its surrounds, the poor girl in a miserable limping fashion, for the free citizen's hats. When each one had been recovered, the group hobbled stiffly away in a straight line behind the friar, who guided them to the shade of a huge chestnut tree.

Under the arbour, the *pulque* was passed around again, but this time everyone took a swig, even Doña Rosa: "For my heart," she said.

A brief cool breeze wafted across the shady spot, inspiring meditation. For some time, they all sat or crouched very still. Hands were lifted to shade squinting eyes, and contemplate the stillness of the yellow, solar bleached land around them. No one seemed to worry that the slaves were sitting pathetically in the sun, the girl still rubbing her ankle, or that the driver and his assistant had disappeared. Some of them closed their eyes. Fernando nodded off into a siesta. But eventually the cool breeze was replaced by a caustic current from the opposite direction. The shock of it took their breath away and inspired a certain panic.

Fr Pablo felt a dizziness as if a cosmic hiccup had rocked the world. He gulped, shook his head, and let the beads on his rosary slowly drop onto each other. Then he leaned toward Sarmiento: "I imagine Golgotha would have had a similar air," he murmured.

Sarmiento's reply was equally arid: "A good place and day to be crucified, verily cousin," then through a melancholy wheeze: "But which of us, marry, will receive the first nail?"

The friar sighed and frowned. He picked himself up and shuffled to the trunk of the tree, as if the centre would be cooler. He had not so much been surprised by Sarmiento's response as by his own initial statement.

Any further ideas were quickly drowned out by the piercing ring of the cicadas. This became so intense that Doña Rosa had to put her hands across her ears. She looked across at Sarmiento who caught the pained veiled gaze – *Yes, most definitely exciting* – he thought, and licked his lips. She wriggled and let out a rumbling, muffled complaint. Her ruffed husband, expecting some kind of fit, grabbed her in a tightly restraining embrace, and when he lifted her face and the veil over it, he located a bruise. He licked his handkerchief to rub this in case it was just a smudge of dirt.

The agitated wife twisted her neck to catch Sarmiento's reaction. Her husband's licking was mimicked bawdily by the alchemist. Doña Rosa could take no more of what she assumed was provocation. When she glared, however, Sarmiento felt it like a thud in his heart. A gurgling rumble rose from the woman's throat again. Her husband complained:

"Did ye not learn corporal control when yer were in that nunnery o'yers?"

Which did not gratify her at all. She writhed in his arms, slapping him until he relaxed and she could break free, mumbling a curse and flicking her crimson cloak. This flapped like a blood red manta ray as she stormed away from them, into the blistering glare and the field of dry scrub that it was toasting.

Sarmiento laughed to himself as she raced past, but the unnerving image of her eyes stayed with him. It was an ambiguous, bewitching look. He shook his head to remove it, scratched his groin and burped *pulque*. But she remained with him.

Don Gabriel, a disgusted look on his face, spat on the ground before shouting after her: "Don't be a fool now ... it's awful 'ot ... Get back in the shade before yer brains 're shrivelled." She kept trudging, so he threw a stone which fell several metres to her left and cursed her under his breath: "Then get ye ter hell, me darlin' hussy," and sat heavily down again, reaching out to grab the sack of *pulque* while signalling to the slave-girl to follow her mistress. So the poor girl had to lift herself tenderly up and hop off after the woman, while her male companion went to his master who needed someone to rub his neck.

Eventually the driver and his assistant came back with three of the horses: "One of the mares got away," they reported, tying up the sweating animals they had retrieved before immediately beginning their next chore, gathering up the luggage which had been thrown about with the crash. The younger assistant went toward a trunk that had rolled upside down in the ditch.

When Sarmiento's drowsy mind, still full of the woman's gaze, recognised what was happening he pulled on his red, wide brimmed hat, picked up his folder and went out into the sun to stroll casually over. It was *his* trunk that the driver's assistant had located. From a distance he yelled and ordered the young paid worker to turn the rusty iron chest over. The lad shook his head as if to say – *What do you think I'm doing?* – He cupped his arms under it, but it could not be budged and he had to find a thick branch in order to lever it up. The case creaked as it slapped over, but another sound, a jingling rattle, was clearly audible.

Sarmiento swore and ran to it, pushing the young fellow aside. Then, panting and spitting, and throwing his folder of notes to the ground, he isolated a thick iron key from a ring of them on his belt, thrust it into the lock and turned. When the lid was pulled open, the revelation inspired an anguished, beastly roar. He kicked the chest and it jingled again. Then he kicked the boy, and, panting and whining like a madman, tore off his shirt and knelt down, reaching into the trunk to pull out a handful of jagged shards, squeezing them until they cut his hands. These he lifted above his head. Blood streamed down his wrists.

Fernando and Fr Pablo, who had followed, stood over the crazed alchemist. The friar gazing in horror at the bleeding hands. Each saint's stigmata-cut slashed his own mind. He clutched his crucifix and mumbled a prayer, then: "There is evil in this place."

But the engineer remained phlegmatic. When he peered past Sarmiento to look into the chest he gasped, then whistled, before exclaiming: "Oh, I say! A laboratory, marry." Sarmiento swore again.

Fr Pablo soothed by the engineer's calm, also looked in. He sighed, then gulped to find the strength to inspire. He patted Sarmiento's shoulder: "Most of the instruments are safe enough. And a new retort will be obtained ... surely."

But it only served to further fuel the alchemist's rage. He reached down, picked up a leather satchel, shoved his folder of notes into it, then looped the strap over his shoulder and marched off. He trudged up a wide but rocky path, which turned out to be a dry river-bed, rising into parched mountains.

The driver suddenly bellowed. He was in the ditch where the coach had toppled, his assistant and Don Gabriel's slave-boy next to him, their hands under the chassis. They needed help. A constipated grunt, then: "If your lordships'd but gi'us a bit of a hand."

Fr Pablo lifted his cassock and trotted over, but their *lordships* turned away. The physical task was abominable and unnatural to them. Fernando hobbled back to the tree and his *pulque*.

Fr Pablo threw his arms up in imitation of his crucified God and bellowed a plea: "To escape this arid spot we must all push. If not, who knows how long we will have to remain."

But the two drunk *lordships* continued to ignore the necessity, just as they also ignored the fact that Sarmiento and Doña Rosa, as well as the limping slave girl, were all already out of sight ...

I gathered altitude, looking for them. The valley broadened. They became specks. Sarmiento trudging to the left, Doña Rosa to the right. They looked absurd in that rocky landscape, wrapped in their European clothes. Unnatural, I thought, and that was probably the first time I realised what an anti-natural thing the human race is. Doña Rosa had to lean forward to lift her long skirts in order to make room for her short but rapid strides. She looked ridiculous with her veil and shawl covered head. Sarmiento equally so in his wide red hat and red pantaloons. No matter how high I got they never blended. But when I did go high I sensed the presence of others.

Four of them, on horseback, wrapped in dusty cloaks. The man in the middle was familiar: the same one who had been searching for Sarmiento in Galicia. They looked down to the carriage in the ditch, tugged on their reins and descended ...

I threw myself back into the valley. Sarmiento stumbled forward, leaning on a thick dry stick, head heavy; deeply within himself, in his own dizzying fever. He walked over white, scorched rocks; his breathing parched and hoarse. He rubbed sweat from the tingling red skin on his neck. At times he had to walk through tall, dry and seemingly dead grass. There was no wind then to bend it, only his tramping tired legs that cut through it like the wedged-prow of a ship. He lifted his stick forward as he advanced, like a trembling bow-sprit, pointing direction through the dry ocean of his grief.

In the same instant, Doña Rosa reached out and clenched her fingers around the tawny crests of dry flowers, pulverising them before lifting their detritus to her nose and inhaling deep. Her slight smile was made even more ambiguous by the veil. Was she imagining some long dead aroma, or had the perfume been preserved in the drying process to be unleashed by the pulverising act?

Sarmiento sniffed and smiled as if the aroma had reached him as well, for an instant at least. He coughed, and his features quickly returned to their agonised frown.

He hardly noticed the searing heat anymore, nor the biting, scorching wind that was unperceivedly eroding the floor of rocks. He hardly noticed the pain from the bruises on his feet. His was a transcendental agony. His heart, pumped cruelty and anguish into the blood; infecting his brain with ghastly images of a savage world – *A world* – he thought – *Designed to cripple me, abnegate my every ambition* – Then, looking straight into the sun – *So be it!* –

Afterwards, when the low sun was orange-red – *As if it were wounded, and had shed blood* – he came to an almost romantic inspiration – *I have shed blood* – Tears welled in the dry corners of his eyes. A large carrion bird shrieked and flew across the sky. The moon was full, and rising, directly facing the drowning sun, golden in a gold and pink sky. He sighed, his left hand open, as if pleading innocence – *My blood is the blood of my sister* –

Red rocks around him. Rocks that seemed imbued with life. The scaly back of a huge dragon. A shadow swept across his brow. The surprise made him look up. A black mass filled his range of vision. He toppled backward, the darkness dropping at his feet where it took form and became recognisable as a cloth. A cloak, he realised. It was crimson now that it was on the ground – *Doña Rosa's cloak* – He realised.

Then she was there herself, squatting like a Bedouin, with a thick black stick, beating it, until she was sure of something. She turned to look at Sarmiento and lifted her veil. Her face was moist and anguished, an eyebrow up, and a curling lip revealing the crooked teeth. She stared at him.

"What?" he mumbled.

She said nothing, just sat back, lazily prodding the cloth with the stick; pushing it, as if massaging it, before pressing down hard. Then the fabric was wound about the wood and lifted. This produced a kind of unveiling sensation, performed with a sardonic grin. As the cloth gravitated toward the spinning pivot, a snaking, tapering, rubicund form became visible on the cupreous, sunset tinged sand – snaking it did and a snake it was, now lifeless, its neck squashed, its head flattened.

She threw the crimson cloak aside, releasing the stick to slide it under the scaly belly to balance it on the tip. It was definitely dead, but shivering. Then she turned it, and as she did the ruddy hue of its skin blackened. She flicked it three times, its rattling tail whipping its own dead head, then presented it to Sarmiento.

He reached out and took it in one hand, reached forward to stroke her cheek with the other. Her head drooped. He put a finger under her chin. But it was she herself who lifted it up again.

And it was she who grasped the back of his neck, pulled him to her, pressed her own open mouth into his.

So, he sighed and snaked his tongue into the mouth in his mouth, lapping at the refreshing, bubbling well and its reservoir of sweet saliva ... A rock fell and they stumbled apart. They could hear Don Gabriel's slurred and drunken voice, but still a long way off, the falling rock had been closer.

Something moved behind a boulder. It was hard to discern; the light had dimmed considerably. Doña Rosa trembled and Sarmiento squeezed her arm with his own jittery, dagger drawing hand. Then he hobbled cautiously forward, around the other side of the boulder, his knife poking forth, his other hand on the pommel of his sword.

However, the danger was above, on top of the rock. Sarmiento's own instinct threw him onto the ground to roll away. His knees bent automatically and he sat up, peering into dim light, through the dust his rolling had unleashed. He coughed. And then he saw it, or them.

A pair of otherworldly figures, spindly white limbs poked from rough, cloth smocks. Crouching supernatural monsters, like hobgoblins, they were squeezed together in each other's arms, but fidgeting.

Sarmiento dropped his guard and stood up. The creatures on the rock clutched themselves tighter.

Doña Rosa stepped forward too, calling to them, gently. The figures immediately responded, pushing themselves and sliding down the rock, but too fast and they fell over. One of them, a hunchback, half-lifted himself on his feeble legs by leaning on a creaking, bent stick. His smock was long and torn, shivering as his companion yanked at it to pull himself up. When he had he was a head taller than the hunchback, whose deformed lump he leaned on in such a way that they seemed to create a happy equilibrium, moving in a clumsy waddle. Knees and elbows creaked and the hunchback beneath moaned. The taller one was clutching a bulging sack in his left hand, while he reached out to Doña Rosa with the trembling-bony, thumb-empty right. Nor were there big toes on his bare feet, but despite all their miserable deformity and obvious poverty, when they had arrived they were grinning and giggling as if they were about to embrace some long lost friend. Their strange mirth exposed toothless gums, while their bald heads nodded in a gay rhythm that seemed to coincide with their quivering arms.

"What creatures are these?" mumbled Sarmiento: "Not unlike the living dead."

"They are my saviours," the lady murmured: "They found me, parched and gasping, and gave me water. If they are strange and ancient creatures, if they be alive, and not spirits," she whispered: "They must have seen nigh on a hundred springs."

"One hundred cold and bitter *winters*, I'd say," said Sarmiento, louder, and he spat.

Then Doña Rosa turned to stare at Sarmiento. Not long before they had been so red and hot. She struggled to catch breath: "Three frights this same day," and then laughed, flicking back a drooping fringe: "What does your almanac predict for the rest of the evening?"

Don Gabriel's shouts reached them again, this time more distant. They shouted back. The remote voices grew excited. Eventually they could see them. Five flickering flaming torches approached, each one leaving a trail of sparks, and the hob-goblins backed cautiously away.

It was Doña Rosa's husband who arrived first. With a demented ape-walk and wheezing breath, he led a chestnut mare. When he saw his wife he waved his torch in a frantic gesture to the coach driver, who was jogging behind, to take the torch and mare's bridle whilst he embraced his wife and wrapped a blanket around her. He gave her water from a gurgling canteen. She gulped. There was no dialogue, merely gasps through slurps. But when she had finished drinking he slapped her face.

The chilling flat-echo of that blow silenced the night lively valley. The histrionic contrast in the pause prolonged it, and it was threatening to become eternal, until a resumption of panting breaths broke through.

Then the husband looked at Sarmiento, who had observed the violence with incredulity; shivering and sweating again while the spouse snorted and advanced. Don Gabriel put his arm on his hip, near his sword.

Sarmiento remained incredulous, staring at Doña Rosa, whose nostrils dilated, her bottom lip quivering. The husband cleared his throat: "Me many thanks, señor," then sniffing, there were actually tears welling: "Yer more a gentleman that I'll ever be," which inspired even more incredulity, but the husband lifted a hand to stifle any possible objection: "No, señor, no modesty from ye, please. Me wife had an attack of cholera and I watched her go ... did nothing ... while you, señor, went lookin' for 'er. I sat waiting and drinking, thinking the servant girl would fetch 'er, while you did what I should've done. Yer an example to me ... I was sure she would've turned and come back ... and I had another drink," and then he spat and started thumping his own breast hard with his clenched fist.

The others finally arrived too. The driver's assistant ran to them, then the slave boy with the slave girl drooping from his shoulder. Fr Pablo and Fernando arrived on trotting mounts and bobbing from opposite directions. When he saw them, Don Gabriel composed himself, but he opened his arms and wrapped Sarmiento in a hearty embrace.

Fr Pablo slid down off his horse and also hugged Sarmiento: "I thought you were lost. There was such a melancholy hue in your face."

Sarmiento squeezed his cousin hard: "And it's still in my soul."

"Aye, Pedro," and he put his arm under Sarmiento's and lead him away from the others.

The driver and his assistant also moved apart, to gather sticks and tumbleweeds in order to build a fire.

Fr Pablo's voice lowered and became conspiratorial: "You don't know how lucky you are."

"Lucky ... I feel like shit, cousin."

"But your sojourn away has saved your life."

"How is that?" and sniggered sarcastically.

"Don't mock, I do not talk in jest. When you went we had a visit. Four riders, clad in black. Speaking Portuguese."

Sarmiento clutched his jacket over his heart: "Oh, but were I there!"

"You would be dead."

"Or they ... In any case the anguish in my suffering soul would be quelled." And he turned wildly: "We must go ... get them."

"No. They'll be well away. They stopped here and our driver pleaded with them to help us lift the coach out of the ditch. When they dismounted they spent some time inspecting things. They're most definitely searching for something ... searching for you."

"Then we'll let them find me."

"All right, but not now. You'd never catch them, and you are weakened by your ordeal and your fever. You must rest. We've brought some food. I beg you, eat."

Then Fernando was brushing the dust from Sarmiento's back and offering him wine: "All the *pulque* is now drunk I'm afraid," and he laughed, nervously and ridiculously.

Sarmiento was wild: "What would the Portuguese be doing here?"

Which sounded absurd at first to the engineer. Until he recalled the accents of the strange riders: "Selling, señor. Without a doubt."

Sarmiento screwed up his face: "Selling?"

Fernando nodded, a jerking smile: "Slaves, señor. Negroes. From Africa."

And Don Gabriel, who had also neared, spat a curse at the competition.

Very soon they were sitting around the blaze with a warm glow on their faces. The driver's assistant dragged over a sack and pulled out some potatoes which he lay in the coals and faggots. The men were drinking again and laughing, even Sarmiento, but Doña Rosa had returned her head to a drooping posture, slightly turned away from the fire toward the two ancient figures who had crawled down from the rock and were standing pathetically away from the blaze in the cold moonlight. Unlike the absurdly anti-natural arrivals they were chameleon-like. Blending, but shivering and staring at the gentlemen and their lady.

Don Gabriel had still not noticed them. When he did follow his wife's gaze the sight of them startled. He pulled out a dagger, wrapping his other arm around his wife. Then he was pointing and ordering the drivers to search the strangers: "These vermin 'ave been up to no good, sirrah. Look at the sack the taller rogue lumbers wit'. Bulging with their booty, aye!" And as the driver dragged the indicated man toward the firelight: "Look at it, it's soaked in blood. Must be full of kids' hearts, ripped out in pagan sacrifice, I wager. The cowards. Vomit of all prisons!"

But instead of frightening Doña Rosa, she pushed her husband's arm away, lifted her chin and called out to them, making signs that they should open the bloodied sack. The thumbless one understood, and he reached in and pulled out a dead hare: "They've been hunting," she said: "For their supper. And then stumbled on me. I was lost and they found and protected me."

Don Gabriel looked across at Sarmiento, making a gesture that expressed incomprehension. Sarmiento shrugged his shoulders, while Doña Rosa ordered the two hobgoblins to come nearer the fire and rest beside them: "Let us see if the dead can speak."

The pair half-affirmed expectations. The taller one spoke Spanish, although badly, while the hunchback could do no more than expulse haunting moans and groans.

Don Gabriel put one hand over his nose and mouth, and reached forward with the other. He poked his finger into the hunchback's mouth, levered it open, looked in and sighed: "It seems like some turkeycock's been very free wit'is knife on ye."

A burning branch popped.

"That was but a long time ago, señor," explained the mute's thumbless companion, brushing a moth from his trembling lip: "My poor friend's true name is long and I have long forgot. Now I call him Hilario. As for my real name, it seems to be Acamapitchli, though acquaintances now know me as Carlos," and he curtsied: "At your service, señor."

"A happy pair of deformed fools," mumbled Fernando, also brushing away an insect. Then he gurgled something else to the ragged ones in what was almost certainly the old Mexican, Nahuatl language. It was probably an insult or a threat. It made them shudder.

Doña Rosa reached into the coach driver's sack and pulled out some corn pancakes. She passed them around. Carlos clamping his hands as if to utter a prayer, stammered: "You are too kind m'lady 'n' lords."

"And you are most wretched."

"Oh wretched m'lady, yes. Both of us born on unlucky days, in *Nementemi*."

Fernando laughed and explained that this *Nementemi* referred to the five days that had to be added on to the eighteen months of twenty days of the Mexican calendar: "Which are regarded by the pagans as useless days," he elaborated: "For they are the only ones not dedicated to any pagan god."

Don Gabriel, his spirits picking up, laughed too: "Wretched vermin!"

"Wretched señores," echoed Carlos, and spat into the flames: "Wrought from dung we are, señores. Aye! Dragged forth into a most dark and dimly pagan world, wrought forth in the times, prithee, when Montezuma were still Emperor, until the arrivals of his most kind lordship, Cortés, and his conquering Christians. But we are but a pair of wretched vermin *tlatlacotin*."

"The slave class," explained Fernando: "Tlatlacotin: the name given to those who had forfeited freedom by committing some heinous crime."

"Oh aye señores 'n' m'lady," moaned Carlos, while smoke blew into his face: "My crimes so heinous! The reason, prithee, why I have lost these digits. For, alas, I have not always been so incomplete."

Don Gabriel, who was sitting closest to the fire, wiped a handkerchief across his brow and coughed: "Then out wit' your tale, whelp."

And Carlos began ... But I saw more than heard that story. His mind opened and transported me to another dimension which was *his* time and world, and in *his* memory. We were moving through a crowd, men mainly. Aztec men. Naked chests and limbs, pudenda wrapped up in loin-cloths. Carlos looked downward to the feet of the passers-by. Many were moving barefoot, but some possessed sandals. Looking up again, faces moved past, close enough to discern jewellery. Most of the ears that flapped past bore pendants, cut to represent jaguars, serpents or hummingbirds. Lips were pierced as well, and pulled down by labial ornaments, wood for the poor, gold and silver for the wealthy, plugs of various thickness that were worn as naturally and comfortably as any ring.

Some passers-by were drunk and tottering, guzzling pulque from terra cotta jugs, singing and chanting. One of these thrust his face forward. Great, bulging yellowing orbs of eyes illuminated an otherwise dark and sanguine complexion and the bottom lip of his mouth was dragged down to reveal a line of brown and rotten teeth. Carlos screamed when hands suddenly fell on him. They went under his arms, around his waist and beneath his legs; lifting him. A circle of men, perhaps friends, laughed hysterically and began to shake him. They clutched his wrists and ankles, and threw him back and forth in an arching swing which became looser and longer with each pull. When the movement reached its zenith, they let go, flinging him skyward, to be caught again in a mesh of entwined arms.

This brought jubilant roars.

Carlos clapped his hands, but at the same time I could feel his sadness and there was a lump in his throat. He was recalling a birthday celebration that he had never enjoyed and the word *Nementemi* resounded. *Hands, still with thumbs.* The image accompanied by a rush of grief: "*I had been a poet... once*"

And his then thumbed hand, soft and young, was scribbling with a writing cane. An elderly man was beside him, leaning over the smooth, strip of bark page. This observer scratched his chin and mumbled something which seemed to be criticism. The hand stopped. It lifted the pen, paused, then swept across the characters. When bad ones had been eradicated he scribbled others, beginning an inspired rush. This was interrupted by the arrival of a woman. I could feel his heart leap. She carried a bowl of food that she lay on the writer's desk, then she took the old man's hand and kissed him. But as she did she caught the writer's gaze ...

"My true love's eye cries out to me
the rest of her body screams ..."

Then he was alone with her, naked with her, examining the intricate designs, the curling jaguar's tail tattooed on her skin, over her breasts. Breath blew her long black hair, uncovering her folded eyes, as he lapped at the flesh, drawing moisture from the crease of her closed mouth.

"My teacher's wife, such a dangerous initiation..."

Don Gabriel was laughing: "So this old bull 'as no thumbs, but he had balls a plenty!"

Old Carlos whined: "Pray, good señores! Nothing to laugh about. What's to be described is a life of ruins. Tragedy, not comedy. But that woman were a real beauty, and would've inspired any poet señores. She inspired me!"

In his mind again, his pen was frantic:

"My song!
Sing my song and dance to it
let us gladden the Giver of Life together"
I lay flowers and quetzal plumes on your soft breast

after I have removed my excited head,
I scatter your valley with kernels of maize
after I have drunk from the sweet waters of that deep lagoon
which thy river, the river of love pours from..."

His unknowingly cuckolded teacher read it, hand on heart, congratulating.

"Then I was to enjoy a brief but magnificent glory. Oh aye, señores! My verses found its way to the Emperor, who approved them no less. Such a privilege: and with no god to bless me, it seemed a miracle. Little did I guess that it was but the beginning of my damnation. For the Emperor called for me, and I went, leaving my true love behind. The object of my passion would stay wit' her husband, in Texcoco, where I were from, señores.

"At first I did cry, but I thought no more than once upon this separation. Even the most ardent passion has its price. I, dreamed of glory. So I was removed unto the capital, that most magnificent city, Tenochtitlan, to write poetry for Montezuma..."

His mind was full of noise and colour. Tenochtitlan. An enormous market place. Cries, shouts and gesticulations between buyer and seller. In most places exchanges were bartered and a cocoa-bean currency was passed from hand to hand. Men with cloaks flapping over paper loincloths, bare footed women, their hair tied back with braid or coloured ribbons. Someone was exchanging corn kernels for a turkey while a group of men lumbered bundles of beans. He recalled a crash: turning and bumping into a pole that was one of the props of a clown hobbling into him on stilts. The clown toppled, and they both collapsed on the ground. He was dazed by the blow and had closed his eyes. When they were opened again, there was a huge, almost toothless grin, in a simian face ...

"The first time I was to see my dear friend Hilario. Love at first sight. I needed a laugh, and he was in search of a poet's genius."

There were stalls of polished beans, cocoons of maize and shining tomatoes. Chocolate sellers were standing before steaming pots dishing out the hot, brown cocoa sweetened with honey and consumed in painted cups made from gourds. There were women with flat maize cakes and thick maize porridge; salt stalls, and stalls with live birds and dead birds' feathers. Green iguanas had been strung up and there were pickled newts and chilli rats, worms and salamanders, frogs and even tadpoles. Merchants with the finest cotton cloth spread out cloaks and other elaborate feathered gowns. Others presented pottery and cooking utensils. A jeweller offered gold and silver rings, broaches, lip-plugs and earrings. Gold dust was also sold in goose quills. There was jade and turquoise, obsidian daggers and axes.

As they walked by, Carlos winked at a woman who had her hair tied up into black horns. Her face was painted and she had reddened cheeks. She smiled and beckoned with her head, while she twisted a thick stalk between her fingers and nibbled on the fat, fleshy cap of a magic mushroom. But when the young clown, Hilario, farted, she cursed and spat at them.

They ran away, laughing, around a corner into another square. The cacophony increased. This came from several large groups of people who were singing and shouting, rattling gourds, dancing, and hurling flowers from baskets. The clown was quickly amongst them and ironically imitating them, bawdily lifting up his loincloth flap and blowing raspberries.

And, towering above all this, was a pyramid. Hilario suddenly ran to it, clambering up some steps, beckoning young Carlos to follow. The poet looked up. At its summit were two platforms of stone, each with its own little temple sanctuary ... "One for Tlaloc, the god of rain, the other to the sun god, Huitzilopochtli."

At the feet of its cold stone steps was a line of stakes, each with a naked man or woman, with each neck strapped in a leather collar. He shuddered. His memory escaped, fleeing the square to fly down a narrow street of high buildings with flat roofs. This eventually opened out at a lake, where it was calm after the bustling market. Little waves lapped the shore.

Carlos walked hand in hand with Hilario, pausing to skim flat stones over the water. There were fishermen with harpoons and others with snares and nets. Canoes jerked past, to and fro. Paddles dipped. They were strolling down a wide avenue of well-beaten earth. A canal with walkways on both sides ran down the middle. Carlos invited Hilario to come home with him and they went through a gate in a white-washed walled compound and crossed a patio. His home was mostly bare inside. They sat talking for a while on a reed mat on the clay floor, discussing poetry. Until Carlos stood up and beckoned Hilario outside.

He sat down on a bench at a table and unrolled a strip of bark. There was a writing cane. Carlos took it and assumed a scribe's attitude, while the buffoon Hilario watched over his shoulder. But Carlos merely sucked the bottom of the cane, and wrote nothing ...

"My gift had abandoned me. Or I had left it. The goddess of poetry is a goddess of love and I had forsaken her. So Hilario made suggestion that I should partake of the peyote root and magic-mushroom. Oh, heathen he were señores. As I was, but we are perfectly converted now, oh aye."

"So you no longer indulge yourself with such herbs?" Sarmiento asked, wafting smoke away from his face.

"Oh no señores. I did not mean that. But now we make our hallucinations with Christian purpose instead of pagan foolery," and he let his tongue wag out while Hilario went down on his hands and knees in the dust and started panting like a dog. A pantomime pursued until Fernando passed the wine sack to them. Carlos took a mouthful and sighed: "Ah. But none of those medicines did my poetry a pinch of good, so I used logic and philosophies to cure my ills, deducing, señores, that the only way to renew mine art was to return my heart unto those perils I had before so languidly belaboured in. In short, señores, I had to become an adulterer once more."

He recalled a pair of squinting, knowing eyes. A mature face. The mouth a thin and stern line, opened: "*I will squeeze the verses out of you ... my little jaguar...*" A pain in his groin, followed by an intense burning pleasure as the jaguar girl sat up on him: arching her back, her breasts lifting. Her head flicked, breasts bounced, then she turned and crouched over him. A symbol of the smoking-mirror god, the lord of night, Tezcatlipoca, snaked down her back and wound around her spine. She wiggled down and he was inside her...

"'Twas sublime. I began again. Poems were writ. But creation is an incessant process, oh aye. Sacrifices had to be made. Virgins and other married women had to be caught for my cuckold art to prosper. So Hilario it was who volunteered for the distribution of my verse. Hypnotic lines which would have the fairest maidens and most noble men's wives cowering under my loincloth. Oh marry señores, such were our most innocent intentions."

A hand on his shoulder. The tight grip accused ...

"One of our missives fell into a cuckolded lord's hands ..."

Then the obsidian axe falling. He recalled it in slow motion, remembered the pain. His mind screamed. He did not see the actual excision, could not see it, but he felt it, and he had the rest of his life to contemplate the useless stumps on hands and feet ...

"Mexican law was harsh!"

Another pain. In his spine. Aching limbs. Exhaustion. A huge brick strapped to his bent back. Bow-legged toil up stone steps. The pyramid temple. So many steps. Knee-caps, seeming about to burst from the legs.

"The thumbless, toeless poet became a thumbless, toeless slave. Then I would have been happier to have suffered sacrifice."

Another black, obsidian knife was lifted high. Naked arms stretching out of a billowing cape of quetzal feathers.

"The temple ... the friar"

An anonymous slave on the altar screams. Unwavering descent. Thuds at contact. Squelches on entry. Carving. Flesh, bone. A hand dives, pulls, and extracts a still pumping heart. Crowd roars ...

And then I was out of his mind, facing Sarmiento again. His twisting lips: "Were you there when the conquistador Cortés arrived?"

Carlos whined. He watched a tiny scorpion scramble over hot stones near the fire: "Aye, señores... Most definitely there. Though escaped we were and living with Montezuma's enemies, the Tlaxcala, señores."

Don Gabriel suddenly grabbed the old man's chin, turned his right cheek toward the firelight and poked at a scar: "This mark betrays the cheater's lie. It's a brand. Given by Cortés' men to those Mexica captured at the battle of Tepeaca. He's been a slave to Spain. Sold for ten pesos."

Old Carlos, wiping Gabriel's saliva off his face, still whining: "Oh, it's true milord. You've found me out, you have. Yes, I was there. At Tepeaca."

Don Gabriel a theatrically sweeping gesture: "In this valley Cortés faced an army of a 'undred thousand men. And smashed 'em.'"

His wife shuddered, she had also seen the scorpion. She pointed it out to her husband, who stood up and put his heel on it. Then Doña Rosa wrapped the blanket tighter around her and sighed: "Why were the Mexica such terrible soldiers? Or were ours so good?"

Don Gabriel kicked the scorpion's corpse into the flames: "Not terrible, no. Better said they were too brave. Brave, but accustomed to a different kind of war. The mongrels were more interested in the capture of victims for sacrifice than killing on the battlefield."

"Most unwise decision," sighed Carlos. Then added: "And killing from a distance was most dishonourable, señores, or such is how we stupid Mexica reasoned it."

Fernando drank more wine and sniggered: "Of course the Castilians also had horses, which the Mexica had never seen."

"I was told the Mexica had a tradition of head-on combat," this was Sarmiento, poking a stick into a smouldering log: "Only the front ranks fought, the second rank waiting until all their comrades had been cut down."

Doña Rosa rubbed a red cheek. Her pitch gloomy: "A noble gesture."

Don Gabriel slapped a mosquito and scratched his throat: "Dearly appreciated by Cortés' men," then: "Provided they'd the stamina our knights could cut down 'undreds, even thousands."

"And they *did* have the stamina," moaned Carlos: "They did cut down thousands."

Sarmiento turned away, spat, then turned back to the wretched Carlos: "You said you were at Tepeaca. Cortés was supposed to have ordered the deaths of twenty thousand men there."

The old man also spat, but into the fire again, then croaked: "Oh, truly señores. A most sad and terrible day for us. In a maize field we were. Horses came at us, and dogs. As if from hell they came. Tore men, women, children, to pieces. Afterwards, they took us to the town and threw many of us off the roofs of the houses there, just shoved men off to their deaths. They gave the dead to the Tlaxcalans to eat. Oh yes, because the people here, we were all of us cannibals before. And yes, they killed at least twenty thousand of us, señores. Which was probably the right thing. We sinners, consumers of human flesh, we deserved to die. Violent, cruel and treacherous people we were ... and just like the stories in the Bible, we were punished for our perversions and arrogance. We deserved it all. Willed by God, señores, it most certainly was."

Don Gabriel sniggered: "And did ye tremble when yer saw the conqueror."

"Oh verily señores, in a fashion at least, for we had been trembling long before the conquistador came. When Malinche did come ... Malinche is what we called Cortés, señores ... When he came we asked ourselves, is this the fatal day? 4-Motion in our calendar, when the Mexican sun would end; when there would be a mighty earthquake and all would die? Was this that day? Oh yes, señores, the Mexican tragedy had long before been expected: it was writ, as they say, and that very same year was also the year of the Reed, the year when it had been ordained that kings would perish. Montezuma was expecting it as much as we were, m' lords. There were no surprises. No ends of sacrifices would redeem our debts. And when we were pagans we thought that Quetzalcoatl was the feeblest of gods, 'cause he forbade human sacrifice, so we ignored him. And because he was ignored he made himself into a great god, your god, and called himself Jesus Christo. And this Quetzalcoatl-Christo sends Malinche, señores, and pays us a real nice lesson, forsooth. When Quetzalcoatl was banished he went east, they says, on 'is raft of serpents. But he had to come back. Naked and crucified."

The image must have offended Don Gabriel. He slapped Carlos.

Sarmiento however had become agitated, but thoughtful. He begged Don Gabriel to be more considerate with their mad acquaintance. Then he stood up, and, shivering again, began to pace. So Carlos, recognising that he had a supporter, continued, now directing his words at Sarmiento: "It was writ:

'Though you art carved in jade, you will break.
Though you are made of gold, you will crack.
Even though you are a quetzal plume, you will wither.
We are not forever on this earth...."

(c) the twins

Francisco Arizmendi's visit made me recall so much. I sat back in my chair, the wide window-wall exposed the hot plain outside - *will they truly let me?* - But I had no real will to move. I was waiting for Estrella to rescue me. It had to be her, not Arizmendi. Then the verse in Inma's poem became sound, her voice, music, blown through delicious lips ...

i imagine your distant pain,
from the barren centre
of this dry land
you are an oasis,
liquid and sad,
like
a termite queen
your
fecundity robs
no physical liberty
but you are freer than any of them
outside the tyranny of time,
which is where we will meet,
and kiss again...

In my room there was a video machine. I inserted a tape. The same one I had watched a dozen times. Dr Hilario de Coca, become a trembling old man, lying up in bed, a toothpick wobbling between his teeth, nodding his head stupidly at the camera.

His croaking voice: "Val. It's been such a long time, hasn't it? Of course I wanted to thank you personally. Don't be bashful. The doctors here have attributed most of the breakthrough to the fruits of your invaluable research. The Ambrosia drug. A miracle. Oh, I know you must be saying to yourself that Ambrosia hasn't been marketed yet? (*laughs*) No, it hasn't, but it soon will be (*anticipating my distress*) Oh, you're wondering how I know! Didn't they tell you? I volunteered Val. Was a guinea-pig. There was not the slightest reservation (*pulls the toothpick out*) Well **volunteered** is not exactly the right term, I *ordered* my guinea-pig role. When they told me that Ambrosia was the fruit of *your* research I jumped at it (*sadistic grin*) Yet they didn't tell you? That must make you very angry. You should take more care over your work, control it better (*sniggered*) The doctors say you've grown lax and have lost interest, which is a terrible shame. If you're not careful they'll take the credit away from you. Oh yes, they're capable all right, I know scientists well enough, mark me (snorted) But I have always believed in you Val (*the toothpick snaps between his fingers*) It's awfully sad that you regard me with such disdain. Perhaps if you had had known that I was running this ship you would've tried to get away. I'm sure old Enrique would have (*his eyes rolled*) Oh, Enrique. He called me a Nazi once. He shouldn't have done that. But in any case it's still such a shame that the old chap couldn't have stuck to his own business (*straightening the collar of the shirt of his pyjamas*) I was harsh on you, wasn't I. But that's all in the past (*deep breath*) I've always believed in you, in what you see, in the importance of it. Of what you're looking for (*slight cough*) When they told me I had cancer, I told them to get in touch with the sanatorium (*rubbing a finger-nail between incisors*) Not a trace of it now and I'm getting stronger very quickly. It's the *aqua vitae*, Val. Within ten years, our people are telling us, we'll have eradicated *all* disease. Mono-atomic medicine has begun in earnest (*claps his hands*) Of course it's ironic that I am one of your first patients (*snorting mucus)* With all the enmity you and Don Enrique had for us. But you misunderstood our motives. We never wished you any harm. Quite the contrary (*sniffles*) In any case the important thing's not the past but the future, and ensuring the success of your future work is imperative. If the quest for Omega's to begin in earnest, then research can no longer be confined to us, we have to expand, organise the expansion. Eventually it'll have to become more than a private concern. We'll have to break out of this cover, involve governments."

I turned it off, unmoved. I did not care that I had saved the human race, now I wanted to save myself. I no longer believed in Omega. They had told me that I had tried to commit suicide. Possible, it seemed like a nice idea, but I could not remember the attempt. I recalled the conversation with Francisco Arizmendi. The idea of a dead de Coca made me shiver, not because I didn't want it, I just couldn't believe it. I felt deep concern for Arizmendi and Estrella's lives: that the story of de Coca's death was a trap set by de Coca himself.

But then, as always, whenever reality became oppressive, there was my escape. My Guardian arrived with my afternoon dosage of drugs. He sat down beside me and turned the tape recorder on, and began counting, and then Inma's voice was resounding through my dull mind ...

come to mexico my dear,
there is a wind blowing which curls within us,
lifting us -
the gates of tlaxcala are open...

Tlaxcala. Mexico ... It was late afternoon. I had entered the scene on a streak of orange sunlight, thrusting between half-closed shutters, falling on a friar and spotlighting him. He had bright young eyes, but the rest of him was harrowed. His pale but blotched skin sagged off the skeleton, a real wizened rake gnarled by carbuncles. His tonsure, a wispy white ring, encircled an enormous pink protuberance that looked like a budding horn. He snorted, moving mucus, and his hand trembled violently whilst dipping a lump of brown bread into a bowl of steaming chocolate. This sat on a round table, and there were six other men there. But all attention was towards the friar and I had the impression that I had arrived in the midst of some conversation which had just sunk into a moment of pause.

Looking around the table I found familiarity. Fr Pablo, fly-catchingly dreamy, was sitting beside Fernando, now spotlessly clean. The engineer wore an immaculate white suit, hanging wrinkle-free off his stiff, straight back. His wide ruddy face, gleaming out of it like a polished apple, had a dimpled-smile ignorance to it and he nodded insistently. In front of them was the landowner, Don Gabriel, dressed in purple, his fingers heavy with gold and enormous gemstones. He was also looking cleaner than I had remembered him on other occasions. His shoulder length hair had been brushed, his long moustache waxed, and his unshaven chin rustled against a high white ruff.

Each had their own bowl of hot, thick chocolate. Some of them scooped it up with spoons, others used bread. Then the older friar pointed a tremulous bony finger at one of the Mexican servants perched behind the merchant. The young factotum was obviously uncomfortable and anxiously waiting to clear away an empty bowl: "Slaves," hissed the old friar, admonishing, but not angry: "Still they be used as slave."

The Mexican butler grinned and Don Gabriel mirrored the expression. His voice was as coarse as it had ever been: "Pray, you insult me, Father. I pay me Indians."

"A pittance," mumbled the old friar.

"They're paid that which is needed to motivate 'em to work. Why should they 'ave more?" and the landowner's mouth and hands stretched open with his eyes, exaggerating incomprehension. Fernando nodded, but Fr Pablo hung his head sheepishly, obviously perturbed.

I gravitated towards the younger friar's anxiety and nestled in his mind. He was struggling over attitudes, especially those regarding the merchant. Emotions and ideas flashed past and it soon became clear how much Fr Pablo's opinions had altered since the last time I had seen them. Then the friar had considered Don Gabriel to be a noble fellow, a good Christian who had forged a catholic stronghold in a world of pagans. He had been more worried about Doña Rosa and her obvious lack of faith, and had spent many hours visiting her, trying to persuade her to embrace Christ again. But then certain events revealed that the problem in Don Gabriel's house was not the wife, but the nobleman himself. While I was still in his mind a memory flashed passed.

It was mid-morning, and he was walking in front of Don Gabriel's hacienda on his way to see Doña Rosa. But while he was passing the stables his attention was drawn by a human noise, a cough, and he saw the landowner stumbling out, half naked and pulling up straw covered trousers. In the shadows inside, next to the haystacks, a woman was lifting a white dress over her dark skin. She flicked back her black hair and caught the friar's eye. She smiled. Then, when Don Gabriel realised that the friar was gawking at him, he laughed, and greeted him with a snarl, while he scratched his arse and spat.

I looked through Fr Pablo's eyes as he shook the memory away. Don Gabriel was snarling again, as if he had never stopped. Perhaps he had also guessed where the friar's thoughts had been. Then, as if to rid himself of the holy-man's moralising gape, he dipped a large wooden spoon into his chocolate and scooped up a brimming serve that he slurped, rubbing each elbow against the men who were flanking him.

These were obviously twins. On the initial glance they seemed identical. Two, roundly huge fellows that I had never seen before. And, by the way they waved their arms at the servants, it was clear that they were their owners. It was not difficult to deduce that they were also the hosts of the gathering.

I looked into Fr Pablo's mind again and discovered that they were his landlords, the Bishop of Tlaxcala's nephews, and that they had given lodgings not only to him but to Sarmiento as well. Their names were Saturnino and Dionisio. One of them then leaned across the table and tapped his fat fingers on the harsh fabric of the older friar's soutane. His voice was squeakily pitched: "Come, come señores. We must not anger ourselves now, must we? Such an old argument and, if we submit not, our divers logics will have us hateful of each other."

Then I realised that there was another figure standing silently in the background. At that same moment the sunlight struck his eyes and made him squint and retreat deeper into a dim corner. It was Pedro Sarmiento. Apart from the servants he was the only one standing. His back pressed up against the wall, hair brushing against the toes of an emaciated Christ dangling from a hefty cross. He curled his fingertips and cleaned his nails with a small dagger. Then yawned. One of his tubby hosts heard it, and turned and frowned. But Sarmiento ignored the admonishment and yawned again.

"If a case be true and just, then it needs to be championed," the old friar said, licking a tooth: "Even if it puts a distortion on the argument."

Don Gabriel lurched in again: "I'm sorry we are so run in your displeasure, Father, but those Indians 'ave been as forced labour used since time anon." Then, grinning. Made pathetic by insincerity: "They were slaves unto our predecessors, them barbaric Mexican tyrants. We, Father, are their liberators, and most benevolent ones too. All that be asked by us in return: that they live and work alongside us, in a Christian way, to build a more perfect, God-blessed world. We do not torture their babes and wrench out their hearts. We do not eat 'em. Their Mexican lords did. We've abolished bloody, pagan sacrifice and cannibalism, and for this kindness, we be accused that we seem bad Christians!" and he laughed. Equally pathetic.

"To speak truthfully, you grieve many. Why señores, you have made slaves of our good King's vassals," spluttered the old friar, spitting out a tiny shard broken off his rotten tooth: "You regard the Indians as nothing more than a cheaper way to have your work done. They break their backs in your fields and you call them idlers. They express true Christian virtues and you call them pagans. And when they refuse to work for you, you call them sub-human and try to deny them of all rights. And now you tell me, señor, on top of all that, that you be good Christians."

Don Gabriel ran a finger under his collar, exposing a hot red neck: "But why do ye complain so about *slaves*? Yer so dearly admired Fr Bartolome de Las Casas himself supports the nigger trade. And how many black men do ye 'ave toiling in yer own monastery?"

The old friar shook his head: "Negroes, señor, are a different question! They are the descendants of Ham, living under Noah's curse. Lawless, ungoverned wretches. More beasts than humans. And, more importantly, not subjects to the King of Spain. But these Indians are! And because of that they must be protected."

Sarmiento's head throbbed. He rubbed his temples, which evoked a vision, something like a dream. A smouldering, smashed village enclosing a group of huddled, squatting, half-naked figures. Adult arms clutching infants. Before them the threatening gesture of the poking harquebus. Then the clap of a slapping hand, a hard flat palm against a soft cheek. Long black hair thrashed impotently against a thick arm. Another hand; stubby fingers tightly clamping a woman's emaciated limb. She was naked. He was dressed, but with his pants down. She sobbed, wriggled, writhed and tried to push away. The hand slapped again. The large man, famous: old Columbus himself. The woman, his native wife. Then another scream. Another woman. The name Catalina bellowed past. Catalina: Cortés' wife. The scream was muffled by a pillow. The great Cortés, an abominable Othello, smothering his Catalina, his Desdemona. But more vicious than the Moor. When she squirmed no more he released the cushion and lifted her dead head, caught the chin, and twisted. Already dead, vertebrae cracking in the neck. Already dead, muscles ripping. Already dead. Her head drooped in his hands. Let it drop. No remorse. He is Cortés, not Othello. Historical, not fictional ...

"The Franciscans are right" Sarmiento had told Fr Pablo on another occasion: "The New World is an abomination. So much ruin in such short time, for what? So a few failed Europeans can rise, impose themselves."

At that moment there had been no chocolate. Instead of sweetness Fr Pablo had scooped an insipid morsel of boiled snail out of its shell. He slurped at it but his grimace indicated it had been no delicacy: "Ultimately, only failures are condemned. The ones who were unable, finally, to adapt unto the new course." Then froze and held his breath, obviously considering the complete lack of Christianity in what he had just burbled.

But Sarmiento did not seem to register his cousin's dilemma, or perhaps he forgave the cynicism as ironic expression from a lucid mind. In any case it served as a stepping stone on to an even deeper pessimism: "What does it matter? History in the Americas has been made, the New World is already more corrupt than the Old. The friars too will fail. But hadn't it been discovered for that very reason? To corrupt it? – *If it can be profitable?* – they all ask before embarking. And is my ambition any greater? Is my soul really prepared to embark on a spiritual quest?"

His cousin sighed. His voice quavered as if struggling against welling tears: "Perhaps you should not have come."

Sarmiento turned away from the debate and looked through a doorway into an adjacent room. A group of women were around a table, also sipping chocolate and chatting gaily. All of them had pitch black hair - the *Mexican* wives - except for Doña Rosa. She had put on weight since the last time I had seen her, but was still in the same dress with the bees. That was too tight and slightly frayed, but at least it was clean. The colour, crimson, was now discernible.

Sarmiento caught her eye. She did not turn away but stared back with a challenging look. Nostrils opened and her chest heaved up, fell, heaved up again. Sarmiento sucked on one of his rings. She stood up, waved her African slave girl away and approached him to whisper: "Keep your distance. My husband is after your gizzard."

Which inspired Sarmiento to lean closer. His breath against the tiny hairs on her neck: "I thought perhaps you'd like to see me."

She made an umming noise: "You promised to bring me a book."

Sarmiento licked his top lip: "Not here."

Her own top lip curled into a smirk: "But you've forgotten it, troth?"

"Oh, surely no madam," pushing his groin against her dress, which was not substantial enough to rub. She pulled away, but playfully rather than fleeing: "Oh surely yes, señor," then spinning around with a shining pout: "Or tell me what it was called?"

"You were asking for Aristotle."

"I was. But you promised to bring me poetry. My husband forbids it. It will give me great pleasure to hide it from him," then after a melodramatic sigh: "You will have to deliver it to me in a secret place."

Sarmiento gazed into her bosom and bit his bottom lip: "Oh yes. Boccaccio it is. Women should never read such things. But, if you are feeling strong."

She became anxious, rushing: "Strong enough. But, just in case, perhaps you could include a little of one of those potions you make that maintains the heart excited and f..." Her eyes flashed, full of emergency, as a hand suddenly descended upon Sarmiento's shoulder. Her breast rose and her calm smile looked absolutely false within the frame of repressed agitation that was her body. The hand became a jerking claw pulling Sarmiento around into Don Gabriel's electric stare. Hot eyes above a smile that was as huge and insincere as Doña Rosa's: "Pedro, I want you to meet Doña María."

And he guided him from his lip-chewing wife towards a woman dressed in a widow's black who held out a pale hand. Sarmiento took the proffered fingers and kissed them as he bowed.

Meanwhile Doña Rosa collapsed into a chair. She was trembling, but more from the excitement of possibilities than fear. If her husband's jealousy did explode, she felt confident that the alchemist could win the brawl. But those thoughts were swept aside by the rustling cloth and dazzling colour of the other wives who pounced on her with chatter and cake, as if a bright stage-curtain had dropped to mask the show.

Sarmiento looked up again into the woman in black's veiled countenance, and as he did she peeled away the dark shroud. The features underneath were drawn and marked by exceptionally dark eyes. She smiled, revealing a chipped incisor and a missing canine. When Sarmiento smiled back she leaned closer: "Don Gabriel tells me you and an engineer called Fernando are involved in some industry together. The refinement of gunpowder into something magical, he said. A fantastic idea, prithee." Sarmiento sniggered – *the sulphur mine* –

Sulphur … the volcano … lifted him into a memory … high up off a mountain cliff edge.

The wind was bitter ice. The pack bearers made a fire and huddled into a close circle protecting the blaze from the wind. It occasionally blew over or broke through them, ripping into the flames. Sparks and flaming ash spurted, choking smoke stinging eyes. They sat, heads bowed, warming fingers and toes, toasting cornbread in a pan.

Sarmiento was away from the fire, invisible to the rest. He stared upwards at the clear night sky. With his back to the circle of light he could easily distinguish constellations. A notebook, with a thick, lit candle was stuck in the earth next to it. He turned and took his writing cane, and sketched, and wrote.

The pack bearers urged their patrons to break camp. It was important to embark while it was still dark. They needed to make their way up whilst the fine, sandy lava was still frozen. Solidity made ascent easier. A streak of white light on the horizon was the only sign of morning. But Fr Pablo was exhausted: "It's too high. I was not made for this sport."

Sarmiento prodded him with a stick: "Get up cousin. With each step you are closer to God."

Fr Pablo took a deep breath and nearly choked: "This is no Godly air. It hardly sustains at all. I smell devils here."

It was the beginning of their fourth day on the volcano. Fr Pablo had hardly slept. On the first night he had been woken by a terrible rumbling and trembling. Fernando gave the friar some cacao nut to chew: "This was a Holy Mountain to the Mexica. So perhaps there are devils here. But you are a friar, Father. If you are lost, what hope have we?"

The friar swallowed hard and looked at his bandaged feet. His soles were blistered the previous day when his sandals had snapped. Now, the sight of his companion's thick leather boots made him feel stupid rather than envious. He grimaced as he lifted his knees. The broken-bubble flesh that had to support his bulk protested as the black lava rubble crunched. He prodded forward, gingerly at first. Then the flesh seemed to toughen, or perhaps it was his soul, and sharp pain dissolved into a more constant and therefore duller molestation. He climbed.

At times Sarmiento felt sorry for him. Pablo had no interest in nature's cauldrons. He had come because Sarmiento had pushed. An urging which had had a purely selfish motivation.

Sarmiento had been fascinated by the volcano ever since he had caught his first glimpse: that same day when the carriage had toppled into the ditch. Then the huge, smouldering bulk had emerged and Sarmiento had gasped while an inspired Fernando began narrating its history: "Popocatepetl," he proclaimed: *The mountain that smokes.*"

The engineer's father had been assigned the task of organising the extraction of sulphur from the crater to make gun-powder for Cortés' army. So Fernando had heard many stories: tales of his father's adventures as well as the native myths. How the volcano was believed to have been a god, with slopes occupied by troubled spirits. Because of this an ascent had always been professed to be impossible: "Mortals cannot cohabit with demons."

Sarmiento saw an immediate association between the smoking peak and the ruined pyramids that this same engineer had also pointed out to him on their way. Microcosms of the macrocosm. Temples to Quetzalcoatl, the father of alchemy. He had recalled Rodolfo's advice to ignore nothing. In the New World everything would be significant and profound. The volcano; symbol of the alchemical kiln. He knew he needed to scale it, to look inside, experience it.

Fr Pablo gasped and groaned. Eventually he collapsed, falling into a foetal position, his screwed up face squeezing the pain out of his body, while he suffered the agony of the defeat of his Christian will. They erected a blanket on jutting poles, as a shelter for him, then left him there with a pack-bearer to wash his bleeding feet and lance his blisters.

From the summit Sarmiento descended with cautious crunching steps into the crater. Around his waist was a cord, attaching him to a windlass which Fernando had assured him would be strong enough to reel him back up.

When the mountain boomed it was like a cannon shot, taking the alchemist completely by surprise – *The bellow of the Fire Dragon in the Hollow Mountain* – he thought. The Mexican fire god, in the form of a dragon who lived in the depths of the earth – *I have arrived at the Omphalos* – he decided – *The umbilicus of the world. And, from the Alpha, I will set forth to discover the Omega!* – From just under the lip of the crater's rim he had contemplated the distant horizon lost in a haze – *Perhaps my last glimpse of the world* – he considered as he leapt a metre down.

The hemp rope was pulled taught as he briefly flew then crunched into the lower level of slope, his feet digging and pushing the rubble surface. This rose into its own small crater's slope, before avalanching away on the other side in a short tumbling rattle with Sarmiento threatening to follow. Inertia and gravity dragged him forward and he would have probably hurtled right down into the hot mouth of the crater had not the umbilicus rope held him up. He was jerked to a standstill, then rocked and swayed with dangling heavy arms.

The winch he was attached to creaked and when it cracked Sarmiento looked anxiously back. Fernando was smiling down at him, waving cheerfully and slapping the windlass. So he turned his head back to face his vertigo and stare ahead and down. Black, sulphuric mud bubbled and spat – *Heat sulphur over a fire* – he remembered – *and it becomes a clear yellow liquid. Heat it in a kiln at great temperatures and it grows viscous and darkens until it eventually turns dense and black –*

With each inch downward the air became warmer, but acrid, noxious. He put a scarf over his mouth while he let his hand pass over the steaming fumaroles to feel their heat. The walls of the crater were coated with the mineral he sought: yellow, green, red-brown, black – *The second death* – he remembered – *the lake which burneth with fire and brimstone* – Yet as he applied the chisel and chipped the sulphur away, gathering the flakes in a sack tied to a belt around his waist, he started to choke and feel faint.

Dizziness whirled him into an unconscious realm, his memory melting into a recollection of a vision ...

The rock walls sharpened into intricate and extravagant detail and became the sitting-room of a palace. But then, just as quickly, the wall in front turned transparent, revealing a teenage girl, naked, budding breasts and a smudge of red hair between the crease at the top of her crossed legs. She stood, surprised, at the end of a long hall. But instead of covering herself she turned around, bending towards an enormous mirror which she veiled with a long, lace curtain drawn up from the floor. Little clam, bristled red; opening slowly, slightly to reveal the rose pink flesh within.

Sarmiento's stomach rumbled. Then three younger girls appeared. White smocks shrouded by black hair dangled down to the backs of their knees. Between them, cradled in the arc of their bent arms, was the wooden skeleton of a full-sized man puppet. The naked girl's arm stretched forward and fingers scooped the air, beckoning to Sarmiento. Then the three younger ones lifted their smocks and turned, revealing long legs that skipped away and Sarmiento realised that all of the girls had now become women.

He trotted behind. Long locks of hair, black hair, and the curly red hair of the first girl. Dreadlocks bobbing as the naked one hopped up, jumping out of a window.

Sarmiento groaned then took a deep breath and the same leap. The scene opened into an exterior landscape; green and forested. They ran down to a stream. The girls, now enormous goddesses, their whiteness prominent before the verdurous background had stopped and took deep breaths that made breasts heave.

Then they began to move their hands, fingers slipping across the surface of the doll in their arms. Sarmiento felt his skin tingle. He reached out, but the segmented doll was dropped into the stream and he fell.

They had dropped him. He was the doll. Not floating but bobbing, half-submerged. A tremendous pull was dragging him. His ears filled with a roar as he floundered in rushing water that was no longer a stream but an ocean.

A prodigious ebb-tide was tugging him out. Coughing, spluttering. His mouth and lungs filled with a salty brine. Panic, until he realised that he was foreseeing and pre-living his own last moment.

The ineffable concept calmed him. Fear turned to bliss and the ghastly tentacles of ghostly cuttlefish stretched forward and curled around him, to hug and gently stroke him, laying him down on a wavering blanket of tickling sea anemone. A parrot fish kissed his bloated cheek, then nipped a morsel from his swollen bottom lip

– *I am surely most well dead* – he thought, while contemplating the sensual violence in the spasms of a writhing nurse shark, giving birth to an enormous, pulsating seedpod.

When his soul had finally abandoned his vision and returned to the sweltering, smouldering reality of the crater, he felt at first sublime, then anxious ...

He was out of the water, but still could not breathe – *like a fish* – he thought. His body, his real body, twisted into violent, spastic throws, almost hurling him into the fiery depths. A distant voice yelled. He twisted his head back and looked up. The figures at the rim were a blur, but he remembered where he was and who was up there. He coughed, the heat was unbearable and he knew he had to move. He reached out, caught the rope with the slippery-wet palms of his hands and gave three desperate tugs. At the other end of the line a nervous Fernando ordered the pack-bearers to hoist ...

This memory flashed past in an instant, leaving him back in that house in Tlaxcala, holding that woman's hand – *What woman?* – he thought, and had to struggle to remember her name. She looked up at him, aghast. She could sense something was wrong. Then he remembered: Doña María. She was whispering: "The sulphur mine, will be operating soon? If I may be so impertinent?"

Sarmiento shook his head: "No," he said, regretting his return. He scratched his forehead. Don Gabriel was eyeing him from behind the woman with a snake-eyed snarl. The alchemist felt his throat dry up and he looked for a tray of drinks while his explanation dribbled out hoarsely: "No... Our industry, alas, is becalmed just now," he explained as his own eyes fluttered to escape the serpent-eyed assault: "Some annuity is requisite," then fixed his gaze on the sparkling necklace around Doña Maria's neck: "But if a wealthy damsel, or her husband should wish to be a patron of this venture?" and his own audacity made him feel stronger.

Doña María frowned: "I know nothing of business, let alone such an ambitious industry as alchemy. As for my husband; I'm afraid he has been missing for some long months. Returning to the colony from Spain, his transport, caught in a storm, was wrecked. We assume him to be dead."

Sarmiento shook his head and moaned softly. Doña María squeezed his hand: "Don Gabriel told me that you have no small knowledge of men's stars."

Flattery made his eyebrows jump: "True madam. A part of my art is called astrology."

"Then pray, speak to me of my husband," and she passed him a ring while wrapping her hands around one of his and rubbing it. Her dark eyes were imploring: "Please. What do you see? They say you have a gift. A tremendous prophetic eye."

"They do?" and Sarmiento frowned. The extent of the adulation was verging on the absurd and he began to sense the trap: "I said I was an astrologer madam. That is a Godly science, not a black, pagan art."

"Yes, but you see, don't you? Prithee, please. You see."

Her gaze seared him. He sighed: "Are you looking for the truth, or for a balm for your cankerous doubt?"

"The truth is a balm for doubt."

Which was whispered with such sensual commitment that the alchemist could not resist. He closed his eyes and squeezed the ring. Took a deep breath, sighed again and used a memory of his sister to fill his actor's heart with grief: "I see your husband. A grey figure, like a seal on an empty beach. Pale. Oh, so pale!" and then pulling the woman to him to enjoy the rub of her heaving breasts: "Crabs ... I'm sorry, madam. He's a corpse."

Tears actually welled in his eyes, and he apologised to the lady for grabbing her, but that it had been her husband's ghost reaching out for her.

However, rather than shocked, she threw back her head to open her throat and let loose an enormous and outrageous belly laugh that attracted the gawking attention of the other women there.

Between the foreground and the gossiping backdrop, Don Gabriel's snarl had curled into a sneer as he considered the woman's hand slapping Sarmiento's cheek. A slap that was echoed by an oval mouthed, ohhhhh, from the wives.

The shock of the blow opened the alchemist's fist and Doña María reached in and took back her ring: "You are a cozener, señor! A shark. But your sharking stops here. Undone, señor! Let all Tlaxcala know it, just as they know, all but you and your so-far-seeing eye, that my husband is here in Tlaxcala buried, a year hence. He died far, far, from any beach." Then retreated. Don Gabriel's sneer was now a glare. Sarmiento shook his head. Another deep breath: "So you've been organising a witch hunt, partner," and drew phlegm to make the following insult gurgle: "You quat!"

Don Gabriel's voice was a deep monotone: "Yer a cunning man, Don Pedro. But in cursing us your bad tongue has bewitched yer own enterprise!"

"My bad tongue, by your bad language made, señor!"

"You've bewitched our corn, our servants, our babes at nurse. You've cursed us all."

"Do not blame your impotence on me. If your cock does not rise, that is not my fault. It's not my fault if the devil strangles your balls while he makes your wife's sex hot. But if you cannot manage, perhaps you are in need of an exorcism yourself. Find a friar, whelp!"

The latch clanked loudly up and the door creaked open, but the only one paying any attention to Sarmiento's exit was Fr Pablo. He had not witnessed the scene in the sitting room, so it was without prejudice that he lifted himself from his chair at the table and followed.

Outside, Sarmiento looked down the street, to the end where it dipped away. Further on was the other side of the valley and the horizon, the setting sun painting a breathtaking sky. He had been in Tlaxcala for over a year, the monotony gnawing at his patience. He sighed and wondered about his boat; his freedom. A man on horseback had appeared, a black silhouette in the distance. Sarmiento watched him dismount and harness the steed, which reminded him of the real enemy. Then the grinning, obese faces of his *hosts*, the Bishop's nephews, invaded his mind's eye as well – *Indolent* – he thought, which seemed a sufficient abstraction for them both.

On another occasion I had seen him in the tiny cramped space of his Tlaxcalan laboratory. It was a cellar, candlelit with no windows. There were candles under the still too, heating bubbling liquid. A round face, made rounder by the curve of the retort it was reflected in, made Sarmiento jump. Saturnino. The combination of permanently half-closed eyes and a huge fleshy grin made him seem diabolic. Behind him, his twin brother Dionisio was the same. The first one tilted his head and pointed at a beaker at the end of the still that was slowly being filled: "What's this, pray?" squeaking like damp leather rubbed against glass.

Sarmiento ignored him. He was pouring liquid from one flask to another. This gurgled. It was Dionisio who answered his brother: "They call it Alchemy," and clasped his fat fingers together as if in prayer: "Our guest is searching for the control of God's universe."

Saturnino clicked his tongue: "Blasphemous practice."

Which inspired a squeal from the other twin: "Aye," and clapped: "But our good guest would argue that what he's searching for is not domination but rather empirical knowledge of our good Lord's work."

Then Saturnino's pink-slug fingers were sliding over Sarmiento's shoulder and his sanguine lips hung at the alchemist's ear whilst blowing irony to his brother: "Oh surely, good Dionisio. 'Tis just another way of saying *control*. What will he do with the universe's secrets once he understands them? It seems to me that our beloved guest is lusting after a chance to partake in the process of eternal creation itself."

Sarmiento did not flinch. He continued transferring the liquid from receptacle to receptacle while Saturnino pushed his face closer to the beaker: "They say, brother, that these alchemists can perform miracles."

Dionisio was languid: "Miracles? Oh no, brother. It's science that's performed here, not magic."

"But, it's been said, that an alchemist may excite lust for the heat of love in an otherwise cold and dry heart," and Saturnino slipped his hand under his shirt and began to rub his hairless chest.

Dionisio sucked his top lip: "It is a possibility within the grasp of such a science, so they say, marry."

Then Sarmiento exploded: "Why gentlemen! For the love of God…"

The twins: "Ah! The alchemist is a Christian!" and they laughed.

Sarmiento hissed: "And will you have the neighbours hear all of it?!"

Saturnino sucked in his cheeks: "Your anger, señor, implies some crime."

"Why, pray, I thought I'd been favoured by you."

"Oh certainly good fellow. You're well countenanced. But we would hope that you'd likewise countenance us."

Then Dionisio: "A favour, señor. Not too much to expect. Haven't we been so kind as to give you these lodgings?"

Sarmiento was cold: "Lodgings I can find in a hundred homes. If you want my help, you must provide a real favour."

The twins grinned: "Speak, señor. We will try."

But at first the alchemist picked up some tongs and clamped them on Saturnino's button-nose, pinching another squeal from him: "I have a secret," and pulled the twin towards him: "A secret plan," then released the nose with a jerk: "To go to an occult place."

Saturnino squealed again, and rubbed his smarting little protuberance. Dionisio clapped his hands: "Tell us more, prithee."

"That I'll not. Knowledge of the mission would be the death of you."

Saturnino still rubbing. His tone dulled: "Then what do you want?"

The alchemist pinched his shirt: "That you arrange audiences for me, with wealthy landowners, bishops or viceroys."

Dionisio's eyebrows lifted and his jaw plummeted: "In order to sell them this *secret* plan, eh what?"

And Saturnino sucked his cheeks in like a fat fish: "You   want   us   to arrange an audience to sell a secret!?"

Sarmiento licked the top row of teeth: "A secret audience, aye!"

And the twins became squeaky again: "Troth señor, what you're asking is absurd."

"No more absurd than a potion of love," and he leaned forward as if about to pounce on them: "Do we have a treaty, señores?"

Dionisio began to pace, as if thoughtful: "Yet you say you want some rich man's gold," then pointing an accusing digit: "But why do you not make your own?" and the finger curled through the air: "You have this most beautiful still, señor. A retort most recently imported, and a crucible. There is much base metal in this town. If you were to turn it all into gold."

"If I had three lifetimes I would," spurted the alchemist: "But I'm impatient, and so is my secret plan."

Saturnino was rubbing his belly: "How many lifetimes, pray, would a love-potion take to brew?"

Sarmiento paused before answering: "That   would   depend   upon astrology, the position of that fair star Venus."

The serious tone used by Sarmiento excited the twins. Dionisio: "How long, pray?"

"Let me have a month, baboons."

Dionisio laughed and rubbed his thighs: "Then shark for us. But an amorous swindle, bringing women to our beds. When we've pried open that first maiden's clam, then we shall look for your patron."

The friar's hand on his shoulder made Sarmiento's heart miss a beat and he gasped, Pablo's gentle voice in his ear: "Why do you leave us? You've not discussed your plan with the landowners. Their purses bulge with gold. Do you not want finance?"

Sarmiento took his cousin's hand, stroked it, and then pulled a ring off one of his fingers: "I cannot see them capable of appreciating the exorbitance of my quest."

"Is it so righteous? Or does the probity come from you yourself? Oh, how the demon sinner has so quickly and absolutely reformed!"

Sarmiento twisted his golden ring: "Did you know that the Indians never used gold as a means of barter?" and licked the rim: "It was never a symbol of power. Only strictly religious attributes were applied."

"You mean pagan."

"Oh yes, pagan, if you like cousin. But less pagan perhaps than the greed of the conquistadors," and he looked through the ring to a murrey patch of setting-sun sky: "You and I are here in this distant slice of the empire because there is gold and silver here. If Montezuma had not had gold, Cortés would not have risked his life in the conquest. Towns and villages would not have been ransacked, men would not have been tortured and killed, tombs would have remained uncovered, the dead left to lie in peace. Can we call ourselves *good?!* *Better?!* Is the spirit of the conquistador a Christian spirit?" He clutched the ring firmly: "For these pagans that were here, this gold contained the blood and spirit of the Sun," and held up another of his rings: "This silver was the spirit of the moon." Pablo was dumbfounded. Sarmiento, trembling, mad: "A very alchemical dialectic, sirrah."

The friar hissed: "You'd do better to hold your tongue."

"Can I not speak freely with you then cousin?"

"Yes, you can, with me. But others'll not be so obliging if they overhear you preaching alchemical virtue. It could be mistaken for necromancy, and you may find yourself troubled by the inquisition."

"But let *us* talk openly, metaphysically cousin. The Mexica believed that the duality of Sun and Moon blew the spirit of life over the earth."

"Pray, who told you all this? Wretched Carlos?"

"Probably, or some other old poet. These Indians are interesting creatures."

"They are men!"

"Oh yes, they're men. And interesting, if one takes the time to listen to them."

"That's why I'm here."

"You're here to persuade, not to learn."

"You're also here to persuade."

"But not to persuade them. I find the Mexica to be a poetic people. Don't you?"

"Perhaps. But I'm a friar, not a troubadour."

"And therefore must close your ears, if you suspect the beautiful verse you hear does not conform with our God."

"If the ideas are truly beautiful they must conform."

"Then listen to this," and he unrolled a parchment and began to read: "*... we are only here to sleep ... only here to dream ... 'tis not true, not true, that we are here to live on the earth ...*"

But the friar merely sighed, turned and returned to the house.

Sarmiento picked up a pebble, rubbing the surface as if trying to absorb the hardness of it. Then he walked away down the sandy track out of the town, to the Indian settlement on the outskirts.

A swarm of emaciated, barefoot creatures materialised from the shadows, forming a brood of stumbling kids. Miserable, wide, yellow eyes out of dark skin screamed silent pleas, but the stranger's coldness made them droop and become even more withered before they dropped away.

Then there were only women in the street. Happily rotund after the gnarled-sad children, they were all breasts and bellies in front of doorless entries, solitary perforations in the walls of windowless homes. They were also barefoot, but some had their heads wrapped in rainbow coloured shawls, dulled by lack of illumination. The daylight diminished, but they remained, still, and most of them silent, ghostly vigilant at the entrance to their humble cells.

Three yellow-brown and crippled dogs pranced out. Motley mongrels, hungry with fangs bared through slathering jowls. They hobbled straight into his path, growling, to hold their ground, and block the invader's way. But the alchemist did not waver. Instead he began mumbling some indistinct guttural verse and advanced straight into them. Jaws snapped, ears pricked ... then shivered, and their growls turned into sharp yelps of hopeless canine insanity when the intruder crossed the frontier they had imagined. They twisted, contorting, accompanied by a cacophony, as if they had been kicked by a flurry of hard leather boots. Dust rose from an emergency of slapping paws as they darted away; sad tails between wobbling hind legs.

Sarmiento seemed hardly to notice. He entered a long, narrow lane that curled downward. Music could be discerned: drum and flute. At the bottom was the red glow of a bonfire which was on the other side of a low arch. He had to cower going through. As he did, silhouettes of men emerged. Shuffling, tottering figures moving in circles around the fire. An intoxicated revelry. He pushed his way in, arrogantly shoving any drunk who crossed his path, making an almost complete circle around the bonfire until he came to a scaffolding of sticks acting as a flimsy throne for a ruddy effigy.

He reached back into the crowd, grabbing anyone who passed. Yanking hair to pull up heads and examine faces. Glazed, uncomprehending eyes shone back at him. Then his pulse raced, he saw a bald head on an immediately recognised body which had a more pronounced limp than the other shuffling figures. The head turned. A stupid smile in the familiar face of the old and thumbless Carlos. He was obviously drugged, but he soon recognised the Spaniard. He grinned, laughed and reached forward: "Don Pedwo... Don Pedwo, señor..." and patted Sarmiento's shoulders.

Sarmiento pointed to the effigy on the scaffolding: "What's that?!"

"Ah, Don Pedwo. Welcome, welcome. You're always welcome, señor."

The alchemist shook his head, violently: "The idol. What is it?"

Old Carlos gasped: "A Saint, milord. Santiago, *Matamoros*. The Moor-killer, señor."

Sarmiento grabbed his cotton smock and shook him: "A new name for an old god. It's Huitzilopochtli."

The Mexican pressed a finger against his lips: "Troth. But you are such a clever man, well versed in our religion ... tell no-one, pray, please, no ... Not even your friary friend ... please ... You know it ain't allowed, señor. If they ask you, say you that it were Santiago, I beg it."

The Spaniard's chest sank, dragging his shoulders. He sighed and stretched his neck: "What's happening here?"

Old Carlos's expression became even more pitiful. His voice depressing: "Oh! A funeral, milord. A man you also knew. For me old friend it is ... The blind and crippled Hilario ... Oh! We'll miss his jokes, and his farts. His arse was a trumpet."

Sarmiento shook his head to hide an involuntary grin and snigger at Carlos's shameless but fraternal irreverence. Then spitting he wrapped an arm around the old poet and guided him closer to the idol. His voice dropped and calmed with resignation: "What's it made of, this *Santiago*?"

The Mexican sniggered, stupidly: "A dough, made from amaranth seed."

And the Spaniard reached forward and stroked it, tentatively, as if daring to fondle some precious jewel: "Amaranth," he whispered: "Which symbolises eternity."

This excited old Carlos: "Aye m' lord! It do! It do! You are most wise ... Immortality..."

"Because of its long lasting flowers."

"Aye, señor ... you know too much ... Have learned too much too quickly."

"And the arrows mean he is a god of war."

"Oh most certainly. God of war, he is, let us not deny't, but a god of much more as well m' lord. He's also god of the sun."

"Maintaining the vital cosmic energy. The principal recipient of Mexican sacrifice."

He opened his arms as if offering his own heart, but Carlos looked away and his voice became gravely cautious: "No longer practised. I promise you. The dough of our amaranth seed was kneaded with a good goat's blood, no longer a handsome youth," then staring back into the alchemist's eyes: "We are Christians now."

Sarmiento slapped his fingers, like squid-suckers, on the old poet's cheeks: "Aye, Carlos, Christians. But perhaps even for us the shedding of blood should be necessary," then lifting his head in search of stars: "Is it not written that God did not hear the children of Eve, Cain and Able, until blood was shed?"

Carlos looked down at pebble-pocked dust: "If you say it, señor. But I think that you are not a Christian. You are possessed of a pagan soul, and should a poet be, or a hermit priest."

Which did nothing but make Sarmiento thoughtful-sad: "...or a conquistador with blood on his hands."

The image of blood seemed to waft across the Mexican's face, reddening his eyes with a cruel image: "...or a god with a bloody club."

"Aye!" moaned the Spaniard: "I should be a god. Will not rest till I am," then became solemn, until he remembered his invigorating purpose: "Carlos! I came here for some of your drugs. I want to meet God tonight. Huitzilopochtli, or any god!"

And Carlos also grinned, huge, which was dragged into a frown by realisation: "Oh sirrah! All the mushrooms be eaten, milord. I wanted more meself," he slurped: "Yet I know a place, near here, where medicines can be got," stroking Sarmiento's leather doublet: "There is a priest, a Tlaxcalteca, most strong he is. He will open the door for you ... make your acquaintance wit' a god or two. Wit' a demon or three." And laughed.

Sarmiento grabbed the Mexican's smock again. His voice seditious: "Then tell me where."

Following the instructions given he kept close to a wall, at the end of which was a corral. In the middle of this was a white-washed, windowless bungalow, half in ruins and muddy in the gloom. He stared into it but it was pitch, so he yelled. His shout had a brief, stifled echo. There was no real reply so he squatted in the doorway to wait. After a while he fell asleep on his haunches.

When he awoke there was more light. A full moon in a clear sky bleached the square. He shuddered and gasped. Right in front of him was a funny face, creased like a prune. A dark fold opened revealing two peeled almond teeth pushed into the prune-skin flesh. A cloud of smoke was burped out. This stung Sarmiento's eyes and burned his throat, making him splutter. The prune-face laughed then backed away slightly. Sarmiento sensed something move – *a limb* – he supposed – *an arm* – Then a red glow, the tip of a fat cigar that had settled between the creases that were the prune's lips. From somewhere far away came a pan-pipe melody, a melancholy tune, but relieving the discomfort generated by the face and the cigar smoke. The prune-faced man laughed again.

A cool wind had risen and Sarmiento shivered. Dust and leaves blew across the corral. The sound of the flute seemed closer, embellishing. The two sat and watched each other. After a while they talked, in the Nahuatl language, impossible for me to understand. But I did recognise the name *Quetzalcoatl*. The guttural sounds of the sky god's name, flung back and forth between the protagonists. Sarmiento scraped a shard of charcoal across a slip of paper: *Quetzal...* he wrote. And then directly underneath scribbled: *bird* ... and then underneath that: *spirit* ... Creating another column he wrote: *Coatl/serpent/immortal* ... Then: *Quetzal-coatl* = *Immortal spirit...* Followed by: *The bird = the will to live/The serpent = Abraxas = the will to die...*

Then he stopped writing and concentrated on the Tlaxcalteca's finger as it slid through the sandy soil in the doorway, tracing a circle filled in with a pattern. Sarmiento stared into it – *a map* – he told himself, although if it was, it was too ambiguous to be a functional tool. But he copied it anyway, scraping a shard of charcoal across a slip of paper. The line that snaked out from the centre was vague, but Sarmiento recognised that it went in the direction that Rodolfo and the copy of the Dauphin map had told him it should go: to the west and to the south ...

And I suddenly stepped into a new world, or an image of one... A long, low, wooden boat was being rowed into a natural harbour of glowing, golden, metallic cliffs. At the helm was a sturdy, dark skinned man with a parchment dangling from his fingertips, open. I examined it. The same pattern that the Tlaxcalteca had sketched; Quetzalcoatl's map.

The vision was convincing, as if there had been revelation, but to whom? Whose mind was I in? Mine, or Sarmiento's? The prune-faced man's, or the dark man at the helm? It produced vertigo: a thousand places at the same time, a thousand minds, in a thousand heads, in a thousand places and a thousand different times; at the same time. Atomised, I was becoming part of everything; exhilarating and horrifying. I reached out. By concentrating I managed to compose myself and surface again in one place, but still with Sarmiento and the Tlaxcalteca ...

The latter moved brusquely, pulling a yam out from under his tunic. This was twisted into a peculiar almost anthropomorphic form. Then he reached forward, ripped some hair from Sarmiento's head and tied it around the root. The Spaniard did nothing to resist. The Tlaxcalteca's voice droned, moaning a phrase which he had Sarmiento repeat several times in order to memorise it. Then he uttered it again, this time waving a stick over the yam and finally he lit a piece of dry bark with his smouldering cigar. As soon as he had, Sarmiento doubled over. There was a sharp pain in his liver. The Tlaxcalteca laughed. The pain increased, suddenly stopping when the torturer had extinguished the flame.

The old man handed him his cigar. It contained a herb with soothing properties, but Sarmiento puffed too hard. Too many times; perhaps deliberately. His mind became light while his head grew heavy. The prune-face opened wide and the constant laughter was deafening. Sarmiento squinted, trying to focus on the blurring image of the man in front. He reached out, but the blur was an illusion, the man had vanished.

Stumbling to his feet he staggered into the ruined hut where he supposed the old Indian had gone. The stench of urine inside made his stomach churn and he had to suddenly spin around in order to direct his vomit out of the doorway. Then he collapsed. Another sharp pain dug into his groin, but that was because he had fallen onto the pommel of his sword. He groped for it, unsheathed it, then collapsed again. The ground in the hut was cool and he submitted to the relief, dropping into a deep sleep ...

Despite the effects of the drug it was his reflexes that saved him. He still clenched his sword and the instinctive need to cover his face deflected the falling blade. The black figure, distorted by the hallucinogenic, appeared as a stalking demon. Jaundiced glowing eyes, scaled and reddish skin, and a thick bone structure that made it seem horned and saurian. Sarmiento's defence was unconscious but effective. He raised himself, blocking a second sweep, then slashed back. His own sword dragged, there had been contact. His foe groaned and feet shuffled as he backed away. Another groan, then he ran.

Sarmiento had an itch and scratched his arm, only then realising that he had his dagger in his hand and he had been taking aim to throw it.

Breathing was difficult. The exertion, the dust and the drugs. He wheezed, gasped, then remembered the prune-faced man and dropped to his knees to run his hands over the dirt floor, feeling for the scrap of paper he had sketched the Tlaxcalteca's map on. He patted around but found nothing. It had obviously been taken by the assailant, but – *Why would a demon take a map?* – Then he realised that it was not a demon – *How long must he have been following me?* – he wondered, and staggered onto his legs. Shaking his head to get the intoxication out of them.

They knew exactly where he was, he realised, and they would be back – *Yet it's good enough luck* – he thought. In the darkness of the hut the thief had probably imagined the slip of paper to be his copy of the Portuguese map – *Thinking they have it will delay them. But how long?* – Until cruel vengeance inspired more foolish-brave internecine ideas and he stroked his dagger's double edged blade across his lips – *Hurry on friends. I'm waiting for you –*

VIII. Separate and Wash with Vinegar and Salt

(a) the winged serpent

So many years have I been in this sanatorium, so long it was since I had seen Estrella, and I had forgotten so much again. Forgotten, yes, my amnesia is now considered to be a chronic condition by my doctors. According to them I am condemned to an eternity of broken life-cycles in which I will die and be reborn. How many times has it been now?

It was Arizmendi who brought it all back, making me so funereally conscious again of my loss. Inma's disappearance, he reminded me, had complicated an already complex situation. The police had begun, I remembered, what seemed to be a very bogus investigation, but they had never questioned me and I never dared approach them. What would I have told them? The truth? That I had been with Inma some months before her disappearance? That I had been crazy-ill in her bed in her old teacher's flat in Galicia? That I had been astral travelling? That Inma was a witch who had practised a *Walpurgis night* on me in order to extract information about the subject I observed on my astral journeys into the past?

The weeks following Inma's disappearance had been difficult. Reality had become an ambiguous term for both Estrella and I. The possibility that Inma was dead was excruciating and Estrella began to blame herself for not sensing Inma's despair and having allowed her brother to leave his weapon in her flat.

Our relationship with Sarmiento had also waned: we drank more, travelled less and wrote next to nothing. And then, with the autumn came a new problem, more mundane and purely material, but nevertheless it was also pressing. My original grant from Australia to write the Terra Australis had expired, and I had nothing concrete to show my patrons which could give them any reason to renew it. It was a perfect reason to jump overboard and begin a new life. But instead, it was that very clear option that actually inspired a renewal of the project.

I remember the letter announcing the cutting of the grant. I read it and tore it up, and as I was doing so Estrella came to me, cradling a pile of books in her arms. But instead of passing them to me she just let them drop on the floor. I reached down and pulled a thick folder containing my notes out of the pile. She handed me a pen. Later she made a puritan gesture and locked the liquor cupboard and we were able to work solidly for the next few days. Until reality stopped us. Neither of us had any money, and we could not live on enthusiasm alone. That would run out eventually, as would the ink and paper. So I arrived at what I thought was the obvious conclusion: "I'm afraid that arsehole de Coca must be paid a visit, our impecuniosity makes his offer irrefutable."

Estrella sighed: "I'd rather burn all this," she said, then blurted her own suggestion: "Don Enrique Villeplein."

There was some apprehension at first. Estrella had not seen her old friend for months. Perhaps, she thought, he would be angry with her. But when she rang him with the proposition he agreed to it right away. The only condition he gave was that we should move in with him.

He had plenty of room at his residence near San Lorenzo, which, he whined, was really so big and lonely: "I've been living alone too long," he told us: "A bit of youth around me will be uplifting."

The house at San Lorenzo was high upon the slope of a mountain, overlooking the monastery of El Escorial, amidst a wood of Spanish oak. We were fetched by Don Enrique's personal chauffeur who drove us up to the granite wall marking the boundary of the property, erected at enough distance to keep Don Enrique's castle-home unsighted from the road. I got down from the car with the driver to help him drag open a huge cast iron gate.

He: "No need, señor."

But the gate sagged somewhat on its screeching hinges as he pulled. A rasping contact as the base dragged against the concrete road.

"Let's walk up," I suggested to Estrella, who liked the idea, but we had to discern the path which was covered, then trudge ankle-high in brown leaves.

Eventually the mansion came into sight. The broad, white front of the building was surprising, I had expected something gloomier. Even the sharply sloping, grey, slate roof was promising.

I was unaware of ever having experienced snow, but the white gravel path leading up to the wide main door made me think of it. It crunched under foot, a happy kind of crackle. And as I reached the silent steps that lead inside I paused to take a profound lungful of the cleansing crisp mountain air, as if we had arrived at a sanatorium.

It was only after we had settled that we felt courageous enough to tell Don Enrique about our full purpose. Estrella brought the project up over dinner. Enrique sitting in front of us, the bow of his cravat huge and bright gold, which seemed to complement his silver hair and moustache. Estrella's fork sparkled as she waved his attention: "Do you remember me telling you about our night with Tomás Puigsegur, experimenting with hypnotism?"

Enrique was carefully isolating a bone from the fillet of hake in front of him: "Yes. You claimed that Val here had enjoyed an out-of-body experience ... most interesting," and then with the fish in his mouth, between chews: "It's a shame that you didn't pursue it."

My own fish exploded with spittle in a coughing fit. A servant came with a glass of water. When I had recovered: "What should be concluded ... regarding what happened to me?"

He shrugged his shoulders and looked down at the bits of fish that I had spat onto the tablecloth: "I imagine it was a bone."

Which was perplexing, until I deduced the confusion: "No ... it was the night with Tomás that was being referred to." It was so hard then for me to express myself, I had to take a deep breath and close my eyes in order to force out a more intelligible question: "What do you think really happened to me that night?"

His fork clunked against the plate: "What do I think? Well, I wasn't there was I?" and he chuckled and began carving the fish again, until he realised that he had not given me the answer I wanted. So he sniffed and: "Well, I suppose even if I had been there, one can only take your word for what you said you saw. Of course you seem like a perfectly honest chap to me, I would find no reason to doubt you."

"But as a s-scientist," I persisted, leaning forward: "What's your scientific opinion? How should out-of-body experiences be regarded?"

His eye-brows shot up in surprise and he laughed: "Scientific opinion? Oh I don't have too many scientific opinions. Let us say that as far as the scientific community is concerned I'm an aberration, an eccentric. But, on the other hand, if you want an opinion derived from what I've seen and experienced in my own life, then I would say that *astral travel* is a most real phenomenon. Why not? There have been many recorded instances."

"But there haven't been many that have travelled into the past."

"No," he admitted: "There haven't."

"But I did ... Didn't you know that?"

He chewed: "No, I don't think I did," and swallowed, and then: "Yes, you're right, it's very unusual."

Estrella nodded: "But there's more," and she swiped a serviette across her lips: "That night was only the beginning. We've refined the process, and we've found that it's possible to send Val to specific times and places. This is why we're telling you this, because the book that you're sponsoring, actually uses that research. Observation carried out during the out-of-body experience. We thought you should know."

And Don Enrique dropped his fork, coughed without opening his mouth, and then: "Yes, thank you for telling me."

Later, after the meal, in the *salon d'estar*. We were sipping wine and listening to records: Schubert, Schumann and Wagner. Estrella and I found ourselves circling the room as we would a museum, studying the archaeological specimens decorating the walls.

"Reflecting the depth of human creativity," murmured Estrella. She was standing opposite me under a votive statuette, probably Egyptian. The feminine figure was slightly inclined and jutting so that it was looking over Estrella and attending to every word from her delicious mouth: "Every time I come here these walls seem to change," she said. I had not been aware until then that she was familiar with the place and I felt suddenly hot, with a strange, hollowing sensation in my stomach.

She crossed the room and threw herself down on an antique sofa, keeping her eyes fixed on a small, painted figurine that I later discovered was a representation of the Hindu goddess Kali. A black and naked woman with four waving arms, bearing a garland of human skulls to cover her breasts. Her mouth was open, as if she were laughing. Her teeth, stained with blood: "The collection grows more and more intricate, more complete."

Don Enrique ran a finger between his lips: "I've added nothing for years. But what you say is interesting in itself. There's obviously been a development of your own inquiring mind. You're seeing things which had been ignored before, that's all. No, no new additions."

Estrella pointed to a small glass cabinet. In it sat the shrivelled, decrepit form of a shrunken head: "That wasn't there before."

"Oh, but it was. That's always been there. Surprising you never noticed it. It's usually the first thing people acknowledge."

It was the first thing I had been struck by. Stitched mouth and eyes. Smashed nose. I felt the thud of the head-hunter's club in my own face. The shock lifted me. I span around to regain my breath. When I turned back I saw that Don Enrique had leaned forward and was stroking Estrella's hand: "But of course, you are Estrella," he said: "My *Estrellita* ... you are unique," and then let her hand go and sat back: "I do you a grave injustice expecting you to act as the common mortals would."

Which was said without any hint of spite: on the contrary, pure flattery. Estrella hung her head to hide a blush. In that instant she looked as young as she really was. As beautifully fragile as I can ever remember her. A beauty which was mirrored by a delicate white, stone chalice that sat before me on a pedestal. When I leaned toward it, Don Enrique scolded me: "Please, don't touch!"

I froze, but could not draw myself away from it: "It's exquisite."

"Absolutely..."

"The stone. So white. And it looks so soft. What is it?"

"Alabaster."

Adorned with black hieroglyphics.

"Obviously Egyptian. Is it authentic?"

"Oh yes," and he sounded offended: "Of course. It's the chalice of immortality. The inscriptions come from the Book of the Dead."

"An ancient Grail. It must be worth a fortune."

"Why naturally, but I got a special price for it," and laughed: "Most of the things you see here were bought as souvenirs. Picked up on my travels. Many years ago now of course. Amazing what you could get in those days for next to nothing."

"Travels," I turned around slowly, grasping the full scope of what he was saying: "You must have seen the entire world."

"Entire ... Oh no ... Not even half of it. I've been to certain patches of it, nothing more. And nothing daring or dirty. I prefer the image of the world viewed from only the most exclusive hotels."

"But you've been to all the continents. These masks must be African. The shrunken head?"

"Indonesian, from Celebes," and then he pointed to a rotting wooden lance dangling from the far wall: "That over there is a seal-harpoon from Siberia ... and this..." and he picked up a curling tusk from the top of the coffee table: "This is a bore's tooth nose-plug, from Irian Java. But do you know I've never been to Australia."

Estrella laughed: "We are waiting for an invitation, Val."

Which sounded accusing and I grimaced. Don Enrique, however, ignored it. He reached into an inside pocket of his coat and drew out a packet of tobacco, then a pipe. Memories had been dug up and his tone became nostalgic: "There's so much left to see, and I've seen so much. Amazing things ... but you ..." and then he suddenly reached forward to me and grasped my wrist, laughing: "You're the first person I've met who's travelled into the past."

The word pierced me, threw me inward, then out. The image of Sarmiento, in his laboratory with the old Mexican Carlos, where he was drawing glowing hot metal from a kiln. But this was a mere glimpse, vanishing as quickly as it had come.

Estrella had wandered away to a bookshelf by the window. She butted in and steered the conversation toward another subject, that which had brought us together in the first place: "King Solomon's mines."

It made me shudder to recall that first day when she had handed me her ring. Her eyes gleamed, then she took a breath, as if sniffing perfumed air: "But it's actually a misnomer to attribute them to Solomon, you know?" She picked up a delicate old book and began thumbing through it. Her tone was mysterious and ambiguous, dry, but sensual. She sipped her wine and looked out the window: "He was merely the sponsor," she sipped again: "And even then, only partly so." Then she looked back at me and smiled, before inviting Don Enrique, who was next to her, to elaborate. It was his theory, she said.

Our patron pressed a wad of tobacco into the pipe-bowl before lifting the spout to point at the wall. To a small, cracked and irregular fragment of grey stone that was fixed there. He said it was Phoenician and told me to go closer and examine it. It was an imperfect bas-relief, most of what was left being undulating lines depicting a sea full of fish, on top of which the rear end of a ship could be clearly discerned. Less obvious were eight tiny oval shapes that turned out to be heads, clustered together within the confines of the vessel. I had to look carefully to make them out, but eventually it became clear enough. Oarsmen with their paddles out: "Like that," Don Enrique said, and began miming a rowing action: "There can hardly be any doubt about it." Then a match flared and he puffed a cloud of smoke which stung his own eyes. He sniffled and it made him sound sad: "It was the Phoenicians who did it ... who sailed, and rowed, rowed, and sailed ... to Ophir." The tobacco smelt deliciously sweet. "It's quite clearly stated ... not the slightest ambiguity ... It's all there ... in the Bible. They were Hiram's ships ... Hiram ... king of the Phoenicians ... who also built the Temple."

Estrella ran a finger across the convolutions of the stone sea. She was radiant: "Hiram was a magician," staring deep into my eyes. I thought she wanted me to kiss her, but then she turned abruptly away. She was drunk: "His secret learning came from India."

"Like all ancient wisdom," added Don Enrique.

"*He* was Solomon's teacher."

" '*Vanity of Vanities*', Hiram told Solomon," suggested Don Enrique. "But there's more ... a much more fantastic story behind all of that." He stood up, stretched his arms and went to the bookshelf to slide out a large, thick tome: "Quetzalcoatl."

He opened the book to a glossy plate and handed it to me. There was a drawing depicting the deity. A short, sturdy figure trapped in an elaborate bulky costume. The sense I had was of weight, although Quetzalcoatl was a sky-god. But the book really just acted as a catalyst, evoking other images of the god, memories from past *journeys* that I had to literally shake out of my mind.

Don Enrique looked askance at me, but said nothing. He went to the couch and puffed on his pipe while I came to my senses. Then: "Does this trouble you?"

I was sweating.

"No," I said. Then took up the book again to study other pictures, drawings and photographs of statues depicting the god as a plumed serpent, or dragon. Don Enrique ran his tongue across his teeth: "What would you say about the idea ... proposal," he sucked the pipe and puffed: "That Quetzalcoatl was a legendary figure, who existed ... was real at one time ... just as Homer and Troy were real?"

"Just as Christ was," appendixed Estrella ...

Then I was suddenly back with Sarmiento and the wretched Carlos again, staring into a simmering retort. Sarmiento's voice was grave: "The Quetzalcoatl who left the Mexica, sailing away on a raft of serpents, invested with a triplicity, the same ascribed to Hermes: with the power and fortune of a king; the knowledge and illumination of a priest; and the learning and universality of a philosopher. Hermes Trismegistus: the thrice-great Hermes."

And Carlos nodding ...

Don Enrique scratched his chin and gritted his teeth: "Well, if we accept that he did exist ... and that ... like Christ ... he must have been an exceptional man, imbued with tremendous sensibilities and occult knowledge ... a miracle worker ... or an alien visitor ... you know the crackpot ideas ... Well," and he coughed: "Well here's another one." Then he laughed and offered me another drink: "By comparing Mexican mythology with Hebrew legends it's possible to contrive ... conceive ... that Quetzalcoatl was a contemporary of Solomon."

Estrella nodded: "There are studies in the Academy's library to support it. One by a French writer called Bourbourg. Hermeneutic or semantics based. He links Quetzalcoatl to the Navigating Serpent in Solomon's

History of the Wonders of the Universe."

Don Enrique was now also nodding: "Now if what Bourbourg and the others say were to be the case, it could very well be that Quetzalcoatl actually visited Solomon."

Then Sarmiento's voice again, as if reciting – *The Quetzalcoatl who left the Mexica, sailing away on a raft of serpents* –

"Around the time of the building of the Temple," continued Don Enrique: "Furnishing Solomon with his own great knowledge?"

"As Blavatsky proposes in her Isis Unveiled," added Estrella.

"Providing the celebrated King of Israel with the impeccable wisdom of a great hermit traveller."

"Who had seen and learned so much."

"Three millennia ago."

"And who was later to visit the Mexicans, teaching them the art of pyramid building that he had learned in Egypt."

"Or Atlantis."

"Leaving such an impression that they made him a god."

Their enthusiasm made me snigger. The theory was nice but impossible. Don Enrique was gaping at me, awaiting my response. I coughed. So many obvious holes in the argument. I told them so: "I'm sorry, it cannot be ... swallowed ... I cannot swallow it ... A terrible chronological error has been made ... if Quetzalcoatl was known to Solomon, he would have to have been thousands of years old by the time he was said to have abandoned the Mexicans ... but that can hardly be regarded as feasible."

Enrique, however, slowly shook his head: "Only if we discard the possibility that this magician possessed the ineffable secret that all alchemists were searching for ... that he was, immortal."

Mexican mid-morning, shadeless and scorching, a parched and hollow lane. I was following a dusty frock coat. Soiled naked feet and desiccated ankles, poked out from under the too thick, but frayed and flapping cloth. The sand's accumulated heat turned each tread into a smarting hop, so he advanced like a dancing crane.

He, the friar. Fr Pablo.

I realised this when his chin had turned slightly and I had caught the sweat dripping profile of his sharp nose. Like a bird's beak then, poking from under an upturned nest. The straggly straw rim of his peasant's hat produced negligible shade, until he wrenched it off to wipe a cloth across a lake of accumulated sweat on his prawn pink tonsure. And then that same head dipped as he bowed under a low, white, horseshoe arch entrance, becoming momentarily adumbrated as he trotted through a dim, short corridor, opening out to a walled enclosure.

The chaos was heard before seen. There was a banging and clanking of metals. A persistent hammering. Dull or sharp blows. Wood, stone, steel. These were punctuated by human voices: orders and complaints, occasional roars and yelps, songs, or piercing whistles. Cacophony intensified by echo which eventually became visual. The twitching arms and backs of sweat-oiled men with buckets and boxes. Knees cracked and muscles tightened to lift baskets brimming with fat chunks of grey rock onto raw shoulders. Some of these were pink from sun and friction, others red, because the same sun and friction had opened a gash. They moved forward with a sad bovine moan, to drop rocks in a shallow trough, producing a hollow clatter and there, other thick arms, like pistons, raised and dropped enormous iron mallets pummelling the griseous lumps into shrapnel and powder. A mixture which other workers shovelled out and spread around a shallow circular pit where the minerals crunched and crackled under the gravity of huge granite mill stones, impaled by a thick beam of wood, which in turn ran between a central rotating post and a mule.

This animal, yoked and shivering, skin wrapped tight around bone, seemed ready to snap. Nevertheless, its exhausted struggle must have been preferable to the smarting slash of the whip received whenever it paused. This was administered by a gleaming brown slave, who in turn bore the brunt of blows from a gentleman's slashing cane. The engineer Fernando's slashing cane. He had developed a belly since the last time I had seen him. This wobbled under his shirt as he flicked his rod.

Meanwhile the rock in that crude mill rolled around and over itself, crushed and converted into a rubble that was shovelled out by another panting slave who spread it over the patio where it was sprinkled with a silvery liquid from a gloved hand. Then other mules were driven. This time, hooves were used to pulverise it into a mud, which was also shovelled and finally slapped into large tubs of water: agitated, sifted, before being collected in buckets again and taken into a cooler interior. I looked inside. Sarmiento was there. Working. It was his laboratory.

The red-faced friar collocated his straw peasant's hat again and flapped over to Fernando, who was swatting slaves like flies: "What's happening?"

The engineer's fat brown cheeks swelled his face into slits of happiness when he saw the friar. The only signs of discomfort were dark sweat patches under his arms, which he quickly lowered: "Oh, good morrow, Father," then remembering he had been asked a question: "Happening?" lips parting to expose still unadulterated teeth: "Something most exciting. Half of the idea is from Don Pedro. If it works it'll make us an enormous fortune, verily so."

Fr Pablo must have been reminded of the gunpowder factory idea on the volcano and he laughed and shook his head. His bird's nest sombrero rustled: "But what is it?"

"Oh, a new method Father. We're separating silver from rock, using mercury."

The friar scratched his chin with a too long and dry fingernail, and frowned: "And that will make you rich?"

The engineer spat on his finger and smoothed down any stray hairs on his moustache: "Oh yes, Father. Very rich. If you knew more about mining you would understand. Ask anyone who understands mining."

But Fr Pablo laughed again: "And what do you call it? The patio method?" and sniggered.

Fernando, however, missed the irony completely. He just scratched his forehead: "Very good, Father. The patio method. Excellent," and became immersed.

Fr Pablo dropped his hand on the engineer's shoulder, his thumb making a tickling contact against hairs: "Is Don Pedro here?"

Fernando pursed his lips and blew air through his teeth: "Señor Sarmiento? He would be with his retort. Making some new amalgam for us." Then, perhaps because the friar did not move or speak, creating an unbearable pause: "You have known Don Pedro for many years I've heard," which made Pablo blush. He nodded so that he could hide the implicating rush. Fernando drew a nostril dilating breath: "Is he a good man, Father?"

Fr Pablo's eyes opened and flickered, too electric to be a pacifier of souls: "Is fire good?" which trembled, suggesting an arson-probability. But Fernando did not have to think of the answer as it came almost immediately: "If one has control of it, it can be most good, yes."

Which was sufficient for them both.

Coming around again, I had to laugh. Don Enrique coughed and grimaced, unaware of my distance. He was obviously insulted by my mirth: "Yes, I know on the surface this Quetzalcoatl-King Solomon thing sounds as crazy as the idea of someone astral projecting themselves into another century," and then caught me with a challenging stare, which I did not understand until I realised that he thought I was laughing at him and his dissertation on the Mexican god. I shook my head and apologised, but did not tell him what I had just seen. He carried on: "But let's stretch our credibility, because ... if we can possibly accept all this, and ... that ... my proposal ... that although Quetzalcoatl gave Solomon a wealth of information about the fantastic lands he had been to ... despite that ... he never gave any clue to the routes he had travelled by."

But I was slipping away again ...

Fr Pablo advanced, inside, to Sarmiento's laboratory. The alchemist was with the wretched Carlos, who was asleep. His scabby, bald and brown head tilted back. If not for the rasping air down his throat he could have been taken for dead.

Sarmiento did not hear or see his cousin enter. He was immersed in chemical procedure, spooning sludge into a crucible.

When Fr Pablo saw and smelled the Mexican, he covered his mouth and nose with the coarse cloth sleeve of his cassock. Fingers reached blindly for Sarmiento's arm, clutched it and pulled: "Really cousin, I warned you. This grizzly fool can do you no good."

Sarmiento sniffed, finding that which was foul for Pablo to be quite sweet. His eyes were glazed and obviously drugged as he considered the prostrate figure being objected to: "Fool!? No. He's touched me," and lifted his hands as if supplicating a god before shaking the wavering motion of his intoxicated mind onto a firmer but still whimsical argument: "I wonder at his virtues, his faculties; his capacity and faithfulness of memory; his swift apprehension and penetration of judgement. Not only worldly wise, but spiritually gifted." Old Carlos snorted in his sleep, a gurgling phlegm filled snore, and Sarmiento, expecting to receive a sneer and cynical laugh from the friar, bellowed: "No Father, he's not a fool, rather a prophet, pray!"

"He's a pagan devil. And you, are bewitched!"

A momentum which exploded back at him: "Oh aye! He is most certainly pagan, and if that paganism implies that he's a devil then he is a devil too!" thumping a fist on a glass instrument covered table. The rattling of fragile receptacles seemed to hush his voice onto a lower, softer register: "Have you heard of Quetzalcoatl?" But the friar's upper lip curled into an expression of disgust. Sarmiento gripped his sleeve and shook him: "If you understood alchemy better you would not screw up your nose like that. This land and ours were created by the self-same god. Here the rocks are the same. There are mountains, rivers, lakes. The people are born with the same number of limbs as we are, the same number of eyes and ears, the same organs. Nature's secrets, God's laws, are the same here as in Galicia," his voice dropping again, his vision expanding: "I look for the same things here to satisfy my science as I had to do there."

Fr Pablo swallowed regret of his impotent intervention and slid a white cloth across his brow. His tired protest reflected his weakness: "Most dangerous task ... anywhere."

Sarmiento tightened his stomach: "Listen to me and you may learn," the last word was a relaxing release. He returned to his instruments and spooned more black mud into his crucible, the tone now matter-of-fact: "I've discovered that there were two Quetzalcoatls. One was a god, the other a priest, a prophet, and a magician. I would call him an alchemist."

Pablo's eyes had moistened. He wanted to cry: "When I talk to you it seems everyone is an alchemist."

"I once had a book," persisted Pedro Sarmiento: "A very old book, in Hebrew, that claimed that the Bible's King Solomon had had a great teacher, not Jewish, but a man who had travelled the breadth of the world. This teacher, said the book, was a magician, dressed in a variegated cloak of birds' feathers ..."

"Quetzalcoatl ..." One dimension, melted into the other. Estrella poured herself another glass of wine, punctuating Don Enrique's argument with her own: "The mystic informed Solomon about two islands, wherein were the gold and silver mines the Bible has situated in Ophir and Tharsis. But this same Quetzalcoatl withheld one crucial detail from his Hebrew host. He never told him exactly how they could be found. Just vague pointers, describing distance and direction."

"The detailed information was given to another."

"Someone wiser and more worthy of it."

"A great navigator, and magician, like Quetzalcoatl himself."

They waited for me to deliver the elucidation: "Hiram. The Phoenician King."

"Precisely," and Enrique clapped his hands: "*He* was given the demi-god's map, a chart describing the only correct route to the so-named Solomon's mines ... and it was he, not Solomon, who went to Ophir!"

"Which was in the Pacific," sighed Estrella.

"The most logical assumption," continued Enrique: "A voyage which lasted three years must have been to a very distant place. Much shorter if one went from the Americas though. And of course the civilisations of the Americas would probably also have known the route. Revealed to them by Quetzalcoatl when he lived amongst them."

I scratched my head and nodded: "Yes, you're right. It *is* a crazy theory: Quetzalcoatl meets King Solomon."

"So crazy, it's absolutely sublime," laughed Estrella.

Don Enrique puffed out a cloud of cigar smoke: "If we can discover the neurological reason behind your gift. Then perhaps we can create a mind affecting drug, administered orally for example, like an aspirin, that will allow anyone to travel into the past whenever they want, as if you were going to the cinema. Why this will be the most important discovery since ... since ..." and his eyes rolled: "Since the discovery of radium!"

It drew a sweet smile from Estrella, and she repeated his conclusion as an interrogative: "Since the discovery of radium?"

Don Enrique sniggered, like a child explaining some infantile joke to an uncomprehending adult: "It's a whim of mine. I've had another theory, for some time, that alchemists discovered radium long before Madame Curie."

"Does it matter?" I whined: "Why is so much importance placed on who was the first?"

Answered by Estrella: "Because it seems more important than asking who was the second." Then she shook her head, as if frustrated: "I would like to think one day I'd be a Marie Curie, but this discovery Val is all yours."

"Discovery? Nothing has been discovered yet!"

"Your *journeys*?"

"Journeys ... journeys to the past ... Rediscovery, not discovery."

Then Don Enrique was thrusting his pipe stem at me: "If we can prove physically what we suspect metaphysically ..."

"We need a scientist. Someone who understands hypnotism."

Which pulled Enrique's mouth into a wide grin: "How old does he have to be?"

Later on that night Estrella got up from the table, straightened her dress and wobbled precariously out. I looked over at Don Enrique. He sighed: "Oh, even pissed she's so beautiful."

"Yes," I affirmed.

"You are so lucky."

I sniggered: "It could be supposed that I am."

"If only she were beautiful forever."

"Oh, she will be. Forever."

But Don Enrique grew stern. He reached out for me. A trembling hand: "No, I mean physically beautiful ... beautifully youthful ... youthful, physically, forever ..." and squeezed my wrist tight.

It hurt, and frightened me: "Yes, if only..."

"If only ... and perhaps ... perhaps Val."

———————

(b) distill

———————

Don Enrique's assertion to become my new hypnotist was no idle claim: "Did I ever tell you that I used to frequent gatherings in which Freud himself put in more than the occasional appearance?" he vaunted.

A bragging which Estrella always warned me to take with a *pinch of salt*, but, whether they were true or not, his accounts were always related as if he were remarking on what he had had for breakfast. He certainly knew more about hypnotism than we or Tomás would ever do.

He explained the different theories. Besides Freud's psychoanalytical applications for hypnosis there were also suggestion and modified sleep theories; the idea of disassociation and conditioned response; hemispherical specificity and atavistic regression; or neuro-psychological theories as well as role plays: "Yet the real question of what actually happens remains an enigma," and then I remember him lifting my chin and squeezing my cheeks forcing my mouth open, and he looked at me as if examining the teeth of a horse: "Always enigmatic," staring hard as if he was looking inside my skull: "What kind of deliciously strange scars does your battered cerebrum bear?" then a paling look of horror spread across his face: "We'll have to be extremely cautious with each blind step we take."

When the sessions got under way they were never dull or monotonous. Don Enrique had a delicious sense of theatrics and he even had his stage, in a conference room in the basement.

He pushed open a pair of heavy, red-leather upholstered doors and flicked up a stiff and clunking switch. This initiated a fluttering of neon that had soon bathed the room with too much too-white light. There were chairs, a curtained stage and a screen: "Usually I watch films here," he confessed and smiled impishly: "It's a very private cinema."

Often the sessions were filmed, although I have only ever seen a projection of one of them, and that only partly. I found the experience of watching my unconscious, but open and flickering eyes unnerving. The physical reaction to the soul's transport through out-of-body fields of time was disconcerting and my lucid-dream observer's voice sounded nothing like my real one, too rough and nasally. Of course, if I could have put up with that it would have helped me enormously to write the accounts now. Estrella *did* watch them, and transcribed them, but that access is now lost.

During those sessions, Don Enrique was always the star of the show. He would appear in top hat and tails, a flashing monocle wedged over one eye, smoking a long cigarette through an ivory stem and carrying a bottle of champagne in an ice-bucket at his side: "The hypnotist must always be allowed the means to relax himself. The subject of course will have no problem, he is in the hands of an artist."

Our first task had been to return to Sarmiento in Mexico, for that tormented sojourn was about to come to its dramatic end. Enrique began by holding up a firm finger, less than a metre from my face, and asked me to look steadily at it. Then he droned an order that my eyelids should grow heavy, so heavy that they would have to close. Having achieved this, he relaxed my arms and legs and then, to get me out of my body he told me to imagine myself floating in a boat on a very wide lake. Afterwards, he took the boat and lake from under me to leave me suspended in space. Then he told me to imagine a certain American place on a certain sixteenth century date according to information we had discovered from research. He told me that I could see something in which there were people dressed in certain ways, and that they were using certain archaic terms when they spoke. And finally he instructed me to look for Pedro Sarmiento and I felt a tremendous rush and I was there ...

A square. The Tlaxcala town square; in a storm. The wind, a dust raising, banshee howl. Sarmiento, drunk and hatless, stumbled. Behind him was a crowd.

Sarmiento's red bandanna flapped. He rolled his head around and the vertebrae in his neck made a cracking noise like a crumbling peanut shell. He advanced towards a pole of bristling wood, toward the blurred shape of a figurine that had been nailed half-way up. The crowd gasped.

The strange shape was a coarsely hewn effigy, carved from a huge yam over which a brown rag had been draped, like a penitential robe, and tied by human hair. A placard had been strung around what represented a neck. Sarmiento read the text to the crowd: "The inquisition herewith condemns this heretic, Don Diego Rodriguez, to be burned."

Then he reached under his shirt and extracted a small tinderbox: "Diego Rodriguez, I banish you to hell!"

He flicked the lid and with one hand open and up as a windbreak, he twirled the flint with his thumb. Under the cloth dangling from the effigy the fire caught and the effigy burst into flame ...

I rocketed away, to a house. Inside, in the dark, was a capped, bearded head on a pillow, with a bandage wrapped around the face between the nose and a swollen mouth.

Then Sarmiento's voice murmured into this scene too; mumbling something: – *Diego Rodriguez, I banish you to hell!* – The head jerked up.

Obviously Diego Rodriquez's head. His eyes searched desperately for the owner of the voice that had come to him. He clutched his heart. A gasping gurgle in his throat …

I zoomed back to Sarmiento. The dust cleared. The sizzling yam was black. The crowd, murmuring behind him. Shocked and indignant. Someone screamed.

Suddenly hands were on Sarmiento. His body resisted as he was jerked forward, but his mind was gone, into another part, recalling a reason …

One day, weeks before, Sarmiento had been returning to the twins' house in Tlaxcala. People were peering through the windows and the open door. Sarmiento's heart raced. He pushed past the spectators.

Inside, furniture had been upturned, papers strewn; there was splintered wood and smashed glass on the floor.

The twins, Saturnino and Dionisio, were sobbing while a surgeon attended to breaches opened in their faces. Fr Pablo was unconscious and had been laid out on a table. He was pale, his forehead split. There was dry blood.

Sarmiento pulled some herbs from a pouch and waved them under his cousin's nose. Pablo came around with a splutter. Women entered with bowls. They went to the wounded men, spooning hot soup between their lips. The twins lapped at it, the friar sipped. Sarmiento wanted news: "What happened?"

The friar was too weak to answer.

The twins had to moan a response: "You told us to fear nothing," they said: "That you would look after us …"

Saturnino: "They said nothing …"

Dionisio: "Did not need to …"

"We knew what they were after. They just began hitting us …"

"Without saying anything. Just pummelled heads …"

"With the pommels of swords …"

"And they kicked me …"

"And me …"

"They kicked all of us ..."

"What could we do?"

Sarmiento groaned: "It was them?"

The twins looked away. Both of them hanging their heads. Their tone was disdainful: "What do you think?"

"It happened so fast ..."

"So unexpected ..."

"We were nearly unconscious before we could realise ..."

And started moaning, groaning and sobbing again.

Sarmiento recalled a spurt of violent images that made him rough and desperate. His memory shifted. Leaping past more weeks into another earlier memory, throwing me there too, though I arrived on my own, out of his mind ...

At first I was blind. Aware only of sound. A whining whimper evolving into a high pitched giggle, punctuated by a rough bellow and an occasional roar. Deep and constant breaths came over a rasping rhythm: a rough palm rubbing cloth. Soft, natural light, early morning or late afternoon, allowed me to discern fat, stubby fingers. A man's hand. It suddenly curled up into a pale, fat fist gathering the cloth to it. A shining, crimson silk. The fist gathered in more material; pulling it up. Uncovering naked flesh. A woman's round thighs. Voluptuous curves.

Then a face poked out. The round, full moon visage of one of the twins. The mole under his bottom lip telling me that he was Saturnino, on his knees, gazing upward past the dropping folds of crimson, toward the face of the woman. She pushed her head back. Long, wavy black locks slapped against the same crimson cloth covering his hands and her arse. She opened her mouth and tightened her diaphragm, letting loose a gurgling laugh.

The other twin was on a chair. He too was hard to discern, being buried in orange taffeta. The cloth itself bore a delicate design. Stylised vegetation twisted and curled as the fabric drooped over the huge man's knees, terminating in his lap where it had been hunched up around straddling thick legs. The owner of the legs and the taffeta had her hand under his shirt, rubbing his enormous aspic gut. Her head was inclined and her tongue out, licking his forehead while he himself gazed, intently mesmerised by the tight and enormous cleavage between her breasts. These hovered just in front of his nose, just out of reach of his own lapping tongue.

Then, as my perspective widened, another man entered the scene. Elderly and stiff, his neck wrapped in a starched ruff.

I had seen him before: he was *Don Diego Rodriguez* whose name had been cursed under Sarmiento's breath, the one who had been startled in his bed at the same instant that Sarmiento had ignited that yam effigy. He sat with one hand flat down on a large table. From there he leaned toward the woman on Dionisio's lap, to give her thigh a hefty slap. She shuddered. The assailant then stood up, a warm light giving him prominence, and his hand and arm looked massive as he reached to grab the twin's ear, dragging it towards his own thin and downward curling lips: "See how these women never complain. Let no man say he was badly treated in Puebla, at least not in Diego Rodriguez's house." And pushed the woman hard between her shoulder blades so that her breasts were shoved into Dionisio's face: "These women are yours for the night. You'll find a room upstairs." There was a twitch in the host's cheek as he nervously flicked long strands of hair away from his own ear: "One bed's been prepared. I've heard you have a proclivity for sharing your pleasure with your brother."

Which inspired a slow moan from Dionisio and his blushing head nodded.

Rodriguez pinched the twin's chubby cheek: "And take your bottle with you. Make certain you've enough sack for the whole night ahead." He twitched again: "I would not like to be disturbed. Your friend and I have so much to discuss," and lifted his head to look back across the long table that he had come from.

I followed his gaze, traversing a surface strewn with objects. Baked-clay dishes, pots and plates, all empty except for the greyish brown streaks of grease speckled with lumps of ignored matter. A clove of garlic in its shrivelled sack, a pair of ragged basil leaves and a dozen or more furry, olive stones, as well as black pepper corns or scraps of bread crusts and shreds of cinnamon coloured meat. Flies hovered and circled, dropping down to suck.

In the middle of the table was an iron candlestick holder. Its stem was a sharp spike bearing two curling branches, each supporting an already melted stump of wax. On either side of this, like round sentinels, wooden bowls were brimming with fruit and nuts.

These had been disturbed and were spilling out. Stones, pips and shards of shell were scattered around the table and floor. A jug stood upright behind the bowls. It carried red wine but was practically empty. There was a flask of water hardly touched, and what seemed like golden goblets inlaid with dull gem-stones or polished glass.

One of these had been knocked over, a stain running from it to the edge of the table where it was still dripping, mainly absorbed by the pages of a book that had been carelessly left open and upturned on the table top.

Resting upon this was a complicated, bronze celestial-globe, implying that at some stage the protagonists had been talking science. A discussion which had obviously been abandoned to favour more physical pursuits.

I was reminded once again of this by the moans, and then by a slurping sound which came from under the table. This belonged to a dog, a black mastiff with drooping ears, its front paws crossed to protect a long bone which its teeth gnawed. Gobs of white spittle dripped.

Pedro Sarmiento leaned nonchalantly against the back of his chair and chewed pieces of fruit. His distance from the three mastodon men and the ample figured women assuaged his own frame, but his sardonic grin was still obvious. He was remote from the orgy, both physically and mentally, buried in the room's penumbra. He rocked on the back legs of the chair and watched how the twins slowly composed themselves before shuffling away like nervous schoolboys leading their virgin lovers up the stairs.

The black dog under the table snorted. Sarmiento spat out a plum stone. It bounced when it hit the floor. The dog shivered: "You seem to know exactly what your guests want, Don Diego," Sarmiento mumbled.

The sun must have still been hot. The big man flicked his long hair away from his ear again. His neck was red around the ruff. He burped slightly and sat heavily down at the opposite end of the table. The feeling expressed in his voice was bitter: "I know what those two want," he murmured: "I knew the moment I perceived the lascivious sketches on their faces," and he reached into the bowl and took a plum: "But as for you? I've been told you have something, some secret, to tempt *me* with."

Sarmiento's grin widened: "Tempted you already are, señor. Is that not why you invited us here?"

Don Diego's lips sagged: "True enough. I'm indeed curious. But let you not be too pleased with yourself. I already know that it's in some way concerned with some El Dorado."

Which froze Sarmiento. His eyes flickered slightly, each blink revealing a hurried thought.

Rodriguez paused for a moment, as if enjoying Sarmiento's distress: "Yet, so many great men have already tried and failed in this enterprise. Even Pizarro himself, with Orellana."

This brought a snigger from Sarmiento and he thawed: "I'm not here to argue the existence of El Dorado, señor."

The sunbeams had angled away from the table and Rodriguez also became shadowy. He smirked back. This turned into a snarl, echoed by a rumble from the mastiff's belly. The man crossed his fingers together and lifted them under several rolls of compressed chin: "No, you're not. Your plan is to go elsewhere. You wish to discuss a nautical enterprise." Sarmiento nearly slipped off his chair: "You believe yourself capable of the most amazing things – the discovery of Ophir and Tharsis and King Solomon's mines."

Sarmiento exploded: "What?!" dissipating into a nervous mumble: "Who told you this? My cousin? Or was it these turkeycock hosts of mine?"

Don Diego scratched his bristly cheek: "What does it matter to you who told me? You've come - have you not? - to tell me yourself."

"But how is it that you've already discerned the particulars?"

"I also know you have a map."

Sarmiento scratched his shirt: "Do I?" which faltered. An image of his cousin's gawking face flashed through his mind.

Don Diego picked up a table-knife and pointed it accusingly at his nervous guest: "Why feign ignorance? Did you not come here to sell it?"

Sarmiento gulped: "No. I came to sell an idea," then became conspiratorial: "My intent is to traverse the enormous gulf that Magellan and Eclano have bridged ... and in doing so visit the silver Isles of Solomon's gold. That is true, pray." The pitch rising with his excitement: "I know where that treasure is, señor, all I need's a ship. So if you, or someone else, will finance such an enterprise – and I'm here because I was told you have the wealth for such patronage – if you'll promote the claim I'll guide you there … to Ophir!"

But Diego Rodriguez laughed raucously and stabbed the knife he was holding into the table top. The thump startled the dog underneath. It raised its head. The master pointed aggressively at his guest: "*You*, guide me," and his chin twitched: "Diego Rodriguez follows no mendicants. If you want my silver, you'll have to make yourself worthy of it. Show me your map, sirrah," and he thrust an open palm across the table. Sarmiento contemplated it carefully and silently. Its lines were deep and dark, but not long. This seemed to calm him. He reached into a bowl on the table and took a handful of nuts. Then he leaned back again in his chair: "I don't think I can take you, señor. You'd not survive such a journey. Your heart's feeble."

Don Diego spat into the hand and wiped it across the table-top: "I've heard of your professed wizardry, your charlatan sharking sorcery. I have friends in Tlaxcala. Your enemies," and he yanked the table knife back out again to jab a tomato, lifting the dripping fruit straight to his mouth. He bit it, oblivious to the red mess that spurted over his ruff and down his white shirt: "You make enemies very quickly, Pedro. As for your friends – what protection can you expect from them? These wanton nephews of the Bishop – what power do they possess? Or do you expect that cousin of yours to protect you? A rather pathetic aspiration I would say. To obtain power, a purse full o' gold is requisite. A treasure map's not good enough, you have to have it locked away. Build a castle or a palace around your wealth to protect it, and pay handsomely for loyalty. Until you have that, you have nothing," and he plastered the rest of the tomato on the table top, leaving a gelatinous mixture of juice and seeds: "As for your secret. It's no secret," and then leaning forward again: "I don't want your map. But I know someone who does, someone who'll pay handsomely for it."

The last phrase hammered into Sarmiento, like a ripping thrust from a beast's horn. But he bounced back, rose to his feet and grabbed the front of Rodriguez's shirt, just under his frilled neck: "You're doing deals with the Portuguese."

Don Diego wrenched the hand away, ripping the shirt, but he was oblivious to that; more interested in a slight shiver that ran across the surface of a large grey curtain covering the wall behind Sarmiento.

His voice was calm. Cold: "I'm talking economies, not politics."

Pedro Sarmiento rubbed his thumb across the iron ring on his index finger, polishing the symbol of Mars. He looked down to the table top; a pair of shivering wasps had gathered around the pools of tomato traces.

Don Diego did not notice: "And even but it were treason, should a shark like you accuse me I have no fear of it. Your faker's tongue will turn no man in my contrary." The wasps' feelers twitched while mandibles jerked horizontally, gathering lumps of red juice: "As for your situation," thumping his fist on the table. The dog jumped up and the grey curtain behind Sarmiento shivered again: "If I were you I'd be wondering how I was ever going to get out of these doors."

But the blow on the table had also angered the wasps. They darted towards the landowner's face. He tried to wave them away.

Sarmiento did not flinch. He had deduced the trap that had been prepared, and so, while Don Diego was occupied with the hornets and his own barking mastiff, he suddenly twisted around and flung his entire weight onto the heavy curtain at his back. There was an audible rip then a thud as the mass of cloth avalanched upon two figures of men that were behind it. Discernible, at first, as wriggling bulges under the curtain. The most prominent of these humps obviously belonged to a pair of heads. Sarmiento stood back and then swung a leg. The kick connected with one of the lumps and there was a dull clomp indicating that this had crashed against its neighbour. The curtain gave a final sag and sank to the floor.

Don Diego, confused through the canine din and vespine attack in front of him, was slow to realise what had happened. When he did, Sarmiento had already advanced and had his sword under the ruff, pricking his throat.

The mastiff growled. Sarmiento's head tilted slightly, catching the dog's stare. This cowered, slowly turned, and almost crawled away to a corner.

Sarmiento lifted a dagger to replace the sword and gently stroked Don Diego's Adam's apple: "Stay quiet," and bit his bottom lip before almost spitting: "There were two behind the curtain... and there are two more of them. Why don't you indicate where?"

But there was no need. The men he had been expecting suddenly burst into the room. They were dressed identically. Black cloaks, faded and worn, were draped over equally black doublets. The pitch of this cloth was only relieved by the brilliance of their baldrics, which had been worked in gold, and the shining steel of the rapiers and daggers that hung from them. They froze when they saw the knife at Don Diego's neck.

Sarmiento manoeuvred Rodriguez in front of him to act as a shield, then slowly edged forward. His sword poked and swayed in front of them like a wasp's feeler, while he whispered his plan into his hostage's ear: "A vile dilemma we are facing, señor. Most vile for you. A knife to your throat ... I cut it, you die ... and the world will be told that you were killed by these Portuguese assassins," and he noticed that one of them had a black scarf supporting his arm in a sling. The one he had already faced and wounded: "They, in turn, are about to have their lives most bravely terminated by your valiant Galician guest."

The wounded one blinked, slow and heavy, and gulped. But his face was one enormous snarl. This increased in intensity when Sarmiento caught his eye.

Sarmiento felt the man in his arms move and jabbed the knife, just hard enough to draw a drop of blood, before whispering again: "And even should one of them, or both, flee, then who'll they tell the true story to? Who'll believe a Portuguese assassin?"

The other one had a pale face, highlighting a pair of black piercing eyes. His nose was a huge puffin-bird's beak under which grew a wispy line of grey moustache.

Sarmiento's words continued to blow into Rodriguez's ear: "What good will all your gold and power do now? Have you confessed today, Don Diego?" his captive's hefty frame trembled: "Let's see your black dogs cower, just as your mastiff did, and let's have them back into their kennels," insisted the alchemist: "You've built a fine palace here, why don't we go and inspect the dungeon? Surely you didn't forget to build some miserable cell where you can torture your lazy Indians in ... ummm?" Rodriguez rolled his eyes, which seemed to confirm it: "And I'm sure these Portuguese know where it is too, don't they?"

The prisoner repeated the gesture, gasping when Sarmiento released the dagger's pressure. As he did, Rodriguez's fat hand darted up, grabbing the alchemist's wrist to shake it.

A sharp pain ran down Sarmiento's arm, and he gasped as he watched the dagger fly from his fist. His free hand shot like a claw, searching desperately for the throat, but made himself content to catch hold of the neck of the big man's shirt. He yanked this, pulling the huge man, who pulled him back, causing a spinning whirling-dervish dance, until Sarmiento let go and pushed at the same instant, sending Rodriguez flying across his table. Clay dishes crashed to the floor. Some of these hit the mastiff, which yelped.

Sarmiento turned. The man with the arm in the sling was almost on him, wheeling his own slashing blade with his left arm. The alchemist lifted his own, just in time to shield the blow, which was clumsier than hard. Pushing under the assailant's blade he was quite easily able to flick it away and surprise threw the attacker off balance. As he slipped down Sarmiento slashed his sling, scratching another gash in his bad arm. The victim dropped to his knees, his free hand darting to the fresh wound.

Then it was the puffin-beak one's turn to lunge.

Sarmiento span around to dodge the new blade. Too fast, he became unbalanced and toppled. The new assailant, realising that his prey was exposed, reeled back and lifted his sword high before bringing it down with such a force that it would have split the alchemist's head like a watermelon.

Luckily there was a black, marble pedestal, supporting an icon of the mother of Christ, which fell just within the arc of the blade's trajectory. The stone cracked on contact and a pulverised indentation was chopped out. There was powder and flying wedges of shrapnel, even a flash of sparks as the metal of the blade submitted and snapped. The upper part twisted and turned over itself, hurtling back towards the swordsman's head, slashing the bridge of his puffin-beak nose.

Sarmiento rolled. The pedestal wobbled under the impact, then came crashing down, the virgin bouncing on its aureate edges over the floor.

The alchemist twisted himself in the direction of his assailant and kicked his legs back, catching his attacker's ankles and bringing him down with a closing scissors like twist.

Collapsing face forward, the puffin-beak nose smashed into the bottom stair, cracked, and the grimacing face reeled back and up, only to receive another blow from a kicking foot. A fat foot. Dionisio's foot.

The twin, after his climax, had descended in search of a bedpan. Saturnino who had heard his brother's squeals also stood aghast on the staircase, contemplating the carnage and Sarmiento's grin. Their accidental return had decided the battle in his favour ...

*　*　*

The dungeon had been dug in such a way that there was a concavity in the middle of its floor. Water gravitated there into a stagnant, foul pool. This reflected candlelight that splashed against the human figures in shimmering golden waves.

Saturnino bore the light while Sarmiento stood armed on guard, and a panting Dionisio bolted the screws in Don Diego's irons. As he did, the prisoner coughed into his ruff which was torn and tilted.

The face next to him was groggy and red with his own dry blood. His puffin-beak nose broken and bent. The one with the sling was conscious, but frowning and in obvious pain. Although his second-time wounded arm had been bandaged, it did not seem to have stopped the bleeding. There were also the two others, they who had been behind the curtain, each with a huge black bruise on his forehead.

Sarmiento was agitated. His knife quivered in his fist as he stepped forward. Don Diego spat on his leg and Sarmiento slapped him, hard enough to inspire a trickle of blood between his lips. Then the alchemist reached down and roughly yanked a handful of that powerful man's long hair, thrusting his dagger under it, to carve away a thick lock. A panting, frantic barber. His eyes; hot orbs in a ruddy, moist face, dripping like the walls as he moved on to the Portuguese.

He stripped the first one, the one with the nose, pulling his trousers down and pushing his knife under the wrinkled sack of testicles. The prisoner's breathing turned into a frantic choking frenzy, his body struggling against the binding chains. The irons cut into his neck, his wrists and ankles, and when Sarmiento finally lifted the blade and sliced his manhood away, the scream was bestial. The blood gushed. The twins vomited while the other Portuguese and Don Diego dry retched.

Then Sarmiento put the blade under the next man's ear, lifting the lobe to blow whispering words against his timpani: "You think your sins will be ignored," and then hissed, loud enough for all of them to grasp it: "You have done my family and me grievous, grievous harm, señores!?" When he pulled the knife it carved through the gristle and he encouraged the dissection with a firm tug. After the last sinew had ripped away the blade arched through the air, the parabola terminating under Don Diego's nose.

One of the twins begged: "Please, señor ..." echoing against water and brick.

But Sarmiento merely leaned closer to the once proud slave-trader, his hot breath blowing against the now shivering weak face: "You invited a host of vermin into your house, and then thought it proper to arrange an insult with this Galician. You thought you'd have a bit of cruel sport to go with your pudding. You thought I'd be a sweet white wine, but, now you must swallow the vinegar," and without the slightest vacillation sliced through the landowner's top lip. The twins turned their backs and crossed themselves.

Sarmiento thumbed the locks of hair that he had gathered from Don Diego, then went along the line carving hair from each of his prisoners. When he had finished, he knotted each lock around itself and put them all into a leather pouch. This he held up in front his writhing, sobbing victims, swinging it and paying special attention to the Portuguese who could not bear to look at his accusing, mad gaze: "Within this tiny sack lies a magical key to the control and power over your pathetic bodies. I have your souls, señores. Now, I am your maker, and I will make *you suffer,* agonise until you come to me on your knees, praying for me to cut your throats and put a final end to your miseries. You've done so much to anguish *me.* You've killed my loved ones, and now, I want and will have my most terrible revenge. Your livers will burn, mark me, and a worm will slowly eat your innards. Each one will have a different torture. My turn to use imagination. Your turn to endure it, sirrah."

Later, outside, he and the disconsolate twins were saddling their horses. A breeze had picked up. The twins stood in the doorway, a blanket wrapped loosely around one, a sheet around the other. Their lips were sagging, their black hair blown across their faces. Sarmiento slapped Saturnino's back: "Tell your whores to go to the dungeon and treat the men's wounds. I would not want them to bleed to death. My sport is just beginning, sirrah."

When the twin had done this they mounted. Sarmiento slapped

Dionisio's back: "Ride on now, both of you. I'll catch up later or see you at home."

But the twins just stared apprehensively at each other: "As soon as we leave, the whores'll set them free again," observed Dionisio.

Sarmiento shook his head: "Perhaps. But I don't think our bloodied prisoners will be in a mood to chase us. In any case I've let their horses loose. They'll have to walk back to Tlaxcala or get a coach."

*　*　*

A wind blew a lace curtain. Another moonlit bed room. A four-poster bed with white sheets turned down so that soft streams of cotton flowed to the floor. Between these was Doña Rosa, alone and ghostly pale in the moonlight. She was lying on her back in a white cotton nightdress, her head right back on a huge pillow. The collar was untied, freeing her bloodless neck, curling up to a bloodless face. She looked lifeless but her breast rose and a slight snore rasped through her throat. I had caught her in profile, and when I hovered to the other side I saw her eye, swollen and grey.

She shuddered and writhed in the bed, as if anticipating the sudden thump which came and which was loud enough to wake her. Her neck flicked, her back shooting forward, erecting her. She gasped. There were thick soled boots on the wooden floor. Men's boots. She wanted to scream, but shock had clamped her throat shut. Then the owner of the boots was on the bed, with his arms around her. One arm squeezing her, the other flat across her mouth to stifle any possible cry. Her eyes were wild orbs of fear. She blinked. Discerned the silhouette of her captor. Squinted. Focused. It was Sarmiento.

He felt her body melt in his arms and removed his hand from her mouth while relaxing the arm that had encircled her. She leant forward as he did. Her breath blew across his face and he dropped toward her, to kiss her and to run a hand through her long hair before softly stroking her round and pregnant belly. Then a pause, their breathing deep and audible as he leaned slowly away from her. At a distance he was able to discern the blue-grey and bloated eye: "This violence, pray?"

She took a deep breath through her nose, but her tone was matter-of-fact: "My husband. His cholera. When he takes his bottle, which gives him courage enough to whip his woman. Please, Pedro. Have done with him," and she stroked his cheek, only then to realise how damp he was. She turned his face so that the moonlight could illuminate it: "Blood ... My God! ... You too have been in a brawl."

He sighed: "It's been a violent night. Mars in the fourth house explains this discord at home, and the presence of that same red planet in Scorpio facilitates and exaggerates all brutality," then smiled as if he had been making a joke: "We should've been more careful."

Her chest heaved: "Have you come to kill my husband?"

Sarmiento shook his head: "Not yet. Let the potion do its work, his time has almost come," and as he said this he pulled the leather cylinder containing the map out from under his shirt, and handed it to her: "Hide it," he said: "In your safest place. Until I come back for it."

And made a move to go, but she reached out and clutched him: "Don't leave me now ... please ... I've just suffered the most terrible nightmare." He stopped and put his hand to her head to softly stroke her hair. Her voice went on, tremulously: "I dreamt I gave birth. Horrible, painful. I was surrounded by the nuns from Burgos staring at me from over a large white sheet, the whiteness my only comfort. The nuns on the other hand were all grinning and laughing at my screams; poking fun at my suffering, spiteful taunts ... until my baby was born ... They took one look at him, screamed and ran.

"I pulled the new born to my breast. He was ugly and deformed. There were horns on his head. He had teeth and a withered leg. A budding but already wiggling trace of a tail at the base of his spine. And yet, as I cleaned the blood and afterbirth off his face, and he whimpered and reached for my breast I thought him to be the most adorable baby I had ever seen. And yet surely ... he must have been the antichrist ... surely ... surely I am damned."

Sarmiento just sniggered: "Damned? I doubt it. It was just a dream. If anything I'd say you've been blessed."

* * *

More bruised and battered heads. This time the twins. I was back in Tlaxcala, Sarmiento was mopping and rinsing their heads, still trying to get confirmation of the crime from the reluctant victims: "Diego Rodriguez's men?"

Saturnino and Dionisio kept their heads down: "We saw nothing."

Sarmiento with his head bowed, in his hands, rubbing his forehead: "How can you be so frightened? Too frightened to accuse the men that could have killed you!?"

But then Dionisio grabbed hold of Sarmiento's doublet and almost squealed through his tears: "We were lucky were we not, that they did not treat us with the punitive chastisement that you inflicted on them. We are lucky, are we not, that we still have our balls."

The scene exploded, and I was swept forward. When forms returned again, Sarmiento was staggering down a street, stumbling over cobblestones. Before him, the same pole he had burned the effigy on. The black stain remained, accusing. He shivered, dizzy, in front of it.

Rough hands took him. A hand on the back of his neck, pushing him down until he was kneeling before a pole. Hands yanked his forearms, pulled them up, squeezing them, wrapping a coarse, snaking fibre around them and pulling it tight. Splinters from the post speared the fronts of his wrists while the rope dug into the backs of them. There was a rip of cotton and then cold air on his sweating torso that made him shiver. Knuckles cracked beside an ear. His flesh twitched with the contemplation of the imminent blast. A murmur of laughs and guffaws. A crowd: "Blasphemer!" they accused.

Some spat at him, others whispered a chuckling approval: "Bloody brave little joke. Revenge on that fat and cozening bastard Don Diego and an attack on the inquisition at the same time. All in public. Brave man. Got to take your cap off to someone with so much guts, I say, prithee."

"But to use magic like that. Getting his hair and burning it. Old Don Diego Rodriguez died because of it they say. It burnt his heart, searing his soul. The devil's work. They should burn the bastard not whip 'im."

Sarmiento listened, smiled, then groaned. The sting of the first lash was mainly on the back, but curling around and slapping his chest and belly. The second blow must have been a hundred times worse. The skin gave way. The third ripped against the open wounds, gorging, as did the rest, opening new gashes, deepening those that already existed. Jets of blood splashed against the flagellator, some chaotic trajectories even staining the onlookers.

After the eighth blow Sarmiento seemed to be grown used to the surprise and he no longer shouted when he was struck. For a while he enjoyed a kind of consciousness devoid of thought. But eventually realisation returned and there was shuddering pain again.

He bled profusely and remembered the wretched Carlos' words: "Brave, señor? Oh, the Mexica were brave all right: *May your heart not falter in fear*, they told us: *May you savour the fragrance, the sweetness of death by the obsidian knife,* they said: *Desire, long for, the flowery death by the obsidian knife. Savour the sweetness of darkness, the din of battle, the roar of the crowd* ..."

The roar of the crowd made him gasp for air: "You are killing me ..." he spluttered, tightening his throat as he did, to hold back the breath of a scream.

The whip cut again, the crowd roared again, savouring the violent vengeful moment. Sarmiento clenched his teeth.

By the time he was untied his feet were drenched in crimson. Salt was hurled on his wounds. It made him croak like a raven, and he passed out.

IX. Peru (Adjustment)

(a) ascend

According to Sarmiento de Gamboa's biographers, he left Tlaxcala in 1557. The next time he was heard of he was in the City of the Kings, which is now called Lima, in Peru. But the accounts of him there derived from a document dated 1564, creating a limbo of nearly seven years in which nothing at all is known.

So it was decided that my own observations should fill this substantial gap.

But the roads between Tlaxcala and Lima were many and the distance was enormous. Knowing the object's geographical position as well as the day he was there was crucial in Don Enrique's method, so the lack of such concrete information meant my mesmerist had to experiment and several tedious, frustrating days were endured from which I emerged exhausted.

Estrella began to worry about me. She confronted Don Enrique quite frankly about it, asking if he really knew what he was doing to me. My hypnotist stroked his upper lip: "Well I could try and speculate, but they are only theories remember," our gaping pause signalled approval to continue, even if he was only guessing. He closed his eyes to grasp his ideas: "The first thing I do is deactivate your normal sensors. I do this in order to put another part of your brain into play. You see it is a problem of hemispherical dominance. The brain consists of two hemispheres, you know?" we nodded: "Well, what I'm doing is shutting down the dominant right side in order to give the dormant left a chance to function better."

The idea sounded as solid to me as any theory I had heard, but I do not think it satisfied Estrella and she remained worried. Her concern was obvious and Don Enrique in turn became anxious. Later, he took me aside to tell me that he wanted to invite someone else up to the house: "Secretly," he said and clutched my wrist tightly, as if to cement the conspiratorial bond: "I want to surprise Estrella."

The new guest's arrival was to take place on December 13th. It was a very cold morning, I remember, and we had our first snowfall. I was as excited as I've been lead to believe a child is at Christmas. I forgot about the imminent arrival of our secret visitor and dragged Estrella out for a walk in the snow. She was not too happy about that. It was freezing up on the mountain, but when we came back down again she was even less happy.

When she saw him she swore and turned down a different path, dragging me with her. A completely unexpected reaction: "It's Vicente Gomez," she stammered. Her vaporous breath blew into my affirmation and what must have looked like the most ridiculous smile. Her frosted pink face reddened: "He's an arsehole."

I coughed, cleared my throat. The ice-air burnt it: "He is ... has been said to be ... an authority on the conquest ... His second book has just been published."

"Fascist pamphlets."

I gulped, sniffled, became conscious of a sharp nip at my ears. I rubbed them: "Have they been ... Have you read them?"

"No," she was slapping her arms across her chest. As much out of indignation as against the cold: "But, who gets published here if they don't write fascist pamphlets?"

I felt a hot flush through my own cheeks as I prepared myself for the cold confession: "He's going to be accommodated here ... s-staying with us."

"What!?" the hot response seemed to make ice crackle.

"It was thought another expert would be a necessity. It was believed it would be ... would please you. He's considered your friend, isn't he?"

She beat her breasts again: "He was Inma's friend ... and Dr de Coca's," and then almost screeching: "He's an arsehole like de Coca, and a psychopath," and then she squeezed me between her soft mittens: "You know that, you've met him. How could you have invited him here?"

Vicente Gomez was the same Vicente who had been at the first session with Tomás. I had considered him strange, but I had no idea that Estrella hated him. Don Enrique wanted to use his wide knowledge on the conquest of Mexico and Peru to verify what I had seen.

Estrella later took Don Enrique aside: "He's probably spying on us for de Coca."

Don Enrique shook his head: "This puts me in a most unenviable situation. I've invited him to stay for a week. I can't just order him away again." And he wouldn't, so Vicente stayed.

Whether Estrella was right or not; whatever Vicente's own motivations really were, it did not take him long to begin sowing seeds of doubt in San Lorenzo.

When I eventually reached Vicente and took his hand, it was as cold as the ice under our boots. Hardly a handshake. His nicotine stained fingers merely wafted; his freezing dry palm brushing against mine without squeezing: "Valen/tín ... the out/of body man."

And sniggered, cruelly. Sucking a cigarette like a baby its dummy. His pungent black tobacco, sour in my nose.

He had, as they say, a *demonic air*. Perhaps that's what Estrella understood as his *fascist* side. The purity of the snow made his darkness striking. It was as if he belonged to the ice, standing frozen; a charred tree-trunk erect in his black-wool overcoat, its collar pulled tight against his throat. His glasses-goggled eyes constantly drooped. His upper lip always twisted up to one side and the thick mop of curly black hair looked pitch against his pallid face.

Nevertheless, that afternoon he was invited to witness one of my trance induced excisions, and he sat, hunched on a creaking chair only metres away from me, with arms folded. I could also make Estrella out through the smoke standing next to the camera. She also had her arms crossed.

Don Enrique had decided to take a risk and continue with our attempts to locate Sarmiento in the unhistorical void between 1557 and '64. The most probable result would have been failure. In a sense I supposed Don Enrique was trying to cover his ground. If it did not work it was because we had tried to enter a difficult space, but if it was successful the results would be even more impressive.

He used his usual method, but this time he made things more personal.

I was told to imagine *myself* in the year 1562, and that I was with *my* friend.

As Don Enrique's soft sweet voice sent me away, I caught a glimpse of Vicente's amphibian eyes fixed in a brooding, sceptical stare, and then ...

* * *

A cloudless sky. Sarmiento on horseback, cantering up a narrow but paved trail.

Following, at a distance, was Fr Pablo, rocking. The friar's head was tilted back and he had his cassock's hood off. His mouth drooped open like a fly-catcher, snapping shut when he tugged on the reins of his horse. The dappled mare shook its white mane, snorted, and stopped while the friar reached into a satchel dangling from its flank and pulled out a leather folder. He untied it and opened it on his lap, then reached back into the satchel and jerked out a bottle of black liquid and a writing cane. It was easy to consider virgin landscapes to be fair and perfect. He dipped the quill into the ink. The mare dropped its head to graze. Flanking plantations: wheat, and rustling maize. Fr Pablo composed a description of the huge mountains before them. His sentences ran clumsily along, exploding at times into ugly pockets of exaggerated verbiage, but he seemed happy while he was writing.

Sarmiento was already beginning to rise. Because he had sold his alchemist's laboratory in Tlaxcala to finance his escape he would have to find another way of being God. He still dreamed of creating worlds, and of being laid down for an eternity under a patch of long green grass that he himself had sown. But this was not a vulgar colonist's dream, it was differentiated by the detail that his grass would sit under a sky that he had likewise created. He had to grip hard on the reins as his mount suddenly began to clamber through a rockier area, a rough-soft environment where sharp slashes of glistening naked ore rose into wig like tufts of grassy gentleness. He looked back over his shoulder. Fr Pablo was still on the grass, holding a sheet of paper up in the breeze to dry its ink.

Sarmiento did not worry that he was leaving his cousin so far behind. They had made their pact: each to their own pace. They would meet in the next town.

He looked drowsy, perhaps even asleep, but he wasn't. His mind was fixed on the pain in his thighs, his groin, and his balls. His penance.

He needed to forget Mexico. Expunge Doña Rosa from his mind. But he also needed to forget Galicia and efface his entire life. Even the precious map had been put away, shoved into a sack, where it was now well buried at the bottom.

A condor screeched as the trail wound steeply up to a plateau. There, a treeless savannah emerged. Windswept and cool. He stopped at the edge when his black stallion kicked a stone and sent it plummeting over the sheer cliff. He dismounted and looked down into the depth; and shivered because he had the unnerving sensation that it was beckoning him over.

On the other side of the depression, the sharp snow-capped peaks were immovable, irrefutable – *I am perched on the pimple of a perfect globe* – he told himself. At a distance equidistant to the distance of all other pimples from the centre – *and this world also has a soul, like each man on it* – he thought – *and that soul is the centre* –

He turned away to pull out a wine sack and guzzled, not wine or *pulque*, but *sora*, an Inca brew made from maize. He sat, watched, drank, and ate cheese. Until the wind blew another ghost at him.

He was by no means perplexed by the vision, for he opened his eyes even wider, to stare out and therefore into it, as if contemplating one of his own bubbling experiments. At one time he even reached out towards the wraith thinking that he could perhaps touch it.

Touch her: it was a beautiful woman he saw. She had pitch black hair and Asiatic eyes that squinted into gay slits as she smiled back at him and reached out. An aureate crown bore a large golden disk glowing above her head. An Inca queen, he told himself, and she laughed. Only briefly. Her smile disappeared as quickly as she herself had materialised, and she was pulled back. Her soft leather dress – *skin of bats* – was undone and it dropped. She shivered. Wet cheeks. Wet eyes, but challenging.

She crouched and reached down to the earth. Her feet were buried in a mound of gleaming, green-brown shit. She pushed her hands in. Squelching in the viscid matter. She dug it up and lifted dripping portions, which she proffered towards a line of drooling spectators. Her Spanish conquerors, their hands rubbing sex through the fabric of their pants. She squelched the shit through her fingers then smeared her body with it. That was her challenge to the rapists around her – *Take me if you will. If you can bear such filth, you pig!* – Until suddenly she was lifted. A rope twisting around her; tying her to a high wooden stake that had just as suddenly materialised. The tight ropes squeezed her and made her squeal. She shook her head and whispered a bitter order – *Hurry up* – Then another squeal, followed by a dull thud and a slight squelch as an arrow pierced a gap between her ribs. She sighed instead of screamed. Then another arrow thudded into her thigh. Another, and then a hail of them.

Sarmiento cowered as if from a real, material threat; his bending knees folding his trembling legs into his firmer chest, an arm up to shield his face from the vision – *Why do you torment me with so much grief?!* – he yelled, into nothingness, he realised, and, with the hallucination gone, he thrust his chin defiantly out, ready to spit at any concrete manifestations of demons ...

When his cousin eventually reached him, he had composed himself and was sitting up. Fr Pablo dismounted and sat down with him. Together, they looked across the valley and contemplated the stillness of vastness. The snaking river that had cut the gorge was unbelievably silent and the white foam of the noiseless waterfalls seemed like unchanging artists' slashes of white paint. In one particularly quiet corner, tucked amongst the neat lines of terraces, sprouted a town, brown-grey in the mountain's shadow. Then starting from this, other settlements were discerned; hamlets, villages. The peace of the valley was inspiring, and the inspiring valley inspired Sarmiento to give the friar a tight affectionate hug: "How goes your book, cousin?"

The friar shuddered. A subconscious memory of some deeply repressed vice, struggled with the comfort of physical contact, ambiguously rationalised by the Christian idea of love. Horror and joy took his breath away and he felt strangely and suspiciously hot as Sarmiento rubbed his shoulders. The alchemist's mouth was close to his neck and a warm breath trickled down the back of his cassock, along his naked skin. He had to squirm to encourage a loosening of the grip.

He had been asked a question – *how goes your book?* – and there was a flicking pause before he properly appreciated the concern in the query. A hot heartfelt rush of inspiration surged, and he began to hurl histrionics:

"This place," it was almost sung: "No truer marvel of Holy invention could be found. It needs to be described so that those who will never have the chance to see it may experience a part of it. If only an unfortunate part, most debased by my inadequate knowledge of the science of description. Yet at least it'll be something."

The self-adoration disguised in the friar's humility seemed to depress Sarmiento. His own tone was leaden: "Aye, and something good, cousin. You write well, very well. Though at times I wish you were more economic with your vocabulary. Your book's science, not poetry."

Fr Pablo swallowed so much of the thin Andean air that he became even more drunkenly magnificent: "All things created by God's Will are poetry."

Which brought a smile to Sarmiento's gloomy face: "Like Rodolfo, poor soul. Verily, his science was poetic."

The friar, maintaining his pompous affectedness: "And his soul will remain a marvellous line of eternal verse in God's composition." Sarmiento sighed and his cousin, suddenly imagining quite wrongly that they had become close again, squeezed Sarmiento's hand: "And you. Does this land not ease your own spirit?"

The metaphysical idea encouraged the alchemist's sincerity: "Aye, perhaps. But I've much further to go before I'll find myself."

The friar could have cried: "Then don't look for yourself. Look for God."

But Sarmiento thumped his chest: "I do," and then prodded his heart with a finger: "He's in here."

They mounted. Tugged reins. The horses snorted and they went down.

* * *

Our hypnotist host organised what he called a *Moorish picnic*. A couscous in the hothouse amidst tropical plants: "Oh, I do loathe winters," he said.

He was wearing a fez and a *djellaba* and had installed a hookah with various tubes. We lay down by a little pond in which lotus flowers bloomed and sucked the gurgling, water-filtered smoke. Estrella was obviously enthused by the circumstances and had grown out of her grim mood: "'Who are you?' said the caterpillar," she recited, imitating a deep masculine voice: "'I – I hardly know, Sir, just at present,'" she continued in an infant Alice's high-pitch: "'I know who I was when I got up this morning, but I think I must have changed several times since then.'"

Don Enrique was able to pursue the joke: "'Explain yourself, girl!'"

"'I can't explain myself... because I'm not myself you see...'"

"'I don't see... Repeat: *You are old Father William!*'"

"'*You are old Father William,' the young man said...*"

Which was as far as she got, interrupted by one of Enrique's servants who brought out a pile of books to lay them on the hot-house lawn in front of us. They were historical documents concerned with the conquests of Mexico and Peru. Enrique invited us to peruse them while we scooped up semolina and lamb.

Inspired by the arrival of these documents, Vicente lit a cigarette and opened a black briefcase he had with him in order to pull out his own pile of papers. Estrella's smile immediately faded as she realised that the manuscripts that she herself had typed up from my accounts, and which had been passed on to Don Enrique to scrutinise, were now coming out of Vicente's bag. She grabbed our host's arm. Turned him aside, whispering, but violently, almost spitting at him: "How could you be so...? After what I told you?"

But our patron merely flicked a thumb across Estrella's mouth to brush tiny semolina balls from her damp lips. He smiled and dismissed her interrogation with a simple: "We are here to learn; we can learn from him."

Estrella pushed her plate away and folded her arms. I reached out for her but she shrugged me off. Don Enrique gave me an eyebrow jumping *leave her alone, she'll be all right* look. So I did. I scraped my fork to mix oil and onion with the grain on my plate. Took a mouthful. Then I picked up one of the books in front of us. It was a leather bound copy of José de Acosta's *A Natural and Moral History of the Indies*. As I did I glanced over Vicente's shoulder. He was flicking through our manuscripts on Mexico: "Ah, the Mexica," he said (pronounced Mesheeka) and burped quietly, the cigarette on his lip shivered: "Brutal people / they were. Did you know that/ the Matlatzinca/used to make their sacrifices by/slowly crushing the victims/in a net? Babies were made/to cry/so that the rain god/would let it pour."

"Sympathetic magic," remarked Enrique, laying his fork across his empty plate with one hand and twirling the stem of a red orchid in the other: "Not unlike our own catholic church, the church," and the flower came to a drooping standstill: "That our beloved Franco so loyally supports." Which was punctuated by a sparkling, accusative stare. Then his voice became pompous: "Like the Christian who takes the host, the ancient Mexica were also fully acquainted with the doctrines of transubstantiation, and had their own ceremonies for taking consecrated bread, believing that they were partaking of the very body of their god."

Vicente guffawed, semolina and smoke flew: "But/I'm afraid/that's not /the same/as human sacrifice."

"No," and Enrique even seemed to snarl with the negation, although this quickly curled into a knowing smile: "Yet our inquisition also burnt its enemies," pointing the flower like a stick: "That was not sacrifice, but it probably had the same effect on the society," the orchid twirled again: "When there is an institutionalised death penalty decreed, it creates a social catharsis; whether you're sacrificing a criminal or a virgin, the function is to purge the anguish of the masses."

Vicente tweaked the tip of his nose: "So/in this way/you/justify barbarism?"

"Oh no," replied Don Enrique: "I merely object to the western hypocrisy which condemns the so called *barbarians* for practices we ourselves uphold. Don't you abhor the death penalty?"

"It's/not/the same," and he yanked an anemone unconsciously from the lawn: "A terrorist/is scum/and should die. The ancient Mexica were cruel/because/they killed without compunction/just as a terrorist does."

"Just as the State does."

Vicente crushed his flower: "It's not/the same."

Enrique gently put his orchid down and reached forward to take the book I still had open in my lap. It took him a while to find what he was looking for. When he did he passed the book to Vicente: "Read this passage," then lifted the orchid, pushing his nose against the dusty stamen: "It gives a fair description of how, when the Mexica took a captive caught in battle - an enemy, a *terrorist* - that self-same terrorist would not be tortured, but, rather, gratified, by having the name of the god he was to be sacrificed to attributed to him. He would be proclaimed to represent that divinity, and treated in the same manner that they would have treated him if he really had been that god. The condemned person therefore spent a year eating, drinking and fornicating, and at the end of that year they killed him, cut him open, and ate him. Do we treat our condemned so humanely before we put him in the garrotte and snap his neck?"

"If we were to/reward assassins/there would be chaos," another flower was wrenched out of the turf. He turned to me, obviously tired of Don Enrique. He stubbed out his cigarette, then inserted and lit a new one. After the first draw: "And you. You are/ observing your hero/your Sarmiento de Gamboa/in Peru?" I nodded. He sucked smoky air through his teeth, then: "But do you know why/he left Mexico?"

I had to swallow grain first: "There were problems with the inquisition," I affirmed: "A fit of madness. The effigy that had been made of Don Diego Rodriguez was burnt."

Which evoked a slow nod from Vicente: "And have you/any idea/ why/his cousin/the friar/went with him?"

I shrugged my shoulders: "... because he was his cousin?"

Vicente smirked: "Because/he was losing/his faith." And then: "Do you know how/I know this?" The question seemed trivial. I shook my head again: "Because/there is a manuscript/written by/Fr Pablo .... Did you know that?" He tickled his nose with the anemone and glowed: "...and/as far as I know/the only copy of that manuscript/is kept/guarded/and hidden away/in a safe... in Dr de Coca's office..." Estrella glared at the huge trap.

Trap or not, Vicente had guaranteed himself another front row ticket to our next session.

Estrella maintained her protest but Don Enrique was inflexible: "It's of the utmost importance. If we can observe the same events described in Fr Pablo's manuscript, a text that none of us have seen, our technique and its results will be harder to refute."

Creating a tornado: "Except that Fr Pablo's manuscript does not exist!"

Don Enrique closed his eyes against the storm unfurled at him before slowly nodding at the possibility: "Maybe," but his lids suddenly sprung open again and he darted forward to clasp Estrella's wrist: "Or maybe not." His own pace became wild: "But we cannot verify that existence, because if we see the manuscript before we describe it, it is reduced to the same function as any other text we have. We have to discover what we know and then see if we can confirm it or not. And what harm can it do us? Why are you so worried about de Coca and Vicente? What do you think they can do to us?"

Estrella did not answer. She just got up and stormed out. And we did not see her for the rest of the day. So the next session, so important to Don Enrique, had to be filmed by Vicente.

Late afternoon. Long, low-sun shadows. Sarmiento and his cousin were on horseback, trotting toward a town. Sky blue boxes from a distance, splashed with the violent red of their roofs. A drowsy flock of shaggy, long haired sheep ruminated grass at the side of the track. The Spaniards' horses snorted authority and the nervous herd pranced out of the way.

When they reached the town, the travellers had to bend their backs under the cracked arch of a ruined gate. A silent yawn within crumbling, moss-pocked walls that were paled, but also softened, by twilight shadow. Already cold, they both pulled their cloaks tightly around them to keep any breezes out. Sarmiento's nose and beard brushed against the prickling coarse strands of his mount's mane, sniffing the wet leather bridle. His mind was full of anticipation for a clean, straw bed within some warm and smoky inn: "It's weeks since I've been able to wake up with a dry and unfrozen arse," he mumbled, more to himself, or some cruelly responsible god, than to the friar behind him.

On the other, interior side of the gate, the sun was completely masked by buildings. Fr Pablo looked up at a tower, rising like a giant bishop's hat, silhouette-dark, but also dazzling. A golden flash of sunlight shot out through an arch traversing the middle – *It must be the cathedral. The first church that Pizarro had built* – However, the flash soon disappeared whilst they drifted between the peeling paint walls of the low but compact houses along the narrow violet street before them – *What little people must live here* – he thought – *What kind of wonderfully simple interiors must they have?* – As he breathed in an acrid atmosphere made him grimace, imagining cats. The town seemed deserted, and they were almost at the end of that first street before they received any definite indication of human existence. A distant rumble of drums and, listening carefully, the sharp note of some wind instrument. Sarmiento gave a gut-deep bellow. His cousin sighed. They yanked on their reins and turned their horses' snouts up an adjacent lane. The drumming became louder, and underneath it the muffled murmur of a crowd. There was hardly room enough for them now, at times their knees grazed the walls. The horses snorted, and as they cantered forward Fr Pablo coughed and pulled the neck of his cassock up over his nose. The same feline stench that he had suffered by the gate was stronger now, as if they had become immersed in a cloud of it.

There was a glow at the end, the lane rising up to a torch lit, smoky blue square. Children ran down and past them. There were street stalls, covered with canopies. The horses had to nudge their way through the ever thickening crowd and the friar shuddered as a strange red face, with huge white eyes and a tiny black moustache looked up at him. A demon's face, he thought, then realised it was a mask.

Moving into the square they were able to see where the music came from. A makeshift orchestra up on a makeshift stage. Most of them were beating drums: more noise than music. A bustling audience was packed in.

When they saw them in the torch light they realised that most of them were masked. Shouts and laughter, and clapping hands, crammed and swaying together. Many of them were spinning through a whirling dance. Bulky woollen ponchos, bright red, patterned with blue or yellow stripes. Red woollen caps with long flicking tassels, or black European style hats. Men or women? It was difficult to tell under the masks and nearly all of them wore skirts. Leaning, arm in arm, drinking from cane beakers or chewing coca leaves. The only sober sign was that of serving girls, who walked through the mass in groups of five. They carried clay jugs from which liquid was poured into proffered beakers or straight down gaping throats. Everyone it seemed was either drinking, chewing, or unashamedly urinating. Much to Fr Pablo's disgust. The water flowing over his horses' hooves, was piss. He wanted to vomit.

Sarmiento, on the other hand, lifted his nose and sniffed into a cloud of smoke that wafted past: "Someone is roasting mutton." He pressed spurs into his nervous mount's frothing flanks, tugged the reins and he and his cousin guided their mounts carefully through the throng towards a tavern. The drunken rabble parted, without looking at the horses, as if unintentionally, as if forced away by an invisible wedge. Then, over the shouts and laughter, there was a terrible shriek.

Sarmiento's horse reared, kicking out. Sparks flashed as a flaming torch swept in front of the animal's dripping snout and below the flames was a thick but flabby flesh arm. This belonged to a short, swarthy character who was screaming. His head shook, or bounced, as if loosely attached to a spring, poking out from a smock which was chequered. Long and greasy black hair tied in plaits spun around his face. His ears flapped, the lobes of them were huge, stretching down to his shoulders, and the gaping holes in them indicated that he had probably been a *pakoyoc*, a member of the old Inca nobility. He had a long knife in his other hand that was slashing.

Sarmiento's top lip curled and he unsheathed his sword. Beneath him, his assailant's half-closed eyes were mad slits of anguish in the flashing torch light. His fat red lips, moist with spittle, were dripping. They opened wide to release a torrent of curses in his Inca language, while he lunged again and again at the protesting, prodding horse.

Sarmiento raised his own blade and made to cut down the aggressor when another man, equally swarthy, but with long white hair and beard and a deep scar running under a black eyepatch on his left side, had his own blade out and in the way: "A pox on you, sirrah! Hold your arm! Unless you'll spar wit' *me*. Troth do it, señor, if you have the balls for it!"

Sarmiento grunted through gritted teeth, wriggling, uncomfortable in the saddle. Swords crossed. They stared, scowling. The other man's unpatched eye, was promising hell. Sarmiento gasped. His horse suddenly reared again and the frustrated jockey was dizzied by a blur of faint pinprick lights within the violet night firmament. The animal he was rooted to span and jerked and all light whirled into one brilliant space.

Loping behind Sarmiento came a truly enormous figure, also bearing a torch. He reached forward and took the bridle of Sarmiento's horse, steadying the mount with a single pat from his fleshy palm. As the horse calmed down, Sarmiento arched his back and clamped his knees into the mount's gleaming flanks to settle things even faster. When he lifted his head again and looked around, he was surrounded.

Two other interested parties had arrived, clad in red ponchos and masked by demon faces like the other revellers, but instead of reaching for

Sarmiento's horse they grabbed hold of the knife wielding *pakoyoc* and wrapped him in thick arms.

Seeing the provocateur restrained Sarmiento relaxed his blade. The man with the eye-patch reciprocated and laughed: "Lo, you're verily a good gentleman I see. Just as we all are, troth," an ironic, picaresque smile. He even seemed to wink at Sarmiento: "Even this dog-leach, my mad friend 'ere," and pointed to the character still dangling his knife through his fingers although his arms were well secured: "Wretched flea bag mongrel that he seems, he too is a good man. And I'm much indebted to him," scratching his crotch: "He's dragged me out of many a ditch when I've been drunk meself, mark" and spat: "Though the scarab is well sozzled today, well, he must be excused exactly for that; because he's sozzled he knows not what he do," then he turned, slapped the staggering chessboard's knife out of his hand and punched his face in the same movement.

The swarthy drunk rocked on his heels, then fell with a thud beside his little and obviously blunt blade. The huge man holding the reins roared, his round belly rolling. Then he lifted a thick hand and gently patted the horse's wet nose. The animal snorted, slathered. The huge man puckered and kissed its snout, hushing it.

The one-eyed man stepped forward and took the reins himself, staring up at Sarmiento, grinning to reveal broken teeth: "Aye, you're a gentleman, and should defend yourself as any lord would. Though beware, here we're all *your lordship* when we want to be. Even this cur." He beckoned to Sarmiento to dismount, then, when he had, he leaned closer to his ear: "*Chicha*, they have here. Have you tried it? *(laughing)* Lo, a terrible brew it is, mark me. Yet this one *(pointing to the man still unconscious on the ground)* when he gets in a melancholy mood, he guzzles it like it were water from a mountain spring *(slurping)* It's a disease. Makes him all hot in the head. And then he has this stiff-born thing about horses *(slapping Sarmiento's mounts thigh)* He cannot stomach them, pray. Blames them for all his bad luck *(scratching his cheek and lowering his pitch even more, as if revealing some darkly secret plan)* For you see, the Inca wretch would be a wealthy man now, if not for us Castilians *(then smiling, his voice rising again).* Yet mark me, the whoreson fool's really a good man, and I must his protector be. For I told you, he's my friend."

"That I heard, and I can see it," said Sarmiento, dryly.

The one-eyed man snorted, stepped back a little, and scratched his crotch again: "Well let's invite you to at least one drink *(leaning forward to Sarmiento's ear, to whisper again)* And here you'll find that the whores are second to ..."

Sarmiento put a finger to smiling lips: "Shush. I come with a friar."

Pablo, who heard nothing, had also dismounted. The eye-patched man quickly looked him over, then put a thumbnail under his teeth and flicked it: "A pox on you! A friar who doesn't drink?"

Sarmiento sniggered: "Not drink? Him? Why I'd wager he has such a thirst that he'll even have the vinegar."

They roared at this, slapped each other's shoulders and backs as if they had been life-long friends, and tugged at the blushing friar's cassock, pulling him into a tavern with them. They also dragged along the *pakoyoc*, slapping his face, and splashing water on him to bring him around ...

I shivered, as if the water had been thrown into *my* face. A distraction that made me briefly conscious of the voice that was guiding me: "You will find out their names."

"I'm Rodrigo Muñoz de Avila," said the one-eyed host, slamming a mug of wine down on the table. Then, opening his arms and palms like a Christ figure at his last supper: "And these are me good friends." He then lifted the brow of his functional eye and flicked his head in the direction of the barrel-bellied colossus who had been holding Sarmiento's horse's reins: "Leopoldo, *the Bear*, Lopez Ufarte, the deepest gut in the Indies. He could out drink ten of the thirstiest pissheads you could find, and eat more than a hundred of your best swine. A burper and a farter he is, and we should pray he has no gas tonight," then, grabbing a passing serving girl's arm: "Bring us mutton. Stuffed with garlic, and well roasted. Oh, and that excellent ox-tail casserole you have," then squeezing Sarmiento's wrist and pinching Fr Pablo's cheek: "You'll dine well tonight lads. You're the guests of Rodrigo Muñoz."

Sarmiento pointed across the table to the man who had attacked his horse, who was face down and unconscious again: "And who, pray, is he?

You say he's a *pakoyoc*, but really, tell me please, the whole story. Without waking the poor wretch."

Rodrigo Muñoz lifted his bottom lip and lowered his voice: "He, señor, is none other than Don Pablo Huanca Inca, grandson of the last great Inca king. And these two wretches with him are his nephews, they say. Now all of them bear good Christian names, sirrah, Juan and Jesús, but with the family name Yupanqui," and the two masked men who had carried Pablo Huanca into the tavern affirmed it with a nod, before slowly peeling off their masks.

The leather brown faces that were revealed, were at the same time harsh and calm; mirroring sharply torn souls ripped open by the flash of Spanish gunpowder and the slash of Toledo steel. Their wounds had been sealed in scars, but deeper down, in mind and soul, they accepted their conquest, which is not to say they were thankful for it. To them it was a soothing hatred: "The invaders think us stupid," mumbled the one called Jesús. Too low for anyone but his Inca companion to catch. It was drowned out anyway, by Rodrigo Muñoz, who roared: "Aye, each one of them's been Christianised, but for what, pray? To become the thirsty, whoreson whelps you see today," and laughed.

The swarthy heir to an extinct throne suddenly lifted his head and belched. His black dreadlocks shivered in the presence of light air before his gravity drawn face crashed into the table top nadir again. Rodrigo, Sarmiento and the giant man-bear gushed, while Fr Pablo shook his head slightly. Not even his Christ could properly explain the endless, weeping night darkness of that miserable man's soul. The presence of the Incas stirred up his own personal crisis. He was starting to despise mankind.

Meanwhile, the Spaniards' taunts provoked a quiet admonishment from the dull eyed Jesús Yupanqui: "Do not laugh, sirrah," then reaching for the friar's pale hand: "Let it be known that Don Pablo Huanca Inca fought ... bravely ... against Spanish horses and Spanish steel," and he leaned forward. The breath of his hushed voice tickled the friar's nose: "How can I describe the awe we felt when our people first saw the Europeans. Your people seemed like *Viracochas*."

"Ancient name given to a pagan god," rasped Rodrigo, who had also leaned forward to keep in touch with the dialogue.

"The universal creator," added Juan Yupanqui, defiantly: "We thought so because you possessed *yllapas*."

"Thunder," translated Rodrigo.

Juan Yupanqui continued, staring into a space above the head of the friar, as if his ancestors were there: "We thought the harquebuses were bringing thunder from heaven," his voice now a moan: "But the most terrible things were those enormous animals you rode on. On foot your men were awkward in their armour, breathless at the altitude. But on your horses, we could do nothing."

Jesús shook his head: "They cut us down like corn."

"Always up high, striking down. Look at the scars," lifting his poncho.

Jesús grimaced: "We thought more of killing one horse than a dozen men."

"When we did catch a horse we would slice off its head, impale it and arrange branches and flowers around it to proclaim our victory."

"Yes, a dead horse was a great victory, against Pizarro."

"Pizarro, lucky quat," sighed Rodrigo Muñoz, though the thumping fist gesture accompanying it was histrionic. His overacting threw spittle across the table, splashing against the arm of the serving girl bringing the mutton. But the orator, oblivious to his misdemeanour, rattled on: "Lo, if I'd been with Pizarro I'd be a rich man now. But I was not so fortunate. While he was on his way to get the treasures of Cuzco, I was riding with Alvarado's army, in the Quitan campaign. What a debacle! If only we'd had Pizarro's luck; if only we'd had our own Cajamarca and all its gold. But no. Our fate was Quito. And Alvarado, being the impatient cowherd he was, decided that the best road to Quito was the straightest. Straight through the jungle, straight up the mountain. For him a mountain was just a mountain. What did it matter to Alvarado that we'd be scrambling up the slopes of the Andes?"

Then I saw Rodrigo Muñoz in that other time. Much younger, his hair black, riding behind his general. Both were slightly hunched forward on their tired horses, knowing they would have to bow to let the low lying branches of tropical trees flick over them. The rain was incessant. Water dripped from their long hair and beards. Drops formed rivulets, trickling under the collars of their mail coats, under their shirts, down their backs. Splash and patter on the fleshy foliage, a constant rush that deadened their minds.

Then the rain stopped. A gap. Light. Space. A clearing on the hill top. From there it was easy to discern a series of winding roads, all running away, towards the slopes of a serried mountain range within which they all disappeared, swallowed by a rising mist.

Behind them, down the hill, now also shrouded by the mist, was the camp. A pungent effluvium emanated from the oozing glands of the mass of exhausted figures. Thousands of them were Indians; Alvarado's army of Indian slave porters, recruited in Guatemala by throwing them into irons. They lived chained to each other and even slept with their collars on. Too tired to sleep properly they ate grass and soil to mitigate their hunger, while each festering sore on their scab covered skin attracted sucking insects. They were too exhausted to waft anything away, so the flies or mosquitoes gorged themselves and the joyful hum and buzz of well-stuffed creatures contrasted with the constant moan of human suffering.

A pair of sleepy soldiers stood guard. Harquebuses were cradled in their arms over heavy steel breastplates, while stained and rusty swords dangled from groins. There was a certain sensuality, but the sighs, coughs, gasps and groans were evoked by pain not pleasure. The grunts and blows of the African slave grave diggers wafted by. Emaciated, flyblown corpses had been strewn beside them. Dead Indians. Armpits swollen. Buboes.

Gradually the expedition broke camp: "We are on our way," said one – *full of hunger* – thought another: "To Quito" – *so full of desire* – "Their gold and silver belongs to us" – *like it did to the others before us* – "Their women belong to us" – *we will never be hungry again* – "The City of Cities" – *I look behind me and I don't miss a thing* –

The Guatemalan slaves moved only to avoid being whipped, listening to the same motives: "We are on our way," they heard – *full of hunger* – they thought: "To Quito," they were told – *carrying a city on our shoulders* – "Their gold and city belongs to us" – *but what are we struggling for?* – "Their women belong to us" – *will you leave ours alone then?* – "The City of Cities" – *I am so homesick, where is my wife and little ones?* -

Rodrigo Muñoz rose to join Alvarado on the hill top. From there they were to descend into the jungle on the other side. Alvarado shouted at his officers, who were pushing and prodding a group of groggy, machete wielding Africans. These hacked at the thicket until a pathway was opened, quite narrow, but wide enough for Alvarado's steed. There was tension, the heat and the mosquitoes made everyone irritable. But when they reached the road, spirits lifted. The unchained African slaves, only a moment earlier on the verge of desertion, began to sway and chant as they went: "Oouuey-ooey...".

The road had rescued them from the jungle, bringing them to a valley. They found a narrow path following the fast flowing river, penetrating a gorge, but at the end of it they had to scramble up a slippery steep slope. Several fell, a dozen died. The rain came down heavier than ever. Squelching through red mud. And, on reaching a spur they had a new perspective. A new hell to face ...

"We'd crossed Erebus, marching into that infernal Hades itself!" groaned Rodrigo Muñoz, and spat on the tavern floor: "The ground trembled. The earth roared. Billowing smoke."

"A volcano!" blurted Leopoldo: "Erupting."

"Cotopaxi, they called it. Vulcan's own arsehole, opened and farting fire. And the clouds that covered us were smoke. Grey rain. Verily I say, spitting mud ..."

Ashen mud. It dripped into their eyes, into their mouths, was sucked up noses, into lungs. Thousands of coughing dying souls.

"We are on our way (*cough*) to the new city (*wheeze*) the city of cities (*gasp*)"

"The roads were blocked. We had to hack our way up the precipitous slopes. So high. Up in the snow."

It froze them. Hundreds were dying. Half-naked Guatemalans. Purple, chilblained fingers and toes. Gangrened feet. The stench. Dead Indians beheaded so that their chains would not have to be unlocked, so that the headless body could be dragged out from the dog collar. Dragged out, then thrown away.

"Where are we going, fie?"

Snow splattered fingers yanked out daggers and thrust them into horses' necks. Spurting blood stained the would-be conquistadors. They trembled, men as well as the dying horses.

Wide open horse eyes accused and damned all humans. A tacit equine curse, inspiring mumbled moans: "What treasure could be worth this hell?"

Desperate, shivering soldiers, inserting swords between dead horses' ribs. Ripping flesh. Opening. Hands in. Pulling innards out. Wobbling viscera on earth. Then they climbed in, under the stinking ribs, to keep warm. It was cosy inside the dead horse. They were alive inside the dead horse.

And when they reached the top, starving and freezing, the Guatemalan slaves were mostly dead, the horses were mostly dead: "We are on our way (*groan*) to the new city (*moan*) the city of cities."

A voice which drifted and faded away across an immense valley, echoed back as a piercing condor's shriek.

When they reached the road, they stopped and their limbs sagged. Many of even the strongest collapsed. Weeping they were, even the bravest: "We are on our way."

At first they were happy to be on the road. At first, but the mud of that same road ahead was churned and pocked with boot marks and tracks of horses' shoes.

The first to realise what this meant wailed.

The first to realise that they were not the first.

The tracks ahead were quite clearly the signs of an army. Another army. An army ahead of them: "In our city." A Spanish army: "We are not the first!" In actual fact there were two Spanish armies: "We've been beaten!" Ahead were Almagro and Benalcázar: "They've gone to our city. They will get our gold."

"The booty was theirs. All of it. Oh, aye, they paid off Alvarado. Compensated him for his ships. But as for us, we got nothing. After all we had suffered, for nothing."

"Oh, you're such a murmuring man," accused Jesús Yupanqui: "The weight of all lays so heavily upon you, because you took nothing. Yet we had everything *taken* from us!" then through gritted teeth: "If Don Pablo Huanca Inca were awake and sober he would tell you stories of real suffering, sirrah!"

Sarmiento turned to his cousin and slapped him: "Take out your quill, your paper, and scribe, for God's sake!"

Fr Pablo squeezed his eyes shut before stretching them open wide, and shook his head. It was Sarmiento who lifted the friar's satchel and began rummaging in it to extract the pen and notes.

Rodrigo picked his nose and snorted: "So the friar is a pen-dipper!"

"Aye, he is. A chronographer no less. Most noble profession. Not to be laughed at."

"Was I laughing, señor?"

"I would hope it not."

"Then I would that I were not," and while chewing on some stringy mutton: "Who, Father, is your patron, pray? Which bishop, I mean, gives you the gold to write this book?"

Fr Pablo looked up, squinting cautious: "No Bishop."

Sarmiento licked his lips: "By my means, señores. The patron is I."

Rodrigo's eyebrows shot up: "You!?" and the monosyllable extended into a clear guffaw: "No offence friend, but, your thin threaded cloth ain't the finest I've seen. Scarce does it cover yer buttocks."

Sarmiento's own top lip curled up into a snarl: "I work for my silver. I'd work for you, if I thought that you could pay me. I'm an astrologer."

Rodrigo's throat gurgled: "Astrologer? Oh yes, I'm sure the bastard sons of the Pizarro's would pay handsomely to know their cozening destinies." Then lowering his head: "And this occult science o' yours fills yer purse while you tramps around writing yer book." When he looked up again it was straight at the friar: "And so your good and no doubt holy lines are paid for with the devil's own silver." Fr Pablo's solemn, guilty nod inspired an eruption: "Ha! I'll drink to that! Waitress!" then leaning toward his invitees and lowering his voice into intimate depths: "Oh, you seem a most unnatural couple ... most unnatural indeed," and he winked at Fr Pablo, which made the friar blush.

Sarmiento snarled again: "This situation, of course, is only temporary. Here in Peru we hope to find a patron, a Viceroy or a bishop, who will buy a dedication."

"Then good luck to you both," but also snarling: "If yer friend is the important *chronofrogger* that you say he is, then he should countenance me for my 'ospitality and write me story as well."

"He will. And your sad adventure has been listened to, and in due course, with a more reflexive saturnine temperament, the scribe will set down his conclusions and emboss your name in the hallowed realm of literature," which twisted Fr Pablo's face into gaping admiration of his cousin's audacity. But Sarmiento had not finished. He rose, at the same time beckoning to the two sober Incas to rise as well: "Now," he said emphatically: "Let's hear from the Indians." Sitting, leaving Juan and Jesús Yupanqui, dumbfounded up on their feet.

Rodrigo thumped his fist on the table. The two Incas jumped: "Sit down you good baboons!" and they did, terrified: "Tell us your tale, if that's what the good friar'd like to hear."

Juan gulped, then lifted his chest. He leaned across the table and, in a low but proud voice: "Did you see how he made us jump, Father? They have been making us jump for years."

Which inspired the dreary-eyed Jesús: "They took everything from us. If Don Pablo Huanca Inca were sober he'd tell you."

"What would he tell us?"

"He'd tell you about Cajamarca. He was there. Don Pablo Huanca was there, in Atahualpa's army, when Pizarro came ..."

Francisco Pizarro, I saw him. The conqueror of Peru. He lay down for a short siesta, and once in the hammock he fell into a deep sleep and strange dream ... *He was running forward into a lead grey terrain that was wide and open. At first he presumed himself to be gliding over a waveless ocean. On the steady horizon he could discern two mountains, which he imagined to be islands. They were distant, and he only had a vague idea. But then long, sharp stems of dry and thorny grass bit against his legs, carving through the salmon-pink skin of his sunburnt buttocks and he realised he was not racing over an ocean at all, but that he was in a desert. Running naked, he realised. Pushing forward he discerned a thin, charcoal black tree, under which sat an equally skinny and dark man, cross legged like a yogi. The plant was a shabby acacia. The man under it, gathered within its roots, smiled, and his tiny black head became all pearly white gleaming teeth. Then suddenly the same dark figure was moving, his folded legs straightening, and as he did a brilliant and hot orb of light rose, like a tiny sun, directly over him. His skin-tone became much lighter, a milk-coffee brown. And, within the café-crème, his navel was like the last bubbling trace from some recently removed stirring spoon. Wrapped just under this was an orange sarong, which shivered slightly with his ascension. This yogi man was chortling at the dreamer who had arrived before him. Guffawing at the visitor's pale nudity, especially his flapping, moth cocoon penis. Then, parting his sarong, he extracted his own strip of sex, as thick as the dreamer-visitor's arm. Freed, it urinated: a rushing, glowing fountain arching high and splashing against Pizarro's feet. The dreaming conquistador tried to jump back, but he was paralysed, wrapped in something heavy. A pile of metal from toe to chin, which at first he thought was just junk, until he discerned the gleam of gold, silver and precious jewels. But then that sparkling treasure began to steam, dissolved by the torrential excretion from the pissing yogi ...* Francisco Pizarro, awoke gasping and sweating. He clutched tightly to the sides of his hammock, panting. There was something beyond the nightmare which had an enormous relevance: the vague and craggy peaks of what he had thought had been islands, which were really dry mountains – *Very great* – he thought, although unable to remember why, and he fell asleep again.

"Atahualpa," scoffed Rodrigo: "You deemed to call that vomit coloured coward your king."

"Coward he was not, señores," and Juan Yupanqui lifted his nose: "He was a personage of great intelligence, rather."

Rodrigo turned away to ruminate on bile and memory, leaving it up to *the Bear*, Leopoldo, to do the roaring: "Pizarro arrived wit' one hundred 'n' forty men, and At-wahl-pa, wit' 'is thousands, shat 'imself."

Jesús squeezed his eyes shut, as if the Bear's voice had provoked a migraine: "No, señor. You say that, but verily it is not true. Atahualpa knew that if a force so small should dare to march against his multitude, then they were most certainly courageous men, who had to be treated with due respect."

And I was hurled backward again. Shadows indicated that the sun had not long risen. Agitated sentries shouted orders to each other. Pizarro's captain, Hernando de Soto, had to be roused. One of these guards burst into the captain's room. De Soto was still in his warm, straw bed. He shook off his somnolence and wheeled around. The remnant of a dream lingering in his consciousness, provoked confusion. Stiff strands of bedding flew. A terrible, because absurd, question flashed through his mind – *Where am I?* – The vision of the armoured sentry coupled with the smell of his body seemed to hurl him back to a proper perspective of time and space – *The day has arrived* – he told himself – *The day that I am to act as Pizarro's envoy. The day I meet the Inca king* –

He screamed to his squire to fetch his armour and the shuffling feet on the powdery floor turned the room into a dustbowl. I remember registering a hardly discernible crack, de Soto did not realise it. It was the chitin of a horny weevil crushed beneath someone's feet. Pink elytra stretched apart and twitched pathetically before crumbling into tiny particles quickly lost in the rest of the rising dust.

Captain de Soto snatched his leather baldric from his dresser and buckled it himself before sheathing a sword. At first the act of piercing the tight gash was slow, but when he was sure of having achieved a straight and certain entry he suddenly thrust forcefully downwards, grimacing. He was ready.

Taking his harquebus and two taurine powder horns from the thin, outstretched arm of the factotum, he flipped the cloth flaps in the doorway apart and stepped into the street. The soldiers waiting outside straightened themselves. Captain de Soto's squire ran behind. Where they were, inside the city of Cajamarca, they were surrounded. In the valley below and around them, Atahualpa's general's armies were camped in tents. Thousands of tents.

Captain de Soto mounted his horse. His gaze was firm, controlled, unblinking. He had the airs of a madman which infused him with an almost supernatural confidence. There were only fifteen other horsemen that went down with him, descending into the multitude of the enemy camp. Fifteen against thousands. But it was the thousands that trembled, not the fifteen. The sight of those strange animals, those horses which they thought were giant dogs, made them gasp. And the sight of de Soto and his men in their polished, gleaming, amber coloured armour, also filled them with more than some doubt. A passage opened for the Spaniards. No one dared to touch, as if contact should promise an instant and gruesome death. It was a strange day.

Jesús Yupanqui dropped his head into his hands. His voice became a triste wail: "And if you saw a monster tonight, what would you do? Even though there were a hundred of you, you'd all run ..."

Captain de Soto paused for a moment and mumbled a prayer in Latin. Then he gave orders that he should be accompanied at the head of the line by his translator, Felipillo. The bi-lingual bastard led his horse through the barrier of pure bloods and trotted up to his lord. As they cantered the translator babbled, explaining that the Incas had already heard all about Francisco Pizarro's expedition. When de Soto asked if they were not therefore afraid of them, the translator replied that they were, but not as much as they would have been if they had not been expecting them. De Soto told him to tell Atahualpa when they met him that they came in peace, but the interpreter argued that it would have been a waste of breath. Atahualpa had already made up his mind. He already knew how the Spaniards operated ....

Juan's voice, rasped through gritted teeth: "Atahualpa was no fool. When he invited the Spaniards into Cajamarca, he was preparing a trap."

"Oh yea!" screamed Rodrigo: "Verily a trap you say! Yet we all know what happened there to your most great king's sly plan ... Go into the town, stay there for a while. And he, the coward, went to his bath house twenty leagues away, to wallow in the hot springs with his concubines ... What kind of king!?"

Eventually the wash broke against an unmoving figure. A *pakoyoc* envoy from Atahualpa himself. He was a short, dark man, wrapped in a long cotton smock covered by an enormous cape of black and white plumage. He clasped a feathered fly swat in one hand, a long copper staff, culminating in an elaborately carved alligator-head in the other. From his neck hung a heavy but brilliant collar of gold and gems. This contained hundreds of emeralds, rubies and variegated stones girdled by tiny and exquisitely crafted bells, each bearing its own intricately worked figurine.

The envoy and Felipillo conversed. The translator turned to de Soto: "He wants to know if you be Pizarro."

De Soto sniggered: "And am I?"

Which perplexed Felipillo. He scratched his head: "No, milord ... You are Captain de Soto, Pizarro's envoy," then, shaking his head: "You want to talk to Atahualpa. You have a message from Don Francisco."

De Soto slapped him: "Yes, but I know all that. Tell him!"

Through the translator the envoy asked de Soto to let off his rifle.

The Captain flicked open the operculum of his dangling horn and dripped a stream of gunpowder into the breech. Without bothering to add a projectile, or even use a rifle support, he lit the wick with a taper and fired aimlessly into the air. Many dropped to the earth screaming. Only the strongest stood their ground.

"'Tis a funny game for them," said the translator. "They think you very much brave."

"Idiots," mumbled de Soto.

The envoy stepped forward, until he was standing, quite calm and still, only inches away from de Soto. Neither of them moved, neither spoke, and a new tension rose from the uncertainty of prolonged inactivity. Then the envoy clapped his hands and a score of slaves stepped forward with trays of roast duck and mutton. The translator informed de Soto that Atahualpa wanted Pizarro to accept this new offering and return the gold and silver that they had stolen ...

Juan squeezed Fr Pablo's cool hand: "You are a holy man, you must understand. For us, pray, the wealth of gold and silver is not the same as the metals that your people lust after. Its importance was not as an exchange of goods, but spiritual. In gold resided our sun god, just as in the host is found the body of Christ. And in silver was the moon-goddess, her white light."

"But now you are Christians."

"Yes, of course, good Christians we are too, but that does not make good of the terrible evil that was done to our people ..."

Finally, de Soto and his men were riding through the pillared gates of the small town of Cajas, into a square. Before them the Sun Temple, the buildings around it replete with *acllas*, the holy women. De Soto's men lifted their visors and drooled.

Thick hands grasped tiny arms and dragged the trembling weeping women, hundreds of them, out into the square. There the prettiest ones were divided up. Each Spaniard took one. And the square filled with the sounds of tearing fabric, screams, sobs, moans. Then thuds. Fists against complaining faces ...

"And that upstart dared to do that with Atahualpa's thousands only twenty leagues away! ..."

Atahualpa sat before de Soto on a low stool. He was fresh out of his bath, smelling of sweet herbs and wrapped in a splendid azure cloak. His head was crowned by a large golden disk and a series of tightly wound cords, one of them dangling from the front, off the disk, as a tassel. This wobbled and tickled his brow even though he seemed to remain perfectly still. Surrounding him were a dozen women on one side and a score of stern *pakoyoc*s, with dangling earlobes and golden plugs, on the other. Captain de Soto stepped forward, bowed and began to explain Pizarro's pretensions ...

"They lied to us. Said they wanted to help Atahualpa in his family feud. They invited him to go to Cajamarca to talk to Pizarro. It was a trap ..."

They were laden with hefty, gleaming objects. First, twelve images of twelve kings, in tin and copper, over gilt with pure gold. Then a solid gold chalice, inlaid with intricate bands, delicate mosaics of precious jewels. All of it brought from another land. Two great islands far away ...

The image vanished. Juan's speech was cut by a whack on the table top. As the cane came crashing down, Jesús' hand fled and his top lip curled. Rodrigo angled forward: "Lay aside, wretch!" then to Sarmiento: "I do feel the fool does fancy your rings, sirrah."

Jesús shaking his head, an upward-curling top lip expressing recognition of a much used and dirty tactic: "N-N-No..."

"But I saw your wanton eye."

"Y-Yes señor... I was admiring them."

"Admiring the gold."

"No, señor ... I was admiring the designs."

Sarmiento lifted his arm and signalled Rodrigo to sit back. Then he propped his ring laden fingers up before the Inca's face: "Look closely then friend. Beautiful?"

"Yes, señor."

"You understand it? Can read it?"

"Yes, señor; the sun, the moon ... Yes, señor ... they are magic rings."

And Sarmiento slowly nodded. Not taking his eyes off Jesús Yupanqui. Jesús, his gaze fixed on Sarmiento.

(b) Avachumbi and Ninachumbi (the islands of the sun)

Vicente remained unmoved by my description. Fr Pablo *had* written about Xauxa, but that, he said, did not prove anything. I would need to find out more specific details.

"Is ... er ... Was no mention made of Rodrigo de Avila in the document de Coca has?" I asked, almost pleading. But he shook his head. There was nothing to coincide with the reports except for the name of the town.

"In his text/the friar/also championed/the Indians' cause," he admitted: "But that doesn't/prove/you really saw him."

We had a snack with some wine before continuing ...

In my next immersion, I emerged in a room. There was a grey, dawn light. The tables were plastered with cooled melted candlewax. Three men were there: Sarmiento, Rodrigo de Avila, and Leopoldo the Bear. They were all miserable and red-eyed after being up all night drinking. Rodrigo was in a large and rickety armchair beside Leopoldo, who was naked from the waist up and rocking slightly on a flimsy wooden stool. Each seat exaggerated the physical size of its occupant, Leopoldo made enormous, Rodrigo puny. They were deep in conversation, if you could call their slurred complaints conversation: "Whoreson Indians ..."

"Insolent slaves ..."

"Vermin ..."

"Cow-herds ..."

"Lead by the conjuring church ..."

"Cheaters ..."

"Abominable stinkards ..." etc.

Which seemed to lull them into a sense of contentment. So much so that the Bear closed his eyes, fall asleep and dropped off his stool. Unleashing a resounding explosion of air from his arse as he did.

Rodrigo turned his nose up: "Ah shite! We'd better move," and he struggled out of his chair: "Before the gas has us vomiting."

And he and Sarmiento made a sudden drunken scramble for the door. But, on opening it, they found their exit blocked by Fr Pablo who was trying to make an equally desperate entry: "Let us out!"

"Troth, still drunk," jeered the friar and pushed the door hard, the edge of which slammed into the bridge of Sarmiento's nose.

He toppled backwards against Rodrigo, and the one-eyed man slipped so that the drunken pair collapsed together.

Pablo stepped over them with waving arms, but stopped dead in his tracks when slapped by a faceful of Leopoldo's methane: "What?! Is there something dead here?"

No one heard. Sarmiento was unconscious, Leopoldo was still asleep, and Rodrigo too exhausted to move.

The friar looked for water, found only wine, and threw a jug of this in Sarmiento's face, who came to with a gasp and a flick of claret soaked hair.

Fr Pablo was uncharacteristically rough: "Lift yourself!"

Sarmiento rubbed his aching head and prodded the smarting red bridge of his nose: "You would have been wiser letting me sleep, sirrah!"

"Something has happened, I've seen someone. We're in danger."

"Danger?"

"The thugs from Tlaxcala," he whispered: "The Portuguese. Or at least one of them. He's here, flexing his blade and asking questions about you no doubt."

Sarmiento, obviously wrestling with a judgement, shook his head again: "Fetch my sword," which was grunted.

Fr Pablo sighed through a smirk: "You're wearing it," and put his own hand onto the hilt: "Have we not been wandering these last seven years to avoid precisely this?" and looked up with a loving stare into Sarmiento's dripping, long face.

The alchemist, moved by an urgent need to be sober, pushed him aside. He reached for a frayed, leather bag, fished into it and yanked out a dry root with a wisp of black hair wrapped around it. Then he went straight to the table, slamming the yam down, while at the same time unsheathing his dagger and frantically jabbing the effigy: "They are supposed to be all of them dead," he gasped, adding spittle to the drips from his hair.

Fr Pablo grabbed his wrist, his eyes widening. The threat to his soul implied in the voodoo act was more frightening than any prospect of death. Tension in the throat made his pitch high, and it shot out, rapid: "I told you this witchcraft does not work," then deeper and slower: "You cannot kill a devil with his own craft."

Startled by a resounding thump on the door, and submitting to instinct, Sarmiento suddenly dropped to the floor, his sharp dagger up and wavering, his spurs rattling as he crawled noisily away from the sight lines of the window.

The thumping continued.

Pablo's knees clamped, but his shoulders sagged and his head was light. Had the killers come already? But if the worst happened, he reasoned, he was happy to die.

Meanwhile, Sarmiento had intuited a strategy. Simple rather than subtle. The safest form of defence. It was a cliché, but the obvious means, he convinced himself, were often the most effective. He would attack.

So he pulled himself up beside the door – *Preservation through violence, or a bloody internecine end* – He wiped the cold sweat from his trembling hands, then considered the lines on them. He could see no reason why he should die. And thus, assured by a hand that failure was forbidden by destiny, he unsheathed his sword, and pulled the door open in one dramatic, huge, hinge squealing yank, his sabre whooshing and cutting an arch before falling in the space between two men. These collapsed backward, each face shielded by an arm: "Mercy!"

The plea was uttered in a shrill rough harmony.

Sarmiento groaned, also granular: "A pox," and reached for the reclining figure closest to him, pulling the protecting arm away, revealing an eye. It was a little moist blinking gash, but it was instantly recognised.

The arm was jerked and there was a short slight popping noise as a ball of bone slipped out and back again into its socket. The owner of the bone grunted as he was pulled to his feet. His back was slapped and then Sarmiento flung him through the door: "Fie, man! Come inside."

Fr Pablo gasped when he saw the hurtling figure and opened his arms to receive him. An engulfing embrace and the relief after the shock wrenched high pitched laughter from them. It was Fernando, the engineer.

Sarmiento stretched his own arms around the embracing couple. Fernando in the middle laughing. His relieved, polished apple face gleamed optimism despite the rough welcome, while Sarmiento and Pablo stood back to contemplate him.

Business had obviously been kind to the engineer. A bulging purse dangled from his belt, jangling as it swung and tapped against the delicate, filigreed gold tracery of his sword hilt. His hair and beard had been groomed with vainglorious precision. His handkerchief was snow white lace and his violet doublet was an intricate, heavy looking garment, buttoned so high up his neck that he had to stretch himself, and this made him seem taller than before. Sarmiento took out his dagger and prodded an intricate sleeve roll coiling on the engineer's shoulder: "Most fine cloth, pray," mumbled the alchemist, his voice tinted with a slight waver of envy. The sight of Fernando's obvious good fortune evoked ideas of squandered possibilities.

When Fernando returned the miserable alchemist's inspection he grimaced, as if Sarmiento's rags and bitter mouth had challenged fundamentals. Pity evolved into guilt and he had to turn away, toward the man who had been with him, a stranger, who stood timidly in the doorway. The engineer, by nature considerate, realised an impropriety done and wasted no time in introducing his dazed and forlorn companion: "My new friend and good associate, Pedro de Ahedo."

It brought a slight and seemingly honest smile to the now named stranger's simple face. That was creased, but not in a bitter way. He had narrow, pale grey eyes.

Fr Pablo gravitated towards such gentleness, and held out a trembling hand to whom he hoped would be a new friend: "Most pleased to meet you," then to the engineer, with much more exuberance: "Oh, it's so nice to see you again, Fernando. And I'm oh so sorry about this rough reception, but, we have a little problem."

Fernando sniffed and perceived the gas leaking presence of the sleeping Leopoldo: "Is that your little problem?"

Sarmiento explained: "The bloated mongrel you see there, a most mephitic beast, he farts in his dreams, so it's better to keep him awake and hope he'll control himself, which he should do, for not even he can bear his own ejections when he's conscious," and began slapping *the Bear*'s bristly sea-lion face.

Fr Pablo helped the still prostrate and paralytic Rodrigo up, sitting him at a table. The one-eyed man groaned as he rose, clutching his head: "Fie, what a pox-ridden, dung-heap of a world this is!"

But this time the complaint was contested by the friar: "Have you never considered that the enormous iniquities you suffer were sent by the just anger of God?"

When they were all around the table Fernando pulled out a block of cheese and began carving while explaining himself, cheerily at first: "I told you, troth, before you had left, that we would one day meet again," then sincerely grave: "Only when you had gone did I realise what an irksome, gloomy tomb Tlaxcala was." He pulled out a loaf of bread that he yanked apart: "I worked on with those wearisome whales, Saturnino and Dionisio, trying to win countenance from them and convince their wealthy uncle to invest in a proper factory, where gold could be refined on a significant scale," chewing so that the following was muffled: "But they were such an insipid couple. No nose for enterprise. They insisted upon an absurd bargain. Petitioning a formula that they proclaimed to be in my possess," swallowing: "Some secret algorithm for a sweet potion of love," swallowing again: "Protesting most hotly, señor, that it had been left, by you, with me."

Sarmiento sniggered: "Oh aye. Because I *had* told them. I had to lie to free myself, of their baboon tongues and monkey-lust folly."

Fernando ignored the confession. Fr Pablo filled a mug with water, sipped then spoke: "But why, pray, have you come here, señor? To Xauxa?"

Fernando laughed: "Oh, I've no want for staying here!"

Sarmiento, rubbing the front of his negating head, grunted through a cynical smile: "Don't *you* worry ... It's not our intent to stay either."

"Good," continued Fernando and licked his lips: "You can come with us. Let our destiny unfold together."

Pablo clapped his hands. His own smile idiotic, his pitch high and bright: "But where are you going?"

Fernando's face opened: "Obvious, isn't it?" but, when a general landscape of raised eyebrows implied the negative: "Have you not heard?" The eyebrows remained up, heads wavering on necks: "They have uncovered quicksilver ... *argentum vivum* ... mercury, if you like. To the south of here, in Huancavelica. An entire mountain full," and he gave Sarmiento a hard stare, demanding recognition of the news.

The alchemist's red head nodded slightly before shaking again and he reached for the water jug to drain a beaker full in one gulp. Fernando maintained his stare but Sarmiento just dragged the back of his hand across his lips and turned away.

The engineer's pitch and pace rose into a more urgent area: "My intention is to apply our," and his face suddenly lit up: "Our *patio* method," and then slapped Fr Pablo 's shoulder, reminding the friar that he himself had invented the term: "There's tremendous profit to be made ... extracting gold from ore." And leaned back toward Sarmiento who looked peeved: "But don't misinterpret my intentions. I have no will to shark this idea from you, señor. I'm no cozener. Quite the contrary, in fact I've been searching for you, to ask you to join us in this enterprise, and if you want, to lead me. It's your system, yours."

Sarmiento twisted, but only to shrug his shoulders. He kept his gaze toward the table top: "No, I've other ambitions."

Low enough to deaden all excitement, until a suddenly reanimated Rodrigo blurted out a drunken: "I'll go wit' yer. I can smell a fortune, I can."

Fernando's bright face darkened. He looked to his companion Pedro Ahedo, who advanced and put an arm lightly around his shoulders.

Fr Pablo tried to brighten things again by extracting gossip from Tlaxcala: "What of Don Gabriel and his lovely wife?"

But Fernando closed his eye and hung his head, disappointment brushing against the boundary of depression: "Don Gabriel, bless his soul, passed away last year," which brought Sarmiento's head up: "He had been ill and in bed for months." The alchemist's eyes flickered. Fernando continued: "Doña Rosa has also left Tlaxcala and I have heard she's in Lima," which brought Sarmiento onto his feet and he began to pace. Fernando's gaze followed him: "She really did come from an important family it seems, for she has integrated herself in the court of the Viceroy, and has wedded his cousin."

Fr Pablo was obviously determined to renew the engineer's optimism: "This Xauxa is an absolute den of iniquity (*Rodrigo nodding emphatically*) full of dangerous temptation, just look at my poor cousin here, and his scurrilous mates (*Rodrigo and Leopoldo shocked by the sudden betrayal*) Two days solid they've been drinking (*brought smiles; interpreted as a compliment*) perhaps Huancavelica will be more salubrious."

Sarmiento was sitting at the table again, but he had been dragged far away, into his own thoughts. Memories of his ex-lover, a hot image of her nakedness ... abruptly wrenched from his consciousness by his cousin's following line of implicating argument: "We were, just this minute before you arrived, making ready to depart, to no place in particular, so we might just as well join you. A bit of serious enterprising will do us all very much good, troth."

Sarmiento kicked out under the table at the friar's shin. Pablo grimaced, but did not yell. Sarmiento stood up and, knocking over his stool, stormed out, slamming the door. Followed by the friar, his head flicking.

Outside it was cold and grey and it had started to drizzle. A llama shivered and pricked up its ears. Clucking hens were fleeing. The friar slipped on moistened clay, making his question vibrate as he fell: "What's w-w-wrong?" His palms hit the ground, stinging, but they protected his face.

A sharp whisper shot back at him through rigid lips: "Wrong? What's wrong?" his hand was rubbing the hilt of his sheathed sword: "You clerical baboon. What are you telling these people?"

The friar, carefully lifting himself. Crucifix dangling: "I'm being nice to an old friend. Nothing more."

Sarmiento advancing: "And you'd have us killed?"

"If the Portuguese and his cronies attack it'll be better to have more men with us."

Sarmiento sniffed, fresh llama shit: "But don't you see what you've done? We want to run away from the cat and you invite the mouse."

"What do you mean?"

"Can you not see it? The Portuguese's sudden arrival was no accident. He's following the mouse. The mouse with the cheese." Then, after taking a deep breath: "You see, cousin, I made sure it was well known before we left Tlaxcala that I'd left my map with Fernando."

"You what?!" Fr Pablo was fuming: "He could've been killed!"

"And the strangest thing is that the dapper quaffer is still alive," and he rubbed the rain from his bottom lip with his thumb: "How, cousin? For if this Portuguese thug thinks he has the map, he wouldn't have followed him all the way down here from Mexico. There would've been ample opportunities to relieve him of it on the way."

Fr Pablo shivered: "Are you sound?" he mumbled.

Sarmiento was oblivious: "I suppose they must've lost track of him somewhere. Or perhaps he just doesn't care. Perhaps he's just using him, pray. Using him to find us, and get his revenge by getting my balls."

The friar grabbed handfuls of Sarmiento's shirt: "But Fernando didn't know where we were!"

Sarmiento grabbed the friar's throat to silence his passion. His own low and rasping voice was sardonic: "Yet he found us ... just as the Portuguese knew he would. For he's being watched, by a spy ... this Pedro de Ahedo!"

Fr Pablo, croaking: "Ahedo? You really are not sound. How can you think? He's so shy."

"Shy!? Shifty, I'd say. Downright maleficent!"

The friar sagged: "So, you're not going to Huancavelica."

"No. And neither are you, cousin."

"But we cannot let Fernando go."

"We have to. Don't worry, they won't kill him now."

"And what are we to do?"

"The first thing is to get supplies. You stay here and keep Fernando and his sly friend occupied. In the meantime, I'll gather provisions. But don't tell them that."

"What shall I tell them?"

"You're a friar. Make up a story. Tell them that I've been vomiting and that you've put me down to rest out here in the stable, on the hay. In any case, keep them busy. I'll be back in an hour. I'll give you a signal."

"What signal?"

"I don't know yet, let me think. I'll give three raps on the front door, the second blow being the hardest," and he demonstrated on the friar's forehead: "Don't open the door yourself. Wait for one of them to do it. After that slide out the back as quickly and unnoticeably as you can. I'll be waiting with the horses and the provisions."

"But where will we go?"

"Obvious isn't it? To Lima. To meet the Viceroy."

Mad was that morning of drizzle. Sarmiento was half in sleep, half drunk. An image of some huge, flapping sail, made him shiver. He examined the vapour blown from his lungs, remembering that he was hot and still alive. He had to trudge across the square, which exposed him. The open space had turned into a slippery mud rubbish dump after the fiestas and rain and he imagined a crossbow, jiggling as he moved, trying to fix a line between the arrowhead and a point in his back. His hand shot up, wrenching his shoulder to scratch a future possibility hole between his hard, bulging horn omoplates. Figures leaned, ominously half hidden in the brown grey shadows under the awnings of the town hall. They were propped up, but not by crossbows or harquebuses, they had simple wooden poles under their armpits, simple straw brooms. Not assassins, cleaners: waiting for the spitting rain to stop.

The stalls flanking the square were dripping and abandoned. Sarmiento's head throbbed. He imagined a remnant of music. It filled his mind. Loud enough to make him shake his head. His focus was on a stable. A young lad was sitting wrapped in a white wool warm smock; his head bowed, asleep. The horses snorted when they sniffed their owner. One had a mouthful of hay, and chomped. More hay behind them rustled and moved, and a stiff figure emerged, slowly, as if some zombie rising from a grave.

It was Juan Yupanqui, his hair flecked with ubiquitous strands of straw. Bubbles of saliva popped between crooked yellow teeth in a huge parting mouth. He clambered out of the hay and advanced from the stable with a parabola drawing arm indicating to Sarmiento that he should change his intention and course and follow him. The alchemist stopped, struggling with the concept of entrapment. In the pause Juan approached. His lips curled and he hurled voice at the wavering Spaniard: "We want you to meet someone. Someone special. We've told him about you. That you read the stars. He too understands astrology."

Which made Sarmiento suddenly look up into clouds. He munched the flesh on the inside of his cheek, then looked down again: "Inca astrology?"

Juan's eyes widened, expressing ineluctability: "He wants to see you. Has something to tell, something you need to know." The drizzle stopped, symphonic timing it seemed. A sun-beam shot through a breaking fluff of cloud, instilling optimism and trust. Juan Yupanqui leaned closer and stretched himself, nearing Sarmiento's ear as he did: "This is a secret," then suddenly flicked his head away to consider the surrounds. Turning back, he was anxious: "You must swear. Swear to keep it secret." His voice was hopeless: "You won't destroy us, will you?"

Sarmiento's stomach was pinched by a sharp cramp. He nodded affirmation through a grimace. The Inca flicked his head and then turned. Sarmiento followed. Two scampering figures stumbled across their path. Drunks. Wrestling. Impotent violence. But a tied up mule shuddered when they bounced against it. It kicked its legs back and up, attacking air. Sarmiento sniffed. There was a perfumed smoke smell of burning pine resin, of baked cereals and simmering sugar sweetened chocolate. It was a fleeting pleasure, his hangover pinched his brain, twisting it from the inside, twirling it and then gnawing on it. His gut churned to accompany the torture. He had to stop and vomit.

"We will give you something for that," said Juan, thrusting a supporting limb under the alchemist's damp armpits. Then they stopped before a door: "The name of the man you are about to meet is Señor Urco … Urco Huaranca … but the Spaniards know him as Don Chepo," he said: "Your people think he is one hundred and forty years old." Then, seeing Sarmiento's eyes widen, he lowered his voice to express an exorbitant finale: "Really he is much older still."

Sarmiento blew out sceptical air: "Then we should be delicate with him," rich with a sarcasm that Juan ignored.

"Oh," he laughed, thumping on the door: "There will be no need for that. He is sounder and stronger than either of us."

The sincerity of this seemed to affect Sarmiento and the next sentence was expressed with a certain melancholy: "He must be like a king to you."

Juan's face glowed with the idea: "Yes," and he nodded: "Yes, he is."

Dry-hinges shrieked as the door scrapingly parted. It was Juan's brother, Jesús, who was pulling it. He bowed to the alchemist and made pathetically servile gestures indicating that he should enter. Sarmiento stretched his leg and disappeared inside, to be ushered down a dim passage while Juan crossed his arms and remained out.

At the end of the hall Sarmiento had to dip his head to pass into a cave like room, but bright, cheered by abundant candlelight. A pair of very short, seemingly neckless men looked bewilderedly up at the unfurling stature. Something about them made Sarmiento's heart jump. When he had taken a breath and realised they were human he grinned. Their hands, disproportionately wide for their stubby arms, were covered in a dripping grease that they had been rubbing into the skin of another tiny figure, hardly visible at all under a cloth – *And that is their ancient king* – and he squinted – *their fairy king who never was* – which inspired horripilation – *Could he really be so old?* –

Linen flapped away and a long, emaciated arm rose, slowly, to greet Sarmiento. Double joints in his fingers allowed them to bend grotesquely back. Unwrapped, his skin shone smooth and warm in the candlelight, brilliant but also grizzled flesh that was stretched tight over the skeleton. Although this betrayed an apparent absence of muscle, he was able to sit cross legged and straight backed in a loin cloth. He looked up, smiled with a taught but wrinkle free face, and nodded a greeting to accompany his wavering fingers. The massive skull of his shining bald head tapered behind him, as if he carried an egg on his long saurian neck. He tilted this up to catch the visitor's eye. His own moist gaze was obsidian black and he croaked something out of a small and toothless beak-like mouth.

I was reminded of figures I had seen etched in stone at Don Enrique's. Representations, I had been told, of ancient Egyptian kings. But if this old Inca had levitated off the floor and hovered through the roof into a waiting flying saucer, I would not have been surprised. The strangest thing was that he was human.

The midget masseurs draped another clean, blue cloth over the old man's shoulders. Meanwhile Jesús also beckoned to Sarmiento, who remained fixed in a trance in the entrance way.

"Please señor, sit down," said the young Inca, his open spatula hand indicating a brightly coloured rug. Then he clapped his hands and the little men stooped their backs and scurried away.

The alchemist gaped. His knees cracked as he himself crouched: "Does he speak Castilian?"

Jesús shook his head: "No, not a word. He hates the Spaniards," which froze Sarmiento. Jesús laughed: "But don't let that trouble you, señor. You're an initiate ... and that makes us kinsman, does it not? The soul is thicker than blood or water."

Sarmiento's stomach gurgled audibly and he remembered that Juan had promised him a palliative for his aching gut. He turned, looking sheepish. Jesús laughed. At the same time one of the little men appeared again with a bowl of simmering broth: "Ah..." sighed Sarmiento. He took it, gulped it, and sighed again.

A spurt of sound rattled from the narrow gap between the old Inca's hardly moving lips. This time Jesús translated, leaning towards their alchemist visitor: "He says he knows you."

Sarmiento ran a flicking, excited tongue over his top lip: "Then let me know how."

Jesús' eyes rolled as he absorbed his ancestral tongue to spit out Castilian: "He saw you in a dream."

Sarmiento could not resist the joke: "The poorer for him, when I dream, troth, it's of pretty girls with long waves of golden hair ... not ugly men like me."

Jesús glared at him: "He does not jest, sirrah."

Sarmiento blew an equine expression of boredom out through vibrating lips: "Then let him reveal the purport of this dream. What did I do in that nightmare of his, pray?"

"That is of no importance. The rub is that he knows you because he has dreamt you, and that is why he's going to tell you his secret." Sarmiento made a scooping gesture with his hands. But Jesús became suddenly grave: "Although, he says, he also knows that one day you will betray us ... betray all the Incas." Then his eyebrows lifted to express relief at the munificence of the next palliating idea: "But you will never betray the *secret*," that last word being hissed with a hurricane-snake assibilation.

The old man hung his head as he spoke, staring into his open, uplifted palms. Jesús wrestled with the translation, his face at times screwed up, as if trying to evacuate a difficult constipation: "The Incas considered the stars and saw, in that celestial book, their own destruction ... the destruction of our civilisation."

Sarmiento blew out more air, suspecting a political motive behind his invitation: "You've brought me here to tell me this?"

Jesús rattled faster: "But we've also seen the eventual annihilation of the universe," which was almost screamed at the final syllable: "We know when this will take place, and that is why Señor Urco is telling you this. We've been unable to save our culture ... you yourself will be instrumental in its ultimate demise ... but we must still try and preserve the universe. For that we have more time, more time to evolve, strengthen ourselves ... become gods!" Which had Sarmiento shaking his head and laughing. "Scoff not! Señor Urco knows why you are here, that you've been sent to us to go further. He knows about your map."

Sarmiento jumped: "What does he know?"

"The land you look for is already familiar to him," which had the alchemist now urgently attentive: "The great Inca emperor, Topa Inca Yopanqui, embarked on a voyage that lasted an entire year, one year on a balsa wood raft of nine long logs, strapped together with hemp. Señor Urco knows, he says, because he was there, reclined on a deck, on mats of plaited bamboo reeds. He recalls the voyage well, he says. The emperor sitting straight in the middle of the ship, in his lordship's bamboo hut, banana leaves tiling his roof. And he says, it was a terrible journey, sirrah. Unimaginable, he affirms. But eventually they reached the place that had been revealed to him in an oracle. Two great islands ... magic islands ... the islands of the sun ... residing off the coast of a huge continent, on the other side of the enormous ocean. The same isles that you seek, Spaniard. These islands are called Avachumbi and Ninachumbi. The place you Europeans call the Isles of King Solomon. Your map. He wants you to show it to him."

Sarmiento paused at first. He dragged the parchment out from its protective tube in his satchel, but with one hand, maintaining the other on the hilt of his sword. With one hand and a knee he unravelled it. Urco sighed before continuing. Through Jesús: "It's a true enough chart, but distorted. You'll not find the Terra Australis there," and rubbed a finger along the coastline: "You must sail much further west ... much further," and prodded an empty space.

Sarmiento made to rise, as if insulted, but the old man grasped his arm. The fingers were strong, he realised, they bit into the skin threatening to leave a bruise. Jesús stammered out the next part of his translation, trembling with emotion: "He says he will see you again. But after many years. And when he does, he says, you will kill him."

Sarmiento turned wrenching the clawing hand away, violently: "Ask him how he manages to keep himself so young, if he's really so old?"

The old man gurgled an answer. Jesús turned back to Sarmiento: "He says that he knew you would ask that question, but that you need not worry... you are blessed and protected by a powerful god, more powerful than the god of your king. As such you will learn the answer to all your questions in good time. There is no need to be anxious. The road to truth is so vast that one does not seem to move along or through it. One must be patient. Only with time will you realise the landscape has changed. All he will tell you now is that the secret will have to be swallowed. Swallowed with blood to change your blood. And that you will learn that secret when you reach Avachumbi and Ninachumbi. That will be the beginning of your incredible destiny." And then: "As for your other problem. That has already been resolved," and the two midget servants re-entered, carrying a wicker basket between them.

They lay this down in front of Sarmiento and opened its lid, but it was Jesús who reached into it. Sarmiento's eyes widened in horror and his throat became a spastic twitch of dry retching that pumped the still warm broth in his stomach without evacuating it. Swaying before him was a severed human head. Black hair dangled around a ruddy skin streaked with hard red-black rivulets. One open eye, bright white around a sharp brown orb with pin-prick black pupil. The other eye was missing. Sarmiento stared into the black hole that had been left and coughed. It clued him to look beyond the intrinsic horror and recognise the Portuguese soul that had once animated that dead face.

Jesús grinned: "Urco Huanca ordered the execution. He knew it would please you, señor."

Sarmiento gulped. A tear dribbled down his cheek. He was crying, out of joy.

X. Theory and Methodology

Callao, the port town of Peru. Sweltering sad. Its straight streets, roaring with commerce surf, ran hurrying seaward into jutting jetties, propped up on mussel heavy pillars. These were phallic foundations of breakwater architecture from which purple shells dangled like bunches of crusty grapes above the constantly inconstant tideline. Water against wood. A sensitive chaos sea surface slapped, as well as caressed, the timber of men's piers and vessels.

Such proximity to ocean, reduced restless humanity to pensive calm dreams and I was bombarded with sound and images from their minds. Some on board the anchored and hemp tied ships fantasised an imminently full and brilliant, heavy hull departure. To them, their triple mast ship was a rolling Golgotha that promised paradise for the enduring faithful. Some leaned against the splinters of pillars like silent, stoa philosophers, asking themselves how much gold would be needed to find perfect happiness. A full purse would bring satisfaction, a treasure spilling chest absolute contentment. But while some men smiled, others frowned.

They had their bulging purses, but a gloomy thought made them unbearably light – *Should the heavy Emperor's treasure constipate our ship's bowels? It is we who will sink with it, not the King* – And the idea of ragged, red crab claws scooping their eyes out on some kelp covered seabed made the pessimists shiver.

Yet most of them were more bored than hopeful or fearful. Too much thinking about gold had already dulled their minds and killed their spirit. These ones leaned with folded arm contempt over the ships' rails, gazing down on other members of their species whose boots clomped against boardwalk planks, or sat gloomily on pierheads. Such minds were cloudy and heavy with alcohol, miserable enough to forget about any Inca treasure dreams.

And punctuating all the thoughts was the croak of stretching ropes pulling timber. Thick fibre ties, a criss-cross of umbilical cords still attached to floating womb pregnancies that promised rebirth to both the hopeful and sullen alike. That was why they had been drawn there, gravitating to the melancholy avenue of escape. To live or die, or continue in the same miserable direction as always?

Sarmiento and Fr Pablo were between it all. Like everyone, in their own centre. Their legs dangled from a wharf, their footwear removed, stinking toes wiggling, catching the cool breeze off the cold-current sea.

A red-footed shag stretched up on a seaweed speckled pedestal, like an aquatic phoenix resurrected from a drowning.

Sarmiento watched untied ships disappear. These were slowly masked by wind pushed progress and the earth's curvature. It filled his mind with physics – *If the world were flat, would we see horizons?* – but any answer was impossible to calculate on a jetty. The sinus clearing salt sea air, so refreshing after years of dust, helped him remember the future – *I came here with a reason* – and a ghost memory of Rodolfo smiled at him, while smaller hollow boats knocked against poles. This made his soul leap and fill his throat with a lumpy anguished hope.

A modern soul, I thought, would have grieved the time he had wasted on years of aimless wandering, but Sarmiento, though Renaissance-awakened, still had a medieval lack of contempt for time. Life expectancy was much shorter than now, but each of his days unfolded more slowly than they do for us. One could say time dragged, but another interpretation would be that it lingered.

Such long lingering was even more acute in Fr Pablo's mind. He had changed. As his heart had indurated, his soft face features had dried and crusted also. His eyes were now black-bagged and shaded by drooping tired lids. Fed up of looking outward, too ashamed to look in. His mouth line tended to pull itself from the top front rather than out from the sides, expressing disgust rather than joy. Even his tonsure had been left unshaven grey. Sarmiento ran his palm across it and whined: "Clean yourself up, cousin. We'll need you to look friarly again, if we're ever going to shark anything in this town."

The friar's face became more sullen than ever: "You've tossed our rent away again with the dice. Instead of gambling you should be looking for an audience. Instead of being cutpurses in this pirate port we should be acting as gentlemen in the City of Kings."

Sarmiento looked from the wharf at the lapping water below: "We are here because the lodgings are cheap."

Pablo shook his head: "Oh, the beach we sleep on is economic enough, but you will not gain an audience with any Viceroy while you're covered in sand."

"Then pray for us."

"I stopped doing that years ago."

Sarmiento slowly shook his head: "I think I preferred you when you were a happy friar. Now you do nothing but chew bile."

"Would it have helped you in your thieving if this cross I carry still meant anything to me."

"Oh it still means things. Otherwise you wouldn't feel so guilty bearing it."

Which made the friar spit ...

And I was transported.

Into a blackness. But before my vision could adjust to it, an illumination suddenly flashed into being. A whooshing flame devouring a rushing gust of air. The flame of a torch, I realised, the light from it revealing the sweat damp, downward tilting head of its bearer.

This was orange red except for an ash grey and straggly natural tonsure and a grizzly smudge of days old bristles. His brow was creased, his nose an aquiline slide for dripping sweat. Downward tilting because he was on a stair and looking back to the friar and his alchemist cousin. He nodded to them, as if confirming a promise of something, then turned and stepped up.

The friar kept close behind him, lip up in a snarl of disgust. One arm was steadying him, the other straining with the weight of his pack and satchel. Then the torch-bearer, as if sensing the snarl, stopped on a landing and stepped back to let them pass.

"A gloomier place I could not imagine, even in the most Spartan monastery," moaned the friar.

The torchbearer mumbled back: "If you want something better you'll have to pay for it."

Sarmiento wheezed, struggling with his own pack: "But it is superb, Landlord, a perfect place. Ignore the friar. He has a good, catholic church taste for finery, but the purse of a martyr. If there's really a bed here with firm legs to hold us, we'll both be grateful for it."

"Good. There's your bed," he said, pointing into a lightless space: "And if you need a hot tub, you can 'ave it. Just a matter of asking fo'it. The charge is ..."

But before he could finish Pablo had stumbled against something unseen. He banged his shin and yelled, a sharp shriek, which was echoed by a higher pitched squeal.

The landlord blew air and thumped his beacon against the landing, a swift movement dragging oxygen to it so that the flame roared again and spat gold. Then he was lifting his legs and thumping up the stairs. The wavering flame threw flickering light and shadow against the bed.

Occupied. Naked grey breasts bounced and pitch black hair flicked. A bristly pair of buttocks tensed.

The landlord roared: "Out! You thieving loafers. Out!" and wrenched a towel from his shoulder to flick it and slap the hirsute arse.

The man whose buttocks were smarting red rolled over, his hand covering his naked sex while he spat at his assailant: "God's teeth, man! Fie upon you, you bastard!"

"Only those who pay can have a bed, sirrah!" and he slapped the towel against the man's cheek and nose while he grabbed the woman's wrist and wrenched her arm.

The friar turned his back to such immodesty while Sarmiento grinned: "She can stay if she wish. I would not kick her out of bed."

Which made the landlord laugh: "You'll be thinking yourselves lucky if you don't catch her crabs," and he started throwing the naked couple's clothes and other belongings down the well of the stairs, missiles and feet clomping as the man and woman scurried bow-legged down.

When satisfied that the free loaders had gone the landlord turned back to the new arrivals, pushing out a fat fingered hand: "The nights are paid for in advance."

Fr Pablo's facial features suddenly opened in unison, his skin paled and his fingers began to flick around his waist. But Sarmiento remained calm and pushed a finger into a leather purse under his sandy doublet. He wormed out a coin: "We'll have the bed for three nights," and the landlord nodded and hobbled briskly down to leave them in darkness, making them mere voices.

Pablo was livid: "Where did that coin come from?" Silence. "You sharked it, didn't you?"

"I found it."

"Did you find the whole purse?"

"Well, as a matter of fact."

"For the love of God, you'll be the death of us, troth."

Then I saw the room in golden morning light. There was a tiny attic window and Fr Pablo was coming from the stairs, bearing a bowl of frothy soap water on which a mirror and a knife lay crossed. His cassock, ungirdled, hung heavily off his shoulders, revealing a long neck. After coming solemnly forward he perched himself on the edge of the bed: "The landlord must've taken a liking to us. He boiled the water for me without charging any extra. Perhaps we could even get a free bath."

Pedro Sarmiento, displeased because still sleepy, leaned his arms on top of the staircase and looked coldly at the nescient smile: "Would you like me to do your tonsure for you?" he asked lazily.

"When I've finished with cheeks and chin," replied the friar and blew a gob of lather from his top lip before setting the knife to the soap on his neck. Then after clearing a clean line: "At times, when I'm with you, I feel like an Icarus whose flown too close to the sun."

A wry smile broke quietly over Sarmiento's lips: "I am no sun god, cousin. But perhaps one day I could be an old and wise Daedalus," and he pulled open the tiny window and inhaled with a grimace: "The sun is already baking the last tide's deposit of kelp. Nicely pungent."

Fr Pablo had started on his cheeks: "Preferable to the stink in here."

Which made the alchemist's head spin. He was fed up. His lips pursed and his throat gurgled as if he were about to spit something substantial: "Ah, what's wrong wit' yer...?" hurled on one breath.

Fr Pablo's pitch became a whine: "We left Xauxa for the City of the Kings," and then scratching his top lip so that the rest came out half-whistled: "And we drop into this foul port"

Sarmiento's eyes rolled, his voice rasped: "From this port, sirrah, I'll sail one day," which seemed to calm his spite. He dipped a sponge into the soapy water and began to lather his cousin's scalp: "As for why we're here. 'Tis a much cheaper place and, until I obtain an audience, we'll have to watch each miserable centimo."

Then he drew out his dagger and shaved circles around the priest's pate, leaving a creamy dob in the centre which looked ridiculous enough to inspire a laugh.

The friar pushed him away and reached for his pack, to pull out a towel which he ran across his face and head. But as he unfurled the grubby rag a pair of tiny objects hurled out and hit the wall with a clunk.

Sarmiento scratched his arse then leaned down to retrieve one of the fragments. A small and jagged shard of rock. The friar also stretched himself in order to reach the other piece, which was similar.

"What're these then?" chirped the alchemist.

"I picked them up years ago," and lifted it, as if examining it for the first time: "When we were riding through Yucatan," and he twisted the face of it to catch the streaming sunlight: "I thought it curious. It has some pagan scrawl," then, as if recalling an idea that had been formulated years ago and forgotten: "Which shows that the natives here had some sort of writing, at least at one time."

And he handed his piece to Sarmiento who slotted them both together: "But cousin, this is a most interesting find, marry. And you've kept this as a secret from me all this time."

"I did not think it could be of any interest to you, other than a magical one."

"Magic no. But as science, it's most curious."

– Science and magic – thought the friar – One day the two will be confused and we'll need an apocalypse to save us – An idea which drew his head drooping down, but only to quickly flick up again.

Sarmiento, meanwhile, was drowning in the broken mystery in his hand. Imagining an occult sense, it opened gates in his mind, dropping him into a choking well of sublimation. Sensing his cousin's heart stopping rapture Fr Pablo inserted pragmatism: "It was one of several stones. I gave the other to Father Bartolome de las Casas. I thought it would help him argue the natives' cause."

Sarmiento thrust the friar's own rocks under his nose, as if revealing them to him: "Does this calligraphy not resemble the alphabet of the Greeks?" and his tongue pushed against the interior of his cheek, making his mouth seem egg-possessed.

"If you want it to," and then with surprising cruelty: "It could resemble anything," then pushing his own tongue, but under his top lip, which he flicked, so that the rest was expressed on a slapping sound: "They seem as demon images to me."

Sarmiento's throat gurgled with wet disgust: "Your good friend Father Bartolome would not be pleased with that conclusion."

Pablo was full of a back-straightening conviction-strength: "And it would not be the first time the great defender had been wrong."

Which made the alchemist's eyes gleam. The show of strength was promising. His head tilted down enough to be considered an expression of submission, emphasised by a full circle return interrogative: "So, do you think it resembles Greek?"

A circumnavigation which exhausted the friar, made him tired-fierce: "Resembles, yes. And it resembles Chinese!"

Which in turn animated the alchemist: "No, Pablo, Greek! Greek!"

Greek. Sarmiento wanted it to be Greek. He had a theory. Later explained over a lunch of pickled whitebait, bread and water. They were at the wharf again. Cloudy again. Legs dangling again. Fish, much larger than the minnows they were eating, darted; green, brown shadows just under the surface. It made Pablo dream of cod fillets.

Sarmiento however, had his mind fixed to sand sea bottom depths: "Atlantis, Pablo, have you not heard of it?"

Which drew a guffaw: "Do you think the only knowledge possessed by friars is that what's in the Bible?" and when the alchemist did not answer: "I doubt the existence of such a place though, if that be what you're asking. I think it no more real than Zeus or Poseidon were."

But this did not dampen Sarmiento's enthusiasm: "If Socrates had lived to Christian times he would have been sanctified. As would Plato. I think the story of the sea-drowned continent is as feasible as Noah's ark. Or would you like to tell me now that there was no flood?"

"All right," sighed the friar: "Let us assume then that Atlantis was destroyed in the deluge, but there is no trace of it now. Until we can make a machine that will transport us through the dimension of fish, we will never know."

Inspiring a protesting smile: "Oh, but you are wrong cousin. There are traces. The very stone that you found in Yucatan has helped me fit the final piece of this puzzle."

"Then please tell me, I'm all ears."

Sarmiento stopped eating. Theory became sufficiently nourishing: "It cannot only be said where it was. It can be described exactly."

The other preferred to chew on crusts: "Well, let us start with where it was, shall we?"

Sarmiento actually rubbed his hands as if preparing to lift a weight: "Plato tells us that his account was derived from the venerable Solon, and that he received his information from an Egyptian friar at Delta."

"Yes, I know that," and he licked a grey slither of skin from a tooth.

"According to that account Atlantis was larger than Asia and Africa together," if he had had gills he probably would have done better, but because he hadn't he was forced to gasp: "The eastern end was just beyond the Pillars of Hercules which is near Gibraltar, and from my calculations I would put the eastern extreme of Atlantis within two leagues of the mouth of the Gibraltar Strait," leaving him on the verge of a cough, which he resisted by breathing through the nose: "And in front of the Gibraltar Rock was a port with a narrow entrance." Then he changed his tack and pulled a notebook and a piece of charcoal out of his satchel. To give visual substance to words he drew what looked like a turtle head: "Spain," he explained when his cousin's face screwed into perplexity, and scratching a teardrop under the turtle's beak: "Gibraltar," and then another line running down from it: "Africa." Then millimetres close to the African line he dragged another one running up again: "The coast of the island then turned north, close to the coast, and was joined to the Island of Cadíz," and he slammed the charcoal into the page, forming a thick black dot: "I've seen evidence of this with my own eyes." Leaning back, his voice drooping into a low-deep proclamation: "More than a league out at sea from Cadíz, under the water, the remains of very large edifices, constructed from a cement which must be almost imperishable."

Fr Pablo swallowed hard and shook his head. His own tone raised and jocular: "This is all very interesting, cousin, but what has it to do with the rock I found in Yucatan?"

Sarmiento returned to his sketch and the line that had run into the black spot he called the Island of Cadíz, dragging it up and around. A big circle: "Well, as Plato said," he explained: "Atlantis was bigger than Asia and Africa," and made a sweeping gesture across the page: "Which means it would be at least two thousand three hundred leagues from East to West," then sweeping his hand around in a wide circle, the twisting force of which seemed to pull the pitch of his voice up with it: "Seven thousand one hundred leagues around its coast!"

Which crashed into a wall of cynicism: "You've made these calculations yourself?"

"I have," but this just drew an unfriarly, wry smile from Pablo. Sarmiento gritted his teeth and continued reinforcing the charcoal lines with a pointing finger: "South from Gibraltar the continent ran close to Africa and included the Canary Islands," then thumped the boardwalk wood on which they sat, imaging it were land: "These Western Indies' lands that we've been wandering over these long years past," and paused to lick his lips, as if about to bite meat: "Were once united to the antediluvian-Atlantis ... and the people here are the descendants of European colonists," screwing up his face because he was unsure that he had expressed himself coherently.

Fr Pablo attacked the obvious weakness with a dry: "But if these Americas were a part of the continent of Atlantis then the people here should be regarded as ... as survivors of Atlantis."

However, Sarmiento was shaking his head, trying to re-establish his confused drift and dropping his voice to establish significance again: "According to these people's own stories of creation there was a great flood, caused by the creator. The same flood that Noah survived," and his eyebrows lifted as he began to rub the eastern half of the Atlantis coast off his map: "The same that sank Atlantis," when he began again he was excitedly urgent: "And this flood, according to the Incas, killed all life in their known world, a world which was later re-populated."

"Repopulated? By who?" with the jumping pitch of incomprehension.

"By Europeans!"

"The Incas say their ancestors were Europeans?"

"No, they say their god, Viracocha, created them. But I believe it was Ulysses himself who came here. That's why your stone has Greek inscribed on it!"

And the circle had curved right around once more, this time on a far more outstretched circumference. Too far, Pablo could not accept the revelation: "It's not exactly Greek," he pointed out.

Sarmiento nodded slowly: "Not exactly. But it's evolved from Greek, that is most clear."

"Derived from Ulysses' pen, that's not so clear."

Sarmiento was drawing with the charcoal stick again. Filling in the east coast of North and South America: "According to Plato the mountains of Atlantis were in the west running from north to south," and he began scribbling a series of sharp, upside-down ticks: "And the highest peaks were in the south. Mountains exceeding in extent and height and beauty any that existed in Plato's world. Troth man, can you not see it!?" and he jabbed a pair of taught fingers into the page: "He was talking about the Andes!"

"But what's this to do with Ulysses?"

Sarmiento sighed and crossed his arms while he chewed the inside of his cheek: "Have you read Dante?"

"Dante?"

An interrogative that infuriated the alchemist. He began waving his arms and showed his yellow teeth: "Dante ... Dante Alighieri ... The Inferno ... Purgatorio...???"

"Yes, yes. I know who Dante is."

"Have you read him?"

"Yes!"

"And do you not remember what he said of Ulysses?"

"Hardly, other than he was in Hell ... being roasted."

"Well, Ulysses spoke to Dante and told him the story of the last years of his life," and he went back to the page to add the Mediterranean Sea to his map, with the boot of Italy and a squiggle which was supposed to be Greece: "After his return he grew tired of his homeland, Ithaca," and made a black dot as he had in Cadíz where he supposed Ithaca must have been: "He left his wife Penelope, and sailed off again in a simple ship with a group of friends," and he pulled the charcoal to reveal Ulysses' path: "They went beyond the Pillars of Hercules to a world which has no inhabitants. To these Americas, cousin!" thumping the page with his fist this time.

"Dante wrote that?"

"Yes!"

"That he went to the Americas?"

"No ... of course not ... but ..."

"Well let me tell you that I do remember something about Dante's Ulysses. He was burning in Hell because he was guilty of *prostituto nostrae virtutis rationalis* ... the sin of intellectual promiscuity ... for using his wits and cunning to persuade other good men to commit foolishness ... or worse, follow him to the end of the earth where they were swallowed up. That is the lesson that Dante wanted to impart, Pedro. Not to instil such vain notions that Ulysses discovered the Americas. I think you'd do well to read Dante again, from a more Christian perspective."

* * *

And it was as if the young priest sucked me into his black throat and spat me out into my own time. I came back gasping with Don Enrique and Vicente standing over me with very concerned looks. Vicente suggested we get some air. There was still enough daylight for a walk but Don Enrique declined, he hated the cold, and Estrella had still not come back, so Vicente and I walked out alone together.

We trudged up the hill across snow, Vicente sucking his cigarette: "A terrible vice. Devouring my lungs," he coughed: "But it takes/so much/effort/to stop/I think myself/incapable."

He threw a little cone at a squirrel which leapt onto a trunk and rose in a swift spiral. The violence of the act made me moralistic: "If the squirrel is ... was ... had been hit?"

But he shrugged this off, reached out and dragged me toward him. His hand, sticky with resin, brushed across my cheek as he wrapped his arm around my shoulder. The thick lenses of his glasses over his bulging frog's eyes were moist. He was panting. A strong scent of ash on a vaporous breath blew across my face: "Estrella/doesn't like me/does she?"

"What?"

"We could say/that/she hates me."

"No..." I lied.

"And/it's obvious/that you/love her."

"Yes."

He shook his head and hurled away another pine-cone down the hill: "If/you knew/the danger."

"Danger?"

"There is so much/you don't/know."

But he soon made sure that I did. Swiftly and straight to the point he told me that he knew of the existence of photographs in Dr de Coca's office at the Academy. Photos that he had not actually seen, but he had heard from someone who had that they were incriminating. Finally, he thrust the knife all the way in, so to speak; blubbering through a cold, blushing pink face that the photographs were, *pornographic*. After which he released me and slipped away into the pines.

I suppose the idea should have revolted me: that was why he had told me, wasn't it? But instead I actually began to try and imagine what kind of things incriminating pornographic photos would have depicted. I tried, got nowhere. I could not imagine Estrella posing for de Coca. Impossible, I told myself. Unless, he had drugged her. And I received the horrible image, of Estrella, glassy eyed from some barbiturate, staring into a distant point in her subconscious, while a grunting de Coca ...

But before I could imagine anymore I was suddenly swept away, to my other world ...

Sarmiento and his cousin were in a difficult spot, between trees. I had to fall down through branches to join them.

Three horses were tied up. These were pulling fetters, sweating from the exertion with foam on their flanks.

Pedro Sarmiento was agitated, Fr Pablo nervous: "This is too dangerous. We shouldn't."

Sarmiento rubbed his thigh: "Because of the danger?"

Pablo's bottom lip shivered: "Because of the spiritual danger. That's the only real danger there is."

"You will not be damned for tethering horses, cousin. Not even the cruel Hebrew God would be so unjust."

"My presence here makes me as culpable as you yourself. Because I'm a friar."

"And your damnation will be worse, because you're a friar. But they are fine friarly sentiments cousin. Why are you so certain that I'll a sinner now be? I told you, it'll be but a short interview."

"The interview will be short, but the rest will be long. I know you."

Sarmiento slapped his cousin's back: "Don't worry, sirrah. Just keep your eyes directed through that gap in the trees. Study the road down there. If you see someone come, then you know the signal ... *hoot-hoot* ... like a Galician owl."

And he turned to push through the dense copse behind them to open a difficult passage and rise up the wooded slope. The trees and bushes resisted, thorns slapped his cheek. At the hill top was a rock. A gnarled, poking breadstick with thick tufts of spiky grass to adorn it. He reached out, touched the stone, and leaned on it as he moved around it. The area was encircled by trees and he didn't see her, in fact he almost tripped over her.

Doña Rosa was absolutely naked and stretched out on the red, silk cloth of the dress she had unburdened herself of. The reverse side was pink. Her milk white skin looked ever so soft and her wavy brown hair was severely dark and even rough against the skin. But the general impression was that she seemed younger than the last time I had seen her. Her head rested on an arm, the arm resting on a boulder. Her armpit was shaven smooth. The other arm ran down like a white serpent to her lap.

Sarmiento ripped a leafy twig from the rock and tickled her armpit. She breathed in deeply through her nose. With the inhalation came a smile, but she did not open her eyes. Sarmiento sucked his teeth: "Do you not want to look at me?"

She smirked: "If it were not you, I would be terribly disappointed."

"If it were not me you'd be raped, milady."

"Which is why I keep closed my eyes. In my mind you must be you."

"In *my* mind I must be me."

"Then that's good. And you may kiss me," and she leaned in the direction his voice came from.

He crouched over her and began untying his shirt: "You are most

309

forward today, milady."

"And you, señor."

"I still have my trousers on."

"Then you are a damned fool, sirrah."

"You speak like a whore."

"I speak like a man."

"A man who knows what he wants."

Which inspired her to open her eyes: "All men know what they want, or at least pretend to. They want that a wife won't know what she wants, but that their whores will."

"Are you my whore?" and he leaned to kiss her.

"Yes," and she slipped his trousers down, and began to stretch his already firm cock. Sarmiento began to tighten his stomach, bending his back and thrusting his buttocks, forward, back, rubbing his sex through her fist. She gasped: "I am your whore, your filthy slut, sirrah" and then clasped his balls and squeezed them tight as she spat out the last clause: "And the mother of your son."

Which drew a yell from him, and he fell back.

Afterwards she ran her long brown hair across his face: "We are Gemini-souls, are we not?"

"Tell me of it."

"Our bond is our common hate, unnatural hate, for both of us despise our family. I, for the lack of love they offered me, for their treason ... you, for their betrayal of your sister."

"And for other things."

"Oh yes, other things. What crueller collective than the family?"

"Yet despite this common hate we are really very distant. This need of yours, so common, which is to engender. It's the lust of very mortal beings, an instinct-whim for perpetuity. But mine is a Titan's soul. I yearn for eternity."

"The vainest desire of all. Don't let your alchemy blind you. No man lives for eternity. Not even gods, despite their boasts, are really eternal. Men will always look for newer deities to satisfy their own forever changing needs."

"So, you don't believe in my quest?"

"The idea of it charms me, and I can think of no better purpose for your life. But do not fill your spirit with your ambition before that ambition has been fulfilled. To call yourself a Titan and belittle all others is a vainglorious thing until you are a Titan. It'll only make men bitter toward you ... men ... and women. As for your lack of engendering will, you should have considered more on that before you filled my belly with your seed."

Then they both lay, face up and panting. Staring at the sky. Silent ...

Until I realised it was me that was lying down and staring up. Something cold bit my cheek. Ear nipping snow. My back was wet and starting to grow numb. I struggled up. My mind lurched and I remembered Vicente's accusation against Estrella again. But as my consciousness moved into one space the universe span and I was dragged into another

Pedro Sarmiento was shoving his cousin's back with his boot. The friar stirred, he had been snoozing under a tree. Stirred, but not startled. He turned to look groggily up, to see Pedro advancing to his horse and lifting his foot into a rusty iron stirrup.

"That was quick," he murmured.

The saddle sighed under Sarmiento's arse: "Long enough to give you time to snore," he clutched reins: "I thought you were my sentinel."

Fr Pablo sat up and rubbed his face with his hands: "Did I fall asleep, pray?"

Sarmiento had to yank hard to keep his horse steady. His reply was strained and dry: "Fall ... I doubt it ... I'd imagine you more likely laying yourself down and rolling up comfortable on a nice patch of soft leaves."

The friar stretched himself and yawned: "You should have let me sleep. It's much better and softer here than that slab we sleep on in Callao."

"Slept on, cousin. We're not going back there. We are heading forward. For the City of the Kings."

Fr Pablo clapped his hands and laughed: "Ah, you have won your audience, troth!"

"If you move your arse. I'll have it when we get there, yes."

The friar's ignorant smile returned as he brushed dry but sticking leaves from his cassock: "And how is Doña Rosa?"

Sarmiento's mount's head flicked back, baring yellow teeth. The rider's voice rasped: "You should ask her that yourself," becoming sandpaper rough: "At her confession."

*   *   *

My leg stretched. A step. I was hallucinating as I walked. My space was still outside, but the world of my vision became interior. A room … It was well swept and well lit, there were windows with lead frames and glass in them.

Fr Pablo's skin was washed pink. This poked from a new and unfrayed smock. He was hunched over a solid table, scratching a quill to describe their new home, that Lima that they called the City of the Kings. He sketched its buildings, mainly churches and convents; its people, the faithful. But that was a nauseatingly optimistic scribble, most unreal.

A door facing the friar was suddenly flung open, crashing against the wall and making the window panes shudder and rattle. A hand caught the door on the rebound, slamming it back shut. It was Sarmiento. He was drunken and wobbling wild with hair sticking up. He crossed the room and slumped into a chair. Blood was on his white shirt.

Fr Pablo's heart raced, his eyes wide open: "What happened?"

Sarmiento, examined his bloodied shirt: "It was a nose bleed."

"Nose bleed?" then the tonsured head shook: "No. I mean what happened with the Viceroy?" and his soft face opened wide.

Sarmiento sniffed, then sighed: "What do you think?" an angry groan: "The world is the same, everyone the same. Here, New Spain, Old Spain … what difference does it make? No vision, no one … nowhere!"

The friar's eyes bulged even more: "But did he see you?"

The reply came loud: "Yes, of course he saw me," then softer, but rattling quick: "He fornicates with my lover doesn't he?"

Pablo gulped: "I beg your pardon."

The rattle turned into a hiss: "He's dipping his wick, isn't he?"

The friar slumped back down again in his chair: "You mean Doña Rosa?" the obvious affirmative answer was not given but the friar continued with what he would have preferred to have remained ignorant of: "With the Viceroy?" then the morality: "But she's married to his cousin."

Sarmiento prodded his nostril to see if all the blood had properly dried:

"Her husband is a busy man, troth," then adding his own morality: "And *she* needs constant attention."

Pablo hung his head to think and try and grasp the full meaning of what he was being told. Then, looking up again: "So the Viceroy didn't like your plan."

Sarmiento refused to catch his eye: "Like it. What's there for a man like him to like? He can't see beyond his own prick!" getting up to pace: "His job is to govern Peru, he said, and we have some pressing problems at the moment, he moaned," and lifting his arms: "I fear the colony is on the brink of rebellion," then dropping his hands dramatically at the end of the phrase: "Blasted *curacas*."

"*Curacas*?" and the tonsured head flicked.

Sarmiento slumped on to another chair at the table. His voice became slow: "The old Inca chiefs ... they want more rights."

"And what did you tell him?"

"The truth of course," and the pace picked up again: "I told him that I thought the Incas were restless for good cause and that he should appoint native judges ... after all the Incas did very well at administrating things before we arrived."

"And what did he say to that?"

"He said it was interesting advice and that he would think about it. Then he asked me if I knew it through occult means."

The friar shook his head: "Why did he ask you that?"

Sarmiento's tongue flicked lizard like across his upper lip: "Because Doña Rosa had duped him into believing that I was some great astrologer."

"So what did you tell him?"

He laughed: "I lied of course. I told him that I had foreseen a dark future unless drastic measures were taken."

"And what did he say to that?"

"He offered me the post of the court astrologer. Insisted that I could not deny the position."

Which drew a tremendous clap: "So, you're in the court. You will have to succeed," but realising that Sarmiento's spirits had not picked up at all: "Why are you so angry?"

"I don't give a damn about the court," which came out through gritted teeth: "I want to sail!"

Pedro Sarmiento's mind was full of images, of Doña Rosa, who was seated in the palace next to the Viceroy. In her red dress, a hairy hand clasping hers – *Can I possibly love this slut?* – The Viceroy's lascivious grin – *a sweeping blade would quell that smirk* – He ran a red ribbon across his palm, which was a bitter reminder – *Love me, she said, and she killed her husband for me, but for what?... so that she could marry this other turkeycock* – Her second husband ... Rich and violent – *She married him and invited me and her husband's cousin to her bed ... yet she says she loves me. Can a slut love one man?! ... And if a man were to love her, he would have to be a fool, so I will not love her ... Love died years ago; with Magda; with María Dolores ... Now there is only need ... And I need to leave ... To have my boat –*

* * *

Estrella did not get back to San Lorenzo until after supper. I was angry with her and revealed Vicente's accusation about the photos. Her cheeks reddened and she hung her head. I caught a glimpse of her mind. There was a sense of excitement.

Estrella looked up at me and saw that I had seen her thoughts. She slapped me, accusing me of violating her most personal intimacy. I blabbered my own apology. I had not purposefully looked into her mind, the image had been flung at me. I was sorry, I said, over and over again. I did not want to interrogate her, but then came another accusing question: "Have drugs been experimented with by you and Inma. I mean, not just hash, but hard drugs?"

"What are you insinuating?"

"Nothing. It is being asked if you took drugs."

"Yes, sometimes."

"And how were they obtained?"

"From Tomás."

"And they were purchased by him from Vicente, right?"

"Yes."

"Who got them from Dr de Coca."

"Perhaps. I've really got no idea. Inma got the drugs."

"But that's why Vicente wasn't wanted around here, because of what is known by him, what has been seen. You knew what was going to be revealed to me, didn't you?"

But she was furious: "Did I? You tell me. It seems you've got it all worked out," then an excited, infuriated burst: "But if you really want to learn something interesting, why don't you ask me where I was today? You know I didn't spend the whole day watering the plants. So, who was I with?"

XI. Fortunes Change

(a) the secret

Who was she with? I didn't care. Jealousy is pathetic. I watched her as she carefully set up the camera for the next session. I watched from my chair, feeling onerous and inferior. She was so much better than I. Intellectually. Morally. Physically. I could not imagine a more complete person. What right had I to judge and accuse? I was lucky to have her attention at all, never mind her affection, perhaps even her *love*. She was a Venus who had deigned to smile on this Vulcan cripple, and for that reason I was blessed. That was enough ...

*　　*　　*

Sarmiento was gazing over papers. Beside him was the book I recognised to have been taken from the hermit Canches' house. He pondered this while scratching his own writings, or creating and comparing astrological charts. It was obvious that the patterns emerging in front of him enthralled.

A man was with him. He had a wide and fleshy face bordered by a ring of white wavy hair, a long at the chin beard resting on an equally white ruff, and a moustache, almost imperceptible because hidden by a bulging red nose.

I remembered it because I had been expecting it. It was the gaping, white dead face I had seen on that nightmarish flight so long ago: the Viceroy, the Count of Nieva, Don Diego Lopez de Zuñiga y Velasco.

He ripped open and chewed figs pulled from a silver bowl, his bright and happy eyes peering over Sarmiento's shoulder as he dropped four ringed and trembling fingers on the alchemist's collarbone. Then he inclined his head towards Sarmiento's ear, and whispered: "Tell me astrologer ... What do you think of sin?"

Sarmiento swallowed, but hardly paused from his work on the chart. His reply was non-committal: "Whatever the Pope tells me to think."

The Viceroy scratched the interior of his nostril and gurgled: "Aye, pray, what the Pope tells you. But are you a sinner?"

"Is there anyone who is not?"

Which set the Viceroy moving, hobbling from arthritis and gout: "Most certainly not, which is why I ask. We are all Catholics here, and sinners," and his hand started to wave around in the air: "Yet *you* look into God's plan," and he clutched his count's medal as if it were a crucifix: "If He dreams that we'll be dominated by the yearnings of the flesh, as your chart describes, what can one do to save oneself?" and paused to rip out seedy fruit with the few good teeth he had left.

Sarmiento lifted his own teeth over his upper lip. His answer came with its release: "A friar would say *pray, confess.*"

The Viceroy skewered another distant fig with his dagger: "But you're not a friar."

"A Viceroy should be a good Catholic."

"Oh, aye, and he is. But, as you see here," pushing a shaky finger onto the chart: "Scorpio rules my lust," then through a smile: "Would it not be unnatural for me to resist that?"

"But?"

"I am old..." and his eye sparkled brighter: "That's what you're thinking, isn't it? That the Viceroy is too decrepit to have a working cock. But, let me tell you, this bull has a good, thick tail between his legs and while his back is still strong enough to push he'll use it when'ere he can, marry."

Which made Sarmiento put his writing cane down, then turned to the Viceroy and smiled: "Destiny is written, but God gave us the chance to change even what is written."

"And the flesh?"

"It was created by God. It should therefore be adored, should it not?"

The ringed-fingers dropped on Sarmiento's shoulder again: "I like you better than the friars."

The alchemist looked up and smiled. False ingenuousness: "Thank you, your Excellency."

Then the Viceroy was hobbling again, fondling the gold on his fingers: "Doña Rosa told me that the rings you bear give you power." Sarmiento shrugged a non-committal reply. The Viceroy persisted: "I would like to see how they function." Sarmiento remained silent, breathing deeply. The Viceroy twisted the end of his moustache: "Your friend, my cousin's wife, she is a marvellous woman, delicious. Of course our position makes it more than difficult to pursue such an affair, one would say nigh on impossible, wouldn't one?" An image of the Viceroy clutching Doña Rosa's hand flashed – *But now he says that they aren't lovers* – then – *Not yet* – he shuddered – *Perhaps it would be in my interest to quell my jealousy and help the brock* – The Viceroy rubbed his hands: "Or perhaps impossible is too strong a term. Miracles have been performed before," and then the crux of the matter: "What help, I ask myself, could an astrologer offer?" and pushed against Sarmiento's chair to spin it around, as if trying to demonstrate virility. It scraped a little and left the old man panting.

The pathetic attempt shocked Pedro. For a moment he looked askance, but then looked up at the Viceroy and smiled: "Give me a week, your excellency, and you'll have your answer."

*   *   *

Afterwards I went to Estrella to apologise. In return she gave me the explanation for her absence. That she had gone back to Madrid, but that when she arrived she found a message from Francisco Arizmendi that had been slipped under the door. My eyes must have rolled or something because she slapped my cheek: "Are you reading my mind again?"

I shook my head and burbled a negation. Then: "What was contained in that message?"

She sighed: "He asked me to call him. He said he had something important to show me. We arranged to have lunch together. He had a little photo album with him. Pictures of Inma, him and I.

"He told me that he had gone to Inma's flat. The landlord had been in touch with him. Someone had to either pay Inma's rent or collect her things. Francisco decided that the best option would be to move her stuff into his own flat. But first he went there to talk it over with the landlord and try to convince him to wait another month. However, when he arrived at the building he saw someone familiar leaving." Then she stared at me, as if expecting me to suggest who. She only finally volunteered the information when I shook my head: "My brother, José María," and lifted an eye-brow indicating the seriousness of the revelation: "He came out of the main door of the building with a shoebox and a book under one arm, and a roll of paper under the other.

"My brother didn't see Frank, he was too wrapped up in his own sinister meditation, or at least that's what Francisco assumed. He had a strong hunch that José was coming out of Inma's flat. He got a good look at the book and it was very similar to Inma's diary. Also the shoebox was from Inma's favourite shop. He told me he even thought about stopping José María in the street, but by the time he'd decided my brother was well down the road.

"Anyway, at first he thought José must have been up to see Inma, that she was back, and that she had given him those things. But at the entrance he saw the porter. He asked about Inma, and the porter replied that as far as he knew there was no news. Then he asked if he'd seen a man leave the building and the porter insisted that he hadn't. This implied, Francisco deduced, that José had sneaked out.

"When he entered he could smell traces of cigarette smoke. Someone had been there all right. He did not think that José had been stealing, I had told him lots of foul stories, but he couldn't believe that a brother of mine would be a thief. Nevertheless, after thinking about it, if the book under his arm had been Inma's, then it had been taken ... although he still did not suspect anything insidious, and assumed that José had been picking it up for me. He even assumed that the shoebox must have contained a pair of Inma's boots that I had probably asked José to fetch. As if I would ask for such a thing?

"In any case, he checked Inma's jewel box. She had some diamond jewellery that was worth quite a bit, and that was still there, so he assumed from this that nothing was missing. But at the same time he was sure, instinct told him, that something had."

"Something which can ... could be carried in a shoe-box."

"Precisely ... but not her diamonds. What kind of thief would ignore diamonds? Frank didn't realise what had really gone until a few days later. He was looking at photos of Inma at home, and he noticed that in almost every photo Inma was wearing jewellery that always bore the same design, the Greek letter Omega. In fact, there had been a poster bearing a huge Omega over her bed. So he went back. The poster had been removed."

"And there had been a roll of paper carried under your brother's arm."

"Exactly. Then he looked in her jewel box again. Diamonds, pearls, gold ... but ... nothing bearing the Omega sign."

"Yet it can ... could have been taken with her when she left."

"It could have, but Inma didn't pack anything remember, because all her suitcases were left behind. If she had taken her Omega jewellery she would have had to have grabbed a handful of them and thrown them in her handbag. Illogical. And why take the poster?"

"But, likewise, why should it be taken by José?"

"We also remembered that her notebook had gone too... under José María's arm. He was clearing away incriminating information, and Omega is a tell-tale sign," which was left to hang for several seconds on a pair of arching eyebrows. When these lowered so did her tone: "Francisco then showed me a page of photos he had of us all which had been taken some time when we went on a fishing and hunting trip. There had been a photo of the *boys* with their prey. José María was in the foreground with three hares and his shotgun. Frank brought out a magnifying glass and indicated the gun. The same one that José said Inma had been asking for, and had disappeared. And in the photo, quite clearly visible through the glass, engraved on the butt, was ..." and she licked her lips, leaving me to round off the obvious deduction. This seemingly irrefutable clue wet her eyes and she hung her head to mask any seepage, but continued, through sniffles: "Afterwards Frank brought out an Academy newsletter. There was a picture of Dr de Coca sitting in a high, square-backed armchair. In each corner of the back of the chair was Omega, engraved in gold." She threw her head back again and flicked her fringe.

Such problems seemed impossible for me to fathom. I started to stutter again: "B-b-but what has been p-proven? Has any law been established to prosecute someone collecting trivia once collected by a dead person?"

"No, but it points in a direction. Francisco is convinced that Inma was killed, and he's determined to find out why."

"Killed? And you?"

"I don't know," a heart-broken murmur: "I don't know if I want to know," dissipating into a whisper: "If it's better not to know."

* * *

When we told Don Enrique Villeplein about Francisco Arizmendi's story, he put a podgy hand over his lips and became thoughtful: "Perhaps Vicente knows something about this?"

Estrella shook her head disparagingly: "Maybe, but even if he does, you don't expect him to tell us, do you?"

I was nervous: "It is not still assumed that we're being spied on, is it?"

She was blunt: "Yes."

My reaction, ingenuous: "Then why were we told about the manuscript?"

"Because it's a lure. De Coca wants to do a deal with you, so he sends Vicente to reveal his part of the bargain. He knows how badly we would want to see such a manuscript."

Then Don Enrique came out of his meditation: "Very well ... If Vicente's a trap, let's use the trap to catch the hunter. Let's find out what Vicente really knows about Dr Hilario de Coca."

Estrella shook her head again: "I think you're underestimating Vicente. He's no fool. Why do you think he would suddenly just tell us everything we want to know about de Coca?"

"Because we'll give him no choice. We'll hypnotise him!"

But there was one drawback, one cannot be hypnotised against one's will. We had to seduce Vicente into the trap.

We began another session. Vicente started coughing as he always does. We were expecting it. I complained that I could not concentrate and Vicente apologised and made his typical affirmation that he really wanted to give up the foul habit. At this moment Don Enrique insisted that he could help. Hypno-therapy was a proven method of curing bad habits.

Before I realised what was happening Vicente was sitting in my chair and Don Enrique had his finger up in front of his nose telling him to close his eyes: "You will tell us what you know about Omega."

"It is/the last letter/of/the Greek alphabet..."

"You will open a door ... the door to Doctor de Coca's office ... You will see de Coca inside," and then: "What is Omega?"

"Doctor/de Coca/can tell you better/than me."

"You will ask Doctor de Coca."

"He says/it is not/important."

A cul-de-sac.

Estrella made a proposal: "Ask him about the manuscript."

"You will ask Doctor de Coca to show you Fr Pablo's manuscript."

"That manuscript is/a lie ... It does not exist."

Estrella: "I told you!"

Don Enrique waved his arms to settle her, while he droned on: "Ask Doctor de Coca what he wants from Valentín."

"It is about/Omega,"

"What about Omega?"

"I don't know/anything/about that."

Estrella: "Great!"

"Why is Doctor de Coca interested in Sarmiento de Gamboa?"

"He is interested/in/his alchemy ..."

"In his alchemy?"

"In his/discovery."

"Is it so important?"

"Yes."

"Why?"

"Because of/Omega."

"Who else thinks it's important?"

"General/Franco."

"General Franco? Why?"

"Don Enrique/knows." Which made the hypnotist silent.

Estrella threw the next question: "What does Don Enrique know?"

"He knows how/to make/gold ... He makes gold/for/ Franco ..."

Which left us speechless. Don Enrique looked sheepish, a childish smile: "I think there is something that you should see ..."

(b) the secret internal fire

Vicente finally left us and then Christmas was coming and Estrella also left to return to her family home in Galicia. Of course she never invited me there again, she knew I would not have gone anyway.

José María came to pick her up in his car. He was as bigoted and irreverently jovial as ever. And as bitter; making sly remarks and eventually erupting into a sermon about our living together and sponging off poor old Enrique's hospitality to indulge in our own sinful debauch.

I was going to accuse him there of our suspicions of his membership to the sect and his role in Inma's disappearance, but Estrella must have sensed it and hushed me. She was forlorn when she left, knowing she would have to endure an ear bashing the whole way from the man who, though her brother, was suspected of having murdered her best friend.

Don Enrique's personality changed when we were alone. He became more serious and sober, even dressed more reservedly. He insisted again that there was something he needed to show me. A factory, he said, in Toledo.

We were driven down on Christmas Eve, to a steel and concrete construction, sprouting ugly and absurd amidst a field of low, leafless vines, smattered with olive and cork trees in the middle of the flat and freezing *La Mancha* plain.

"My little secret," murmured Don Enrique, though that statement was either ironic or ridiculous for the building was neither small nor clandestine. Spewing billowing clouds of foul smoke from its three tall chimneys it could not have possibly gone unnoticed.

Stepping out of the car we were blasted by the freezing air and even under our long woollen overcoats we shivered. The heat in the factory was, at first, a nice contrast, but it soon became an uncomfortable inferno. The hot, dry air rasped my throat and lungs and we immediately struggled out of our outer garments which disappeared with Enrique's chauffeur.

The first impression was that we had entered a small steel foundry, all hissing steam, roaring flame and whirring motors. Red and boiling liquid metal was being poured out of the lips of huge cups into immense vats. We crossed a wire mesh ramp, an elevated rattling passage over humming conveyor belts, transporting shivering fragments of grey rock that were dropped onto long deep trays. This rock was steaming under an artificial rain ejected from sprinklers.

At first I thought this was just a cooling process, but when we were given masks to slip over our noses and mouths to protect our lungs from the *noxious fumes*, I realised the liquid was not water.

"Cyanide," affirmed Don Enrique, who would occasionally slip his own mask off to explain the process: "The rock is recycled," he said with a grin: "From slag heaps of old mining sites. The cyanide reduces the rock to a shiny, viscid substance, a kind of plastic membrane and this is pumped and filtered through carbon." We followed a piece of metal along a conveyer belt, taking it through a corridor of cleansing showers. At the end was a lump of grey matter: "Lead" said Don Enrique.

He lifted it to show us. Sliding a finger along a streak of something brilliant running through the middle of it. Golden.

"Should it be assumed that this is real?" I asked.

"Oh, yes," he coughed, cyanide fumes biting his lungs: "Pure and solid gold. We are refining a hundred grams per tonne here."

I lifted my brows: "Which is to be regarded as good?"

"Summum bonum, if one considers that the most effective gold mines in the world only extract ten or eleven grams. And we're improving on it all the time."

I rubbed the soft metal between finger and thumb, held it up, to the light. Reflected it. It shone: "Beautiful rock."

"Yes, isn't it. But this is not so remarkable. It's not why I brought you here," and he lead me into an air-conditioned laboratory: "The next part of the process is carried out here."

He gestured towards a large, iron, egg-shaped apparatus at the far end of the room: "My alchemist's kiln." He fitted the rock into a crucible, also egg-shaped, then grappled this with tongues in order to insert it into the scorching interior: "We have to fire the rock in order to isolate the pure gold from the lead."

The temperature was raised until the rock became liquid. This was lifted out for me to see: "Notice how the brilliant gold is still discernible from the dull lead, even in its liquid form." I nodded.

Then he tilted the crucible and poured the liquid gold out: "The heavier lead remains in the crucible."

I stared in. Some gold remained. I was going to protest but Don Enrique lifted his hand to retard the complaint, and grinned. Then he tipped the crucible right up and the lead fell out onto a cooling tray. He ran it under a tap. It steamed, squealed, and turned grey: "Where is the gold you saw now?"

There was no trace: "It's sunk to the middle," I speculated.

"And why would it do that if gold is lighter than lead?"

I shrugged my shoulders. He patted them: "No, Valentín. It's not in the middle. I know, I've looked. I've spent years looking for it. The answer to this little mystery is far more incredible."

It was evening when we arrived back at San Lorenzo. We had supper in silence and Enrique suggested that we indulge in another session. I shook my head and complained that I was tired.

"Tired..." he echoed. There was something about the timbre of his voice that startled me and I looked up at him aghast. His eyes were burning hot and I was suddenly away... It was as if I were floating in a huge bubble that very suddenly burst and I toppled onto something, which, by the smooth undulations, must have been soft. A mattress, I realised. A pair of grey figures were beside me. Grey in moonlight. Pedro Sarmiento was in the bed with Doña Rosa. Naked, he on top of her, whispering: "You must take him."

The woman's monosyllable reply was drowsy deep and thick: "What?"

The command contained urgency: "Make love to the Viceroy."

Which electrified: "Fie, señor!" and she pushed him hard away.

Sarmiento reached out, to calm her: "And if I had not told you, you would've gone to him anyway. I've seen how he's been trapping you. Don't tell me you haven't felt it. Help me, and you preserve your own free will."

She dug her finger nails into his arm: "My will, señor, is to lie in my own bed with whom I choose."

"You chose your husband, yet you bed with me."

"Because I like you. But the Viceroy is a lascivious granddad."

"With power and money ... He'll have you."

"He will not."

"He will. He has ordered magic to capture you."

"*Your* magic?"

"Yes. You yourself blabbed it to him. Of course it's done me much good, and could do me much better, if you'll co-operate. If you don't, I'll have to look for a way of drugging you. That'd be harder for me, and more dangerous for you."

"Are you insinuating that I have no choice?" and laughed nervously.

"My advice is sound. You need only lie with him once."

"He will not settle for that."

"No, but once will be enough to prove to him that my magic works and make it easier for me to convince him of the importance of the Terra Australis."

"Convince him through his cock," and she shook her head: "A most dangerous way, Pedro. Remember Saturnino and Dionisio. They did not leave you alone. The flesh is addictive. He will not leave me alone. It is too dangerous," and sat up.

"Then you'll not do it?"

She sighed: "Not without something in return."

"Anything," and he dragged his finger-nails down her back. She slapped his hand away: "I want some more of your *husband's medicine*," transforming Sarmiento, making him grave. She grasped his throat and squeezed it, her pace became locomotive: "But increase the potency this time. My first husband took nearly a year to die. I would be rid of this new one more quickly, pray."

Sarmiento pulled her hand away, rubbed his neck and sighed: "But you hardly see him. How can he have time to annoy you? He is always away."

"I want to be with you," through gritted teeth: "Go with you," as if about to pounce and devour. But then she took a deep breath and her passion became beatific: "To the Terra Australis," then gritting the teeth again: "I must," and her fingers and nails curled ready to clutch, like bird claws: "Be rid of my husband and take me," and then her eyes wild-bright: "As your mistress."

Provoking a vapid response: "As the future Governess of the richest continent on earth."

She turned her back to him: "All right, yes! Why not?" then beatific again. Her hands clasped almost in prayer: "Do you not have ambition yourself? Is this great plan of yours designed for the glory of our king or for yourself?" becoming pleading sure: "You will take me, won't you?"

Sarmiento's upper-canines scraped the bottom row: "Take the Viceroy to bed with you and I will."

And she grabbed his beard and pulled him to her ...

Then Don Enrique's voice pushing me with its drone: "You are moving in the right direction ..."

A garden. Lush green. In the midst, under a vine entwined portico, there was a wine and food laden table with a group of men around it. Three men. One of them was the Viceroy. He was chewing and slathering indecently. Each of them had a hand full of cards. To the back of the Viceroy was another man, dark and Moorish looking, obviously a slave.

One of the players, a thin faced man with long white hair and a grisly handlebar moustache licked his lips and muttered on a whining breath: "You're not really going to take these pagan loving friars seriously, are you your Excellency?"

The Viceroy picked up a card from the central pile and grimaced: "I take them as seriously as the king does?"

"But are you not here to advise the king?"

"Everybody advises the king?" and he made a wide fan of his cards: "He did not send the commissioners on *my* request."

"And they will soon be back in Spain, marry ... spreading infamous stories about Peru."

"Oh, do not worry yourself about that," and he picked up another card. This one drew a smile: "Their report will be in the custodians' favour," and threw down: "... most definitely so." The man to his right threw down also then knocked, which made the others' eyebrows twitch.

This third man was of a similar age, but his hair, though receded, had not whitened much and was still predominantly black.

The Viceroy scoffed: "You don't think we're going to return power to the Incas just because some fussing friars are backing them, do you?"

"These *fussing friars* made many inroads into the old king's heart," insisted the handlebar moustache: "Filling it full of humanitarianism," and he also threw down: "What's humanism got to do with the Church?"

The Viceroy slipped his next card cautiously down and the darker haired man next to him slammed his own on top. His last card. He had won. The Viceroy sighed: "What was the wager, Doctor?"

Which just drew a grin from the winner.

It was the mouth beneath the handlebar which had to moan the answer: "We bet our youngest daughters against your help to acquire an allotment."

Then the grinning one, the doctor: "So I get a night with your little Elenora, Don Luis, and a good deal on some dead conquistador's property from you your Excellency. Well friends, I marry you'll both have some hard convincing to do to pay your debts off this time."

The Viceroy shrugged his shoulders: "I could seal the documents now for you if you like? But personally I'd prefer to wager another hand. Double or nothing. But if you lose, Doctor, then I'd prefer to relieve you of Don Luis' daughter than appropriate your own dear one." The handlebar moustache that belonged to that Don Luis, twitched and he frowned, but he was not really listening to the Viceroy. His Excellency however was fantasising: "You know I prefer them creamy. Don Luis' Elenora has a lovely milky texture." He rubbed his tongue against the inside of his cheek and made a sign to his servant to shuffle the cards.

Don Luis sucked his lip: "I'm afraid it's not so straight forward."

Which shocked the Viceroy and drew a snarl from him. His pitch became violent: "Then you'll have to talk to your daughter man, a wager is a wager!"

The grisly old man was stunned by the tone. His eyes rolled as he started to comprehend the misunderstanding: "No ... I ... I mean the business with the friars and natives," and then, when the tensed Viceroy thawed, he continued with his own obsessing theme: "You know the curacas have offered the king a bribe? They will pay ten thousand ducats more than the Spanish landowners."

The doctor: "But there's a catch."

Don Luis: "Oh yes. They want concessions, but the king is tempted by their offer. Spain is bankrupt and our good king, Felipe, has demonstrated no great love for his subjects in the Americas."

The Viceroy grunted: "Hold your tongue. If you landowners would offer more, you could easily top the *curacas'* bid. And you would've been sharking too good a deal if the king had bought your original proposal, isn't that right, Doctor?"

Who nodded without taking his eyes off his cards: "People here are used to getting very good deals."

Don Luis was looking bitter: "Now his Royal Highness is trying to get a better bargain by playing us off against the natives. We've got more pride."

The Viceroy was obviously getting bored by the landowner's persistence: "Look, man. I told you there is no cause to worry. I assure you, the commissioners will not give the natives a favourable report."

And he winked at Don Luis, who was able to smile for the first time: "So you know what they'll say?" The Viceroy gave a coquettish shrug of the shoulders. Don Luis was insistent: "Come on, your Excellency. The news won't get past our lips."

Drawing a loud ironical laugh.

Don Luis persisted: "What will the commissioners' report be?!"

The Viceroy took a gulp of wine: "Well ... They'll be most disparaging about the natives."

"The stupid natives," added the doctor.

"They will say that the Incas are really a people with neither identity nor will," continued the Viceroy: "According to the commissioners, the idea of returning power to the *curacas* would have disastrous consequences, the natives have no idea what to do unless they are given direct orders."

Then he shouted to the African servant to bring more wine.

The doctor was complaining that they should concentrate on their cards when a heavy footed, thick set, frowning man approached. The Viceroy made a tut-tutting sound with his tongue: "Ah, but here comes my dear son, Juan. He'll want to sit down with us and watch the game. If he does let's not talk of our wager. He's such a moralist."

Then, as predicted the son bowed to the men and sat himself down at the table: "What are you drinking father?"

"Water, Boy," the Viceroy lied.

"Ice cold," said the doctor: "He freezes it with snow. Oh marry, I've told him not to drink so much, so cold. If he keeps it up, troth, he'll be dead within a few days, gasping through an apoplexy."

The Viceroy pulled a theatrically sad and sheepish face at the scolding report. The son laughed, but sarcastically, and his voice was dry as if to match the doctor's irony: "We would hope my father not to die, he would have half of the city weeping." And stormed away.

Don Luis twisted his moustache: "Well that got rid of him."

But the Viceroy was obviously affected by his departing remark: "Only half!?" he growled: "Only half the city would weep at my grave?"

But instead of humouring him, the doctor nodded: "The rich half," and then to mollify it: "You wouldn't want to be liked by the riffraff, would you?"

Another servant rushed hurriedly up to the table to explain that a man had arrived asking for an urgent audience. At first the Viceroy told him to let the man wait for he was playing cards, but the servant insisted and revealed that the man's name was Don Antonio Gomez. The old Viceroy shuddered slightly and then stood up: "Duty calls. But feel free to have as much wine as you like while I am gone," and then turning to his slave: "Get them drunk. It'll make it easier for me to shark them later."

The man sitting in the antechamber had a sea-slug nose, a large mole on his left cheek and a huge ruff that sat high at the back to encompass his entire head. He jerked up when the Viceroy entered, making an equally jerky bow. He did not hesitate to announce his reason for being there: "Your Excellency, I come with bad news."

The Viceroy waved a handkerchief in the air as if to dismiss the panic: "What is it? A revolt? Have you alerted the military?"

"No, your Excellency. There's no revolt. This is for your ears only..."

Which caused blood to rise to the Viceroy's face. There was another flourish of his handkerchief and the servant backed away out the door, closing it as he departed. Then: "The commissioners?"

Antonio Gomez nodded.

"What happened?"

Gomez sighed: "During their voyage back to Spain. It seems ... that they took with them some papers ... most of them signed by you."

"Papers? What papers? They went back with their report."

"And a number of receipts ... illegal ones ... Implying that your

Excellency had done some deals with them."

"What deals?"

Another sigh: "The selling of lapsed allotments. Crown land that was seized and sold. By your orders, your Excellency."

"Fie! What lies!"

"I'm afraid you signed the papers, your Excellency. They appear to know everything."

"Who?"

"The king. It seems there was a spy on board that ship."

The Viceroy slapped a fist into his other open hand: "The friars."

"What can we do?"

"God's teeth! Do? You tell me. What can we do? What fools!" then he shouted down the hall to his servant: "Fetch my astrologer, you brock!"

Antonio Gomez looked aghast: "Your astrologer, señor?"

"Yes, Antonio, when all seems lost, it's time to trust in our destiny, and enjoy life while we still can. Go and sit at my table and finish my cards. You can drink the excellent wine and bet whatever you like. If you win you take fifty per cent," which made Antonio smile. Then, as if to wipe the same smile away: "If you lose you pay half as well."

Antonio Gomez hurried out with his head down. He did not seem to notice Sarmiento who passed him at the door. The Viceroy clapped his hands. He was beaming: "Oh, Astrologer, how dull and dreary politics are, and depressing. Have you got any news for me?"

"The astrological chart is a complicated thing, your Excellency."

"Yes, yes. And the other commission I gave you?"

"That progresses with greater ease," and he pulled a small flask from inside his jacket.

"What tonic is this?"

"No tonic, your Excellency. This is ink."

"Ink?"

"Magic ink, señor. A letter written with this will secure the heart of any woman. Even your cousin's wife, your Excellency."

"That lovely white rose. And you're sure that it works?"

Sarmiento nodded and began tip-toeing toward the door, which of course puzzled the Viceroy: "Did the tonic I give not make your cock as firm and tall as a Cyprus tree?"

"It did."

"Then why do you doubt your alchemist," and he wrenched the doors open to reveal a handsome, dark woman who had been crouching and listening at the door.

The Viceroy made a melodramatic gesture of tragedy, the back of his hand flicking up over his mouth: "A spy, fie!"

But Sarmiento slammed the doors shut again: "No, señor. She is your servant girl, Payta."

"Spying on me!"

"No, no your Excellency. Let us say she's spying on me."

"What?"

"You see I wrote a little note to her," then holding up the little flask again: "With this ink."

"Oh, I see."

"Now she follows me everywhere."

"So it seems."

"And should it not work for you, señor, there are other drugs ... tonics ... Like the one that keeps your willy up."

"Yes, and you must certainly give me more of that when Doña Rosa comes running after me. Yes, I've had enough politics for one day, come and share my bottle with me. I will call the servant girls, you bring your tonics to control them ... and the rest of your instruments ... I want to see Hell tonight!"

Then this vanished in a flash of brilliant light, replaced by a similar room, probably in a different part of the same palace, undoubtedly the room in which Sarmiento was lodging.

He was there with silver goblet in hand, the rim against lips, but motionless and pondering a spread of tarot cards on a table before him. He was smiling too, until a door slammed open and Fr Pablo shuffled in.

Quickly and noisily, through gasps: "What's happening here!?" bending forward, swiping the cards from the table: "Have you lost all reason? The town is full of talk, about the palace ... an orgy ... and there is rumour of devil's magic. The Inquisition will soon enough here of it. Do you think the Viceroy will protect you from them?!"

Sarmiento, who was drunk and jubilant, embraced his cousin: "Ah, an orgy. Yes, we lay with a dozen whores. But who threw the first stone? What friar hasn't done what we did, cousin? Excluding present company, of course ... Yet you also were a bad boy when you were still young and virile, were you not? No, no cousin, don't be angry, it's a most pleasing morn and I have excellent news ... The Viceroy has agreed to finance our voyage ... Four ships he will give us, to find and conquer the islands of King Solomon and the great south land known as the Terra Australis, which will soon no longer be *Incognita!*"

Yet Fr Pablo remained stern and agitated: "Four ships! Now! And where will the money come from," then turned his back: "We have no need of four ships. Not when so much is pressing," and he took a deep breath before turning to face Sarmiento again: "Here, Pedro, look around you. We are in the promised land *here*; this is our gift from God. The Conquest was a miracle; how could it be explained if not? A most bountiful bestowal that we abuse. The colony is sinking into a quagmire of human chaos, and once the world has been sullied enough we lust for other paradises. We are a plague, Pedro. It's not right that we look for the Earthly Paradise until we have done our utmost to clean up the hell we have created; eradicate the suffering; the poverty. What the colony needs are reforms! Now! We need more churches, not boats."

Which transformed Sarmiento. His smile dropped. At first he turned away, agog, as if trying to comprehend, but then he was suddenly all whirling arms and battering the friar, who dropped. Sarmiento did not let up. He kicked his ribs then yanked him up again, pushed him out the door, slammed it shut, and swore.

*　*　*

Don Enrique never really acknowledged the audacious violation that this *enforced* session had been. I felt confused and betrayed. When I came back I was exhausted: "You were told... I was tired," I moaned: "So why was I sent?"

He was unrepentant. He just sat and stared at me. I suppose he saw what was coming, my eyes must have been flickering strange. I sensed it too: the gradual electrifying of my soul that began to surge through my body. It was better not to resist and go with the flow. Once the epileptic process has begun it is impossible to retard it.

When I did explode it did not perturb Don Enrique, he had probably seen many such attacks in his long life. But while he was trying to settle me and stop me from biting my tongue, my inward journey was dragging me through an intense and violent nightmare.

I returned screaming, my hands all over my body, trying to rub the blood off me. Blood that I had imagined splattering over me. Don Enrique seemed to interpret the desperation in my actions and he had a servant help me into the shower.

I probably spent an hour with soap and hot water before I felt *clean* again, but I could still smell that imagined blood for days afterwards.

Christmas turned into a series of anguished days, tormented by the same sanguinary images evoked during that attack. For weeks my ears were humming with the tacit reverberation of the victim's mute screams.

I still have a very clear image of the scene. Wrenched back by epileptic claws to the City of the Kings and to Pedro Sarmiento in the Viceroy's den. He was kneeling, on the floor, his chin on the fist of an arm resting on the upright knee. His eyeballs were huge hallucinogenic, drug-glazed, dilated pools. When he moved, he did so groggily. Charts were laid out in front of him, illuminated by thick, short candles.

The Viceroy was opposite, lying on his belly; pale and depressed and staring equally groggily into an empty wine bowl.

Sarmiento spread his Excellency's cards, sighed and, opening a bottle of imported Castilian vintage, emitted a slurred cry: "Live loud and fully, my Lord. Time to enjoy your life, it's not destined to last much more."

Between them lay destiny's abstract mirror. In the middle, *La Muerte*, with its reaping skeleton, and this had been dropped directly over *La Torre*, the crumbling tower, in flames and exploding under the impact of a bolt of lightning.

Sarmiento suddenly took the Viceroy's hands, roughly forcing his podgy fingers open to stare into his palms: "Both the right and left corroborate it," and as he said this he clumsily unravelled a roll of parchment from under his shirt. A sidereal chart. A wheel was sketched there, with the symbols of the zodiac drawn into the rim.

He lay it down and compared it with the other charts spread out on the floor. Squares and triangles were depicted between planetary symbols: "Mars is in Scorpio this week, which is not good for you, and in opposition to Venus, which is worse. The probability is enormous; you must take the utmost care. But everything, every sign goes against you. Prepare yourself," and then the realisation of what he really meant forced a groan from him.

If the Viceroy died, he would lose his boat.

But the Viceroy, on the other hand, remained quite stoical. He even managed a grin. The following admonition was flippant: "Do not invent such things, Pedro, unless you are sure of it."

Sarmiento clenched his fists and pressed them against his temples, while the muscles in his neck and face tightened into an expression of absolute anguish: "I tell you this because I love you, your Excellency," he lied: "Only an enemy would hide the truth from you."

The theatrics were inspired by the drugs, but the Viceroy seemed oblivious to the falsity and the performance made him serious.

After a moment of silence and thought, he gulped his wine, and looked up, reaching for Sarmiento's hand: "I do not doubt what you say Pedro," staring into the alchemist's flickering false eyes: "I have the utmost faith in you. But it was you, remember, who told me about the possibility of controlling and altering nature's course." The absolutely vain idea tickled his own profound vanity and drew a smile: "If I am condemned by the stars, and by God's Will, then we must use your occult knowledge to find a way out. Now that I am to bed Doña Rosa I do not want to die."

Sarmiento actually sobbed, hardly convincing. He amplified this with a tragic question: "A way of escaping death itself?"

But that ridiculous interrogative was precisely what the Viceroy had been wanting. He reached forward and grasped the alchemist's hand in a ridiculously supplicating posture: "Yes, Pedro. There must be a way," and the stupid smile became a demanding snarl: "Forge a magic ring."

Sarmiento shook his head: "It's an ordained death," which would have satisfied the Viceroy, who would have been perfectly happy cutting his own throat. But the final mad idea began to form in Sarmiento's drug crazed brain and he took the first step in his advance into the most impossible terrain. He bent his head and groaned histrionically: "The struggle for eternal life, is just that, a struggle. It takes many long years to prepare oneself – you do not have the time."

The Viceroy rolled over and murmured: "Then I am killed."

Sarmiento stood up, went to a table, uncorked a bottle of wine and then returned to fill his bowl. He paced the room, a hand wringing his red beard until he suddenly spun around and dropped to his knees, almost brushing noses with the Viceroy: "I have it," he said, and kissed him: "The idea is remote, something I learned once, but I've never practised it myself. It's incredible, and requires enormous faith. The suffering, like the abbreviated time, will be intensified." His breathing increased in depth and rate as the impossible took hold of his nerves. He took a mouthful of wine, drinking straight from the bottle: "Of course you shall need a collaborator ... But I could ... it's monstrous, yet it's the only hope. It has to be emphasised, I've never done it before. We should experiment first. Find someone. Someone equally wretched to try it out on, first."

Whether Sarmiento himself really believed in it or not, it was still the most ridiculous and brutal plan imaginable. But when I first saw the scene I had misunderstood it ...

(c) citrinitas

Don Enrique knew of the ritual. Fantastic as it may seem he provided the only interpretation I can find to explain what follows ...

It was a dim cellar and the lugubrious light made them look grey. The young girl was kneeling naked in the middle of the room, bent forward, wrists and ankles bound together, her neck traversing the sanded surface of the high *chopping* block. Her breathing was irregular, gasping, her larynx being placed too flatly upon the heartwood, stifling access.

Sarmiento stood over her. His biceps and flexors bulged under the strain of the enormous broadsword wielded high over his head. The Viceroy watched. He was horrified, but did not look away. Both men were drenched by sweat. The Viceroy had soiled his trousers and he was joking about it, apologising through his gasps.

Sarmiento let the blade drop.

The time it took to slice through the girl's neck was probably less than one tenth of a second. Within two-hundredths of it the blade had severed the first nerves which sent the primary impulses of pain to the brain. This received those impulses about three-hundredths of a second later and immediately began the complex reaction.

The dramatic increase in the palpitations of the heart pumped the adrenaline which would have urged the rapid advance of the hands to the afflicted area in order to defend it, if the same hands had not been bound as they were. As such only the fingers were able to move. Only the fingers were able to express the agony.

Then: a retroactive spasm from the torso pulled her away from the immediate danger. A bending, expanding and pushing impulse from the toes, to lift the entire body and begin a more purposeful retreat. A filling of the lungs, afterwards a dramatic contraction of the same organs to expulse the air which would project the scream.

But none of this was immediate enough, the blade had already severed the neck, cutting off all routes.

The head dropped into the basket, its lips mouthing repeated mute screams or gasping for the air which the brain sensed was no longer being received.

On the other side the torso fell away. Blood spurted from the opened veins as the heart maintained its automatic pump for several seconds more.

Nerves sent frantic messages to a brain they could not locate and everything became a twitching, spastic mess, stabilised by Sarmiento's stamping boot.

Pushing his other foot down on one of the arms, he chopped at it as if it were a branch. The flesh opened, he hacked through the bone. The arm came away.

The other arm he dispatched with one blow, like the head. The legs were more problematic but they were soon off too.

Afterwards he rolled a huge, empty oil jar over. He lifted and squeezed the torso in first, then the limbs, and finally the head, pushing them all firmly down in order to fit the lid on.

"...An alchemical act," explained Enrique: "There have been several recorded descriptions. It seems madness to take it literally. I've always assumed it had to be regarded symbolically, but you have seen it with your own eyes."

"My third eye," I protested: "It's not the same."

"Well, if you want. But, believe it or not, its purpose was supposed to be the reincarnation of the victim. If Sarmiento really did take the idea literally, he would have then buried the jar in a mound of fresh manure..."

Which he did. In the garden of the palace. At first I was confused. I thought I had slipped into another time zone, for instead of observing Sarmiento cover the jar I watched the girl herself, in perfect health, shovelling the horse and cow excrement ...

"Well, if we take the literal interpretation of the experiment, then the woman would have been Sarmiento," Don Enrique argued: "If the magic worked, it would have transformed him. The tradition says that the alchemist would adopt the victim's form as long as he wore the victim's hat."

A hat, no, but the digging girl had been wearing a shawl. I felt sick: "Don't ask for this to be believed by me, please."

Don Enrique shook his head and laughed: "I'm not asking you to believe anything. The story is yours. All I'm saying is that there have been recorded instances of such an occurrence. According to the myth, after nine months the dismembered body in the jar dissolves and turns into a foetus. The jar becomes a kind of artificial womb. Nine months later the collaborator digs up the jar and frees the newly born being. But that is the legend. Now *you* are telling me that you saw it take place."

Saw it? Did I?

I recalled the scene witnessed now long ago. The first time I had seen Sarmiento, when he had been in bed and I had looked into his mind.

That night he had seen the Viceroy's corpse in the street. That scene I have already described: the mutilated body, amidst Hessian sacks, gobs of blood soaking in sawdust, and his corpse entwined in that of another. A woman

– *The same one that they had cut up* – I realised.

And then I remembered what had happened to that body, that they had carried her away, but then the body had become that of a dog. A huge black bitch.

"There had never been a girl," Don Enrique proposed: "You imagined it. Or you didn't. You saw it, *he* imagined it. You were too close to his mind. His drugged mind. You saw what he imagined. But really, the experiment was carried out on a dog."

"And the shawl, the dog would not have had a shawl."

Enrique: "Of course not. There was shawl on the floor. Left by one of the servant girls who were prostituting themselves. He picked it up. Imagined it was hers. He imagined the whole thing."

"But they killed the dog?"

"It would seem so."

"But who killed the Viceroy? Or was he not dead either?"

"No, he was. You told me yourself. And it's a recorded fact, is it not?"

Then I saw the Viceroy. He was in Doña Rosa's room.

They were arguing in the dark. He tried to grab her. She slapped him and screamed.

The door flung open and another man, her husband, the Viceroy's cousin, came in sweating: "Señor, you have dared to make a cuckold of me, unlocking this privy-chamber door with your counterfeit key," and pulled his sword out, sliding its tip under his wife's dress, pushing the fabric up her moist and shining legs: "What you have put in here displeases me," and the blade whooshed as it cut the air, squelched as it slashed the Viceroy's throat.

In the street, the square. A horse drawn cart, the same that I had seen before, was rumbling up a lane. It carried the same load; Hessian sacks, and buried under them a mop of white hair, the Viceroy's hair; and another mop, the dog, the bitch that Sarmiento's drugged mind had imagined was a girl. Imagined: then I had been lost in his vision, but now things were clearer.

I hovered around the cart. Moonlight fell on the driver's face. I recognised him. At first I could not remember where. He was only vaguely familiar, but mnemonic process linked him to the engineer, Fernando.

Then I remembered. He was the one called Pedro de Ahedo, the man Fernando had been taking to Huancavelica to establish a gold and silver refinery. But what I still did not know was that Fernando was also dead.

It felt as if a hand had grabbed me, holding me back by pulling at my shoulder.

I turned and saw a face level with my own. Rodolfo's old and haggard face, his toothless mouth, a gaping gash like the hole in María Dolores' throat, yet his voice was soft: "Antimony is a mineral ... participating of saturnine parts ... and agrees with *sol* ... containing *argent vive* in itself ... in which no metal is swallowed up ... except gold ... and gold is truly swallowed up by this *argent vive*..."

(d) the devil's pact

I opened my eyes and Don Enrique was there, embracing me in his old but gently-strong arms. He was wiping spittle from my mouth, and hushing me, begging me to stay calm. Other unknown faces stared down on me also. The servants, and judging from the horror expressed by some, mine must have been the first epileptic fit that they had ever seen.

After showering, I was given a cocoa with cognac in it, and Enrique interpreted what I had experienced. He even recognised the words of Rodolfo: "They come from *The Secret Book of Artephius,*" he said: "A twelfth century alchemist."

"Why do you know so much about alchemy?" it wasn't meant as an accusation, not at first, but I remembered Vicente's comment, that Enrique had been working to uphold Spain's tenuous economy, and I could not help myself: "This gold that is being produced by you, it's not really meant for Franco is it?" I was expecting a denial, but I wanted to see his reaction and form an opinion according to that. He staggered towards an armchair and slumped into it: "Oh yes, it's true," and he sighed: "But ...

yes … of course … it upsets you, doesn't it?"

I shook my head not as a negation, but as a critical statement – *Of course it did!* – he seemed so naïve then, almost childlike. I could not believe that he was actually admitting it. Nevertheless, it was me who was the naïve one, as always.

His spirits picked up and he called for one of the servants. Some scotch was ordered. Glasses were poured for both of us. Then, after a sip: "I should have been frank with you I suppose, although it's quite irrelevant." I did not think so and told him so. He laughed: "But why are you so sure it's important; you don't know anything about the background of it. I had to make a decision, just as you did when you let yourself be drawn into the Academy. You have become a member, but I'm not, and if we were to compare the two, you would probably find the Academy more pernicious than Franco."

"Wars are not fought by the Academy … people are not tortured … are not killed."

"Oh no, not exactly. They don't exactly torture, don't exactly kill. But you know very little about where you've thrown yourself, and this Omega group, what do we know about that? I know very little too, yet I have my suspicions about a lot of things. But let's not waver, we were talking about me, my gold and the Regime." He took another sip and began stuffing his pipe bowl: "I didn't go to Franco; he came to me. They found out about my work, probably through the secret intelligence service, or perhaps through an informer. Oh yes, there are informers even at the Academy, I know that for sure. Not just Estrella's brother, but people inside the Academy, people you would never have guessed. Anyway they were going to close the factory and have me imprisoned," and he struck a match and held it over the pipe bowl: "You see making a bit of your own gold on the side is not an absolutely legal business," puffing, the flame brilliant: "I was arrested, but never tried, and the whole thing was hushed up." He shook the match, extinguishing the flame: "Next thing I knew I was in Franco's palace. He wanted to find out exactly what I had been doing, was very interested in it, in alchemy," puffed: "Interested, no, he was fascinated by it, in some sense obsessed. But frustrated that he could not properly understand it," pulled the smoking pipe away, licked his teeth: "Although he understood the gold making side of it well enough, he was desperate to know anything about the philosopher's stone and the prolonging of life, so eventually we came to an agreement," sipped his whisky: "He would allow me to continue my work, even facilitate the acquiring of special tools and machinery, if I would provide him personally with my results. And bestow a certain amount of gold each year," puffs: "So, as I said, I had to make a choice." Then he lay the pipe down and began to gesticulate: "What alternative did I have? Go overseas! But to where? I've seen the world, its governments; the governments of the free-world. Are they so much better? Oh, for some they'd be a lot better I know, but for me? I could have gone to the United States, could have offered my services to free enterprise, or worked in secrecy until the FBI or CIA caught me. Do you think they would have been sympathetic about my gold production? Do you think they would have turned a blind eye? Of course not! They would have crushed me because I would be undermining their whole system. Do you really think I could have made gold for capitalism? And even if they did let me, should I have? Think about it: the United States, Britain, France. These so called democracies have been responsible for more of the world's misery than any other single dictatorship. Or perhaps I should have gone to the Soviet Union? Communist ideals are very noble, but the country is only run by people. Men and women hungry for power, like Franco. Like all leaders in all countries, all of them run by the same people. Obdurate beasts with slavering jaws and grappling claws, reaching out to grab. An insatiable will for dominance, and rule. That is politics. So I stayed here, despite the trap. But remember that all of this was supposed to be between Franco and I. I didn't know that Hilario de Coca knew, let alone Vicente. How much do they know?" I shook my head. He sighed: "But I'm not a political man. The only way to change the world is to change human nature, something which no politician will ever do. Only science, a science motivated by strong forward looking philosophical notions will ever manage that. Science. A science that will transform humanity, physically, genetically, spiritually. Alchemy! That is what I took you to see. But it's late and you are exhausted. We will return to Toledo tomorrow."

_____

(e) albedo

_____

That night I saw Sarmiento again: drunk, depressed and staggering down a filthy street. He squelched some excrement and wavered, holding himself upright – *The faster you rise the harder you fall* – He sniffed, groaned and scraped the sole, spreading the mess like mortar between the gaps in the cobblestones. He reached for his shirt, which was open, his bare chest under it; no map!

He recalled how the man, Pedro de Ahedo, had come at him out of the shadows, how he had pressed his dagger to his neck, threatening to skewer him while a gloved hand opened his shirt and took the chart – *That bastard!* – he thought and stumbled to a drinking fountain to plunge his head under.

I looked with him, at his face reflected in the trough: pondered it as he saw it.

He was ugly. Ugly and red. He spat. Too ugly to be a hero. His ruddy features now expressed bitter failure as well as passion. So many scars. He groaned, but the water invigorated him, and renewed a desire to drink something stronger. He pushed himself up and staggered, wet, but with dignity, toward the only tavern in the square.

The wood of the door inspired him, and drew a sudden vision of his ship, which just as quickly depressed him again. Without the Viceroy and without the map it was the wood of a vessel that would never be, supporting a captain that would never be.

Now that the Viceroy was dead he had to accept his own failure.

He ran his palm over the teak, stroking the entrance. Nostalgia for the future, as if by sympathy he could change everything. But those failed dreams resurrected tragic memories, and he had come out to forget.

Inside it was noisy. Everyone as drunk as him. He made a sign to the innkeeper and a jug of wine and a plate of sweating cheese were slammed onto his table. Afterwards came stale brown bread. He cut some mould off, rolling it into a tight ball to throw at the waitress. She looked appetising, more appetising than the food. Nevertheless, he still squeezed a big slice of the cheese into his mouth with an equally large lump of bread and tried to dissolve it all with the wine. He nearly choked. He thought he could taste blood. Not his own - *His*!?

Blood on the bread, in the wine. The image came back: the dead Viceroy's haunting head.

Of course the murderers would accuse him of it. They knew he was at the palace the night of the murder.

How long would it be? He had no defence. They would have to find him guilty.

He looked around and caught the stares of others. They seemed blank to me, but he imagined them accusing.

The tavern was buzzing with opinions. A balding, sallow and grubby head bobbed around: "Paco's wife," it croaked: "Told him that she had heard of someone. Yea, mark me it's true they say. Someone who'd seen his bastard lordship stiff as a board. Yea, stiff alright enough, and flat-face down in the street with his dead bitch dog. Both of 'em covered with sand to soak up the blood. And his penurious highness did bleed, said them that saw't," already smirking in anticipation of the joke to come: "He gaveth oh so most generously in the end."

"Then why was it told me that he died in his bed? And that 'twas an apoplexy?" a thinner, scruffy figure with an incredulous face said.

The original speaker seemed offended by the doubt: "Marry, I would not know what that would be, señor."

A third member explained: "Apoplexy? 'Tis what they call *the will of God*, 'cause no turkeycock doctor knows what it is either."

Then the first again: "Right you are. You die of apop-ele-sy when some brock don't want us to know what you died of. If you get the rub?"

"I heard it was the ague," said the thin one.

The original speaker, incredulous: "Nah, the ague don't kill so sudden."

It was the third who summed up: "'Twas 'cause his poncy majesty wouldn't have no wine, just iced water they say. Marry, that's what did 'im in. Lack of fortification."

Sarmiento couldn't help but snigger at the insinuation. His pulse raced. Disparate images of their orgy were recalled – *We were striving after God through gluttony –*

They had been demonic nights. The Viceroy's home a Venusberg, and nostalgia for the palace absorbed him. So much so that he did not notice the ominous hush that had descended, nor the ensuing reboant thump of heavy boots on the floorboards.

When three men, all armed and uniformed, stopped beside Sarmiento's table, a great but silent expression of relief wafted through the tavern air.

Sarmiento slowly lifted his head and grimaced. Before him was the gleaming breastplate of an Inquisitional Guard.

He had to retard an impulse to clutch hold of the belts and buckles adorning the belly and pull himself up. Then he sneezed as his nose rubbed against an enormous ostrich feather flapping from the helmet clutched tightly under an arm.

He had been waiting for it, even hoping for it. Despite their incomprehension he would welcome their justice. Now that he had lost his map he had nothing left to lose.

The figure inclined forwards, squinting and sniffing, as if he could vaticinate identity by analysis of odoriferous emanations, then leaned back, patting the ample belly plate and nodding his head: "That's 'im!"

The other guards smartly grabbed their man, who did not resist. They lead him out of the tavern to the square and the court on the other side where they locked him into a dark and narrow, vaulted prison in the basement.

Lying in that windowless cell, staring pointlessly into blackness while contemplating a slow and steady drip of water, his stomach gurgled and burned. He tried to force himself to vomit, then gave up and lifted his knees and pushed them in. The pain persisted and sharpened. He twisted over, one side to the other, rolling until he fell off the bunk. Then he writhed, an agonised grub on the stone floor. At first the chill through his damp clothes was soothing, but soon it became unbearable and, shivering, he had to wrap himself in a blanket.

With the warmth he finally started to doze, dreaming that there was nothing, that he was dead. The prison's blackness invaded his dream, imagining, in his dream, that he had fallen asleep and dreamt another more intense blackness. An infinite journey into nothingness – *I die, falling into the sea, dragged under by an eddy. That is my fate. I plummet with someone else's foundering ship –*

When he woke again he was desperately thirsty – *A furnace inside my gizzard: eternal fire ... but at least I am, my pain confirms it –*

Then a loud bang on the iron door. The rattling of keys squirming in the lock before another bang, then a scrape. The door jerkily opened. Exterior light blazed in. Painful contrast. It took him some time to distinguish the grey, bearded guard who shuffled, a lantern held high. His free hand was withered, but he reached out and laid it on Sarmiento's damp head.

The crisp air and open space of the bright court was a relief. Sarmiento took a deep breath and looked past the tribunal members to a tapestry draped against the back wall. A streak of direct light diffused the image, but he could still recognise a hunting scene: a pack of lithe hounds, teeth embedded firmly into the flesh of an agonised stag, one wide open eye, gaping deer's mouth gasping. Until his view was blocked by the Viceroy's son, Juan.

Sarmiento groaned. It was the youngster, Juan, who had denounced him.

But the prosecutor, fingering a pile of papers pressed tightly to his chest, was more nervous than the accused. He dabbed his brow with a handkerchief, swallowing a large lump of air to puff himself up. His black jacket, too tight, restricted his breathing and made him uncomfortable. Underneath the jacket, a white shirt frilled out. His voice, likewise frilled, was delicate and wavering, but he tried to seem strong: "You made our happy home your hell."

Happy home? A nice lie - thought Sarmiento. Home for the Viceroy's son had always been hell. Yet he bore no compassion for his dead employer's orphan. Not that much was needed, Juan was happy enough that his father was dead. We do not all love our fathers. This son, tortured by his progenitor for being prudish and unimaginative, had loathed him.

Sarmiento looked into his eyes, so much squinting hate directed at himself – *Oh, how you long for justice! To discover the incredible sordid truth* – he thought, while anticipating the prosecutor's inevitable plea for absolute, capital punishment.

What would his defence be? That he had been forced to do it? Who would swallow that? No, he had made a grave mistake, and now he was perfectly resigned to the logical consequences.

He imagined the probable auto-da-fé. His flesh peeling away, seared off by an intense heat from climbing flames as the crowd roared. Brief infamy – *What will it be like to endure real agony?* – He grimaced, but then nearly choked as a hand dropped onto his shoulder.

He turned, his nose almost brushing against his cousin's face. He whispered into it: "Thank God you've come. You'll defend me?"

The reply, also a whisper, but blunt: "No."

Sarmiento swallowed: "So be it," then through a half closed throat: "And Doña Rosa, is she not here?"

The friar sighed: "She's no longer a resident of the City of Kings."

Sarmiento nodded, slowly, gravely: "You mean she's been removed."

Fr Pablo was surprised. Became curious: "Removed? Why?"

Sarmiento put his arm around his cousin's shoulder, pulled him closer: "Because she's the only one who can prove my innocence. She was with the Viceroy that night. She knows who killed him."

But Pablo pulled away, bewildered: "Who killed the Viceroy? Pedro you are deluded. What do you think you are here for? Please cousin, your mind is baffled by the devil himself and the accusation against you is just that, that you are in league with Lucifer. There is no charge of murder! Not yet," and laughed: "Oh no, you are to be tried for..."

But then the actual accusation echoed across the court from the magistrate's desk: "Thaumaturgy!"

It was delivered, and that was it, nothing more. Sarmiento sat up straight. His eyebrows up, mouth gaping. Air was involuntarily expulsed from his lungs and he had to press his lips shut to retard the guffaw. His cheeks filled. He needed to explode.

It all became suddenly so ridiculous. No talk at all of murder, as if no one had died. The prosecutors were putting forward their petty recrimination so seriously and sternly. Accused of possessing his three magic rings which had been used to obtain influence over people in power, and control over women. Only that.

Of course he was guilty, everybody knew it, he had often boasted of it himself. While he had been with the Viceroy there had been nothing to fear from being pompous. Why defend himself now? What did he care?

For a moment he suspected divine or diabolic providence. He hardly listened to the rest of the accusations. His heart raced, mind emptied. His attention fell on one of the red-robed judges, a cardinal with an index finger well up a fleshy nostril. With each twist the cardinal's eyes rolled and his thin, white lips sucked in and out. Sarmiento laughed softly, infuriating the Viceroy's son, who yelled: "V - I - L - L - L - A - I - N!!!!"

The drowsy cardinals stirred to give an admonishing look at the hysterical prosecutor.

He lifted his nose and puffed up his chest, then pushed out a stiff arm and an open hand, demanding that the *beast* hand over his magical rings for inspection.

Sarmiento dropped them, into the prosecutor's palm: "Power over women," he whispered.

But none of his victims appeared before the court. Only their signed testimonies were read.

The maid Payta's confession was the most damaging.

The Viceroy's son was triumphant: "Her most lucid and willing affirmation told us of a mysterious ink that gave any man or woman that should be in the possess of it, a satanic control upon the loves and desires of whomsoever should read what had been written wi'it, and that you had used the ink to perform unnatural sex acts upon her."

Sarmiento raised his eyebrows and grinned. His voice was thick, superior, cruel: "And said she exactly what we did?"

When the judges read their sentence Sarmiento had to restrain his laughter again:

> (i) condemned to be stripped half-naked and attend a mass with a burning candle – *an absurd sense of theatrics* – he thought – *or perhaps they think I'll accidentally immolate myself by setting fire to the hairs on my chest* –
>
> (ii) to be obliged to fast on Wednesdays – *I'll have to gorge myself on Tuesdays* – and
>
> (iii) to surrender all his books on witchcraft – *the most dolorous stroke* –

Afterwards he sat with Fr Pablo: "You have been lucky this time," said the friar: "Terribly lucky. Or not. For I fear the punishment will do nought to cleanse your putrid soul."

* * *

The next day, Christmas day, Don Enrique took me back to the laboratory. We were alone, the staff being on holiday, and he repeated the experiment with the gold in the lead. The refining process separated it, just as it had done the day before, leaving a grey mass at the bottom of the crucible with a brilliant streak in it that disappeared when the crucible cooled.

"We call it *ghost-gold*. No one is really sure what it is, but I have a good idea." And he opened the kiln again, reinserting the crucible: "Now we'll turn the temperature up a bit."

The next time he brought it out the lead had disappeared, the metal turning to a dark, greyish substance: "Materia Prima," he said and transferred this to a kind of saucepan before returning it to the kiln, increasing the heat even more until the powder turned white: "Do you remember what Rodolfo told you? Argent vive?" I nodded, but I still didn't understand it: "Argent, means silvery-white. V*ive*, living ... now watch carefully." When he heated it again the white powder began to literally levitate: "Does not that argent powder seem to be alive to you? If we were to weigh the pan and the powder now, while hot, we would find that it weighed only a third of the weight of the pan when it had nothing in it," and then he squeezed my arm: "What you are seeing here is what the alchemists called *antimony*. It is the penultimate stage of the alchemist's quest. Just one more step and the Philosopher's Stone will be obtained. What do you think?"

I shuddered: "Has it been assumed by you that Rodolfo got this far?"

"Perhaps. But I doubt very much that he got any further."

"Why not?"

"If he had gone further, if he had found the Philosopher's Stone, he would have been splendid, perfect. He would have been immortal."

"But it's thought by you that Sarmiento *did* find it."

"De Coca says so. Perhaps he's right. We have to set sail."

(f) toreador, en garde

A few days later Estrella was back, with tickets to the opera. To a performance of *Carmen*.

It would be my first opera. Not only that, my first experience of a grand orchestra in a grand theatre. *Carmen*: the tremendous power of the overture.

"Patriotic power" whispered Estrella: "Thank God the composer wasn't Spanish."

Then the first instance of the tragic theme: the timpani punctuation thumped against my heart, and from then I was lost in the chaotic fray of emotions. When I heard that soprano, that Michaela: her sweet suffering evoked María Dolores' beauty and innocence; her virgin aria, the delicate kiss on Don José's innocent lips (*as if they were mine*). The marching soldier-impersonating street-urchins filled my heart with a childhood never known, and I have never been able to bear the image of any child. When Carmen sang her song of seduction I wept, because a million knife deaths suddenly flashed before my eyes in that moment of sublime passion: sublime-passion-deaths consumed by a sublime-passion-universe.

The universe is cold, they say, but also so hot when everything gathers. Frozen cold or incinerating, a knife-blade universe: such cold steel, yet when it pierces flesh it burns.

...*l'amour*

sang Carmen

...*l'amour*...

such a hot-cold voice I wanted to scream.

But I managed to suffer all the grandeur, until the third act. Until the finale; the bull-fight. Then I could hold on no more, and I was lifted.

Up. Out. Away ...

A bull-fight. Real: it had been real. In the City of the Kings.

The music remained but I was in another part, there, one hot day in

Lima, high up in the heavy air. Made heavy by its enclosure from thick cumulus clouds. Their blue black underbellies had recently opened their sluices. The hot earth had sighed and sucked.

Below me was the stadium. Circular. Circles emanating from other circles. The circular order of all utopia-universes. Sand in the centre. A ring of sand, darkened by the shower. Around that a black mass of pinprick points, until I dropped and the dots became dots of heads. Black dots of black hair or black hats. Thousands of particles packed into the bullfight-scene molecule. And I was looking for one particular particle; the Sarmiento particle.

This time I had to feel his presence rather than look for it. The crowd was a seething mass in mask and costume disguises. Masks and cloaks and the horns of *Carmen* blasting through my head. Timpani again... Escamillo in the opera, singing the famous – *Toreador, en garde* ...

I went down, dropping into the city, solid with people. And there was my particle.

He was unrecognisable yet I knew him. His wet glare through almond shaped cracks in a black half-mask. A sackcloth dangled from his shoulders and he held a long pole with a long curved blade, like a reaper's scythe. The black reaper, I realised, Thanatos, the spirit of death.

His eyes, flickering brown sensors within impelling white frames. His right hand reached out, his fingers longer and paler than ever. Trembling, feeling, guiding. When the other particles saw him coming they quickly moved away, not wanting to be touched by such a fatal being.

So a path opened before him in the crowd, like Moses parting the sea. Death was looking for his victim, reality a flashing blur, he would also have to trust sensors more sensitive than sight.

Then ... Down. In the bull-ring.

The horned beast, death threatening black-tipped horns. The crowd roared in fear and admiration, but the bull's eye was bovine sad.

Black capes, wafted by men in grey suits and black hats, twisted in the air. They flapped, an audible slap that encouraged applause as once again the chorus of the opera wafted across the centuries to fill my astral ears with ...

à bas! à bas! ...

I turned. The Thanatos-Sarmiento again. His victim was also in fancy-dress; in a plumed cloak and full of the colour of an Inca king. A leather satchel dangled from his shoulder. Definitely the man Sarmiento was looking for; the map thief, Pedro de Ahedo ...

une autre quadrille s'avance / voyez les picadors ...

A shriek as the taurine monster, tail up, arse exposed, crashed into flesh. A round, fat belly squelched. Fragile flesh of mare's gut. The picador's horse. The bull lifted its head and the neighing victim collapsed then flipped over with an agonised eye onto its back. Twitching, helpless legs wavered in the heavy air.

Ahedo was immersed in the spectacle and he laughed when the gored horse's belly ripped apart and the red-blue intestines slid slowly forth. Beside him were his allies; an elderly fellow posing as a Harlequin, and another with a cruel mouth in the white suit of a pompous cavalier ...

comme ils vont du fer de leur lance / harceler le flanc des taureaux ...

Sarmiento stepped forward, dragging out his dagger to cut the strap of the dangling satchel and pull it away at the same time ...

l'espada! Escamillo! ...

At which moment there was a shrill scream and the crowd buried their faces as another gored horse's abdomen opened, and more gizzards spilled out in the blood on the sand ...

Vivat! la course est belle...

Ahedo had hardly noticed the removal of the satchel, so enthralled was he by the horses' agony. It was an unconscious movement that revealed the theft. Fumbling. Gasping. He turned, just in time to see the blur of the slashing blade; just in time to instinctively move back as the blur swept past his throat and the grinning figure of death struggled away into the screaming crowd ...

Toréador en garde! ...

So Ahedo unleashed his own sword.

Unleashed in the solid crowd as if he were in some airy open field.

The blade had hardly begun its hyperbola rise when it stammered, thumping against the limb of a girl standing in front of him. Not in costume or mask, this was a simple peasant girl. The iron pierced and then dragged, slicing a hot gash in the girl's arm. The heat made her flinch, groan, which turned into an almost immediate wail as she caught sight of the crimson gush that escaped. She tried to squeeze the opening closed, but it was a torrent and it spilled through the thin cracks in her closed fingers.

The girl was with her family and her father turned with the wail. He made the immediate association between the thick mess and the gleaming, steel blade now wavering high in the air above Ahedo's head. Lest the criminal escape, he leapt on Ahedo, dragging him down.

The commotion aroused Ahedo's own allies to action. The one with the cruel mouth in the white cavalier's suit lifted a boot. The leather thumped into the peasant's head. A nearly fatal blow on the temple and the victim wrapped his arms around his skull to protect brain enclosing bone against a repeat attempt. But the one in white was then punched by a second peasant, whose thick fist knocked Ahedo's ally off his feet.

Meanwhile, Ahedo was thumping the peasant holding his legs hard in the middle of his back. A rain of blows until he let go. When he had, Ahedo was jerked to his feet by his Harlequin friend who kicked and connected squarely with the poor peasant's nose. Bone snapped and the nose twisted, showering those nearby with more blood.

This offended the crowd so much that even unconcerned parties unsheathed their own swords and set on Ahedo and his band.

Ahedo himself, however, was an excellent jouster. He smiled and encouraged the challenge, flourishing an arrogant blade in front of paling faces which opened a tremulous circle around them. This prodded tentatively inward against Ahedo's jousts, but the latter was able to occupy three swords at the same time while the Harlequin and his friend in white fenced another three.

One of these was forced backward and tripped down the steps of the stadium, his toppling momentum catching hold of a dozen others, who, when they had reached the bottom decided to punch each other.

Very soon the entire stadium seemed to be in revolt ...

By this time, Sarmiento was already well away from the arena. He turned into a narrow deserted street and threw off his cloak and mask, then ran. And it was only when he was well out of sight that he actually opened the satchel.

He took a deep breath. Years of disappointment told him that his abrupt assault would bear little fruit either. He did not really think what he was after would be there. But it was. His map, rolled up in the same leather pouch that he himself had always carried it in.

He unravelled it, kissed it, and even said a short prayer of thanks.

Then he went into a tavern, drank a shot of *chicha* and bought some Castilian wine and cheese. At a table he waited for the arrival of his cousin.

Their relationship had been strained after their own fight, but when Ahedo's plan had come to Fr Pablo's attention, the friar had decided to return to his depressed cousin and offer help: "I've heard a story, more than a rumour," he had told him one breathless morning: "That Pedro de Ahedo, and your map, have had an audience with the new governor, Lope García de Castro," then desperate, as if his own life depended on it: "He's had the audacity to inform the governor of his own intention of mounting an expedition, invented by himself, the lying brock says, in search of the Isles of King Solomon."

Pedro de Ahedo would have been a notable actor, thought Sarmiento. The *sharker* had played the role of an inspired patriot with great gusto. His proposition had inspired the governor, who had never guessed Ahedo's real purpose.

In fact, Sarmiento did not know that real purpose either, but he was fully prepared to invent one.

He would have done anything, the whole of his destiny was threatened by this upstart who had taken his map. He decided to use the impeccable voice of his cousin to explain Ahedo's treacherous scheme: "You will go to the governor, Don Lope, yourself cousin, and denounce Ahedo. Why would Don Lope not believe the testimony of a priest?"

"The plan," Fr Pablo whispered to the ambiguously interested new governor: "Was not even formulated by himself, but by his original employers, the Portuguese."

Which drew an interested frown from the governor: "Why would the Portuguese encourage a Spanish expedition to King Solomon's Isles?"

The friar considered the frayed sleeves of his own coat and carefully crossed his fingers. He was a terrible liar and he knew it. But the story he was about to tell, he assured himself, although invented, could very well have been true: "Because they knew that with their man, Ahedo, in charge," he gasped: "The fleet would never reach its destination." Then drawing spittle to moisten his lips: "Their spy's task is to convince the colony to embark on the expensive enterprise of gathering a fleet for him," and then looking sternly at the governor: "Which it seems he is on the point of achieving," then after a slapping wipe from his tongue: "This expedition will be a great waste of time and money, because the fleet will never discover anything." The governor wriggled and Fr Pablo's voice deepened with a growing belief in the possibilities of their invention: "The Islands of King Solomon exist, but Ahedo will never go there, would never have gone there even if he could, even if you gave him the ships. He doesn't even have a map," which was a bluff. Fr Pablo felt the blood drain from his face as he uttered it – *and if the Governor has seen the map?* – yet bravely ignoring the possibilities of incrimination, he continued: "The only map of the Solomon Isles belongs to Pedro Sarmiento de Gamboa," and then to give some verisimilitude to his invention: "I've seen the chart in Sarmiento's possess myself," but looking down because he felt himself blush, until the governor insisted that he get to the point of his argument: "Ahedo's vile plan, is to assume the role of admiral; take control of the fleet, and lead his men into a career of unexcelled piracy, plundering the American coasts in order to ferry Spanish gold to the iron deposit boxes in Portugal."

Such was the story. Although there had been no evidence to prove it, it had convinced the governor not to back Ahedo.

– *And now* – thought Sarmiento – *the second part is complete. I have the map back* – and he squeezed the parchment which had returned to what he considered its rightful place again, under his shirt ...

When his cousin arrived he had already drunk the jug. He smiled a remonstrance: "What took you, cousin?"

But Fr Pablo was agitated: "Get up, pray..." and lifted him to his feet: "It's best that you make yourself scarce for a while," and pushed him towards the door: "Do you know what an uproar you caused today?"

"I should, cousin, I was there," and described his own view of the adventure as the friar hurried him up, pulling his arm to usher him out of the door, into a narrow lane, already quite dark. Fr Pablo stumbled and almost slipped into a waste water conduit that ran along one side of the lane and was about a metre deep. He groaned and clutched Sarmiento's supporting arm.

"The wild drunk must save his sober friend," laughed Sarmiento: "Be careful cousin, the next time you slip, I might leave you there for the night."

Fr Pablo hissed: "You don't realise, do you? We are in danger."

Sarmiento shrugged his shoulders: "Danger ... What danger, I have my map again."

"And Ahedo's hatred," which came through clenched teeth: "He's wild mad and after you. He's already been jousting with practically the whole city. He's like a wild and cornered boar. He's not going to run away until he has your spleen, I'm sure of it, troth!"

But Sarmiento was more intrigued by the gossip he had missed out on: "Jousting with the city?"

The friar shook his head, realising he would have to now explain: "Yes. Well, the governor, on hearing about your disturbance, and hearing that Ahedo was involved, assumed the capital was in rebellion against him and sent out the guard to restore order and arrest Ahedo."

Sarmiento slapped his fist into his open palm: "All the better for us. I tried to cut his throat, but the fox has a million lives."

Fr Pablo sighed: "Well his life was spared again. The guard found him but he fought them off, wounded a sergeant in the arm. Then ran."

"Bad news, pray."

"Yes."

The friar still had the last sibilant in his mouth when a sword, invisible in the dim light, came shooting from a ghostly white mass out of the ditch.

The sharp metal squelched up through the ribs and impaled a lung and the heart of the friar; thrusting through, and poking out of his chest.

The friar looked down at the bloody point trembling below his chin, then fell back in the ditch. He had not the air to yell.

Sarmiento roared and unsheathed his own weapon, but the white assassin seemed to vanish like some occult spirit. The alchemist groaned and stumbled. He leapt into the ditch to lift his cousin's now limp body in his arms. He was already dead.

Part Three: The Alchemist Explorer

"If I ventured in the slip-stream
Between the viaducts of your dream...
Could you find me?
Would you kiss-a my eyes?
To lay me down, in silence easy
To be born again..."

Van Morrison
"Astral Weeks"

---

let us not restrict ourselves to the solitude of singularities,
our existence together is a complete narrative, intricate and replete with
thousands of verbs,
tens of thousands of substantives
                              rejoice
in the epic poem,
          the verse is our story
          and the story
is a life progression of trivial steps toward enlightenment
each step its own crystal junction
          reflecting infinite possibilities
                    implying that the infinite can be realised once it is
learned how
it will open all the sticky sliding drawers of your
          mind and soul
                         when you learn how to pierce the steadfast
relationship betwixt time and space
madness can be a blessing
                    when it is learned how to rejoice
remove yourself:
          their world is the illusion,
the sublime is real...

XII. The Voyage

It was about a month after Francisco Arizmendi's visit that Estrella arrived at the sanatorium.

Life there was already changing, just as Arizmendi had promised. The experiments on me had stopped; that month I had no blood transfusions, and I was not obliged to take any more drugs. Even when I asked them to sit my Guardian outside and remove the security cameras from my room, the request was carried out with a compliant smile.

Estrella was nervous at first. Her face gleamed with the same brightness the young genius had always had, but it was a much sadder sheen; tinted with the melancholy deep woe of knowledge and experience: "I really am so sorry, Val," she finally said, lifting me back into my wheelchair: "You have suffered so much because of me."

I wanted to offer her a whisky or a cognac, or some *hash*, but alcohol and cannabis were forbidden in the sanatorium: "Could I interest you in some Valium?"

This encouraged the desired laugh: "Oh Val, if I'd known you were going to end up here," and took out her own handkerchief: "Neither of us, of course, knew that." I peered gormlessly back at her, my glasses, sliding down the bridge of my nose, had to be pushed up again: "You don't think I sent you here, do you? I mean we did ... in a way ... when we called De Coca, but we had no choice." I must have blinked slowly as I tried to comprehend the reason for her fanatical defence: "What do *you* remember?"

I shook my head: "Remember, of what? What is to be recalled?"

"Of the last day. The last time we saw each other."

"The last time?" the concept made me shudder and I thought it better to prepare some tea for us both. The electric wheelchair hummed into my little kitchenette. There my words whooshed out over the jet of tap water as I filled the kettle: "You were back at San Lorenzo, from Galicia," the whoosh becoming a gurgle as liquid replaced air: "The New Year ... I suppose it was 1972. Experiments were still being carried out at Don Enrique's." I had to concentrate to find the strength to twist the tap tightly closed, my voice suddenly resounding: "but we were particularly excited," then went to the stove: "You'd been given something." I reached for the gas-lighter gun: "a drug." I turned the gas tap, the hiss: "Mescaline ... It was assumed by you that it would help me," metal clicked: "It was taken by me," the tip of the spark-gun wavered precariously until persistence managed to get a spark to hit the gas. That exploded with a *pluff* and a surge of blue flame: "Then I was hypnotised again."

For a moment I found myself gazing irresolutely into the controlled stove-fire, my mind drifting in a liquid-gas nowhere. I had to blink to return to time and space. Remembering the kettle, I lifted it rattling to lay it on the flame. When I turned I caught her grimace. I was more monstrous than ever and she knew it. Her own voice was deep and drawn: "And you fell into a coma."

Which made me shudder and return to the preparation of the tea, rummaging in the cupboard: "What would be preferred? By you?" packets rustled: "Earl Grey?" I lifted boxes to inspect them: "But they're only tea-bags, leaves are better ... What about Prince of Wales?"

– *You fell into a coma* – I tried to hold the memories at bay. What she called *my coma* was another world for me. A world that was constantly begging me to return to it. Once resurrected the temptation was impossible to retard. I turned my back to Estrella so that she would not see my eyes roll up, back into my head.

*   *   *

– *The ship is an egg* – thought Sarmiento – *The ocean a womb ... the journey before us a gestation* – and he sniffed the salt sea air, listening to the inhalation roughly rub across the hairs and dry mucus of his nostrils. There was a gurgle in his lungs when they filled, and his eyes suddenly widened. His neck cracked as his head turned; toward tar and hemp.

Sailcloth flapped slightly, but not enough to excite anyone. The planet was blue that day, and breathing, and the bay's calm undulations soothed those on the sighing ships. Destiny depended so much on winds and weather; which is why it used to be so easy to believe in.

I looked into the other men's minds. Perhaps it was the calm, but no one seemed concerned about the enormous emptiness ahead of them. There seemed to exist a presumed security, as if tragedy was something foreign or had become obsolete. Many yawned, exposing dark oesophagus-pits of boredom. It was adventure that most of them wanted, not this false start.

They had set sail the day before, but the wind had suddenly dropped, hardly giving them time to raise the anchors. Then they had drifted stupidly, because hardly at all, only a hundred metres from the wharf. There the families and friends who had come to see them off had stayed, camping all night with guitar, pipes and wine; lest a liberating wind should suddenly gust again and drag their loved ones invisibly away. There was a rumour, that had quickly spread, said to have been started by a moaning *mestizo* woman. She had claimed that by catching the image of the ships disappearing over the horizon and holding it in their memories, the safe return of those same vessels would be ensured.

Eventually the planet's breath became a sigh blowing from the land, and those on board looked up at the sails. This made some of them anxious, but it was still too soft to fill and push. Blinding flashes from rippling water, catching and projecting sunlight, made them squint.

"Had the wind blown us out yesterday, the moon was in opposition to Venus," murmured Sarmiento into his sidereal charts. It was the 20th November, 1567, and he was explaining the configurations to the ship's notary, Catoira: "This would've emphasised the possibilities of losing ourselves. Which is not to say that today's the best day to mark our destiny with. In fact, it promises many problems. But it's a better day than yesterday. The lagging wind has saved us from disaster."

Catoira smiled: "Even if the stars had predicted total disaster I would've still climbed aboard, Captain."

Which made Sarmiento's eyebrow arch – *Was that an optimistic nature expressed, or a suicidal one?* – In any case he was glad to have found a sympathetic passenger; capable of grasping the occult dimension of the universe. He scratched his groin. Perhaps it was the excitement of potentials, or perhaps it was a herpes. How much dirt had built up on him?

Then the chief-pilot, an old sea-salt, Hernán Gallego, approached. A ruddy cheek under a grisly beard twitched: "Good morrow, Cap'ain," and he chewed the inside of his lip as he stared out over the bay, looking for aberrations on the still surface: "The tide'll soon be turning."

Sarmiento's eyebrow arched again. He had been apprehensive about the old navigator's presence ever since their introduction through the governor.

Gallego began sniffing: "The wind'll blow and we'll sail," then his chewing reached the top of the lip and began on the exterior side: "Yer instructions to me 'ave been read and will be adopted. A west south-westerly course, until we reach twenty-three degrees south. Can it be confirmed, Cap'ain?"

Sarmiento nodded, a slight movement, but severe: "That's the route."

When he caught Gallego's eye again, he suddenly comprehended something that had been gnawing at him for weeks. He had seen the old sailor before. A churning rippled through his stomach; in the City of the Kings. Then the old-salt's eyes had been glazed from drink. He remembered him, wobbling precariously on a stool, one hand clutching tightly to the table in front of him. Around him there had been a boisterous scene, a tavern, and sitting beside him another familiar face with a gruesome smirk. An irksome name had to be attached, Pedro de Ahedo, and the old Gallego had had his arm around his shoulder, patting it.

Sarmiento cracked his knuckles. He pulled a splinter from his thumb and spat and looked away from Gallego and Catoira, across the *Almiranta*.

The *Almiranta* was the second and smaller vessel of the fleet. It had been named the *Todos Los Santos* and was the flag ship commanded by the captain-general, Don Alvaro de Mendaña. A young commander, only twenty-five – *with a complicated sidereal chart* – At that moment he was stiffly clamped between his uncle's embracing arms.

The uncle, Lope García de Castro, was the Conde de Nieva's successor. He was only filling in until the new Viceroy could arrive, but he already glistened with gold and made jangling-coin melody when he moved. He pecked his nephew's cheek, tickling his nose with his beard, and there was a smirk of satisfaction as he patted his back.

The nephew Mendaña, however, was looking away to the brown line of shore. To an empty patch where he imagined a solitary figure, becoming sharp in his wilful mind's eye. It was the ghost image of a young *mestizo* girl, very pretty in his imagination, with an apron to her nose as she sobbed into it. Two hot wet nights before, they had been naked and making love. She had promised to come to the harbour, risk splinters in her bare feet on the rough pier, in order to wave her captain-lover off.

But that was an image and she was not really there. Mendaña felt choked.

The governor sensed his nephew's despondency and slapped his back again, harder this time, to distract rather than encourage: "Do not disappoint me," he mumbled through gritted teeth, repressing his viciousness.

A passion that quickly passed. Lope Garcia de Castro was really quite happy; gratified with his own cunning dexterity in co-ordinating an expedition that he himself regarded as a tremendous and profitable farce. His persuasive art had fooled everyone. The whole town had been buzzing for months with the idea of the Solomons and the wealth it would bring. Ever since that whelp Ahedo had come to him with the idea, he had been carefully plotting its outcome. For, as far as he was concerned, this moment *was* its outcome. He had made his profit even before the doomed ships had raised their anchors.

As soon as Fr Pablo Martín had entered his court with his report, the whole complicated plot had unravelled before him. How to make a fortune out of the most fatuous scheme – *One day* – he told himself – *there will be men who'll possess a perfect enough grasp of money-making to comprehend the genius of my profit making imbroglio –*

First of all, Ahedo's plan was approved, but under the stipulation that it had to be ratified by the king. This, the governor knew, could last several years, in which time he would take control of the idea and put his own puppets in charge. The commissions he had taken from each contract were scandalous. The expedition was declared to have cost double its real price, one half of the cost going into his own pocket. Yet no one had ever complained, except for that fool Pedro de Ahedo, and he had had *him* run out of the country.

While they rowed him ashore, the governor thought about how quick the foolish fall. He stepped out of the boat with an inflated chest, his nose pointing at the sun.

The day before he had delivered a speech. A boring and improvised discourse that had turned into a long lecture on bravery and patriotism. Throughout the sermon he made an all too obvious effort to invent virtues for his nephew.

Blank expressions in the crowd had expressed scepticism; Mendaña was a complete novice. It could only have been the governor's perverse imagination that had put such a delicate young man in charge of such a portentous voyage; into regions whose winds and currents and lurking hidden dangers no one knew.

Then, no one had expressed their doubts, but now, when they saw the governor approaching the jetty, the crowd became a blaring megaphone of sarcasm.

Lope García de Castro smiled stupidly, twitched nervously and grimaced. He was impatient for the ship to be off, for the complications to be out there, far enough for him to forget ...

Now at his station, the novice-commander Mendaña looked back as a wind gushed up from the land, stinging his eyes enough to draw tears out of them. The *mestizo* girl who had never been there was now imagined struggling with her ex-conquistador father and her brother who would not let her leave the house – *She would be waiting for me, I'm sure, if she were allowed* – he thought – *Why will they not let her?* – He lifted his green, felt and feathered cap and ran his fingers through his fair hair. As he did someone shouted that the anchor should be raised. His pale and freckled face frowned in anguished thought – *Who gave that order? Am not I the commander?* –

When the pilot Gonzalez suddenly appeared behind him, it made Mendaña jump. The navigator smiled at the reaction he had caused and a slight whistle was blown through the gap of a missing tooth. Then he tweaked a golden ring in his ear and lifted a rubbery arm to wave to Sarmiento's ship. Hernán Gallego was alert and waved back. The crusty anchors were raised.

Mendaña gulped – *Just as my uncle had told me it would be* – he thought – *Others will make the decisions* – His only role – *To discern betwixt one or the other in case of discrepancies* – But then and there the pilots were in complete agreement; nothing to be done. And if there was, and he had to make a decision and something did go wrong, he could blame his advisors.

The ship suddenly groaned and lurched and Mendaña stumbled. Gallego roared across the water: "Heave ho! We sail lads!"

A band at the wharf, kettle-drums and long horns, stirred and blew and thumped. Behind them were the crowd, most of whom were at that moment sitting or lying on the ground, many with their backs to the ships. They clambered up and applauded. Some lads had flags on long poles and they pushed through the band, to the front, where they began swinging their banners, as if writing coded messages in the air.

But after the initial excitement the atmosphere in the crowd became gloomy: "A tragedy," someone said, and loud enough for others to hear it. They punctuated the sentiment with sniffles.

"Off they go," shouted another, in the direction of the governor: "To a destination that they're all so sure about, even though not even a fly has been there," and then reaching up on tiptoes to look over the crowd and catch the governor's reaction: "Because a little birdie has told them so!"

"Columbus didn't know where he was goin' either."

"But Columbus was a bloody sailor. The governor's nephew, on the other hand, wouldn't know how to get across Lake Titicaca."

This provoked more sobs than laughter.

"Don't worry mum," a bright young voice insisted: "Our Diego's gonna come back a rich man."

An optimism which was not ignored by another cynic: "Rich! That's what they think! I'm glad I'm not on board."

"But you could've been an 'ero for once in yer life."

"Phhh ... Hero? This world is full of heroes. We were heroes for comin' here, to this hell-hole Peru," an anti-patriotism which caused a disapproving murmur: "I mean, we may be better off here than we would have been in Castile or Galicia, but how many of yer still feel like heroes? Eh? ... Bah! And what happened to Columbus? He was a hero ... as were the Pizarros ... look what happened to them. Were they happy? Did they die happy? Not on yer life. What's the point if there's no peace to get from it?"

A philosophy that inspired other stoics: "The hero lives in a world full of his neighbours' envy. Nobody really likes the winners. Let me be a loser. I'll stay here," which even generated a bit of applause.

Out in the bay on Sarmiento's ship the men waved slowly. Many of them sensed the gloom ashore and shivered. The abyss that they were sliding into suddenly became apparent. A murkiness that spread. Sarmiento perceived the damage and screamed to one of the African slaves who was a trumpeter: "Blow! Blow!"

The slave took a deep breath, filled his cheeks and his horn blurted. Then cannons were let off. Sarmiento ordered other crew members to raise their own standards and pennants and signal back to the snaking flags ashore. A ceremony which made even the cynics clap. It was a slow dribble at first, but with a steady increase of momentum, until they all erupted with a stirring cheer. Rational despair was mitigated and the prophets of doom at the harbour began to dance and scream while, on the ship, sailors raced to and fro, tugging at ropes, yelling, waving, becoming monkey-men clambering up stiff masts: "Let out the top-sail!"

Hunched figures in rufous coats mopped the worn and wrinkled decks: "Heigh-ho my hearties, get to't lads!"

And the Gemini fleet slapped the sea.

I flung myself outwards to get an objective look. There the ships became more decrepit than inspiring. Dark, egg-shaped hulls, stained and draped with green, furry folds. And the design of them seemed hopeless. Tiny, rough and rounded vessels, bulging pregnant bellies that were ample in width but short on length. Bobbing eggs, they were, difficult to manage and manoeuvre, so easy to crack and break apart. Tall towers fore and aft threatened to tip the ships over rather than guarantee any stability. They advanced clumsily, only as well as such egg-ships could, according to the winds, which were always encouraged: "Blow!" the crew yelled, to either their African trumpeter or some invisible cherubim angels: "Blow!"

But if there had been statisticians they would have known the grim odds that I had seen: eighty per cent chance that the ships would sink.

Mendaña grimaced and rubbed his temples. So much sun and noisy activity had given him a headache and proximity to the sweating crew made him quake. Not that he was frightened of them, it was more the quivering effect of a gentleman's repulsion for what he called *the ugliness of ordinariness*. The youngsters aboard were full of racing enthusiasm for adventure, but the older men carried heavy, dubious features. Scarred and bitter faces; ugly masks for even more decrepit souls.

If Mendaña did look into those roughly hewn countenances, he found a hot reflection of disgust and undisguised animosity. If he caught their eye they would openly snarl; as if daring him to give an order. But he was not only frightened to offend or be offended, he was also repulsed by the essence of them. By the way they ate, how they spat bone and fat back onto the plate with the rest of the food. If they did use their blades at the table it was to pick gristle out of the gaps between teeth or drag black filth from their fingernails – *Such pigs will be hard to control* – he realised.

I caught the thought and followed Mendaña's gaze, across the deck to Don Pedro Ortega de Valencia, the *maestre de campo*, who was the officer in charge of the troops. He was an old, but still sturdy and corpulent man, prowling the deck with a stick. His suit was black, except for a bright yellow girdle around an immense belly: a protuberance which emphasised the thinness of his stockinged-legs and his knobbly knees. He stiffened, sensing someone staring and turned, then acknowledged his captain-general by raising his staff. He seemed to try to smile too, but the features of his face sagged into drooping sacks of fat, except for his bottom lip which was held firm against the downward tendency; giving him a grouper personality, ready to snap.

– *He's your mastiff*" – Mendaña remembered the governor saying – *Mastiff?* – he thought – *I'd think him more like a decrepit bumblebee* –

But then Mendaña did see dogs. Two of them, both huge and straining forward, although retarded by strangling chains. These were clenched by the thick hand of their master, who was himself a slave; Ortega's slave. An African, bare-chested with gritted teeth, his arms bulging while the dogs' fangs also revealed themselves in twitching, dribbling jowls. They passed in front of Mendaña, who gulped – *The bumblebee has a wasp's sting* –

Meanwhile, while Hernán Gallego was guiding his ship out of the bay, Sarmiento was in his cabin, inspecting navigation instruments spread out on his bunk and flicking through the pages of a thick book. This was full of illustrations and diagrams; a guide to the craft of sailing.

He went to a chapter called *Direction Finders* and tried to match the pieces on his bunk with an illustration or description. There was a lacquered box that looked something like a rough drawing on the page. He twisted the book around to examine it from all angles and, when he was convinced they were identical, he voiced the term printed under the illustration – *box-compass* – as if he were learning a foreign language. Then he spread out some rolled up parchments – *portolans* – he whispered. They were embellished by flower-like designs which were markers called – *wind-rose rays* – he assibilated. He also uncovered the name of a star-shaped board which looked like a blocking game with holes and pegs. It was called a *Traverse Board*, and it was used for counting *the legs of the tack*. He scratched his head – *bearing and distance* – he reminded himself. Then – *What did I tell them? That I was a great navigator? Greater than Columbus?* –

He had never been in-charge of a boat in his life. As a child he had sailed with his father on their fishing trips, but it had always been others pulling the ropes and turning the rudder – *Thank God that the governor had the brilliant idea of putting Mendaña in command; now he can make the mistakes* – But though he did not have the fleet, he *was* in charge of the *Capitana*. He would have to make some decisions.

So he continued and went to a chapter titled *The Mariners' Chores*, discovering terms like *veering* and *tacking*. There were diagrams explaining the application of trigonometry to navigation – *Mathematics is a magic science, as mysterious as my alchemist's kiln* – He laid out the altitude instruments but just sighed, frustrated – *Angles and angels* – he told himself – *God was a geometrician* – Then scratched his head again – *This can't be any more difficult than plotting a natal chart* – But he quickly grew frustrated and slammed the book shut, laying still for a while, listening to the creak of wood.

When he got up again, he reached into another pile of books and opened an Aristotle. He read quickly at first but then stopped to ponder a phrase – *The primal element is water, and, accordingly, the world floats on water* – not Aristotle's idea, much older, from Thales. It troubled him though. He stared into a goblet of wine, where a crumb trembled on the surface – *The ship rocks; the world shakes. But in what receptacle lies the water that supports the world? And in what goblet universe, on what table, in which ship?* – He gulped the wine and swallowed the crumb, then went out onto the deck and into the wind. He had spent years dreaming of it, now he could smell it.

Mendaña turned up his nose and gripped his stomach as his cabin boy came forward with a plate of sliced cuttlefish swamped in a garlic and brine sauce. He was seasick then, but even when his stomach became more hardy he would still shy away from such emanations. This meant that when practically anybody drew too close he would cringe, a gesture which did not make him any more popular. He tried to restrict his direct communication toward sailors with a *decent* appearance. Those who were not filthy or flea-bitten, and he always donned gloves before touching anything communally mauled. In fact, he felt comfortable with hardly anyone except his servant boy Juan.

Juan López had been placed specifically by Mendaña's uncle. Perhaps that was the only kind thing the governor willingly did for his nephew.

I saw them together one morning. Juan: a short, stout body gave strength to an otherwise insipidly soft face framed by long, brown hair with sun-bleached tips. As he approached Mendaña's cabin, his white cotton shirt billowed open. He was bringing the captain-general his breakfast on a tray. A bucket full of vomit lay by the side of Mendaña's bunk. Juan removed it. When he returned he was gripping a black book.

"Ah Juan," said a mawkish Mendaña: "Thank you for your concern. Verily, I was most ill last night," and he rubbed a crispy smudge of dry bile from his chin with his sleeve: "But that does not make a need for you to read me your Bible."

The servant blushed: "No, señor. This book is not a Bible."

Mendaña gave a hard blink: "Yet you are a licensed preacher."

Drawing Juan's chin proudly up: "Yes, señor, but I would prefer to be a conquistador."

The captain-general's stomach turned with a wave inspired roll: "Like Cortés?" Which rose with his swirling gut.

The servant looked sadly sympathetic: "No, señor."

"Pizarro?" And his knees lifted under his blanket folding his legs into his chest.

Juan took a damp rag and applied it to his leader's forehead, to cool, as did his voice: "No. Like none of them. I would be a Cid, or an Amadis of Gaul, señor," blown whispering warm into the young captain-general's pink ear: "I would resurrect the spirit of chivalry, fight evil and create good by my great example. My fight would be for love," and he wiped a last trace of yellow-green vomit from a dry corner between Mendaña's lips: "Or for King and God, but not for gold."

"Very noble ideas Juan, very noble indeed," which came out languid. The following question was excited by comparison: "But this book you have?"

"It's a book of romantic verse, señor," and he passed the leather-bound tome to his master, who took it in one quivering, white hand, running the palm of his other over its surface as if he were a faith-healer examining a troubled soul.

When he had finished he regained spirit and sat up: "Then let us read," he was actually quite jolly, his voice gathering body: "And I've heard that you play the lute."

Juan's little mouth responded to the joy of recognition: "Yes, señor."

"Then go fetch it, and let's hear it," and flicking through the pages of the book with an excited eye: "And we'll sing," his smile broadening with each new page: "Many of these verses are songs I know."

That was to be the first day of many recitals: *"In Castile there is a castle,"* they sang: *"With a moat of gold, and battlements of silver; betwixt parapet and parapet, stones of sapphire, In Castile there is a castle."*

But the captain-general had the kind of singing voice that had to be endured rather than enjoyed. Nevertheless, it seemed to relax him and no one complained to his face.

At first there was very little for Mendaña to do. The pilots knew which course to set, and the officers which orders had to be given, so the captain-general could spend plenty of time with Juan López and his lute; swapping books of romantic verse and tales of chivalry. This suited him well, for Mendaña had truly had what some would call a sheltered life, what *he* would have called a cultured one: the life of the Spanish *hidalgo*. He had been born into a noble family, in a small village in León called Congosto: "Oh we had less than one hundred neighbours Juan, and more than eighty of us came from noble stock."

But despite all his idleness Mendaña considered even that easy part of the voyage to be a terrible trial. In order to appear to be leading, it was recommended that he should spend at least two hours a day in public, on the poop-deck, with his pilot Gregorio.

Gregorio Gonzalez was a filthy man by Mendaña's standards, suffering a tendency to ooze copiously from the pores that was aggravated by a love of liquid intake and a passion for garlic. When he was with him, Mendaña would soon become gloomy.

On that second day at noon, Gonzalez was there on the poop, with a metre-long stick resting on his cheekbone. He pointed this toward an indeterminate point between the sun and the horizon. Then he closed one eye and looked along it, as if it were a telescope, whilst jostling a shorter, perpendicular piece of sliding iron.

When Mendaña saw Gonzalez with the stick he froze, until he thought he had discerned exactly what his pilot was doing. Then he rushed forward, halting again at Gonzalez's back, panting and wriggling with nervous excitement, as if his bladder were full: "My dear Gregorio," he whined: "For God's sake, you're holding a stick. Put it down please before the crew see what a fool you are making of yourself. I'll get you a telescope, but I would not point it at the sun, for I have heard that many an innocent wag has been blinded for it. Mark me now, I say, put the stick down."

Gonzalez did so. Then turned. His own gnarled and ruddy features curling into an expression of total incomprehension while studying the trembling-pale face of his commander: "Please, Cap'ain, you all right?"

Mendaña's face screwed into his own squinting expression of mystification: "Perfectly, my dear Gregorio, it is *you* that I am concerned with," and pointed to the stick: "You were looking down it, up at the sky."

Gonzalez shook his head. A smirk and resigned sigh: "I was shooting the sun, Cap'ain."

Mendaña bit his top lip and squeezed his hands together as if in a desperate prayer: "I think you should lie down Gregorio, the departure was so busy, and, well, with Mars in opposition to Saturn this week who knows what kind of colic has been unleashed from your spleen? Eh, what? Shooting at the sun! Señor Gonzalez, that is a *stick*."

"A staff, Cap'ain."

"What?"

"This stick's a staff."

"A staff?"

"Yes, a cross-staff they call't. Or a quadrant," and he pushed it up to a gulping Mendaña's eye. The captain-general grimaced as the pilot's breath wafted across. Gregorio seemed to sense it, and he blew as much air into his commander's face as he could: "Close your other eye please, and point the staff midway betwixt the sun and the sea," Mendaña's legs began to wobble. The pilot continued: "And then slide this little iron along until it's lined up with the sun at the top and the horizon at the bottom." He gripped Mendaña's wrist: "Then, when we've fixed the position, we look at where the iron pointer is on the staff and, there you have it, Cap'ain. Now we know what our latitude is." He even slapped the captain-general's back, which shuddered: "At the moment we're sailing at thirteen and a half degrees south."

Sarmiento's ship was a degree higher. They had been at sea for three days, had a good wind behind them and had advanced nearly four hundred kilometres. For the majority of the crew it was easy sailing, but it was precisely that calm which dragged forth memories for Sarmiento. Reflections on what he thought to be his curse.

His own birth chart: Scorpio in the eleventh house, with the moon aligned with Mercury, implying the sudden death of friends, and a sadism; and the moon again in opposition to Venus in the fifth disillusions; difficulty to love; a latent homosexuality – *Did I love him?* – he thought, considering his dead cousin.

Meanwhile on the *Almiranta*, Mendaña was trying to amend his *faux pas* with Gonzalez by complaining about his miserable condition. He ripped a white handkerchief from his sleeve and patted his nose: "Oh Don Gregorio, being a noble is by no means as pleasant as the peasants think, you know. I mean, in some ways it is a curse."

The pilot pulled an exaggerated, ironically sympathetic face: "Really Cap'ain?" his voice full of sarcastic interest too: "You mean that not payin' taxes is a bad thing?"

Mendaña, oblivious to the mockery, became patronising: "Why yes, Gregorio. I would love to pay taxes. But it is impossible for a noble to do so. It would be going against the Will of God. Noble lineage is a gift from the Lord, and if that gift were to be sullied, why it would bring a curse down on us all. Just as Lancelot's sin brought a curse on Avalon, so the whole Empire would find itself sinking into a quagmire of putrefaction."

"If the nobles paid taxes?"

Which was deeper now, with insult, but Mendaña was still oblivious and maintained the condescending lecture: "Yes, Gregorio, if the nobles paid taxes. For our fathers and grandfathers were knights; the same knights who had a dream called ..." and then clicked his fingers, indicating that he was waiting for Gonzalez to finish with the right word.

"Called a dream, Cap'ain," now not only deep but desert dry: "A dream is called a dream, unless it be a nightmare."

"Tut-tut, no Gregorio, the dream was called *Spain!* They built it from the sweat of their own swords."

"Of their backs, Cap'ain. The expression is the sweat of their backs. It's the *blood* of their swords, Cap'ain."

Which was able to frustrate the captain-general and his pitch climbed: "Yes, well, with blood and sweat, who cares? The point is that their chivalry and heroism made our Empire what it is, and they should be grateful for that!"

"Who should?"

"The peasants!"

"Well, if you say so, Cap'ain," and he scratched his bearded cheek.

"I will affirm it a thousand times. And do you know that if we nobles did pay taxes, very soon there would not be a single noble left."

"Oh really, Cap'ain? Why is that?"

"Because of inflation, Gregorio, inflation."

"Ah, inflation."

"Yes, inflation."

"Which comes from the Latin: *in-flatulus,* Cap'ain," giggled the big man, who then burped.

"Oh yes, go on laugh. It's obvious you've been away from Spain a long time, because ever since they started shipping gold over from the colonies the prices have been blown right out of proportion. The price of goods and services go up while the value of the nobles' lands plummet."

The pilot shook his head, making curls wobble: "What a pity, milord."

Mendaña stiffened his back and jaw: "That's why I emigrated," then through gritted teeth: "When my parents died I was left without any inheritance, not a penny."

That brought Gonzalez's head up and he held Mendaña in a hard stare: "So you came to Peru, to rest in the bosom of your good uncle the governor."

Which was unbearable for Mendaña and he had to turn and shake the affront away: "Well, he wasn't governor when I arrived, you know?"

"No, not quite; you were very lucky, Cap'ain."

Provoking a turn, with a raised and jerking finger: "Lucky? Was I? Well, pray, if you think so; but personally I don't regard this post of mine on this worm-eaten ship, sailing into the middle of nowhere, as lucky!"

This made Gonzalez darkly serious. He put a contemptuous finger to his lips: "Hearken my words, Cap'ain. You may think this is all an absurdity, and it may be, but if you want to get yourself back to Peru, or Spain, or anywhere else in one piece, then I suggest you keep those sceptic thoughts to yourself. For really, the office of a lord is to give, and the day that the first knight began to horde his wealth instead of sharing it, was the day that the Grail was lost; it had nothin' to do with Lancelot's lasciviousness. You, Cap'ain, *you* are the commander, and if *you* don't believe in this voyage, marry, nobody will."

Mendaña was at first stunned by the cultured rebuff. His lips began to tremble, unsure of his moral right to condemn the sailor's insolence.

Eventually he huffed and, convincing himself that there was no good reason for a captain-general to be on deck, he went inward to contemplate his mission in the maps he had – *Good or ill guesses* – he wondered – *Let there be no danger* – he prayed – *As long as it is sunny and warm, and that the sea does not get too rough* –

He unrolled a parchment he had locked away in a little chest, but it was blank except for one wiggling line down the right-hand side. After contemplating this for some seconds he screamed to Gregorio Gonzalez: "Where's that blasted map?"

The navigator raced into the cabin, looked down at the table, then looked up at Mendaña: "There, Cap'ain, in your hands."

"This is the map!?"

"In a sense, Cap'ain."

"In a sense?"

"Well, it's not a map yet; we have to draw it, don't we?"

"But I thought we knew where we were going."

Which inspired a squinting-blink: "Pray General, we do. We are going in search of the Isles of Solomon and the undiscovered continent known as the Terra Australis, that are said to be rich in gold and ..."

Mendaña bared his teeth: "Yes, I know all that," and thumped a rigid digit down: "But where are they on the map?"

"They're not there."

"Why not?!"

Gonzalez was starting to lose his own patience: "Because we have to draw'em, when we find'em."

Mendaña stood legs spread, with his fists pressed into his hips: "So, we don't know where they are?"

The pilot picked amber wax from one ear: "Oh, but pray, Cap'ain, we do."

"Then where are they?"

"Well we know we have to sail," and unconsciously licked the bitter oily blob on his fingertip which made him grimace: "Down to twenty-three degrees south."

Mendaña began to pace: "And when we reach the latitude of twenty-three degrees we will find what we are looking for?"

"Umm ... I suppose so, Cap'ain," and he began to play with a dark curl over his forehead.

"You suppose?"

"I don't know."

"Well, who knows, sirrah!?"

Gonzalez shook his head in taciturn frustration: "Captain Pedro Sarmiento. He knows. He has the map."

Mendaña's neck tightened into something tortoise like, which made his voice rasp: "So Captain Sarmiento is leading this fleet."

"Oh no, Cap'ain," and the curls shook again.

"Then who is?"

"You, General," which came with a nod.

"Good," but then he exploded again: "So I am leading this fleet even though I don't know where I'm going," and laughed and shook: "That's very good. Marry, I think I might have a bit of wine to celebrate," then physically pushing Gonzalez aside: "Where's Juan?"

Sarmiento stood alone on the poop.

He, by himself with the ship's smooth rudder in his rough hands. Gallego had gone across to the *Almiranta* for a meeting with Mendaña. Catoira was resting. He gripped the rudder hard and steady, his eyebrows lowered, darkening his eyes, looking to the horizon. A slight haze blurred it whichever way he looked. Always distant, always the same distance from the centre. They had been at sea one week. In the centre, amidst nothing. He looked down at the rest of them, blackened and dried by the sun and wind, rigid at their posts – *Each one of them their own centre* – But then the idea was repulsive. It made him shiver. So vast and empty. His chest ached – *If death should be like that* – he thought – *a vast and empty centre* –

The ship sighed as Mendaña scrambled up onto the *Almiranta's* poop to attend his meeting with Gallego. His white gloves appeared to the chief-pilot first, then a pouting mouth face as he hauled himself up, banging his head on the rail. The pale, sickly grimace that resulted made Gallego shiver, but he smiled, bent his back and held out a hand – *Mendaña is an imbecile* – he decided – *but a close relationship will have to be maintained* –

Mendaña rubbed his head and smiled as he rose. He wanted to be positive. He had learned that a good captain should inspire: "How now good Gallego, marvellous breeze, what? We'll soon enough be where we want to be, eh?" Gallego sucked air through his teeth, which whistled, a signal that Mendaña picked up on, though it puzzled him: "What troubles you, loyal Gallego?"

Gallego took a moment to answer, stunned by the adjective – *loyal*. The irony of it saddened him. Then he had to pause, to empty his mind and abolish self-guilt, before he could assume his role and his actor's lines. It was a spurt: "Our landfall, General."

"Landfall? It'll be short in coming, hark you this, eh?" But having spoken Mendaña realised that he was asserting something he absolutely knew nothing about. His own audacity shocked him. The blind leading those that could see perfectly well. It made him turn suddenly away, to bite his lip, before spinning back. But the old-salt just shook his head and looked away from the probing stare.

Mendaña's mind stirred. The pilot had been offended – *By me* – he realised, but then – *It's my uncle's fault, it was he who suggested following Sarmiento's course* – Suddenly he imagined a deep gash in Gallego's heart – *Poor old fellow* – he thought. Obviously too late, but he had to try something to patch it all up: "Do you think us to be still distant from the Isles of Gold?"

Gallego lifted his head. His feigned humility gave his voice an infantile ring: "Yes, señor. Either we change course now, or we're lost. And as for all that talk of Don Pedro. Well, to speak sincere, I think he be a terrible taborer. All brave noise. But as for 'is tabor tale, as 'ollow as any drum's roll, it makes me stomach ache each time he thumps it."

Mendaña's blood rushed. So glad was he to have so successfully contrived his pilot's sentiments that he embraced the old man: "These miserable doubts should have been expressed before."

Gallego felt himself stiffen in the young commander's arms: "I've no wish to offend no one, señor."

Mendaña relaxed his grip, his arms preferring to draw flourishes in the air. He was beginning to appreciate the histrionics of leadership: "But do not leave this matter so unresolved. Your counsel now is urgently necessitated."

Gallego deliberately paused and feigned thinking, before expressing himself with a solemn pitch: "Then it's best we deduce a more obvious line."

The round ship rolled over to starboard and Mendaña's mind turned with it. He recalled a night with his uncle, in the palace. The governor, flourishing a gold, gem inlaid goblet brimming with fine red wine, lowered his voice as Gallego had just done, to sound stern. In the same breath that he had recommended following Sarmiento's route he had warned him not to be taken in by the alchemist: "If he should fill your heart with sumptuous romances of fantastic lands," he rasped: "It would be better for you to act as Ulysses were obliged to do, and stuff your ears with wax," and he tapped his own earhole with a jewelled finger in case the nescient nephew, who was thinking more of sirens than brave captains, had not understood: "The stories he will tell you of Solomon's Sapient Isles shall serve the mission well to inspire your simple minded crew, but let not the captain-general be taken in by such charlatanry," and he gasped after gulping a mouthful of wine: "His Terra Australis is a dream," which rose almost to a shout, as if to wake the dozing nephew: "It is not *your* cause," then lifting a waving hand as he prepared to preach: "Spiritual paradise is in the heavens, not on earth," which made Mendaña thoughtful: "Sail south, south-west to twenty-three degrees. Then, when no land is found, for there will be none, let me assure you of that, change course," and making sure the nephew was attending carefully: "North-west, towards the Philippines."

Having communicated these imperatives, his tone relaxed into a kinder paternalism: "Your mission is a simple thing. No continents, you are looking for islands. 'Tis not the spiritual gold that we want, but the wealth that can be made from the spice trade," becoming pompous and official: "If you encounter new, economic ports then so be it, you shall conquer them for our Royal Majesty the King of Spain," slurping wine and shouting again: "But none of this Earthly Paradise drivel, I beg you."

Each evening while he munched his supper, Sarmiento scrutinised the charts drawn up by the pilots. This time he choked on the salted ox-tongue he was eating and Hernán Gallego had to thump his back until his windpipe was cleared: "Are you all right?"

Sarmiento was purple: "Fie, no, Gallego. I'm not. These charts you drew are wrong, sirrah. According to this we've turned a quarter of a degree north."

Gallego smirked and coughed through his smile: "Oh yes, Cap'ain. It's for the winds, so that we don't lose 'em."

Sarmiento thumped the table. The plate bounced and the tongue was flicked to the floor: "A pox on your winds, sirrah! The line has changed."

Gallego looked at the chart as if it were the first time he had seen it: "It's a slight correction."

"Correction!"

"Yes, correction. My course is better. If we lose the winds blowin' from Peru ..."

"Then we'll get winds blowing from Chile! You have changed *my* course, Gallego! Without asking permission. And I'm the captain of this ship, marry. Should I not have been consulted?"

"You're the captain of *this* ship, but we sail in a fleet. General Mendaña has ratified me decision. He knows it's better."

The next morning there was a tremendous commotion on the *Almiranta* too. Gregorio Gonzalez and the *maestre de campo* Pedro Ortega burst into Mendaña's cabin. The old soldier went straight to Mendaña's bunk where the captain-general had not even stirred. He cleared his throat and called Mendaña's name, but when there was still no response he actually slapped his superior's back with his walking stick: "General, señor, wake up! There are bad tidings."

Mendaña wriggled before tumbling to the floor. Gonzalez offered a hand to help him up with, but the captain-general refused, preferring to grapple with wood and blankets. When erect he began to stagger, drunk with half-sleep and fading nightmares, he wobbled out onto the deck with a blanket still wrapped around him, rubbing his kidneys and shading his eyes against the morning sun.

Through yawns: "Morning already?" then recognising the anguished expressions on the faces of the men before him: "What's happened, pray?"

Pedro Ortega was wheezing and waving his stick toward the horizon: "The *Capitana* has disappeared."

"Disappeared?" then turning to Gonzalez: "Gregorio!" who trotted over: "Yes, General."

"What day is it?"

"Saturday."

"And did you change course yesterday?"

"No, General."

Pedro Ortega's diaphragm pushed his bumble-bee belly up and he roared: "Change course!? What are you saying, change course? We all know the right line. Very simple. Very clear. Just as it should be."

Mendaña sniffled: "I think I'm catching a cold," and blew his nose. Ortega and Gonzalez both looked aghast. He sniffed again: "Oh really, you are so thick-headed Gregorio. We should have veered north-west yesterday afternoon. Didn't you see the other ship turning?"

Gregorio Gonzalez stuttered: "Y-yes, General, it t-turned, but ..."

"But what, Gregorio?"

"You said nothing about changing ..."

"Oh, Gregorio, so you were waiting for me to order you, were you? That's new. So I should have told you, should I? That's very new indeed."

The pilot noticed that Ortega was glaring at him as well, which made him cringe: "General, please, I had no idea."

"But didn't Gallego tell you?"

"No."

He had the pilot sweating, which pleased him: "And did you not ask anybody when you saw his ship veer away?"

Gregorio Gonzalez felt himself melt: "No."

"Tut-tut, Gregorio. And what are you going to do now?"

"Changing course, General. North-west," which sounded abysmal.

Mendaña sniffed his victory by holding his nose high: "Aye Gregorio, and be quick about it."

And went back to his bunk.

Gonzalez groaned while Ortega grumbled: "No way to run a ship."

When they had recovered and reached the *Capitana*, Ortega pushed on his staff to lean his massive bulk over the rail in order to manage a clean shout at Gallego: "Next time you change course tell one of our pilots, will you, sirrah!?"

Gallego sounded cocky: "I did, pray. I told the general."

"You'd do better to tell an albatross," which came out of what sounded like a potato-full mouth as his thick arms pulled him erect: "Make room for us. We're coming aboard."

So Ortega, Mendaña and Gonzalez stepped into a wobbling dinghy to be rowed across to the *Capitana*. Mendaña contemplated Ortega's prow filling belly while rubbing his own delicate guts. The short traverse was a constant sequence of lurches; and he soon became green and grumbling: "Shouldn't they be coming over to us."

At the meeting Mendaña was surprisingly firm from the beginning, twisting a bright red quill pen between his fingers as he commanded: "If, Captain Sarmiento, you do not show us your map, then I cannot go on *assuming* that it exists. I have one hundred and fifty lives to take care of. If Hernán Gallego tells me there'll be no winds lower than fifteen degrees, then I must believe him, map or no map, because he's the most experienced seaman we have."

Sarmiento spat into a bowl: "Then why did our chief-pilot not tell us about these winds when the course was plotted in the first place?"

Gallego sniggered. His tongue in his cheek: "Because I was not sure then."

"And now you are sure?"

The chief-pilot sniffed, straightened his back and leaned forward: "Yes, positive. I'd bet my balls on it."

Sarmiento smiled and shook his head: "But you've never seen *this*, have you Gallego?" and he slowly dragged his map out from under his shirt. He rolled it out and ran a finger along it, tracing his planned route. It was the first time any of them had looked on it, and they all leaned forward in a kind of silent reverence, as if they had never expected to see it either: "Or did Ahedo show you it?"

Which prompted a sudden snap in Gallego's neck as his head suddenly twisted: "I never saw Pedro Ahedo's map, but he told me about it, and where the islands were, at seven degrees south, señor."

I too, looked closely at the chart. There were details I had not noticed before. Now I was also interested in latitude. At twenty-three degrees south, some distance off the eastern Australian coast, were two dots …

"Here they are," murmured Sarmiento: "Ophir and Tharsis. The Isles of King Solomon and the Three Kings," then comparing his with Gallego's route: "If we keep to your course we will never reach the Terra Australis, no matter how good these winds you promise us are."

Gallego spat: "They'll be better than no winds at all."

Meanwhile Mendaña had become engrossed by the presence of another group of islands mapped off the eastern coast of New Guinea, as if mirroring the Spice islands to the west of it at seven degrees south, just as Gallego claimed. He recalled his uncle's instruction – *Your mission is a simple thing. Spices are what we want!* – The memory of the governor, his wild eyes and thumping-fist-exuding confidence, inspired an aggressive mimicry: "Blast you Captain, you'll have to compromise. The islands the governor wants are these ones, lying off the coast of New Guinea."

Sarmiento croaked: "No señor, we're in search of Ophir and Tharsis, and the Terra Australis Incognita."

Mendaña took a deep breath. His eyes wide open, making a desperate attempt to seem wild. It seemed pathetic against his tremulous tone, but at least it convinced Mendaña himself. He even gave the table a slap to embellish his decision: "The Terra Australis may be a part of *your* plan, Captain, but it's not the aim of *this* fleet," and sniffed, as if the pathetic gesture demonstrated conviction: "We will keep this course, maintaining it at around fifteen degrees." Gallego tried to interject against the absurdity that Mendaña had just pronounced, but the captain-general silenced him by raising his hand: "You too, good Gallego, must compromise. We'll go no further north, at the moment. If I, or anyone else, has any well founded ideas to change our route, or if anyone would like to reveal any other secret map that they may have, then the pilots and captains will meet together with me, on *my* ship. Is that understood?" They nodded. Inspired by the confirmation he immediately modified his own law: "Better still, we shall keep the ships close and meet each day for a briefing, understood?" When Mendaña stood up again, he seemed taller.

Eight days later Hernán Gallego looked up, blocking sun from his eyes to examine a frigate bird that was soaring high on motionless wings. This lifted and dropped with a mocking control, poking fun at the giant, cumbersome, egg floating below it. Gallego grew excited by the presence. Sharp lines of other groups of seabirds were advancing or retreating across the sky. His body creaked with the ship's timber as he bent his neck back, his squinting eyes peering through the wind and sea spray. He was not interested in classifying species and types, for him the birds were all *birds*; what was important was their direction, where they had come from, where they went. That was where the land would be – *It has to be close* – he thought and reached up for the booby above him. But that bird twisted its neck, flapped its wings, caught a current of air and was off – *Retreating or advancing?* – Their trajectories were confusing, a constant crossover from north and south. Leaving with the dawn they returned at dusk, but to and from where?

– *This movement of birds indicates that if we veer either north or south we will have to find land* – he concluded – *yet Ahedo had insisted that we could only ever reach* terra firme *at seven degrees* – and then he was filled with doubts, ending with the sneaking suspicion that Ahedo had lied.

Sarmiento's calculations were also erroneous. He contemplated the same gannets and boobies as Gallego, and wrongly estimated that they were most definitely in the vicinity of the Terra Australis. Imagining an imminent arrival, he prepared himself by re-reading the Greek vision of it.

Aristotle had claimed the Terra Incognita possessed the form of a dream. It was a world reigned over by the brother-gods, Hypnos and Thanatos, beyond the Boundless Sea. But this philosophy threw Sarmiento's mind into a turmoil and he became lost in the monstrous area of infinity. The term *Boundless* bounced into other associations and he pondered Anaximander who said that the Boundless had to be the beginning, because all is either a beginning or derived from a beginning, except for the Boundless Thing. The Boundless Thing is logically unique because it has no limits. It is situated beyond cause and effect, making it impotent and indestructible. The very fact that the Boundless Thing cannot be born means that it is the Beginning in itself. This was the kind of philosophy that inspired Sarmiento to wander in equally dangerous fields, coming to the conclusion that they were headed toward a part of the universe in which the Boundless and the Beginning existed together. The Alpha-Omega.

Gallego went into the captain's cabin with a goatskin sack of wine and passed it to Sarmiento without asking if he wanted a drink. Sarmiento took it and acknowledged the kind gesture. Gallego, when he did speak, was grave: "You hated Ahedo, didn't you?"

"I had my reasons."

"Everyone speaks badly of 'im, not just you. But I found 'im to be a gentleman, honest, and I would've been his cap'ain if they hadn't robbed 'im."

"He got what he deserved."

"Do you know that 'e invested four thousand pesos in this enterprise? Oh, the governor took it 'appily enough, then called 'im a pirate and 'ad 'im run out of the country. Would a pirate've given four thousand pesos out of 'is own purse?"

"If he knew he was going to get two ships fully equipped with cannon and harquebus he might. Even pirates have to start somewhere."

Mendaña sat up on his bunk. Although squawks were filling his head, it did not inspire him to go out on deck and look up. He was hot and feverish and needed to vomit. Arching, spluttering chunks splashed into a pan. The stench was foul, but he hardly thought about it, he was still devastated by a nightmare – *A field full of white poultry. Their mocking squawks were an insulting irritation, their waddling advance, an impudent march towards him. They displayed no fear, although the object they were clucking towards had a regiment behind him. "Beware! You will eat those insults, for I am in command here!" he shouted. But the fowls ignored all of his orders, and continued their steady march forward. Then an officer from the regiment came up to him and informed him that the harquebusiers were ready. He looked back. Impossibly long barrels were pushed up, poking forward, metres long. And behind them, a line of grinning infantry was ready to charge. He hurried behind, crouching behind a bush as he gave the order to open fire: "No prisoners!" he cried. And as the smoke and blasted, floating feathers cleared, the field now carpeted with croaking, squirming birds, he gave the order to unsheathe swords and charge. Soldiers screamed and hurled themselves into the fray, hacking at any surviving chickens' necks. Sweeping arms, slicing swords, a myriad of crimson spurts. Then, neckless fowls, feathered eggs on galloping legs, wings flapping, refusing to die and clucking "Revenge!", charged back. Some were still spurting blood from the severed tubes that were veins in their necks. They ran straight at the dreamer, who thrashed at them with his own sword, but they kept coming, hundreds of thousands of them, throttling into his face. In order to defend himself, he had to catch them between his teeth, ripping flesh off them, devouring it raw. Flesh which suddenly transformed into something pink and tough - and then he realised that he was chewing on a human arm. But this did not stop him. The sweet taste was delicious; it was impossible to put the morsel down. He gulped and slurped, burped - which echoed around a now still and silent battle field. "Have I won?" he asked himself, but felt a burning passion in his belly. He was unable to control himself. He tugged the last strips of flesh from the humerus bone, then advanced to gorge himself amidst what was now a banquet-field strewn with headless, human torsos.*

Sarmiento leaned over the taffrail and looked toward the east. A bright, golden bar flashed, burning the horizon and announcing the inevitability of a new morning. Purple and gold light gushed across the ocean and a breeze picked up. Still cool – *The best time of day* – he thought.

"Señor," the voice, a soft whisper, plunging into Sarmiento's ear. It was Catoira. He was pointing to the south. A cloud bank was reclining seductively, red smears streaking folds of grey and black – *As if it has been slashed* – thought Sarmiento, but then realised the significance – *Avachumbi and Ninachumbi!* – and his hand slapped over his mouth, retarding any compromising expression of joy. He breathed deeply, through his nose, calming the thumping heart with oxygen, then released his hand, cupping it with the other. Arching fingers, tips touching, forming a little megaphone in order to project his order up to the boy in the crow's nest: "What do you see, lad?! Look to the south!"

A pause. A stumbling lump moved.

"A cloud, señor."

Sarmiento's hands went up, fingers splayed. His voice a rasping scream: "Fie, lad! Look closer on it! A pox on you if you cannot see land!" which generated a mute response. He groaned and murmured: "The lad is blind, marry!" then went forward and grabbed one of the African boys:

"You've got a better eye. Go up to the crow, boy. Tell the whelp up there to make room for you. Tell him to get down and scrub the deck."

He pushed him on and then turned and whispered: "The secret," into the wind so that it could be blown at Catoira: "The secret is there," and Catoira looked away, peering out, expecting to witness something exorbitant: "The secret," persisted Sarmiento, grabbing Catoira's shoulder: "Marry man, consider its form. That'll tell you. By location of the essential part, we see beyond God's revealed will to glimpse *it*." Catoira gulped and seemed about to ask: *"What?!"* but restrained himself. Sarmiento's hand on his shoulder squeezed tighter, his voice dropping: "The majority of men are blind to it. Blind, 'cause of their ignorance. Ignorance, Catoira, of essentials," and for a moment I thought Sarmiento was going to kiss the notary. He bit his own lip instead: "To know the essence of yellow, the quiddity of weight, the fundamentals of ductility, fixity, fluidity, solution and so on," then shaking his head and throwing his arms up in the air again: "And, on their discovery, to then cognise methods for super-inducing them, joining them into the one same body."

Catoira tried to tell himself that his captain was not mad, but inspired with genius. He tried to take it in, befuddling his mind with an incomprehensible immensity. It was a mystery that excited him and made him want to be brave.

Sarmiento, his voice crashing into a melancholy moan: "Our secret, Catoira, do you follow? It's by such manner that we can make gold from a lump of shit." He tensed, pushing a clenched fist under Catoira's nose, then dramatically released the fingers, making Catoira jump. The action had revealed a tiny, gleaming, golden pebble, sitting in his palm. But Sarmiento snarled: "Can you not smell how foul it is?" and threw the stone into the sea, laughing disparagingly at Catoira's instinctive gesture to catch it: "Wherever we go," he continued: "The norm will be the obscure. Alike to falling into a dream. To understand true revelation there must be transformation. Prepare yourself for Holy Metamorphosis! Solomon's University lies very near; the nought-meridian. We could become gods ourselves. I hope you are ready. The Great Work; the study." Catoira's jaw dropped and he blinked while Sarmiento laughed in his face. Then he slapped the writer on the back: "Not to worry, friend," he said softly. "The gold will be there, for anyone," afterwards mumbling to himself, unintelligible for Catoira: "Anyone worthy of extracting it."

The rumour of *land* quickly spread, and soon everyone had gone to the side. Gallego groaned. He knew Sarmiento was probably right. The cloud bank was huge and he had noticed even better signs that they were near land: sticks and coconuts in the sea, floating from the south. It seemed to be the final nail in the coffin of his own argument. But then he shook his head – *It cannot be* –

Sarmiento screamed an order to lower the longboat. The crew, sensing an end to the traverse, roared.

"Gallego!" he screamed, gesturing wildly: "Come on, man. We're going over to Mendaña's ship. I want you to be there."

Gallego shuffled sulkily, complaining that the sea was too rough. But two chirpy crewmen came forward with oars: "Not too bad for us, señores. We'll get you across safe and sound, don't you worry. We'd row you to that cloud itself if need be." And they became all limbs as they guided their captain and the rather depressed chief-pilot down into the longboat.

Gallego covered his head with his jacket as the little boat lurched through slamming waves. He seemed like a novice then, preferring not to look until they were within reach of the hawsers of the other ship. But it was shame, not fear, that made him cower. Sarmiento collected a rope and briskly clambered on board, making his way directly to the half-deck and the captain-general's cabin, bursting in without even bothering to knock.

Mendaña was sitting up on his bunk wrapped in a blanket. The cabin reeked of vomit. His servant, Juan, mopped his brow and wiped a streak of bile from his bottom lip. At the end of the bunk was Gregorio Gonzalez, hunched over charts.

Mendaña looked up, straightening his back. He forced himself to smile. His brown eyes were dull: "How now, Pedro," he said, weakly, then sparked up as Gallego also entered: "Hernán, welcome! Although your visit is early today, isn't it?"

Gallego hung his head as if he had been scolded. Sarmiento nodded.

Mendaña's smile brightened and he wafted his hand to indicate that they should approach: "Come, your presence here pleases us greatly," but after ejecting the phrase, his lips regressed into a muted expression: "Coincidental, don't you think Gregorio," and Gregorio Gonzalez grinned.

Mendaña maintained a look of practical insipidness: "We had just been talking about you?" Gonzalez nodded: "We've just come to a very important decision," and the captain-general smiled again, not a real smile, merely an ever-so-slight curl of the lips. He asked Sarmiento and Gallego to sit down, his lips twisting a little more, and, with his visitors' arses on stools, revealed that they had decided to change course again.

Sarmiento sniggered: "Aye, aye, señor."

Gallego looked at Gonzalez blankly. The chief-pilot was still depressed by the idea that Ahedo had lied to him. Mendaña meanwhile maintained his phlegmatic composure until he suddenly sneezed. Then, when Juan had wiped the mucus away, he informed Sarmiento, in a deep, dry voice, to tell his own officers and steersmen that they would be heading west-north-west until further notice.

"West-north-west?" echoed Sarmiento, and Mendaña repeated it.

"West-north-west".

When Sarmiento rose, his hand went instinctively to the pommel of his sword. The sniffling Mendaña could not have helped but interpret it as a mutinous movement, and he quailed. Sarmiento leaned forward: "Have you been outside this morning, señor?"

Mendaña coughed: "No, but I've been told about it. Some cloud they say. A vague possibility I've been told," and then firm: "But we're not here to look for chances!"

Sarmiento took a deep breath, but his eyes rolled: "Señor, we've already been travelling for three weeks with a gale behind us, as Gallego had predicted, but we've found nothing, until now. There is an island to the south of us and you want to ignore it!" Gallego's head dropped. Sarmiento went for the kill: "That the last decision to change course was an erroneous one," Gallego was even nodding in agreement at this. Sarmiento thumped his fist on Mendaña's desk: "And now you wish to amplify the problem by heading north when we should be returning south, we should sail to twenty-three degrees, as my map indicates."

Mendaña, his limbs once more solidified, looked at the down hearted Gallego: "Our chief-pilot said we should have gone north to seven degrees. I was wrong to have ignored him. Now we will rise. I cannot possibly risk this whim of Don Pedro Sarmiento's any longer. You see I am commended. My orders are from the governor himself. We sail for the Philippines. So we must to veer north immediately, despite the *vague* possibility."

Sarmiento already knew of the strategy. He felt momentarily desperate and yelled a defence he already suspected was futile: "Head for the Philippines. Aye señor, but only if we should not touch upon our goal at twenty-three degrees. At twenty-three, señor! We've not been there, so how do we know it's not there?" And he pointed leeward through the hull: "And really we are but a short step away," he growled.

Mendaña whined then used Gallego's old ideas to complain that they were running short of supplies. Gallego's eyes flickered and he looked down to hide his shame: "Once the crew start getting hungry they will become restless. Would you have us all dead? Is that how the sacred islands will be reached? In a pair of floating coffins!?"

Back on the *Capitana*, Sarmiento had to announce the change of course to his men. Brutal but eager faces looked up at him, tongues hanging like excited pups. Each one caressed the hilt of his sword. The two secondary pilots Enriquez and Manriquez acted as spokesmen. A stiff pair, so alike that they seemed like twins. Even their dry, monotonous tone of voice was identical: "The men, señor ..."

"... if you should wish it, señor ..."

"... the men will throw this general ..."

"... throw him overboard ..."

"... and go south with you ..."

"... we are all thirsty, señor ..."

"... thirsty for the pleasure of Paradise," and then they slapped Sarmiento's shoulder, one at a time, as if they had been lifelong friends.

The Captain smiled, lowering his own hands, one onto each of the pilot's hilts: "No, pray, no mutinous thoughts. It'd only damn us. There's no need to rebel. We'll arrive, each one who hopes. Destiny has prepared it for us. As for these fools that command us. They will have to conform, but be patient."

That Sarmiento took it so lightly was an indication of prescience. He had known, the cards had told him.

I often saw him with his future laid out on a table, often with his own card crossed by a man, usually the same character, the Knight of Disks. A black knight, his pitch armour, thick and heavy; the fiery part of earth; mountains, earthquakes and gravity. In his fist was a flail. Over his arm, a thick shield. The person symbolised by it is dull-witted, stupid and slavish, incapable of foresight. They are churlish, surly and jealous, and lack the courage or intelligence to better themselves. Yet they are always irritably meddling and interfering, and inevitably spoiling whatever comes their way. Any success is due to instinct rather than careful planning. Their fire is a smouldering patch in a desert.

– *Alvaro de Mendaña* – Sarmiento deduced, and whenever he laid the cards down he half-expected him. It did not perturb him though. Readings always left him optimistic. He knew that eventually he would set foot in Paradise, and that he would be highly lauded, would meet kings and queens, lead armies and would have books written about him.

Then something did sicken him. One night he spread a group of cards for Mendaña, who was not there, and who knew nothing about it. He did it simply out of idle curiosity, but the result brought out gooseflesh and tingling horripilation. The spread was ominous: dominated by the Tower, that ruined, crumbling, phallic edifice, that had been smashed by a lightning bolt. The eye of Horus was opening. This represented internecine energy at its most absolute. Mendaña, he realised, had to be pitied.

On Christmas Eve Sarmiento was approached by one of the two Franciscans aboard his ship.

He came onto the poop, rubbing his hands. A large insincere smile: "Good morrow, Captain."

Sarmiento's back straightened and he looked to the horizon rather than at the priest: "Good morning, Father."

The feigned smile was maintained: "The speech you gave this morning was quite rousing. Very appropriate. The crew's spirits have been dwindling these last weeks. But, I could not help but observe that you omitted any details about tonight's ceremony."

Sarmiento's head twisted back and glared at the friar through his own faked smile: "Oh, did I, Father? Perhaps I did, because I myself am ignorant of it."

The friar squeezed his rosary and became stern: "You would do well to spend less time with your astrology and consider your calendars. Tomorrow is Christmas day."

Sarmiento leaned back, enjoying the opportunity to apply irony: "Oh really, then you must organise something, Father. We can have one of your lovely masses. We have some wonderful voices aboard you know."

The friar shook his head: "Yes, Captain, yes, we certainly do, and we certainly will have a lovely mass. Three lovely masses to be precise: at midnight tonight, the aurora, and then morning mass. Of course, it is hoped that the Captain of the ship will attend all three of them," and then caught Sarmiento with a vicious stare, his voice turning to a hiss: "Remember, Captain, this is a Christian and Catholic endeavour," and after a deep breath: "Our prime objective is the evangelisation of the pagan aborigines in the immense lands you have promised we will find."

Sarmiento scratched his navel through his shirt, which was almost a disdainful gesture, then: "I'm aware of that Father. Although, calling it our primary objective is debatable," and grinned cheekily: "Your church was against the expedition from the start. *It would be too much of a strain on the colony's economy,* you said. As for these men," and he opened his arms to indicate the motley bunch around them: "You may think they believe in God because you've seen them cross themselves before dinner. Well, you're wrong, Father, these men only think about their pockets and their stomachs."

The priest swallowed hard and seemed about to spit: "Verily, señor, it is obvious how you feel about having God's representatives aboard, but I say to you: *beware.* I know where you've come from and I don't like it."

Sarmiento leaned forward. Blowing the words into the priest's face: "Then I am sorry for you, Father. For we are going to be together for some time still to come it seems. The Philippines are a long way off, and I'll be the captain of this ship at least until then. Now, if you want to celebrate your Christmas, go straight ahead, that is your job. *So do it*, and I will sail this ship."

I followed Sarmiento down, into the ship's bowels. A stove blazed. Flickering, ruddy illumination. He moved awkwardly, bumping his head on jutting beams, clambering towards the naked back of an African slave. The latter was working, on metal. Sarmiento reached out and dropped a hand on his shoulder: "Bubi," he gasped.

The sweating blacksmith twitched but did not answer. Sarmiento had to peer over his wide shoulder in order to divine that the slave had understood his assignment perfectly. That he had waited, as commanded, until a certain hour when the planets and stars were in a certain place. That he had drawn the two six-pointed sidereal designs in chalk within a circle on the floor around the anvil.

A European would have seen the blasphemy in the order. A European would have resisted and told someone. But the African was fabulously taciturn.

Bubi, of the Baleketo tribe. Of the Bubi people. From the West African Island of Fernando Poo. A wizard. But Bubi was not his real name: "You should never give your name to a stranger," he had told Sarmiento one other day: "He could kill you."

Sarmiento took the idea seriously. He had learned about names from Rodolfo as well: "My people are born with two names, a mundane title given by parents, and a magical name written in God's book," he told Bubi: "But the magical name is only known to a very select few, it gives us power."

"What is your magical name, señor?"

"If I told you, you'd have tremendous power over me."

"You see! We have the same belief."

"Yes, with a major difference, your people know their magical names, most of mine do not."

"Then your people are fortunate. I wish I had never known my name. One day a bad spirit heard my mother calling me, since then my life has been cursed."

"And where is this *bad* spirit?"

"He follows me."

"You've seen him?"

"Many times. I saw him before the slave-traders came to my village."

"And does this *bad* spirit have a name?"

Which made Bubi laugh: "If I knew it I would kill him, but of course he has a name, everyone has a name, everything. If you could talk to this hammer he might tell you his name."

"Do you know the hammer's name?"

"Yes."

"It spoke to you?"

"Yes."

"And what is the name?"

"I cannot tell you, señor. If I did, the hammer would get angry. It might kill me. But if you are a friend it will tell you itself. It will go to your dreams and tell you."

"I've heard it said that the Bubi people are the most savage on earth."

"That is because we are brave, but we are not cruel. We fight to protect ourselves. You would be savage too if you were woken in the night by the salve-traders' guns."

"Yet *you* did not fight hard enough."

"I saw many of my friends killed because the Portuguese were offering a horse for six slaves. Killed because they resisted. Because they did not like to believe themselves the same as the hind leg of a horse. But I preferred the certainty of slavery to the uncertainty of death."

"But now you're most certainly a slave. Why don't you fight your way home?"

"Perhaps one day I will. If I want to be *free*."

"Don't you want it?"

"I don't know. I don't understand it."

"You are a slave. I am free. Why is that so hard to understand?"

"And you have to bow to your general and your king. So are you a slave?"

"I'm a captain."

"I'm a Bubi. This hammer is my slave. I know its name. Who is not a slave, señor?"

"The king."

"The king? The Bubi king, you know, lives in the Bubi town of Riabba. That town lies at the bottom of a cold volcano. There the Bubi king sits and he cannot leave. He has forty wives and he cannot leave them. If he left, he would die. He cannot look on a white man or any of the white men's things. If he did this, he would die. Taboo, you know. The Bubi king has more taboos than any man. He may not even look at the sea. Not even from a distance. If he glimpses it, he dies. Who would you choose to be? The slave or the Bubi king?"

But despite this affirmation it had taken Bubi many years to accept the slave's role and in the first month he had tried to take his own life several times. When he did not die he imagined his *bad* spirit was saving him to inflict more terrible tortures. Resigned to the fact that he would not die until his demon was tired of tormenting him, he immersed himself in the palliative of work. Something for which a slave there is no shortage of: "All workers are slaves," the wise-wizard had pronounced one day to the other slaves: "Only the work itself can ever be true compensation for the life consumed by it."

On that day at the furnace his brown skin, bathed by the hot hypnotic light, gleamed. His gnarled hands operated according to the dictates of his eyes. His eyes were wells and just as the well in the village had reflected the faces of thirsty men, so his eyes also reflected the images that floated in different elements and dimensions. The universe existed in the task, he believed. And if the task was art, then he himself was a microcosm of the Creator.

The ivory orbs of his eyes rolled between their ebony lids. His brow and cheeks were disfigured by deep scars that had been cut when he had still been a child: "A Bubi custom," he had confessed: "But very recent. When the slave-traders began taking our children we began to stamp ourselves. If another Bubi sees my face there can be no doubt ... I am a Bubi."

Sweat dripped over the furrows, down the bridge of his nose, over his lips, into his mouth: "My essence is salt," he murmured.

He licked and blinked but did not brush the tickling moisture away, his hands were too occupied with the angle-tongs, clasping something tiny. His feet shuffled, struggling to create an equilibrium forming opposition to the anarchic roll of the ship. In front of him, another African slave carefully pumped the bellows while the slave-creator mumbled instructions. Then he pulled the thing out. Metal, but red hot and impossible to distinguish what kind. He lay it on the tip of the flat beak of the anvil and hammered it. It curled around. He heated it some more then pricked it with pincers, making a ring of it. Afterwards it was returned to the fire. Drawn back out. Hammered again. This time the ship stammered and the smith's mace missed its mark on the first beat. The ring was turned. Put back in. Out. Hammered again. One side flattened. He took the tongs and became a slave-artist to set about on an intricate design. Tiny. I could not make out exactly what it was. Sarmiento hissed with the water when it was finally immersed. Cooled, it looked to be bronze. He lifted it from the tongs that were proffered and held a candle up to it before mumbling a chant. It was a strange language, perhaps Aramaic, but I understood perfectly: *"This is the seal on the ring ...*

... he hissed and waved his hand, splayed like a plane-tree leaf ...

"Seven are her veils ...

... he whispered ...

"Seven her names and the lamps beside her bed
Seven eunuchs guard her with seven drawn swords ...

... the whisper growing ...

"In her wine cup are seven streams of blood ...

... and his eyes rolled, churning expressions of an inward journey. The younger slave laughed.

"Seven are the heads of THE BEAST ...

... his throat tightening to restrain the scream, making both of the Africans gasp.

Then Sarmiento was also gasping, his eyes widening, but his chant softened into a more melodic recitation ...

"And she rides
she rides
The head of an Angel
riding on the rising wind
Head of a Saint
rising on its martyrdom
Head of a Poet
martyred by its verse
Head of a Slut
thrashed by the exercised joy of strength
Head of the Virtuous Man
flagellated by his passivity
Head of a Satyr
unloved because of his budding-horns
Head of the Lion-Serpent
feared for the poison in its claws
Seven letters have her Holy Name

... and he drew the sign of the cross across himself, but starting at the navel, before waving his hand over the seal again ...

"This is the Seal upon the Ring

The Seal upon the tombs of them whom she hath slain ..."

... then threw a handful of some powder which made the fire shoot, enshrouding them all in a pink veil of smoke ...

The ships bobbed on and the atmosphere worsened. The men, tired. Rations were depleted. The water was foul: "It smells like a bean eater's fart, troth!" croaked one of the soldiers: "And the taste! I wouldn't wash my feet in't, never mind my liver, fie!"

The cook tied a large white handkerchief over his face before screwing open a barrel of putrid fish. The mestizo boys who were helping him raced out on deck to vomit. The smell wafted out of the galley with them, snaking slowly on elevating currents of air up onto the deck and up to the poop where Mendaña was arguing with the *maestre de campo*.

Pedro Ortega was ranting and waving his arms. When he argued, he was never discreet. Mendaña shuffled. The old soldier had become excruciating, especially as he championed Sarmiento's route. Ortega wanted to be a Pizarro, he needed a continent, and that was what Mendaña feared the most.

I can remember Mendaña another day with Juan López, who had been equally puzzled by his master's decision: "Why do we not follow the captain's instructions, señor, and go to the Terra Australis?"

Mendaña stroked the lad's cheek, tenderly: "Ah, Juan. Always the romantic. But our mission, as laid down by my uncle, has been most clearly stated. We are to discover *islands*. Besides if we arrived at this continent what would we do there?"

"We would conquer it, señor."

"Like Cortés and Pizarro?"

"Aye!"

"And who would lead our army?"

"Troth señor! Don Pedro Ortega of course!"

"Of course, Juan, of course. But think about it Juan. Don Pedro is no Cortés, and certainly not a Pizarro, poor old bull ... and besides, we don't even have horses. How could we conquer a continent, vaster than Asia itself, without horses?" The servant boy hung his head, so Mendaña pushed a finger under his chin and gently lifted it: "But worry you not Juan. We'll find islands, the Eastern Spice Isles. They were also on Sarmiento's map. A hundred of them. And perhaps Ophir and Tharsis are there. In whatever case you'll have your glory. One day they'll write books about you, I'm sure of it." He had been sipping wine and reclining amidst a bed of cushions on his bunk. Juan López was on the floor, with his lute, strumming softly. Mendaña sighed: "This romance that you read to me, of Sir Lancelot of the Lake, what was the name of that castle in which the Grail was found?"

"The castle, sir? It was Corbenic."

"And this Corbenic ... if you were to imagine it, where would it be?"

"On an island, señor. A solitary rock in the water."

"And could not that water be a sea or an ocean? Could it not be this vast gulf, Juan? Might it not be that *we* are headed for Corbenic? But it would have to be an island, would it not?"

"Oh verily, señor. Most definitely an island."

"And so I rest my case. Our course is good."

"And you are a good general. A good King Arthur, worthy of the Grail."

"And you Juan, will be my Perceval. The Grail will be yours." He took a sword and tapped the youth's shoulders, staring deeply into his eyes, until, realising the absurdity of such solemn histrionics, he burst into laughter.

Perhaps Mendaña recalled this conversation himself. It was obvious that his mind was not with Ortega's argument. He was more engrossed by the shapes of the blemishes staining the old soldier's bald scalp that cut a gleaming path between crinkly grey tufts of lustreless hair – *Marks which must mean something* – he thought – *A microcosmic key to his fate, which is partly mine as well* – Meanwhile, the *maestre de campo* was unrelenting: "Another day dawns, General, and we are still surrounded by the same horizons. The men are getting worried."

Mendaña yawned and Ortega squeezed his staff as if he were about to clobber his captain-general ... And it was at this moment that the stench from the galley wafted under their noses.

Both men shuffled away from each other, but before either could make an accusation, the cook was standing between them, mumbling through his handkerchief: "Most of the fish and meat is putrid, General. We'll have to ration."

Mendaña breathed in and choked.

It was Ortega who responded: "Ration you say, man! But we are given meagre enough portions now."

Mendaña shook his head: "But if the food is bad, we cannot eat it."

The compromise quickly came from Ortega: "We'll ration the crew and soldiers. Officers will be exempt, of course."

Mendaña's jaw dropped: "Shouldn't we make an example?"

"Do you want to make an example?"

"No."

"Then we won't."

The following day Mendaña was pale again with another seasickness. Juan López wiped his hot brow with a damp cloth. The general whimpered: "Oh Juan, did you not say once that I should be the king of this ship, its Arthur, and that this worm-eaten barge is our Camelot?"

"I said you were my Arthur, señor."

"And yet I'm a king without his queen. My beloved Guinevere is so far away, and that fills me with such melancholy."

"The quest for the Grail is, by its nature, a most triste journey. This grief in your heart is a test, more hard and painful than any battle against giants or dragons. On this quest our tournaments and adventures will be different, my dear General, but we'll have our miracles, mark me pray, I'm sure of it."

Mendaña and Sarmiento were antitheses. When the general became tyrannical Sarmiento displayed democratic tendencies. When Mendaña made his officers exempt from rationing, Sarmiento had his own officers endure the rationing as well.

One day I saw Sarmiento, stern, with cheerful Catoira, sitting down to dinner. Catoira always took his rations with a smile. He was a young *humanist* who had read Greek and Roman philosophy as well as the Bible. He had read Plutarch's *Lives* and had imagined the conquistadors as noble

Caesars. Lima had quickly disillusioned him. He confessed this to Sarmiento who was curious about such a bookworm's need to be on a ship: "Pizarro's dead, but his greed remains like a pestilence. It was not at all hard for me to decide to move on."

Sarmiento acknowledged sympathy with a nod. He was contemplating the writer's shivering image reflected on the surface of his wine: "In liquid, the hearts of men are revealed to the wise."

Catoira looked for himself in the cup: "What do you see in my heart?"

Sarmiento pursed his lips: "That you are a man capable of sacrifice." And he poked his finger gingerly into the wine to scoop out a bread crumb: "I've seen you reading Seneca, good Catoira, and I'd say you've become a stoic."

"Do you know what a stoic is then, Captain?"

"Oh yes, verily I do. A man who's grown tired of pleasure."

Catoira scratched his cheek: "Perhaps ... or one who's merely recognised the vanity of it," and poured his own wine into Sarmiento's cup: "The stoics were men of admirable principles."

Sarmiento chewed his beef while pointing to Catoira's plate: "A good stoic would pass on all his rations. He'd be able to draw sustenance from ideas alone." So Catoira tipped the contents of his dish onto Sarmiento's plate, which made him laugh: "You'll one day be a saint, Catoira."

But the young writer shook his head and laughed back. His curly black hair shivered. Then he reached to Sarmiento's dish and took back a bit of the salted beef he had dropped there. He chewed it through sniggers: "No, I could never've been a monk. A cloister would kill me. I was born to be an observer. I need to meet men, travel and prove to myself that the world really is a sphere."

"And that it revolves around the sun?"

Catoira nodded and scratched his bottom lip: "That too, if it's the truth."

"So you do have a vice."

"Many, Captain. Too many," then leaned forward to whisper: "It'd be impossible, surely, for my observer's spirit to constantly manifest a monk's faith. There's something about the God of love that doesn't quite concord with what I've seen in the world."

"You speak like a Jew."

"I think it's called scepticism."

"And do you also doubt there's a devil?"

"Oh no, he most certainly exists." Then stern: "Do you know, sometimes, I've even thought a terrible, blasphemous thing. It's occurred to me that ..." and he suddenly dropped his head.

Sarmiento flicked some fat between his teeth with his tongue: "Don't worry lad, your blasphemy's safe enough. I'll not run to the inquisition."

Inspiring a lift: "Well ... It's occurred to me, after contemplating men's ignoble natures ... it'd seem that perhaps ... perhaps the devil is really God ..." the listener's jaw dropped: "And that Christ is a dissident."

The idea froze Sarmiento. When he thawed, his mouth curled up into a huge grin: "Ah, that's a nice one marry! Just think of it, Christ, a bastard son o' all Evil, protesting his daddy's violence he goes and preaches a love that his father cannot swallow. A nice one Catoira."

But the writer was sweating: "I didn't mean it exactly like that."

The sea was calm except for the occasional swell, pushing a wave into the cutting bow, or thumping the hull's belly and splashing over the side. The sky was cloudless; a mid-afternoon sun, scorching hot. The slight breeze was hardly refreshing. Most of the crew were in an empty-bellied siesta attitude, bemoaning the famished nature of their laziness. It was too hot and they were too weak to work. So they waited for the sun to drop.

In direct contrast, a group of tireless cabin-boys, animated by adult weakness, were out to play, chasing each other. Running legs and little slapping feet drew a dull echo from the hull. It was a shouting, squealing game, a desperate pursuit and escape. A jumping, swinging, climbing, hiding joy. Reality for those boys revolved around a wonderful-terrible fear-lust of the tag. The ship itself became immaterial. The slaps or kicks received from grizzly sailors were irrelevant.

Then with the dropping sun the shadows rose, the game stopped and the boys and men were put to work. Scrubbing, hauling. But with the sun's retreat the slight breeze also choked, until each breath died away and everything became deathly still. Arms slowed and legs moved as if weighted with bricks of lead. And the dusk brought a strange and ruddy cloud that seemed to pull all attention as it rolled toward them.

The slow, hardly discernible unfolding of a mist spreading from south to north, girding the whole western horizon. It was a turbid strip of vapour that looked like a long line of salebrous coast. When the full moon rose, veiled by that fog, it became a crimson orb hanging to starboard, reflecting a bloody hue over the dead calm ocean which was more transparent than usual.

Gallego thought that he could actually see the bottom, and he dropped the lead in again and again, searching for an impossible sounding.

Mendaña struggled aboard the *Capitana*, arriving for the scheduled meeting. He was glad this time to have changed ships, Gregorio Gonzalez and Don Pedro Ortega had been driving him crazy with their barbarisms. But once he had lifted himself he became transfixed by the glowing sea and eerie atmosphere, and instead of going to Sarmiento's cabin he went up to the poop, to Catoira, who was staring silently at the hardly functional flicker of a fading candle.

The writer gasped, ignorant of Mendaña's presence. Sarmiento was also on deck and riveted – *The Terra Incognita* – he recalled – *has the form of a dream* – and he felt his soul shudder.

The whole ship was lulled into a silent trance. But this was suddenly broken by a splash of grim reality.
A cabin-boy running, then slipping on the mist moistened half-deck, fell on his arse, slid, and, as the ship rolled with a sudden swell, he was propelled under the rail and vomited into the ocean.

Hernán Gallego saw the sliding blur and heard the plop: "Man overboard!" he yelled, holding up a lantern and pointing to starboard.

Everyone picked themselves up, shook a dream out of their heads and scurried to the rails, leaning out to stare into what had suddenly become a pitch black sea.

No sooner had he fallen than the encroaching fog smothered the ship, blinding them to all trace.

No moonlight penetrated anymore, their own lanterns only managed to illuminate a feeble radius beyond which there was absolutely no visibility. Perception of the exterior was reduced to a shrill and tremulous: "Help me..."

The crew murmured: "Who is it?"

Then another child's voice: "It's Ceballos, señor."

And one of the officers: "My boy!"

But it was like looking into a black wall.

"Put out the lights!" someone shouted: "Perhaps we'll see better," and all flames went quickly out.

The desperate voice in the sea persisted and they used their ears to perceive direction of motion: "Towards the stern!"

Some candles were lit again, briefly, to locate lines and hawsers, hurl them overboard in order to fish for the invisible lad.

"Hang on boy!" but none of the ropes had reached him. Then someone threw a chicken coop full of birds: "Swim!" they yelled: "Swim to the chickens."

But the boy's voice faded: "Help me ..." and the chickens' squawks also suddenly stopped.

The *Capitana* filled with a murmuring hum: "We're driftin' away from him."

Until another noise, a creak, a splash, and light. Horror.

Mendaña: "My ship!"

It was lit up like a Christmas tree. Lanterns hanging from bowsprit and yardarms. Each light with a double halo, one orange, one blue. Caught in a current or pushed by a freak breeze, the contrast with their own stillness made it seem to be flying straight at them: "Our lights!" they shouted: "They can't see us!" and the ocean filled with their roars.

Roars which came back from the *Almiranta*: "There's a ship there! Fie lads! We're gonna hit!"

A mighty groan as the *Almiranta*'s hull lifted sharply. A sudden swell grabbed it, and it flew directly in front of them.

The boys on board screamed. Riggings were wrestled with. Rope, burning the fingers of desperate hands: "We're done!"

The ship lurched, they fell. The *Almiranta* had nudged the *Capitana*'s bowsprit. An ominous scraping sound. Timber cracked: "Hang on, lads!"

Men staggered as both ships righted themselves. At first their relief seemed to blow across each boat like a sigh. This dissipated into a silent stillness, broken by Gregorio Gonzalez's rasping voice from the *Almiranta*'s poop: "Where's yer lights!? Fie!!"

Mendaña yelled back to his pilot: "We've lost a boy!"

The rest of the *Capitana* forgot about the fear of collision and rushed to the rails. Hand-cupped ears, discerned faint shouts coming back to them:

"I can't hear you," it whined: "Where are you?"

"Turn the ship," screamed Gallego, and then, clambering into a dinghy: "I need two oarsmen and a steersman. Come on! Move lads!" Lower the dinghy!"

Arms tugged and the little boat went down. Oars were out, pushing away from the hull, rowing into the pitch heart of blackness, disappearing into … a miracle.

The watch at the beak was the first to sight it, and screamed. Unbearably uncanny. Some of them actually ran when they saw it and hid themselves in the ship's hull.

Catoira reached out for Sarmiento's hand: "Am I mad!"

Sarmiento took the hand and squeezed it: "If you are, we are both. Mad, or damned."

It was as if a spirit had been born in the blackness. A bright, glowing teardrop of light, like the flame of a massive candle, fulgent through the dense, opaque gloom that enshrouded them. Emitting a noise. A high-pitched ringing. The brilliance of it increased until they were all squinting, their flat hands shading their eyes. A unified gasp until it dimmed again and the blackness returned.

The boy was unconscious, but alive. Hands reached for him. They wrapped him in a blanket and carried him to Sarmiento's bunk.

Then a circle gathered around Gallego, as he prepared to tell his tale: how the light had appeared, through the fog, directly over the floundering youth, its powerful beam revealing the lad slumped over the bobbing chicken coop: "If that was not a supernatural emanation, then God don't exist."

The audience gaped as the boy spluttered back into brine-vomiting consciousness, and while the ocean spluttered out of his lungs and splattered on the deck the priests fell to their knees, to pray.

Sarmiento pinched himself: "Am I awake? Or are we all dead?"

* * *

Estrella stirred me by placing the mug of hot tea in my hand, lifting it to my lips: "I hope it's not too strong," she whispered: "You still have it black with sugar, I trust?"

The heat in my trembling hands and contemplation of the question situated me. I struggled to clutch the handle and get my burning palm away from the cup. I instinctively blew to cool, and vapour fogged my glasses. An aroma of freshly cut wood, and then I was sipping and the smell was on the tongue, become taste – *But I had been making the tea, hadn't I?* –

This realisation did not shock. I had become well used to such lapses. Time and space is not the same experience for me as it is for most of you.

"Of course we were terrified," Estrella blurted. This did confuse me: "We thought we had lost you," she continued and I recalled our conversation. That we had been talking about my coma. That the voyage had been resurrected by the notion of *coma*. My eyes probably rolled around my lenses. Estrella sniffed hard: "Then we did lose you." I gulped the tea which was already cool enough for proper mouthfuls: "We had to call a doctor, but we were scared" – *She's confessing* – I realised, though it seemed of little significance to me then: "It had to be someone we could trust to keep the thing hushed up," the word *hushed* seemed to push my next gulp into the windpipe and I spluttered, my eyes now moist. Estrella however did not pause: "Dr de Coca was the most obvious candidate." Tea had been regurgitated in dollops down my chin. I reached for a handkerchief: "It was he who had sold me the drug." I dabbed my dripping jaw and rubbed my wet eyes: "He came, examined you, diagnosed the coma and before we knew it you were being wheeled out, unconscious, to the ambulance, to be taken to his clinic ... still in your coma."

Why did she persist with that monstrous word?

XIII. First Approach

That night Mendaña stayed on the *Capitana*. He did not sleep but paced the deck, wrapped in a woollen blanket to keep the chill mist out of his bones. He stared outward, though hardly, his vision smashing against the impenetrable wall of fog. But he wanted, desperately to see beyond, to a return of the miracle. And he was not alone. Other aimless, incommunicative figures paced as he did. Each one lost to his own mental ruminations on the mysterious phenomena.

With the dawn the fog cleared. Mendaña shivered until the sun was free of the grey veil and the sky was blue again. Soon it was warm enough to draw steam from the damp blanket and Mendaña became a mysterious angel as delicate wisps curled off his back and shoulders, twisting around his uncovered head. His greasy hair was dark and plastered down over his pink face, which was full of a beatific smile. The warmth eventually drew a sigh from him, and he threw off the blanket and stretched himself. Then he called to one of the African boys to muster the men of *importance* to his cabin. There would be a meeting, not only for the officers and navigators aboard the *Capitana*, but also the priests.

He began by addressing the latter: "What we saw last night was a miracle, was it not?"

Fr Francisco nodded solemnly and clasped his gnarled hands, his sunflower seed eyes squeezed into pine needle slits: "A great portent. We, who are the vilest and undeserving, seem to have been blessed by a sign ... *praeter ordinem communiter observatum in rebus.*"

His companion, Fr Pedro, whose hands were fleshier, his eyes rounder, also stepped forward. Each consonant articulate, the vowels round and clear: "What we have seen has emanated from a divine agency beyond the order commonly observed in nature. We are miserable and wretched, but God loves us."

Mendaña's own face seemed to glow with the joy that the tremendous idea brought him: "And what purpose do you think it had?"

"It was a guiding light," said Fr Francisco, and hissed in before expulsing a whispered but well audible: "Like the star that lead the Magi to Bethlehem, this light will lead us to the Isles of the Magi."

"For it is believed that the Isles of Solomon were the birth place of the Three Wise Kings," carolled his companion.

Inspiring a profound silence. Gallego crossed himself. Enriquez and Manriquez bowed their heads and clasped their hands, to mumble a spontaneous but uninspired prayer in unison. Catoira's jaw dropped. He looked to Sarmiento for his inspiration, but the captain looked more insulted than enlightened. He snarled and shuffled impatiently – *And now the mission is most definitely a Holy and Christian one* – he thought – *How quick these priests do pounce on an advantage* –

A boy appeared in the doorway, drowsy and rubbing his eyes. Gallego turned: "What is it, Trejo? A nightmare?"

The lad sniffled and looked for Mendaña. When he had located him he took off his filthy hat and bowed: "I fink I've seen somefin', General."

Mendaña coughed to clear his throat: "Well boy, out with it?"

The lad wiped his dripping nose with his sleeve: "It's an island I fink."

And all of them were suddenly fighting to get onto the deck.

"A man on the watch! Quick! Come, what do you see?"

When the sailor reached the crow's nest there was a sudden hush which seemed to coincide with the arrival of a gust and the mainsail flapped dramatically. The climber stretched himself, leaning right out of the crow's nest and then, with his hand to his brow to mitigate the sun's glare, he screamed, which evolved into a bellowing phrase: "Land ho!"

Causing an immediate thudding racket as hands released whatever they held. Then, attentive silence. All eyes were peering up the mainmast. The commissioned sailor was hanging from the shrouds, pointing: "An island!"

It inspired a low murmur and a surge to the starboard side. For a time, there was voiceless rapture. Faith in the watch was not enough, there had to be a personal recognition: "I see it."

"D'yer?"

"Yeah, just a thin line now. Under the cloud."

Cloud, which Sarmiento mistook for smoke: "Volcanoes. Probably the two volcanoes we know to be on the east coast of New Guinea."

This made Mendaña peer harder: "New Guinea?"

"Yes, General. This has to be New Guinea and we've sailed too far. Avachumbi and Ninachumbi are much further south and east."

Inspiring a shake of Mendaña's head, who began to consider other possibilities that they may have missed. He took possession of the deduction and turned to Gallego: "We've arrived at New Guinea, sirrah."

Hernán Gallego remained leaden, inspissated by his realism. He scratched his chest and spat over the side of the ship: "It's too low and small," he argued: "And that's not smoke you see, but a risin' mornin' mist which's become a cloud, pray."

Mendaña squinted. He saw nothing clearly: "Verily, good Gallego, I think you're right. Oh yes, most definitely," then to Sarmiento: "It's a cloud, Don Pedro."

Sarmiento scratched the scar on his cheek: "Perhaps."

Mendaña rubbed his hands: "Set our course."

But the chief-pilot, still smarting at the destruction of his own Ahedo-induced dreams, deduced that the enlightened way was to unveil all vain hopes. He shook his head: "That mayn't be wise, m' lord," and lifted his chin to utter proud syllogisms: "Such a trivial spot in the middle of this vast expanse cannot be inhabited," the gravity of his own voice in the conclusion inspiring a perseverance with sophism: "Food and water'll 'ave to be scarce, it's not worth the effort of lookin' for a 'arbour."

Mendaña, who wanted to believe, sighed, while Sarmiento squeezed the taffrail, his arms tensing, as if he were about to rip it off.

Down on the main deck the only sound punctuating the creaking hull and the flap of sails was the churning of men's empty gizzards. They could not have heard what Gallego had said, but if they had looked aft and seen their officers' reactions they may have guessed it.

Though his throat was wet and his stomach full enough, Mendaña needed badly to set foot on this, his first discovery. Yet he was numbed by doubt, and it had to be Sarmiento who reacted first to Gallego's provocation. He released his hands from the rail and they span into the air, whirling him around toward the chief-pilot, who shuddered, half-expecting the captain's contorted fingers to wrap themselves around his throat. Sarmiento tensed himself in order to restrain himself. His voice was rasping: "Have we not come to discover a New World?" he croaked: "I'm certainly not here to tack around the south seas on a barnacle gathering expedition!"

The capacity of his vociferation was deliberately tactless, erupting in front of the restless crew who unanimously comprehended the implications. They began to murmur again.

Sensing this, Sarmiento persisted: "Would you have us die of thirst? We've been eight weeks at sea. Too long!"

But Gallego also became passionate in his defence and his arms began to shoot, flinging sharp digits into the air: "Wind's up again. Who knows 'ow long it'll last?" then the pointers curled in and became a thumping fist: "It mustn't be wasted, sirrah, by explorin' some tiny, lonely rock!"

Sarmiento clenched his own fists, then released one of them to point a trembling index finger towards the island, that had become more clearly defined. The clouds around it had lifted. The sun shone on it. It was green: "He says it's a rock, and yet I see it covered in jungle and palms. I for one'd gladly welcome some sweet coconut milk with my supper," which drew a caterwauling from the crew. Then direct insults began to trickle out, evolving into strident truculence.

Mendaña straightened his back. It was time for him, he realised, to redeem himself with the masses and make a popular decision: "My orders were that we should take possession of any land that we come across," and he span around to the crew: "We go ashore!"

Gallego grimaced. The crew roared, arms went up in the air, and some of them began to sing. A song that petered out as sailors began to sniff and turn, inspired by the scent of burning incense.

The grey smoke wafted over them from a swinging censer as the friars advanced slowly across the deck, clambering up to the poop to fabricate what seemed like a spontaneous speech from the articulate Fr Pedro: "Last night, God sent us a sanctimonious sign of His approval for our mission. Proof that we have embarked on a most pious quest. Today, the day of the Epiphany in our Holy calendar, we have arrived at a new land, and we must offer our thanks to the Lord through prayer. Let us pray." And the deck groaned as its inhabitants knelt: "And let us lift our eyes to the heavens and let us rejoice and sing *Te Deum Laudamus*."

They made a starboard tack.

As they approached the isle and began its circumnavigation it became increasingly obvious how wrong Gallego had been. They were sailing along a coast bristling with coconut palms, peering inland where, within the dark green fabric of a tight jungle, the bright tones of coloured birds flashed, indicating fruit. Mendaña was pacing, nervous and excited: "We are here. But what shall we call it, this virgin place? What shall we call it?"

"Being the first discovery of the expedition it would seem fitting that the name should come from the leader of the expedition," muttered Sarmiento.

But Fr Francisco leaned over Mendaña's shoulder to whisper: "Would it not be the most appropriate thing, General, given that it was discovered on the Epiphany, that it should be given the name of Jesus," which inspired an immediate and excited reaction.

Mendaña went to the front of the poop and shouted across the ship: "This island will be called: *The Name of Jesus!*"

This made the friar wince and Sarmiento chuckle. A solemn Gallego approached, his top lip curling, as if he had chewed some bitter olive. He pointed to the south-east, to a grey spot on the horizon: "We're losin' a lot of ground on the *Almiranta*. What if they haven't seen the isle yet?"

The huge ostrich feather in Mendaña's cap, fluttered: "Gregorio Gonzalez is a marvellous drunkard, but a miserable pilot. It'll take a year before he'll ever make a brave decision on his own initiative."

"Gregorio is captaining the ship?"

"No. I left Pedro Ortega in charge. Although he's worse than Gregorio."

"Then should we not go back for 'em?" mumbled the chief-pilot.

"Oh no, good Gallego. Have faith. They'll catch up when we've reached our island."

I gave myself altitude in order to examine the scene myself.

To the north were slashes of white, the ephemeral climaxes of ocean swells breaking against a large reef. This encircled a jutting point which was almost a tiny island in itself, a protruding knob, bearing four palms that made it look like a three-masted galleon with a poking bowsprit. This semi-islet was joined to the rest of the land by a natural sandy walkway that itself developed into a golden beach, stretching down the western side, protected by other reefs. From high I could see the grey sharks circling amongst the bottle green shallows, dappled by darker spots of verdure that were really blooms of brilliantly coloured coral.

The ship again was on the outer rim of the reef, but near enough to the coast for them to discern a quivering of the low shrubs. These even seemed to open and shut sometimes, as if large ground animals were moving through them. Animals, or shy but inquisitive humans, spying through camouflage.

Their first glimpse of the natives evoked a mystery. Someone claimed that they had spotted something that looked quite white and vaguely human. The *whiteness* encouraged talk of spirits. Someone murmured that they had reached a phantom place. The speaker was Catoira, who at that moment became a prophet and poet: "Perhaps here, at the omphalos, if this is the omphalos, we ourselves will be converted into wraiths."

An idea which had sprung from a conversation with Sarmiento: "This island is not on your map, Captain."

"No, Catoira. I'd thought that we'd now crossed the gulf, but it seems that New Guinea must still some distance lie."

"And this spot could be the Ophir that we seek?"

"No, most definitively not. We are too far north. But that's not to say that this is no equally marvellous place. I've read classical histories that tell of a mysterious floating island, peopled by supernatural beings. A place which is said to sink beneath the sea, or is changed into waves when ships approach," and then: "Sea faring men do oft talk of the existence of magic isles that are wreathed in mystical mists, rendering them invisible and impenetrable. Perhaps that's the reason for that strange, guiding illumination that blistered our souls last night. And then, this morning, when the land was first sighted, did we not ourselves wonder at the strangeness of the vapoury scud that did rise from it?"

So the island became something solemn and secretive. And many of those aboard the *Capitana* felt a gush of acid rush through their bellies when

Gallego gave an order to lower the longboat: "We must find a harbour."

But while making preparations for the reconnaissance another revelation was made: "We're on our own," which seemed profound at first until the speaker expressed more clearly its mundane significance: "Where's the *Almiranta*?"

Followed by a gruff: "Lower the sails!"

There was a groping, grasping movement up high, a tugging of ropes down below, and the grimy sails were dragged in and tied up.

The lowering of the longboat was also postponed.

"It'll be better to wait."

And they did, bobbing on the calm seas of the lee side. Staring out, toward the island, its reef and the breaking surf, until from the topsail an observer spied boats.

A flotilla of canoes crashed into the breaking surf, rising on the white water and flying over it. Seven small catamarans each one bearing seven passengers. A surprised and fearful groan wafted out from the *Capitana* as the sailors backed away from the ship's rim. Sarmiento turned in the direction of Gallego: "Uninhabited, you said," while he grasped rigging and leaned outward: "So what have we here Gallego?" swinging, almost falling: "A bevy of sea-fairies, or mischievous elves that have come down from the wood? Ha!"

Gallego waved the taunt away and shouted to the crew to prepare themselves. Men strained their eyes toward the poop, registering the command but not reacting to it. Sarmiento responded to these obvious and embarrassing gestures of *cowardice* by catching a rope and swinging down to the deck, almost taking a sailor's head off as he went. Boots thumped on wood, his arm waving his sword. Each swipe accompanied by a booming voice. The peons stirred, clumsily pulling on helmets, grappling for harquebuses.

Neither the crews of the ship nor the canoes were eager to arrive, but currents and momentum dragged them together.

Expectant silence, the Islanders gazing up in wonder as the strange, high, creaking bow of the *Capitana* became an enormous wedge, cutting a path straight through their fleet of catamarans.

An amazement dissolving into fear, and there was a frenzy of splashing commotion as the Islanders paddled their boats to a safe distance.

Mendaña clapped his hands and giggled. He had never dreamt of such a spectacle. But he had assumed that the Islanders were retreating, and it was only when Sarmiento screamed the order for the harquebusiers to lift their weapons and take aim that he realised that they had actually been surrounded.

Sarmiento laughed and waved to a sulking Gallego, who ignored him. Mendaña was beside the old sea-salt. He stared silently, trying to think. The Islanders were shouting and banging drums.

The captain-general grimaced, he could feel the drums vibrating in his chest. Although he had become imbued with the vice of command and lusted for the opportunity to give more inspiring orders, this situation left him mute with a shivering lower lip and wobbling limbs. Surrounded, a battle on the verge of taking place, perhaps a massacre. Suddenly his mind was imbued with images surging from his nightmare: the vision of bloody, dying chickens.

Sarmiento repeated his order for the harquebusiers to ready themselves and Fr Pedro put his hand on Mendaña's shoulder. The priest's voice was soft but urgent: "You must act swiftly, my General."

Mendaña stammered. He wanted to command, but felt muted by the commotion and noise. He looked down. The sailors were awaiting his leadership. His jaw dropped and he took a deep breath: "Lay down your arms," he squealed, then realising the pathetic pitch of his voice lowered it to announce: "There'll be no violence." When they obeyed, he felt a warm relief. He took a deep breath and continued: "They can do us no harm," as if he possessed an intimate of Polynesian culture: "We've come to find pagans and make them Christians, not to massacre them."

Evoking a spontaneous protest from one of the soldiers: "And if they should want to massacre *us*, pray? Have you asked them?"

Mendaña turned to the Franciscans, who smiled and nodded. This inspired confidence, and he turned back to sermonise with authority: "We have been graced by God's magnificent light, the star that brought us here. He has chosen us and he will protect us, for *He* does ever guide the righteous to make *His* glory great upon the Earth!" This started the friars nodding. Mendaña pointed to the men in the canoes and then announced the obvious: "We're the first Christians seen by them," his voice reverting to a squeal again: "'Tis a prodigious day," drowned out by powerful chants from the Islanders.

The crew turned away from Mendaña to look outwards, the Islanders' tattooed faces staring back at them.

"Under the strange lines on their painted faces they are quite pale," said Manriquez to Enriquez.

The latter reached a conclusion: "Like us."

These two officers were standing stiffly behind Sarmiento, who was joined by Catoira: "That there are so many of them, here, on such a small and lonely isle, would have to indicate that there is a continent nearby. Yet the natives of New Guinea are known to be black."

Sarmiento nodded: "Their paler complexion denotes an origin from another place. The Terra Australis, marry!"

Then Mendaña called Gallego over and ordered him to fetch a translator.

The chief-pilot squirmed, looked incredulous and reminded the captain-general that indeed they were the first Europeans to arrive, and for that very reason they had no translators.

Mendaña suddenly felt gripped by a nausea. He became hot, his face reddened, beads of sweat formed on his brow. For the first time he was realising where they actually were, that this really was a brand new world, with a brand new language.

The new reality blasted Mendaña who hardly ever envisaged the obvious. Like a child he stalked the poop-deck, leaning over and insisting on finding out what these strange men inhabiting his discovery were saying: "I want to know; I want to know ..." he mumbled.

The Islanders lifted their oars, waving them while they screamed.

"They seem to be provoking us," murmured Manriquez.

"Oh nay," contested an ironic Enriquez: "It is but a show of their pious affection."

"So glad they are that we have brought them priests," and they spat together in perfect unison.

Mendaña chewed the lace of his cuff. The sensible thing, he decided, was to create a distance between them, at least until the *Almiranta* arrived.

So he gave the order to unfurl the sails. This brought a thunderous flap which caused a hubbub in the canoes. Thick arms dipped oars into the sea, and they turned.

Sarmiento beat his chest and screamed to Mendaña: "They go!"

Which made Mendaña jump. Suddenly he regretted their retreat and he pulled a white handkerchief out of his sleeve which he began waving franticly. The fatuous action inspired the entire ship's crew to drag out a cloth to wave, but the canoes did not turn back.

Eventually the *Almiranta* caught up. Ortega, as furious as ever, leaned over the side. His voice full of a bellowing irony: "Thanks for waiting for us, chums! It's nice to know 'ow much yer loved."

Mendaña, eager, his gloved hands flapping: "Ah, but faith, Don Pedro Ortega, my loyal *maestre de campo,* we have just seen men. They came to us in canoes, troth. Savages, and pagans obviously. Completely naked and covered in war-paint. Marvellous, pray, verily señor, marvellous! We have discovered a New World!" and he thrust an open hand in the air, a gesture very similar to the one made by bull-fighters when the beast drops.

But Ortega was totally unimpressed, still smarting at the fact that his ship was constantly obliged to chase. He thumped the rail with his staff: "And should we thank yer for 'urrying on to yer adventure, General? Abandonin' us like some flea-beaten dog. Would you 'ave us be your mongrel, to kick whene'er you feel the urge o' it?"

This dampened Mendaña's spirits, making him blush and tremble. But the tension was quickly broken when the word spread through the ships that the Islanders were running along the beach.

"Waving to us," murmured Manriquez.

"Palm leaves," continued Enriquez.

"But white …"

"White palm leaves …"

"Waving to us as we waved to them …"

"With our hankies …"

"Our white hankies …"

"Imitating us …"

"They want to communicate with us …"

"They want to be our friends …"

Green had become blue, blue turned into grey. A mist rose off the bay and curled over the shore, invading the jungle.

That evening the order was given that all should be on the alert. They were sailing too close to the reefs for comfort, but they could not afford to go far out into the high seas lest they be dragged away.

Nevertheless, it was a calm night. The gentle lapping of the sea against the hollow hulls was soothing. Juan López had his lute and strummed and sang songs meant for his captain-general who remained on the *Capitana*.

The romantic verse and music filled Mendaña's head with memories of the girl he had left behind. Sitting in the shadows, her image, dim but close in his mind. Her soft breasts, her belly, her thighs, that he had licked. Her salty skin, like the sea.

– *The sea is a woman* – he told himself – *and I will navigate her ... for I am now a great captain* –

Perhaps he would have grown excited if the music had not been so slow and soothing. But he did begin to rub the satin shirt that covered his body until, remembering where he was, he stood and paced, pausing to wave to the musician who sat on the *Almiranta*, bathed by the warm light of a blazing beacon.

Under that same torch a guard stood, but slumped against his pike and dozing, until a thick hand suddenly fell on his shoulder and pressed down. The guard shuddered and squeezed his weapon. It was Ortega's hand that had dropped. His low voice: "Stand firm, lad, and attend. Do you not know where we are?" then relaxed his grip. The guard straightened his back and morion helm, and coughed, his inquisitor insisting through gritted teeth: "Well?!!"

"This is an island, señor," gasped out more than said.

Ortega's mirthful reaction was accompanied by a glazed-eyed Gregorio Gonzalez who had moved out of the shadows. His lips had been stained purple by wine. A black bladder dangled on a leather strap from his shoulder: "Our guard's most observant, Don Pedro. He sees water and rock beneath the air and thus, by philosophic indagation deduces, it's an isle!" and laughed.

Ortega laughed too, then his hand darted up and his fat fingers caught the young soldier's whiskered cheeks as in a vice, forcing his mouth to pucker: "Attend boy," rasping: "Though you cultivate a beard, yer drowsiness betrays a green and youthful nature. You're here to watch, lad! This isle's a most unknown place and must be regarded with respect, until we apprehend otherwise. All we know now is that it's stuffed with naked savages. Look ashore lad, what d'you see?" Very little could be discerned other than the flashes of light from fires being lit on an invisible beach: "What d'you make o' that, pray?"

The guard stammered the obvious: "F-fire, señor."

"Aye, fire ... And what'll they do with that fire?"

"Cook, señor."

"Cook, yes, but what? What do they want to cook? What if they want to cook us?" which inspired a deep, Adam's-apple bobbing gulp: "Look on those fires and imagine yer own flesh sizzling there. Well it may, if we're not defended. And who defends us?" The soldier gulped again, unsure whether the obvious reply was really required: "Such greenness in our perilous circumstances makes my own soul tremble, and when that does, well then my voice does quiver too," and he turned the guard's face in the direction of Gonzalez who was guzzling a purple jet squeezed from the black bladder: "Who knows what orders this frightened officer may burble as he drinks his consoling wine? Who knows what'll be understood when he asks a corporal for his flagon? A trembling, stuttering voice, that may be misunderstood as *flog 'im* instead of flagon, by which the corporal enquiring to his officer asks in a low and mumbled voice *who?* While the nervous officer, not understanding seeks verification and asks *what?* Which the corporal hears as the *watch,* and so the dozing guard receives a ghastly flogging ..." and then tightening his diaphragm to make his belly-full voice bellow into the young guard's face: "Troth, lad, is that what you want?!"

The guard was panting, his response hurried: "No, señor!"

"Then open yer eyes!" and he slapped the cheek he had been squeezing.

Gregorio stepped forward and offered the *maestre de campo* the wine-skin. Ortega took it and guzzled, while Gonzalez tried to calm him: "Don't be so rough on the boy, pray. He'll learn," and then, picking his nose: "I bet these savages there are not so fierce, and that they fear us more than we do them."

Pedro Ortega let loose a resounding burp which carried across the bay: "No doubt they do," then accompanying the burp with an almost equally resounding fart: "I fear us more than I do them as well."

On the *Capitana*, Sarmiento stood alongside Catoira, staring outward across the wine dark sea to the shore where bonfires had been lit. Bright orange stains on an otherwise bluish-grey landscape. Catoira was also sipping wine, but from a cup: "This vintage is most fine, Captain."

"It should be. It's been sitting ten years in the jar. I had it brought aboard especially for this day."

"We've not stepped ashore yet."

Which made Sarmiento turn abruptly, his breath deepening. He said no words, just nodded his head slightly and ummed. Catoira leaned forward on the ship's rail. He had not wanted to spoil the occasion and decided to change the subject. He made a sweeping gesture to indicate the extension of the beach: "These blazing bonfires that they made," he whispered: "They are making signs to us, are they not?" The voice was soft and sensual in the still and warm night air: "We waved kerchiefs and they wave palms, we lit beacons and they light pyres," and then, as if stewing over a problem of inference, eventually concluded: "Although their replications are always bigger than ours." Which inferred more: "Are they trying to welcome us, or frighten us away?"

Sarmiento rubbed his chin: "What would you do in their place?"

"Welcome us, certainly."

Which drew a shake of the head: "Would you? No, Catoira, I think you would not. Think on it, you have your religion, your life. Then someone arrives with their own god, an appetite for your best women, and with some terrible blasting weapon never seen before. What would you do?"

The wine gulped down Catoira's gullet: "Drag them onto the reef," uttered with ironic glee, followed by a sigh: "But they don't know us. Don't know our guns."

"Precisely. Not yet. But if we find a harbour they very soon will."

"Poor souls."

Sarmiento licked drops of wine that had remained fixed to his top lip: "This is a magic place," and his lips made a slapping sound.

Catoira rubbed his own face with his sleeve: "Aye, señor," his own lips curling into a slight smirk as the following, strange idea gradually came to him: "And might it not be a mere illusion, inspired by our own imaginations. A manifestation of our own desperate collective minds?"

and then after a pausing moment of recollection: "The noble Roman Cyppus was said to have dreamt that he had horns on his head. Only to wake up with a sharp pair of bony points poking through his scalp?"

Sarmiento laughed: "Ah, Catoira, I've had many of my own terrible dreams in which reality and imagination are indistinguishable; haunting terror in nightmares which has later been confirmed. But I believe that such moments have always been inspired by magic not by imagination. Perhaps its manifestations come from the same supernatural worlds that dreams inhabit, but they are not the same stuff. Magic gives material substance to that which God, not men, does dream."

"And so you think this isle to be bewitched?"

"Perhaps," and he lifted his nose, opened his nostrils: "Sniff the air. Does it not seem thicker in your lungs? Does it not make your head spin, as if you'd taken some benumbing drug?"

Catoira closed his eyes as he took the breath, and smiled. Satisfied: "Aye, it does, Captain, it does. But let us return to these fires of theirs. I'm sorry to have to insist on it, but did you not notice that they began to sprout straight after the *Almiranta* had lit her beacon? As if that were their motivation. Just as our wafting kerchiefs did inspire their flapping, white palm-leaves. They're copying us. But why?"

Sarmiento grinned: "Let's see." Then he stepped back, leaned down and pulled up a Yoruba slave that belonged to Gallego; glowing whites of eyes and teeth, the rest of him melting into the darkness that encompassed them: "Go, slave! To the beacons. Piss on their faggots and extinguish them," which made the slave look askance. Sarmiento grinned again: "Or if you cannot piss then drag a bucket full o' the sea and chuck it on 'em," which the slave did happily.

On the beach there was an almost immediate reaction. Commotion. Tiny figures could be discerned racing around their own fires, which became steam, then white smoke.

Catoira shook his head: "They are watching us, our every move."

"And tomorrow they'll receive our gloved hands in theirs, or feel our steel and fire. They will either welcome us, run, or perish."

Pedro Ortega cursed when he saw the *Capitana*'s beacons go out and immediately ordered his own slave to stay at theirs, maintaining it stoked.

Then he turned to the young soldier on guard again: "Forget about the isle tonight," which brought a look of utter incomprehension on the soldier's face: "There's no threat from there. They're naked and will not attack at night. Look you instead to the *Capitana*. This light will keep it in view."

He moaned quietly to himself. He was searching the other ship for Mendaña, whom he was sure was the one responsible for putting out the lights. He suspected they were plotting something vile against him and he began mumbling to himself, as if emitting a telepathic message to his commander-in-chief: "You are a costive, cowherd general ... but you will not slip away from us again tonight."

Mendaña, meanwhile, was with the friars, barking orders to three slaves who were dragging a hefty crucifix: "Dust it carefully now. Demonstrate that you really could be good Christians and not just lazy good for nothing heathens," and then sweetening his voice as he addressed the priests: "What kind of men do you expect to find on this island, Father?"

"Well, we have seen that they are naked, so I doubt that they will have discovered the enlightenment of the scriptures."

Mendaña patted the cross: "Christ should be the first ashore after me. We will proclaim the coming of the light even before we have announced our claim for the king of Spain."

And the friars nodded. Fr Francisco leaned forward slightly to whisper: "These boys are doing a wonderful job getting the dirt off," and then: "Why don't we have another cup of that marvellous wine you have."

Catoira was drunk and leaning over the rail with a bottle raised high, shouting up to the firmament. It was such a moonless, starful sky that the Milky Way was glittering cream: "Behold, Thales was right – we bob in the sea of an earth that bobs in the eternal gulf of the cosmos. We bob and roll and the infinite cosmos turns around us, an infinite number of concentric circles. The paths of stars are hollow roads full of fire."

Sarmiento clapped. He was also drunk, but tired and prostrate on the deck under a blanket: "Very inspired," he said, and the force of it made it sound sincere.

Nevertheless, Catoira turned and shook his head as if Sarmiento had been cynical: "But you doubt it, don't you?" and then after slurping more wine from the bottle, his drunken mind evoking a memory of an insult he had once received but never championed: "Perhaps you, señor, are more of a sceptic than I," spitting out, vengeful.

Sarmiento, however, seemed happy for it and he laughed: "Yes, but I've another reason for doubting." and he sat up: "Since we've been on this ship I've thought a lot about this very same idea ... that the universe is water ... but my feelings are tempted by a newer, more modern philosophy."

Catoira bowed: "I'm all ears" then slid down onto his arse as well.

Sarmiento took the bottle from him to assist his lubrication: "Many years ago when I was at the university of Alcalá, I'd a long conversation with a Catalan mathematician and astronomer who'd read some polemical text, just published then, by a certain Prussian Canon who'd calculated with mathematics that the earth does revolve around the sun."

The ship's writer coughed: "Which of course agreed with you."

His captain slurped more wine: "It makes some sense."

"What kind of sense?"

Sarmiento became forceful: "It makes some sense to me that mathematics should be applied to metaphysics and cosmology, something which Aristotle failed to do. Just as our navigation's improved with Euclidean application, so our understanding of celestial movement will also benefit from geometry."

Provoking a drunken, wounded dog whine and a shaking head: "And geometry proves that the sun's the centre of the universe?"

"Perhaps. Or perhaps it'll go even further ... perhaps it'll prove that the centre of the cosmos is God," and he pushed the bottle into Catoira's chest.

"This book, if it were true, would have to be quite famous. Yet I've heard nothing of it before."

"According to the Catalan it was a very tedious thing, very difficult to read," then with an incremental passion: "But, from my experience, Catoira, the tedious works are the ones most worthwhile. To indagate in a tract which has hardly been read and hardly ever will, because it's too *profound*; that's a valuable thing. Don't tell me you've no taste for the unique treasure? Is that not why you're here? Or have I misunderstood you? Perhaps you're just one of those vulgar men who's come because he's nothing better to do?"

Catoira sighed: "I've come to escape a vulgar world. But if we do find the Earthly Paradise, I've no expectations of it. If it's worse than the world we know, I'll not be surprised."

"Then lie down and look at the stars. It's the only place we'll never touch. And imagine it as you will, Catoira, no matter what false dreams we have of it, it'll remain pure," delivered in a cantabile tone which suddenly deepened: "This world of ours, on the other hand, will always be subject to our rapacious ambition."

Then minds were lulled, and so was I. I let the ship embrace me; let myself be absorbed by the porous fibre of wood. I surged through it, along the grain, permeating each potential splinter, until it was also embraced by me and *I* was the ship, the men's minds bobbing within me while I bobbed on the sea of an earth bobbing in the eternal cosmic gulf described by Catoira. Bobbing and rolling in the centre, *my* centre. It was from *my* instant, from *my* place, that the infinite universe revolved. The ship and I, and our universe, was one of an infinite number of other universes. Universes that had already existed, born only to enjoy a puny, ephemeral glimpse of the infinity it had emerged into. Eventually dissolving, evaporating, into the amorphous essence of everything. An everything which can be measured, at this and any moment, in any direction one wishes and the result will always be the same. I am enclosed, locked in by the spherical rims of the machines of heaven. Revolving rims of mighty cogs, filled with fire. Fire that can be seen as stars, which are but pin-pricks in the rim. Light which drops onto the still surface of this sea, and stays there, bobbing like everything else. Distorted by surges, pulling and pushing, all energy is decadent ...

They slept soundly and peacefully that calm night, even the guards. However, the weather changed with the dawn. The sea turned choppy and dark clouds brought a heavy shower. This was greeted with applause by the thirsty crew. They dragged barrels out to fill and ran around the deck with their tongues wagging. Only the officers looked perplexed. Until a tremendous wind gusted up which scared them all. The sea became a bubbling cauldron and the rain on the gale came so hard it whipped their skin red. They wailed and groaned, inaudible complaints blown overboard. Waves and surging currents caught the ships, dragging them like children's twigs in a raging full gutter. Orders had to be screamed directly into ears and then relayed.

Mendaña, soaked and scared, whinnied into the side of Gallego's red and swollen head: "Get the sails out!"

Receiving a brutal response from the chief-pilot. His white beard shook a white spray that shot back into the general's face: "Fie! No! This wind'll rip 'em apart."

At first the negation stunned Mendaña, but he took a breath and insisted: "We are leaving the isle!"

Catoira realised that what had seemed like a conflict really had a common aim. He grinned.

Rounding the western tip of the isle the winds were less intense, but the *Almiranta* had again been left behind. Or so they thought, in actual fact it had been blown around in the other direction. They realised this when it suddenly appeared in front of them.

It was Enriquez and Manriquez who announced it, simultaneously, purple faced and clicking their heels: "The *Todos los Santos*, señor..." and pointed together.

When he saw it for himself, Mendaña clapped his hands: "Give them a signal, good Gallego," and then: "We're turning back to the island." The order thudded into the air, which had seemed to calm for an instant as if to allow the words to hang. Gallego looked dumb-founded. Mendaña's eyebrows shot up and he shrugged his shoulders: "That's right. We're turning back," Gallego shook his head, but Mendaña nodded with a stupid smile: "Do not worry about our sister ship. I'm sure Don Gregorio has espied us. They'll be swift to follow, now that they know where we are."

Gallego coughed: "I think not, General. They've got a strong head wind. Look at 'em. They're in trouble."

Mendaña stomped: "But, good Gallego, we'll be in trouble too if we don't go back."

Gallego leaned forward, threateningly. His cholera mounting as he exorcised it: "Why did we round the point then, General? We're on an excursion, is that what you think? Is that what yer noble navigating tool has cognised? Pray! Why are we wastin' our time?"

Mendaña realised that not only Gallego's but all the officers' eyes were accusingly fixed. He thumped the ship's rudder: "Wasting our time? You may reckon so, good Gallego, but I do not. I do not want to lose my discovery," and he clasped his hands, as if in prayer: "Who knows? We may be on the reef tomorrow," then pressed one hand against his chest, his face contorting into an expression of offence. The next sentence was a rapid burst of monotone: "This may very well be my last chance to make my discovery," then moaning, almost tearful: "What would happen if I suddenly died?"

The officers shuffled uncomfortably, restraining the abusive replies they all wanted to give. But the universe replied for them. The wind whooshed and the ocean roared and crashed. Tension in the sky made it flash and thunder. Mendaña found himself dizzy and gasping. Forgetting the debate, he retreated, hurrying to his cabin. Sarmiento took charge: "Bestir, bestir..."

Echoed by a grizzly Gallego: "To your posts!"

The sailors staggered with clenched teeth across the rolling decks, balancing arms flapping out, pink fingers straining to catch shivering hemp, to fling themselves onto the instability of other quivering strands. Breathless heads were stooped into the breathtaking winds and nipping rain. Bowing heads on twitching shoulders ducked under the clapping rocks of thunder that invariably followed the white electric light and the phantom scenes that had been illuminated. Men on the top sail, dizzied by altitude and chaotic motion, their hands at one with canvas and cord through clutching, squeezing fingers, shivered silently. The flapping sails were as constant as their own flapping hearts. Trembling arms tugged brails, hauling and furling canvas, then unfurling it again according to the instructions roared from the hoarse, wind-defying officers' throats.

"Get to it lads, we sail with the jib only ..."

"We'll use the mainsail haul in the others ..."

"Pull them all in lads, we'll have no sail at al l..."

Manriquez and Enriquez a harmonised echo: "Pull them in."

The priests, high-pitched squeals: "To prayers, to prayers!"

Mendaña's scream from below as he stumbled: "All lost!"

XIV. Arrival

Estrella was still standing over me. Concerned. The cup of tea had gone, but that bitter-sweet wooden taste was still on my palate. She brushed the back of her hand against my cheek: "Should I go?" she whimpered: "You're so tired."

Which seemed like a challenge, or even an insult. I pulled myself up, lifting myself, wobblingly, out of the chair: "No," then attacked: "Why was I never visited ... by you ... at the clinic ... in Madrid?"

She blushed. Her gaze turned and the voice came guiltily low and staccato: "We tried, but, at first we were told that you couldn't have visitors, because you were under intense observation, or something like that." Then she did look up, her face tense, teeth clenched, before releasing to expulse a higher, emotive pitch: "And then they told us that you'd been moved." She went over to my bookcase, drew out a fat example on slavery in the sixteenth century: "I see you kept to your theme."

A line of thought that I resisted, I knew it would only drag me back. I replied with a dry: "I've been treated well by them. I've always been fetched any reading matter requested."

She put the book back and slid out another. Her own book on dreams: "You're probably the only one who ever read this," and became terribly sad, but because of me, it seemed, not the book: "It was a nightmare. I thought they'd killed you. Both you and Inma. I was so scared."

"What was concluded by Don Enrique, about me?"

Her chest heaved: "He started to investigate. He had contacts. People high up ... but he started to have problems."

The last word invigorated me. I paced on my shaky legs: "Problems?"

then felt uncomfortable.

Estrella noticed my nervousness, but she was now highly strung herself. She got up and went to my bed. When she sat down the mattress sagged: "Perhaps the Valium would be a good idea. Are you sure you don't have any hash?" I fell on the bed next to her, my gaze fixed on hers, which dipped.

Nevertheless, it seemed that digging was the right course.

She had come to uncover our common abyss and she would not stop, even though it would probably cave in on us both: "Inspectors began investigating Enrique's business. Secret police. Tax inspectors. They found irregularities. Nothing serious, but Enrique regarded it as a definite and ugly message."

This seemed to be delivered as a finale.

I felt relieved, my voice chirped: "So he stopped looking for me."

She flicked her fringe from her brow: "I thought so," then gulped. Her throat was drying again. Her eyes welling: "But then, the next summer," and she had to close the pain with a pause, before tremulously gasping the conclusion: "He was found dead in San Lorenzo." Followed by a rasping bitter coda: "Dead ... On the stage ... Where we had carried out our experiments." Which only really explained the whereabouts. I persisted. I needed more. She started rubbing her hands hard and bowed her head. She was obviously crying, but did not want me to see it: "He'd been crucified ... Nailed up ... He bled to death."

"De Coca?"

Her face came up. Her cheeks drenched. Gasping so hard: "They blamed an organised gang of criminals. Art thieves who took everything," then grabbed my smock and squeezed it: "But it wasn't thieves. I know it wasn't." Her tongue was hanging, desperately fishing for air: "Oh Val, I was so terrified." And the shock also wrenched me.

*   *   *

For four days I watched the ships plod into the wind. A constant gale was blowing straight into them from the north-west, a chopping air that made the dark blue sea white-crested. The boats seemed to gulp at it, a choking slow progress, trying to maintain proximity to the equator.

One day I saw Sarmiento, out and lonely on the storm lashed deck, wrapping himself up in rope and shrouds, neck and head pushed forward into wind and stinging rain like an all-ears Odysseus confronting the Sirens' song. He was staring across the white-capped swells of grey black ocean, his vision blurred by the slap of the elements that distorted perception like a mind numbing drug – *'Tis the Via Lactea* – he told himself, imbuing the natural with an occult metaphysics – *that which is below is the same as that above* – It slapped him and slapped his soul – *There are two ways to reach the Philosopher's Stone* – he remembered Rodolfo telling him – *Over land, which is the safest way* – and licked salt from his dry lips – *Or by sea* – and a wave smashed against the hull, washing over the deck and filling his boots – *The latter is faster* – the wind howled – *but wrought with peril* – and the ship was lifted on the crest of a massive swell, and dropped. Sarmiento gasped and trembled – *You should not treat me so roughly, Señor* – he told himself. His storm solitude mind imagined his mad thoughts projected into direct communication with elements imbued with will and even intelligence – *One day you will be* my *representation, and you'll have to do as* I *bid* –

Mendaña was stretched out on his bunk, his stomach tumbling and churning in clockwise gyrations. He coughed and spat, and vomited into buckets and pans. I felt his fear and heard him curse the sea. So desperately was he needing to stand on solid ground again. And he also began to long for his servant Juan López, still on the *Almiranta*. The boy who had sung romances and wiped his vomit green lips, had been forgotten and he felt guilty for it. The recognition of it drew a grimace and groan, which in turn inspired a soft hand to stroke against his cheek and wipe moisture from his brow. The tactile comfort drew a sensual smile, and his illness delirium gurgled into the impossible reality of himself in the arms of his *mestizo*-girl lover again. He sniffed and believed the memory of musk to come from her golden skin, so he reached forward with a weak, white arm to rub his own fingertips across the succulent flesh of her lips. He turned and stared into what he thought were her sad, black wells of eyes, dry with abandon and wet with the tragedy of their impossible love. The idea inspired movement and he rose, to put his own lips to hers.

But when it felt his tickling breath brush upon it, the face in front of him was horrified and edged back. The brown skin reddened. Ruddy-honey boy's face: "Gaspar," gasped the captain-general when he realised who the real owner of the countenance was.

Gaspar Alvarez was the cabin-boy allotted to Mendaña while the captain-general was on the *Capitana*. He was a *mulatto* bastard boy, who had been conceived when some hot-pricked Castilian had raped his Ivory Coast mum. Yet despite his violent creation, Gaspar Alvarez had the most gentle spirit, and his soft and still hairless face with his massive pink lips and triste brown eyes were feminine in form.

"Can you play the lute?" Mendaña asked him, but the boy just grinned and pinched a murrey nipple on his naked chest.

Gaspar Alvarez could not read or write, and he had no stories to tell his master. He was not an entertainer. He had been ordered to work; to empty the captain-general's stinking receptacles, mop his stinking floor, change his fouled sheets and suffer his constant groans. He was a sprightly thing, but underneath his demulcent appearance was a stoical tough spirit and an iron belly. Or perhaps he had no olfactory sense at all, for he was often seen to be cheerful as he scrubbed and scooped up Mendaña's variegated mess with a song.

Yet Mendaña was not the only one suffering the storm. Sarmiento too had his bad moments and I saw him wake with a scream, not from a nightmare, but because he had been dreaming of a dry brown land and hot women and hotter food. It had been the waking realisation that he was still at sea in a night of wind that had drawn the anguish from him.

Catoira, on the other hand, had real nightmares. He had made the mistake of opening a Bible, and reading Jonah, so that he became possessed by prophets – *Sleeper arise, and call upon thy God* – and he would wake into the bobbing darkness of a creaking, sighing belly that gurgled at times just like a whale – *I found a ship going to Tarshish, and went down into it, to go with them unto Tarshish, from the presence of the Lord* –

Then the wind dropped, suddenly, as if a cord had been cut and the curtain had crashed down to close the scene. Inertia petered out and the cutting wave ships were once more reduced to a slow bob. The contrast was uncanny.

Mendaña staggered off his bunk and stared out at the horizon. The ocean had become a shimmering plate of silver that the setting sun drew a golden path through, from them to the horizon. Mendaña was awed, half-expecting another manifestation of the ineffable. Hardly anyone spoke. All the sails were unfurled but none of them flapped.

The exhausted stripped off their shirts and collapsed on the deck to enjoy the pleasant prick of the low sun on their tired backs and limbs. They could have rested for weeks.

Could have ...

Dusk brought another storm and tired and hungry sailors' groans. Their jelly weak arms had to tug again to furl the sails in the fear of being carried unwittingly onto occult reefs, and for days they struggled like this.

Finally, on the seventh of February, a long pink stain was spied running along the length of a misty horizon. There was no need for the watch to announce it, they had all intuited it and were already leaning over the rails.

The following day dawned into a mist-wrapped morning. The stain now loomed huge before them over a bay, grey-green in the morning half-light. Mountains, embraced by the ashen fluff of low lying clouds, were blurred by sheets of rain that moved down their slopes, into valleys and over the sea.

Frigate birds and then canoes came out to greet them.

These new vessels were bigger than the ones at Jesus Island, some of them reaching around twenty metres in length. They were mainly boarded platforms, like rafts, each one elevated off the surface of the water between two canoes. Sea sleighs, they were, shooting forward on sharp, narrow blades, pushed by the wind blowing into a triangular sail made of matting and hanging from a mast and a long yard. Speed was amplified by the co-ordinated action of a score of oars and I went close to one that bore a string of red feathers blown back from the mast like a standard.

Elaborate carvings decorated its hull: curling vortexes, inter-laced and grouping into an elaborate whirlpool matrix. This was adorned by little nacre buttons which occasionally peered out like the eyes of fairy spirits.

At times I sensed life in that wood; that each canoe was an animate log, and with each forward jerk they caught a breath. My lucid-dream consciousness gasped, zooming around them like a wheeling, plunging swallow, dodging their dipping oars.

When I saw one of the oars held still, it stared at me, for it also bore those disconcerting nacre eyes.

The men who were rowing; thirty of them in most of the boats, their thick arms arching down, their naked sweat drenched skin gleaming as if oiled. They groaned in unison, a deep, brave sound with each push, and they looked towards the strange Spanish ships with determination. Until they closed in on them and realised how huge the visitors' vessels really were. Then, they found themselves gulping and short of breath. They imagined themselves before a huge floating coconut full of wild creatures; hairy half-men, half-pigs, perhaps sharp-toothed cannibals.

When they stopped rowing they stood up in their own boats, slowly and cautiously, lest a spear should spring out at them. When the spears did not come they became more confident, straining their necks to obtain a view of whatever beings were aboard the strange vessels: "And if they should be demons? Monsters with shells like lobsters?" thought one, who shuddered when the first Spanish helmet did appear, gleaming above the rail.

This inspirited them all to lift their weapons. Bows and arrows, green jade axes, and clubs imbedded with sharks' teeth, rattled alert. To inspire themselves further the Islanders began to chant, gruff voices to mitigate doubts and instil courage, its unity imbuing them with a sense of indestructibility.

The powerful voices made the Spaniards nervous: "There's a lot more of 'em this time," said one, as he buckled a neck strap to secure his helmet.

"I'd get the cannons out," said another, fingering the cool trigger of his harquebus: "Fire a round. Shut 'em up, fie!"

The sailors began nervously making other puerile comments and bad jokes in order to disguise their fear: "They don't sound happy to see us."

"M' wife makes the same noise... ha-ha."

"Your wife isn't that big though ... look at the arms on them turkeys."

Sarmiento, however, was fascinated. He even leaned outward to get a better look at an Islander who was busy aiming an arrow at him. Then he became elated and shouted to Mendaña that the captain-general should make his presence known to them: "Make them think they lie in the shadow of a god."

Before Mendaña himself could say anything in reply, a group of sailors had rolled and heaved a huge barrel up onto the poop-deck. Having settled that, their hirsute hands, covered with scabs and warts, took hold of their wriggling captain-general and hoisted him onto the staved pedestal.

Mendaña wavered, thought about jumping down to admonish those that had lifted him, then thought about retreating to his cabin – *Let someone else be God* – But up there all eyes were on him. The Islanders had stopped chanting and were staring at them – *Marvelling* – Mendaña thought – *at our European features. Astounded by our obviously superior European intelligence* –

Yet, to the Islanders, this strange figure, bearing such delicate embroidery and sewing on his nobleman's suit, did not seem to be the demon or anthropophagous enemy they had been expecting. Nevertheless, the stranger did have interesting features, and when they saw the great red feather that fluttered from Mendaña's green cap they became nervous and full of expectations.

Red feathers were a precious commodity to those Islanders, their excellence being gauged according to beauty and rarity. It was like gold for them, and many had taken part in brave voyages across enormous distances to find them.

So they began to murmur and mumble, and enthusiasm made their pulses race. Perhaps this strange vessel had brought beautiful feathers for all of them. It was obviously a propitious meeting. Many actually dropped their weapons and began to yell: "*Tauriqui, Tauriqui!*"

Mendaña responding to the theatrics that the scene demanded, lifted his arms. When he did the crew, spontaneously joining in the performance, fell to their knees and began moving in what became an exaggerated display of ironic awe.

Catoira sniggered a whisper: "If he be God, then who will have pity on us?"

Sarmiento grinned, then he himself kow-towed and groaned, moaning his commander's name: "Men-da-nya-a-a-a".

Catoira laughed, and only Gallego remained steadfast; his arms folded against his chest.

Mendaña was actually enjoying the clown role, which suited him better than any other. He thrust his nose upward and made flamboyant gestures, beckoning to the Islanders to come closer.

"Careful," said one of them: "They're trying to trap us," which seemed to sober the others.

Mendaña began to make the sign of the cross from nose to navel, then across the chest, but none of the Islanders responded to them or his other obvious gestures that they should climb aboard the ship. Frustrated, the captain-general wrenched off his red-feathered cap and hurled it into the sea. This act, considered incredible by the onlookers, created a general hush, punctuated by murmurs of: "They bring beauty ... They bring us treasures."

Then the oarsmen on one of the boats, the first to wake from the dream they had all dropped into, plunged their oval blades into the sea and moved toward the treasure.

A trembling hand reached in, scooped up the cap and lifted it up for inspection, gaping at the large damp and drooping feather before a gruff voice bellowed at him.

He shivered and passed the glorious prize on to a tall and spectacular figure, tattooed from the tip of his shaved head to his toes.

When this one, who obviously their leader, put the cap on his own head, he shouted: "See how the visitors pay homage to us!" and then: "Let them pay more!"

Which brought a tremendous roar from all the boats. The Islanders lifted their weapons, shaking them and chanting again; making signs that more treasure should be thrown overboard.

Mendaña thought he understood – *So easy are these savages to please?* – and he continued his own strange striptease, slipping a delicate white lace handkerchief out of his sleeve to be dangled at an arm's length and waved at the audience around him. Finally, he stretched his back, took a deep breath, stood up on tiptoes and hurled the handkerchief overboard. It flittered out, held up by the air, looking at first as if it were going to fall back aboard the ship, but a wind gushed and carried it so that it slowly dropped near one of the catamarans.

Immediately comprehending the gesture, half a dozen of the locals were suddenly in the water and swimming for the floating rag. When one of them reached it, Mendaña applauded and then flung another feathered hat, becoming an arching discus, plopping in another place for the chase to continue.

That race for the second cap became a desperate clamouring struggle which intensified as the Spanish soldiers and sailors began hurling their own hats, scarves and handkerchiefs overboard. Splashes and screams of joy punctuated the continuum of roaring laughter.

Then one of the Spanish sailors dived in also. When he had resurfaced, others threw a sack down to him, full of sea biscuit, bottles of wine and silver goblets.

Some of the Islanders took hold of him, lifting him into their canoe where the sack he had was opened, the bottles uncorked, and the wine and biscuits passed around for everyone to try: "Let no one say that the Spanish are not a generous folk," he cried.

Mouths opened. Chewing, gurgling, laughing. They tried the wine but did not like it and poured it into the sea. The sailor protested. The Islanders laughed.

On the ships some of the soldiers were fondling their firearms, just in case.

Catoira picked his nose and came to a quick, unsubtle idea: "What cruel gods must these naked savages have."

Sarmiento rubbed his chin: "Cruel?" and then: "And what is the nature of our God, Catoira? Ours is a God of love. So we say. And we prove it with this serpent persuasion, or a harquebus romance. Or both."

Islanders jumped into the sea and swam to the *Capitana*: "Help them aboard," shouted Mendaña, uncharacteristically deep and confident.

When ropes and rope ladders were dangled down, dozens of men climbed up.

The size and novelty of the ship made the Islanders gasp; sailors' hands touched their naked skin and they jumped. One of the natives, a smaller thinner man with greying hair and a whirling tattooed face was inspired to a conclusion: "They have never seen tattoos like ours before."

A younger native sighed: "So they come from another world?"

The older one shook his head: "Perhaps. A world where no men wear tattoos!"

"Then they are cowards, not men. We have nothing to fear."

Clambering slowly and cautiously over the rails, the Islanders felt as disembodied as I did walking into the dream world of this strange apparition, but their vision had a pungent smell to it. They sniffed and turned up their noses. When the sailors approached them they grimaced. Mendaña came down from the poop to embrace them. They grimaced again: "Only devils could smell like this," said one, who trembled.

"I'd rather sleep with my pigs than spend too much time in this foul place," moaned another through a grimace.

The Spanish soldiers grouped in file while the drummer boys beat a rolling call to order. Some of them groaned under the gruelling, tropical, midday sun. The sight of so many naked, skin-painted men at such close proximity made many shudder – *Savages!* – at least one of them thought – *Primitives! Why does our general allow them on board?* – Ignoring the fact that they themselves were the real visitors.

The leader, who had taken Mendaña's red-feathered cap also clambered up.

Firm and erect with his arms folded, he towered above Mendaña, and looked down on him with a theatrical growl that was drawn on. Markings dripped from his lips like black blood, his brow furrowed by angry ink. Patterns slid down his entire body, drawing an X-ray man with a skeleton-skin. A naked body, except for a necklace of tiny shells, bracelets and anklets, a flaxen cape and a loin cloth with a big pink conch attached. The only thing he carried, supported under his folded arms, was a mace, as high as himself; the head of which bore a face. A face full of other faces. Faces in eyes. Face-eyes with faces for eyes. He was a walking work of art.

Mendaña shouted to slaves and servants to fetch food and drink. There were biscuits, conserves and salted meats, wine, which the Islanders sipped again, but never with relish.

"*Vino*" said Mendaña, pointing at the claret that he was offering.

"*Bino*" repeated the Islanders and then shook their heads to indicate that they wanted none of it. They were more interested in adornments than foodstuffs. They wanted feathers.

The Spaniards could not understand. Then the friars came out, holding up bells and beads which were curious enough to draw a crowd. These experts in seduction decided to organise the playing of a game in which any Islander repeating the prayers they mumbled would receive a gift. This primary school trick collected excited adherents, and soon tattooed lips were uttering *Pater Nostres* without the slightest idea of what was meant other that it won them a prize.

Those who did not manage to win, began to pilfer; searching for the treasured feathers. A frenzied exploration that intensified as more and more Islanders climbed aboard. They climbed masts, invaded the hull and cabins. Tension mounted and some of the sailors began prodding the intruders with their harquebuses.

"They seem to think they've captured us," moaned Enriquez.

"Perhaps they have," sniggered Catoira: "They'll take us to their Cyclopean leaders and have the sailors for breakfast."

"And the officers for lunch, fie." mumbled Manriquez.

Mendaña recalled his dream of the chickens again: "Keep your guns down!" and then turned to his officers: "Let's look for a harbour."

Gallego scoffed: "A bit difficult, General. The tides goin' *out*."

A black stain spread itself along the northern horizon; completely unnoticed until, night already fallen, a flash burst from within it followed by a crack and rolling rumble.

The wind worsened, the waves thumped them again. The moon was masked by cloud, the pitch night sea below its blackness only relieved by the occasional glimpse of breaking surf. These wave tips, white, but dull in the gloom, became more regular as the wind's intensity increased and as they neared the invisible reef.

Then, the roaring gale muted the other roar, the surf roar. When it was heard, it was too late. The *Capitana* thumped, shuddered and tilted dangerously. Barrels and hefty chests rolled and slid, pinning sailors against walls and rails.

Then someone announced it, confirming their dread. They were on the reef.

The crew, all yells and wails, groans and moans, imagined leaks in the hull. There were screams for jars and buckets to fill. Luckily nothing had really been pierced, but nevertheless, pessimism still set in. The captain-general was among the worst afflicted – *Only a miracle will lift us off* – he thought, and prepared to die.

He even called for a priest and confessed.

Waves broke over the hull. Buckets were distributed, chains of men passing the pails. Futile; not enough buckets, not enough men. Mendaña trembled.

Until eventually the dawn came.

The clouds cleared and a new gentle breeze replaced the onslaught.

There was a strain, the wood croaked and creaked, followed by a tremendous jerk. The boat stammered. The crew awaited the final snaps and breaks, but instead the whole contraption rose, upwards and sharply out.

A sudden swell had dragged them free.

Anxious for a harbour's comfort, they lowered a dinghy that was shallow enough to move over the reef. This came back an hour or so later announcing that it had found a bay, more than suitable for the ships. But they would have to cross the reef.

Captains and pilots looked down. The bottom could be clearly seen, some twenty to thirty feet deep. Gallego ordered a boy up to climb along the bowsprit: "Cry out if you see a white bottom, lad."

He himself took hold of the ropes of two anchors, ready to drop them if a sudden halt was needed. In his other hand he had the lead and was taking soundings: "All right lads, look lively, we'll get through this."

A gasp.

The bright light, the one that had led them to the drowning boy, was back. This time it was a flickering white flame in the morning sky, a rival to the sun itself.

Mendaña raced to the poop: "Verily señores, we are blessed," and gave orders to the steersman to keep the marvellous illumination in a straight line above the bow-sprit: "The light'll guide us through."

"There's more depth here," cried Gallego from the prow.

Mendaña put a finger to his mouth and chewed it, trying to restrain the fantastic: "Keep the light ahead of us," he murmured.

And then the announcement came: "We're out of the reef!"

Followed by the boy in the crow's nest: "I see the bay."

Sarmiento: "Hoist a flag so that the *Almiranta* can follow!"

The light then distorted, becoming more brilliant, until it took the form of a giant, brilliant star. All morning they sailed like this. It was still visible at midday, shifting in the day sky towards the west, guiding them in: "To Estrella Bay" said Mendaña.

Estrella is "star" in Spanish.

And then, whilst the *Capitana* was already laying anchor and the *Almiranta* was just rounding the point, the sea seemed to boil and waves rose and pushed.

A huge part of the ruddy cliff face suddenly cracked and snapped and dropped into the bay with a terrible crash, tilting the ships to one side, almost throwing them into the sea …

Afterwards an excited Mendaña embraced Pedro Sarmiento and, brushing a tear from his cheek, sighed: "Was not this ship quite presciently called 'The Kings', after the Three Wise Kings? And were they not to write on this stern: *'I am "The Three Kings" because my guide will be the star that guided them'*?"

They gazed out. A slither of white beach divided the bottle green liquid they had grown so tired of from the verdure of the jungle. Proximity to Utopia filled them full of awe. They had arrived, but to where? They had drifted too close and the lack of perspective was befuddling. It was certainly a massive shelf of land. But a continent? Was it a continent? Could it be that they had arrived at the Terra Australis Incognita?

It was February 9th, 1568. Sarmiento, claimed that numerologically it was all significant. Despite their erroneous change of tack, they had either reached or were nearing their end.

Mendaña was deeply affected by the miracle of the star, but Catoira was puzzled, especially when Sarmiento supported the captain-general's idea that they had discovered the islands of the Magi. What relationship could there possibly be between the Three Kings and Solomon's Mines?

"The Magi," Sarmiento whispered: "were Persian Magians.

Zoroastrians. Fire-worshippers," which made Catoira's eyes widen, preparing himself for some incredible blasphemy. Sarmiento kept his voice low and mysterious: "The three Magi from our Bible story ... who were also called kings, and who were said to have made gifts of gold, incense and myrrh to the infant Jesus ... they were fire-worshippers like the rest. And astrologers, for they saw *His* star."

"The Star of Bethlehem," corroborated Catoira.

"Yes," assibilated Sarmiento: "Different from all the other stars. Created at the moment of Christ's birth and situated much closer to the Earth than any other sidereal form."

"'The same star seen aloft of our bowsprit?"

"Yes, Catoira."

* * *

There was a dull clunk as the longboat's oars went up. Some of the rowers were groaning happy with the end of effort. They were Africans mainly, Moors and Ivory Coast Negro slaves and slave sons of slaves. And now they had rowed from ship to proximity of shore. Pulled most of the way by muscle and sweat, inertia would take them the rest.

Between their bare, whip-scarred backs and raised oars was a hefty, dark and prostrate cross. A hoary friar sat at the stern with an arm wrapped around it, but holding himself into the vessel rather than protecting the pole. He had grimaced with each roll of the fragile, small skiff. Now that they were almost on the beach he stroked the smooth wooden surface of his saviour's symbol with long, grey-white El Greco hands, preferring to look up rather than down. The afternoon sun in front of them, made his huge eyes squint.

Sarmiento was squatting at the prow, as if about to leapfrog out. His chest was expanding in a squeeze box rhythm under shirt and doublet, too fast, leaving him short of oxygen and making him conscious of his thumping heart and full throat. Proximity to real arrival filled him with panic, the panic of the culmination of a life. He had to use pessimism to calm himself – *This is not Ophir ... there is no volcano* – And so the real discovery had yet to come. Yet he was unable to rid himself of gnawing hope. What if they *were* there? The strange light had been portentous –

Destiny – and he lifted himself to make the leap after all.

When he saw Sarmiento straighten himself Mendaña was all octopus arms, wrestling with the alchemist-captain's doublet to pull him down again, as if to save a potential suicide. Sarmiento gasped, and there was horror in his bulging eyes – *Reality is senseless* – he thought – *to go so far to be pulled down by a wimp* –

Yet, the wimp Mendaña was already standing himself. Full of the same choking panic as his captain. The dry earth of a New World would soon be crackling under his feet and it disturbed him.

– *The first man* – he thought, as if he were about to step on Jupiter – *The first* – He wanted to scream and had to palliate his own panic by concentrating on ritual.

He turned to the men and began a pathetically tremulous speech to remind everyone of explorers' protocol, proclaiming that he, the captain-general, had to be the first. But there was no one keeping an eye out, and when the inertia of their drifting boat reached its finale and hit the sandbank, the jerk pushed Mendaña over.

Everyone laughed, not even the friars could restrain themselves. Mendaña, dazed at first, splashed through shallow sea to land. His green suit, blackened by water and freckled white with sand, sagged. But the enormity of the situation overcame his own embarrassment and he spread his arms. He looked down, the earth was moving, illusion of course, it was really an army of tiny grey-brown shells, dragged by tinier hermit crabs, scurrying away in rippling retreat.

For a moment this troubled Mendaña who had never seen such a thing, but quickly recalled the rules of protocol: what they had always said Columbus had done. He had to drop to his knees, jab his sword squelching into the sand and kiss the earth before mumbling a prayer. So he did. And while his head was down, his lips on the sand, a crab raised a claw at him.

The friars were the next ones out of the boat, plunging bare legged into the warm sea. These were followed by a miserable Gallego and Sarmiento. Ortega, who was always grumpy, made waves.

Once on the beach they dripped and brushed away sand, then organised themselves to make a line of honour for the arrival of the crucifix.

This was hovering over water on struggling slaves' shoulders. The priests looked severely at these grimacing, wavering cross-bearers. They imagined the collapse before it happened, but none offered their own shoulder to prevent it. The older priest even swore as he watched their saviour's pedestal-ship drown, imagining Christ's own head, green and fish-like gaping under the froth of wave crests. One slave received the weight of the crucifix on his leg. He did not scream, but it was obvious from his silent suffering that he needed help.

Neither priests nor officers took one step forward, the subsequent commotion was generated by Africans, dragging their comrade victim to shore. When they had rubbed his leg he could hobble up with a grimace. Then they were all back in the sea again, and the cross was back on shoulders.

"Now you know why we are Christians," shouted one of the priests.

– *Perhaps* – thought one of the cross-bearers – *but do* you *know?* –

Their water-logged boots slurped and splattered, vomiting sea as the panting, groaning procession struggled across the white beach to an approximate centre. There a sergeant threw spades at them. Enough depth was needed to prop up the weight of wood without roots.

Once the slabs were upright the Christians became reverent. The friars organised prayers and hymns. Afterwards Mendaña gave a speech to proclaim the new land property of the King of Spain and officially naming it Santa Isabel, after the patron saint of the day of their departure. A tedious discourse, yawns were contagious.

The next morning, back on the ship, a panting Manriquez knocked three times on the captain-general's cabin door before flicking up the latch and opening it.

Mendaña was oblivious to the visitor. Kneeling by his bunk with his nose resting on his clasped hands, he was completely lost within himself, searching for his inner light – *Obviously transmitted* – he reasoned – *by divine will* – But so deeply drowned he was, that when Manriquez's hand fell on his shoulder the shock drew a scream: "What?!"

Manriquez staggered back and actually slipped over, upsetting the captain-general's table as he did: "Sorry señor," he blurted: "But it's important." And tried to reorganise the mess.

"What?"

"Visitors, señor," spilt drinking water vanishing into a sucking cloth: "The Indians."

As Mendaña pulled himself up his lofty emotions crashed into a more leaden excitation. He straightened his nightshirt, and screamed for his Gaspar, who came sliding in and bumped into Manriquez. From the floor they both looked up, aghast, at their general's nakedness. He had lifted his nightshirt to his head and was shouting muffled commands through the cloth for the boy to dress him. When this chore was fulfilled and while the cabin boy was smoothing out the creases in his general's doublet, Mendaña turned back to Manriquez, standing again but still with the dripping cloth clenched in a fist, and instructed him to escort him out onto the deck.

The morning light made Mendaña squint. The bay was calm. A sea bird squawked while he scratched his neck and sniffed the still air. Curling masses of fish could be easily discerned, close to the crystalline surface, nibbling at the weed and barnacles that had collected on the ship's hull. Mendaña cleared his throat to draw attention. Sarmiento turned and grinned: "Good morrow, Tauriqui. The Tauriqui is here to see you."

Mendaña's eyebrows rose: "I b-b-beg your pardon, Captain."

"The Tauriqui, señor … the chief … He's arrived, asking to see our own Tauriqui," and thrust his finger forward, indicating another fleet of canoes. The crews were all kneeling or sitting except for one solitary figure; tattooed as the others had been, with a high headdress full of long, black and white feathers. His arms were thick, powerful, arrogant, and braceleted with delicate, white bones and coral; themselves adorned with tiny sharp teeth. Mendaña was tremulous: "Are they the same Indians who came to us two days ago?"

Sarmiento nodded: "It would seem so, General. He arrived making the sign of the cross. I don't think he learned that from the Pope."

When the Tauriqui saw Mendaña he immediately recognised him as his equal in rank. He raised his arms and began to shout what were obviously greetings, then repeated the gesture of the cross.

Mendaña giggled softly and rubbed his hands: "How quickly they learn," he sniggered through an imbecile grin.

One of the friar's leaned towards him, a vulture-beak nose poking as he whispered into his ear: "He obviously comes in peace, and with his heart open to the Lord."

Mendaña was radiant: "I'll make him my friend. His next lesson will be to learn who his God is, and his new king," then he turned back to Manriquez: "You man, give me your hat."

The officer looked obviously peeved, and reluctantly peeled his blue feathered cap from his bald head. When he held it out, Mendaña snatched it from him without a thank you, but just as he was about to hurl it at the Tauriqui, Sarmiento's hand came down on his. It squeezed. Sarmiento's rough voice: "No, let's coax him here ... fish for him ... Dangle the cap from the rail and throw the rope to him. Let's see if he swallows the bait, marry."

The reaction was almost instantaneous. The Tauriqui jumped at the rope without a second thought and scaled the side of the ship, alone; shell rattling as he moved. Mendaña's lips twitched, while his throat went dry. The Tauriqui was huge in his headdress, and his gritted teeth made him demon like in Mendaña's eyes. The captain-general shuddered and started to draw away.

Sarmiento had to grab him again: "I think it'd be best that you take his arm and help him on board, and be firm."

Mendaña gulped. His eyes drawn to the advancing Tauriqui's throat, or to the nacre shield that covered it. This bore a strange, almost hypnotic design, a spiral pattern that began to swirl as Mendaña stared. To save himself he looked away, to the Islander's hand, which was clutching a huge double pointed hatchet; destruction on one side, creation on the other. At first Mendaña could only see the negative face – *He could crush me if he wished* – a terrible thought that made him tremble. With it, imagined like the thought, came a flash; like lightning, momentarily blinding him. He felt his legs begin to wobble. He opened and closed his eyes, tightly. The Islander was already on board, pulled up by Sarmiento and Catoira, his tattoo streaked grin huge as he slid one hand along the handle of his hatchet. Mendaña felt sick.

The Tauriqui showed no fear of the Spaniards at all. No awe for their strange ships. When he was on the deck, he immediately began Island diplomacy. He twisted a bone bracelet off his wrist and presented it to Mendaña.

Catoira cleared his throat: "Take it, General, and smile."

As Mendaña received the offer the Tauriqui snatched the cap from the rail. He stroked it and held it up, which brought a cheer from his own men in the canoes. He waved an arm and several of the rowers stood up and clambered onto the *Capitana* with pandanus leaf baskets hung from their shoulders. These were opened on the deck; offerings of coconuts and breadfruit, which inspired applause from the still hungry sailors. To reciprocate, the friars came with a short, red cloak bordered with gold, and draped this over the Tauriqui's shoulders, while his own men took off his turban and crowned him with the cap that Mendaña had given him. Meanwhile Mendaña put on the bracelet he had been presented with.

When he did, the Tauriqui suddenly lunged forward and grabbed him.

Officers and guards reached for their swords, but the Tauriqui did not falter. He squeezed Mendaña, lifted him and squeezed him some more. Then he laughed, and began patting Mendaña's back. It was a show of affection, although it took Mendaña some time to realise it. When he did, his grimace turned into a timid smile and he returned the gesture, although his was more of a nervous slap than a friendly pat – *The act is forgivable* – he thought through the throbbing pain of his aching back – *This man, after all, is a savage* –

Releasing the captain-general the Tauriqui stepped back and began shouting and pointing at him insistently, repeating the same words until Mendaña realised that he was asking him what his name was. Mendaña told him and then made the same gestures and asked the leader what *he* was called. But instead of answering the Islander merely pointed to himself and said: "Mendan-na."

Which encouraged Mendaña to shake his head and say: "No. Me Mendaña."

To which the Islander shook his head, pointed to himself frantically and insisted forcefully: "Mendan-na." Then he pointed to Mendaña and repeated the words: "Byje Ban Arra."

At first Mendaña thought this was some kind of insult, but after listening to it repeated over and over again he began to understand that it was the Islander's name and that he was playing a game, or a local ritual, in which names were exchanged – *He wants to swap names with his conqueror* – Mendaña flattered himself. So Mendaña became Byje and

Byje, Mendan-na. It seemed innocent enough to Mendaña, seeming to prove the Islander's innocent, *primitive* nature.

Then the captain-general ordered the servant boy to bring out all the spice samples that his uncle had given him before setting sail. This was presented to Byje Ban Arra to identify. There were cloves, nutmeg, ginger, pepper, mace and cinnamon. The Tauriqui poked at them, pinched them and picked them up. He sniffed, licked, chewed, then lied and said that none of them grew on his island. Byje Ban Arra had not yet decided if it was wise to trade. He had seen no women yet on the ship, and that, he thought, probably indicated that it was a warship. He knew that he would have to treat the very strange strangers very carefully.

Mendaña felt uncomfortable. He asked the Islander to try his spices again. So again Byje poked and licked, and again he affirmed the negative. Mendaña grimaced. He looked down at several sailors' incredulous faces. They had just arrived, but many were already asking themselves why.

In order to distract from the general's faux pas, Sarmiento turned to the slave Bubi: "Get out your drum and flute and play something."

Which Bubi did. A reaction quickly came from the Islanders. Byje and the other men aboard caught the rhythm and began lifting their legs and arms, erupting into a dance. Then the canoes also began to sway and the music inspired an exodus from canoes to ship. Dozens climbed aboard to join their chief in his frantic ballet, many of them bringing their own instruments with them. There were pan pipes and hefty conches which punctuated the rhythm with deep bass blasts. The Spaniards laughed and clapped and imitated the Islanders. Officers from the *Almiranta* were also rowed over to join the festivity and Mendaña requested the presence of more musicians, trumpeters, pipers and drummers, as well as his page, Juan López, and his lute. Wine and food were also brought out.

As they mixed the general interest became language learning. The Islanders soon learned how to ask - *What's that?* – and they taught the Spaniards their own equivalent – *Eybeine?*

"They speak our language so well," observed a red and fat cheeked friar.

"Not like the pap the Indians in Peru do mumble," confirmed an officer.

"Destined to be Spanish subjects, pray," affirmed another.

They supped together, exchanging food and drink and then organised themselves into choruses. The Islanders were fascinated by the lute's complexity and subtle music, and even more by Juan López's sweet singing voice.

"Such good folk," mumbled Mendaña to nodding priests.

"If this lot are so friendly, what must their wives be like," sniggered Sarmiento to Catoira, who bit his bottom lip.

At one moment Mendaña hurried over to Sarmiento's side: "Great news. I've been talking to the Tauriqui, and do you know what they call this land here?"

Sarmiento shook his head.

Mendaña grinned: "We are here in search of the Isles of Solomon, are we not?"

"I should hope it so, General."

Then the general's voice hushed: "Surely, Captain, this must be the same place. The same Avachumbi and Ninachumbi which you have spoken so much of. The Ophir and Tharshish, which Marco Polo called Sabba and Cipango, did he not?"

"That is one idea, General."

"Then this is the same I say ... the same ... Wherefore came those Magic Kings? Why from Tharshish, sirrah! *Regno Tharse, del qual vene hi magi.* If it is true that Ophir and Tharshish are Avachumbi and Ninachumbi; and they are also Cipango and Sabba."

"Surely, General."

"Then surely we have arrived. The Tauriqui has told me the name of his land ... it is Sanba."

"Sanba?"

"Aye Pedro. Sanba, that sounds so much like Sabba. Sabba and Cipango; Ophir and Tharshish. Sanba must be Sabba, the proximity is too close to be coincidence. These are King Solomon's Isles. We have arrived."

With this kind of talk the legend quickly spread. Soon everyone was aware that they had reached a special place and that they were at the gateway to an even more magnificent discovery.

Mendaña and Sarmiento started sharing time with each other to discuss the incredible significance, almost even striking up a friendship between them. Ignoring the fact that Marco Polo's Sabba was in Persia and playing deaf to the "n" in Sanba, they were soon able to convince themselves that they had arrived at the spiritual naval of the mundane universe.

Mendaña had been alone with Byje in his cabin, sitting at a small, round table, enveloped by candlelight, they had even held hands, which was significant for Byje. In a world of hundreds of little islands in which each tiny stretch of land would harbour a dozen different tongues; where hundreds of languages circulated on thousands of boats; where one was just as likely to receive a gift from a stranger as a smashing blow on the head ... in such a world one is constantly having to make life or death decisions with men who you cannot speak clearly to. Because of that Byje knew the tremendous importance of reading faces and understanding the language of body temperature.

Mendaña had done most of the talking, in a soft, seductive whisper, but through a tense jaw. Byje listened to the ramble, but he was more interested in understanding what he was not being told. Mendaña's hot, wet palms indicated that he was terrified.

Unaware of how much he was really revealing Mendaña insisted, trying to make the Islander comprehend that he and his people were vassals of the King of Spain, who had been sent to Byje Ban Arra's land to see Byje and the rest of the Chiefs and bring them the sublime knowledge of the one true God and the Catholic faith.

Byje quickly began to understand the farce. He scratched his chin and feigned interest, but he had already come to a conclusion that any tribe capable of being governed by a Tauriqui like this hot flushing Mendaña must have been decadent and weak. He watched the Spaniard lean back and he realised that he had finished his discourse and that he was expecting a question, so he communicated the idea that he wanted to know where that King of Spain that had been eulogised so much was situated.

Mendaña was radiant. It was the first time he felt that he had been really understood. He reached out and lay his hands on Byje's broad shoulders, stroking them, and explained with a silly giggle that the King, whose name was Felipe, was still in Spain and then, lowering his voice and frowning to look serious, he explained that from there he ruled the entire world.

In order to make it easier for Byje to understand what the *entire world* was, Mendaña unfolded one of the navigation charts over the table, running his hand across it and explaining which parts of the map were land and which sea. Mendaña emphasised that Byje's land, which may have seemed like a universe to Byje, was but a tiny island and lied that the entire extent of the rest of the world, so much bigger than that island, belonged to the King of Spain. He explained that all the Tauriquis in the rest of the world were *naclonis,* which meant subjects, of the same king, the King of Spain.

The well-worn diplomat Byje kept his rage at the absurd insult perfectly controlled, and imitated Mendaña's own nescient grin before asking the Spanish Tauriqui where his God was.

This made Mendaña assume a theatrical severity. His voice dropped to Archbishop levels of profundity as he outlined the dogma of an omnipotent God, creator of the heavens, earth and sea, and how, thanks to Him, they and everything else in the Universe existed.

This surprised Byje. Mention of the word God, which was "Dios" in Spanish, pronounced more like *dio* by Mendaña, who had a tendency to swallow his final sibilants, sounded like *io* to Byje. And when he began to understand what Mendaña was actually talking about, the *io* became most definitely Io, which was the name of his own people's creation deity. Mendaña, he assumed, must have been an initiate, for only initiates of the cult of Io knew the real name of the creator.

His excitement boiled over and he leaned across the table to embrace Mendaña. Then he began his own frenzied sequence of sign language. Lifting one hand in the air, he said: *"Yue colhana,"* which meant "this is the sky". Mendaña nodded. Then Byje placed his index finger of the other hand on top of the one in the air and said, in broken bad Spanish: "Aquíd Io," which Mendaña understood as "Aquí Dios" or "Here is God" and that was more or less what Byje really wanted to say. Mendaña clapped and told Byje that what he had said was the truth. He called him his brother and embraced him. Both were convinced they had found a new initiate.

The next morning, I went inland. Into the deep green vegetable flesh of the forest. I rose, up a hill, to Sanba.

Sanba: human slashed scar town. Some twenty huts were there: A-framed constructs of dry-grass thatching on bamboo props, grouped around a huge, central hall. And between them, freckling the ochre earth, fat, brown cane toads, still greedy after the nightlong banquet of rhinoceros beetle, were sentinel still, or crawling like ugly babies, at times pouncing in a flopping fall.

At the lip of the hill a crowd had gathered, their backs to me. The naked backs and buttocks of the men and children, and the black fountains of wavy hair that splashed down the women's spines, slapping against their grass skirts. They had all seen the toads a thousand times, the beetles a million, they were looking out to the novel; to the coconut-ships floating in the bay.

An adolescent boy then suddenly turned and ran, followed by another, and another, creating a dribbling then gushing decomposition as particles rushed to a stronger centre of gravity; to the hall.

Inside Byje Ban Arra and his family were sitting down to a breakfast of sweet potato and spinach cooked in coconut milk and served on a large drooping leaf. His fingers and lips were white with carbohydrate mush when the panting figures arrived at the doorway; brightly haloed, dark figures caught at the shadow-line.

Byje roared an admonishment. The young spokesman was tentative: "Please, sir. It's our visitors, sir. They are being visited, sir."

The stupid sequence of words stretched Byje's face and he put the leaf-plate down, stood up and made a sweeping gesture which drew the other young men up. Then he grasped his jade axe and moved, down to the beach, where his people were dragging their canoes across the sand. They were heaving and shouting, loud enough to drown out parrots and cicadas. Those that weren't pulling were pointing. Towards the Spanish ships, which were now being slowly surrounded by other canoes. Visitors belonging to another Island nation.

On the *Capitana*, Alvaro de Mendaña bit his lip. The cries from the new canoes sounded anything but cheerful. These new Islanders were of a different race to Byje's Polynesian people; darker skinned Melanesians, waving spears and maces.

The deck echoed with the constant clanks and thuds from running feet dragging harquebuses and crossbows. Some of the harquebusiers were already in position and poised, their guns aimed down at the dark warriors' betel-nut splattered faces.

The ships had now been surrounded. Realising the strength encirclement gave them the men on the canoes began to bob with their weapons. Then an occasional spear or arrow shot at the hull of the ship, usually bouncing off it, which brought rounds of applause and roars of laughter from the Spaniards,

Byje was standing fierce on the raised platform of a catamaran which was being pushed through the shallows. He chewed betel and spat the red juice onto the deck of the vessel as if he were blessing it. An army of arms shoved, then suddenly and unanimously they caught hold of the canoe hull's sides to lift their bodies. There was only a slight shake of the platform as the springing legs dropped smoothly into the peapod hulls of the catamaran. Arms plunged down to snatch paddles, thrusting them out and slapping them against the sea. Each stroke was co-ordinated with a deep bellow, as the catamaran surged forward in profound jerks.

Byje, his focus fixed straight, croaked communication from the side of his mouth to a warrior called Gauga, on his left: "It's Meta and his men at the visitor's ships, isn't it?" exposing the betel stained teeth.

"Yes, sir."

Which encouraged expectoration: "The idiot... I sent word to him to wait. Now he thinks he'll impress us all by killing the strangers."

"Why don't *we* kill the strangers, sir?"

"I told you Gauga. Because they are strangers."

His attention was caught by a gliding booby: "They've come a long way," he persisted. The bird swerved in the air revealing its black mask and yellow cap. Byje scratched his own shaven scalp: "They're not pagans, they worship Io, just as we do," while the booby made its spectacular dive, right at the front of the canoe.

The warrior Gauga gasped when the bird hit the surface: "If we were fishing today we'd be blessed."

Byje spat more betel-juice: "We've seen their weapons, tied to their waists, and when they pull them they shine," the booby bobbed up on the surface again, gulping what must have been a huge fish in its throat: "I didn't like the look of that shine," and, as they rowed past the floating belly-full bird: "We must be patient," spitting again: "Meta is a fool."

Gauga gritted his teeth: "Why don't we just let him attack?"

Which made Byje suddenly turn. His face a real growl not just a painted one: "Because he might win! He might kill them all."

Meta's canoes surrounding the ships slowly crept forward. Rhythmically, while the warriors maintained the force of their chants. This was broken when one of them started a chaotic jumping and screaming. The sight of him lulled the others into a silence. Their heads turned, almost in unison, away from the explorers, toward the shore. Then, from each canoe, a murmur, low but expressing alarm and confusion. Black arms tensed, pumped. Rapid anarchic tugging created enough friction to turn. The surface frothed. The canoes shuddered and moved backwards, wobbled then pulled away in a new line, away from the ships.

Mendaña squealed, his cry of joy evolving into a question: "What for this sudden cowardice?"

His shoulder nudged slightly by Sarmiento, who pointed shoreward. Byje's fleet had begun to cut its way across the bay.

As the scene developed, the explorers' excitement grew and they began to shout and clap Byje – *So, we have crossed an ocean to witness a race* – thought Catoira, as a group of scabby sailors around him began to gamble on the outcome of the event.

Byje was at the prow of the leading catamaran. Rigid and plumed. His own solitary voice boomed across the harbour like a regal, rowing coxswain. By moving straight along the coast, his oarsman pulling in perfect time, they soon caught up with the inferior canoes of the less organised Melanesian party.

Vanquished by the mere act of being caught the Melanesians quickly laid their weapons down and stood with their hands up in their boats. Some of them were trembling and jumping nervously. Some of them almost crying. Byje leapt aboard one of the canoes and began marching up and down along it. His shouts were hurled across the bay to the Spaniards, who listened, as if understanding his discourse and the signals transmitted by his waving arms.

"What are you doing?!" shouted Byje to the other chief, Meta.

"What are *you* doing?" he hissed back: "You've joined sides with the strangers and become their protector." When he spat, Byje reacted by thrusting his double edged axe against his throat: "I have joined no-one, and I'm with everyone. Even with you, Meta, if you want. Until the strangers prove themselves our enemies they will be my friends."

"When they prove themselves, it'll be too late."

"And if we kill them now, what profit will we get from it? Do you want to sail in those coconut boats of theirs? Is that what you want?" then lowering and deepening his voice, directly into Meta's ear: "Have you not seen the feathers they wear? Feathers, Meta, that they consider *worthless*. Where they come from there will be many more of these feathers. Our ancestors have crossed the world to get them, now these men come to give them to us. We should not kill them."

Which made Meta bright eyed: "So that is your plan."

"Yes," but then Byje's jaw tightened and his voice rasped while he slowly exerted more pressure on the axe at Meta's throat: "And after a whole day of enduring talk with their stinking Tauriqui, on their stinking ship. After a whole day of lying to them about what good and peace-loving people we are, you go and attack them!"

Then released the pressure, leaving Meta choking and whining: "If you came to see me more often, you could have told me, and the rest of us, your plan."

But Byje ignored his argument and cut it off to continue his own line: "Now I'm going to have to tell them that you're a filthy cannibal, Meta. A flesh eater and a head-hunter, and that you're at war with me. But now you are defeated."

Meta groaned: "It would not be a lie."

"No, but I prefer not to be so honest with strangers. It's better to lie. Knowing that we are not good friends could be to their advantage."

XV. Utopia

Estrella rose from the bed and went to my desk. To a pile of notebooks: "So you are still writing the Terra Australis."

"It's been a long and tormented process, but it's almost finished."

She lifted book from book: "All of these are related to the research?"

"All of them. And there are more. There will be two thousand pages in all to be read. When it is finished."

She opened it and flicked through the pages: "I abandoned my own book. After what happened I lost all ambition. All desire. I had to change. Forget, and begin again."

"Stop," I interrupted: "What page has been reached?"

She scanned the page in order to find the tiny numeration which was lost under the words: "Page four hundred and sixty."

"They are in Utopia," I told her: "The Bay. Please let it be read by you to me now. So much pleasure would be gained ... to hear *you* reading."

(a) the bay

There was a distant clunk; metal against timber. A clonk; pine on hollow banyan. A sharp and repetitious wheeze; steel slicing through teak. Mendaña had given the order, suggested by Pedro Ortega, to construct a brigantine so that they could survey the coast and establish once and for all whether they were on a continent or not. A factory and a camp site were therefore set up on the beach.

The sailors, turned construction workers, were housed in huts thatched with palm leaves, or tents made from old and damaged sails. Soldiers drilled daily for hours, but slowly, lazily. Likewise, the carpenters' cutting and sawing was monotonous. The climate made heads heavy. Heavy feet became difficult to lift. The ring of the blacksmith's anvil was constant enough, but also always punctuated by long pauses. A thud. A coconut struck the sand.

Hernán Gallego, was inevitably in the centre of it all, enjoying the salubrious air of positive purpose again. He had always thought and often stated that if he had not been a sailor he would have been a builder, for he had a carpenter's wood-grain soul. He became the dominant figure on the beach and the base camp grew around him. He organised it all: the regrouping of materials and their removal from ship to beach, supervision of all the packing and unpacking. When inspired he had more energy than most of the men who were thirty years younger, and he was determined to prove it. And when he had the timber before him, a plane or chisel in his hands, and was imparting the carpenter's diligence to his slaves, he was splendid. Even the real carpenters seemed to ogle as he explained the differences betwixt heart and sap or balk and wane. Now he was the true cog in the sluggish machinery, perhaps the only part of it that worked well.

The others sweated, although it was a misleading sheen. Most of them did not have the builders' mettle and avoided toil at all costs. They had come to take, not edify. They would be servile only when watched, and there was only one Hernán Gallego to control them.

Once, after catching a pair of loafing sailors, the chief-pilot had tried to motivate them with a profound phrase: "Suffering's inevitable if you want to make something good."

But those receiving the wisdom hardly even waited until he had turned his back before exploding into a burst of honking guffaws.

The locals were also constantly poking around and getting in the way, or at least the women and children. The women had to cross the beach in order to reach the river where they collected fresh water and washed. The children came with their mothers or alone, drawn by novelty to invent fantasies and new games. They all seemed particularly fascinated by the Bubi blacksmith and his hot forge and the boys were constantly pestering the African to let them bash some glowing red metal for him. The girls and women, circled around with outstretched and splayed fingers, trying to touch the big, moist man. This attention made him visibly nervous and he would shiver, but they enjoyed that too.

For the women and children of Sanba the Spaniards' presence on the beach was a pleasant break to the island monotony. They watched their men grow anxious and wondered why. The strangers were strange, but they had come with presents and there did not seem to be enough of them to pose a threat of invasion. Their odd, blotched skin faces seemed ugly but also quite funny to the children, and some of the sailors made exceptional playmates.

However, when Byje announced that they were going to build a new canoe, a big war canoe, everyone realised that their already fragile situation on an island full of hostile tribes had become even more precarious. When axe lumbering youths trudged into the forest behind Byje's best magicians, many of them tried to open their minds to their ancestors for help and interpret the tingling pin-prick sensation on their skin. At such times they believed they could understand the language of the birds.

Come down you wood-sprites
        leave your thick-branch homes
abandon
    the shoots and roots
      Come out
up, down
    and go
swarm,
      leave
Go there!
    away
There!
    where you can make your noise
where you can scream ...

The pitch of the voice in the forest became a screech itself as a tattooed hand clutching a green-stone axe suddenly hit the trunk of the highest tree. Then an acorn kind of nut was squeezed into the fresh white gash.

Eat! Take this offering ... Eat!
Step down from this tree, old men
This is a canoe, and you would be shamed to sit there.
This is a canoe, from which you are expelled

Eyes rolled and lips shivered, then puckered, and the man uttering the words spat a lump of red betel against the trunk. The mouth was a toothless gash in a trembling wild and tattooed face.

Behind this, a few metres distant, stood Byje, with his arms crossed and solemn: "Do your best, good Mata," he murmured to the chewing, expectorating witch-doctor: "This boat must be strong and swift."

And Mata spat again. Harder and redder.

Still on the deck of the *Almiranta*, Juan López sat staring across the still, green bay to the deeper verdure of the jungle, becoming bluer then grey in the misty mountain tops. His hand wavered over his lap, bobbing, as if tapping out the tune of some melody; as if his mind's ears were humming with solemn, sheep gut strings, some future romantic music. He had a melancholy gleam in his eyes and when I did look into his mind there was a heavy-chested sense of sorrow at the thought that his captain-general had abandoned him. He could guess no reason why he had not been called ashore yet, and his brown eyes widened as he gazed over the mountains, imagining a golden city hanging from cliffs on the other side. A miraculous place that had to exist. Home of a new Grail. Had not his captain-general called him Perceval? - *But why did he not call?* –

For those who were on shore, however, the sweet and creamy dream of Paradise was quickly developing a hard and bitter crust. The oppressive, humid heat. The furious mosquitoes.

Catoira came out from behind a bush he had chosen as a latrine site, slapping and scratching: "Is it not a proof that we were not meant for this Heaven on earth," he complained: "that the mosquitoes hanker for Spanish blood rather than that of the Indians?"

Sarmiento laughed: "How right you be Catoira! We still have much to do before we can be worthy of it. But I warned you."

Yet despite the joke in Catoira's question it evoked a doubt in their capability for making a real discovery. One thing was to sail the seas until they bumped into something that no one had bumped into before; but it was something else to discover something that would change the fate of humanity, and make the world a better place to live in.

Sarmiento pointed to Mendaña, sitting on the porch of his A-frame hut, gazing across the white sands at the bay: "He suspects the potential of all of this to be his fate," he murmured to Catoira: "But he's incapable of acting in a way that will realise it."

In actual fact, for Mendaña, on that tropical coast, the intellectual idea of possibilities was just as vague a concept as the intangibility of spirit. Nevertheless, such a vagueness was less dangerous than the perils of the physical.

Whether as thoughts or urges; when the physical came to him it had to be wrestled with. Through squeezing the essence out of it, the material could become something philosophical, and he became obsessed with the problem of the ephemerality of existence. Why does everything wither and die?

Floundering in such existential seas, he would run his hand over his naked chest and remind himself that he was still young, but older each day. Sweating made his groin itch and that troubled him. How does a Captain get his release on an expedition powered by men alone? Morning, noon and night, he had Gaspar wash him and rub oil on him. He should not be a hypocrite, but what did he really believe in?

As a good Christian and an officer he had decided that the flesh was a swiftly treacherous threat. While his men were doing deals and trying to befriend the native men, as he had advised them to, they were also constantly ogling the women. Sex, he concluded, had become a vulgar menace to stability and authority.

Then, catching sight of one woman's wide eyes and fleshy lips – *Provocative, it will be hard to keep our men off them* – but he himself was too hypocritical to sense the self-accusation.

Then he sniffed, camphor, and turned. Another young girl was coming down a dry path, her feet crushing fallen leaves. It made his blood surge – *Why do they insist on walking past my hut like that?* –

"You are a young man," remarked the young friar, Pedro de Laguna, who had noticed the reaction.

"As you are."

"But I've made vows."

"No vows could dampen the heat I feel now."

Which inspired a quote from the Franciscan's leader: "*Where there is peace and meditation there can be no worry or vacillation.*"

The girl ran across the beach, into the wind, feeling it inside her matted lump of hair, chilling her naked body, stiffening her nipples. Mendaña sighed, the friar coughed. Both of them wriggled.

Sarmiento, Catoira and Gregorio Gonzalez purposefully relocated themselves to sit by a stream under a shady tree to ponder a bevy of women who were giggling and washing prickly conches. Their naked labour excited the men. Gregorio was goggle-eyed: "Have you noticed how some of them pluck the hairs from their little clams?"

But Sarmiento was sullen: "They don't seem shy to show it to us. Perhaps they never left Paradise. Perhaps they never took the fruit of the Tree of Knowledge. And we've come to teach them about Christ."

Which made Catoira chuckle: "Not exactly right, Captain. I don't think *we* will be teaching them *that.*"

"No, but we brought plenty of priests with us."

Gonzalez, however, had his mind full of the mollusc simile: "It's not right, señores, all these young damsels," then biting his top lip hard: "Several of the men tell tales. Of copulations," he whispered.

Catoira slapped a hand on the pilot's balls and squeezed them: "And you'd like to do the same, sirrah."

"O no, pray. Not me," pulling the hand away, which wrenched the testicles and made him grimace. His voice dropped into something strangely sincere: "That's the very source of my complaint. That none of them do naught for me. Not the slightest itch," which was completely contradicted by his slathering jowls.

Sarmiento murmured lazily: "Not to worry man. It must be their nature that does not agree with you," and then, with a meaningful wink at Catoira that the pilot could not see, and with exaggerated irony: "Their savage blood."

The idea made Catoira, rather than Gregorio, thoughtful: "They *are* savages. They know how to kill; we've seen the weapons they carry. This is not the Paradise on Earth. How could it be? In this wretched climate, with all this mud and mosquitoes?"

Sarmiento scratched an insect venom full lump on his chin: "Yet neither the mud nor the mosquitoes seem to bother *them.*"

Gregorio gurgled: "They're naked, that's why the heat does not bother them."

Then Sarmiento again: "They're in Paradise and they're happy. We were banished, now we return, and it seems like hell to us."

"Unless we find gold," smirked Catoira.

But Sarmiento ignored the other pair's ambitions. He kneeled down and thrust a hand into the mud, ripping up a handful which he squelched between his fingers: "Perhaps there's something far more precious than gold here, Catoira. But I doubt that we'll ever find it. We must cover ourselves with leather and cloth. We cover our bodies and at the same time cover our souls. We cover our shame."

The ideas were well beyond Gregorio. He leaned away, not only to escape the depth of concepts, but to catch a better glimpse of a particularly well-shaven mussel. Catoira however felt obliged to persist with Sarmiento's ethnological theology: "And these washing girls are shameless."

"No," insisted Sarmiento: "They've *no* shame, but that's different. You look at their naked bodies and you see all their evil and all their goodness at the same time. There's something noble in such naked honesty. A nobility which we've lost. Their fathers' fathers, I tell you, pray, did not come from the womb of Eve."

Gregorio picked up on the mention of Eve to return him to the same complaint he had had before: "If this be Paradise, then shouldn't the women be ... well ... I'd imagined them to be ... more ... exciting."

Catoira laughed at the obsessiveness and patted poor Gregorio's shoulder: "Exciting yes. But to have the pleasure of it, you have to try it first."

"But, how can I try if no inspiration urges me hence?" he lied.

Sarmiento scolded: "It's you that's imperfect, sirrah. Your catholic blood is full of a leech that tempers the furnace. Strip yourself naked, good Gregorio. Embrace the nature that surrounds you. One week like that and your pointer will rise at the proximity of any warm flesh: regardless of its toastedness."

Gregorio, suddenly perplexed by the response, did not like it at all. He turned away to the sailors' barracks, head tilted down, in silence.

Sarmiento also moved away. He was always happier on his own. In loneliness he forged his soul. In company, expressed it. As for the ideas just elaborated, he had formed them one day when, bored by the noise of men, he had hobbled off by himself in search of the voiceless.

Armed with dagger and sword, his torso stiff in his rusted metal breastplate, he had ascended a sharp hard salient, a tongue of dry rock that licked out from the corner of the wide bay's mouth into the sapphirine sea. Even the dull iron of his armour seemed to gleam and his leather sheathed sword flicked like a stiff tail, rattling against the challenge of rocks that he stumbled over and squeezed between. Wavering-clumsy, he had been, balanced by only one irresolute and hovering arm while the other cradled his rusty helmet. His eyes flickered from side to side, focusing out and down. His top lip curled up, expressing disdainful amazement. Occasionally he had stopped to catch an energising breath, or admire a landscape, or stoop and pick up a stone. The granite side of his soul had grown tired of the capricious liquid world and the weakness of wood, it now gravitated to mineral obduracy and he fondled any rock he had the time to ponder on.

After a while, he reached a kind of summit and perched himself on the edge. There he took a deep breath and thought about their goal – *Already the air is fresher* – he argued to himself – *It becomes cleaner the closer we are* – a romanticism that was quickly tempered by an experience fed pessimism – *It's like a bubble of pure oxygen floating in the liquid excrement of a universal cesspool* –

Below him had been the bay. Their camp; a dark stain on the gleaming white beauty of the beach. A misanthrope's complaint from his hermit-alchemist psyche made him grimace and look away from it, over the stretching sea to a smudge of pink that was the horizon. Nature, the antithesis of man, could inspire – *And we transgressed that line, in search of the limitless, and arrived here* – Then, turning round, dense jungle running to the base of the high, craggy mounts, implying impenetrable barriers.

Impenetrable? No. Merely other limits to be transgressed. But nevertheless thick and resisting. In order to enter one had to slash and cut, or burn. Destroy it. Which saddened him for a moment, gripped by a premonition of a woodless world infected by the virus of men and their insipid civilisation. Yet the conservative was not his true nature and, dropping the just gathered stones and straightening his helm, he chopped his way through, until he found a trace of an inward path.

Of course his slashing presence was disturbing to the rain forest and each chopping frenzy would silence the insect-bird opera, creating the deafening silence of jungles. But an awareness of his protagonist role inspired the alchemist – *The forest is full of such fearful life* – he thought – *The entire wood trembles at my presence* – And he spat provokingly, waiting until the insects and birds found the courage to start up again.

Then parrot plumage smashed through high clusters of foliage with such anguished squawks that Sarmiento's heart jumped. He expected to feel some fanged, vampire-bird's beak clamp into his jugular. And there were other avian communications: haunting, ringing, occasionally melodious but usually rasping tortured calls. Some of them threatened, others were desperate pleas for succour.

After a while he realised that he had lost the path and became anxious. The forest seemed to be growing around him as he watched and he had to use spiral vines to hold him up on the slope. But these twirling branches became a curling cage, green and rubbery and hard to cut, and his arm had less and less room to make a sweep. Also the moisture gave the vegetation an unctuous fabric that further inhibited progress. Sticky stems brushed against his face leaving his skin smarting from some stinging acid, or scratching him with pin-prick thorns. Effort and atmosphere had him sweat soaked and gasping and his stroll had turned into a frantic push. At times the insects would also manifest themselves, in swarms in front of his face, clouds of tiny flies fluttering into it, up his nose, into his mouth and ears, eyes, crawling in his beard.

The complexity of the situation inspired panic. These and other insects crawled under his shirt, sometimes leaving their own smarting sting. Thinking himself hopelessly lost he suddenly roared and began madly slashing a clearing around himself, an egg-like hollow within the vegetable womb. Then he dropped, exhausted, dripping wet and wheezing like an asthmatic, on a bed of cuttings, some of them thorny. The stems of a bright green plant dangled in his face. Purple bracts at their ends. It evoked horror at first, until he made an effort to relax by considering details. He reached forward to yank tight buds off the stems, peel leaves apart, and for a little while the clandestine violet petals that the dissected buds revealed brought him pleasure, until a beast arrived.

It was a long, thin black wasp hovering before his face in search of sweetness or moisture with a strange attraction for his neck, and it kept darting in that direction. This forced the alchemist to wave a hand. The wasp resisted. Returned. No explicable reason. Frustrated, Sarmiento pulled out his dagger and lashed at it. Which actually seemed to work. But when he had disposed of the hymenopterous creature he had hardly time to relax, his legs were covered with a trail of ants who had advanced to explore the inside of his boot. He wrenched this off and slapped his leg. Most of the ants hurried away, but at least one stayed long enough to sting his naked foot. Vengeance made the boot a hammer and he battered leaves and grass. Then he sighed and paused before preparing the boot's return to his foot. Again he shivered. On the brown toe of the muddy boot was a twitching, arching worm, dragging its body upward toward the lip – *a leech* – he realised. But this confirmation soothed his panic, and he smiled as he picked it off, then deposited it in a leather pouch dangling from his belt, happy now to have found a future palliative for some fever.

Yet his nerves were still not allowed to settle properly. A sudden loud rustling, low, at ground level, made him breathless.

His hand settled on his cold sword's hilt and he squinted to peer through branches in the direction of a thicket where something had moved. The sound implied heaviness. A large mammal or huge reptile. Thinking of food, he summoned a madman's courage and crept closer to the screen of foliage separating them. The vegetation that brushed or slashed against him was moist. The red-clay earth was slimy. His boots squelched. His breathing rasped.

Then, a faint mumble of human voices coming from amidst the thicket could be discerned over his own wheezes. His hand, flushed and freckled with black and ochre dirt, was still on his sword's hilt. His red face dripped. Bushes cracked, grass swished and, crouching behind a fern, he parted a veil of delicate pinnules and arching fronds.

At first the revelation was unexpected and it shocked him. He fell flat. Mud splattered his cheek and something dripped into his eye making him grimace and squeeze both of them shut. Then he blinked hard again. The dirt was out of his eye and he could think about what he had just seen. The reconstructed image drew an impish smile from him, which melted into a subtler curl depicting curiosity as he lifted himself, uncomfortably and therefore shakily, to stretch his neck up, his hand carefully parting the ferns again.

The reality returned much as he had reconstructed the image. A surge of blood made him squirm, uncomfortably hot. The fingers that were still clenched tight upon his sword hilt, unravelled and moved from the cool metal to the damp cloth over his groin. He rubbed it, massaging the flesh underneath as he made a lizard movement, stretching his neck to push his head even further through the ferns. His gaze too was saurian in its intensity and his tongue, purple in that dim jungle light, flicked.

Inside the green frame was a pair of young, naked bodies, spread out on an apple green blanket of fresh grass, at the bank of a gushing stream. The rhythm was unmistakable, the gasps and grunts universal. They were wrapped in a most perfectly natural fornication.

He had to restrain a cough which made him gag slightly. He could not see their faces but their bodies were athletic-trim, tight and adolescent thin.

The boy was rough and hurried. Each breath a pig like grunt. The girl squeaked, a mouse like timbre. Her head flicked from one side to the other, blackened by her long hair and forest shadows. Impossible to see her face. They did not kiss.

Sarmiento rubbed harder as the male arse in front of him bobbed faster. Empathy had placed his own penis out there and he had to swallow hard to retard his own groans.

– *Free of our civilisation-sodden perversions* – he considered, almost whispered audibly on his breath as he untied the crotch in his trousers to release his bone-hard penis and tight balls. He closed his eyes to imagine a more graphic image of the couple, pornographic backdrop to a spurt of aesthetics – *There should be no art or philosophy beyond the sensual and real* – and he began to recall his own history of flesh – *Fantastic because it is so natural* – then opening his eyes again, the boy was up on his knees, the girl turned round and on all fours, her breasts wobbling, fat-flesh pendulums between her taught, force bracing arms – *So close to creation. So far from the petty ideal* – then she pulled away, pushed the boy over and straddled him. Her massive peach arse tentative at first, pushing down in a slowly coiling corkscrew motion – *All are equals under the eyes of God and Satan* – then grinding – *Paradise ... ugggghhhhh* –

Blood was pumped to where it was most needed and he shuddered. His penis turned a dark shade of burgundy, bulged, throbbed. His head ached and his arms tingled. His legs became numb. He felt dizzy and collapsed into the bracken. He could have died then, he thought, clutching his heart, and when another ant crawled onto him and stung his neck, he slapped the aggressor into a mangled dead mess.

But despite his sympathy and excitement for the natural act Sarmiento still looked at the young couple's love making and saw a pair of *savages*. His observations were ambiguous. He, like the rest of the invaders, imagined them as a wild and lawless, hedonistic race. But unlike the others he was capable of grasping the complexity of a society whose purpose was expressed in magic ritual. For the alchemist, the hedonism and magic cults were a projection of his own wild will. Even the idea of cannibalism had a perverse attraction for him.

My own perception of them was quite different. I observed a well-mannered people and strongly organised, governed by authority and its laws. Laws in both public and personal relations which allowed for very little improvisation. Under the control of extremely complex kinship and clanship ties the Islanders seemed closer to suffering an inhibiting dictatorship than enjoying the natural freedom that Sarmiento fantasised about. The chief and his magicians had more direct power over their subjects than any European king or pope. If the idea of the *savage* implies anarchy and chaos, it was a more fitting adjective for the European society; especially the one that had been created in the Americas.

Yet it is easy for me to preach my clear sightedness, most of us like to see ourselves as the more enlightened ones. Enlightened by our position in time and space. Enlightened by my objectivity, which is really my subjectivity. If someone were to tell us that we lived in a dark and primitive corner of the cruellest and most savage culture that has ever existed, could we accept it? We talk about the dark ages, what if our time will be known as the black ages; could we accept such an idea?

Later on I saw Catoira come out from behind another bush he had chosen as a latrine site, much as he had before when the mosquitoes had attacked, but this time instead of slapping and scratching he was red faced and pulling at his skirt.

Gregorio Gonzalez saw him and laughed: "What be wrong wit' yer, Writer? The mosquitoes been bitin' yer arse again!"

The scribe lifted an arm to point but stumbled as his skirt slipped down. Gonzalez and Sarmiento roared. Then, clutching his skirt, Catoira stammered: "The t-t-trees down there ... They're full of women! Hanging from the branches. Like a tribe of Amazon banshees. They wouldn't leave me alone. Kept trying to get a g-glimpse of my p-private parts. Then one of them actually jumped on me and started p-p-pulling at my skirt ... Can you imagine it?"

Sarmiento shook the mirth out of his head and spoke seriously: "We must look so different to them. We act so different that they doubt our humanity."

"Yet if that were the case wouldn't they be frightened?"

"That would depend, would it not? If you believed your visitors were gods or demons that would terrify you. But if you considered your invaders a peculiar type of ape. Would you run from them or study them?" and he squashed a tiny spider under the folds of his shirt.

But really the women had had a ritualistic reason for pouncing on Catoira. Unknown to the Spaniard he had gone to shit in one of the villagers' gardens. The women, who were garden magicians, had been performing a series of rites and casting magic spells which would assist in the growth of the crop, which in this case was taro. When Catoira stumbled in he was committing *taboo*. In fact, it was taboo for any man to cross a field at the time of the important ritual, and according to local law the women were expected to humiliate the man, exposing his genitals and ridiculing his sex.

"Here comes one of the red-skinned men," said the first woman to notice his violation.

"One of the women with beards," laughed a third.

"Let's see what he or she really has," insisted the first: "For if he's a man, then his little willy must be slapped," and they had pounced on him from the tree and pulled at his skirt. Yet they had no intention of fornicating with the smelly red-skin, as Catoira himself had supposed.

But Catoira was not a vindictive man and I had also seen him speak well of the Islanders. He had been sitting at the edge of the beach, sharing the milk of a coconut with Sarmiento and Gregorio Gonzalez while watching the servant boy Gaspar playing a game with some native boys. They were trying to balance themselves on a floating log. A game which Gaspar invariably lost.

The three men were, as usual, discussing the nature of the Islanders. Gregorio had referred to them as *barbarians* when Catoira recalled a quote from the Greek general Pyrrhus: "*I know not what kind of barbarians these may be.*"

This was uttered in obvious praise. The rest of the famous quote, which Catoira had no need to complete, went: *The discipline I see has nothing of barbarity in it.* This seemed to display some ethnological objectivity after the mauling he had received from the women.

* * *

Stone cutters were pushed along the length of the felled tree, lopping away the final branches. It had taken one long day to bring it down and many men's labour. While some wielded axes, others were rubbing stone against stone to sharpen the blunted or broken blades. But now at last the trunk was ready to be transported to Sanba. Tough creepers were looped around it, umbilical cord links to the shoulders of the tattooed workers. Back muscles rippled as they heaved. Beneath their feet wooden slips had been laid down to slide the tree over, although progress was slow and clumsy. A loud moan of anguish suddenly ripped forth: "It's heavy! There are spirits here still. Too heavy!"

The shout was directed at the witch-doctor Mata, who was squatting under a tree, in a sensual mood, twisting his nose-piece. The rub of the polished shell against his flesh, as delicious as a sweet slice of roasted pork, inspired a tweak of the white pubic-leaf between his legs. He obviously did not want to shift himself and his reply to the shout was a moan. But duty bade. He would have to move. So he slowly straightened his legs and, picking up a dry banana leaf, adopted a snobbish stance as he ceremoniously approached the croaking log. Those that were pulling let the creepers drop and they stood back to allow Mata to perform his magic. The witch-doctor lifted the banana leaf before laying it carefully and histrionically down on the log. Then he blew a whooshing sound from his mouth and reached down to rip up a handful of long grass which he began slapping against the fallen tree, chanting as he did: *Down, come down*

Out rot! Out! Let the canoe tremble with speed...

Women could be heard, then seen, hurrying up the track from the settlement bearing platters of food. Women from Sanba but also other women and men from the other settlements around the bay who had come to help in the construction of the canoe. They were excited. Not so much by the idea of the canoe, but that one of the pigs they had been transporting from their own village on the beach up to Sanba had been robbed from them by the strangers.

Byje calmed them with promises that he would talk to his friend, the strangers' Tauriqui, and demand compensation. The breathless workers were hardly stirred by the debate. Only when the smell of barbecued pork and baked sweet potatoes wafted up to them did they muster themselves and reach out with trembling tired hands, as if in supplication. The banquet began. With their mouths full of sweet potato and gobs of pork fat clinging between the gaps in their teeth, smiles emerged, and they began to sing, some of them gurgling music between long gulps of coconut milk or slurping sucks of sugarcane. Despite the aching limbs and the stolen pig, they were satisfied.

* * *

That night, down on the beach, Toledo-steel slashed under the surface of hot meat. The peeling grey pork curled, staggered then dropped or was flicked onto metal plates. Daggers jabbed, pierced, impaled, and then lifted chunks to mouths. Calcium cutters snapped and masticated. A spasm in the neck and the flesh was gone. The air, also swallowed, had to be expulsed, reboant proclamations of satisfaction. The men were reddened by the glow of dying embers that were the remains of the bonfire around which they had sat. The remnants of the stuck-pig, an ugly, half naked skeleton, which was torn and broken apart.

Around them the world was black, so they were unaware of the presence of spying eyes. A group of Islanders, all men, were squatting between or leaning on trunks of trees on the hill. They who considered themselves to have been the real owners of the now no more pig. But how would they receive their retribution?

Mendaña, a moderate eater and drinker, was content to see the others patting their full stomachs. Opposite him Gallego was still chopping his portion: his knife preliminarily performing the duties of the teeth that he had lost. Next to Gallego was Ortega, immersed in the labour of his tongue, trying to push stubborn strings of gristle out from compact incisors. Then Catoira, lying back, staring at, but not contemplating the stars, and Sarmiento, wiping grease and specks of flesh off his dagger.

Mendaña turned and caught the eye of young Gaspar who was behind him, and smiled. He so appreciated this bastard boy and his sad humility. Such a rare virtue amongst so many self-opinionated, would-be heroes. Meanwhile, what had been quiet, good natured conversation, slowly evolved into angry debate.

Hernán Gallego was complaining about the Islanders' presence in the camp. With each of their visits something would inevitably disappear, usually a tool. Also, the more serious workers had found the constant milling around oppressive. On several occasions his patience had run out and he had had to wave his sword and scream at them to get out.

Sarmiento remonstrated the idea, arguing that it was no way to treat the Islanders, who they needed as friends.

Gallego ignored him and pointed out that the constant interference was slowing progress on the construction of the brigantine. Mendaña nodded, it was important that the scouting vessel should be completed as quickly as possible. Sarmiento shook his head. There were indications that the Islanders were planning a combined offensive, if they wanted to they could muster thousands. Alliances were needed and had to be encouraged and respected, and Byje's people were the only allies they had. But excluding them from the beach camp would taint their apparent faith and good-will, and Byje would have no option but to doubt the Spaniards' intentions. Mendaña nodded again, of course he agreed with Sarmiento.

Then Ortega joined the side of Gallego: "This story from the Indians," he snorted and his bottom-lip wobbled: "About the good Indians and the bad Indians," and rubbed his teeth with the gum inside that same wobbling lip: "It don't make much sense to me," shaking his head as if in desperation: "I've never known a good Indian."

Mendaña looked thoughtful but could only manage the obvious: "But we don't know these people still."

"Precisely, which is why I don't think we can trust 'em," and then: "You say that the yellow men," by which he meant the Polynesians: "Are at war with the blacks," the Melanesians: "Yet we've seen black-men standin' with the yellow-men. The villagers at the end of the beach are blacks, but we see their children playin' with the yellow ones who come down from the hill."

Mendaña had a theory to explain it: "The villages around the bay seem to be vassals of Byje. That one at the far end of the bay, full of *blacks*, as you say, good Don Pedro, although they seem more like *mulattos* to me, for they are not black like our Negroes and some even have the most beautiful golden hair. We have seen from that village a procession of men and women carrying pigs and yams to Sanba. I'm sure that is a form of taxes or retribution."

Inspiring a bellowing confirmation from Gregorio Gonzalez: "Which is where this lovely pork came from, fie!" and he sniggered repulsively.

This formed frowns on the faces of Gallego and Pedro Ortega.

Mendaña wriggled and his face reddened: "The pig was taken!" he squealed: "Was I not told that it was hunted?"

Sarmiento's opportunity had come.

He argued, scoldingly, that Byje was an ambitious man and the Spaniards' presence tipped the balance of power in his favour. As long as he thought he could trust the Spaniards he would be a loyal ally, but, their own camp was in the middle of the bay, the people's route to the river. Cutting them off from fresh water would only provoke an inevitable war, if stealing their pigs did not do so beforehand. The important thing, Sarmiento entreated, was to stay as long as possible where they were, and explore: "It's time to go inland. Divine who Byje's allies and enemies really are and determine if this really is a continent or not, not by sailing around it but by scaling," and his finger was thrust through the wall of black night to where he supposed the misty slopes of the interior to be: "Climb the craggy peaks, establish an overview that will divine the mystery of the land we're on. If we are at the centre, then the *real* centre has to be the mountain."

Mendaña nodded again, although more tentatively this time: "You want to go *there*?"

The idea, though practical, terrified him. As a child he had wandered into a forest surrounding his village at Congosto, had quickly become lost and had even spent a nightmarish, freezing cold night out there. They had found him the following day, damp and shivering and half-dead from fear. He shuddered when he thought of himself in the jungle, but then remembered that if he had a job it was to delegate and so he appointed all responsibility to Sarmiento.

*   *   *

In Sanba the men of the community – Byje's Polynesians as well as their Melanesian allies – formed a colourful circle around the log. Herbs were wrapped around Mata's axe as he began the task of scooping out the centre. As he did the men erupted in song and began to stand and sway and then jerk themselves into a rhythm, to dance. The magician also began to move and work in a ritualistic way:

I strike you with this canoe-cutting axe
The boat is within you and I will drag it out to make you fly
Like wind we shall disappear in the mist
then hurl out of the clouds, sea-weed wreathed,
and bring our bravest warriors' spears
to the cold hearts of our enemies
Our cult is Io
    and Io is our totem
Io is in my arm,
    my axe,
        and now in you,

canoe

It is Io who will make you fly...

* * *

That afternoon there was a short, but violent storm. The first of many. The rainy season had begun.

At first the change was refreshing for the Spaniards. Men stood out under the cloudburst to cleanse themselves. But once washed the water became undesirable, its constancy annoying, its consistency insalubrious. Bodies and minds were dampened. Bones began to ache while minds fogged and became depressed. Life would be monotonous again. All activity had to revolve around the plugging of holes, protection of beds from drips, of food from the suddenly surfacing plagues of ants or from the advancing legions of ravenous crabs.

Sarmiento's appointment was significant enough to drag Gallego's attention from his builder's purpose. He had been watching the captain-general and the navigator growing closer each day. From Gallego's point of view, Mendaña was entrusting too much to Sarmiento, while his own influence had diminished into something insignificant. Mendaña never consulted him anymore. His advantage had been completely lost.

But if Gallego did have anything on his side it was the slow labouring of tropical time and the boredom it created. The awe inspired by miracles is quickly mitigated by the mundane, and Gallego tried his hardest to undermine all of their dreams. He began to apply his scepticism even to the most dramatic miracle of them all, openly questioning the 'guiding star' itself. Why had it to be assumed that it had been a positive omen? Perhaps it had been a warning. He even dared to wrestle metaphysics with the friars: "What do yer think, Father? That this is the Paradise our captain-general 'as proclaimed."

"Without Paradise, God would be unbearable," grunted an old priest.

Gallego picked his nose: "Yet if it were, would any of these men deserve to be 'ere? It's vanity that fuels their lust ... for im-mortality. Thinkin' themselfs significant, nay, important even, thus death becomes incompre'ensible."

"And *your* vanity? Have you none?"

"Long gone, with youth. Age and infirmity makes us 'umble."

Yet, there was little humility expressed when discussing Sarmiento. Whether it was authentic hatred that plagued him or a mere tool that he used to satisfy his pact with Ahedo, he was quite open about his enmity, its virulence being demonstrated that stormy afternoon by another snippet of dialogue.

He and Pedro Ortega were sitting on a hollow and rotting log, under a rough lean-to erected on the outside of the camp, facing the sea. The storm water gushed off its lip. Ortega was cleaning the sand from his harquebus, Gallego sewing the perished leather of his belt. I caught their conversation in mid-stream. Gallego was upset: "Salt is an abrasive element, señor Ortega. And an old sailor is full of it."

"If salt engenders bile, you'd do well to swallow it. Sarmiento's a rancorous man."

"Not given to diplomacy."

"You know 'im well enough."

"Know? I loathe 'im. But I'm too old to fear 'im or anything else on earth. It's not fear that inspires me anger, but the pride of an old man ignored," an idea which seemed to motivate a pause, as if it were the first time he had thought of it. It was certainly the first time he had admitted it. Then he blinked to regain the track of his argument and turned to face Ortega, who was immersed in the mechanics of his gun. His tone was plaintive, his look sheepish: "What would you 'ave that I do? Cower in the penumbra of me sad distrust? Hardly more than 'ad our ship unfurled its sails was I off-capped to 'im," and he reached forward, grabbing and squeezing Ortega's arm, demanding intimacy: "And I speak not just o' me; you've also been off-capped in his new enterprise, this jungle expedition," his voice a whisper, but an angry one, spitting conspiracy: "You're the *maestre de campo*, and yet, who leads our troops?! Off-capped to 'im, señor Ortega! And why should yer forgive any more than I? He, lovin' in his own bedevilled pride, stuffed with epithets of his Holy Mission to mask 'is true satanic purpose. Bewitchin' our infant captain-general with his alchemy-hope. It bodes no good, no good at all," then released Ortega's arm and renewed his sewing. Inserting the needle with more virulence than dexterity it seemed to calm the violence in his voice: "And so what're we to do then, señor Ortega? Outface 'is bragging, we must. We're too far from 'ome and Christendom to allow ourselves to be led by pagan generals."

The allegations hit their mark. Pedro Ortega lapped his tongue along the barrel of the harquebus, then grunted, disgorging phlegm.

(b) the village

In the mangrove swamp the soldiers were green with the weed that they had dragged with them. They were already almost beaten by the squadrons of mosquitoes, but fear of a brutal death in some flesh ripping crocodile's jaws kept them from complaining. Ortega's slaves lead them, pushing in jerks through the weight of water, ripping their feet from the sucking mud bottom, their arms strained up to hold food and gunpowder supplies dry. The men behind them were the same, but with harquebuses over their heads rather than bundles and from a distance they looked like an advancing field of crucifixes.

Once out of the swamp they had to climb. A steep, red ridge. Sarmiento looked sympathetically at the stiffed hipped *maestre de campo*, but worried about how long it would take for them to get him up.

Ortega, however, read the alchemist's face and growled: "I'll be at the top long before you, sirrah. Unless your magic can fly you there," and he jabbed his staff into mud and moved.

There was a narrow path up the slope. Treacherous, not only because of its lack of width, but the red mud was squelching and slippery soft. They rose in single file, the slaves managing better because they were barefoot and they could dig their toes into the clay to support themselves. The others however seemed to think slave wisdom a degrading thing and so preferred to suffer the encumbrance of perpetually sliding soles.

But no sooner had the first soldiers set foot on the path than an echoing and reboant blast of conch horns rang out. Byje Ban Arra had placed sentries. The pig thieves, the Islanders realised, were on their way.

As the Spaniards advanced the path became more difficult, narrowing into non-existence at times, and they had to stretch themselves like spider monkeys to move from one rock to another; clutching the black and rubbery life lines of erosion-freed roots, or holding themselves up on prickly, stone clinging shrubs. The vanguard grimaced and kicked their legs up until they were squirming over the top of the ridge.

Ortega was breathless. His massive bulk needed the support of three of his slaves. But when he was up on the edge he did not collapse panting on the ground like the others did, he straightened his back and erected himself. He was the first to compose himself and have the audacity to suggest to Sarmiento that they should keep moving. It piqued the alchemist at first; the competitive arrogance of the fat, old pig would have to be chastised. But then he realised why Ortega was so adamant.

The Sanban welcoming committee rattled at a spear's throw from them. There were at least fifty men, each one with a mace and spear, or bow and arrow, though none of these were aimed. They were observing. Some of them were catching their first, close up glimpse of the visitors: "It's true," said one staring dubiously into the Africans' souls: "They have head hunters with them."

Then another low voice: "And how do we know they're not all head hunters? Why is Byje so sure?"

"Because he has spoken with them, and with their Tauriqui," affirmed a third and more confident orator: "He says they are good men who worship our gods."

"Yet their totem is not the same as ours. They stuck it on our land without asking for permission. That should be punished."

"And they steal our pigs. That should be punished."

"We could push them off the cliff."

"No!" shouted one who seemed to have authority: "Tauriqui Byje told us not to fight. Just to keep them away long enough to hide the food. He says they just want food. The garden magicians have cursed them. They're very hungry and don't know how to feed themselves."

A preposterous idea, which evoked raucous laughter.

The Spaniards and their slaves were quickly up on their feet. Sarmiento looked down behind him. The sheer thirty metre drop made him dizzy:

"We'd better be away from this edge."

Inspiring a nervous shuffling forward, hastily gathering packs and maintaining their backs towards the wall of trees while they loaded their harquebuses.

The African slaves trembled. They had quickly picked up on the Islanders' animosity directed against them in particular: "Perhaps they think we're the leaders. After all, we always go first."

But the joke fell on deaf ears. The idea of violence and death was too prominent to encourage laughter.

Sarmiento kept his hand fixed firmly to the pommel of his sword: "Keep your calm lads. If there's a charge, we'll give them shot. They won't stay long once they've heard our thunder and smelt our sulphurous smoke."

Eyes on both sides were attentive. Anxious. Deep breaths tried to submerge their racing pulses in oxygen. Sarmiento fished a necklace of beads from under his shirt and held it up in front of him, like a vampire-dissuading crucifix. He gestured to Catoira and Ortega to do the same as they approached the Sanban line.

Some of the Islanders groaned indignantly before the offerings. One of these I recognised to be the one called Gauga, who had stood beside Byje on his catamaran. He had two huge green feathers pushed into a headband: "So they come with their little gifts."

"Hardly compensation for the pigs."

"Hardly ... but something."

Then one of the original owners of the pig whined and whispered to Gauga: "Ask them for a headdress with a red feather. That would compensate ... or with two feathers ... No, it'd have to be three. That sow they took was pregnant."

Gauga stepped forward and slowly lifted the beads from the out-stretched hands, passing them quickly behind him to the claimant. Afterwards he pointed to his head and to the feathers there and held up three fingers.

The Spaniards picked up on the frustrating gesture. The expedition had not set out with feathered caps, but with steel helmets, and they were not going to part with those. Sarmiento shook his head: "Byje..."

Gauga turned and issued a sweeping glance. The men moved with it, opening a lane through them. Sanba and their Tauriqui were on the other side.

As the Spaniards advanced, the army of Sanban warriors melted away into the forest. Air became thicker and stiller and the village of Sanba seemed deserted except for a pair of brown and drowsy, fly-magnet dogs.

"This smells like a trap," whispered a nervous Catoira, but Sarmiento just grunted and grimaced at the too obvious affirmation as they softly stepped into the flat area of the village. The thirty huts there were arranged around an inner circle of rougher little cabins on stilts. The latter were the storage spaces, where the villagers kept their coconuts and yams. But at that moment these seemed to be empty.

As they advanced, the Spaniards began to sense the eyes that were on them. Although women and children's eyes they seemed to have a skin penetrating power. The visitors became prickly hot and sweating damp. Not that the eyes' owners were conscious of such a power, they themselves were panting breathless. Only minutes before they had been running and humping and the village had been an ant-nest of activity in which all food and drink and any other valuables were taken away to a safer place.

Then suddenly Byje was standing before the Spaniards, arms folded, in front of half-a-dozen other huge men with their arms folded. His top lip peeled up into a snarl, a blasting coldness that froze Sarmiento and his mud heavy boots.

Catoira's eyes and mouth widened as his disaster sensitive stomach sank, weighed down by its own muddiness. Pedro Ortega, however, who had suffered heaviness all his life, waddled goose-like into Sarmiento's forward place. Once fixed at the front line he began a mime, shovelling air into his mouth and rubbing his bumble-bee belly.

Byje maintained his snarl, but clapped his hands, indicating the fetching of food and water. The water was brought in hollow cane, while coconuts and yams, arrived in swaying, soft baskets. Ortega took the cane bottle offered him, sniffed its contents and, when assured of its cleanliness, drank. Then he passed it to Sarmiento who also took a mouthful while the *maestre de campo* made signs for them to bring more.

However, now Byje shook his head as the rest of his warriors, some of them with their spears up, reappeared, surrounding the Spaniards.

Ortega's face was all twitches, his head flicking, his hand wafting as if a squadron of biting flies had attacked. He bellowed and waved his stick. When he did the soldiers quickly formed a rattling, harquebus bristling circle. Sarmiento was sucked to the centre, while Ortega waddled into its gravity.

Byje also backed away. He knew nothing of harquebuses but their strangeness troubled him. He gave his own warriors a shout and the spears slowly began to droop. Then he stepped forward again, flicking his arm and waving his hand in a beckoning movement to the Spaniards.

Sarmiento snorted and buckled the strap of his helmet. Then, turning to Ortega: "I'm going to see what this painted brock wants," and flicking his head in the direction of the huts: "Investigate. Locate the food he's so reluctant to give us. And bring it out here. When I return we'll decide what to leave the villagers with."

Then he signalled to Catoira, to follow.

Byje made a sweeping gesture and in a deep proud bass: "Sanba."

Afterwards he squatted down and screwed a finger into the soil so that it left a deep imprint before he repeated the name. He kept the finger in the soil, dragging it to draw a line. When he stopped he stood up and pointed southward: "Tiarabaso," he said, and returning to the soil he pushed his finger in again at the end of the line: "Tiarabaso," he repeated, and then in Spanish: "There you eat ... Much food ... Tauriqui name Baso ... Is country of Baso in Baso," and he tapped his tongue with his finger: "You know? Much food," then pointing again, more forcefully: "You go!" He was indicating a track.

Sarmiento nodded his head as if agreeing, then asked him how far it was.

Byje understood and he pointed to the sun making a sweeping arc in the air before holding up one finger which they understood to mean one-day's march. Sarmiento nodded: "Good, good," and reached forward to take Byje's arm.

They embraced each other and then Byje ushered them towards what was the largest building in the village. Sarmiento assumed the bamboo building was a temple, and vain positivism imagined an interior brimming with the golden artefacts of some new Temple of the Sun. But really, despite its much higher, double sloping roof and the paintings of sharks, snakes and crocodiles on the doorway, Byje was merely showing the strangers into his home.

Inside, a host of heads on prostrate or squatting bodies flicked up and the Spanish gazes crossed the path of a dozen others. Curious they were, and a sense of something deeply unnatural pervaded. Sarmiento caught a woman's eye, grey under a tangle of long, grey hair. Her bottom lip lunged and a snub nose accused, as if she had seen the ambitions of his culture in the emanations of his soul. She was Byje's mother. A quiet, meditative type, who had long ago learned the futility of talk and the spiritual benefits of enduring boredom.

Behind Sarmiento, Catoira shuddered. He was also with the old woman, but the inspissation of her all-seeing passivity was choking him.

Byje's rattling shells re-caught their attention as he moved toward the centre, to a group of women, his wives and daughters, with dark tattooed streaks running from their lower lips down their chin.

Catoira's first shuddering impression was that they had been drinking blood and he imagined his own heart ripped out. But these vampire-women scurried away as Byje approached, across mats, revealing an even more startling figure.

A man ... ancient and powdery. Pale green white, as if he had been mummified in chalk. Over this ghostly epidermis there were the same tattooed hieroglyphics that all Sanbans had, but his had faded into pea green. His fragile limbs were tremulous, sagging from a stooping back that had to yield under the weight of a proportionately too large head. That was completely bald, although his chin supported a mighty long and thick, white beard. So long that his knees were tickled by it. Yet, despite his ancientness, his eyes were bright and young, and when he opened his mouth he had teeth; albeit splashed red over a jaundiced yellow, but they were real and only slightly chipped.

"What withered wild creature is this?" murmured the ship's scribe.

And Byje, as if he had understood the question, thrust a pointing arm forward and pronounced: "Salacay," and then blinking to recall more of the Spanish words learned from his sojourn with Mendaña, he said: "Salacay father Byje," and: "Me son of Salacay."

"Let's assume he means that the old man's name is Salacay and he's

Salacay's son," said Catoira with a smile.

Sarmiento, however, remained perplexed and serious – *just like Señor Urco* – he told himself, that ancient old creature who had informed him in Xauxa. He looked around them. At the rear of the hall was a kind of altar.

Catoira followed his captain's eye and fixed his own. A marvellously carved green stone axe in front of a black god effigy: "Strange, isn't it?" he murmured: "We've crossed an ocean, coming from a place where the pagan natives also consecrated these stones."

Sarmiento nodded: "In Mexico the black obsidian was sacred to Tezcatlipoca; jade for the winged-serpent god Quetzalcoatl," and then gasped, his hand shooting down to his leg which had been clenched: the ancient Islander's ghost-white claw. The tissue-paper face was tilted up, wide eyed, and he suddenly opened his mouth and croaked.

Sarmiento's own face reddened and curled open into its own state of shock. He looked to Catoira who looked puzzled, registering his captain's anguish but not appreciating why. He looked back down again at the green-white face looking up at him. Green-tinged beads of sweat formed on his chalky brow and his eyes were full of panic as he reached up to grasp Sarmiento's dangling hand while he croaked the same message again. Sarmiento screwed his eyes up as he analysed it. The language coming from that withered man's hole was intelligible and in his mind he repeated the words like a poor translator – *He asked what I said* – and then, his head involuntarily nodding – *and I understood it* – followed by the tremendous conclusion – *He spoke in Incan. And he's heard of Quetzalcoatl* – and then replied in Incan himself, asking the trembling creature kneeling before him to tell him where he had heard that word before.

The croak continued: "Legend says that he was one of us," and he rubbed one of the rings on Sarmiento's finger. It was one of the new rings, forged by Bubi, the one with Jupiter and his symbol.

Sarmiento crouched, pulled down by the old man's gravity rather than his hand. As he did he turned his head to Catoira who was gaping. He signalled him to sit, then caught Byje's eye. The Tauriqui was equally confused.

The ancient man continued. Low and intimate: "Quetzalcoatl was a rebel. He broke our traditions and laws and was sentenced to death, but escaped," gasping: "He preached our secrets." His eyes were rolling as he searched for details in some ghostly distant memory: "He used our science to baffle people into believing him to be a god. He was worshipped in some distant land, taken for a god or a magician, and he spread our secret across the world, as if the magic belonged to him."

Sarmiento peeled the clawing hand from his own, then took it gently and stroked it. They had become immersed in their own bubble, isolating them from time and space in a way that opened the doors to all time and all space; to the eternal and the infinite: "How do you know this language you speak?"

The old man's eyes' glowed: "How do *you*?"

"It's the language of the Incas."

"Yes," then with squinting, accusing eyes: "But you are not Incas."

Sarmiento flicked his tongue across his top lip: "Neither are you."

The croak became a voice, but monotonous, with staccato breaks: "My people were ... we were once ... a powerful civilisation. But were enslaved by the Incas ... Yet, how is it that you ... speak their language?"

Sarmiento ignored the question and insisted with his own: "How did you come here?"

"I sailed ... with Tupac Inca Yupanqui."

Which inspired a scream retarding snort of phlegm: "Then this is Avachumbi?" and his hands lifted as if he wanted to pull the old man's jowls to him and kiss them.

Salacay, however, slowly shook his head. His long beard wafted: "No..." and his eyes flickered again as he rummaged for memories: "Avachumbi was called Ambrym by these people. It was a volcanic isle. The natives there were very dark skinned, and very wise." Then through a wheeze: "Magicians," followed by a wide-eyed flash of grief: "The volcano exploded ... the isle," and the air itself seemed suddenly sad: "Was destroyed." Then remembering that his own earlier question had not been answered: "But how do you speak the Inca language?"

Sarmiento snarled his answer: "We were their conquerors," which made Salacay's eyes flicker. Sarmiento remained firm: "But tell me, you escaped from Avachumbi ... from ..." then trying to recall what he had just been told.

"Ambrym," the old man nodded: "I foresaw a disaster ... left ... As far as

I know I'm the only one who did," and then with his face curled into something terribly triste: "I came here ... have been here for ... a thousand full moons."

Sarmiento shook his head: "No man can live so long."

The old man's head also shook, and he looked down at this thin arms: "Perhaps I am no-man," then he lifted his eyes again while he pointed to Sarmiento's ring: "Byje told me that your people were initiates ... members of our cult. Now I see that it is true," and he pulled his thick beard aside and pointed to a tattoo on his breast under his left arm. There was a symbol, identical to the one on Sarmiento's ring. The sign of Jupiter.

Sarmiento's mind raced. Fantastic ideas surged that he had to retard in order to remain coherent: "Where did you obtain these markings?"

"They have been sacred to us since the beginnings of time ... when we still lived in our ancestral home ... on the other side of the world," and then: "I brought the cult here. My own ancestors brought it with them, when they came ... from the other side ... of the world," and squeezing Sarmiento's arm: "That is where you are from ... isn't it?" but Sarmiento was too shocked to answer: "My ancestors left your world ... after the deluge."

"Deluge?"

"Destroyed, by the flood. That is our legend."

Which made Sarmiento's mind run madly through his own Atlantis theories.

Salacay gasped and persisted: "I am a Chachapoya."

Sarmiento had heard of them. A pre-Inca civilisation. Famous for their white skin and European features.

The old man leaned closer to the alchemist-explorer and whispered in his ear: "We were conquered by the Incas ... but ... the cult of Io remained safe from them. Our magic is very old."

Sarmiento could not resist. He squeezed the old man's age withered arm: "But how have you lived so long?"

The question made Salacay suspicious. He paused and wrestled with the question before deciding to answer: "These islands have a secret," and then as if reading Sarmiento's mind: "As you know," and he winked at Sarmiento: "There are many ways ... jade is one of them." Then, after swallowing hard: "Like gold. By treating it properly, then you can drink it

... and you will live as long as jade." Sarmiento nodded, but disappointedly. Rodolfo had drunk gold and it had been killing him. He had thought it preserved him, but it was obvious it only made him ill. Salacay saw this deception and nodded: "Yes, you are looking for something else ... something more certain." Sarmiento lowered his head, tilting his ear closer to the dry lips: "These people have treated me like a god."

Not the continuation that Sarmiento had been hoping for, but close to the old man's chest he spied something else through a wispy veil of beard.

Another tattoo, under the right arm. Greek. The sign of Omega.

Sarmiento licked his lips and gulped.

Another thing had grabbed his interest as well. A tiny blue pouch that seemed to be made of some animal's bladder was tied around the man's neck.

He tried to keep the excitement out of his voice. His thespian pitch came out boy-like: "Will you help us?"

Salacay laughed: "That depends on your purpose ... Why have you come?"

Sarmiento rubbed his ring: "I do not know yet."

"You are warriors. You conquered the Incas, and you come with slaves. How can you resist these people? You will destroy them ... and me ... I don't need to be a soothsayer to see that."

The alchemist sniffed and shook his head before lowering closer to the old man's ear again. A huge ear with enormous long lobes. He whispered: "The quest of my colleagues is not mine," and then with a snarl, unseen by the old man, but felt: "Do you really care about these savages?"

Salacay trembled as he began to realise the depth of this man's ambition: "They have loved me as a father."

"Adopted father," and Sarmiento grabbed his wrist, squeezing it hard: "You have no sons, do you?"

"No."

"Then tell me your secret. I'm an initiate."

The old man was strong enough to wrench his arm free. His voice lowered and croaked less: "Your impatience is a nasty worm, nestled in the core of your soul. First we must extract it. If you want to know what I know, tell your people to go away and stay here alone with me. Then I will show you. But you do not want to stay. I think you are incapable of making the ultimate sacrifice."

Which infuriated Sarmiento and he reached for the man's neck, grasping the chord of the little bladder he had tied there: "What's this then?" he said and wrenched it off. Salacay hissed and his face was wide with horror and hate. Sarmiento reached for his dagger. But before he could put his hand to it there was a tremendous roar and men came into the hut, trembling and waving their spears, shouting to Byje.

Outside, Pedro Ortega was carrying out Sarmiento's orders. His men were in the huts, hurling anything they discovered out. But they found next to nothing. This made Ortega and the men he was commanding rough, snatching the wrists of children, the passively resistant arms of women: "Where's the food?"

The men in the Sanban army around them were restless and nervous.

They reached out with an arm to tug at a stranger's shirt, but when they touched the steel they shuddered and backed away, waving and poking their spears, but no one dared attack. No one dared be the first to discover how much strength the stranger warriors really had. Not until their Tauriqui would command them, or a witch doctor or some spirit voice in their heads could advise them how they should act. Nevertheless, the tension and excitement mounted and soon the entire village were jumping about, taunting the invaders and screaming the words they had learned in Spanish: "Away! Away!"

Sarmiento ran outside shouting orders to Ortega, contradicting the previous ones: "Don't touch anyone! We're leaving."

Then to Catoira: "And we'll take the old man with us." To a ruffled, angry Ortega: "Go with the scribe and arrest the old man inside." But when they looked back in the hall, Salacay and everyone else had vanished: "As if it were a dream," murmured Sarmiento. Then, turning to the soldiers: "In line, lads." And as he uttered this he uncorked the bladder he had ripped from Salacay's chest. He smelt it before sipping a little. It was bitter and he grimaced. He had to talk to that old man again. He gestured to the slave Bubi to come to him: "I want you to look for tracks. We're going to hunt these people." The black face opened into a pearl white crescent and Bubi nodded. Then Sarmiento turned to the soldiers and waved an arm: "We march," and finally, as if responding to a question mumbled from some inner voice: "Toward the future..."

*　　*　　*

"Future..." the idea reverberated.

Estrella sensed my cringe and stopped reading.

"A headache," I mumbled. A pitiful apology. Then: "Was it known by you that Dr de Coca believed that God had not yet come into existence?"

She shook her head: "That God is in the process of becoming and will only exist at the end of time?" She seemed to sense the accusation inherent in what I was saying: "Was it known by you that Inma believed the same thing? Was it known that Don Enrique was another adherent?"

Until it peeved: "What are you getting at Val?"

"The Kingdom of God was announced by Christ as something that was to come, not as something already existing. But that is not believed by you, is it?"

"Perhaps. But first I would have to believe in the same God that Christ believed in."

"Was anything concrete ever discovered by you, about Omega?"

She frowned: "No. Francisco tried to follow it up, but always came to a dead end. It was always a gnawing worm for him. Then when he found out that Inma was alive I suppose it became unimportant."

"But what about you?"

She hung her head: "The whole thing was so ugly I didn't want to know anymore ... What do you know?"

I opened a drawer and pulled out a thick pile of letters. She lifted the top one.

"This is from Inma," she observed.

"Brought by Francisco Arizmendi ... Just as you ..."

Her fingers began to fondle the opening of the envelope. Her eyebrows lifted: "May I?"

"Yes, of course." I noticed her cringe when she saw the verse: "They are poems mainly ... sometimes prose," and I pointed towards an ink ant-trail running down a sheet: "Let that one be read."

She licked her lips and took a deep breath, before sighing a sad dirgeful recitation:

the ultimate and primary miracle,
...she read:
it's time to talk in dry whispers about
the ultimate and primary miracle
preceded by a slowly unfolding series of uncanny events
> *the first:*
the unearthing of glowing quartz-rocks
wrenched out of black-brown soil
from the thirsty gardens of so many scorched homes along the entire
sun-burnt coast
it was devastating, tragic:
> *the magnetic energy generated,*
drawing sensitive creatures,
> *whales, dolphins and other cetacea*
toward the parched land
> *a kamikaze attraction,*
that decimated...

a calculated operation
but no link was ever officially made
between
the glowing rocks
and
the suicide squadrons of marine mammals
to those few of us who were informed
the somnolent island continent became ever more significant
as more and more beautifully insidious details of the Omega Day
project surfaced
it was imperative to be there
to experience creative involvement
bear witness
ensure that we too would have a say in the creation of the Espiritu
Santo
the interior of the somnolent island continent,

such a dry but happy place
- we would have to walk there -
                i told you
and you
immediately pulled on your thickest soled boots...

When she finished she folded the letter away.

"It's a message," she said: "When Inma and I were at University, when Franco was still in power, we used to write such messages. But do you understand it?"

I nodded: "Now it is understood, yes ... Do you?"

"No," she said: "Not really, no."

So I passed her the next notebook.

(c) the march

Dry lips, cracked and poking between bristles, were parted by a curl of personal bitterness. The lips of soldiers are by definition cruel, at least in their potential as paid assassins, no matter what their ideal is. The soldiers there that day were greedy brave. Theirs were free spirits, but bitter. Sour spirits that the governor had preferred to be rid of, shipping them off with his marshmallow nephew to get them out of the colony.

Although the governor had had no intention of cleansing anything more than his own back yard, the endless space of sea and the tightness of jungle had silenced those masculine loud natures. In the damp and dark confines of the rain forest they peered through sharper eyes and treaded carefully. When free of the city's cacophony and the tavern's frivolity they became more astute. Unseen danger silenced them, arousing the attentive intelligence of the stalker.

Ortega, sensing the atmosphere of the hunt and fearing all its tragic potentials, warned them to remain calm. He himself would have felt much safer if he had had his dogs with him, but the prudent captain-general had ordered them to remain on the ship with the slave who had trained them, and who seemed to be the only one who could control them – *I would give more for one of those faithful mastiffs than any ten of these men* – he thought, then made an angry sweeping gesture with his arm to attract the attention of the puffing soldiers. If they heard movement they were to prepare the harquebus, but not to shoot until ordered.

The instruction, absurd in the jungle, where the harquebuses were rendered ineffective by denseness, was not contested. Soldiers keep their criticisms well-guarded. Theirs was a parrot personality, not given to the forming of opinions.

As for their pride; their mighty tradition fitted their bravura as tightly as the invulnerable armour of their selfishness. The Spanish *tercios* were the most feared fighting force in Europe, as were the ersatz armies of conquistadors afterwards in the Americas. Not even Alexander himself, or the Caesars, had been as effective conquerors as the Castilians. The Aztec and Inca empires had crumbled to a handful of Spaniards, so what was there to stop *them* from seizing the empire of Sanba and any others that had formed on the vast continent of the Terra Australis? Kill and be killed. A cruel world and a cruel god owed them something for their sacrifice.

A gentle exception to all this was Juan López. His educated spirit gave him a mountain goat's air, but his meat was mutton. His lips were softer and brighter, settling gently without a snarl. He did not hate life, but in those marching days the presence of so many hot souls had seared and blackened his own pearl smooth essence. His ambitions, that had made him always so light, were choked by the viscosity of this new claustrophobic reality. He trudged along, jelly-legged and bewildered under the weight of his harquebus and the leaden shackles of contempt from the other soldiers' stares. Disillusion dragged. The sodden trudge was nothing like the glorious march he had envisaged when he had received Mendaña's call to go ashore and join the troops.

When the captain-general had met him on the beach with the embrace of a long lost friend, announcing that he himself had recommended Juan's participation in the expedition, Mendaña had squeezed his shoulder and called him Perceval again: "Go with my good blessings fair Perceval, and God's love," and then: "And hurry back ... I will miss your music," which despite the enormous smile sounded insincere, especially as he had spent the last few months quite happily with Gaspar.

A soldier behind, a rum pickled sergeant called Simón Arragocés, prodded him with the butt of his gun, complaining about his clumsy dawdle: "Move Midnight, you slug!"

Which peeved the gentle Juan: "Why do you call me Midnight, good señor?"

The sergeant laughed. A jocund, rotten teeth smile with a fly attacking shake of his hirsute and helmeted head, but he did not answer the question. However, when Juan stumbled, gasping in mud, and needed an arm to lift him, there was a continuation: "*Midnight* I call you, because there be no daylight between yer ears," and laughed moronically: "You could lie and rest, sirrah. But we won't wait for ye, Midnight," a whisper that was rasping through a fixed snarl.

For Arragocés the violence of the infantry was a sweet catharsis for all his own suffering under the master's stick of his peasant class childhood. Now he would make this *posh-boy* "Midnight" find out what life was about. And when the youngster was on his feet he shoved him with his mud caked boot just to see how he staggered.

At such times Juan wanted to cry.

The situation seemed impossible, and yet he was the only one who seemed to suffer – *What if my body were simply to refuse to go any further? What if I were unable to will motion anymore? Would I be left to the mercy of cannibals?* –

He had never imagined he would tire so quickly, but the sultry, tropical heat and Toledo-steel that he carried were tremendous burdens and he had to clear his mind of everything in order to palliate the pain of the march. Not only the physical demand and the insufferable comrades, but the harsh and hostile land which seemed nothing like a Paradise on Earth. Neither had the contact with the Islanders impressed him. He had imagined the people of a magic place to be more extreme. He wanted demons, dragons and giants in his romance world.

These thoughts were thumped from him by another slapping stick. This time it was Pedro Ortega: "Alert, lad! I saw your eyes closing. Get drowsy and you're a dead man. Fight it, lad. We'll need yer wide awake shortly anon, and you'll need yerself," and he waved his hand, scanning the slopes around them: "Have you not seen 'em? The hills are crawling, pray."

Which brought Juan to a standstill. The forest surrounding them was alive with creeping natives, silent and maintaining distance, some of them positioning themselves in the branches of trees above them.

As for the Islanders' intentions, Catoira was the first to divine them. To their right was a deep gully, green with ferns drooping down to a muddy stream, full from the previous day's storm. The Islanders, Catoira realised, were racing ahead to cut them off. Gasping, he unsheathed his sword and screamed: "Onto your toes lads! They're trying to fence us in! We'll be trapped, if we don't sprint for it, pray!" and then with his sword high like a standard, and thinking of Caesar: "*Avaunt!*" Which inspired a rattling, gasping charge, Pedro Ortega hobbling last, peeved by the ship's scribe's audacity.

Sarmiento was almost oblivious to this. His mind had been spinning with the conversation with Salacay. He fingered the rubbery texture of the bladder between his fingers, uncorked it and sniffed it – *Jade-juice* – he thought – *His ambrosia, no matter how foul it tastes* – After taking a swig, he immediately felt the heat of it singe his gullet and bite his stomach. A tingling sensation floated back up his spine and through his limbs, numbing his brain for a while and making his immediate interrogative – *Am I poisoned?* – irrelevant.

The stomping charge had thrust Sarmiento into a groggy sense of the time-space around him. Like a cockroach he shut down his five senses and concentrated all energy on the instinct to run. He had no idea why, until he saw the Islanders dropping like dripping candle wax onto the path ahead, grouping into a teeth clenching, chanting pack, that stomped their feet and waved their hands like hawks' wings hovering in breezy air. As they did the momentum of the charge was reduced to a dribble.

Ortega hobbled up to Sarmiento: "Well, Captain? Will we blast 'em?"

Sarmiento blinked. The drug in his blood made his tongue seem thick and swollen, his stomach churned. He saw a mighty sea swell and reached for a rope. The jungle whirled around him. Again. He felt a panic grip his benumbed body. He pushed Ortega aside, then shoved the others forward, straight toward the chanting line of warriors. In no-man's land he stopped and blinked. Colours intensified, the jungle glowed and the racket of the warriors lowered. He stared into them, searching for the white beard of Salacay, or Byje. But neither were there. This was just a hunting party from another village.

"The strangers are strange," murmured one of the islanders.

"Tauriqui Byje says they're his friends," whispered another.

"He says we shouldn't kill them. He says they're good men."

"They don't look like good men."

"They are strange."

"We could push them into the river," and they laughed.

Sarmiento screamed. This silenced men and jungle. The alchemist stiffened his body and heaved in air. Then, from his full chest, without thinking why, he expulsed a mighty: "Narria!" which was the word for *war* in Sanban tongue.

It evoked shock, to hear a familiar language hurled back so aggressively at them. Sarmiento's eyes were wild, his lips and arms trembling. He shouted again, even louder this time: "Narria!!!" He did not think, used animal instincts to judge, and with the stench of fear blowing at him from the line in front, he advanced to grasp one warrior's limp spear, lifting the tip to his own throat. With the spike pricking his Adam's apple he yelled again: "Narria!" Expressed with such violence that the Islander shivered like a child emerging from a snowy mountain stream. The horrible potential made his stomach churn. He let go of his spear and backed away, a gasp that evolved into language, mumbled, but frantic, on gut-tight air: "This red-man is not a man ... a d-demon ... The red in his hair ... it's the red blood of his victims ... I have heard the spirits of his v-victims ... They have talked to me ... Told me that we are doomed ..." Which rippled through the group.

Sarmiento picked up the spear that had been dropped and smashed it over his knee. Then holding up the two broken pieces he yelled again: "Narria!"

Which was enough. The line of men parted before the red demon. And once the density had been broken the individual particles became more liquid than solid and dribbled back into the forest.

Catoira clapped his hands and ran to his captain-friend, who had become liquid legged. When the scribe arrived he collapsed onto him, gasping to get his breath back and calm his pounding heart. Catoira thrust an arm around his back and lifted: "Hercules could not have done better," he laughed.

Then Ortega, as if nothing had happened: "The men are thirsty."

Sarmiento's eyes flickered. The whites of them seemed bleached. A rush of water blew through his brain like clean air into his lungs: "This river is running full. There must be streams that feed it. We'll soon have water."

And they did. In more ways than one. Clouds slipped over. The sky opened. And they were drenched.

The squelching pack bearer groaned. His legs wobbled and gave way. The great, water logged weight on his back pulled him down and he collapsed into bracken.

Their arrival at the shallow bend in the river did nothing to inspire him, in fact it depressed. They had crossed it already so many times, marching most of the day, six hours at least, trudging through constant rain and mud. And they had been there before. Five hours ago they had stopped there, built a fire, barbecued smoked sausages on it. A grey-black patch of earth and some tell-tale discarded skins betrayed the truth. They had been walking in one huge circle or a series of smaller concentric ones. No progress at all.

Another slave yelled out his pent up frustration, and then to cloak his audacity and avoid corporal punishment from an officer, he turned his wail into a rasping, guttural song. When the sergeant looked at him he shrugged his shoulders: "From the village, señor. In my master's house. An Andalusian lament. Bemoaning the tragic fate of our Lord."

But the spirit of the team had been destroyed. When they were told to break ranks they slumped exhausted onto any patch of flat ground they saw, too tired to worry about dryness, too wet for wetness to matter. Some had thought about building a fire, but the complication of finding dry kindling quickly killed the idea and they slumped too.

Meanwhile Catoira, with the faith of his familiarity, approached Sarmiento to complain: "It's the same river, Captain."

Sarmiento spat into it: "How Catoira, no river is ever the same. Forever changing. Heraclitus, remember?"

Of course such a metaphysical evasion convinced no one, and if it had been a joke, no one laughed.

Sarmiento waved Catoira away to rest with the others, then he crouched down and dipped a hand into the stream.

Everything was now so clear to him. He had taken too much of the drug, but now that the initially distressing effects had waned he felt perfect. Younger, more vital. Whatever was in the potion it was a miracle. The only side-effect was an insatiable thirst.

He drank the handful of water, then dipped his head for more, but as the disturbed surface settled he found himself staring down at something on the bottom. Something gleaming. He rolled up his sleeve and scooped silt up from the bed. Sifting it through his fingers he was left with half a dozen tiny pebbles. He searched, but the gleaming substance had vanished.

Thoughtfully and silently he crouched at the bank bending over the stream to stare hard through the diaphanous but light distorting element, further skewed by the crashing drops of rain. He was alone. The rest of the expedition deliberately turned their backs on their commander lest he should order the march to resume. So they did not see him suddenly spring up, his sword out.

He had glimpsed a reflected image. A blur, becoming a grinning, painted face. A man, covered in leaves, with a garland of aromatic herbs around his head like a Bacchus. He smiled and offered this to Sarmiento which was an obvious gesture of rustling good will.

The other soldiers were dozing while a dozen Islanders staggered into the stream and began to cross. All were armed, some with bows and arrows, others clenching long spears that they leaned on as they stepped, tentatively, over the rocks. It wasn't until a lizard ran over a drowsy soldier's knee, making him yell, imagining it to have been a snake, that they were all roused and one of them glimpsed the warriors. The harquebusiers immediately had their muzzles trained on the assumed enemy while the slaves fumbled with tinder boxes.

Ortega had his arm raised and poised to give the order. But groaned. Sarmiento was blocking the line of fire. In any case the Islanders hardly flinched. They were looking outward and upward into the jungle around them, their arrows aimed into the drooping, dripping tree tops.

The man at the river leaned forward and lowered the leafy garland onto Sarmiento's head. Then he patted the alchemist's shoulder with a tensely splayed hand before lifting him up onto the bank where he laughed and hugged the Spaniard: "Sarmiento," he said pointing to himself: "Me, Sarmiento."

Which was befuddling at first, but then the teeth in the face became familiar and the alchemist soon remembered where he had seen that shining calcium before. He was one of Byje's men, who had changed names with him on that first day on the boat. His real name had been Seseboco, and he was actually Byje's brother.

Then the face became serious stern and whispering. He explained, half in his own language, half in Spanish, that Sarmiento's men should look into the jungle. He started pointing to the trees around them and then began miming the action of firing arrows. The forest was infested with an enemy. Then a name was applied to the evil – *Baso*. They were in Baso's territory and his men were scouting that area with a formidable force. He pushed his wrists together and held up his arms before pointing down a track: "Byje." He said. "He go Tiarabaso."

And then through signs indicated that his Tauriqui had been trapped while out hunting and had been taken as a prisoner to Tiarabaso.

"And Salacay?" stammered Sarmiento.

Seseboco pulled a sad face, bent his head and nodded.

Sarmiento persisted: "If you take us there, perhaps we could be of help."

And Seseboco nodded again, as if he had understood the complicated conditional sentence.

Sarmiento beckoned to Catoira, who came, tilting his head to lift his ear: "No time to rest. We're going to Tiarabaso."

That would not be well received by the exhausted men. Tiarabaso was another four hours of tough hiking away.

Ortega puffed and complained: "Did we not want to climb a mountain?"

Sarmiento nodded. He had no sympathy for the moaning men. He felt marvellous and marched with a smile.

It was some consolation to Juan López that all the men were miserable now. But the jungle was still particularly dark in his mind. Dripping, grey-blue grim and reeking with a putrefaction. His boots were painful heavy with snowballing mud, his head heavy with snowballing self-pity. His gaze, always down, at the ochre bricks on his feet, to the red-brown ooze in which they advanced, at the gaping foot prints left by those ahead in which he would deposit his own bricks. So heavy. His soul, withdrawn into the faculty of pain, oblivious to any power, made him seem to sink deeper than all the others. He did not even notice the gap through which they climbed. So absorbed. The light had to be felt to be realised. Only when the sun pricked his skin, slapping his neck, did he look up to see the blue gap betwixt retreating clouds. Squinting blind he became – *The lamp of the world* – he thought, and felt a fresher air clear lungs and mind – *I am lifted with your light* –

Catoira at the front had also gasped that air with a wonder expressing breath, while Sarmiento, who had cut a hiking staff for himself, leaned. His helmeted soldier's profile made him look like a worldly wise Ulysses. The metaphysics that spurted seemed integral: "Everything that's created is part of a natural order. If this is as perfect as it feels, then it must resemble God's own garden."

Catoira knelt and the sceptic even crossed himself: "Then we are in the vicinity of the beginning."

The slaves, who were all trying to prove themselves devout Christians, and several of the other soldiers, followed Catoira onto their knees, Juan López was no exception. Their guide, Seseboco, bowed slightly and nodded his head: "Tiarabaso," he said, and grinned.

The verdure of the valley was splendid. An intense and shining apple green carpet, brightened by its contrast with the steep, dark, mist shrouded slopes of jungle. The gleaming river that ran through it, forking around a grassy hillock bearing a tidy, brown village, had already quenched most of the men's thirsts. And the presence of organised gardens and orchards, seemed to promise food a plenty.

"Let us rest our weary legs in these green pastures," murmured Juan as if reciting scripture. He turned to Simón Arragocés with such a beatific smile that it made his cruel sergeant exaggerate his own snarl to compensate. Experience had told the soldier that such general contentment could bode no good. The hilltop position of the village, protected by the river, was a strategically difficult and dangerous one. If there was a God, he was a cruel old bastard, and the hopeful were His favourite victims.

When they were down in the valley, an eerie silence and stillness transformed Paradise into Purgatory.

Smoke did indicate life though, rising in an almost clinging way between the houses and yam stores. The settlement was circular, fringed by betel and coconut palms. Seseboco put a finger to his lips to hush the Spaniards, and crouched, as if to hide. Which was absurd, for they were standing in the midst of an open field and had been perfectly visible from the other side of the river since they began their descent into the valley. But Seseboco looked so serious and concerned that the Spaniards followed his lead unquestioningly, and gazed along the line pointed out by his trembling finger.

In the circular midst of the village, veiled blue by the smoke of a sadly simmering log, some equally sad and pale figures could be discerned. They were sitting in front of grey stakes that they seemed to be tied to.

A long white beard intimated Salacay. This was confirmed by Seseboco who insisted that the man next to him were Byje and his captain Gauga, whilst the other figures present were their women.

Then he sucked his teeth and licked his lips, making gestures that indicated that they were all to be eaten.

Ortega hobbled up to Sarmiento. They were advancing across a narrow strip of turf. This was spongy underfoot due to proximity to the fast flowing river: "It's the most obvious and pathetic trap I've yet to have seen."

To which Sarmiento nodded, and then, through a grin: "Tell the men to have their harquebuses ready. And tell them they're going to wet their feet, or better still, we're going to wash the mud off our boots."

Ortega's eyes rolled: "We're going to walk into it?!"

Sarmiento licked his lips: "Yes, Don Pedro. Are you afraid, señor?"

The old campaigner snorted, then turned sharply and shouted the order.

Seseboco's face shivered, holding back a smile.

The sudden manifestation of warriors behind them when they had crossed over the river, came as no real surprise. Neither did that of the men who sprouted in front of them like giant mushrooms, in a shell rattling murmur from the earth around Byje and Salacay. Obvious, it was, that Byje had joined forces with Baso to surround the invaders and ensure a massacre of the Spanish squadron.

Ortega grabbed Seseboco, yanked his hair and thrust a dagger to his throat: "Shall I cut his gullet out now, Cap'ain?"

Sarmiento shuddered as the rest of Seseboco's men fled, then shook his head: "Give him to a slave to tie up. There'll be no killing just yet."

Meanwhile Byje had jumped up from the stake he was supposed to be prisoner to, lifted his arms, twisting his wrists to show the Spaniards that his bonds were air. He lifted a wobbling spear and laughed, filling the valley, before turning in the direction of the spindly ghost that was Salacay: "Now we'll show these idiots the meaning of respect. Tomorrow the Tauriqui Mendaña will have their heads returned to him in a nice big sack. Afterwards he can go back to his king and tell them that there is a greater king on earth ... and his name is Byje Ban Arra."

The ancient man was ripping up the leaves of herbs taken from a pouch to sprinkle into the simmering hollow of the burning log in front of him. He blinked and croaked: "But let it be known," monotonous: "That the one called Sarmiento," punctuated by wheezes and his whispering cape: "Is to be taken alive."

The men on the river bank behind them were Baso's men, darker skinned Melanesians. About a hundred. They pranced and danced like giant birds of paradise. Huge headdresses of wafting plumes. Their faces were painted red and yellow, with black beards whitened with some chalky mud. Their palm-oil smeared black skin was shiny smooth, as were the long black spears and ebony clubs they wielded.

Sarmiento ordered a slave to get the drum ready. Then, turning to Simón Arragocés: "What do you think? Do we have a chance?"

"There are a 'undred behind us, Cap'ain, but they'll be easier than the fifty on the hill."

But then, as if cursed by the boast, there was a rattle of bone on shell as another squadron of Baso's men came flying out of the forest to join the others on the bank.

Ortega snorted: "They're lookin' for a good brawl, verily enough."

Sarmiento's voice was sceptical: "I'm not so sure. Look there," Ortega followed the line indicated by Sarmiento's finger: "A savage comes!"

And a tall and robust man, wild-eyed and tense, advanced with a splash into the river. His grass skirt sagged and the huge club he had dangling from one shoulder slapped against his back. Behind him came a grey-smeared boy, completely naked, without even a pubic leaf, and cradling a pandanus basket in his arms. This was full of yams.

Sarmiento glanced back up the hill to where Byje was. The chief was obviously nervous.

"What's Baso up to?" the Tauriqui spat red: "He sends his son with an offering."

Gauga slapped his thigh like a nervous child and groaned: "A peace offering. He's going to deal."

"Double-crossed."

"Unbelievable," sighed Gauga: "We're sitting in his own village and he has the audacity to betray us," and he reached to pull an arrow out from a sling. But Salacay, blue behind the smoke, had the thin fingers on his thin hand up: "Wait first," and wafted the smoke with a banana leaf up to his nose: "Let Baso experience their rudeness," and after inhaling the herbal aroma: "Then we'll see if he still wants them as friends."

Sarmiento lifted his sword and walked along the front line of his men: "Be ready lads. But hold your fire. Nothing rash remember. Let's try and come out of this war without a fight, eh?"

Which seemed to please even the most bellicose ones.

Baso's son approached with his skirt dripping and club raised as a cautious gesture. Sarmiento decided to take similar precautions, fastening his shield and unsheathing his sword.   Face to face, they paused, scowling at each other, until the Islander made a grunting noise, indicating the grey-smeared lad to come forward and lay the yams down on the grass in front of Sarmiento. The captain-alchemist returned the gesture, calling to a slave to bring a copper necklace wrapped in cloth.

With the gifts in front of them the two men lay their weapons down in a mirroring action like a pair of mime actors, then picked up the gifts. The Islander excitedly lifted it like a great trophy in the direction of Byje, and spat.

Byje shuddered: "The pig!"

Salacay dipped a bunch of whispering grass in a tube of water. It gurgled. He let his tongue snake out. The red betel dye had turned it purple: "Bring the leader man here."

"What?!"

"Beckon to him," and he yanked the soaked grass out of the tube: "Invite him here." The drooping bundle dripped, then he slapped the grass against the air and mumbled some kind of spell: "... *wet the palm-trees, wet the tall and short grass* ..." before slapping the air again, this time over the embers in the burning log so that it hissed: "We cannot fight now ... not against two armies ... We must win back his friendship."

Sarmiento twirled a yam between his hands and grinned at Baso's emissary who was waving his spear in the air to excite his men. Then he signalled to Pedro Ortega to come forward: "What do you think?"

Ortega sniffed, phlegm moved. He stroked the iron breastplate over his belly: "The black man seems sincere enough, troth."

But now it was Sarmiento's turn to sniff. He looked up at the sky because it had suddenly darkened. Deep purple clouds.

"What does he expect us to do? Massacre Byje? What would our good General say, if we went back with the head of his best Indian friend?"

Ortega's jaw cracked: "It'd not be a good idea, Captain."

"No, Don Pedro, it wouldn't," and he scratched his chin. But then, after a sudden eye opening flash of inspiration he turned to the slave who was guarding Seseboco: "Unleash the hostage," and then to the rest of them: "Right lads. To arms. We move," raising his sword tip in the direction of the town.

Ortega coughed, as if to conceal a guffaw of disbelief: "There?"

"Yes, señor. The only way to the mountain is through the village," and then: "If the mountain won't come to us, we have to go through the town."

Ortega wheezed and signalled to the men to gather themselves into a delta formation: the shield bearers on the flanks, the harquebusiers inside with the officers.

Juan López felt his heart crashing under his breastplate: "Do you understand what's going on, Sergeant?" and shuddered because there was a sudden clap of thunder.

Arragocés, who was probably expecting the thunder after the lightning, did not blink, just laughed. At last the boy had asked a question that he liked: "It's as if everyone were enemies and allies of everyone else at the same time," and then grinning: "A fairly normal situation really. You fight a war against the Pope one day and he's sittin' in yer general's chair the next tellin' yer to bring down the wall of the castle of some king that ye thought was payin' yer goddamn wages," the last part of which had to be shouted, for the sky suddenly opened up and let a deluge drop.

Breathtaking warm wall of rain. Men had to gasp to get air through it; had to bellow to be heard over the whoosh and roar of it. Some of the harquebusiers panicked: "It'll be hard to light a taper in this, Cap'ain."

Sarmiento was adamant: "Keep moving, fie. And keep the harquebuses up and pointing. The most important thing is that they look like they can be used. *That* is our deterrent."

As they edged up the slope, however, Baso's army crossed the river below them.

"Now we *are* vulnerable," gurgled Ortega to Sarmiento, low enough for it to be private: "If they are to push from both sides at once, we'll be like grapes in the wine press."

Sarmiento was busy trying to reply to signals from Byje that he wanted to make peace. Then: "All right, hold the men here ... but tell them to be ready to charge when I give the signal." He unfastened his belt and gave his sword and dagger to Catoira, before pushing his way through the wall of shields. Out of the delta phalanx, he paused. But to fill his lungs rather than think. He had already decided what had to be done and he marched unhesitatingly up the grassy slope.

Byje's lips, adorned now with hanging droplets of gleaming rainwater, widened into a spectacular grin: "He comes," followed by an abrupt flick of the head and a shrieking: "Seseboco!"

The hostage, now free, was sprinting up the slope. The Sanbans began whooping and cheering and waving their spears as their compatriot collapsed in their arms. Byje embraced him and wept. Joyful tears of reconciliation from red faces which suddenly turned back, to Salacay.

His croak was unmistakable: "He's stopped," he said pointing an ivory-white and bony finger at Sarmiento, who had paused half-way between his men and the village.

The alchemist's arms were open, one cupped hand making a wafting gesture to Byje to join him in no-man's land.

Salacay threw the water logged bunch of grass to the ground, as if angry with it, then grasped a long thin staff and slowly rose in a rib thrusting, wobbling straightness: "He wants you to go to him," and lifting his spider-leg arm: "Or one of us..." then taking a cautious, cartilaginous step forward: "I'll go," raising his arm again to silence any protest: "We speak the same language."

Byje gasped and turned to his brother, Seseboco, who nodded back: "He'll be treated well. They're honourable men. They did me no harm."

Salacay bobbed stiffly down the hill like a stringed marionette, constantly shrinking into the realm of the lonely stranger. Sarmiento received him with a forced smile and stiff, open arms. They embraced, but Sarmiento's arm was taught around the islander's neck, locking it in a choking clamp. Then Sarmiento yelled and the soldiers charged forward, enveloping Sarmiento and Salacay before regrouping the phalanx into arrow head formation.

Byje's shocked mind had hardly time to stir itself. The men around Byje began to scream. Seseboco buried his face in his hands and then started beating his breast. Byje felt his legs liquefying beneath him.

Adding to the shock of Salacay's capture, two black streams, like busy ants, were creeping up the flanks of the slope, emerging behind the Sanbans and closing in on the village from the sides. Baso was shaking his spear. The Sanbans were surrounded. Byje also knew that there were more of Baso's men hiding in the huts of the village with bows and arrows awaiting an ambush on the strangers. Now it was the Sanbans who were to be caught in their own trap. He looked up at the sky for inspiration – *Had Salacay not invoked the rain for our advantage?* –

The Sanbans screamed for Salacay's fate. Many of them jumped in a wide, frog legged gesture expressing a frustrated reluctance to leave the field, while others shook their spears in panting fear of whatever could happen next.

The Spaniards cried victory, but Sarmiento raised a halting arm. The Sanbans were still in front of them and would have to be directly challenged if they were to get to the mountain. To avoid a bloodbath, they would still have to confront Byje and his men. So he put his dagger against Salacay's throat and advanced with Byje's father straight to the Sanban line.

Byje shouted to his men to hold their ground. Then he went forward to stand before Sarmiento and his adopted father. They stood in silence and stared, flickering eyes caught in a reciprocal rigid gaze, and they began nodding to each other as if they were communicating telepathically. Salacay's eyes flickered and Byje nodded.

Behind them Baso's men were getting restless. In front the harquebusiers' fingers were very itchy.

Then Byje turned to Gauga, and gave him some instruction. Gauga too started nodding, then darted away.

Sarmiento prepared himself to bear the brunt of a sudden attack.

However, when Byje finally lifted his arm again, it was to raise his mace, but upside down ... the signal for a general retreat. His people gasped, a slight pause, followed by a sad sigh of grass skirts ... and the Sanban's ranks burst open like beads poured from a sack, dissolving into the jungle.

Baso's men looked on in impotent disbelief. They had come for a fight, had come to join one or other army in smashing the third party. This outcome, however, was absurd and unmanly. The emissary who had exchanged gifts with Sarmiento began to scream and curse and spit at the Spaniards. Sarmiento squeezed Salacay's throat a little tighter and ordered him to translate.

The old hostage smiled: "He says you must leave the Island now. He says you are great cowards. If you don't leave, he says his people will eat you. He says there are more of his people in this land than the beach has sand."

Sarmiento grinned: "He's obviously never counted sand," and then: "Can you count old man?" Which made Salacay crunch his teeth.

Sarmiento jerked his thin arm and hissed: "Where is the mountain path?" And the thin arm slowly rose and stiffened, a thick yellow nail pointing into a thicket. Sarmiento smiled: "Take us there. To the mountain top. We need to see what this place really is."

Salacay grinned: "Happily, I will take you there," he said: "But that does not mean you'll ever find your way back again."

While Salacay lead the Spaniards on a circuitous route around the mountain, Gauga clambered up a steep short cut. Even when the heavens opened once more and made the track mud again he did not pause. His toes dug, like spikes. Water gushed off the wide leaves of tropical trees, but such showers were refreshing.

Since he had been a small boy, Gauga had run up that track and he knew all of its idiosyncrasies. He reached the plateau at the top before nightfall and raced into the village.

A group of boys chasing a chicken saw him first, and assumed he was a demon fallen from the sky. They screamed. Three men, who were sitting on a veranda carving crocodile images, stirred from their work and raced for their spears. Gauga stopped in the street and through his desperate panting shouted, in the Melanesian dialect, for an audience with Ubi, their chief.

More men came and crowded around him, each of them demanding an explanation for the intrusion and audacious request, until one of them recognised the warrior from Sanba. He was recognised as an ally. The two provinces had carried out an exchange ceremony that year and he himself had swapped armlets with the intruder. He embraced him, and they ushered him to Ubi's hut.

There they found their chief sitting on his porch with an elaborate piece of wood carving in his lap. It was a *tabuyo* the oval prow board for a new canoe. Engrossed in the task of chiselling, knocking a shark's tooth into the grain with a wooden hammer, he did not deign to acknowledge the presence of the crowd, and he merely shrugged his shoulder when one of the elders announced the arrival of Gauga.

The Sanban stepped forward nervously. Ubi, although their ally, had the fame for being a capricious man, and it was obvious that he had caught him at a bad moment. There was a slight tremor in his voice: "I've come from Sanba," he began: "From the great Tauriqui Byje Ban Arra, ally of the people of Tiaraubi, to announce the news of a battle in Tiarabaso, between ourselves, allied with the people of Baso, and the strangers who have come over the sea and are marching through the land in conquest of its people. I come to warn the great lord Ubi and his people that Baso has allied his nation with these strangers; that they are coming here, and will most certainly arrive after dawn tomorrow."

Ubi flicked his head as if there was a fly. A droplet of sweat dripped off his long nose: "What weapons do these strangers possess?"

Gauga's eyes flickered with the question. His mind was struggling for an answer – *Weapons?* – He realised he did not know. Realised that they had not fought. And then reached a monstrous conclusion: "They use no weapons, but their magic is powerful. Their men turn themselves into a giant turtle, sometimes a crab. They move across land like a crab. They do not have weapons, they do not kill, but they cloud our minds with magic and make our bravest men tremble. That is their power."

Ubi rose. A tall man with powerful limbs: "Then we must make magic too. The witch-doctors will be ready. Our warriors will be ready. We're going to hunt and kill a turtle!"

XVI. The Summit

I pushed myself up from the squeaking sad bed, into my iron side chair, and propelled myself: "Is it recalled that you thought I'd been seen by you before, in a dream?"

Her reply was murmured back at me through a sagging wall of hair: "Yes," delivered slowly enough to sound mysterious: "It was a feeling that always haunted me."

"And is it known by you that Inma had been affected by a similar impression."

Which jerked the head, and the long fringe wafted.

I leafed through Inma's letter and passed on another poem:

the first time we met it was a dream
   you, naked under sun, on the boulders of a rocky coast,
the green-brown sea splattered your battered head,
   lightless,
      lips so red
   i held my breath so that i lifted,
a human hydrogen balloon,
   and hovered over you
my skin much whiter than yours,
   floating in your mind's eye,
desire made you want to turn,
spread your arms,
part your crossed legs
   so still and dead,
you could have been dead,

and i was a ghost,
　　dead,
but warm under the sun on the other side,
　　looking away from the sea,
the brown sands stretched,
　　brown desert rising to dry mounts,
grey street running through,
　　thick stone slabs sunken in dust
leading to the ruined palace
　　rubble:
indiscriminate lumps, igneous rubbish
　　- a warning of past disasters -
the fallen statue limbless, in the middle of the way
　　- but from where had she toppled? -
we had to ask
　　no good answer -
any good answers?
　　the ruined palace,
venetian villa, hard,
　　you shivered, and shadows encroached as the sun set
until i felt sorry for you
　　naked, in essence,
but becoming used to the cold, even enjoying it
　　i smiled,
sensed you wanted to wake up
though you were not asleep...

Soft sound whooshed from Estrella's lips. Distant, as if drifting in the rushing liquid of her own thoughts.

I, too, was full of my own reality. The poem dragged up a detritus from the oily bottom of my most distant soul: "She was transported there, before, when I was in my coma. Yoga and astral travel were practised by her, even before. In a sense, when you met me I was already possessed."

The last word startled Estrella, tugging her into my own reality: "Possessed?"

Realising that I had her, I found myself stammering into the impossibility of keeping her: "It's explanation is difficult ... very hard ... to be r-really understood."

*　*　*

Pedro Ortega, took off his helmet and peered over the top of the jagged rock. Wisps of hair blew up from his bald head and his bulging frog eyes were squeezed and squinting into the wind. He gritted his teeth, then suddenly relaxed, and the bullfrog orbs were opened with a bullfrog grin.

He turned and turned again, each time more slowly. On each side was the same stretch of lead coloured ocean. There could be no doubt. It was an island: and there, in the distance, poking from the waves, the jutting summits of more islands. But not a trace of anything more substantial.

– *Yet I saw this first ... before Sarmiento* – he told himself and ruminated on the antipathy he had for the navigator.

Mendaña should never have put the *turkey-cock alchemist* in charge in the first place: he himself was a much more experienced campaigner; he was a self-made man who had marched and fought with conquistadors; he had massacred pagans and made them Christians; he had received lands in Panama and servants to turn forested hills into fertile money making plantations; he had policed the land and learned the rituals and rules of corruption.

Protecting the rich he had become richer himself. But gold never mitigated his ambition. He knew that the key to greatness was risk. So when he had heard that the Governor of Peru was seeking investors in an expedition in search of the Great South Land.

But reminiscence of his own importance was stifled by a sharp tug on his shirt sleeve. It was Sarmiento, panting and pointing downward.

Running along the flat of a treeless spur was a long line of well-armed warriors.

Sarmiento spat: "A nice welcome, sirrah."

"They seem to like to dress for the occasion."

Sarmiento's index finger bobbed up and down in the air. His lips were moving, silently counting each particle of the human stream: "At least five hundred it would seem. That means we're outnumbered nearly twenty to one." He sighed: "What says you, good Don Pedro? What are our chances?"

The old campaigner put on his helmet, and straightened it, as if the friction of rusty steel helped get his mind working: "We could break through, if, as before, they come at us without shields," and ran his tongue through a gap in his teeth, tasting meat: "But we would 'ave to use the 'harquebuses, and this treeless plateau makes a battle very comfortable for us ... if they resist, there'll be much blood spilled. Their blood." Then his thick voice softened, becoming almost dreamy: "On the other hand, if we stay where we are, on this higher ground, we can fend off any charges without need of a massacre. But we've only enough provisions for another three days. So if our captain-general forgets to send reinforcements, which is more than likely," shrugging his shoulders: "I can see no other option but the spilling of Indian blood."

Sarmiento scurried down the steep slope grimacing when he reached the men. His last step off the slope had been an awkward one. His right foot had been placed too obliquely and body weight had jerked the tendons in his ankle. The spasm of pain made him limp to his men, but he pushed his way through to where Salacay was being held. The old native sat cross legged and grinning, even though he had a machete held over his head. Sarmiento slapped him: "You planned this, didn't you? This winding path you brought us on, slowing us down, whilst the trap was set for us."

Salacay turned his slapped and smarting face away from the accusation: "You asked me to bring you to the mountain," and he rubbed his cheek: "I have," then turned back. His eyes, squinting animosity: "You said you wanted to see if this was an island," and licked his red teeth, his pace increasing in urgency: "Now you have seen for yourselves. Although there was no need. I told you last night all that you needed to know. Why did you not believe me?" and his throat tightened so that the voice rasped: "Why did you have to come here?"

An image of the scene beside the campfire returned to Sarmiento's mind. They had been huddled there, wrapped in a thick fog. Old Salacay's voice had been much softer then, revealing so much, as if he had been desperate to impart knowledge. He had begun with geography, taking a straight stick for a pen, and he had drawn a representation in the ash of the cigar shaped island they were all on: "This island is called Mulu-Mulu. A big island, I don't know its extremes myself, but an island it is. Many have circumnavigated it," and then: "There is no need for you to climb now," and smiled.

But Sarmiento had shaken his head: "We cannot leave this place until we have confirmed it ourselves," as if he were asserting his culture's nature.

Salacay had deliberately made a wry smile and applied his stick to the ash again, sketching similar shapes around the first representation: "There are many other islands here that we trade with," and he had jabbed the heart of one of the drawings: "This one is called Malaita." Then he waved an open hand across all of the islands, as if blessing them: "We have some friends and some enemies on each one. Many of them are cannibals. To the south-west is a very large land, not an island at all. Protected by an enormous reef. I have only heard about it in legends. They say that Paradise is there."

But then, on the mountain top, Sarmiento crouched down to his cross-legged prisoner's level, laying his arm around his shoulders and, whispering: "This liquor I took from you. That's what prolongs your life, isn't it?"

"Is it?"

"I have tried it and I feel exulted."

"And if you set fire to it, it would make a pure and bright flame, emitting no smoke, and would burn forever. But it's all that I have. And I cannot make any more, not here."

Then Sarmiento put his hand under the old man's beard, to his throat, and squeezed it: "What is it?"

"If you kill me you'll learn nothing." The hand withered, the neck widened: "It was made on Ambrym. It's an amalgam, reduced to fluid and filtered seven times through white sand with fire."

Sarmiento slurped: "Amalgam of what?"

Salacay's face became a wrinkled squint: "You shouldn't have taken it. I would've given it to you. But you're a thief."

"Amalgam of what?" and the alchemist squeezed the old magus's throat, forcing a gasp.

"It's made from the amber of a certain tree."

Sarmiento's soul jumped: "What tree?"

The reply was full of insincerity: "If you were to be more civilised, I could show it to you."

"The trees are here?"

Salacay maintained his hoarse whisper: "No. They are further west and south. A vast land. Difficult to find."

Which brought the hand to his throat again: "You're lying. You said you'd never been to that land."

A creaking croak: "Very well, it is all a lie. And the liquor is a lie."

"I'll kill you."

"No, you won't, but perhaps I will die."

The last word made Sarmiento freeze. A second of stillness. Then erupting: "Stop talking in riddles!" and he pulled a dagger, thrusting it in front of the old man's face: "If you've got nothing important to say, I can cut your tongue, then perform a thousand other amputations before I rip out your heart."

The old man gnashed his yellow-red teeth: "What I've said so far is true?"

"And you've been to the Great South Land."

"Aye, but long ago. I went on an Ambrym ship."

Sarmiento stared deeply into the forehead in front, as if reading the old man's mind: "And there is something else."

Bringing an immediate submission: "Yes."

"Something that is here, on this island."

"Perhaps, it's hard to find."

"Where should I look?"

An arched eye-brow: "You, or we?"

"Where?!"

Salacay shook his head at the violence: "It's found in nature," then conciliatory: "But if you want me to show you, return the flask to me."

"There's very little left, and I've grown quite fond of the taste."

Now, the old man's turn to express rage: "You stole it!"

"If you want more, you'll have to show me."

But Salacay just spat at him.

Sarmiento wiped the mess from his cheek, stood up and looked around. Ubi's witch doctors were preparing the battlefield. Painted white with ash mixed mud, they looked ghost like, and they slapped the earth and air with banana leaves as they chanted:

Let the spears of the strangers be heavy, let them fall short
Let the clubs of the enemy be heavy, let them fall from their hands
Let the axes of the enemy be heavy, let them fall
Let the arm of the enemy be heavy
Let their legs be heavy ...

Their warriors began putting arrows to their bows or jostling their spears and gradually a uniform shout came from them.

Ortega came hurtling down the slope: "Ready!"

The Islanders' drum beats quickened, and the men with bows and arrows seemed to be suddenly vomited out of the line into the space between armies, racing around the Spanish phalanx, who were saurian tough under their shields.

Sarmiento remained calm, but with fingertips rubbing hard against the hilt of his sword: "Keep your arms up, lads. Harquebuses ready. Hold your fire."

An Islander screamed as he ran and let go of his tensed string. The arrow left at an awkward angle, shuddered in the air and slapped obliquely against a wooden shield. Others followed. Occasionally one would clunk against a helmet, but they were fired too hastily, from too great a distance to do any damage. Whenever one of the Islanders stopped to crouch and take proper aim the tortoise-phalanx would shuffle towards them. This terrifying image created a trembling arm, and the missile let loose would quiver hopelessly.

Some of the Spanish soldiers were laughing at the wobbling, slapping missiles, until there was a sudden chilling cry. One of them fell with a dart lodged under the side of his helmet, in his cheek. When a friend kneeled to help, another arrow whistled down and stuck in the earth between Ortega's legs:

"Who opened that gap?! You boy! What are you doing, fie!"

"Please, señor. He has an arrow."

"Your shield, whelp! Get it up!"

Sarmiento peered out through the gaps between the shields. One of the Islanders, who seemed taller with more paint and adornments than the rest, was making daring approaches and had a much firmer aim than any of the others.

The alchemist looked toward Bubi and told him to put Salacay in the charge of Juan López. Then he lifted his arm, indicating that the slave should follow him: "We're going hunting," reaching at the same time for one of the harquebusiers. He pushed his ringed fingers under the sharpshooter's breastplate while he pushed their way out of the phalanx with the other. They emerged in the same area into which the audacious warrior was running: "Come on lads. We've got a real, feathered turkeycock to fry." And caught an arrow on his shield. This pierced the wood, contesting the insult.

The warrior screamed when his arrow struck and threw his thick arms in the air as if celebrating a bullseye. He could sense the admiration of his men and his ancestors. What else did he need? He had no fear of death because he had no concept of it. He had seen dead bodies but he knew that the body was only an illusion and that souls did not die. He had a name, but he knew that he was more than a name, he was part of the universe. He heard countless voices in his head, and when he spoke it was a voice, but not one voice: when he was angry it was a particular voice, when he was content it was another. He was part of the universe and the universe was part of him. When he was fighting a battle, as now, it was the spirits of his bravest ancestors guiding his arm; or the spirits of the men he had eaten. Cannibals were not only eaters of flesh, they also devoured souls – *Come on turtle* – he thought – *If you eat me I will be as you ... if I eat you, you will be with me ... Only the strongest body will survive ... but the ultimate destiny of all existences is to become One* – On the battle-field he was exorbitant, and he cried to his men to follow him: "This turtle is great. A demon or a dragon. But do not be afraid, it spits no fire. If we kill it, we'll be exulted. If it eats us, we'll be exulted."

And he waved his bow and arrows as he ran. The gasping gash of his mouth, mightily open to expulse a gurgling roar at those demons that had dared abandon the protection of the shelled phalanx. Veins in his arms bulged over bulging tendons. One arm up, groaning under the weight of his double-edged axe held high and swinging over his head.

The sharpshooter was kneeling, lifting his gun. Sarmiento slapped his shoulder: "Aim for the heart."

And ... Bang! The warrior dropped and the entire mountain top went suddenly silent still.

Fire and thunder. Gunpowder had arrived.

The Islanders gaped. Their brave warrior twitched as a shudder of incomprehensibility surged through him. His ivory eyes were pumped full of terror and he opened his mouth to roar but was unable to. His chest was open and bleeding as he collapsed to the ground - *What had he said about the turtle? That it was a dragon that spat no fire?* – The irony as much as his wound made him numb.

When the harquebus went off the shields were lowered to get a better look at what had happened. They saw the shock and expected the army to flee. They all thought that the native was dead. He had been shot from close range and all had heard Sarmiento give the order to aim for the heart.

Sarmiento himself wandered panting over the field. His wild expression had returned, staring into the colourful stream in front of him. He lifted his arms and shouted: "Teo magu!" which meant *don't be afraid.*

But as he staggered around, mad-drunk with sulphur, he accidentally stepped on what he thought was the corpse of the warrior. A hand suddenly wrapped itself around his tender ankle and an arm tugged at his leg. He grimaced and screamed more from the shock than the pain. It was as if Lazarus himself had clutched his soul. He shook the zombie off and jumped back.

The sight of their hero's revival, however, renewed the Islanders' confidence - *Our man is alive... The stranger's magic is weak* – they told themselves. And sensing the help of their own gods the stream of warriors roared and charged.

Shock rippled through the Spanish and broke the order of the phalanx. Catoira and three other soldiers ran out to defend Sarmiento while the sharpshooter and Bubi staggered back into the protection of the group. Ortega shouted orders for the phalanx to reform. The soldier with the arrow in his face cursed. He was still on the ground trying to unhook the barbed point embedded in his cheek, and they were trampling him.

Ortega cursed back at him, grabbed his arm and pulled him up: "Are you not dead yet?"

A pale face streaked by the crusty rivulets of dry blood could only stare stupidly back. The arrow bobbed, pulling his cheek and mouth down.

Ortega grabbed it and snapped it near the base, fresh blood spurted: "Put yer helmet back on. Doctoring will be done after the battle. Meanwhile, if yer living ye fight!"

The pained soldier felt the shark tooth barb with his tongue, and, ignoring Ortega's order, he reached in and screwed it out from the inside. There was a squelching pop as the hole closed behind the retreating wood. The slapping gash smarted and he grimaced, but then laughed when he saw the bloodied but otherwise perfect shark's tooth, like a cruel joke extracted from his own rotten tooth mouth.

Through the shouts and curses Salacay edged away to the side of the huddle. Juan López moved with him, but he was oblivious to the efforts being made by the old man to slip away from his captors. Salacay was using his magic arts to confuse the soldier boy, and distract his gaze from what he did not want him to see.

Meanwhile Sarmiento was struggling to wrench his leg free again from the wounded warrior who had dived back onto the ankle trying to yank him down, but also manoeuvring himself closer to where he had dropped his axe. The shot had gone through his shoulder and the blood was streaming tomato red over his shiny black skin, but Sarmiento's own display of discomfort and shock when he had grabbed his ankle inspired thoughts that his opponent was weak. He breathed deeply to fill his damaged chest, and crunched his teeth together as he lifted himself and reached for his axe.

Sarmiento's heart dropped. The charging Islanders had stormed forth cutting him off from the phalanx. Only Catoira and the three others were on his side of the battlefield, and now the wounded warrior had his hatchet again. The alchemist did not think twice. He heaved and lifted his sword.

The Islander looked into the wild-alchemist's assassin eyes and thought he saw them spit fire, although that was probably the sweat and spittle spraying from Sarmiento's purple face. He knew then that he was standing before a demon and that his soul would soon leave his corpse. The Toledo-steel seemed to also shine as it drew its arch, finishing just below the resigned native's breast bone. The blade squelched as it opened a gash down and through the belly. Blood spurted from an opened artery and showered the alchemist who slashed at the stomach again, cutting it open in a cross that released internal pressure and allowed red intestines to push through.

Catoira grunted as he took the thud of three charging warriors on his shield, then yelled as he swiped indiscriminately with his sword. One of them felt the iron slice against his arm and squealed. The others saw how the steel so easily snapped a spear, and awareness of their dangerous proximity to such a formidable weapon had them backing away.

Sarmiento looked past the choking, dying man at his feet. Catoira and the three others were swatting in the air while the natives made tentative advances. But the real danger was now at their rear where a thick line of feathered warriors had formed between them and the phalanx. Realisation made them huddle.

"Catoira, good friend. So nice to see you here," Sarmiento gasped.

"Nicer were we not surrounded by nervous Indians."

Sarmiento smirked: "Ah Catoira, trust me, I feel splendid," and swirled his blade through the air while his tongue curled over his cheek, licking up the blood that had been splashed there: "Verily señor, right now, with a sword in my hand I can think of no man better than myself."

"No man, but there are thirty between us and our squadron."

"We are five, so there are six each," and wafted away a fly: "What can we do, but fairly try and force our fortune ..." and bellowed: "Come, whelps!" So they ran with him straight into the line, pushing their way through it with the shields ...

When they emerged on the other side the squadron jerked into motion and pressed the phalanx forward to absorb them.

Juan López looked anxiously around. He was trying to hold Salacay up, but he was being pushed franticly from all sides because the phalanx was swaying all over the place. They were shoving and trampling each other while they made room for the men being incorporated, at the same time thrashing back at the prodding spears and thumping clubs of the enemy.

Juan López looked at the old magus he was guarding and Salacay returned the young soldier's gaze with a sheepish stare. So old and feeble he looked that Juan felt sorry for him and loosened his grip on the neck, wrapping his fingers around his necklace instead. This hung down the old native's back and Juan used it as one would the leash of a dog enabling him to push away his shoving comrades with his free hand. So much so that while he felt the old man suddenly drop to a kneeling position on the ground he never noticed that his prisoner's wrists were free of their bonds, nor even that he had lifted the leash over his head.

It was only when he tugged at it to inspire a rise that he registered the escape, and by then the magus Islander had become dust in his own magic wind and blown himself away under their very feet.

Sarmiento wiped his blood splattered face and pushed into the tight huddle of the phalanx shouting orders to make room. Catoira and the other soldiers also slipped in behind him. The whack of arrows and spears against their shell of shields was now constant. He caught a flash of white out of the corner of his eye. At first he thought it was one of the ash-smeared witch doctors of Ubi's tribe, but looking back he recognised the immense beard. Salacay, alone at a distance, was waving a taunting bone.

Sarmiento span around. Juan López, gormless and pale, was standing with the necklace drooping between his fingers, shaking with a sad rattle. Sarmiento yelled, but the young soldier suffering the shock of his pathetic failure seemed not to notice – *Bewitched* – concluded Sarmiento, who turned back to the bearded escape artist.

There was too much noise to hear his chant, but he could feel it in his brain. Hot words that pierced and made his vision blur.

To save himself he pushed himself out into the field again and charged toward the feeble white figure, one arm bearing his sword, the other reaching to catch. But Salacay, who was standing at a cliff edge, stepped back, becoming a flash of white, evanescing into the grey sky backdrop behind him as he fell.

Momentum almost took Sarmiento into the griseous void with him. He wavered over a sheer drop of some twelve-hundred feet. His eyes were trained down into the dark verdure of the jungle below, straining for a semblance of something pale and red and twisted, but saw nothing.

The harquebuses flashed and roared, natives fell, and Sarmiento limped back to the squadron. Exhausted and depressed at first, then hurrying because the islanders were charging again.

They thudded into the phalanx. Each man had to push forward to hold their ground. Impossible. The phalanx was shoved back, toward the ridge. Then suddenly a rain of arrows and spears and stones, hitting harder now because they were coming directly from above. The Spaniards looked up through the gaps between the shields. A group of warriors had appeared on the ridge above them. The clamour was deafening: "They're throwing the mountain at us!"

The barbed points of spears and arrows began to break through the wood of the shields like stiff claws.

"We're lost!"

Someone screamed.

Ortega was purple-wild: "Load your pipes lads, we're going to give 'em some more smoke."

The next round was organised in such a way that half the guns were fired toward the charging army, after which the phalanx suddenly turned and the rest of the guns blasted the men on the ridge above them. As always the thunder and smoke provided a respite and in that pause they charged the high ground. But the slope was steep and muddy and the natives regrouped while the Spaniards were pulling themselves up the slippery track. A soldier called Alonso Martín caught an arrow in his thigh and had to be dragged up while the harquebuses were fired again.

But once up on the top, steel was able to push the natives back and make room for the positioning of the instruments of thunder and fire. Without shields the natives were helpless, and, in the open field, sitting ducks. Swords hacked. Guns blasted. Arrows, stones and spears slapped against shields and armour.

The phalanx advanced, but into a village replete with snipers. Each hut had one small opening from which a flurry of arrows or spears would come. Nevertheless, this was futile resistance. Those natives that sensed it fled. Those that did not were burned alive when Sarmiento gave the order to set fire to the town.

Red flame and billowing black smoke. The former intensifying, the latter blending invisible into the encroaching night. Silhouettes of men staggered around the fires like sad, black demons, whooshing, flaming torches dangling from their hands, illuminating kerchief masked faces.

But then, over the screams and through the stench of burning men, Sarmiento announced that he wanted a prisoner.

In one of the huts a man had armed himself with what seemed like an inexhaustible collection of spears, which he used with such dexterity that he had managed to beat back several attempts to set fire to his hut, slashing one soldier's cheek with a spear which he had then lodged in a slave's thigh. Then, just as they were about to blow him out with the harquebuses, Sarmiento decided that he wanted the brave fighter to be their new hostage. Ortega was ordered to organise the capture, but as the old officer advanced he himself received a whooshing lance that clipped his brow, opening a deep and bloody breech. He looked up at Sarmiento, half his face masked by a squeezing hand: "We're not going to be able to take this brock alive, Captain. The savage is resolved to die rather than fall into our civilising hands, and he'll have no compunctions about taking us to hell with 'im, pray!"

But Sarmiento just blew a neighing air through vibrating lips: "Have you never tamed a horse, Don Pedro? One needs rope!"

And so they tempted him far enough out to get a lasso around his neck, then pulled him to the ground and bound him.

With this spirit quelled and the burning buildings now smouldering charcoal the mountain had been won. So it was decided to descend.

"The moon is full," it was argued: "There will be light enough, surely."

One of the exhausted men protested: "Why not camp here the night?"

"And if the savages come back? If we have to fight a morning battle? Without breakfast, with parched throats."

Another supported the rebellion: "We have to rest."
Sarmiento was adamant: "But first we go down."

XVII. Collapse

(a) the descent

The night jungle: a dense, trapping, invisible net. Flashes of lightning were momentary illuminations that only served to reinforce the thickness of the jungle wall reality, and augment their desperation. The young, sobbing pack bearers went first, machetes flaying blindly while the older slaves and infantrymen followed close behind. Swords out, shields up, hardly daring to breathe.

Alonso Martín, still with the arrow in his side and more exacerbated than the other wounded ones who had been patched, was being dragged by Juan López. The ex-cabin boy was happy to fill this nurse's role, but Alonso's groans were perturbing; not because of the expression of pain, but for their tell-tale resonance. The Islanders had to be close, watching, stalking, and ready to pounce.

Ortega, his own damaged face swollen at the eye, which looked like a fermenting plum about to burst its seam, grasped Juan's arm: "Shut him up will yer."

But when the youngster merely gawked back he realised that he would have to demonstrate and thumped Alonso Martín with such dexterity that it left him unconscious. This of course doubled the burden and Juan himself collapsed, until Catoira offered his own shoulder.

Sarmiento remained upright against the thorny stems. His confidence was assuring, but misleading. In reality his mind was wandering between the material and the fantastic, and he had a sharp pain in his side. Sucking his ring with its emblem of Jupiter mitigated the pangs and his fear, he thought, and, because he believed it, it did.

Ortega was panting behind and dabbing his festering wound, and behind him Bubi with one arm wrapped around the neck of the hostage they had taken. This Islander was gasping and trying to move his legs at his captors' pace. He clutched the Bubi's shirt for support while the African dragged and jerked him along, as if he were already dead.

Then one of the soldiers at the vanguard cried out with joy.

Then another.

They had reached a path. Progress could now be a steady, though staccato, descent. Attention now fell on the feet whereas before they had been concerned with their faces and heads. The relief of the change evoked laughter that had to be hushed up. The track was steep and had its slippery dangers, but the descending men were not afraid of falling, happy enough to have found the fastest way down. Until their wish was fulfilled with a muffled cry from the vanguard. The path had suddenly dropped away from under him. Only a metre, but the poor lad had collapsed and twisted a knee.

"Careful..." he whispered to the next one as he pushed himself up from the mud.

"Careful..." repeated the other as he slipped down on top of the first. Then the third was also wavering over them.

"Careful..." they stammered, then looked ahead of them. They had tumbled out of it into a flat and open space, the clearing around a village.

Smoke from hidden, smouldering fires gave the moonlit scene the scent of roasted pork. They sniffed and their bellies rumbled. Their feet were shuffling whispers as they staggered forward into the circular centre, surrounded by the dark, sloping silhouettes of A-framed huts.

Gravitating towards one which glowed red inside and emanated a gurgling murmur of rational animal life, each soldier's mind was full of his own pirate purpose. Any polite ritual in search of an invitation to dine would be absurd. Experience had blazoned them with a simple logic that the Islanders were a savage race of liars. Only Juan López advanced with any idealistic illusions of peaceful settlement. This stemmed from his religious education. As a licensed friar he had learned something of the concept of Christian peace that a life of realism had not yet fully extinguished.

The first of the residents to step out and see the creeping invaders screamed and ran back inside. Then the pulsating red gash was full of black figures, black bobbing heads and wafting black limbs. The voices were suddenly loud, a hopeless echoing in the valley that evolved into a fuller but also more specific cacophony of yells and shrieks which became words, a chant ... in Spanish. The invaders shivered. It was as if the whole world had learned their language: "Away! Away!"

Black forms pushed out from red light to blue, kicking up dust to add density to the exterior atmosphere while their own darkness paled. They also shivered as they drew closer to the sagging weary and ghostly white invaders. Preternatural. This sensation was amplified in the villagers' minds by rumours of spirit invaders who worshipped a dragon god and were capable of metamorphosis. Some of them saw massive snakes and huge white lizards erect and creeping forward and they had to rub their eyes and shake their heads to get the vision out.

The Spaniards also peered. Too tired to think for themselves they awaited their captain's command, but he himself was transfixed by the magic of the night, his gaze trapped by a hunched and stalking figure who had danced bravely around their flank, drawing dangerously close. In reality a local witch doctor, the spider-man could have been Salacay, Sarmiento thought, and a swaying beard seemed to affirm the idea. The magus stared at him and his eyes seemed to glow – deep, penetrating and hypnotic – and Sarmiento suddenly had a vision of himself tied to a stake on a burning bonfire. He heard himself scream and watched his own skin, red and shrivelled by the flames. He looked away, but it did not break the spell – *It is Salacay* – he deduced – *But a ghost or real?* – Yet when he turned back to the phantasm, it had disappeared.

His other senses also came back and he shuddered. The villagers' frenzy had mounted and they were throwing rocks at the leaden-legged invaders. A large specimen bounced off Sarmiento's breastplate. His head felt clogged – *Salacay?* – He screamed – *Where are you, fie!?* – Another rock hit his helmet. His head was so hot, swelling and full to bursting. He vomited, which brought relief to the stomach and head. He had to react, he realised; he had to give a command: "Together, lads ..." the voice rasped through a tight throat: "Shields up!"

The men moved and grouped while a thick, masking-moon cloud crept past. The villagers, hysterical, were a writhing mass of shadow again in the barely lighter general darkness. Though still cautious, they pressed forward, closing in. Torches were lit by both sides so that pockets of glaring, frightened faces became visible. Bright teeth in gaping mouths.

Sarmiento wiped bile from his chin and stretched himself, waving a commanding arm: "Infantry! Draw swords! Harquebusiers!"

The first arrows whizzed past.

"Shields up!" he yelled, although most had already been lifted instinctively.

More arrows. The occasional spear. Clanking against helmets, breast plates. Then a whiz and a scream. An arrow scratched the throat of one of the infantrymen. Sarmiento ordered the harquebusiers to fire. The flash of flame.

The residents backed away. They were stunned. Several had fallen. The wounded groaned.

Sarmiento received another vision of himself on the pyre, brief, but long enough to make him gasp. He trembled then gave the order to charge.

Soldiers guzzled air to clear their minds and oxygenate the adrenaline that would lift their limbs. Swords hissed out of scabbards, drawn into an air full of blood curdling yells. The shield bearers gritted teeth and raced into the mob, while the harquebusiers reloaded.

Their iron slashed into yielding, cracking poles. Steel clonked through wood then squelched into flesh. Cut and bleeding, the residents were quickly scattered, their screams soon deadened by jungle.

To confirm the victory, the breathless Sarmiento waved his arms, a frantic but silent communication perfectly comprehensible to the panting, sniffling pirate squadron. The scattered individual parts staggered around or dropped.

The wounded Alonso Martín, still unconscious, was dumped into one of the huts, where Juan López, in the heat of torch light, extracted the arrow and dressed his wound without disinfecting it.

In other cases, empty bellies ruled, making connections with the smoking oven. This was a pit with hot coals and a yam covered pig. The original owners had still not started their banquet, now it was all theirs, and so that night the villagers' huts were occupied with full-bellied Europeans, snoring over each other's snores, their own bloated stomachs pouting upward as if in joyful reverence to the fullness of the moon.

Sarmiento shivered in his sleep. Perhaps it was the digestion of pork provoking a strange dream. This began in front of a tree. *Although it looked like an oak, it bore a singularly huge and solitary pomegranate, ripe and ready to pick. He dreamed himself reaching out for the red fruit, egged on by a handkerchief waving Mendaña. However, he himself was unaware of the snake wrapping itself around his arm until it was squeezing tight. He roared but the reptile merely yawned before clamping its jaw tight. One long stab. The hypodermic fangs, cauterised, injecting a poison which had its own searing sensation upon contact with the blood. Bubbling blood and steaming poison erupted out of the wound, gurgling, blue vapour, itself toxic. Sarmiento had collapsed screaming in a spastic fit, until the poison reached his nervous system, paralysing him. The coward Mendaña turned and fled. Then Ortega arrived in a suit of gleaming armour. Picking the fruit, he took it to the captain-general who was now swimming naked in a huge, grey-green gelatinous pond of frog's spawn. Mendaña reached up from the black freckled mess to accept the offering. His own skin had turned green and his blonde hair had tints of blue in it. He smiled as he scooped up the red fruit and gobs of spawn dripped from his arms. Then Ortega reappeared, this time pulling a leash with a dog collar wrapped around a thin, pale neck. Half-expecting to see Salacay the self-dreamed Sarmiento miraculously overcame his paralysis and ran to the figure, only to quickly comprehend that it was not the bearded old man at all, but a red-haired maiden, his beloved sister. Ortega pushed the girl into the pond with Mendaña, whose eyes turned a brilliant gold and became bright new coins. A long red tongue slipped out and wrapped itself around María Dolores' neck. She did not murmur, just sank silently into the jelly...*

Awaking from this, Sarmiento crawled desperately-hurriedly to the doorway. The moon had already sunk and the night was now pitch. His bustle and rattle disturbed the other soldiers who were peering through the blackness, trying to divine the source of the disturbance.

Sergeant Arragocés was the first to demand an explanation: "What, fie, is happening there?!"

Sarmiento put his hand in mud and shivered: "Where am I?"

Arragocés recognised the commander in the voice: "Still on the mountain, Cap'ain. On its slope."

A grey light, that seemed to be brushed on rather than streaming in, indicated the encroaching dawn. Sarmiento sighed and a gentle breeze came off his breath. A breath which misted.

They were buried in a fog. Sarmiento looked for his boots, tugged them on, then stood and stretched himself.

He emptied the night long accumulation of urine and started to rouse the other men.

He jostled Bubi and their prisoner, but as he did he noticed that their Islander hostage had almost unravelled the rope binding his wrists. Without speaking he grabbed his beard and pulled him up, then took him to a tree where he called his men to bind him with a thick rope. Then he called four harquebusiers forward. The rising sunlight bleached the grey fogged atmosphere white. He whispered to the squad, then turning to their hostage gave the order to fire. The blast was deafening, the prisoner trembled, but when the smoke cleared he was still alive and Sarmiento ordered him to be untied while he grabbed him by the beard again, demonstrating that the tree beside him was full of shot: "Next time you try to escape, the shot will go here ..." he said and thumped the native's belly, knocking the wind out of him. Then he had them tie him again, with a cord from the wrists to the neck. The Islander shook his head and spat at the humiliation. While his spittle sizzled on the ground the opaque atmosphere dissipated and streams of gold began to filter through.

"Ah," sighed Catoira: "At least today it will not rain."

The track down was rough. The Islanders attacked from behind and above. Defence was frustrating, the harquebuses were rendered useless by trees and the shield bearers' arms ached.

Stymied, the order was given to fire the harquebuses anyway. Futile. Although, in difference to the ersatz firing squad, the purpose this time *was* to kill men; but still only trees were hurt.

So the Islanders crept closer, their arrows striking each time more forcefully, hard enough for their barbs to pierce the wooden shields. They looked like demons as they raced, painted and plumed, through the jungle. When they ran out of arrows they threw rocks. When there were no rocks they threw dirt. When no dirt they threw their bows. And when they had thrown everything they spat at them, pulled faces, and poked their naked arses at them.

Until one Islander got too close. He suddenly appeared from behind the thick white trunk of a tree in front of a rear guard soldier with a loaded harquebus. The Islander's arrow slipped off the string at the crucial moment and he was desperately trying to put it back when the soldier's own shivering hand applied the taper and blew a gaping hole in the warrior's head. Brains dripped from a smoking skull. Stench of singed hair.

The Spaniards decided to exploit the gory details and they strung the corpse upside down in the fork of a high tree for everyone to see.

"So, the turtle-dragon will burn and sting when it wishes ..."

And the Islanders thought it better to leave this capricious enemy alone that day. They retreated into the jungle, abandoning their village, but not before hiding their supplies of food.

Exhausted soldiers and slaves staggered into the relinquished huts in search of things to ingurgitate. When their dinnerless fate became an inevitability, they hardly complained. Most were too exhausted to be hungry. But when they had collapsed under bamboo and leaves the sleep that was needed was reluctant to come. It had become another undesirable chore to most. At the lower altitude the heat and humidity had worsened, as had the mosquitoes. And because of the natives in their minds, they lit torches to keep the night away, and sentries had been posted, but most were heart thumping jumpy whenever they heard a rustle. One of the lucky ones, a young mulatto shield bearer, not only fell immediately unconscious but began to snore resonantly. This added to the other hut members' insomnia, but no one complained of their comrade's good fortune.

In most of the huts there was a similar pattern of the fortunate-few and the unsleeping-majority. Juan López lay beside a now febrile Alonso

Martín. Both of them slept, but poorly, for sleep only brought more terrible nightmares. Juan López screamed out of visions, always culminating with the spectacle of a hefty spear plunging into his own bare chest. There was a dull thump and sharp crack as the breast-bone snapped and a second later he was awake, his cheek smarting from Sergeant Arragocés' slapping hand.

"Give the lad some rum," the sergeant moaned to one of the other soldiers: "They've not the mettle for stuff as this, poor boys. They're used to a more docile folk like them of the Americas. This savage race torments them."

Juan grimaced. Being plagued by this imbecile sergeant was excruciating, not only because he was a brute. Juan was also repulsed by his physical appearance, for Arrogocés was the epitome of infirmity. Any good doctor would have to have recommended a change of diet. He had a xanthic complexion, caused by a liver dysfunction, and his face was creased into an almost perpetual grimace due to an overactive pancreas. His eyes were large, ochreous orbs with splashes of red and a brown-black centre that seemed to seep. His voice would have been a belly-bellow had not his throat trapped it, making it gurgle in phlegm and rasp.

Then Bubi burst in with a torch, frantic, panting and crawling straight up to a dozing Catoira to yank his sleeve: "Please, señor... It's the Captain. He's fallen into an epilepsy, señor."

For most of the descent Sarmiento had been enduring a dull ache in his liver. This occasionally intensified, becoming a furnace. At first the pain seemed to make his vision blur, which was gradually to sharpen again, but into impossible hallucinations. The old wizard Salacay, he believed, was still in his mind. Eyes, gigantic monstrous, floating; and as they widened Sarmiento's innards were scorched. Terrible ideas generated an image of themselves; consider a monster and a monster would appear.   When the spasms began, Bubi abandoned Sarmiento to find more proficient help. As he sprinted away he caught a glimpse of his captain-master extracting his dagger from its scabbard. The African stumbled and wept, terrified by the image of the writhing figure desperately trying to jab himself, to skewer and lever out the incubus imagined to be within. Yet luckily the same spasms also gave Sarmiento a spastic lack of control, so the blade hit dirt and cloth, sometimes wood, but always missed the flesh.

Catoira shouted to the three who had accompanied him and they threw themselves onto their captain, holding him still. Catoira himself struggled with the hand clenching the knife. They tried to soothe him, Catoira rubbing his temples and mopping white foam from his lips. Meanwhile Sarmiento wrestled within himself; in the invisible depths, where he struggled against his ghosts and Salacay's tremendous will.

Later, partially recovered but exhausted, his head resting on a nervous Catoira's lap. A miner bird's monotonous metallic "tink" reverberated from the jungle, relieving the constant undercurrent of rain. This seemed to annoy Catoira who groaned. A crack of thunder made him shudder. It had been lightning annunciated, but he had not expected it to be so harsh: "There'll be another deluge. Perhaps it'll do us a favour and wash us out of this jungle." But the thunder and lightning got inside Sarmiento's head and made him convulsive again.

Eventually a sweating Juan López came and lay a crucifix across Sarmiento's heart and began to chant: "Amara Tonta Tyra post hos firabis ficaliri Elypolis starras poly polyque lique linarras buccabor ..."

When Sarmiento came suddenly smiling out of his trance, Juan López wrongly believed the exorcism had cured him. As for the captain's grin, that derived from the solemn priestly etchings on the soldier's face.

"Ah yes, López. The soldier-monk," he laughed: "When you're sick o' the sword, you unsheathe your cross," and then: "How many men have you killed this week, Monk?"

"I'm no monk, Captain. Though I would've been, had not the hermit life been contrary to my adventuring spirit."

"The hermit life? Hermit life of the monk? Ah yes, sirrah, that's a good one. They talk about their vows of silence and the virtues of the solitary, meditative existence, and yet we see and hear them all over the place. Hermit life ... yes, very funny!"

Which offended Juan. He had been educated to have respect for the church. His captain's outburst sounded like humanism and therefore blasphemy.

"I'm a good Christian, Captain."

Which lifted Sarmiento and had him reaching for the neck of the soldier-priest's shirt: "Then you should not be soldiering. A good Christian does not kill! You're a demon, lad ... I can see your horns."

And the poor boy shuddered and had to pull himself away. His face, horrified; as if Satan himself had just burped on him.

(b) surrender

Sarmiento and his squadron finally did emerge from the jungle, collapsing onto the beach.

In the right spot, for a longboat was scouting the coast there. The sailors greeted them as heroes, pulling them into the boat with cheers, claps and a lot of back slapping. The soldiers vomited their exploits and the sailors rowed them with a song that was really an improvised eulogy, condensing and magnifying the adventures they had just heard.

Even Juan López felt proud then; his jungle suffering, fading into the brighter world of heroes of which he had suddenly become a part.

However, once on board ship the reception was quite different. Mendaña greeted Sarmiento and Ortega with a cold stare and ordered them into his cabin.

Drizzle or storms, the maddening dampness had had an insalubrious effect on Mendaña's mood and several times he had expressed a suspicion that it would bring disaster with it. His mind had been full of an unseen, creeping enemy. The wall of noise of the rain, blanketed any otherwise tell-tale sounds to give away an ambush, and that terrified him. He had posted more sentries, and chastised any sleepiness or neglect. Sudden noises made him jump and in his sleep he had been haunted by nightmares that had become "recurring". Now he was furious: "What have you been doing up there?"

Sarmiento and Ortega were both shaken by the impertinence of the accusation. Ortega touched his suppurating sores and Sarmiento grimaced at the bite of his liver, then they both slowly dribbled out as much of the story as they could immediately recall.

Until Mendaña intervened: "I heard the shots, señores," shots which he had taken as a personal affront to his immaculate plan of peaceful conquest: "There were shots," he insisted: "We heard them from here. We saw the fires. From here, señores. The shots. The screams. The fires. We saw and heard it all, from here!"

Sarmiento swallowed hard: "On the hill. At the summit. The first shots were made when the situation was already unsustainable."

Ortega also spurted: "If we hadn't. Most of us would be dead now," and his blue-slit damaged eye was festering as the pairs of stories merged into the same soliloquy.

"Our mission was to scale the mountain..."

"Which we did..."

"And we were attacked by a thousand Indians," Sarmiento exaggerated.

"But we saw..."

"Saw for ourselves..."

"I myself was the first up..." emphasised Ortega: "To confirm that this is an island."

Mendaña's cheek twitched: "You were also ordered to do no harm to the Indians. And yet it seems you conducted a massacre."

"Hardly that, señor," rasped Ortega.

"Why did you ransack Byje's village?"

Sarmiento was now snarling: "We were sent without provisions. Ordered to obtain food and water from the natives, señor!"

But Mendaña shook his head and guffawed: "By bargaining with them, not by ransacking and burning their homes!"

When he had finished with his officers, Mendaña went to examine the hostage they had brought back with them.

He had been shoved into a bamboo cage that sat in the middle of the deck. It was a small and narrow enclosure and he was pressed like a sandwich in the slot of a toaster. Mendaña pushed his staff straight through the bamboo bars into the mouth of the hostage, to lever up his lips.

"Christ will forgive you," he whispered: "Even you," and he reached in and rubbed his hand through the specimen's curly hair.

The prisoner, thinking he was being teased, spat in Mendaña's face, but the now Christian Mendaña merely turned his cheek, while the always attentive Gaspar wiped the spittle away.

Bubi felt the hot gaze of the hostage slapping his back, adding to the general terrible heat of things. That heat from the fire and from his pounding hammer that rose up his arm. He was crafting a thick chain that would be wrapped around that poor fellow's cage – *Black, like Bubi* – he thought – *Soon you will be a slave like Bubi* –

In the cramped confines the prisoner's chin was pushed up, which made breathing difficult. Existence had become a cramped yoga position, only air could save him. Though he knew nothing of yoga, instinct indicated the importance of breath, that he could inhale hope and exhale fear and pain, and that reality was beyond the body and in the black back of the smith in front of him.

Eventually Bubi had to turn, but as he did his mind was still assaulted by an image from his deep Bubi past, when as a child, and still free, he had stumbled on the stinking aftermath of some African war. A black heap of burned bones. An image that was projected into the prisoner's mind and he suddenly began tugging against the bars. The cage rattled, inspiring curses from the sailors, until one of them got up and silenced the protest with a jab in the ribs and a wrap on the knuckles from a thick stick.

Bubi winced. He had felt the same pain – *If you had my scars I would believe you were my brother* – he thought, and then gasped as he perceived a red figure clambering onto the cage. This was his own tormenting spirit, reaching down to grab and pull the prisoner's hair. It made Bubi hopeful – *Could it be that my bad spirit has found a new victim?* – But before he could rejoice he felt a sharp slap across his belly, as if a flying jellyfish had stung him. Out of the corner of his eye he could see the source of the pain.

A sickly sailor, glowing with a malaria fever, the leather of the whip dangling by his side: "Back to work nigger," he eructed through a snarl.

Bubi squeezed the handle of his hammer. He could have easily smashed his flagellator's head, but he had found the means of retarding such thoughts of justice years ago. In fact, the stinging whiplash meant very little to him, no more than a curt remark from a superior. So, he just shrugged his shoulders. He was still immersed in the image of his bad spirit jumping on the cage. When one has a harpy the rest of existence is all a dream. He mumbled some magic, something to bind the evil thing to the cage as well. A young slave working with him, however, was able to imagine a greener road to revolution: "I heard it said that our masters had a rough reception on the mountain." Bubi nodded – *And our masters' slaves* – "Good don't you think." Bubi shrugged his shoulders again. He had long forgotten what the word *good* meant. The youngster looked offended: "Of course it's good."

Which made Bubi stir: "What do you think? That these Islanders will kill our masters and free us? You think, because he is black," and he thrust a shaking finger toward the prisoner: "That he is a brother. I've suffered just as much from my black brothers as I have from these white-masters. As for these people here. If they catch us, they will eat us."

The cabin boy Gaspar was rubbing Mendaña's sword when Juan López walked past: "Please, señor," he spluttered: "If you've time and could sit wit' me while I finish our general's commission, I'd love to hear ye tell of yer adventure, señor. Me general has told me of yer bravery."

"He has? And what did he say?"

"That there's been no fairer nor more gallantry knight since Lancelot."

"And what do you know of Lancelot?"

"What the general's told me, señor. He often tells me stories, when we're alone and I'm attendin' to 'is toilet."

"So who's this Lancelot, pray?"

"Lancelot, señor? The bravest knight of all."

"But he's but a figment of some dreamy writer's pen."

"Then how did the writer know what he said?"

"It was imagined."

"And yer bravery?"

"Any man who'll walk in that jungle is brave."

"Really, señor. How?"

"It's a terrible dark place, terror oozes as sap does from a broken twig."

"They say it's a magical place."

"Oh verily, good Gaspar, very magical. if you imagine Hell to be magical."

"Did you see monsters, señor?"

"Most certainly did."

"And killed?"

"Aye, lad."

The wide leafed branches dripped softly and the hot earth turned tree tears into a pungent rising gas. No breeze. The air sagged and the jungle was whipping whistle, chirping still. Only the occasional rustle of vegetation when a parrot or a pigeon dropped or hopped.

As he trudged back into Sanba, Byje Ban Arra was sullenly conscious of his tremendous failure and the hopeless faces of the people greeting him were gloomy mirrors of his own despair. Baso's betrayal was a lump of burning pepper paste in his belly.

It had taken him two days to return. Baso's men had been everywhere. He had been a trembling, crouching witness through a veil of shivering leaves to an ambush on a pair of his own guards. He had seen them speared, their throats cut, their lifeless wrists and ankles tied, while a pole was slipped under the bonds to lift and carry them off for the cannibal Baso's supper.

Byje paused to consider the village his own mother's father had built. Palm trees formed a palisade around it – *Like a cage* – he thought then, and his miserable spirit considered the idea of exodus. His forefathers had come in their long ships, navigating from a distant place: why should they not consider another emigration? What right had they to call this unwelcome land home? But it was a matter of honour. An emigration would seem like they were fleeing. To run would imply a feeble mettle, and his people were the bravest on earth.

The women of Sanba knelt on mats or squatted on dirt. All of them with their eyes averted from the grim reality of men. In times of war it was better to look inward. Sons and brothers would soon be changed, reduced to spirits by some swinging axe or heart jabbing spear. By looking into the liquid gas reality of their own souls they were preparing themselves for the inevitable melting of the material world. They looked down at sprouting green grass and twisted dry dead leaves, and felt the aching transition between all metamorphosis. The garden magic was true magic; the cruel image of life was an illusion. The universe was tragic, but for that reason beautiful. One day they too would become trees.

But while the women languished in liquid to gas metaphysics, the men's minds were full of flesh. Skin which could be cut and ripped, meat which could be carved. Their universe was hard and sharp calcium. Cutting and burning could reduce it, and that was their hope, for reduction meant power. Reduction and annihilation. Death did not exist, only power made any sense. Power to reduce the universe into a dry bone singularity. One day their bravery would turn them into rock. Such was their will to solidify, rather than become air; to become stone rather than wood.

The village was swollen with their mumbling. They were the people of the province of Sanba, a Polynesian people in the Melanesian dominated isle of Mulu Mulu. The men rumbled around the exhausted Tauriqui. They shoved forward then rested, leaning on their spears. Most of them were tired, their limbs and heads with crunchy dry scabs and red line grazes. Some bodies were patched with pandanus bandages. The road back from Tiarabaso had been difficult for all of them. They had had to fight, run through jungle, avoid the paths patrolled by Baso's men. There were also other Tauriqui's there, who had come from other allied settlements. Hands flicked before shivering faces. Lips flapped and cheeks twitched. Their situation, which had just been beginning to stabilise, was now more precarious than ever. As more warriors trickled in, so did rumour. Baso, shouted one, had formed a treaty with Meta to make war on Sanba. Others argued that the New-men, as they called the Spaniards, had destroyed Baso's army, although Byje's own experience negated this. He shook his head and sucked hard through his nostrils drawing his face into a wild bulging-orb stare. If the New-men had joined with Baso and Meta then Sanba was doomed, he realised, and although he never said this, a suspicion of it seemed to surge from that anguished countenance and sweep over the bobbing, shivering mass. Luckily this most pessimistic premise had still to be ratified, and until it was there was still hope. More rumours gurgled down, mouth to mouth from the mountain top. First Gauga arrived, explaining his recruitment of the Ubi, and that the New-men had walked into their trap. Byje sighed and embraced his general, but his own thoughts were with Salacay. The old man would be in danger. What measures had been taken to ensure his safety?

But before Gauga could even attempt a reply, a wounded witness, survivor of the battle on the mountain, staggered in. He had been lost in the jungle. His shoulder was an open, suppurating wound covered in sucking flies. His report was abysmal: "A turtle-dragon god with a hundred eyes, crawled up the mountain, wreaked havoc and destruction on the province of Tiaraubi. The dragon spat fire, made men's skin burst open," and he pushed his shoulder forward so that those immediately around him could witness the effects of the dragon's wrath: "It also had fierce claws sharper than an eagle's," he said: "More like the teeth of a shark. They slashed."

The report drew a groan. Byje buried his face in his hands and then began tugging his bottom lip: "Where is Salacay?!" he shouted.

The witness knew of the strange old man and had seen him with the New-men, had seen him fall over the cliff. The mass of men moaned. The women wailed. But the bad news snowballed. The Tauriqui Bene had come from the west and gone to Tiarameta in the east. Baso and Meta had talked and exchanged gifts. All of their enemies were gathering their men. Sanba, like it or not, was at war ... with almost everyone.

Byje Ban Arra sat cross legged at a fire surrounded by the elders and chiefs, their generals and war-magicians. Next to him, Seseboco, his brother, his tone firm: "Salacay was wrong, we should not have mistrusted the New-men. They worshipped our same totem. The cult of Io. They are our brothers," and then lighter, more vigorous: "We must go to these brothers, to their Tauriqui Mendanna, and prove that we are real brothers. Show him that we worship the same totem, and that they must join us in this war. Our men must stay to defend Sanba. The Tauriqui Mendanna can go to Tiarameta in his ships. Make war on our enemies there. The New-men have a powerful magic, but it is the magic of Io. The magic of Io is pure and it has befuddled our own magic of Io and our own warriors because we tried to turn our magic against them. It threw Salacay over the cliff because he tried to use his own magic, tried to use the magic of Io against the magic of Io. Salacay is dead, and the magic and the warriors of Ubi are defeated. But if we can make our brothers, the New-men, our allies again, we cannot lose this war."

(c) reconciliation

Dull black hair brushed white skin. Fingers slid across the surface of a flat belly, tickling the navel. When the virgin sailor boy Trejo opened his bright green eyes, he gasped. He had dreamed himself in the hands of golden haired angels, but all he saw now were harpies. The quivering flesh bodies around him terrified, and he was uncomfortably damp and hot. His penis was hard and he did not know why, when it suddenly exploded he felt tremendous shame.

It was not the first time that it had happened, but it was the first time there had been witnesses. He could feel himself cowering, his limbs curling involuntarily into his torso and the girls laughed as his face reddened. His first instinct was to spit at them.

They began squealing and cowered away from the flying gobs of sputum. A giggling little one whose breasts were just beginning to pout held out a leaf for him to wipe his belly. When he looked down to the spot indicated he thought it was his own spittle dripping there, or that one of the girls had spat back without him noticing it. But when he wiped he caught the unmistakable scent. He blushed again while some of the girls ran out of the hut, babbling through giggles what had happened to the outside world, encouraging other girls and boys to poke their heads in and catch a glimpse of the New-men's boy's shame.

Trejo was in Sanba. The idea had come from Seseboco, but it was really a Sanban custom: Sanbans and New-men were quarrelling because they did not understand each other, and there could be no better way to gain knowledge than to eat at the other's table. Therefore, it was decided that a swap should take place. One of the boys from Sanba would go to the ships and learn the New-men's culture and the peculiarities of their particular way to worship Io. This would be reciprocated by one of the New-men coming to Sanba, who in turn would learn how the Sanbans worshipped their common deity. Byje's people had delivered their proposal to Mendaña with gifts of coconuts and breadfruit.

The boy the Islanders chose to represent them was called Mahnu. He was Seseboco's own son and Byje's nephew. A handsome boy, with a body that seemed sculpted by Michelangelo himself. Proportion and elegance. Juan López blushed when he saw him. Mendaña moaned and ordered that he be clothed. Then, without thinking about it, he recited scripture: *"Behold, the man is become as one of us, to know good and evil,"* bringing a lip pursing, anus clamping pleasure to the friars.

Then came the problem of who should return with the Sanbans. Mendaña's immediate decision was vindictive. A dandruff infested sailor called García had been plaguing him all day about their precarious position and about the need to return to Peru. Mendaña thrust a cruel finger at him: "García," and all eyes fixed themselves on the white detritus glowing from a black jacket. The captain-general's mouth curled into a slight but definitely cruel smile with a pitch to match: "You're hungry, aren't you?" The sailor's bottom lip dropped as he reluctantly affirmed it. Mendaña's nose dilated when he spat the penalty: "I'm sure the Islanders will fill your aching belly," delivered with enough obvious spite and received with such a shiver that the witnesses shuffled uncomfortably.

But fortunately for García, while he was standing precariously on a hawser just about to step foot into the undulatory dinghy that would row him ashore; his mind still stewing over the idea that Mendaña's decision amounted to a kind of banishment and wondering if he would ever see Peru and his wife again ... At that moment, the boy from the crow's nest, Trejo, who had realised there was a better solution to the problem, clambered down from his watch and threw himself over the rail, diving into the bay and pulling himself into the little boat where he shook the sea off like a wet dog. Then raising his arms in a dramatic, clothes sagging gesture before the captain-general, he elaborated his proposed compromise: "Please, señor," he blurted: "Let me go with the Indians," and his wet lips curled into an innocent pout: "I came here to see the world, but 've seen nothing but the views from this deck up to now," and shook his spiky hair head slowly while the sailor García, still wavering upon the ship's ropes, nodded so frantically that it seemed to snow over him: "This Sanba will be a good start for me, surely señor it will," delivered with a tremulous but mighty whimper that Mendaña could not resist. He quickly acquiesced and allowed García to pull himself back up onto the ship.

And so the exchange was made.

Trejo leaving the ships, wide eyed stupid, to march up to Sanba with their representatives.

At first the villagers had taken great pleasure in feeling the fabric of his clothes. But now he stood dreamily naked in front of his naked hosts who were laughing at his nakedness. Laughing, firstly, at the idea that the New-men's boy could be naked too and, secondly, at the boy's pied skin; his face, neck and arms being milk chocolate brown, while the rest of his body was lily white. Trejo clumsily pulled up his trousers. His embarrassment brought an uproar which further terrorised the lad until he found the wit to look out and at himself and understand his own ridiculousness. Then he was suddenly laughing too, as he kicked the trousers back off and ran out and around the camp, his unbridled penis flapping.

In case Mendaña did not fully appreciate the importance of the exchange, Fr Francisco Gálvez explained: "This Indian boy is an ambassador," he whispered with an awe-inspired tone and eyelid expanding gesture: "He should be treated as such."

So the captain-general decided to honour the native lad with his personal endorsement: "Mahnu will have free passage to go wherever he wants on this ship," he proclaimed, standing on a barrel to give him altitude, chin forward and hands clasped against his back: "If he asks for food or drink it'll be given to him," bringing a stir from the hungry-thirsty crew that forced modification: "Within reason of course," then, chewing the gummy inside of his lip as he recalled the vital information the priest had passed on: "He's an ambassador and should be treated with the appropriate formality." Realising he was about to embark on something long and in need of a deep breath: "And he's also here to learn, which makes it necessitate for him to observe you all closely, for he, señores, is here to learn from *you*, fine men, so your behaviour must be exemplary."

This generated a cheeky sparkle in Sarmiento's hot eyes and, turning to Catoira, the alchemist exuded anthropological speculation in order to demonstrate his private philosophy: "Look at that lad. We call him a *savage*. He's certainly more ignorant than us. He hardly asks any questions at all."

Catoira nodded, although the affirmation could also have been expressed with a shake: "Ignorant, most definitely."

Sarmiento continued through teeth: "He absorbs what his senses tell him, but does not wonder at them. He feels heat, but doesn't wonder why."

Now Catoira's head had adopted a horizontal motion: "Ignorant."

"And it's his ignorance that makes him noble."

Which pulled eye-brows up: "Noble?"

"Yes, Catoira. Noble. He's not yet chewed on the fruit of the Tree of Knowledge, his soul's still not corrupt."

The scribe became incredulous: "He's a savage."

"That's what we call him. We, whose souls are putrid with wonder."

"Now *you're* sounding like a priest, marry."

"Am I?" and he laughed before his pitch lowered to a more dejected tone: "Perhaps. Each one of us is a contradiction to himself. Even God, Catoira," which drew his chin up: "Only these noble savages are perfect, because they are consistent."

The writer scratched a wafer thin scab from his scalp. His voice was a drone: "If they're consistent and God is a contradiction, then they must be anti-natural."

Sarmiento's hand wrapped over his jaw: "Ah, but didn't you yourself say that God is the Devil."

This seemed to thump into Catoira. It took several seconds for him to respond: "It'd seem that you did love these people."

"No," which thumped out like a fist: "I hate them," then under the breath: "But for that reason, I am filled with awe."

Talking to Sarmiento made Catoira feel extremely lonely. He had thought he had found a friend, but each day the captain became more difficult to understand. Very soon he found himself trying to avoid him. But his writer's mind needed intelligent company and his sceptic's soul lusted for irreverent tastes, and there was no one who fitted these conditions as nicely as Sarmiento did. The relationship therefore evolved into something sweetly torturous, a love-hate thing, so he persisted: "Awe is the last thing I have, if anything I pity them. Their ignorance makes them slaves to nature and God, eventually they'll be slaves to us. I see nothing awesome or noble in not being free."

Sarmiento guffawed: "Freedom is one of our words that I doubt they possess an equivalent of."

Which made Catoira explode: "So you've become an expert on these men," then calmer, but full of bitterness: "One day, when they creep behind you and cut your throat and have your brains for supper, then you'll understand their savage souls."

But the spiteful rivalry just made Sarmiento laugh: "Well matched, good Catoira. Let us then do as noble Socrates did and admit our own ignorance of everything, and to help us overcome our philosopher's shame, let us share a bottle together."

But when he slapped Catoira's back, the ship's scribe did not smile.

On another occasion, one night, I had seen Catoira approach Sarmiento who had been with Mahnu imparting some of his science. Alternating between the symbols in a candlelit book and the heavens above them, he was trying to teach the lad the names of the planets and the constellations. Catoira had been head shaking incredulous: "Do you really think the lad capable of cognising such a subtle art?"

It did not dampen the alchemist's enthusiasm: "Oh, Catoira, of course. Much more capable than you or anyone else on this ship. *Magic* to these people is as important as gold is to us. Take it away and they'll become insignificant. If these witch hunting priests have their way, their Christianity will reduce these noble Islanders to the most insipid race."

"But their magic is not an art, nothing more than superstition. You don't really believe these chants of theirs do them any good, do you?"

Which made Sarmiento close the book and wave the boy away. When he turned back to Catoira his tone was marked by a bubbling violence: "I don't believe in anything, Catoira, and for that reason I believe it all. That is where our difference lies. You stop believing and the universe becomes an evil-cruel place ... but I, Catoira, have seen that Hell and I've risen from it. Now I choose to believe whatever you disbelieve."

Catoira rubbed the hair on the back of his head: "To torment me."

Sarmiento blew out the candle: "That's up to you," then stood up, but before abandoning the scribe: "I'd say I was saving you."

When Mahnu was able to escape his teacher-hosts, he would run across the beach to the point and immerse himself in his favourite world, the unparalleled paradise of the submarine reef. There he would dive and, eyes wide open in the smarting brine, search for magic. He was sublime amongst the ersatz flowerbeds of the animal plant coral; the variegated, crusty bloom universe where clown fish would brush stripes against craggy, white knobbed branches, or nestle within the dandelion petals of venomous anemones. The sea breathes and the boy pushed through the breath, carried by currents toward twitching stelliform polyps on giant fungiform structures. Fish faces mocked him. Laughing clown masks with parrot-beak mouths came to his hands, snatching away offerings of baked yam. Yellow, tubular snouts poked at him while he contemplated schools of transparent minnows darting from the snapping jaws of zebra striped angels.

Yet, despite his awe, Mahnu was well aware that this was not his universe. After three minutes the pain in his lungs would demand a return to the surface, after thirty he would return to the shore exhausted and lie on the beach, dreaming of the world he had just left, of glowing cuttlefish vibrating before his presence.

On one occasion when Sarmiento had observed the boy crawl out of the surf, he had turned to the friar who happened to be next to him, and whispered in a kind voice: "The philosopher Anaximander said that the first animals were born out of liquid, covered with a spiny shell. And this boy should have been born a fish."

Which the friar misinterpreted as an offence: "You'd do better quoting the Bible than your precious pagan Greeks. The boy, thank God, has a soul which no primitive animal has. And thanks to our provident arrival, his soul will be saved." Then scurried away, his soutane swishing over sand.

Sarmiento however went to the boy, who jumped when he opened his eyes and confronted so much redness above him. Recognition quickly calmed him however and he laughed, not at Sarmiento as such, but at the comparison between the waking world, the world of fish, and the world of his dreams. The world of fish and the world of dreams were so similar that this third universe, by his logic, was rendered unreal.

At the camp on the beach, Gaspar held his arm stiffly stretched out of the window, catching water for his captain-general in a coconut shell cup. He looked toward Mahnu, who was kneeling before Mendaña. The native returned the glance with an enthusiastic smile. Gaspar sighed. Mahnu was dressed in his clothes. These had been fetched for the ambassador when it had been decided that he and Gaspar had a similar build. The cabin boy seemed peeved, not only by that order, but by his obligation, by proximity, to befriend Mahnu: "If it be your wish, General," he had stammered when Mendaña had ordered it. Then turning to the native prisoner sandwiched between bamboo: "But I don't understand why that particular savage should be treated like a prince, while this other is pressed so tight into that cage."

Virtues when expressed before him always pricked Mendaña's conscience, for, though he was good at observing them in others, he still had no virtues himself. As for this latest rectitude, it became a seed which would lead to his eventual decision to free their hostage; after all, now that the boy was with them, the nameless prisoner seemed irrelevant.

Then, Mendaña was actually ruminating over this same incident as he reclined in a gently swinging hammock. They had come ashore to peruse the finished brigantine and instruct Mahnu in the fine art of European carpentry: "Our good Christ's mortal father was a carpenter." And he ordered Gallego to show the boy how to cut a dove-tail wedge.

But this had meant they had to spend an afternoon with the old sea-salt, who had taken the opportunity of being with Mendaña to air a thousand grievances.

A cloud had burst and they had to protect themselves huddled in a little hut. The carpenter had squatted at Mendaña's side, fingering a chisel and stroking and picking at his beard. Too close, Mendaña grimaced – *The old salt's pissed himself again* – At that moment Pedro Ortega hobbled past the doorway. Gallego stirred. He had been waiting for the old soldier and so he excused himself. Mendaña happily waved him away and Mahnu, who was intrigued by the movement of the New-men in their heavy water-logged boots, followed the pilot's curved form.

That was blurred by the downpour as he trotted out through the mud to catch the *maestre de campo* up at his hut.

Gallego yelled to the soldier, a salutation that was answered with a croaking hoarse moan: "Aye! How this foul weather makes me old bones complain whene'er I oblige 'em to move! Listen," Ortega said, holding his arms up and letting out a slow fart: "They groan." Gallego laughed and the old-soldier beckoned him into his hut. Inside he poured some rum: "Sarmiento's been a naughty boy. The sentries say he's been talkin' magic to the native lad," but the enthusiasm in the last phrase dampened again: "Of course it'll remain a rumour, the general 'asn't got the balls to castigate him."

Gallego scratched his damp groin: "Oh, I wouldn't say that. Captain Sarmiento's been most tedious since his failed sojourn in the jungle, and Mendaña's still not forgiven 'im."

Ortega grimaced as the rum cauterised his oesophagus: "Nor me."

Gallego's goblet had not reached his lips. He did not want to drink because he did not want to piss himself. But neither did he want the other to notice and force confession of reasons. So he struggled with his private conundrum for a delicate dozen seconds, then recalled that he had come not to drink, but to inform, and he had good news. The lightness of it made him smug: "I've talked with the captain-general concernin' yer satisfaction."

"And...?" Ortega's heart thumped. Impossible to keep the monosyllable solid.

Gallego's rotten teeth munched air: "And he's agreed to the importance of another expedition. But this time wit' you in charge," tone jerking and jumping with an excitement: "You're to circumnavigate the isle and discover whate'er else we come across," and then he was laughing: "What's more, Mendaña's decided to release the native hostage, and send him back to his village ... escorted by ... Don Pedro Sarmiento de Gamboa."

Ortega peered through the message with puckered lips while he ruminated on all of its possible significances: "So the general puts the alchemist-upstart in his rightful place at last. Runnin' the shameful errand of apologisin' for his own brutality. Fie, I like it!"

"Aye, and I'm proud to think that me own proddin' 'ad somethin' to do with the change o' tact."

"Well done, señor."

The news inspired a desire for inebriation.

Gallego, whose fear of the likely return of his leaking curse had almost diminished, sipped the rum while Ortega gulped. They drank and joked until Ortega lost consciousness, just when the jocund colloquy was turning toward drunken mate sincerity. Thus, old Gallego found himself in need of soliloquy.

On his own and sozzled he could dare to try philosophy: "So many new lands 've been seen in this savage life," he spurted at the snoring conquistador: "Now nothin' amazes," and he sniffed, unaware himself to what depths his grog inspired mind could take him. He suddenly felt his chest full of heavy air: "Nothin' is new and never 'as been," then into the soddening wall of rain, which seemed to draw an unwanted seepage down his own leg: "All's repetition. Nothin' matters, not even the grog in this cup," and he threw the remnants out through the door, before actually starting to cry: "What'll we find? Gold? Do you think so?" wiping away tears and runny mucus: "We're too old to be 'eroes, fie! Too old ..." gasping on what was as incontinent an excretion as his own urine: "Too old to be loved. They 'ate us Don Pedro ... and we're too old to love them ..." which petered out in sobs as he cried himself to sleep.

Age, or guilt, had made Gallego a depressive and an insomniac, so sleep became a precious commodity to him.

But then, in one of the rare moments when he could drop off, he was enveloped in nightmare. The ships were under attack from a savage sea monster. A giant luminous squid. Gallego, who had evoked the creature himself, was the last to die, his head being shoved into the monster's shellfish stinking beak.

He gasped when he awoke. He was lying on the beach, in the open. So now he could add somnambulism to his list of infirmities. For a moment he had mistaken the wet sand for sea - *If only ...* – he thought. He was tired of land, and of the monotony of earth. The ocean was all he wanted, even *death* by water was desirable. For a while the carpenter's trade had sufficed, but now; the brigantine was finished and it had to be launched.

At first they were three black specks on a white beach. Later, sprouting, craggy rocks. With time they were impregnated with motion. Proximity made it possible to verify life and distinguish the humanity in them. Men who were already familiar. Proximity enabled specific identification. Mendaña, Mahnu, and the young friar. They looked down as they strolled, hands clasped behind their backs as Mendaña contemplated the ubiquity of sand – *Finite, but impossible to reckon with any exactitude* – he thought, and then – *Yet where is the centre of this beach? Which grain?* – But his mind became full of another screaming debate. The settlement was full of it, divided between those who thought they had arrived at a significant place and those who rejected it.

In order to judge for himself he decided to consult the friar, proposing the argument most favoured by the opposition: "This place cannot be the gateway to the Earthly Paradise, for if it were there could be no cannibals. How could God permit it?"

The friar was radiant: "His mystery."

"But cannibals?" and he kicked some sand – *Calculate where each grain will fall: impossible, yet if God is perfect he could manage it* –

The friar stooped, reaching down to the sand to pull out a piece of dry, white, dead coral which had been protruding: "The Indians think that these rocks be endowed with miraculous powers, in accord with their shape." He dusted the sand off: "Does this not look like a man?"

Mendaña grimaced at the horny specimen - *Like a Spanish captain-general with a knife in his back* –

He had grown to despise his officers. Gallego's motives were easy to deduce. He had done nothing but mope and pester ever since they had arrived. Relations became strained, not only a struggle for power, but, on the mundane level, Mendaña was sick of Gallego's increasing fetidness, every day filthier and always drunk, while Ortega had started to prance arrogantly around the camp, as if he were already captain-general. Each day they showed less respect and more obvious animosity, and each day they gathered more adepts to their cause. But the worst of them all was Pedro Sarmiento – *They tell me the devil is in him. He has become so solitary and strange* – His audacious approaches to Mahnu – *Taking the matter into his own hand as if there were no authority above him. Everyone knows he tries to corrupt the boy. I should have him flogged* –

That morning he had called the meeting to announce his magnificent coup. His ingenious plan; to rid himself of the stinking Gallego and the cocky Ortega and humiliate Sarmiento; all at the same time. As he recalled their nescient faces and Sarmiento's snarl, a shiver ran down his spine. He reached out, grabbing the friar's hand. He needed a true friend. He felt terribly alone: "What do you think of my resolve?"

The friar in turn was inspired by the compassion expressed in the dampness of the captain-general's eyes: "Our driving force is our faith."

"And our reason?"

"A reason born from that faith," but then, seeing he had won the young general's confidence he decided to instruct as well: "You should not abandon your officers, General."

A statement which took Mendaña completely off guard. For a second he imagined it was his governor uncle scolding him and his face drooped with the heaviness of its reception: "I have tried to love them, Father," then shaking his head: "But it is they who have failed to love me. I paid my deepest respect to good Gallego, but ... he has become foul."

Which was delivered so bitterly it made the friar cringe: "He is the navigator; he should navigate. It is obvious that the landlocked life troubles him, and he's often seen with the bottle."

But contemplating his men's souls only affirmed the vanity of psychology for Mendaña: "Can one man ever know another? Take our good Sarmiento. There is a true enigma. You think him not a good Christian, yet I have seen him pray."

But the idea, instead of satisfying the friar, agitated him: "Some prayers emanate from anguished wretchedness."

Which was almost spat out. Mendaña felt the animosity and decided to abandon men and indagate in exorbitance: "And are we really at the eastern gates of the Earthly Paradise?"

"If God wills it, it shall be done."

Mendaña did not register the leaden tone. Ignorant of men's music he had merely heard words, and these inspired his own green, because budding, scientist-philosophy. He lifted his head and looked across the sea – *Progress through discovery* – he thought – *we must be here before we can go there, be there before we can go on. We have come a long way, and it has been a far too long and monotonous journey to say now that we have hardly seen nought but we have seen enough* – A conviction which momentarily took his mind off his loneliness and he even looked happy for a while for having deduced such a reasoning. But his meditation only removed him more and this made him lonelier than ever. Constant proximity made them all lonelier than ever. The disease ran rife amongst the men, and even Sarmiento became afflicted.

Drums. The crowd. Applause. Sarmiento in the background, wane. The humiliation was obvious. The cheers for Ortega and Gallego's expedition were enthusiastic, more than they had ever been for Sarmiento. When they looked at Ortega they ignored his arthritis and saw stone. They ignored all the defects so they could stop believing in the fire of Sarmiento. Fire was dangerous, they needed solidity. But Sarmiento hardly cared; he was more worried about his own frustrated search. The drummers drummed and the captain-general waved from the ship as the brigantine departed. The spectators dispersed, at first slowly, but then desperately, when another heavy shower suddenly fell.

Sarmiento was hankering after a conclusive sign. He sat on the floor of his hut, in the doorway, depressed. Before him was a wall of water. He reached out, grabbed a handful of mud and squelched it in his fist so that it dribbled out through the gaps. Then, after washing and wiping the sticky brown mess away on a pandanus leaf, he dragged his map out from under his shirt. This was his faith, but it also filled him with doubts.

He ran a finger along the lines and recalled the image of old Rodolfo doing the same. The ancient alchemist had been right in the first place, he told himself, the Terra Australis lay further south. They were close, but not there. Sarmiento had committed the worst of crimes, only believing half-truths, only heeding half of his teacher's words. The easy half.

He went back over their journey, back to the boy, the one who had fallen overboard whilst they languished in a fog. Then the light had appeared to guide them, but to guide them away, away from the Terra Australis which Rodolfo had warned had to be found first.

It made sense. The Isles of King Solomon could not be found from the sea. The strange star which had convinced them all had been crafted by gods to fool them all. Like a nesting bird it flies away from its eggs.

Then a cloud must have parted. Daylight suddenly streamed through dripping cracks into the hut. A parrot squawked and a drenched rat scurried past. Sarmiento grunted. They had to advance. It was time to leave.

However, this was followed by an equally sudden sagging of the spirit again. Lack of intellectual kinship had made him sullen and removed.

Since his falling out with Catoira the only gratifying company was Bubi.

He, at least, could speak a common language of heat and metals, a simple object or design was capable of communicating more than a week of conversations.

But Bubi was only a slave. Sarmiento needed free followers if he was to truly lead, and that seemed impossible. It was part of his nature to gravitate away from large, conglomerate bodies – *I have trafficked enough with men* – he told himself – *have felt the satiety, gloom and loneliness that it brings. It's better to suffer the solitude of distance than the emptiness of the crowd. Minds are so full of subjective nonsense that they don't know how to live, not in this universe; and how pathetic are their own universes, the universes of men's minds –*

Not even these arrogant thoughts replenished him. Unless he found what he had come for he had failed, and the proximity of failure made him dry. He became snappy, even with the friends he had almost established – *They're all such innocent fools* – he thought, as if by diminishing men he could redeem himself.

Only the enigma nature held any interest. More and more often he stayed alone, collecting rocks, shells, herbs, amphibians, insects; the minimal becoming ever more significant. Observe and feel, then meditate. Lift the veil, understand. Understand his own failure.

Eventually the order came from the lonely Mendaña that the miserable Sarmiento should return their anguished prisoner to the village in Tiaraubi from where he had been sequestered. Sarmiento took the stoical Bubi, nine other reasonably happy carriers and twenty irascible soldiers with him. The peeved Catoira's exclusion was deliberate and seemed mutually satisfying. But as the cage was unlocked it was Bubi's turn to be upset, mumbling under his breath in his Bubi language: "And so this nigger goes back to the jungle. Only the Africans, it seems, are fit to be called slaves," but then reconciling himself to the hopeless condition: "Only the African knows how to work."

Sarmiento stared in between the gnarled, bent poles that enclosed the prisoner who was squatting, quite still, in a corner. The wooden gaol creaked as the prisoner's head inclined to the left. His sad, dry face was so dark it blended into the still night, so that only moon reflecting eyes and teeth were clear. But to Sarmiento's fevered mad mind it suddenly became a vivid, haunting head. A pale shivering face. Salacay.

He shuddered. He could smell the old magus again, and it made him nauseous. He shook his head and the doubt away. It was only an illusion, he told himself and it angered him, enthusing a will for tragedy. Then another hand passed a flaming torch to him. He lifted it and the prisoner tried to turn from the blinding light, screwing his eyes tightly shut.

Sarmiento took an oily key that slid easily into the padlock, which made a cracking noise of release. Unlocked, the now gnarled and bent segments of the bamboo press sprang apart. The flaming torch whooshed and Sarmiento reached inward with his free arm toward the infirm, squatting Islander to run a finger along a deep wrinkle dropping down from a corner of an eye. He traced it, following its connections, like a child trying to solve a maze in a puzzle book.

The Islander shivered and gulped a thick lump of catarrh. When Sarmiento grabbed his wrist, the other man's pulse suddenly throbbed through his own body. He dragged him out, pushing him into the arms of two helmeted men who received him. These gagged him and then pulled him across the deck.

Below, beside the ship, a moonlit longboat. Silvery helmets gleamed. An order had been given demanding silence, and the clonking of wood as oars were gathered made many of them jump. The prisoner grimaced around his gag as he took the proffered rope to clamber down. The coarse hemp burned his palms.

Where were these cruel men taking him now?

Juan López was at the prow of that longboat, peering desperately toward the beach, his mind a confused rumble. Next to him stood the soldier who had received the dart in his face, still with an unhealed hole in his cheek.

He closed his eyes and saw the arrow flapping again from that soldier's bloody bloated cheek. And then a more gruesome image: Alonso Martín receiving the missile in the leg. Alonso, who now lay dying on the deck. Juan had seen his infected leg seeping a brown, foul smelling pus. The flesh of it was swelling, and gas bubbles were forming under the skin

– *Gangrene* – I knew the word, Juan did not. I knew of the necessity for amputation, Juan did not. He could do nothing, merely smell again the putrefying flesh, hear again his wails of suffering and see once more

Alonso's death door eyes staring into the auxiliary dimension. Juan López shuddered. An antithetical soldier's mettle – *Perhaps the next arrow, the next spear, will be for me* – he told himself.

A thought that Simón Arragocés could smell. He taunted the boy: "They're out there waitin' for us, you know. I 'ope you've been keeping your sword well sharp."

Juan wanted to cry, but the soldier with the hole in his cheek turned to attack the sergeant's arrogance and defend the novice: "You should not wish the war on us, Sergeant. It could bring bad luck."

Arragocés spat: "Bah! Let it bring whate'er it wants. The only thing I'm afraid of is fear. As for you youngsters, you've got a lot of fightin' to do before you can call yourselves real soldiers."

Which the hole-in-cheek soldier took offence to: "I volunteered for this mission despite my wound, a proof of bravery which you seem ..."

An obviously evolving provocation which was silenced by Sarmiento. They were going ashore under the cover of dark, a ridiculous notion if they were to announce themselves with roaring argument.

A heavy thick fog delayed the dawn, limiting vision to less than a few metres. The sharp pain had returned to Sarmiento's liver. He marched with clenched teeth, at times tight shut eyes. Hot with his fever, the world seemed to be unearthly still around him, even the movement of his own troops, and he knew them to be moving, but they were perceived like the pixilated images of some jerky framed animation. An arm would hang by someone's hip, then three seconds later it would be touching the man's beard, but without any apparent progression in between. After a while the captain had to stop and hold himself up against a tree. The thick fog slipped around him as the troops and slaves trudged on up the track. His removal, he realised, had gone unnoticed.

The idea generated a second of panic, dissipated by the realisation of the texture of the tree. His palm was rubbing it when a vegetable inspired wisdom held him suddenly still, gaping, like a cod in some murky, weedy shallow. He had sniffed something. An unmistakable odour, lingering on his palate.

The tree he was leaning against was massive. Thick vines ran like snaking veins up the trunk. The fog masked the enormity to him, but I could trace its rise into an arboreal flying buttress.

His mind was obsessed with the odoriferous emanation. It was so familiar, and he could taste it. Bitter, yet desirable. Then he remembered. The potion he had taken from Salacay. The same smell.

He looked closer at the trunk of the tree. White blobs seemed to glow. Snow white blisters on the black trunk.

They were slimy to the touch. A kind of fungi. Scratching some of it off he held it to his nose.

Unmistakable. This was undoubtedly the ingredient that had been in Salacay's potion.

He licked it. It numbed his tongue. A sensation that spread. First freezing the senses, then reanimating them, much sharper than before.

He grappled for more. The trunk, he realised, was oozing great lumps of it.

He had a pouch that he filled, then stuffed more into his pockets.

Meanwhile, the mist had deepened instead of clearing and when he had harvested enough and wanted to move on he found himself grappling through it, surprised that such a thick cloud did not have any tangible substance.

He needed to catch up with the rest, but he also had to step carefully. He knew that to his right, just off the path and invisible, was the steep drop of a cliff.

But as he edged forward, his head throbbing with his own pulse, he became aware of a rustling sound – *My men* – he thought, but then considering again – *or an enemy* – confirmed when a figure, a grisly blur through the opaque air, flashed past.

Reason froze him. His magician's logic convinced him that it had been a ghost, Salacay's miserable spirit in search of its revenge, teasing him to set chase, tempting him over the cliff.

His pulse raced the breath out of him, and he was just about to shout for help from the platoon when a real material mass thumped into him, knocking him off his feet.

The diminishing of the fog made most of the men in the platoon moan or sigh. They had been staggering forward for unbearable hours in grey regions of solitude, but when the fog lifted, it merely increased their trepidation. The fog had been a pleasant cool invisibility. But now the heat of the climbing sun had sucked their cover into gas, stripping the platoon bare and slapping them with the silent screams of its morning light. Now they could see how narrow the track they were clambering along really was. They had been marching in Indian file. But this meant that no one noticed the disappearance of one of their members; that their captain was not with them.

The prisoner wondered where he was being taken, and why.

Balls of moisture shivered and then dropped from leaves of ferns. The teeth of a palm plant seemed to bite his naked arm. He shuddered, but not because of the scratch, rather because the valley was suddenly filled with a scream. It was distant, but the platoon murmured and clattered as they pressed together into a huddle. There was a crack. A harquebus shot.

Then Sergeant Arragocés barked: "Where's the captain, pray?"

Streaks of colour, the reds and yellows of the warrior's war paint, became a blur in Sarmiento's drugged mind. The colours suddenly flew forward and Sarmiento had to un-befuddle his senses in order to discern the awful reality that was coming at him. Squinting into his hallucination revealed the real shape of an authentic wooden hatchet that was about to drop.

Once the real had been grasped again, he realised that he was slipping over backwards and that his harquebus had dropped from his shoulder. Instinct inspired him to reach for the charging assailant's wrists and insert a boot into his stomach. Then he lifted the leg and flicked the attacker over. Vegetation ripped as the Islander's body hit stems and thorns.

Sarmiento rose, turned and reached for his assailant, who was awkwardly lifting his own scratched and smarting body. Grabbing the Islander's ears, he thumped his helmeted forehead into his yellow painted nose, which cracked.

The assailant then became an all-rattling victim as he pushed away and fled, but Sarmiento was quickly after him, knocking him off his feet with a diving tackle at his ankles.

The Islander fell into plants again, a wall of tall, yellow reeds that cracked around him. His brow was cut, adding to the mess of his nose, he spat, began to shout.

Sarmiento kicked him in the ribs, under the heart, which silenced him, and a sudden wind sighed through the dead grass.

There was a gasping pause for several minutes, listening, watching, sniffling. Sarmiento slid his shining steel dagger between his teeth and fixed the native with a hate exuding stare. The Islander trembled, resigning himself to his conqueror's intense gaze. But the harder Sarmiento was staring the more the brightly painted man paled into the transposed, hallucinatory image of Salacay.

Sarmiento's arm trembled as he gritted his teeth against the sharp steel, to bite through the pain in his liver like a baby on a teething biscuit. A ghost from the drug now possessed the warrior, who had become a Salacay with enormous arms.

Meanwhile, Sarmiento was fishing with a trembling hand in the long grass for his harquebus. He had carried it loaded. If he could maintain the other transfixed long enough to light the taper he could be rid of the attacker, could be rid of his ghost.

Bubi had told him: "*The only way to enjoy deliverance from a haunting spirit, is to tempt it into some other human form and then kill it. Its soul will be carried with the newly dead soul, away into the other world...*" He could sense the other's freezing fear, but he knew that he would have to move sooner or later.

The Islander swallowed, he could taste his own blood and feel a strange energy surging through him, but he retarded the immediate urges to attack. He had to think, he told himself. He had dropped his own dagger leaving him no other option than to jump the New-man. If he could leap and pull the dagger from his mouth he could stab the Invader with his own blade. He had noticed how the metal shell of Sarmiento's breast plate gaped open under the arms. If he could manage a lucky, accurate blow? If he could pierce his heart?

Sarmiento saw it coming, his harquebus was already up. The Islander fell back. The image itself had knocked the air out of him. The alchemist grinned into the explosion as the lead thumped into the gasping target's kneecap. The subsequent scream was silenced by smashing the butt of the harquebus against the jaw.

The bone cracked. The victim's eyelids dropped and his limbs sagged.

Paralysed as he watched the invader push powder and shot with a poking rod down the barrel, horrified as he helplessly watched him light the taper.

The next shot in the other kneecap could have been considered unnecessary, but for Sarmiento it was part of the ritual. It meant that Salacay's ghost would stay with the cripple there, in that spot, with his agony, until he died. Bubi had promised it.

Sarmiento turned away then returned again to slash the Islander's throat, just to make sure. As he did he felt a sudden wind blow into his face that he was convinced to have come from the dying man's navel.

He gasped and prodded his hip for the fungi-full pouch.

It was still there.

For a second he thought he had heard Salacay's voice, a gurgled scream, then the fog seemed to whirl and part, as if the spiralling force of that rising spirit had dug an escape hole through it. Sunlight slapped his cheek, his eyes squeezed shut and he dropped to his knees. The victim's blood was hot over his hand, soaking his trousers.

Sergeant Arragocés, who had suddenly realised he was the senior in command, took ten soldiers and five slaves and returned down the track in search of Sarmiento. The rest of the men stayed by a grassy clearing they had found. Huddling.

The prisoner, meanwhile, shivered. His mind was full of confused sentiment for the village of his home that lay so close. He had deduced that the New-men were taking him home, but had no idea why, although he suspected these cruel people's motives to be cruel – *All men are cruel* – he thought, and he remembered how, as a child, things had been different.

Then their village had been close to the sea and they had lived as much from fishing as from farming. Until a couple of canoes had come, from Meta, he remembered.

The visitors had appeared on a trading trip, they had said, and his own people had brought out shells to swap for the yams in the boats. But when the palm leaves covering the supposed yams had been lifted, those who were gazing in were caught by the damning stare of a dozen decapitated heads and very soon their own blood was gurgling out of their necks.

The people from Meta raced through the village killing everyone they caught.

The chief at that time was Toraya, a generous and happy man. He too was killed and his head was hacked from his body. The torso was then thrown into the sea while the head was stuck on a stick in the head hunters' canoe.

After that the villagers moved their home inland up the mountain slopes. There they had always been surrounded by potentially hostile tribes, but none of them were head hunters and their lives had been relatively peaceful until the night the turtle-dragon god had arrived.

He looked up and shivered again. The hill tops had darkened with trailing clouds.

By the time Sarmiento and Arragocés had found each other it was raining again. Pouring by the time they had returned to the others. Arragocés had expected fury from the commander, but instead they found Sarmiento in good spirits. The drug from the fungi was taking effect and the constant pain in his liver had vanished, as had his fever and headaches. But the captain's smile and mirth perturbed the sergeant even more: "We heard gun shots, Captain ... and screams."

Sarmiento slapped the nervous Arragocés's shoulder. Water logged fabric squelched: "An ambush, fie," which was expulsed through an enormous grin: "But don't worry yourself, there are none of the savages left."

Which left the sergeant awestruck with a dripping, drooping lip.

When the people of Tiaraubi realised that the turtle-dragon god was returning they abandoned their labour of reconstruction and prepared for an exhibition of strength. None of them wanted to fight, none of them wanted to be heroes, but they felt they had little choice.

The turtle-dragon god, they deduced, was an evil spirit. Like the head hunters they had come to pillage and kill. In the last raid they had taken all, so this time there could only be lives to take – *They want to eat us* – it was deduced – *Our souls are the only things left for us to give. They will enslave our spirits with their magic and we'll be made eternal servants to their dead ancestors* –

Conches were blown and spears and bows were gathered. And when the turtle-dragon god advanced into their ruined town they formed a similar huddle in the square. But with each step forward from the turtle-dragon the Tiaraubi army retreated two. Until Sarmiento took the prisoner by the hand and stepped forward, smiling. He began waving his hand, indicating that they should come to him, but they were too scared. So he pushed the prisoner forward, making another waving hand motion indicating that he should go to them. When the prisoner understood this he suddenly turned.

Realisation that he was not going to be killed drained him. His arms sagged and he became full of choking emotion. He cried and then went to Sarmiento and embraced him.

It was a grey but dry morning on the beach. Mendaña was kneeling, Mahnu beside him attending to every detail. The sun became tentatively apparent, like a torch light through a grey cloth. The sand was a damp rug below a wafer thin surface of dryness. After a short while it chilled Mendaña's knees – *The priests are right to complain, we must build a church* – he thought, then clasped his hands and bent his neck and tried to concentrate on the mass he was attending.

He made a concerted effort to be fervent. His reverence was new, but imagined by himself to be a profound, intense bond. Nevertheless, his mind wandered to and fro from the preacher's delivery to the imagined sermon he would have preferred.

While the friar's homily droned monotonously, John 6:55: "'*Whoso eateth my flesh, and drinketh my blood, hath eternal life...*'" Mendaña mumbled thanks, to their saviour, for delivering them to the promised land and relieving him of his pestering officers.

Mahnu mumbled with him, without expressing anything intelligible.

Mendaña smiled. Now the work of God - *the one true God, the God of love* – could finally begin in earnest.

The friar, Francisco de Gálvez, knelt with a bible in one hand, an aspergillum in the other and sang a Latin prayer. The simple pyx was opened. He pinched the Host, lifting it, before dropping it onto Mendaña's proffered tongue: "Corpus Christi."

Mahnu's own tongue wagged like a dog.

Mendaña sighed – *The poor lad, how can we make him understand that he cannot taste our Lord's body until his own has been purified* – and then – *When Byje hugged me what he really wanted to do was embrace the Lord* – competing with the friar priests' voices droning in the back of his mind, until all his new fervour and passion was suddenly blown away by the frantic beat of a sentry's drum.

Mendaña groaned and shook his head. There was chaos around him. Soldiers jumping to officers' screams and the steady rhythm of drums, kicking up sand as they ran to form lines. Officers pointing out to sea. Canoes. Eight of them. Long and brightly painted. These were rounding the headland and approaching rapidly. Each one was replete with warriors wielding bows, spears and wooden maces.

Mahnu screamed and started to run.

Mendaña had to grab his arm and call a sailor over to restrain him. Then he reached for Gregorio Gonzalez's sleeve. The brute suddenly seemed attractive: "Do you think their intention is violent, good Gregorio?"

Who chewed the inside of his cheek and shook his head. Tinder-boxes began clicking frantically. Sparking tapers fizzed.

"No!" shouted Mendaña to the harquebusiers.

One soldier spat. Another scratched his groin. Gregorio Gonzalez had sand in his boot which irritated.

At the prow of the most advanced canoe stood a strong, singular figure with a long spear. He jumped unswervingly from his craft to crunch his bare feet into the beach and walk directly up to Mendaña. The Spaniard pushed his chin and chest out, but, when the warrior thrust his spear into the sand, a spasm shuddered through his gut. The Islander roared and threw his arms in the air, waving and screaming what seemed like a harsh monologue in a language they had never heard before. Nevertheless, he was soon able to make it understood that he came from the west, and that he was at war with Sanba.

Mendaña turned to where Mahnu was struggling in the sailor's arms. His heart sank, but he did not dare issue verbal orders, instead he looked around and tried to communicate with facial expressions, querying looks that seemed to ask if the order to fire should be given before things became complicated. He even started to raise his arm and the harquebusiers' fingers began twitching in anticipation. But, before Mendaña's command could be confirmed, Gregorio Gonzalez had shuffled forward.

"It seems that 'e desires a pact, General," interpreted the sailor: "He'll make 'is peace with us, then an alliance to crush Byje and 'is people."

Mendaña looked askance. Something in the tone used by Gregorio Gonzalez made him suspect a plot; as if this rude visit had been planned.

Meanwhile the Islander was gesturing to his men to come forward with gifts. Several stomachs rumbled in the ranks of hungry soldiers. Some Islanders laid yams wrapped in edible leaves on the beach, while others dragged a large woven basket from their canoe. They built a fire. Slabs of meat were brought out.

The soldiers and sailors began licking their lips. Until one of the slabs, which had, from a distance, seemed like a leg of suckling pork, was seen to flap. At first they wondered what the loose flesh was. With proximity understanding evolved. They were looking at dangling human fingers, quite obviously a child's arm.

The Melanesian chief himself proffered it under Mendaña's nose, yelling: "Naleha, Naleha," which was in the same language that Byje had spoken, and Mendaña knew it meant: *"Eat, eat!"*

The captain-general's first instinct was to give the order to fire, but then common sense and the numerical superiority of the Cannibals encouraged a subtler reflection.

He yelled for a shovel which he took himself and began clumsily digging a hole in the sand, more as catharsis than vesting the leader's role.

He slid the back of his sweating arm across his sweating brow and pushed back his long, blonde, dishevelled hair. This stood up, adding to the pathetic aspect of his exertion.

The little dead limb, lying in its black armed cradle, was still fresh and soft, and quivering, evoking images of the child who had not long carried it: of the horror it had suffered; the horror of the anticipation; the horror of the ripping, cutting contact just before the desperate soul had abandoned it.

Mendaña imagined the arm once attached to Mahnu's shoulder. He saw Mahnu's mouth-open face, heard Mahnu's screams, Mahnu amongst the headless chickens of his dream, their nipping claws running over Mahnu's feet.

Mendaña himself jumped back out of the nightmare. He had wanted to believe as the Franciscans had told him he should, to have faith. But not just in Christ, but in humanity, in all of humanity, in all of the nature that was God's creation ... but this was too great a transgression – *These savages were spawned in Satan's den* – he thought – *Anything that eats the flesh of its own has become another* – and he imagined the taste of blood in his own mouth – *Sweet!* – he realised and then roared at his own transgression. That he could be capable of such a thought meant that the demon before him was trying to bewitch him.

The idea made him brave and he wrenched the infant's limb out of the chief's hands, flinging it into the depression he had just dug, whilst screaming: "Teo naleha arra!" (I won't eat it) "Teo naleha arra."

(d) the other Solomons

i Moving On

The brigantine, with Ortega and Gallego, was away for thirty days. They reached the largest of the Solomon Islands and called it *Guadalcanal* after Ortega's hot and lazy hometown in Andalusia. They arrived and put names to it. *We are the centre*, they deluded themselves, filling their boat up with whatever they could, and in the afternoon they returned to Santa Isabel.

At the home base in Estrella Bay, that month was thirty long days of apprehension.

After the encounter with the cannibals, Mendaña had not left the ship: "Hang out flags," he had said, pushing a heavy chin into the back of a hand that drooped from its limp articulation: "The ship's becoming such a drab place." He was tired of that island. He wanted to move on.

As such, Mahnu was also told to return to his village, though at first the Islander had refused and wrapped his arms around the main mast, like an infant on its mother's leg.

Mendaña was not surprised by the boy's attitude. After all, they had been trying for more than a month to seduce him into the Christian world that they deluded themselves to be actually living in. However, diplomatically it was undesirable that he stayed. So they tried to persuade the boy to return with realism: "The life at sea is a slavish one. Here you've been our guest, prithee, and treated according to your noble standing, but if you were to journey with us, you would have no acknowledged rank and would labour like any other common sailor. And the voyage would be endless for you, across uncharted seas, fraught with hidden, unexpected perils. You would be a year older before you could ever see Spain. Could you really endure such a sojourn? No, lad, it would be better for you to respect your country and your name."

A conclusion which had probably filled Mendaña with more sentiment than it did Mahnu. And when he had watched the lad, still clad in Gaspar's suit, trudging mopishly across the beach, he felt a wave of tremendous loss grip him and even shake a tear from him.

Finally, Sarmiento was sent with twenty soldiers to escort Mahnu home, bring Trejo back from Sanba, and gather supplies for their own homeward voyage.

When they arrived, they found Byje's settlement completely transformed. The village had expanded into a huge town, swelled by the other Polynesians on the Island who had flocked to the *centre*. A centre which was now fenced, as the Spaniards had fenced their own settlement on the beach. The dusty squares, however, had been filled with groaning Melanesian bodies, tied to stakes or pushed into bamboo cages which were obvious models of the prison that had been built on the ship. Pigs were being rounded up and slaughtered, chickens chased and beheaded. When the Spaniards entered, the Sanbans made the same bowing gestures that they had seen the New-men do amongst themselves.

Seseboco came out grinning under a large, wide brimmed and feathered hat that had once belonged to one of the pilots. He looked for Sarmiento: "Welcome," he said in Spanish: "Welcome to feast. Yesterday Sanba won big battle."

When Sarmiento and the others were ordered by the thunder of Mendaña's cannon to return to the ships they took twenty food bearing natives with them and retrieved Trejo. The soldiers with Sarmiento laughed at him, for he was naked, having lost his clothes, and had developed a barbaric taste for painting his body and face.

They all said fond farewells to Mahnu, but they would not be rid of him so soon. As they descended the boy trudged behind with two of his young friends. They had decided to run away from their homeland forever.

"I speak Castilian now," Mahnu argued when they found him, like an abandoned dog with two mongrel pups, once again on the ship: "You will go to other islands. Meet people. How will you speak? I will be the translator. And I will teach these boys to speak your language too. They will be translators too."

Mendaña could not help but admire the lad's stubborn determination, and he let them all stay.

Then the brigantine drifted slowly into Estrella Bay. So tired once they had reached the bay, no one able to row, they just drifted. Those aboard it who were conscious had sighed when they saw the harbour and called it home, for then it *was* home, and they had returned.

Other, more bored than tired men on the *Almiranta*, lifted themselves off the deck and staggered to the rails to wave welcoming arms at the returning expedition. They hurled ropes over the sides, to let them dangle and be caught by the arms bobbing upward from the battered boat below. There were exhausted cries of joy. Old Pedro Ortega had been the only one with the strength to climb himself, the others had to be lifted. But once they were aboard the mothership again, with their throats wetted and their stomachs filled, the vanguard explorers' tongues were wagging and busily relating their adventures and discoveries.

"We sailed around this isle ..." one of them croaked.

"Sailing eastward for six leagues," whined another.

"... and rounding the coast we saw many new isles ahead of us ..."

"We approached one in which there was a canoe and three houses ..."

"Seven soldiers were sent ashore ..."

"We took food, chased away the savages ..."

"Killed one of them ..."

"The rest of the Indians fled ..."

"We sailed on ..."

"There was a storm ..."

"The mainmast nearly snapped ..."

"We navigated through reefs at night guided by the phosphorescent glow of the coral ..."

"Sometimes we went ashore ..."

"One day we were attacked by a hundred savages ..."

"We saw a very large island eastward that the natives called Malaita"

"But we didn't go there ..."

"We sailed south ..."

"Discovered fertile islands ..."

"Where the people go completely naked ..."

"Don't even cover their private parts ..."

"Completely naked ..."

"And cannibals ..."

"We were attacked ..."

"There must have been seven hundred of them ..."

"We killed many savages that day ..."

"That was Florida Island ..."

"We called it Florida Island ..."

"Then we discovered a very large island ..."

"Guadalcanal ..."

Byje knew, when he heard that the brigantine had returned, that the New-men, his protectors, would soon be gone.

The idea made him nervous. The New-men's magic was powerful and it had won them many battles. He gathered his weather magicians and canoe magicians and told them to prepare spells to keep the New-men in the bay. Then he went down to the ships himself with these magicians, bearing an offering of coconuts and breadfruit and a huge turtle.

Once at the side of the *Almiranta* they began chanting their spells and rubbing yams against the ship's hull so that it would take root itself. None of this magic worked. The next day the wind blew up in the right direction and the New-men set sail with Mahnu and his friends, without even saying goodbye.

Mendaña had decided to increase his empire by conquering Ortega and Gallego's Guadalcanal. Byje had become irrelevant.

– The essence of Christ's teaching was forgiveness – Catoira concluded one day *– and yet the Church is full of vengeful Jew and Moor haters who have never forgiven their enemies' mothers for giving birth to them –* Forgive and forget they say. Forgiving is noble, forgetting is easier.

With the turtle-dragon god gone, the allied Melanesian tribes on Mulu Mulu gathered and prepared a combined offensive. Their revenge was implacable. Within a week Sanba no longer existed and the souls of Byje and his people became slaves to Meta and Bene's spirit ancestors.

---

ii Guadalcanal

The ships reached the island of Guadalcanal on a bright sunny morn. The still, blue sea was freckled by silver flashes and the *Capitana* and *Almiranta* looked tall and imperial, anchored in a sheltered port behind a point. The soldiers were already on the beach, gathered in groups, not only happy to be there on such a perfect sun-drenched day, but relieved to be still alive after the nightmare crossing they had made from Santa Isabel to be there. Between them and the ships croaked the longboat. The officers and priests inside were huddled and silent, enjoying the still air and the view of the new place that seemed like Paradise after the Hell that had just been endured.

Gallego was conspicuous in the bunch because of his grimace. He was not only hapless and exhausted like the rest of them, but also fierce. When he caught Mendaña's gaze, his became a bitter attack. The voyage from Estrella Bay to this Guadalcanal had been a knife blade crossing, perhaps no worse than the rest of the voyage, but with this stupid boy general *– If not for me we would be on the reef –* he told himself. If they had been lucky, it was only because the captain-general had not sunk them yet *– The assassin general –* he considered, and decided that Mendaña was trying to kill off all his enemies *– He put Gregorio Gonzalez in charge of the brigantine because he hated him –* he recalled *– Hates his kibes, so he put him in the creaking vessel with four sailors and two soldiers, hopelessly undermanned, and told him to sail! –* "If not for a full moon!" he had roared to an unwitting ally, Sarmiento: "We would've had an arse full of coral, fie!" Which was probably true. Gallego had been up all night, keeping the watch alert, guiding them around the patches of white bottom sea. Then he remembered how Mendaña had squealed when they lost sight of the brigantine: "That fool Gonzalez!"

Fool – remembered Gallego – *He thinks all of us to be fools, yet how could such an idiot know what intelligence was, or even common sense* – and he recalled the force by which he had had to deliver his arguments to convince Mendaña to wait for the brigantine.

Then when the boat finally caught up, he himself had thrown a rope to Gonzalez so that they could tow them. An act which would later become *reprehensible*. Reprehensible, because later in the gale, a gale that had blown gradually up against them, but growing stronger by the hour, Mendaña had panicked and given an uncorroborated order to tack, suddenly – *A stupid tack* – recalled Gallego. The brigantine was wrenched right past the prow of the ship – *We almost ran right through it!* – The *Capitana's* anchor became caught in the boat's rigging. The ship shuddered and they thought at first that they had run aground. At every third roll of the ship the sea spilled over the decks. The rails went under and broke. Only when one of Gallego's slaves had managed his master's order and cut the ropes was the ship able to right itself. The men in the brigantine had to throw themselves out into the swirling soup sea, clutching the hawsers to haul themselves up. But when the brigantine thumped against the ship's hull the men had their dangling legs smashed. At the same time a boy dropped from the mizzen mast and was swallowed by the ocean, a sight which sent Mendaña screaming at Gallego: "Why did you tie that boat to us?!"

Gallego remembered how his heart thumped and his hands had clenched into fists: "Should I have abandoned them, fie!"

- And we would have lost the brigantine if I hadn't been sharp – he remembered. If he had not had his slaves jump into action with grappling hooks, fishing for the swirling boat, as if struggling for a huge bonito. They held it, and saved it – *Because of me* –

Mendaña registered the obvious animosity, but took little notice. He had grown accustomed to such grizzly expression. Though Gallego was unique that perfect day he knew that in the afternoon it would be someone else who was peeved. To console himself he remembered a friar's advice – *A leader will always have enemies. They will despise you when you are weak, love you when you're strong, or hate you when you're strong and love your weaknesses* – but then shocked himself with a question – *What is my strength?* –

When they bumped into the shore there had been a rumbling that evolved into booming shouts and the bellowing of drum. Then the chirp of the fife as the happy soldiers shuffled over sand into lines. Slaves jerked a cross onto their collarbones, becoming black Christs on their way to a low lying Golgotha.

Perhaps it was the music that brought the Islanders out. They kept their distance, wondering at the real significance of the effigy that the New-men had brought: "Our gods will not be pleased," they murmured, and wondered how much provocation would be needed before the Octopus-spirit would be insulted enough to stir itself, wrap its giant tentacles around the crouching bunch and sweep them out to sea.

But when no cephalopod or any other sea creature revealed itself, one of the war magicians there expressed the idea that the gods expected them to defend their honour. The New-men were only men after all: "So why should gods be expected to intervene?"

For the Christian friars on the hill it was the devil's possession of their pagan souls that inspired the Islanders' attack: "Satan cannot bear the sight of the Holy Cross," said one.

"Let us pray," roared another.

"Vexilla regis prodeunt."

But before the first strophe could be finished, the first arrows had dropped at their feet. The Islanders were taking the offence against their gods seriously and some three hundred of them had gathered around the hill to push the New-men into the sea.

Sensing the seriousness of their intentions, Mendaña issued the order to fire.

Within seconds the first tapers had been lit and, after the smoke had faded, the first two Islanders had been killed. But instead of scaring them away it inspired the natives to charge. This forced the New-men into a circle of shields, which they were able to shove down the hill, using their own mass. Once the New-men had been pushed out to the way, the Islanders uprooted the cross and carried it away.

* * *

In order to recover their crucifix Mendaña forgot about Christian forgiveness, ordered Sarmiento to prepare an army for an expedition into the jungle.

Mendaña himself went ahead of the ranks, in the role of the brave leader. He carried his plumed morion under his arm and his ornate breastplate had been polished. They marched across a flat plain through palm groves, then up a steep ridge. From the top they could discern a cool valley. Some thirty neat villages were on the slopes, amongst trees and fields of crops, organised in such a way that they could easily be watered. Each slope had a stream and was full of orchards and gardens of breadfruit, yams and paw-paw trees. Before one of these settlements, a larger one with some seventy houses, the troops were ordered to run ahead and form ranks. Sarmiento ordered the drummers to sound the battle roll.

Stirred by reverberations, Mendaña traded his morion for a harquebus and once more placed himself at the front of the troops. There he raised his arm, a signal for the drummers to cease. All remained still, swamped by an eerie calm apart from the shrill and constant chirp of the cicadas, and a monotonous cuckoo.

Mendaña ordered the march forward into the confines of the village. Sarmiento advised caution, but it was only when all were completely within the compound that they caught their first glimpses of the Islanders. These had always been there, hidden in the jungle. Realising that they were surrounded, Sarmiento made silent gestures, understood by the troops who formed a tight block around their general. All eyes and arms were aimed outwards, while Mendaña cowered into the middle. However, the expected attack never came, or not in the expected way. Instead, a painted figure, naked except for a grass belt with a gourd tied to it, leapt out alone, brandishing a spear.

Sarmiento ordered the men to hold their fire.

The Islander prodded his spear into the ground, dragging it around to draw a circle. Then he began jumping, shouting, screaming and taking mouthfuls of a liquid from the gourd which he subsequently spat, always in the direction of a gasping Mendaña. The other Islanders, hidden, joined in the vociferations, forming a terrible chant. Mendaña felt giddy as did many of the other soldiers. Sarmiento wrenched a smouldering harquebus from one of the groggy troops and fired into the flaming circle. As he did, the witch doctor leaped and screamed. The noise made Mendaña jump, he shook his head then squealed the order to fire. The ranks exploded, and when the smoke had lifted all the Islanders had gone.

Ransacking the huts, they found a number of clay pots, the first they had seen on the islands. These bore curvilinear motives which resembled eggs and fish and people's faces, and which fascinated Sarmiento who was reminded of Greek pottery designs he had seen in Cadíz.

Afterwards they ate breadfruit and slept a siesta before leaving along another wider, shady path that came out on a flat ridge. Most of the natives encountered fled from them, only one was curious enough to endure the aliens. Mendaña rewarded him by presenting a handkerchief. The Islander grinned at the gesture and put it on his head to keep the sun off.

After walking another two and a half miles in the shade of the trees, the Spaniards came out into a gorge with a fast flowing river. They stopped to eat some cake, then returned to the ships without the crucifix they had gone looking for.

"Don't worry," whispered Sarmiento to Mendaña: "These pots we've found are far more significant than planting crosses. Where do you think these ceramics have come from? From the south, señor. From the continent. The Terra Australis Incognita. Where else?"

The young Alvaro de Mendaña had grown very old very quickly and his chivalric romanticism had faded into a realistic vision of authentic glory. He started to realise who he really was: the captain-general of a fleet that had crossed the Great South Sea to discover a brand new world – *My name* – Mendaña considered – *will soon be as famous as Columbus* – But, in order for the Solomons to be as important as the Americas, something of value had to be discovered there. He had been lazy, he realised. He had overlooked the most important thing, which was to find the importance – *But what is important in a world of savages?* – Yet, when Sarmiento insisted on the importance of the clay pots, it made him consider that other greater discoveries had still to be made.

"What if there should be gold on these isles, marry?" he announced, standing open legged with his fists on his hips. It was a passion inspiring conditional, blurted in front of his priests and officers: "The fact that they do not *seem* to possess any precious metals does not necessarily imply that none exist here," he said, whilst his fingers ran over a gold chain. Then he began to pace the deck as his tongue and lips struggled to turn his racing thoughts into voice: "They *seemed* to have very little pottery here also, yet we have discovered examples, enough of it to indicate that they are aware of the technology, which may imply that there is a civilisation in this region, comparable to the Aztecs or Incas," and he looked to Sarmiento, who assented by raising an eyebrow and slowly nodding. The general slurped air into lungs: "Aware, and for that reason there should be a thriving enterprise," dropping his voice into an indicative gravity: "There is certainly an abundance of clay," then lifting his nose and with it his pitch: "And yet the examples are scarce, pray," becoming exorbitant: "So, I say, that the argument that they've not found any use for gold does not certify that there is none," and he even thumped a fist against wood to punctuate the end of his ratiocination.

In order to put his theory to the test, Mendaña announced two decisions at a general meeting: The first was to send one of the younger military captains, Muñoz Rico, with Hernán Gallego, away again in the brigantine in search of more land. The younger man grinned at the news, but it only made the old pilot groan. He had still not recovered from the last storm and his breath whooshed like a gentle surf when he received the order: "Have we not found enough, General?" Delivered with so much cynicism that Mendaña started to pull at his glove, and for a moment I thought there was going to be a face slapping challenge.

Instead the general lowered his pitch, until it sounded sadistic: "You'll take thirty men with you. Fourteen harquebusiers and some shield bearers. And one of the Sanban boys as a translator." Forceful enough to quell any rejoinder.

The second decision was to mount a prospecting expedition in search of gold: "I've decided, pray, that the venerable old trooper, Andrés Nuñez, will lead that expedition," which came as a complete surprise to everyone, especially Nuñez. This military man was a slower, stupider version of Ortega and, although he had some supposed experience in the mercury mines in Peru, this new arthritic leader was more comfortable with harquebuses than spades. His main expertise lay in designating the punishment of lackadaisical slaves, a listless and capricious job for a lacklustre man. Nuñez's arthritis, made grave and constant by humidity, inhibited his ability to march. Like Ortega he was a stiff hipped wobbler, but *unlike* Ortega, he was completely lacking in any sense of self pride. Pedro Ortega would overcome his disability with gritted teeth will, but Andrés Nuñez, on the other hand, was happy enough eating, sleeping and defecating.

Out of respect for his age he had, until then, been allotted a sentry's post, and he had escaped all the expeditionary ventures and any combat. But now Mendaña was making him a leader and sending him off into the jungle.

As if to confirm the inherent madness in the decision, the captain-general made a further slip: "You'll take twenty-two soldiers with you, to guard the miners."

The poor old soldier, now stirred out of his chronic somnolence by the attention and the sudden, painful intrusion of the future into his otherwise present-continuum life, echoed the last word: "Miners." A gruff, unnatural voice that almost sounded like a question.

Others were more definite in expressing the interrogative: "Miners?!"

Fr Francisco was sympathetic: "We didn't come with miners, General."

Leaving Mendaña trembling dumb.

It was actually Sarmiento who saved him: "What the general means, is that, many men here have campaigned in Peru, and have thus done much prospecting. Though we may not be engineers, we know something of their craft," and then with a gleaming eye: "I for one do volunteer my service to explore for gold."

But the idea jerked Mendaña: "No!" he squealed. He could not bear the idea of the godless-alchemist uncovering the Magi's gold: "Captain

Sarmiento will stay with me," and, as if to obliterate any need for explanation, he nominated the first eyes he caught: "Francisco Gutierrez, the apothecary. He will supervise the digging."

Then he dismissed the meeting, but kept old Nuñez and the apothecary Gutierrez for a more detailed briefing, or, more accurately, to brainstorm ideas that he hoped would come from them.

Fortunately, Francisco Gutierrez was a thinking man: "You say we should dig, General, yet would it not make more sense in this land of rivers to pan for the gold?"

A most sound observation which deflated Mendaña's anxiety into a state of sighing soft relaxation.

Francisco Gutierrez was already well known to Mendaña. A quietly spoken gentleman who had a passion for botany expressed through whispers. Although he had enlisted himself as a soldier, he spent more time examining the plants in the jungle than wielding his sword. It was also he who had discovered or identified most of the spices that Mendaña was looking for. But Gutierrez's main job was a doctoring one. With his knowledge of the properties of herbs, he cured wounds. He was not a geologist, and certainly not a miner. Nevertheless, once given his appointment he put his clever mind to the task.

"What is this process you will use, then, good Francisco? Explain it to me, pray," murmured Mendaña, who had no idea.

"The idea, as I know it, is most simple, señor," and his head bobbed with the lightness of that same simplicity: "We go to a river and scoop gravel from the river into a pan. Then the pan is gently agitated like this," and he mimed the motion with his hands: "With the swaying, any water and the sandy gravel is washed out of the pan, leaving the heavier pieces of stone at the bottom. Any gemstones or even gold powder would stay at the bottom of the pan, señor," and grinned before tilting his head to the side and sucking his bottom lip under his teeth: "The difficult thing, however, is to find a suitable river in which to look for the gold. But, if there be gold in these mountains, we should find traces in the streams."

This was enough to assure Mendaña that he had appointed the right man for the job. He slapped good Gutierrez's back and told him to gather all the pans he could for the prospecting expedition, and to leave as soon as he could.

* * *

The young captain, Francisco Muñoz Rico screamed the order to unfurl the brigantine's sail, and when it flapped he felt a warm joy at the prospect of the new lands to be discovered – *I'll name a mountain after meself* – he thought – *the difference betwixt me and old Gallego, who has but a river with his name* – and sniggered behind the pilot's back.

Gallego, however, was miserable and it was infectious. He was no longer interested in his role in history, too tired now to listen to any more dreams. The wind was against them and the boat became a vacillating bastion of moping gloom.

Nevertheless, the Solomons was an archipelago, with hundreds of islands, and they soon had to stumble on one of them. Gallego took them in the direction of a large island that he had already been to, and which had been christened *San Cristóbal*.

There, Muñoz Rico felt a need to re-instil enthusiasm for the cause and began to impart his own pragmatic, capitalist fantasy to the others. A dream of owning a vast plantation in those fertile isles. He cast a waving hand toward the serried profile of the blue-green mounts climbing from the coast before them and proclaimed that: "These hills will one day be replete with grazing sheep and cattle, fattening beef and mutton for the whole empire."

But the gale force wind and looming cumulus cloud, and the presence of enormous crocodiles, excited by the promise of storm and racing across the mangrove mudflats, made such bucolic idealism absurd.

Seeing that the men were not inspired by his vision of farms, Muñoz Rico ordered the slaves to sing, another pointless chore, for appreciation of their reboant voices was impossible against the gale.

Later, when the wind had dropped enough for him to be heard, Gallego nudged the young would-be-capitalist: "And how, perchance, will ye carry yer cows to this purgatory place, Cap'ain?"

Which only reinforced Captain Muñoz's conviction that he hated the pilot.

For a whole day they made no progress at all, but eventually they managed to reach a harbour with a village only some eight leagues down the coast of

San Cristobal.

There were only twelve huts, all on stilts and erected on the beach, but the welcoming committee had obviously been swollen by people from other settlements and soon there were almost five hundred souls on the small stretch of sand.

Captain Muñoz went ashore with the soldiers, asking for help to pull the brigantine in. This the Islanders gladly did, and soon a hundred arms were hauling rope. More Islanders came down and embraced the New-men as if they were re-encountering long lost sons. But when the Spaniards made it understood that they wanted food, the spirit changed.

After the Islanders refused, the soldiers went through their huts, but found nothing except four not so fresh tunas.

"It's a fishing village, Cap'ain," whinged one of the soldiers: "And with this wind and waves I don't think they've been out at sea much this week." Muñoz Rico spat and shrugged his shoulders: "At least we'll have fish soup tonight."

*   *   *

By relieving Sarmiento of his duties, instead of humiliating the alchemist-captain, Mendaña effectively liberated him.

Freed from command, the necromancer was able to find space to explore the occult secrets of what, for him, was a fundamentally magic place. He had spent a life time studying the occult arts from books. In the Solomons there was no writing, but that did not mean that arcane knowledge did not exist. Quite the contrary, its secrets were stamped in the form of the islands themselves, in the trees and leaves, buried in the roots and carved in the rocks of the mountains.

Thanks to Mendaña's decision to hold him back from exploration, now he had time to look for what he himself knew was important.

To help him, he recruited Mahnu: "Come, good lad. Let us go and see this place and meet its people. If you can find someone who understands your language, I'm sure they will be full of stories to tell us."

But though he took Mahnu, he hardly needed him. In the jungle, Sarmiento led the way. The jungle fascinated him. He could sense beings that could not be seen but were there; entities that were too tenuous of nature to be perceived by a human eye, but not too intangible to be apprehended. In the jungle, the division between the visible and invisible, between the physical and supernatural worlds, is not sharply marked. The jungle encloses a thick undefined and undefinable atmosphere that promises marvels for anyone trained to see, as Sarmiento was. Figures moved for him, like shadows in mists. Figures that were both real and imagined, and that needed an eye that could understand how those antithetical concepts could both exist at the same time. An alchemist's eye: Pedro Sarmiento's eye.

* * *

The old, invalid soldier, Andrés Nunez led his expedition on a tardy advance toward the highlands. Nuñez himself could manage no more than ten minutes at a time before pain and breathlessness demanded a rest.

Eventually he came up with a grunting compromise: "Four harquebusiers (*cough*) and four of yer wit' shields will stay by me and me slave and the dogs, pray, whilst the rest of yers go on." When some of the men seemed to look anxious he smiled warmly and actually became philosophical: "Reason, methinks, directs that we should go the same way," and snorted phlegm: "But there be no obligation for us to always go at the same pace." When some of the men shook their heads, he became most forceful: "I'm takin' charge of the rear guard, sirrah!" Then loud, as if the others had already marched away: "When yers find a village, wait for me there."

* * *

After leaving San Cristóbal island, and sailing in a north-westerly direction for five days in moderate conditions, the brigantine reached the southern tip of another large island. The Sanban boy with them told them that it was called Malaita.

They were greeted by a small fleet of huge canoes. It was a slow and cautious approach.

The men on the brigantine were made nervous by the complexity of the approaching vessels and the proliferation of weapons on them. Not the same canoes that they had met so far. Even the young Sanban boy was awestruck – *Men of Ambrym* – he thought, recalling stories that Salacay had told him of that proud magician race with their white ships of nacre. A people who lived for hundreds of years. Mortal men and women but god-like, who had all perished when the island's volcano had burst – *Could it be* – thought the boy – *that some of those people survived?* –

Had the boy explained, or had Sarmiento been there, the others would have discovered the significance of this casual encounter. Had they been sensitive to the refined gestures and soft voices of this race of islanders; had they opened their eyes and minds and thought about the symbols tattooed on their chests, patterns which could well have been Greek or even Egyptian hieroglyphs; if just one of them had considered just one of the astonishing details, then perhaps their lazy minds could have suspected a profound meaning.

But neither Gallego nor Captain Muñoz were capable of grasping the exorbitant.

*   *   *

And while the Sanban boy was gasping at the incredible rendezvous, his mate Mahnu was leading Sarmiento along a jungle path to where another rendezvous had been arranged.

A local artisan was squatted in a green clearing, in front of him a semi-circle of smooth rocks.

"I thought you said the brock wanted to trade magic," spat the alchemist: "Where are his idols, pray?"

Mahnu shuddered: "There, Captain." He pointed to the lumps, arrayed in an alternating pattern of blacks and golds, dagger heads of shiny black obsidian between golden eggs of polished amber: "Sacred, they are."

"Sacred? Why?"

"Because they come from a magic place. The island of Ambrym."

"And has he been there?"

"No, no one has been there. Only Salacay. But this man says that men from Ambrym came here and gave him this magic. He says the rocks contain powerful spirits," which inspired Sarmiento to lift one of the smooth amber specimens and rub his palm across it. The old artisan burbled a monologue that Mahnu synthesised: "If you knew the spell."

Ah, so I must divine it myself! – thought Sarmiento, but as he did rub the fossil-resin his suspicions of fraud were blasted away. A sudden electricity rushed through him. The energy had tweaked his testicles, amplified by a tightening of the anus to shoot vertically up the spinal column. A powerful charge that had gushed from the amber itself.

When he saw the alchemist shudder Mahnu reached for him, expecting him to explode into one of the epileptic fits he had seen on the ship. But calm was restored by deep inhalations and Sarmiento rested a still hand on the boy's head and stared heavenward whilst sermonising: "There is an ever changing force in the universe which can fecundate anything by infusing it with its own celestial properties." His breathing increasing again, his eyes radiant: "This stone has received the gift of communicating cosmic power to us, pray," grimacing as he stared into the sun: "It's sufficient to hold it to feel God's energy," and then to himself, with his eyes tightly shut, revelling in an interior revelation – *And if I were to apply my will to this conduit, would not the power be mine?* – an idea which found an immediate answer. A voice, deep but soft and feminine, invaded his mind – *"the truth, even the future, can be made present to the eye of your soul ... time and space vanish before the third, inner eye, of the immortal soul ... she can shoot through space and envelop the subject no matter what distance, plugging and perpetuating, and make you hear the voice of the person you belong to ... now, you belong to me"* –

Mahnu shook him when his head began to sway: "This man says he has something else to show you."

The artisan grinned through betel nut stained teeth, carefully unwrapping a pandanus-leaf bundle to reveal a short, but very ornate and seemingly solid gold staff.

* * *

As the men from Ambrym approached the brigantine, the Sanban-boy translator sighed. The men and women aboard the nacre boats did not look noble at all. They were tall but undernourished, their faces wane, sharpened by trepidation.

Aboard, one of them began a dialogue: "Look at these men."

"The New-men we've heard rumours about."

"They've been called gods."

"They do not look like men who eat men."

"Yet, do you think they could be wise?"

"The men-eaters say they are cruel."

"Cruel to men-eaters. There is a complexity about their fashion."

"It is different, and they are lonely here like us."

"Why do you think they have come?"

"Our oracles have mentioned nothing."

"Then perhaps they will not stay."

As those precious boats softly lapped closer, Captain Muñoz and his men's eyes widened. It certainly looked like gold. Gold around the approaching men's necks, and each of them carried their own gold staff.

The Spaniards assumed the wands were some kind of clubbing weapon: "They use this lovely stuff to smash heads with!?"

When the wood of the brigantine bumped against a nacre hull, Muñoz Rico unsheathed his sword and lifted a feathered cap onto its tip, indicating with a stiff, prodding digit that he wanted to exchange it.

*   *   *

The prospecting vanguard led by the apothecary, Francisco Gutierrez, soon lost sight of the rear. They themselves had not noticed the presence of the Islanders, but there were a hundred eyes on them. And when those hundred eyes saw what a small group had been abandoned, they decided to attack it.

However, the ambush on a jungle track was not particularly effective. They could fire arrows from the hill tops, but most of them hit branches or tufts of leaves, breaking the trajectory. Another method was to run down the slopes and fire at the turtle-dragon from its own level. Yet the sharp descent through forest made such a noise that the shield bearers invariably knew where to expect the missile to be coming from.

Andrés Nuñez hobbled and panted. The shell of men around him had borne the brunt of the constant sallies from the Islanders. There had only been one scare, when one arrow had squeezed through the defence and caught Nuñez on the chest. This had merely bounced off his rusty breast plate, but when a shield bearer saw what had happened he suddenly became a member of the vanguard. Swearing and screaming he ran into the jungle, vanishing in shivering verdure to emerge some seconds later, his hand full of hair as he dragged and kicked the lean and writhing figure of the supposed would-be-assassin. To cover the shield bearer, the harquebusiers fired a round, even though their hobbling commander remained mute, and when the archer had been brought within the rear guard circle, they all decided to stick their boots in.

Ribs cracked and blood spurted from the native's nose and mouth. The shield bearer turned to the commander, mucus dripping from his nostrils: "Let the mastiffs have 'im," he whispered: "Let 'em eat meat."

Andrés Nuñez neither affirmed nor denied the suggestion, and so it was taken for granted that he agreed to it. The soldiers stood on the Islander's limbs while the dogs ripped open his belly.

The adventure had suddenly evolved into the purest form of sadism.

*　*　*

When he felt the rod in his hands Sarmiento realised it was not metal but stone: "For a moment..." he began, then realised the absurdity of talking and shook his head.

"This is a storm-rod," whispered Mahnu: "Its magic is very powerful."

"Storm," echoed the alchemist. And then, as if he had always had such a wand, he slammed the base of it hard against the ground: "Rain!"

*　*　*

At the same moment Muñoz Rico on the brigantine took a mallet and smashed the rod he had taken from the Ambrym man in his hands. As he did the sea swelled and a huge wave rippled up, lifting, tilting and almost capsizing all the boats. The Ambrym people screamed and when the swell subsided they started paddling away. Meanwhile the rock in Captain Muñoz's fist started to crumble and flake. Stone flakes. More green than yellow. He hardly worried about the stirring sea: the hope of metal, becoming rock, had eroded into dust.

*   *   *

Andrés Nuñez breathed into the pain in his hip as he and his battalion of prospectors struggled down the steep slope of the gorge to the rest of the party and the gushing river below. At the bottom, on a flat patch of spongy grass, Nuñez's slave lowered a stool from the huge pack on his back and set it up to receive the old soldier's arse. As the decrepit man felt the sting of his squashed piles, a nervous Francisco Gutierrez was quickly beside him, advising, while unpacking instruments and unfolding charts: "A channel must be dug," and a shovel was dragged to indicate where, but the march had exhausted Nuñez and he was already snoring.

The apothecary grimaced. He wanted to finish the job as quickly as possible. He did not care about utopias any more. To hurry things up he ordered the distribution of tools and commanded those with shovels to alter the river's course. Others with picks and mallets were ordered to smash the face of the gorge in case a vein should be found, while those with axes and saws were told to get timber from the rainforest.

In the jungle around them the invisible multitude seethed. Perturbed by this foreign magic, a magic that defied the river phantoms and attacked the rock spirits – *If they persist the world will groan and the earth will move* – they thought – *The sea will swell and waves will be sent to swallow the earth* – they knew – *If such a desecration of nature is allowed to persist, the whole universe will collapse* –

Suddenly the island warriors realised the tremendous significance of the moment for them. The gods themselves were under attack. They would be the champions of those gods; protectors of the universe.

Oblivious to the attention they were drawing, the Spaniards took up positions by the gurgling stream. Prospectors perched or kneeled in the sandy bank of the river, heads down, peering into pans that sifted stones from silt. One of these suddenly shivered, then a voice murmured something which attracted a soldier close by. This one stooped, then another figure turned, rose, and went to it. The group of three were agitated enough to attract others who expressed themselves with bellowing voice that made men run to them.

It was only a few snippets, but bright enough to be veracious, and soon the name of the object had become an echoing roar, smashing against the rock of the gorge: "Gold, lads! It's gold!"

But that last consonant crashed into another wall of noise. The champions of the gods had unleashed their arms.

Their position at the bottom of the gorge made the Spaniards an easy target. When stones and arrows poured down on them they had to abandon it and move back up the slope.

Not even the greediest ones wanted to stay. Gold makes men brave, often stupid, but not insane.

Inspired more by the violence than the precious pebbles they had found, the old soldier Nuñez lifted himself: "We'll scale the mountain and blast their rear guard," he chortled. The kind of order which meant very little for hardly any real fighting was done. The attackers maintained their distance, and retreated away from the Spaniards when they advanced. But in doing so, the Islanders unwittingly led the Spaniards into their village.

As soon as he saw it, old Andrés Nuñez gave the order to set fire to it: "To dissuade," he croaked. Francisco Gutierrez gaped back, demanding a better reason. Nuñez chewed his bottom lip: "The savages must be taught good manners, fie!" Which ended with a cringe as an arrow clanged and bounced off his helmet.

Torches were lit and the shield bearers sent to ignite the huts before them. They ran like flaming spirits, pushing their torches under the leafy skirts of the huts. The buildings ignited quickly. Burning wood popped and flaming strips of pandanus leaf rose and floated, breaking into smaller glowing pieces and becoming last gasps of tiny sparkling brilliance before disappearing forever.

Eventually the frustrated owners of the sizzling homes charged. Futile. Pedagogic steel hissed out of scabbards and the massacre conclusion was foregone.

---

iii Escape

On that same morning the *Almiranta*'s storekeeper, Juan Perez, decided that he wanted to go ashore for fresh water. Mendaña was reluctant to give permission, but the storekeeper persisted until the general flagged: "All right," he surrendered: "But be careful. Listen to the horns and drums, the Indian's are restless. Take soldiers with you. And some strong slaves."

As Juan Perez turned from the captain-general he bumped into Gaspar. The mulatto cabin boy had his shirt off as he sat in the sun. His sweating moist chest seemed to inspire a smile from the storeman: "Aye, and what are you up to then," he murmured in a deep, almost seductive tone.

"Nothing," the boy replied, and his fleshy lips slapped: "Just dreaming of the day when they'll take me to kill savages."

"Oh, a nice lad like you wants to be a killer, does he?"

"A soldier, señor. It's not the same."

"If you say not," then grinning: "I'm going ashore now and I need to find five soldiers to accompany me. Why don't you come with me?"

"If the general would allow it, señor."

"Ah, but he has lad. The order came from him himself."

One of the African slaves told Juan Perez that he knew a spot where there was fresh water and lots of coconuts lying on the beach. To reach it they had to row westward around two points, but the sea was calm. It would be more like a picnic than a chore.

Nevertheless, the skirmish willing Gaspar, sat up and clapped his hands when he saw a group of natives come down to the beach. The others laughed at his impetuosity and unfeigned desire. The *savages* just seemed to be resting. Nothing unusual in that. They would pose no threat. Juan Perez laughed out loud: "We're going for water, lad. Not the meat of hapless Indians."

At the other extreme of the beach was another group of Spaniards who were caulking a dinghy.

Juan Perez whistled and waved at them: "You've got guests, lads," he yelled with sarcasm, pointing to the Islanders that Gaspar had been so eager to spar with: "I'd be on me guard!"

Which inspired laughs and waving arms from the others. It was too nice a morning to be worried.

But on the ship from the height of the masts they could also spy another patrol of some seventy men crossing over a hill. They thought that these were heading towards the beach to join those already there, for as the day progressed hundreds had started to assemble. Yet then it was deduced that they were really moving in the opposite direction, and quickly.

Now, however, they calculated that the squadron of warriors was advancing toward the same cove that Juan Perez had gone to.

Men cupped hands over mouths, to become megaphones, blasting instructions to the men on the beach caulking the dinghy.

Bring it back. Bring the dinghy back.

When the little boat finally did reach the ships, hearts were pounding and everyone was gasping desperate: "What took you, whelps?!"

"We had the tide against us. You try rowing into that!"

Mendaña climbed into it with as many men who could fit. There was hardly room for the rowers to stretch their arms, and the rescue mission was an uncomfortable displacement full of constant complaint.

As they rounded a second point they were greeted by a whooping cry and an Islander was there brandishing, what at first looked like a pair of little logs, but was really a thick black severed leg and arm.

Then another cry came, this time from a dry skerry that was poking out of the little bay.

But this time the shout was in Spanish, and they looked to see one of the slaves who had gone with Perez waving at them. He told them that he had swum to the rock, but that all the others were dead. Beaching the dinghy, they raced inland to where it was estimated the river should have been. They came onto a flat plain but could see no one.

Only when they had reached the summit of a hill did they realise the extent of the activity on the other side. Warriors all over the place. Many more than had been originally estimated. A large squadron were moving down the river, brandishing the white cloth of the New-men's underclothes as a victory banner.

Mendaña and his men doubled back to the beach and the dinghy, but half way there they ran into Ortega and his squadron who were returning from an exploratory expedition.

The old soldier's lips were dry and drooping. His report was short, his tone grim: "We've found the bodies ... Nine men ... Chopped into pieces ... We put the pieces in our boat."

*   *   *

The men on the brigantine had estimated the cove to have been uninhabited, so the new attack came as a complete surprise. The first spear: right through the back of the sentry's neck, coming out through his mouth. The charge. The harquebusiers did not even have time to take aim. Swords had to be unsheathed: "Rip their bellies, Lads!"

Blood. Lots of blood. The Islanders pulled back, but from their distance they hurled spears. One smashed a Spanish head, another pierced a thigh. The Islanders charged again. Now the harquebuses were ready and exploded. The attackers retreated, some badly wounded. More spears were hurled. One, well aimed, hurtled through a shield. Terrible scream. Inspired, they charged. The defenders' swords slashed, guns popped. More blood.

A febrile Gallego screamed the order to retreat. They staggered, heavy with blood and sand, lurching into sea, through darting white fish, swimming groggily to the brigantine, struggling to pull themselves up, out.

The Islanders dragged out their own canoes, paddling to the Europeans, surrounding them. A prickly pear fleet. Spears shivered while the starving and exhausted Spaniards contemplated their end, but nothing was thrown.

Enough, they had all sacrificed enough.

The Spaniards left, never to return. And the Islanders could roar victory.

*   *   *

On Guadalcanal the fresh, chopped meat was taken to the river to be buried. Men wafted salt hungry flies away from the tears on their own bloodless faces as the slabs of mutilated flesh were laid by shivering hands onto the dryness of sand. Torsos without legs or arms, some of them headless as well.

If a head did exist it had had the tongue cut out of it and the canine teeth extracted and had been smashed open like a pomegranate. Hollow shells inside, the brains had been scooped out probably to be eaten. In many cases tiny green ants had already swarmed to lap up the remains.

Sarmiento shivered at the sight of Bubi's limbless body. Mendaña vomited when he realised that he could not discern the flesh of Gaspar from the other flesh – *They've taken his lovely head* –

All the meat was buried together in a communal grave.

The sole-surviving slave: "The long boat had run ashore," he told them: "and we were trying to free it when the Indians were suddenly on us. We looked to the harquebusiers, who were in the boat fondling for their weapons. We were expecting them to fire at any moment, to save us ... but while they were trying to load their guns a big wave washed over them, wetting the match. The blacksmith Bubi fought like a Caesar, brandishing a machete. He cut the arm off one of the assailants. But eventually they overpowered and killed him. All was lost. So quickly lost. I saw blood everywhere and ran to save myself ... and swam for the rock ... others ... three others, managed to climb into the boat and push themselves out ... but they were attacked and killed."

Mendaña ordered a new expedition. An expedition of revenge.

Iron cuts better than wood. Iron stops wood better than wood stops iron. Flying lead does more damage than a shark's tooth tip. Fire. The villages burned. In the flat lands and the hills, three hundred houses burned.

The turtle-dragon had risen. Battle lines were drawn up. Lead shot into flesh. Blood. Limbs collapsed. Naked feet slapped earth and men and women fled.

Escaping into flashing flame ambushes, into the grey blurs of soldiers' sweeping swords, stabbing after the slash to rip bellies and backs, pushing them towards the beach.

There the cannons were trained. The victims were rounded up. Forced to huddle. Hell was let loose.

Cannon and harquebus. Fire and more fire.

The dead fell. The pile mounted. Dozens of dead. Scores of them.

Machetes were applied to hack at necks and quarter bodies. Heads removed and impaled on stakes. A fence of fly enticing, horror struck countenances.

Only a few escaped. One. Wavering. A bullet through his shoulder. Blood drenched back and chest. He leapt into the sea. Swam.

"Fish him out!" was the order. "Put irons on him. Squeeze and burn him till he blabs. Find out who gave the order to kill Juan Perez and his men."

"Lunga," came the reply when his bare balls had been wrenched and his soles slapped. This was as good a response as any other.

So the avengers set out to the province of Lunga. Mendaña, Ortega and Sarmiento. Together. Three hours before daybreak. they went to the mouth of a river. Ortega organised the battalion. Mendaña was in charge of the vanguard, Sarmiento of the rear. They marched up the river.

In the red light of torches and the blue hue of smoke they beat their drums and advanced on the first village with shouts and cheers. They washed through like a wave, leaving nothing but flaming huts behind.

Dawn broke as they advanced. Wading through swamps. Clambering over paths. When they appeared before the next village the Islanders saw them and fled. Abandoning two hundred houses, and two hundred houses were burned to the ground. Then the next village, then the next.

The full skirts of Fr Gálvez's soutane swept across the beach. His arm was up, covering his nose with a sleeve to guard it from the stench of burning flesh. Mendaña, seeing him coming, knelt in front of his private altar – *All soldiers* – he had decided – *should confess after a war* – But, instead of demonstrating friarly calm, the Franciscan fell down to his trembling knees and, spluttering, almost in tears, he grabbed the captain-general's hands to supplicate: "We must leave this place, verily General, before its infernal nature damns us all."

The unnatural procedure made Mendaña shudder: "Yes, Father. I was thinking the same thing myself," and then with a madman's cold simplicity: "As soon as the cleansing is finished we will be quickly on our way, troth."

Yet, despite the weakness of Fr Gálvez, the days of genocide had been more cathartic for the Spaniards than morally damaging. Thus the men who returned – the explorers from the sea, the prospectors from the mount – though exhausted and infirm, were able to sustain their battle weary souls with images of their dead enemies. There was no need for these men to devour the flesh of their victims, sustenance was drawn from the vengeful act itself. They did not even have to be a killer themselves, the mere idea that their own kind had murdered a dozen *savages* for each one of their dead friends was enough. The fact that the whole island was trembling in fear of them added to the compensation. For the first time in months Alvaro de Mendaña slept soundly. His dream of the headless chickens had ceased.

As for the Sanban boy, Mahnu, although he felt no particular sympathy for the dead Melanesians, he was starting to question the nature of the Europeans' power. He quizzed Mendaña: "If this gulf you have crossed is really so big, why did you cross it?"

"We are looking for something we no longer believe in at home ... that we believe can no longer be found at home ... the further we voyage, the more likelihood there is that we will find this ... *elusive* thing."

"And did you find it in Sanba?"

"No."

"Did you find it here ... in Guadalcanal?"

"No."

"So, why are you leaving again?"

"Because we are tired ... and the people here do not want us to stay."

"So you will not come back?"

"Oh no, we will be back."

"Why?"

Which drew a pathetic smile from the general, who was happy to splash in the shallows of his own logic: "To finish what was started ... To make the King of Spain, and our beloved Pope, the Kings of the World."

This made the boy think carefully. But before he deserted the ship, he sought one more opinion to his question, and approached Sarmiento: "Why did you come, Captain?"

The alchemist, who was drawing a sidereal chart, was deep in thought. The question only managed to poke at his depth: "What?"

"Why did you come?"

Stirred, Sarmiento turned to him. For a moment he was going to say something about gold and the Philosopher's Stone, but his tongue seemed to suddenly thicken in his throat. He thought again, and then the more terrible reason gurgled out: "Rage," he croaked: "Rage, and ambitious envy."

Which Mahnu appreciated more by the images created by the tone than in the meaning of the words themselves. It made him shiver – *As if he had spat a malaria at me* – he thought, and that same night he stopped considering and stripped himself of his European rags and clambered down, dropping into the warm sea where all the infirmities of Spain were washed away.

Although he could not appreciate it intellectually, he *knew* that it was his nakedness that sustained him. If he had had boots he would have drowned.

After watching Mahnu's escape, Sarmiento turned back to his chart. However, the idea of such a premonitory thing had become absurd – *If I am to live forever, what interest can the future have now?* – he realised – *The future is only of interest if we consider what we must do before the end comes* – and then – *But does the fact that I cannot stop mean that I should do nothing?* – gradually realising the tremendous pressure of the gravity he had hurled himself into – *I have taken the drug and I will not age, will not wither, will not die? But how will I live?* –

It was too early to reach conclusions, but he could sense them; sense a message too subtle to be revealed by astrology.

Through all its symbolism, esoteric language is a blatant hammer. It was a heavy heart in the throat message that he received: that he was not *more* but *less* free now than he had ever been. This great prize was really an enormous encumbrance – *I am no longer human* – he would eventually realise – *Unique, a singularity* – and then even further – *I am anti-nature, this is not my universe* – Yet those ideas came afterwards, at first he caught but a mere glimpse of his damnation, and his reasoning led him at first to exorbitant conclusions – *My gift demands a titanic effort. These islands are too small for a giant-spirit like me. I am destined to trample continents* – an idea and spirit which was suddenly drowned by Mendaña's squawk, announcing that they were having a meeting.

On the deck of the gently rocking *Capitana,* life's tragedies were reduced to comfortable simplicity and the decision to depart came unanimously. Most were ready to forget the Hell that was their Paradise, or accept its ephemeral nature and return to the more solid comforts of the mundane world.

The decrepit Gallego stirred his flagging spirit, wiped the sweat from his malaria fever brow and became the champion of return: "These aren't no Solomon's Isles," he croaked: "Nor those of the Magi. Instead of two we've encountered a dozen demon infested lands, yet on none is there any substantial trace of either gold or spices."

Some thought of Andrés Nuñez's expedition's find, but no one wanted to contradict the desired conclusion by suggesting such a petty detail. A few snippets of gold were no palliative.

Sarmiento himself tried to interrupt but was ignored. He found himself being shuffled away from the front of the pack. People talked over him: democracy, insulating itself from dissension. At first Sarmiento interpreted it as typical sailors' rudeness, but as his interjections increased the cold shoulder treatment became increasingly insidious and conspiratorial. His temper began to boil.

Mendaña was equally galled by the enthusiasm being heaped on Gallego's pessimism. He had foreseen a debate and wanted to ensure that it took place. When no one else suggested an alternative he found himself playing the role of devil's advocate, to reveal his deepest, most real anxiety: "If we do return now, our expedition could be misconstrued to have been a failure."

A gasp and a unanimous: "No."

"And perchance we'll be welcomed as heroes?!" This time Sarmiento was heard by all.

Mendaña cringed. He had allowed the alchemist back in, which was not what he had wanted. Sarmiento, knowing what a weak spot he had pierced, stuck deeper, with a passionate oratory: "To have come this far, for nothing, when the truth is just around the corner." And he pushed through the mob, to the table in front of Gallego, thrusting a finger down into an empty space on the navigator's chart: "That is where we should be!" he cried. "Our goal is a continent, the Terra Australis. That's our final aim, and it's in the south!"

The passion of its delivery inspired some brief applause which dissipated into a general murmur.

No one said it, but all of them wanted this kind of conscience shut up. Gallego spat at the map and embraced the debate: "To founder in seas where none have foundered before! What kind of bubble ambition's that?"

The dry crust of Sarmiento's cold lava crackled: "The same we had when we set sail from Peru."

Gallego's malaria made him tremble and gave him an ardent sheen: "*Then* our ships were not riddled with worm."

Making the volcano explode: "Our *souls* were not riddled with worm you mean!"

The force stirred the mob and the crowd shifted behind their champion Gallego, pushing him forward. But the old-salt, unable to bear the volcano's fire, shied away from Sarmiento's stare and looked for the softer eyes of the young Mendaña. When he had found them his gurgling voice lifted into an almost pathetic pitch: "Marry, señor, we've discovered enough lands to warrant any mission. Lands won, not for ourselves, but for the glory of the King of Spain. It's an 'umble, but great and 'eroic chore. Mark me, our toil will be applauded across the length and breadth of the Empire."

Mendaña felt sorry for those sad, old eyes, and suddenly all of those around and behind Gallego seemed full of triste want and desperate need for a general's leadership. So, with a benevolent tyrant's resolve: "It's decided," he said: "We head home."

Cheers, as if the matador had killed his bull with the first stab. Sarmiento was shoved from all sides. The captain-general continued: "We'll set a course, but south-eastward, heading for the coast of Chile."

"Chile!"

The massive groan collapsed from the mirthful scene like an avalanche. As the general roar mitigated into murmur, individual protests became discernible. Each one of the navigators was against it. *Suicide* whispered the most pessimistic.

But Mendaña was adamant. By his way they could kill two birds with the same stone. Go home *and* discover the Terra Australis. It pleased no-one. Sarmiento grumbled, the Terra Australis was to the south-west, not east. Gallego and the other navigators all recommended a northern route, towards Mexico. The debate turned into a debacle.

Everyone against him, Mendaña's pride forced him to persist: "Heading north, even if we get good weather, we won't reach Peru in less than six months. Your route is back to front, marry. We'll be heading into winter weather in the north and all the bad weather that that season brings."

Eventually there was a compromise: "We'll stay close to the equator and use the brigantine to scout nearby isles to fetch food."

But not a single suggestion pleased the navigators, or the soldiers and sailors, who preferred to trust any officer other than Mendaña. The captain-general, on the other hand, pushing against the weight of the mob was exercised and made stronger and firmer the longer he resisted, until finally, with an uncharacteristic fist thumping gesture, democracy failed and Mendaña imposed his rule. They went south-south-east.

XVIII. The Return

Weeks later Sarmiento scratched the final line of the triangle on the surface of the silver plate. This encompassed an inner circle that had also been scratched. On each point a fat candle burned.

The image of Mendaña was fresh in his mind. His smirk as he had found the audacity to *banish* him to the *Almiranta*, as if publicly stating that he could no longer bear his presence: "I will take charge of the *Capitana* myself," he had said.

Sarmiento shivered with the memory. The young alchemist-god had learned to disdain the mortal nature he had evolved from, and that repugnance had begun to ooze from him like a garlic supper. Those who were still not immortal found the lofty air emanations more than unsavoury, but even if it had been explained to them, they would not have understood the miracle.

If he was a deity he should have been sweet, Sarmiento was foul – *Man is a microcosm* – he thought – *Destined to become its own macrocosm* – and then – *What they would give to know my enigma!* – tempered by a cruel paradox – *Yet if they knew I were a god, they would crucify me* –

Destined to know and be silent, his hot lava soul cooled into a crusty cone that even the most basic life forms found too dry. Too barren on the surface, too violent within to be worshipped. But why should he have expected anything else from the human herd? Even when they knelt before images of Christ the only true faith most of them had was in their conformity.

They had left Peru hoping, but never believing, and they would return, still not believing, still faithless, and now without even hope. Only Mendaña had *changed*: leaving without any faith at all, he had discovered a faith in himself; the faith to lead.

In order to start the process, Sarmiento had merely to murmur the name *Vepar* over and over again. This evoked a whirling blur within a triangle above a plate. There, a phantom of air slowly solidified into what seemed to be a tiny, legless homunculus, its little pink arms sadly reaching for this world that it could obviously sense but not feel.

At first it seemed ugly and monstrous, but with time the figure began to twist and swell into womanly curves, at least from the waist up, below that it had a fish's tail. Twist and swell: a metamorphosis that the creature seemed to suffer more than enjoy, and it grimaced whenever its body ripped through its own limitations to expand into a double dimension of what it had been just before.

The ghostly mermaid's skin had a gummy, wet texture that dripped at times. Gobs of goo that became whirling smoke again and evaporated. Sometimes the flesh would slap and the mermaid would even sigh, letting out a deep moan when it, or she, achieved her final metamorphosis and achieved a proportion larger than Sarmiento himself. Yet, despite the final size, she remained within the confines of the triangle.

When she moved her lips for the first time, Sarmiento grimaced and his head snapped back on a cracking neck. He thought he had felt a hand thrust into his brain. This had permeated with a terrible screech, although he soon came to recognise words through the cacophony. Her voice: not sweet, rather it whooshed, like a thudding wave into a blow-hole: "Why am I summoned?"

Sarmiento threw his head forward again and clenched his fists: "I want a storm," he yelled.

The morning had dawned well, a fair wind in a fair sky. Sarmiento's *Almiranta* was behind Mendaña's ship, bobbing in line. Gregorio Gonzalez's complaint to the alchemist-captain was bitter: "He dispatched you to this worm eaten barque to sink wi'me, Cap'ain. Now he runs away from us wit' Satan's own speed. For the swine hates us both."

But Sarmiento only smirked. His voice creaking with the groaning wood of the boat: "Let them run. Race into their storm. It'll do us well, good Gregorio, to dawdle."

It was only when the *Capitana* had completely dipped below the horizon that Gregorio realised what Sarmiento had ordained. It began as a slight breeze, becoming squalls, evolving into a gale that churned. The separate ships rose and dipped, but their courses were changing.

"Turn west, Gregorio," commanded the alchemist: "And south if need be. Always keep the storm to the north, and it will not engulf us."

"But we'll lose the others for ever."

"Are they not already lost?" and actually expressed this through a subtle grin.

* * *

For Mendaña and the *Capitana's* crew, each fall of their ship was always sudden and sickening, leaving stomachs in throats, heads dizzied.

Foam sprayed like brief blizzards across the deck, the bubble-craft rolling from side to side before sharply diving into dark abysses. Every crashing wave was a crack of thunder and even Gallego trembled; in forty-five years he had never seen such a storm.

The pounding, the crashing, the wail. Walls of water tumbling over them, bursting into them, through the gaps, into the hull. Those on top were just hanging on. Nothing to be done. On each shroud was a sailor, twitching under the sting of spray, too frightened to complain. They shivered miserable in their drenched rags; were suddenly pulled beneath the waves, then up again, open-mouthed and vomiting sea. For me it was pure exhilaration, but them, poor things. The spectre of death, blown at them. Alone, each ship alone, each person alone. Each one of those on deck was exposed, each one of them under it imprisoned.

And during all of this Mendaña was unable to shake the alchemist's image from his mind's eye. Realising he had lost the *Almiranta* precisely when he may have needed it the most he screamed, and then they were all crying out.

Inside the hull the ceiling was a fountain and the men inside were clinging or swimming in a freezing pool. Waves were generated within, as the vessel rolled. Hollow thuds echoed, as men and things were caught by anarchic tides and hurled. Furniture, plates, tools, bedding, floating, rubbing against the stroking arms and parting hands of swimmers.

Obstacles, some hefty and dangerous. Barrels crashed against them; pinning them, crushing them. Screams. More water crashing down, as if someone were emptying barrels onto them.

On top, there was a massive lurch, flinging sailors over the side within another drowning waterfall.

"It's going!" someone shouted.

"The tempest, aye, the tempest."

"Stir yourselves, stir!"

Presentiments of death. Optimists yelled orders against the roar, but these were hardly audible: "The foremast, lads. Let out some sail!"

The idea, from whoever, caught on. Haggard figures, desperate for life, crawled forward, risking atomisation. The sail became a symbol; let it out and they would be saved. They reached for shrouds, jerked ropes. Tremendous friction bit their bare hands, dug through flesh, made them bloody. Sharp, burning pain. Then a sudden, even more intense gust blew up and ripped the sail. It went with a thundering flap: "They were the devil's own wings," said one.

The jerk had made shreds of it, a burst of fluttering rags, sucked into outer space on Satan's own breath. When the terrible consequences of the dismal truth were realised, moping men let go of the ropes. These whipped up, slashing sailors, who screamed; not for the lashing they had received but at the realisation that their life supporting umbilical cord was dangling loose.

The ship tilted even more. More screams of anguish. Now they were foundering, and would for half an eternal hour more.

Mendaña, muted by fear, watched the skiff tear free and disappear. He would have preferred it as a coffin, to have had a more personal death; for to have to perish together with all these others in a communal grave was a repulsive thought. Orders. He should have been giving orders. But who was in his right mind to obey them?

"It's going!" The realisation, dreadful, stirred even the pessimists. Action. Who?

"Cut the mast! The mast! The main mast!"

It was Mendaña. The tardy order; so drastic yet so obvious. The final hope. Men slid at it, thumped axe blades into it, made it crack; the storm did the rest. Another crack and then an explosion as the erection hurtled off, smashing the rail before sliding away into the brine. And the ship sighed, as if it had defecated, and straightened. Shouts of anguish became cheers. They had risen a yard over the water line.

"Up here lads!" screamed the captain-general, and the axe-men scrambled up to the poop where Mendaña indicated. To the cabin on the poop. A useless construction.

So they struck and smashed until the walls splintered, cracked and split into shards.

Mendaña hardened with his power, that he could wilfully destroy even in chaos. The next shout roared another order from his indurating chest.

This was for Catoira, to bring him a blanket, which, when completed, was followed by a stone clonking call to two African slaves to take that cloth up to the bowsprit and tie it there.

These went fore, the wind behind them, at times lifting them. Clasping shrouds, they put the bowsprit between their legs and shinnied along it, on the edge.

The ship flew over watery cliffs, dropping, rising. Waves smashed the slaves, but they held on, their fear had become such an absolute it had vanished.

Mendaña wept and wished for an entire ship of slaves. They wrapped their legs and tied the blanket, which filled with air, stretched, and pulled. They sailed. All night and all next day. Away from Sarmiento's ship.

*   *   *

The alchemist's mind was future-full. Flush of life that he had not yet lived. Text and imagery, the knowledge that he was still to learn – *I am eternal, with as much memory of the future as of the past* – He stepped off the world into a sea of dark matter, reaching for stars. He flew to them, cleansed himself in their cauterising heat, transformed himself in radiation. He dived, swam in spiralling galaxies, renewed his power on the horizons of swirling black holes.

Until he was coughing conscious, the taste of Gregorio Gonzalez's foul breath in his own mouth. The bristly cheek of the pilot was rubbing against his forehead and he was in the man's arms.

"It's been another epilepsy, Cap'ain. You were shakin' so. But now it's righted … it's passed."

But despite the pilot's good intentions, Sarmiento was claustrophobic cramped and had to insert elbows to free himself from the man's maternal hug. When he had he lifted himself toward the rail, looking north; the cloud on the horizon was less dense, less dark.

As his own mind had calmed, so would the storm abate.

* * *

Mendaña sucked his finger before thrusting it into the wind. That had changed, east-north-easterly. But hardly had he registered this before it gusted and blew his cap off.

Gallego was roaring into the gale: "We've a head-wind, lads. We'll have to tack!"

Ten days later they were still tacking. Continuous, desperate, turns, a monotonous drudge, and futile, all the time losing ground, all the ground they had gained the days before.

Then, thunder and lightning – *God's wrath* – they thought – *The end of the world.*

They had to draw in the sail. Half a metre of water slapped in the hull. Always half a metre, no matter how hard they worked to empty it.

They undid the spritsail and attached it to the foremast, and for a while they ran with that until a south wind blew so hard it ripped it away.

"More blankets!"

Their only hope. A north-easterly course, drawn by billowing blankets. More wind. More rain. They whirled around, were pushed around, reaching an altitude of twenty-nine degrees. Then a fierce north-easterly shoved them south-west: "Back from where we've come!"

Seven days, to twenty-six degrees. Eventually a westerly, pushing north-northeast. They erected a pole as a mainmast, a fluttering blanket mainsail, and rose to twenty-seven degrees, a new wind blowing up: "From Hell!"

Pushing them back, the whole thing a waste. Starving men, thirst and exhaustion. A quart of stinking water and eight ounces of putrid ship's biscuit.

Mendaña looked seaward – *If only they had listened to me* – His consolation, that he was right. They had not listened. They had forced him to change course, made him cross the equator. The fatal mistake was theirs.

The men groaned, feeble, half-dead, many had gone blind. No one had the slightest idea where they really were. Only latitude could be measured. Despair inspired risk. The emaciated men gambled their rations and the decks echoed with the moans and pleas of starving losers.

They sailed up to thirty degrees, into a north-easterly that brought intense cold and enveloping fog, forcing them to drop down again.

Some soldiers shivered and moaned and cried out to make an emergency call at the Philippines, as if they were anywhere near the Philippines! But any idea in times of tremendous crisis brings infectious hope: anything had to be better than the course they were on. Mutiny was in the air. Thick and stifling. Men coughing complaint to clear phlegm clogged lungs.

Mendaña, now skeletal hard, received admonishment with a calcium tenacity: "As if this route were my fault?!" he complained back before ordering the chaos with the comfort of calculation. He had proclaimed his own computation that the half a quart of water that remained could be rationed out for twenty days, and that this would be long enough to reach land.

The mutinous minds were dulled, too heavy with misery to verify the general's arithmetic, further muted by the contenting thought that they had at least tried to change their destiny.

And then real hope ...

The wind changed and they drifted against a pole made of pine. There were indications of land: strong currents, seagulls, even ducks. The wind came from the north. It started to rain and they gathered enough water for three days. The weather cleared, but with their shabby sails they moved at a snail's pace. The currents were strong, but not strong enough. Each day seemed like a year. The storms stopped, the wind picked up again. Waves. All night they sailed and at dawn they were between two islands, and on the horizon they could see an enormous streak of grey mass. The continent. The Californian coast.

* * *

Sarmiento smiled as he stared into the pages of Canches' book; scabrous pages, corrugated by ocean atmosphere. He flattened surfaces then took a deep breath and lifted himself back.

The fire in his soul cooled and he felt lighter, more smoke than flame – *"God is cruel"* – he remembered Catoira had said – *No* – he thought – *not cruel, because he does not exist. He has to evolve* – The resurrection was an end-of-universe future when all men would be reborn in God – *But a God that we will make* – his drugged mind affirmed – *That I will make* – and he clutched the flask around his neck, to tilt it and let drip three drops into another mixture of oil, sperm and blood in a golden goblet, combining it with a stirring dagger – *The profit of my intoxication* – and then – *I have a thousand arms, and my face is more terrible than the storm around it* – Thoughts that burnt like a phoenix.

As he drank the potion it bubbled in his mouth and oozed from his lips like blood from a punctured lung.

To his imagined eternal soul, the material universe was a dream state – *Nothing ends* – he told himself, and then – *The next time I return I will come alone* – even – *Perhaps I should kill them all and turn the ship back. Return to the Terra Australis on my own* –

The magic in front of him roared and in his madness he actually whispered back to it: "Demons, soon you will all bow to my will. You have the power, but you need a guide."

Canches' book was full of seals, symbols that were demon trapping prisons. Prisons that could only be opened by a chanted key. Sarmiento began to flick through pages, reaching for the half formed faces of more spirit slaves.

The form of a woman, her face veiled in blue, came to him and wrapped her arms and legs around him, tightening the fingers of one hand around his throat, while the other dropped to his groin, releasing a tempest. Scream of ecstasy – *I am torn asunder* – he thought – *Nerve from nerve, vein from vein, atom from atom, and at the same time we are crushed together* – A line of thought which was quelled before it had time to gather, first by the cold heat of the clamping caress, and then by the sweet sounds of his captor's delicious, husky voice – *"Drown your rapturous voice in mine ... let your sublime eternal matter drown in my eternal-soul ... drink from me, and love me ... your destiny, eternity"* –

But then he was looking down in horror at his own wavering arms. Thin, pale and naked arms; stretching calamari tentacle fingers, reaching for Canches' book. And when it was caught the rubbery digits scooped under the cover, pinching it with index and thumb, the delicate wrist, a pink, silent hinge, lifting leather, to drop it, a dull thud ... and the magic was shut.

*   *   *

Estrella screamed and her own hand shot, involuntarily away from my own closed book. Her breast heaved as she stared in anguish at her own pale thin and naked arm.

Voice came gradually, air that gushed like a wall of rain: "When will you finish this?" sadly, as if anticipating my answer.

"That has not been my intention."

Perhaps I looked bitter then because her gaze could not bear to stay on me. Her fringe was flicked away from her eyes as her hand turned, finding comfort in an exploration of the room. Until she reached a conclusion: "There are no mirrors here."

No, they were not allowed; but I could tell from her grimace that she herself had made an erroneous deduction as to why.

"You have b-been upset ... by the b-book," I stammered.

She shook her head, but now an idea of rejection hung solemnly between us. Instead of a relief our mutual silence thickened the initial problem of explaining the absence of mirrors.

"'What is the use of a book without pictures or conversations?'" I said as I lifted a copy of *Alice in Wonderland*: "This edition is illustrated," passing it to her, open at the picture of Alice peering into the mirror: "You see: 'Looking-glass milk is not good to drink.' The mirrors were removed because my health had been severely affected ... my mental health ... I started to drown in them."

She flicked through the pages of *Alice*, which warmed her with nostalgia: "Are you still troubled by the Red King's snores?"

An idea which, despite *Alice*, was too dense and it gurgled within me:

"It's not known by you who I really am?" I challenged: "Were you not told?"

Estrella shook her head. She put Alice down and reached into her handbag for a packet of cigarettes.

Having her look away from me encouraged an increase in my own melodrama: "This whole life is ... has been ... a farce," I spat, while she slid a cigarette filter between her lips: "I was lied to about my father and mother," she squinted at me through a spiral of smoke: "I was lied to about me ... myself ... about who I really was," smoke blew out, not only through lips, out of nostrils: "They knew ... always knew ... who I really was. That is the cruellest thing."

She stubbed the cigarette out on a saucer: "But why? Why lie to you?"

Her eyes accused. I looked to the crumpled stem of cigarette. Tawny tobacco sprouted like fur from open gashes: "Information was desired. Information from me ... that I would never have given them. My accident was provoked ... no accident at all."

And I slapped at a fly that I had noticed twitching on the table. It escaped, buzzing past Estrella's face, but she was oblivious, had me fixed with an intense stare: "What do you mean?"

I sighed: "It was said by de Coca that a great favour had been done for the World. That a monster had been reconditioned into a normal, quite pleasant human being," and I slapped at the fly again: "My amnesia was provoked. A complete brain-wash. But after the slate had been wiped clean it was then decided that they wanted to know things ... to know how I had lived so long. My secret, I was told, would be the panacea for all human ills."

Which obviously made her uncomfortable. She shuffled in her seat and looked away from me again: "What secret?"

I pulled at the cloth of my pants, twisted it: "The Terra Australis."

She turned back. At first with her eyes trained down, but lifting before she stammered the question: "The astral travel?"

My jaw was tight, teeth gritted: "My memory."

Which drew a frown: "What?"

My own tone was so cold it crackled: "My real memory," then attacking with a frozen stare, which was reciprocated: "I don't travel. I recall," this brought a reaction. Her eyes flickered. I paused, enjoying her mounting anxiety before the imminent revelation: "I've been alive for more than four hundred years."

She exploded, laughed: "De Coca told you this?"

Cruel disdain, I had not expected it and it stabbed: "Yes."

She shook her head and the disdain was replaced by condescension: "But you don't believe him, do you?"

I froze again: "It's been confirmed by others. The letters from Inma confirm it in a way."

She grimaced: "You can't confirm *in a way*."

Then my mind was full of Inma's poetry: "Hers is a metaphysical verse, but it says the same thing that de Coca said." There was a distant banging. Estrella was startled by it and turned: "It's the lift," I explained: "It's being repaired," then struggled to return to the original revelation: "De Coca's story is affirmed by others as well," then straining to recall evidence: "I've been met by some of the doctors who originally treated me? They all maintain it," and after gulping phlegm: "I was born in 1524 ... and I have never died."

Disdain returned. Her flicking fringe, whipping my soul with her violent frustration: "They told you that? Doctors told you that?"

Voice through clenched calcium: "Yes."

"Val ... You're not well."

"Mad."

Then after a sigh: "You seem to be trying your hardest to prove it."

My icicle voice cracked: "This story, was not invented by me. I was told it. Even the session with Tomás Puigsegur was planned."

Which made her thump the table, and she rasped through her own tight throat and gritted teeth: "Planned by me."

She was all open-mouthed stupefaction. I stared into it, trying to freeze it: "But the meeting with you was no accident either."

Which converted stupefaction into simple incredulity: "No ... that's impossible."

My explanation was slow, treacly: "The ring you had ... bearing the Seal of Solomon. From where was that obtained?"

She had to search her memory before she could manage it: "Inma gave it to me."

"And where is it now?"

She looked frightened: "I lost it."

"Where?"

"I don't know ... I had forgotten ..."

Then I rushed: "Your mind is ... has been tampered with too!" Which drew a head shaking denial: "Inma was also working for them. You were a pawn and she was the White Queen."

She exploded: "Who got taken very early on in the game."

My turn to twist away from her: "I think it would be more correct if it were said that she retired. Which of course went against all the rules."

When I turned back I realised that she had been hurt. Although she did not sob, tears were streaming down her cheeks. After blowing her nose: "Perhaps I should go too, Val, before you have me believing any of this."

"Is there ... can there be found any other explanation?" I snarled.

"If you look, you'll find it."

"Let me be heard first," and then I did become hot: "What I'm telling you may have been told by mad men, or maybe I am mad myself, but it's my reality, and explains what happened. Please listen. It's time it was known to you what Omega was, what Omega is."

She blew her nose again: "And why Don Enrique was tortured and killed?"

"Yes, perhaps that too. It's not known by me. I don't know what these people are really capable of. All that is known is that Omega is a very long term plan ... very long ... let's say the longest you can possibly imagine." I watched her light another cigarette: "Has the name of Teilhard de Chardin never been brought to your attention? Pierre Teilhard?"

She shuddered, she obviously had: "Why do you ask?"

My voice cooled and dried into a monotone: "His book is here. On the bottom shelf."

An index-finger tripped across the book-bindings until she had come to it.

"*The Human Phenomenon*," she read, blowing smoke across it as she did: "Did Don Enrique give you this?"

"Yes. Did you know that he knew the man?"

She looked away again, into the book: "Yes."

"But you still affirm you know nothing about Omega?"

She shook her head: "I remember he had some ideas about a universe of tangential and radial energies," then, as if using the smoke off her own breath to gather her thoughts: "Don Enrique thought that they would be useful in context with my work on dreams," and she shut the book and pushed it away: "I tried to read it but I found the arguments hardly convincing."

"But the connection was never made by you? Was it not found to be surprising to you ... that Don Enrique took it all so seriously?"

She was lost in the smoke again: "Not really. Don Enrique liked to believe anything."

"And it is ... has never occurred to you, that my condition might be explained by Teilhard's ideas?"

Which infuriated: "I told you, I only tried to read the book. I don't think I got past the second chapter."

Then I ran my own finger across the cover: "The book is basically eschatological. The Omega Point is announced by Teilhard ... but this has now become the Omega Plan and you are sitting in the heart of it."

"The heart of what?"

"A human challenge to the universe's entropy."

She shrugged her shoulders and her jaw twitched: "What are you saying, Val? That it'll be possible, through human intervention, to transform the matter of a dying universe ... modify the topology of space-time so that the Universe will exist indefinitely?"

I kept my gaze firm: "Yes."

"And the Kingdom of God will be created then, in the Omega point."

"Yes."

Then it was time for her voice to chill into cold monotone: "I don't think I'll be hurrying to join the team."

I laughed: "Oh Estrella, now so cynical. Twenty years ago your eyes would have been made to sparkle by the idea and..."

"Twenty years ago I was a fool."

I snorted: "Were you? You were considered a genius by all of us," which galled her. Nevertheless, I persisted: "De Coca's objective. I suppose. Let's start with the primary one. It was a scientific plan really."

"To create God, in a Godless-universe."

"Yes, yes ... the plan *is* known to you ... Stay, work with me ... The opus is sublime."

But then she was on her feet and reaching for me: "Let's get you out of here."

"No, please," and I had to slap her hands before they clutched: "Was work not carried out by us, together, for a year? Was love not felt? For us, for that work ... our experiments in other spaces, imagining other times. This new madness is not so really different to the old."

Making her step back: "So you're going to stay here."

"In a sense, yes. In another sense, I'm not really here, not now." I tried to explain to her that I wanted to change things, wanted to change her, to change her in order for her to change things, but it was futile: "Whoever is in control is far too powerful," but I could not explain that, I realised. She would never have accepted the real truth. My *existence*, my *madness*, was more complicated than Estrella would ever now be able to fathom. She was not the same Estrella who had introduced me to the Academy. She had escaped, or been rejected. That was why they had taken the ring from her. The idea saddened me, all hope that I had had of our reunion was lost. But instead of gushing with the emotion my voice hardened: "It's been lovely for me that you have been able to be experienced again. It is desired by me that you should stay, but it's known by me that you can't. So it's probably better that you leave now." And then, the cruellest statement of all: "Of course you can never come back." Expressed so firmly and coldly that it frightened her. She left trembling, with me staring at the seat of the chair she had occupied.

*   *   *

Now my Guardian sits silently in that same chair. I know that he has been drugged. I know exactly what is going to happen, it will be the same as it always has been. Not even this final realisation can change things. Not that changes do not happen. In a sense a thing is never itself. Each new time I think about myself I am different. Even this book. This is not the same book that Estrella read, that you have read, that your friend read. It is always different, but, in its essence, always the same.

My guardian has surrendered to sleep. I could slap his face, throw water over him, but it will do no good. The drug that has been administered is strong. Soon they will be here. Who it is exactly I do not know. I will struggle with them and the blow I will receive on the head, as always, will be badly dealt. The damage it will do to my brain will take sixteen years to be remedied. When I am resuscitated, *resurrected*, as they will say, they will fill my head with a brand new lie, with a brand new Terra Australis. What year will I wake up in this time? Does it matter? Everything will soon begin again, a clean slate, back on page one.

Epilogue (Espiritu Santo)

the guide woke us just before dawn, advising us to make our way up onto the deck and to take our cameras with us ... we would be entering the bay with the sun rising behind us ... the conditions for photographs would be picture-postcard perfect ...

at first it was a disappointment ... everything was a dim grey mist ... but the fog quickly lifted and then the island-city was right before us in a breath-taking pose ... its most characteristic landmark, the seven, mighty, metal sky-scrapers of the "health-district", sprouted out of the city-centre like a huge candelabra, gleaming in the morning light ...

disembarking, the brass surface of the pier was already hot under foot, but it was by no means an unpleasant sensation and the guide told us that it was therapeutic: "the whole city, not just the health-district," he said: "is designed to heal."

dozens of colourful stalls greeted us at the end of the pier where the water sellers operated ... there we watched the richer tourists spend fortunes on mugs of a brown, bubbling broth that they claimed rejuvenated them ... even as they were still swallowing the brew they said they could feel themselves becoming sprightlier ...

as we approached the city-centre the huge wall that encircled it loomed before us, a kind of opaque crystal ... the jasper walls, it is called ... streaked with thin splinters of brilliant colours and soft shades, it must be twenty-storeys high ... we passed through one of the twelve gates that gave access to the metropolis and marvelled at the city itself ... on the other side, everything is made of a finely-polished gold, so smooth that it seems like a metallic mirror ...

you asked me where we were, what time this was ...

you thought we had been propelled into the future, or to another side of the galaxy, but this was the same planet and the same time ... (of course this is confusing and it will take you a while to understand it, but you will, don't worry ... if you persist you will understand everything) what we experienced on that trip was a mere psychological twist, opening doors for us - doors which had always been locked before.

that was the first time we ever discussed infinity together ... do you remember? ...

it was actually the guide who brought it up ... he said that each instant is unlimited in itself, that time is really an unlimited succession of infinities ...

the golden city is, judged from our reality, merely a possibility ... in that sense it is another world, or another dimension if you like ...

it needed an effort to reach it ...

we made that effort - doesn't that satisfy you?

we walked through the treasury district of Avachumbi crossing the bridge into residential Ninachumbi ... and i took you to the museum to see the exhibition on the "founding fathers" ... do you remember?

then you remembered ... you laughed ... you were so wonderful then

they were all there: Quirós, Sarmiento, Mendaña, and all their cronies - Gallego, Isabel Barreto, Torres, and Diego de Tovar

"wasn't Sarmiento the first?" you asked

"oh yes," i said

"so why do you talk about Quirós so much?"

"because he was the last," i told you ... "don't worry, you will understand eventually ... i'll tell you anything you want to hear ... but don't forget," i warned ... "this is the perfect end of something incredible."

and you whimpered and then sighed, and we kissed...

Brilliant burning white light. Total light. White universe. Cold, but comfortable, this new re-birth. How many have there been to get to this point? This final point? I think and my mind is ablaze with memory. If I concentrated I could achieve it all. Re-live it all. And as I remember *them*, they will come to life. But wait, do not get lost. This is the Omega Point. I am the centre. The universe is created through me. Call me God. The Omega and the Alpha ... call me ...

Or is this not the end?

White light. My eyes adjust. Fluorescent bar. A hospital. Men and women around me. They stir, make me dizzy. Distorted forms with tiny heads and huge chests. Massive hands reach out for me. Clamp. Not on me, there is a shield. I try to call to them. No voice, but bubbles ... bubbles ... I am drowning in liquid. No, not drowning ... comfortable in liquid. Then I do feel the hands on me, lifting me. I feel the air, hot air. I want to struggle but I cannot move my arms. I cannot move my legs. The hands raise me, high over their own heads. I see everyone more clearly now. Doctors. Obviously doctors. Why does that reassure me? Briefly reassured, until I catch a reflection of myself. Of the face. I can but barely recognise it. The face of the head that is mine. The bodiless head that is mine. From my neck hang heavy tubes. Coloured, plastic tubes. Ersatz arteries keeping this head alive.

If I search my memory I should be able to recall what happened. But do I need to know? Do I want to know? What nightmare tale has my eternal life become? This is still not Omega. Just another beginning. Unless this is but a memory itself. They say everything will be recalled at the end. The miracle of Omega. Everything will be remembered. But if this is but a memory, why can't I shake my real head and think about something else?

Eternal, I am, but also a prisoner to eternity. A prisoner to them. In a state of eternal return, but always to be resurrected into an existence which is worse than the one just suffered.

I am in purgatory. Damned. There will be no reprieve, not for me.

Close the book. Now! I do not want you to know any more. I cannot bear it. Close the book and I am dead. That is what I want. To rest-in-peace. Now, please. Perhaps it will work, perhaps not. For me there is no other chance. Consciousness is killing me. I want to know nothing. This is the end... Close it!

END OF THE FIRST ATTEMPT

OTHER BOOKS BY PAUL DAVID ADKIN

ART WARS
WHEN SIRENS CALL

COMING SOON:

ETERNITY
(THE TERRA AUSTRALIS INCOGNITA SERIES)

NON-FICTION:

DISMANTLING THE PARADIGM
(TRACKING THE PENDULUM)

www.pauldavidadkin.com